To Pete

KARL E. CAMPBELL

SENATOR SAM ERVIN, LAST OF THE FOUNDING FATHERS

THE UNIVERSITY OF NORTH CAROLINA PRESS

CHAPEL HILL

This book was published with the assistance of the
Fred W. Morrison Fund for Southern Studies of the University of North Carolina Press.

The paper in this book meets the guidelines for permanence and durability
of the Committee on Production Guidelines for Book Longevity of the Council
on Library Resources.

Library of Congress Cataloging-in-Publication Data
Campbell, Karl E.
Senator Sam Ervin, last of the founding fathers / by Karl E. Campbell.
p. cm.
Includes bibliographical references and index.
ISBN 978-0-8078-3156-4 (cloth: alk. paper)
1. Ervin, Sam J. (Sam James), 1896–1985. 2. Legislators—United States—Biography.
I. Title.
E748.E93K36 2007
328.73092—dc22
[B]   2007026913

Portions of this work appeared previously, in somewhat different form, as
"Senator Sam Ervin and School Prayer: Faith, Politics and the Constitution,"
Journal of Church and State 48 (Summer 2003): 443–56; "Claghorn's Hammurabi:
Senator Sam Ervin and Civil Rights," *North Carolina Historical Review* 78 (October 2001):
431–56; and "Preserving the Constitution, Defending the Status Quo: Senator Sam Ervin
and Civil Liberties," *North Carolina Historical Review* 78 (October 2001): 457–82.
Used with permission of the journals.

A Caravan book. For more information, visit www.caravanbooks.org.

11 10 09 08 07   5 4 3 2 1

FRONTISPIECE
Sam Ervin delivering a speech at North Carolina State University, 25 February 1975.
From the *Raleigh News and Observer* negative files, North Carolina State Archives.
Used by permission of the *News and Observer*.

for my parents,

RALPH *and* HELEN CAMPBELL

CONTENTS

Preface   xi

Acknowledgments   xv

Introduction   1

1. Tar Heel Born, Tar Heel Bred   11

2. Just a Country Lawyer   43

3. Senator Sam   82

4. The Soft Southern Strategy   108

5. Claghorn's Hammurabi   132

6. Conservative Civil Libertarian   161

7. Privacy and the False Prophets   184

8. A Time of Doubt and Fear   210

9. Rehearsal for Watergate   246

10. Truth and Honor   278

Notes   303

Index   403

ILLUSTRATIONS

Sam Ervin speaking at North Carolina State University (1975), frontispiece

Television cameras covering the Senate Watergate hearings (1973), 3

John Ehrlichman testifying before the Ervin Committee (1973), 5

West Union Street in downtown Morganton (1913), 14

Burke County Courthouse (ca. 1912), 16

Samuel J. Ervin Sr., 18

Laura Powe Ervin, 19

A summer outing in 1916, 23

John Witherspoon Ervin, 27

Ervin and friends at Chapel Hill (1915), 32

Ervin's graduation picture and cartoon in the *Yackety Yack* (1917), 33

Sam Ervin in uniform (1917), 37

Laura Powe Ervin (1918), 41

Margaret Bell at age seventeen, 45

Sam Ervin in his hometown law office (1944), 67

Ervin family arriving at the Union Station (1954), 87

Senator Ervin and Vice President Richard Nixon (1954), 88

Cartoon supporting Ervin's role in bringing down

    Senator Joe McCarthy (1954), 95

Senator Ervin (1950s), 100

The Southern Caucus in the U.S. Senate (1963), 109

Richard Russell, John Stennis, and Sam Ervin (1957), 121

Cartoon satirizing Ervin's amendment to the civil rights bill of 1957, 123

Cartoon depicting debate between Sam Ervin and Bobby Kennedy
    over civil rights (1962), 145

Senator Ervin and Lori Wagner, the 1966 March of Dimes Poster Girl, 163

Senator Ervin at Cherry Blossom Festival (1962), 181

Senator Ervin and Rev. Billy Graham (1959), 196

Cartoon lampooning Ervin's Bible quoting (1973), 197

Senator Ervin watches President Nixon's speech, 216

Cartoon illustrating Ervin's challenge to executive power, 241

Cartoon depicting military domestic spying, 262

Senator Ervin frowns during Watergate hearings (1973), 293

Cartoon depicting Ervin giving Constitution to the public (1974), 298

Sam Ervin enjoying a good laugh in retirement (1981), 299

Sam Ervin and Miss Margaret (1973), 300

Anyone thinking about writing a biography should consider the following cautionary tale. In 1761 a young English historian chose a topic for his book. "At last I have fixed on Sir Walter Raleigh for my hero," he wrote in his diary. "His eventful story is varied by the characters of the soldier and sailor, the courtier and historian, and it may afford such a fund of materials as I desire which have not yet been properly manufactured" (the last word meaning something more akin to "processed" than "made up"). Raleigh certainly offered a wonderful subject for a biography, but just one year later the scholar changed his mind. "I am afraid of being reduced to drop my Hero," he concluded. "I must embrace a safer and more extensive theme." He had discovered that other scholars had already written on his topic and he wondered "what I should be able to add." Furthermore, he worried about how his book would be received in the politicized climate of his times: "I should shrink with terror from the modern history of England, where every character is a problem and every reader a friend or an enemy: where a writer is supposed to hoist a flag of party, and is devoted to damnation by the adverse faction." Finally, the young historian concluded, "The events of his life are interesting: but his character is ambiguous, his actions are obscure . . . and his fame is confined to the narrow limit of our language and our island." Thus Edward Gibbon abandoned his biography of Raleigh and began work on his classic *History of the Decline and Fall of the Roman Empire.*[1]

Gibbon's decision has weighed on my mind during the years I have worked on this project. There are many similarities between his experience and mine. As with Raleigh, other books have been written about Sam Ervin and I, too, have wondered if I could add anything new. In addition, Ervin's fame has decreased over the years and, like Raleigh, he is sometimes thought to hold a rather specific place in history. The senator is certainly remembered by the generation of Americans who experienced Watergate, and by many North Carolinians who revere him as a hero, but even they might incorrectly assume that his historical significance is limited to a narrow section of recent American politics. And just as Gibbon worried about a political backlash from his biography of Raleigh, I have wondered if this book, which deals with many controversial subjects such as civil rights and government domestic spying, might inspire emotionally charged reactions in our overheated contemporary political environment. Maybe I should have followed Gibbon's example and found a "safer" topic.

But Sam Ervin turned out to be far more important and interesting than I had initially expected. The senator's story is much more than just Watergate. Early in my reading I became intrigued by how this conservative, Bible-quoting, southern segregationist became the "liberal" chairman of the Watergate Committee. The more I looked back down Ervin's road to Watergate, the more fascinating topics I discovered. Then came the lucky, or fateful, coincidence that the Southern Historical Collection at the University of North Carolina at Chapel Hill opened the senator's professional papers (and several years later his personal papers) just as I began my research. But even that good fortune quickly turned into a major challenge given the immensity of the Ervin papers and the number of other presidential, congressional, and regional archives that had to be consulted.

Instead of giving up on Sam Ervin, I made several decisions to tighten the focus of the book. First, this volume concentrates more on Ervin's road *to* Watergate than on his role in the scandal itself. The first two chapters discuss his life before he went to the Senate in 1954, chapters 3–7 examine his record in the Senate up until the election of President Richard Nixon in 1968, chapters 8–9 review Ervin's escalating confrontation with the president that led to his appointment as chairman of the Watergate Committee in 1973, and the last chapter analyzes the scandal and Ervin's constitutional philosophy. The book does not retell the full story of Watergate. The senator himself wrote about his involvement with the scandal in his book *The Whole Truth: The Watergate Conspiracy* and in his autobiography, *Preserving the Constitution*.[2] Ervin's contributions to the downfall of President Nixon are discussed in many other publications as well. As more time passes, and as more sources become available, Sam Ervin and Watergate will certainly deserve a new book-length study in itself.

Second, I decided not to write a full biography but a more concentrated biographical study on the central theme of the senator's career—the apparent contradiction between his opposition to civil rights and his support of civil liberties. Ervin lived a long and full life (1896–1985) and he participated in some of the most important events of the twentieth century. Not only did he play a very significant role in the civil rights struggle—a role that has been overlooked to the detriment of the standard civil rights narrative—but he also contributed to the rise of the New South, the fight over Darwin in the 1920s, the general textile strike of 1934, the downfall of Senator Joe McCarthy, the Senate Rackets Committee, the debate over school prayer, the investigation into the military's domestic surveillance during the Vietnam War, the Senate hearings on the right to privacy, the defeat of the equal rights amendment, and Congress's opposition to Nixon's imperial presidency. Because this book focuses on the paradox of the senator's record on civil rights and civil liberties, and on his road to Watergate, some of these topics are covered in more depth than others.

Third, the methodology behind this book distinguishes it from earlier studies of Senator Ervin. In the 1970s, during the peak of his popularity, two talented authors—one a reporter and the other a novelist—wrote biographies of Ervin. Both these works are based primarily on interviews the authors conducted with the senator and those who knew him. My early interviews added little to the popular picture of Sam Ervin that we have today. Indeed, the oral tradition about the senator is so well established that I abandoned further interviews and decided to build this book on the expanded documentary record that had not yet been explored. This approach has reinforced some interpretations, challenged others, and raised new questions about Ervin, the southern opposition to civil rights, the historical context of Watergate, and many other topics of recent U.S. history.

ACKNOWLEDGMENTS

This book has benefited from the work of other scholars and the assistance of numerous institutions, archivists, colleagues, and friends. Paul Clancy wrote the first biography of Sam Ervin, and I have depended on his perceptive review of the senator's life to guide my research and inform my analysis. Christopher Pyle's work on military surveillance was essential to my understanding of Ervin's rehearsal for Watergate. Dick Dabney's book on Ervin is more of a historical novel than a biography, but I have found his research and insights very helpful. William Chafe's work has had a profound influence on my understanding of recent North Carolina history and civil rights. I owe a special debt to Sam Ervin, who made this project much easier by writing several books and many articles about various aspects of his life. I must confess, however, that at times I wished he would have produced just a little less in the way of books, law articles, pamphlets, speeches, judicial opinions, *Congressional Record* statements, committee reports, minority statements, historical tracts, press releases, interviews, and letters. The senator, his staff, and his family did historians a great favor by keeping his voluminous professional and personal papers intact and donating them to the Southern Historical Collection at the University of North Carolina at Chapel Hill.

I would never have thought about writing on Sam Ervin if it had not been for a meeting I had with William Leuchtenburg during my first year in graduate school at the University of North Carolina at Chapel Hill. When I was overwhelmed by the challenge of choosing a paper topic for a seminar in recent U.S. history, he asked if the Ervin papers in the Southern Historical Collection were open yet. I wandered over to Wilson Library and started nosing around in the letters Ervin wrote and received during Watergate. I was hooked. Bill Leuchtenburg stuck with me when I did not have the faintest idea how to write a seminar paper, let alone a book, always providing kind but firm advice. He taught me what it means to be a historian and challenged me to strive for the highest professional standards.

I count my years in graduate school at Chapel Hill among the most rewarding of my professional life. George Tindall directed my master's thesis and inspired me with his love of history. He always had time for a good story. William Barney, Peter Coclanis, Otis Graham, Jacquelyn Hall, Michael Hunt, John Kasson, and Donald Mathews provided encouragement and wise counsel both in their classes and in the early stages of this project. William Leuchten-burg, William Chafe, Jim Leloudis, Robert Moats Miller, and George Tindall all had a profound impact on the development of this book, and if I had taken their advice this would have been published years ago. Among my classmates at Chapel Hill I am particularly indebted to Glenda Gilmore, Odd Arne Westad, Karen Leatham, Bruce Kalk, Sarah Wilkerson-Freeman, and Leah Hagedorn. Their friendship and support in good times and bad means more than they will ever know.

Research for this book would not have been possible without the generous financial support of several organizations. I would like to thank the Graduate School of the University of North Carolina at Chapel Hill, the Everett McKin-ley Dirksen Congressional Leadership Research Center, the Lyndon Baines Johnson Foundation, the North Caroliniana Society, and the University Re-search Counsel at Appalachian State University for making possible trips to numerous archives. The Center for the Study of the American South and the United Methodist Wesley Center, both in Chapel Hill, provided professional and personal support during extended summer research trips.

Thanks are also due the many archivists and librarians who patiently di-rected me to valuable information at the Southern Historical Collection and North Carolina Collection at UNC–Chapel Hill, the North Carolina State Ar-chives, the National Archives, the Library of Congress, the Richard B. Russell Memorial Library at the University of Georgia, the Nebraska State Historical Society, the Joint Collection of the University of Missouri Western Historical Manuscript Collection—Columbia and State Historical Society of Missouri Manuscripts, the Louisiana and Lower Mississippi Valley Collections at the Louisiana State University Library, the Allen J. Ellender Memorial Library at Nicholls State University, and the Seeley G. Mudd Manuscript Library at Princeton University. The book would have contained far fewer photographs without the assistance of Gale Benefield and Dottie Ervin at the Morganton Branch of the Burke County Library, and Daniel Smith, Nancy Daniels, Becky Stragand, and the other librarians at the Sam Ervin Library at Western Pied-mont Community College in Morganton. The wonderful staff at the presiden-tial libraries also provided excellent support, including archivists at the Dwight D. Eisenhower, John F. Kennedy, Lyndon B. Johnson, and Gerald R. Ford Presidential Libraries, as well as the Richard M. Nixon Presidential Materials Project at the National Archives in College Park, Maryland.

I owe a great debt to the academic institutions where I taught during the many years I worked on this project. The History Department at the University of North Carolina at Charlotte provided a supportive environment during the year I served there as a visiting assistant professor. Pfeiffer University generously provided release time for me to write, and I am especially thankful to Juanita Kruse and Gene Earnhart for covering my classes during my absence. At Appalachian State University I have benefited from many thoughtful discussions with colleagues in southern and recent U.S. history and from the encouragement of many good friends in the Department of History.

I am indebted to a number of individuals who helped to make this a better book. Glenda Gilmore, Sheila Phipps, and Tim Silver read sections of the manuscript and offered sound advice. Stephen Ambrose, Joan Hoff, Steven Lawson, Hugh Graham, Bill Chafe, Tony Badger, David Chappell, Tim Thurber, and Jack Roper provided helpful critiques on conference papers. Ben Lea, Angela Kindley, and Pam Mitchem offered critical help when it was needed.

At the University of North Carolina Press, David Perry never gave up hope, although I think I finally exhausted his stock of supportive anecdotes. He has been a source of encouragement from beginning to end. I also want to thank Paul Betz, Mark Simpson-Vos, Zachary Read, Eric Schramm, and the rest of the staff for their patience and guidance.

Friends and family have helped in countless ways over the years. Mac Nelson and Allen Speer have spent many hours talking to me about history, politics, and especially Sam Ervin. When I needed a quiet place to work, the First Presbyterian Church of Fredericksburg and later Lees-McRae College provided me with wonderful office space. I also have to thank the wait staff at two friendly establishments in the North Carolina High Country where I occupied a corner table for hours on end scribbling notes and marking up drafts—the Grandview Restaurant and the Banner Elk Lodge.

My greatest debt, as always, is to my family. My wife, Kathy, has endured "the book" for much of our married life, yet she believed in me always and loves me still. My daughter, Joanna, has never known a time when her father was not working on "the book," but the warmth in her eyes has inspired me through many long nights. My parents encouraged their only son to believe that he could do anything he put his mind to, although I do not think they ever dreamed it would be writing a book.

This book is lovingly dedicated to my mother and father with deep gratitude for all they have done for me, for our family, and for so many others.

SENATOR
SAM ERVIN,
LAST OF THE
FOUNDING
FATHERS

Senator Sam Ervin interrupted his questioning of a witness during the televised Watergate hearings in the summer of 1973 and, with a twinkle in his eye,
slowly drawled, "I just can't resist the temptation to philosophize just a little
about the Watergate." Then the old country lawyer from North Carolina
launched into one of his famous impromptu political sermons: "Men upon
whom fortune had smiled benevolently and who possessed great financial
power, great political power, and great governmental power undertook to
nullify the laws of man and the laws of God for the purpose of gaining what
history will call a very temporary political advantage."[1]

This was live television. No one could stop him. Ervin's fellow senators, the
committee staffers, the witness, the press corps, the restless spectators packed
into every spare inch of the historic Senate Caucus Room, and the thousands
of viewers in the national television audience watching from homes and offices
across the country all had to wait for the seventy-six-year-old chairman of the
committee to finish his ruminations before the Watergate investigation could
proceed.

Sam Ervin was a disaster on television, at least by the standards of the slick,
sound-bite world of broadcast journalism in the 1970s. His eyebrows twitched
nervously up and down his forehead when he became excited and he tended to
stumble over his words as ideas passed through his mind faster than he could
explain them. On camera he came across ruffled, almost archaic, and very
southern. He seemed to be a walking, talking anachronism, or as one reporter
described him, "a last lingering elder from the time of pre-technological man."[2]

"The laws of God are embodied in the King James version of the Bible," Ervin
continued. He was becoming agitated and his voice was growing stronger. "And
I think that those who participated in this effort to nullify the laws of man and
the laws of God overlooked one of the laws of God which is set forth in the
seventh verse of the sixth chapter of Galatians, 'Be not deceived. God is not
mocked; for whatsoever a man soweth, that shall he also reap.' "[3]

There was a short pause, an awkward silence of a second or two. Bible
quoting was not fashionable in 1973. Popular culture, especially on television,
was secular, youthful, and dominated by the esthetic of cool. Ervin was none of
these. The contemporary myth, if not the fact, suggested a nation defined by
anti–Vietnam War protests, civil rights demonstrations, and the countercul-

ture's famous trinity of drugs, sex, and rock 'n' roll. Where did Sam Ervin's old-fashioned moralizing fit into this liberal context? For those few seconds of silence no one seemed to know exactly how to respond. Ervin, sensing the awkwardness, added an uncomfortable nod of his head as if to signal that he was done with his philosophizing and it was time for the committee to get back to work.

Then came the applause. It exploded from the public galleries and enveloped the whole room. Clapping, laughter, and cheers rolled out of the hearing room and over the airwaves into the nation. Even some members of the press and committee staffers joined in. The senators and the witness smiled awkwardly as some of the spectators rose in a standing ovation. Sitting there in the blazing light of the television cameras, Ervin, too, let a slight, knowing smile slip across his face before gaveling the hearings back to order.[4]

No doubt they were not smiling at the White House. The hearings were not going as they had expected. When the Senate announced that Sam Ervin would chair its select committee to investigate Watergate, President Richard M. Nixon and his aides thought the old North Carolinian could be handled. Chief of Staff H. R. (Bob) Haldeman assured the president that Ervin was "not the great constitutional authority he sets himself up to be." Charles Colson, special counsel to the president, reported that Ervin was "bordering on senility" and "a phoney." But Ervin's investigation began to unravel the cover-up that Nixon and his men had worked so desperately to maintain since the botched break-in of the Democratic National Committee in the Watergate office building on 16 June 1972. The Senate hearings revealed evidence of political dirty tricks, illegal campaign contributions, an administration "enemies list," a secret "Plumbers unit" for conducting illegal espionage, hush money payoffs, and other attempts to obstruct justice and subvert the democratic process. And to make matters worse, the charming, Bible-quoting chairman of the committee was skillfully shaping the revelations into a devastating indictment of the administration and even the president himself. By the end of the summer the opinions, and language, in the White House had grown harsher. Nixon's aides leaked complaints to the press that Ervin was out to get the president. In private, the new chief of staff, Alexander Haig, began referring to Ervin as "the sonofabitch." To the president, Ervin had become "the old incredible bastard."[5]

While Nixon and his aides fumed behind the secretive walls of the White House, Senator Ervin and his hearings were becoming a media sensation. Television, newspapers, and radio were filled with accounts of the latest disclosures and explanations of the expanding plot. The major networks carried the hearings live from gavel to gavel. Public television stations replayed the

The Senate Watergate hearings made Ervin a national celebrity during the summer of 1973. Note the television cameras surrounding the committee members (seated from left: Senators Weicker, Gurney, Baker, Ervin, and Inouye). Sam Ervin Library and Museum, Western Piedmont Community College, Morganton, North Carolina.

hearings at night and the most exciting segments were part of the evening news. For thirty-seven days the nation watched as present and former government officials testified before Ervin and his committee.

By all accounts Ervin's Watergate show was a hit. Worried network executives who had taken a big risk replacing their popular soap operas and game shows with live Senate hearings were delighted when the Watergate coverage earned higher Nielsen ratings than the regular daytime programming. By the end of the summer a Gallup survey reported that nearly 90 percent of all Americans had watched some part of the hearings. Over one and a half million Americans had written letters to the Ervin Committee expressing their concerns about Watergate. Never before had so many citizens written to a congressional committee. Richard Nixon, who had received the third largest mandate in the nation's history when he won reelection in November 1972, had the lowest public approval rating of any president in twenty years when the hearings recessed in August 1973.[6]

As Nixon's ratings fell, Ervin's popularity skyrocketed. The senator's moonshiner stories from "down home" in North Carolina, his quaint verses ranging from Aesop's fables to Shakespeare, and his earnest lectures in defense of constitutional government endeared him to a disenchanted public suffering through a long national crisis. As the Watergate hearings progressed, the national press increasingly portrayed Ervin as a genuine American hero. The senator's craggy face seemed to be everywhere—from the front cover of *Time* and *Newsweek* to the "Senator Sam" T-shirts worn by surfers in California. "The Watergate [scandal] has given us a person we believe, and believe in," explained Rob Coughlan, founder of the National Sam Ervin Fan Club. "He says he's just an 'old country lawyer,' but when he talks about the Constitution he makes you want to stand up to pledge allegiance."[7]

Almost every day of the hearings provided another example of what one reporter called Ervin's "genial blend of con law and corn pone." Ervin's confrontation with John D. Ehrlichman, Nixon's former domestic policy adviser, demonstrated how effective the senator's style could be. Ervin asked Ehrlichman about a blatantly illegal incident in which the White House "Plumbers"— the same team of undercover operatives that was caught breaking into the Democratic National Committee's offices in the Watergate complex—attempted to steal the psychiatric records of Daniel Ellsberg, a prominent member of the White House enemies list. Ehrlichman confidently answered that the president had an inherent power to break the law and violate a citizen's right to privacy whenever he deemed it necessary to protect "national security."[8]

An outraged Ervin delivered another of his famous extemporaneous lec-

John Ehrlichman (left, at witness table) testifying in the Senate Caucus Room during the Watergate hearings, 1973. Ervin is seated third from the left at the committee table. Sam Ervin Library and Museum, Western Piedmont Community College, Morganton, North Carolina.

tures. He drew his initial arguments from theology and history. "The concept embodied in the phrase 'every man's home is his castle' represents the realization of one of the most ancient and universal hungers of the human heart," Ervin began. "One of the prophets described the mountain of the Lord as being a place where every man might dwell under his own vine and fig tree with none to make him afraid." Next, he recited from memory the words of William Pitt the Elder before the American Revolution: "The poorest man may in his cottage bid defiance to all the forces of the crown. It may be frail, its roof may shake, the wind may blow through it, the storm may enter, but the King of England cannot enter. All his force dares not cross the threshold of the ruined tenement." Staring across the witness table at Ehrlichman, Ervin snapped: "And yet we are told here today, and yesterday, that what the King of England can't do, the President of the United States can."[9]

The senator was just getting warmed up. Turning to constitutional law, he discussed the famous Civil War case *Ex parte Milligan*, which he proposed to be "the greatest decision that the Supreme Court of the United States has ever handed down." Ervin reviewed the case history like a teacher in a beginning law class. He explained that President Abraham Lincoln had arrested citizens during the Civil War whose only crime had been to exercise their First Amendment rights and criticize the war effort. But in *Milligan* the Court rejected the president's argument that during an emergency, even one as great as the Civil War, he had an inherent power to suspend constitutional rights. Quoting Justice David Davis, again from memory, Ervin recalled the wisdom of the founding fathers:

> The good and wise men who drafted and ratified the Constitution foresaw that troublous times would arise, when rulers and people would become restive under restraint and seek by sharp and decisive measures to accomplish ends deemed just and proper, and that the principles of constitutional liberty would be put in peril unless established by irrepealable law. And for these reasons, these good and wise men drafted and ratified the Constitution as a law for rulers and people alike, at all times and under all circumstances. No doctrine was ever invented by the wit of man than that any of its provisions can be suspended during any of the great exigencies of government.[10]

In only a few minutes, Ervin had undercut Ehrlichman's national security defense and challenged the entire notion of Nixon's imperial presidency.

On another occasion Ervin applied his down-home wit directly against the president. After the committee's dramatic discovery of a secret taping device in the White House, Ervin and his colleagues voted to issue a subpoena for the tapes. These secret recordings seemed to be the perfect means to answer the famous question posed by Senator Howard Baker during the hearings: What did the president know and when did he know it? But Nixon wrote to Ervin claiming executive privilege and refusing to surrender the tapes. Discussing the president's letter the next day during the hearings, the senator reduced the complex legalities of the situation to simple and understandable logic. "The president's message is rather remarkable," he suggested tongue-in-cheek. "If you will notice, the president says he has heard the tapes or some of them, and they sustain his position. But he says he's not going to let anybody else hear them for fear they might draw different conclusions." Once again the audience laughed, the senator beamed, and the television cameras kept rolling.[11]

Ervin became the darling of the print media as well that summer. Journalists had a field day describing Ervin to their readers. "Sam Ervin smiles, grins, chortles, guffaws and harpoons witnesses with barbed anecdotes," reported the *New York Times*. The *Los Angeles Times* portrayed him as "the shrewd, jowly

Tarheel [*sic*] who looks so much a senator that he seems almost a caricature." The *Virginian-Pilot* praised "the fellow from Morganton, N.C. with caterpillary eyebrows, a querulous expression and a down home voice that drawls from a pair of cheeky jowls that appear to be stuffed plumb full of grits." In its cover story on Ervin, *Time* magazine defended the media's obsession with the senator: "On the uptight scene in Washington, newsmen flock to any Ervin-chaired session because there are few genuine colorful characters around. And besides being totally fearless, incapable of intimidation by anyone, there are those stories."[12]

Sam Ervin well understood the power of a good story. He told them frequently during the Watergate investigation, as he had throughout his career. The *New York Times Magazine* quoted him as joking (in exaggerated southern accent), "Mah wife, of course, says ah haven't heard a new stowry in ages, and she's gettin' tired of laughin' at these old ones." Ervin added, "Ah have always found if you got a good stowry that sort of fits things, a good stowry is worth an hour of argument." Ironically, however, the senator could have been speaking of the media's own use of him to frame the story of Watergate. Just as Ervin told cracker-barrel stories and home-grown similes to illuminate his points during the hearings, so did the press tell Sam Ervin stories to shape its reporting during the summer of 1973.[13]

The Watergate scandal was very complex. It did not emerge in one storyline all at one time but came out in bits and pieces at uneven intervals. Reporters struggled to make sense of the scandal, to fit all the pieces of the puzzle together. They searched for stories and symbols that would catch the essence of the unfolding scandal and grab the attention of their audience. Ervin's witticisms made for good copy, but so did the senator himself. Thus, as the Senate hearings wore on, Sam Ervin the storyteller became Senator Sam the character in the emerging Watergate drama.

All stories have an internal structure or organization, and in the summer of 1973 reporters trying to tell the Watergate story tended to follow one of three basic forms. First, in some news stories Ervin served as a foil to the president, or in the words of journalist Mary McCarthy, "the humble, 'low' reality principle." McCarthy thought Ervin to be "virtually Shakespearean, and showing the Bard's own fondness for character parts and honest common-sense rustics."[14] The media also drew from a second dramatic form in its presentation of Senator Sam and Watergate—the morality play. Dating from the Middle Ages, these stories featured characters who personified various abstract vices and virtues. In some newspapers Ervin became the embodiment of "the stern values of another age" and "the voice of truth seeking." In others he was portrayed as "the graven image of Congress" and "the symbol of the wounded institution trying to recover its strength and self-respect."[15]

Eventually the press settled on a third dramatic form, the classic tragedy, to organize the story of Watergate. By the time the president resigned in 1974, a year after the Ervin hearings, the main plot of Watergate centered on the president himself and especially on the dark side of Richard Nixon's moral character. Nixon became the archetypal Oedipal hero who rose to the pinnacle of power only to succumb to his own fatal moral flaws. In this classical tragedy Senator Sam still played a leading role, but he was demoted to one of several Nixon challengers—including investigative reporters Bob Woodward and Carl Bernstein, and Special Prosecutors Archibald Cox and Leon Jaworski—who each played a part in bringing retribution to the corrupted president. This classic tragedy has become the standard historical narrative of Watergate.[16]

But history is not theater. The past can certainly be dramatic, and historians often write in a narrative style, but history cannot be reduced to fit theatrical contrivances. Life is indeed messier than fiction. Watergate was not Shakespeare, or a morality play, or a classical tragedy about the rise and fall of Richard Nixon. It was a complicated constitutional crisis that revealed deep and systemic challenges to the nation's democratic form of government. Likewise, Sam Ervin was not a character actor chosen from central casting to play the role of the old country lawyer in the Watergate drama. Sam Ervin, the man, was never as simple as Senator Sam, the Watergate hero. He was much more complicated than the folksy caricature the news media created for its Watergate drama. But as Watergate developed into a blockbuster of epic proportions, the media fell victim to its own simple caricature. The sensational outcome of the story—Nixon's dishonorable resignation and Ervin's triumphant retirement occurring within months of each other in 1974—only served to cement the semi-fictional Senator Sam character in the press, the public mind, and history.[17]

Yet even at the height of the Watergate frenzy a few columnists sought to correct the emerging Ervin mythology. Tom Wicker of the *New York Times* urged his readers not to be deceived by "the Watergate Chairman's new clothes." Wicker wanted the public to remember that the likable head of the Watergate Committee, who was being praised nationally as "the Senate's champion defender of civil liberties," had also been the intellectual leader of the South's crusade to deny African Americans their civil rights. Wicker, a fellow North Carolinian, pointed out that Ervin had one of the most conservative voting records in the Senate, having opposed not only civil rights, but also Medicare, Medicaid, consumer protection, the minimum wage, health and safety regulations, and the equal rights amendment. Wicker expressed gratitude to Ervin for "his great part in the Watergate drama, for his personal rectitude, occasional grace, and undoubted learning." But he suspected that underneath Ervin's new liberal clothes there still beat the heart of a conservative southern constitutionalist. To Wicker, the most significant aspect of Ervin's career was the challenge of trying to reconcile the record of "ol' Massa Sam" with the actions of "Uncle Sam, the last of the founding fathers."[18]

From the beginning of his senatorial career, Sam Ervin defied definition. He was a man full of paradoxes. An opponent of labor unions, he nevertheless fought for the rights of professional basketball players to switch teams against the "economic enslavement" of the "giant sports trusts." A hawk on Vietnam, he defended the rights of anti-war protesters to distribute literature on military bases, and he opposed the Army's domestic surveillance of peace marchers. A law-and-order conservative, Ervin led the fight against Nixon's tough crime control package that gave the police new preventive detention powers and allowed no-knock drug raids. As one North Carolina journalist observed in 1967: "If stereotypes are always misleading, they are downright laughable in the case of Sam Ervin. After 13 years in the Senate, Ervin still regularly enrages first the liberals and then the conservatives. He defies all the easy generalizations of political journalism."[19]

Ervin explained his seemingly inconsistent political behavior by claiming to be just "preserving the Constitution." He argued that he would oppose any government action that threatened to interfere with an individual's constitutional rights, no matter if it was a liberal proposal to guarantee civil rights or a conservative program to protect national security. Ervin distrusted government power. "When they drafted the Constitution," he explained, "the Founding Fathers accepted as verity this aphorism of the English philosopher Thomas Hobbes: 'Freedom is political power divided into small fragments.' " Above his desk Ervin hung a sign that read, "No man's life, liberty, or property are safe while the legislature is in session." Ervin contended that all of his political actions reflected a single consistent theme: his vigilance against the excesses of government power in order to maintain maximum individual freedom.[20]

Ervin's defense of his seemingly contradictory record fit nicely with his heroic image during Watergate, and it became the orthodox interpretation of his career. The vast majority of both journalists and scholars have, to varying degrees, accepted the senator's portrait of himself as a consistent civil libertarian and constitutional purist. "Sen. Ervin's apparent inconsistency does not stem from want of conviction," one reporter concluded, "but from the reverence with which he regards the Constitution." Another writer observed, "Whatever the current fashion is in liberal or conservative, you won't find him on either side. While everybody else is running from right to left and back, he's following an inner-directed course, [which is] . . . the straight line, solid concept he holds of what the U.S. Constitution means."[21]

But not everyone accepted such a positive interpretation of the senator and his career. Many of the senator's critics—especially activists in the civil rights, labor, and women's movements—saw more contradiction than consistency in his career. Some disputed his reputation as a great constitutionalist, describing him as "an overblown constitutional lawyer" who had stopped reading cases in 1936 and whose limited view of the Constitution did not go past the Tenth Amendment.[22] Others grudgingly admired the senator's legal abilities but considered him a "rational segregationist" who knowingly misused the Constitution as a convenient cloak for his racism as well as his anti-women and anti-labor agenda.

But neither the orthodox defense of Ervin as a consistent constitutional libertarian nor the critical attack on the senator as an inconsistent southern obstructionist can withstand a close review of the historical record. Like the simplistic old country lawyer caricature created by the news media during Watergate, these interpretations are more mythical than substantive. They served the political needs of their adherents more than they help to resolve the contradictions of Sam Ervin's career. The first interpretation of Ervin as a consistent civil libertarian rests on the simplistic theory that political ideology is the wellspring of all human behavior. The second interpretation is ridiculously monocausal in assuming that any white southerner who opposed civil rights can be dismissed as a racist and no further analysis is necessary. Both of these theories are too presentist, static, and incomplete to resolve the central paradox of the senator's career—his unrelenting opposition to civil rights and his uncompromising defense of civil liberties.

The key to understanding Sam Ervin lies deeper in the past. While some of the issues that led the senator down the road to Watergate first emerged soon after Richard Nixon won the presidency in 1968, others had their genesis over a decade earlier during battles over civil rights and civil liberties. Even before that, as early as Ervin's first year in the U.S. Senate, the basic outlines of his conservative civil libertarian and race-based ideology became apparent. But the core beliefs of the man who would eventually lead Congress's counteroffensive to Nixon's imperial presidency had been formed long before, down home in North Carolina.

CHAPTER ONE

TAR HEEL BORN, TAR HEEL BRED

Standing on the front porch of his home in Morganton, North Carolina, Senator Ervin liked to joke with guests by pointing across the street to an old white house surrounded by oak trees. "Yes, I was born right over there," he would say. "So you can see I haven't gotten very far in life."[1] The irony was obvious, but so was the truth behind his self-deprecating humor. All his life Ervin held fast to the "eternal truths" he learned in his youth. In spite of his long and successful career in the U.S. Senate, neither his heart nor mind ever strayed far from his North Carolina home. Ervin lived in his native state for fifty-eight years prior to going to Washington, D.C., and he epitomized its political culture and its dominant ideals. "Senator Ervin is the most North Carolinian of North Carolinians," a reporter explained. "This kind of man seems to be an ornament of Tar Heel History." As Sam Ervin himself explained, quoting the lines of Chapel Hill's favorite song: "I am a Tar Heel born and a Tar Heel bred, and when I die I'll be a Tar Heel dead."[2]

The world in which Ervin was born in 1896 was drastically different from the world in which he died in 1985. He experienced so many remarkable changes during his lifetime that he seemed to be constantly struggling to adapt to new conditions. The often repeated fact that Ervin's generation witnessed both the first flight of an airplane at Kitty Hawk, North Carolina, and the landing of the first man on the moon remains a remarkable symbol of the extraordinary transformations that the senator and his contemporaries experienced. But change came to Ervin in both profound and simple ways. Common items of daily life during Sam's boyhood—buggy whips, pickle and cracker barrels, ice trucks, horse collars, washboards, outhouses, corsets, high button shoes—had become quaint relics of Americana by the time he was an adult. Over the course of Ervin's lifetime he went from riding a horse and buggy to driving a V8 Chrysler, from muddy roads to superhighways, from water wheels to atomic reactors, and from hand-carved pencils to desktop computers.[3]

The pace of change was especially rapid in the South. The Civil War had ended slavery only thirty-one years before Ervin was born, and Reconstruction was only two decades in the past. Emotions from both events still ran deep. Young Sam grew up knowing many former slave owners and Confederate soldiers, including members of his own family. During his boyhood North Carolinians struggled to transform their economy from the precapitalist, slave-based Old South to the free-enterprise, industrialized New South. Such a transition did not come easily to a region mired in poverty and resentful of defeat. In North Carolina, however, the traditional staple-crop economy grad-ually gave way to a new economy dominated by textile, tobacco, and furniture factories and the banking, transportation, and marketing industries that sup-ported them.[4]

The industrialization of the postwar South brought revolutionary changes to nearly every aspect of southern life, especially to race relations. Everything dealing with race, from law to language, underwent traumatic and always contested change during Ervin's life. For instance, not long after Sam was born the North Carolina legislature passed Jim Crow laws dividing public space into black and white sections; years later as a senator he fought and lost numerous battles to sustain that segregation. As a boy Sam had black house servants whom he called "nigras," but by the time Ervin retired he had congressional colleagues called "African Americans." Senator Sam was not the product of some sleepy solid South, as the media so often suggested. He lived during a tumultuous era of radical southern transformation.[5]

Historians, however, have found both change and continuity in the twentieth-century South. As the rapidly modernizing southern economy and an in-creasingly activist federal government challenged traditional social relation-ships, the South's white leaders fought to maintain control over their local communities. In spite of the numerous challenges, North Carolina's ruling class struggled to keep white men at the head of their households, businessmen in charge of their workers, traditional leaders in control of state and local govern-ment, and whites in power over blacks. As the old saying goes: the more things changed the more they stayed the same—at least for a while.[6]

A central problem for North Carolina's white leaders during Ervin's life was reconciling their traditional ideology with the new ideas that accompanied their evolving capitalistic economy. Key remnants of antebellum southern thought, such as the importance of social hierarchy and the inequality of people (based primarily on race and gender), did not conform with the basic tenets of a market economy, such as individual rights and equal opportunity. In the Old South, elite white men justified their complete control over slave society by claiming a God-given superiority in a naturally unequal world. How then in the New South could they rationalize their exclusive access to opportunity and power in a modern society supposedly based on fair and equal competition among all individuals? How could they harmonize modernity with their fears of runaway individualism, instability, and social equality? These contradictions between the past and the present, between the nostalgia for the Old South and the opportunities of the New South, between embracing individualism yet fearing the loss of social hierarchy, had a profound impact on Ervin's boyhood and coming of age in North Carolina.[7]

Sam was born in Morganton, a small town lying below the Blue Ridge Mountains in the western part of the Tar Heel State. In 1896, the year of his birth, it had fewer than 2,000 residents. "It was a small town then," Ervin remembered, "so small that you not only knew all the people, you knew all the dogs and cats."[8] During Ervin's boyhood Morganton had a distinctive character that derived, in part, from its unique geographical setting. Like Ervin, the town was part old South, part Carolina hill country, part New South, and part Appalachian mountains.

Morganton has long been the political and commercial center of Burke County, which is located on the western edge of the Piedmont region of North Carolina—an area of wooded, rolling hills and valleys that covers the vast middle section of the state. The Catawba River flows through the county and down into South Carolina. Its fertile river bottoms and lowlands attracted Scotch-Irish, English, and a few German settlers who established successful farms, some of which grew into large estates supported by African and African American slave labor. Later arrivals built smaller homesteads in the surrounding hills and hollows. These mostly self-sufficient frontiersmen made periodic trips into Morganton for their furnishings, but the townsfolk and wealthier planters looked further south, to Charleston, South Carolina, for their supplies. So significant was Charleston in the minds of Morganton's early civic leaders that they named the original roads of their frontier town after the streets in that historic low country city.

As the North Carolina Piedmont developed in the late nineteenth century, Burke County reoriented itself eastward and closer to home. By the time Sam

Ervin was seventeen years old in 1913 when this shipment of new Fords was displayed along West Union Street in downtown Morganton. Courtesy of R. M. Lineberger, Picture Burke Photographic Collection, Burke County Library.

Ervin was born, the railroad connected Morganton to the growing industrial centers of Greensboro, Winston-Salem, and Charlotte. During his boyhood a cotton mill, a hosiery mill, a furniture factory, and a new bank began to change the face of the little town. In the twentieth century Morganton increasingly became drawn into the nexus of the urban-industrial center of North Carolina and began to reflect the culture of the New South.[9]

While first Charleston and then the North Carolina Piedmont shaped the economic culture of Ervin's hometown, it was the mountains that gave the community its special appeal. Two-fifths of Burke County is located in the rugged terrain of the southern Appalachians. The Blue Ridge Mountains rise just beyond Morganton, providing a temperate climate and spectacular views, especially at dusk when the darkening silhouettes of Grandfather Mountain, Table Rock, and Hawksbill dominate the evening skyline. According to Ervin, "Burke folks know that the most beautiful pictures painted by the Lord are those of the sun setting behind old Table Rock."[10]

Townspeople trekked up into the mountains for fishing, hunting, and "mission work," while the mountaineers came down to Morganton to buy necessities and sell what they could, including farm produce, natural products such as holly, mistletoe, honey, and firewood, and homemade items ranging from quilts and hand-woven baskets to moonshine liquor. Susan Graham Erwin, who was a few years younger than Sam and later married his brother Joe, remembered one particular mountain woman named Polly Malindy who rode an old mule named Jake through the town streets calling out "Kindlin wood and hand wove baskits! Galax leaves—holly berries and mistletoe! Come and git 'em whilst ye may." The children adored the old woman and would run up and down the streets ringing everyone's doorbell to help her attract business. Then, as now, the mountaineers' hard poverty was sometimes romanticized as being folksy by local residents and visitors. During Ervin's childhood it was still common to see poor mountain families camping in vacant lots or on the outskirts of town in old-fashioned wagons, especially during court week.[11]

Morganton was born a court town and much of its history revolved around the courthouse and adjacent public square. The law was important to the town's identity, and its legal culture had a large impact on the Ervin family. The North Carolina General Assembly established Morganton during the Revolutionary War to serve as the court for a new judicial district. During the antebellum period Morganton hosted the County Court, District Court, and Superior Court terms, becoming the legal center for the western Piedmont and northwest mountains. Between 1847 and 1862 even the North Carolina Supreme Court held its August term there, abandoning the heat and humidity of the state capital in Raleigh for the cooler mountain breezes of Morganton. The town earned a reputation as "the Western Capital of North Carolina" and was nicknamed the "little gem in the wilderness."[12]

Some of North Carolina's most celebrated nineteenth-century legal dramas took place in Morganton's courthouse, including the sensational trial of Frankie Silver in 1832. Frankie, a young bride with a newborn child, was charged with killing her husband in their remote log cabin and hacking his body to pieces with an axe to hide her crime. According to Senator Ervin, who later researched the case, she should have been acquitted. He believed that if the law at the time had allowed her to testify in her own behalf the jurors would have heard evidence that her husband abused her and probably would have concluded that she acted in self-defense. Instead, the jury found her guilty of murder. Frankie Silver was the first white woman to be hanged in North Carolina.[13]

Another famous event occurred in 1851 when a local lawyer and politician, William Waightstill Avery, got away with a murder he committed right in the middle of a session of the Superior Court in Morganton. A few weeks earlier, in

This photograph of the Burke County Courthouse from approximately 1912 is believed to be
of a gathering of the local Democratic Party. Both Senator Ervin and his father
practiced law in the old courthouse, which was originally constructed in 1837
and was covered with stucco in 1885. Courtesy of R. Douglas Walker,
Picture Burke Photographic Collection, Burke County Library.

the nearby town of Marion, Avery had vigorously defended a man accused of cheating a merchant named Samuel Fleming. After the trial Fleming accosted Avery outside the courthouse and beat the unarmed attorney with a bullwhip. When Fleming later came to Morganton on business and entered the Burke County Courthouse to talk with another attorney, Avery calmly pulled a pistol from his pocket and shot Fleming dead right in the courtroom. A biased local jury found Avery innocent by reason of temporary insanity.[14]

Incidents such as these became part of the legal lore that helped attract throngs of visitors to Morganton during court weeks. Lawyers and their clients converged on the town from adjacent counties. Town residents, would-be jurors, mountaineers, farmers, peddlers, and musicians gathered in the square where, according to one witness, "they would swap horses, drink, sing, drink, tell tales, drink, and in general catch up on all the news and gossip."[15] Inside the courthouse the lawyers matched wits before the bench and bar. The attorneys and judges were among the most recognized and respected members of the community. They were the stars of the court week show, sometimes playing to packed galleries as much as to judge and jury.

Near the end of the nineteenth century one of the most respected local attorneys distinguished himself not only through his knowledge of the law and spirited legal argumentation but by his distinctive appearance. A serious and stern man, he dressed in such an outdated fashion that children sometimes mistook him for the character pictured on the front of the Prince Albert Tobacco can. The dapper gentleman who wore a neatly trimmed goatee, old-fashioned white cravat, and traditional Victorian cutaway tails was Samuel James Ervin Sr., the senator's father.[16]

Samuel Ervin had come to Morganton from South Carolina in 1874 with his mother and father when he was nineteen. He found an entry-level job in the post office running errands and carrying bags of mail. Whenever possible he took on extra jobs to make a little extra money. At night he began to study law under the tutelage of a local judge who had been impressed with his enterprising spirit. But Ervin proved to be a stubborn student who had his own ideas of how to interpret the law. His disagreements with the judge became so heated that he quit his lessons and taught himself by reading in various lawyers' offices late in the evening. He passed the bar in 1879 and soon built a successful law practice.[17]

The elder Ervin epitomized the term "southern gentleman." The local newspaper observed that "his gracious manner, his dignified appearance, even to his long-tailed coat—all combined to link him in the mind of fellow townsmen with the graces associated with the Old South."[18] Mr. Ervin adhered to a strict daily schedule. He rose early, worked in the garden before breakfast, dressed and ate, walked the mile or so to his law office downtown (he never once accepted a ride), walked home for lunch, took a ten-minute nap, walked back to town, came home at 5:30, worked in the garden again, ate supper, and sat on the front porch in the swing or out in the yard until bedtime.[19]

At home, Ervin maintained a strict but loving countenance. His family remembers him having great integrity and an intolerance for dishonesty, as well as a soft spot for his children. "My father was a rare combination of austerity and jovialness," Senator Ervin remembered.[20] "He had the external dourness of his Scotch ancestry," but was "extremely kind and genial."[21] He did not laugh readily or play games, but he loved to spend time reading aloud to whomever was around the house in the evening, usually from his favorite authors such as Shakespeare, Scott, Dickens, Byron, Browning, Tennyson, and Kipling—many of the same writers his son later quoted from memory on the

Senator Ervin's father, Samuel J. Ervin Sr. (1855–1944). Ervin Family Papers, 4498, Southern Historical Collection, Wilson Library, University of North Carolina at Chapel Hill.

Senate floor. When his legal practice took him out of town he wrote home daily with instructions for fulfilling family responsibilities, tending the garden, and caring for the babies: "Kiss them all for me," he would conclude.[22]

The children waited anxiously for these letters and would complain if they were not each mentioned by name. According to family legend, the first letter Sam Jr. ever wrote came out of a tantrum he threw at age four when he did not get his own letter from his father. With the help of his older sister Catharine, Sam wrote: "My dear papa. Bring me some chestnuts. Samuel J. E."[23] When the children grew older their father took each of them on a trip to Washington, D.C., to see the nation's capitol. Senator Ervin later remembered his father standing in front of the Supreme Court and explaining in a tone of reverential awe: "The Supreme Court will abide by the Constitution though the heavens fall." It was a story Ervin repeated often in his many battles with a more activist Supreme Court in the 1950s and 1960s.[24]

Back in 1874 when the Ervins had first moved to Morganton, the Powe family (pronounced "Po") lived across the street. Their daughter, Laura, was ten years younger than Samuel. One Sunday evening in the summer of 1886 Morganton was shaken by tremors from a major earthquake centered in Charleston, South Carolina. As Samuel ran out of his house he noticed that Laura had the presence of mind to blow out all the candles before leaving her home. He made up his mind that such a sensible young woman would make a fine wife, and they were married later that year.[25]

Known to her neighbors as "Miss Laura," or "Mother Ervin" later in life,

Senator Ervin's mother, Laura Powe Ervin (1865–1956). Ervin Family Papers, 4498, Southern Historical Collection, Wilson Library, University of North Carolina at Chapel Hill.

Laura Ervin complemented her husband's awkward formality with a comfortable warmth. One of her contemporaries suggested that if there had been a vote for the most loved woman in Morganton, Miss Laura would have undoubtedly won. She was, in many ways, the embodiment of the nineteenth-century ideal of southern womanhood. She volunteered in the Presbyterian Church, supported mission work, became the first president of the town's Red Cross, and shared in the personal lives of the families in her community—all while raising ten children.[26]

Laura was a very strong individual who managed her household without compromise, yet always referred to her husband as "Mr. Ervin" in front of both family and friends. None of the Ervin children could recall an instance of their mother ever telling them how to behave or reprimanding them in any way. Jean, the youngest of ten children, explained: "All the teaching, I think, in this family was by example." Sam Jr. later wrote: "She taught much by example, little by precept." Sam revered his mother. In his autobiography he described her in glowing terms: "Her quiet strength, gentleness, and patience seemed illimitable. She was utterly unselfish and completely self-effacing; spoke no unkind words of others, . . . [and] endeared herself to all who knew her by her encouraging and gentle ways, her compassion for the unfortunate, and her sympathy for the bereaved or hurt; and accepted life's heaviest blows without complaining or losing heart."[27]

Sam's mother suffered with her children through a series of tragedies. When Margaret, her third child, came down with tuberculosis at the age of nineteen, she cared for her alone during the last few months, isolating and scalding all her dishes and clothes to protect the rest of the family. Edward, the fourth child, suffered from a virulent strain of asthma until his death as a young man. Joe, the eighth of the Ervin children, was only a young boy when he fell from an apple tree and broke his left leg. Osteomyelitis, a painful and debilitating disease, developed in his left thigh, leading to repeated operations and physical disability. Psychological illness and drug addiction also touched the Ervin family. Yet Miss Laura retained her optimism and faith in the future. She expected much from her children, and they responded with great accomplishments. Many years later, when Sam was appointed to the U.S. Senate, a reporter asked Mother Ervin what she thought of her son's outstanding success. With characteristic graciousness she responded, "I am proud of all my children."[28]

Sam's mother and father built a traditional two-story white frame house in 1877. They called their homestead Fern Hill because of the numerous wild ferns that grew on the thirty acres the family owned on the outskirts of town. It had a fireplace or pot-bellied stove in each room for heat, a separate kitchen with a large woodstove for cooking, and an outdoor privy that the Ervins politely referred to as the "Garden House." By the time Sam was born in 1896 the family's growing numbers and rising social status had led to the addition of more living space and several fashionable Victorian-era renovations, but electricity and indoor plumbing did not arrive until he was a young man in the 1920s. The house fronted a well-maintained village street that ran about a mile into the heart of Morganton, but the backyard rolled out into the countryside. The Ervins had a barn for their milk cow, Daisy, a henhouse, a smoke house, a sixty-foot deep well for drinking water, a large vegetable garden, a small cornfield, an apple orchard, a pigsty off in the distance, and a woods with a spring-fed creek in which the boys could go skinny-dipping in the summer.[29]

At the turn of the century, before the conveniences of modern living, every member of the family had to pitch in to keep the household running. The chores were generally divided up by gender, with the five girls assigned to housework such as washing clothes in a big black pot over a fire in the backyard, cleaning, shucking corn, snapping beans, and canning vegetables and fruits for the winter. The five boys usually worked outside the house hauling wood, weeding the garden, hoeing corn, and caring for the animals. Family legend holds that Sam was the only boy who never learned how to milk the cow. There is some debate as to whether his lack of ability was natural or intentional. He also never became much of a gardener. One story relates that as an adult during World War II he spent an afternoon planting potatoes in his victory garden. When his brother Hugh asked if he had made sure to have an eye on each piece of potato that he buried in the ground, a bewildered Sam asked, "What's an eye?" Sam had a reputation for being the child who spent more time reading than working, but he insisted that he still did his fair share. "While I must confess that I was not too fond of physical labor," Ervin later admitted, "I had assigned tasks which I performed. My mother and father believed that everyone should be taught to work, but did not require any of us to work very hard."[30]

As was customary among upwardly mobile southern families in the early twentieth century, the Ervins hired African American servants to help them maintain their growing household. Jean, Sam's youngest sister, remembered that "there was always a cook who reigned dogmatically in the kitchen, usually a nurse for the current yard baby, someone who came in to do the wash on Mondays and the ironing on Tuesdays, someone to work the garden in the summer and chop the wood in winter."[31] The black help usually remained in the employment of the Ervin family for years at a time; a few stayed with them for most of their lives. Sam especially remembered Betty Powell, the tall cook who ran the kitchen as her personal kingdom. Her daughter, Polly, inherited the job when her mother died and continued to rule the Ervin kitchen for another fifty years. One summer afternoon a very agitated Polly blamed the growing number of ants in the kitchen on "Mr. Sam." He had stolen some flour to sprinkle around anthills in the yard because he thought they were hungry. Evidently, Sam liked to imagine the ants carrying the food to little houses under the ground with miniature furniture and little frying pans. Another servant, an elderly black man whom Sam called "Uncle Settlemyre," cleaned the outhouse and the pigpen. Family members remembered Miles Tanner as the "old darky" who came to cut the firewood during cold weather.[32]

The Ervins considered these servants as friends and even referred to them as unofficial members of the family, although both blacks and whites carefully followed the intricate social strictures of the Jim Crow South. Sam Ervin grew up believing that this racially determined world was the natural order of things and that the folks on both sides of the color line were equally comfortable with its restrictions. He later insisted that during his childhood "Negro discontent was not noticeable in Morganton."[33]

Every Sunday morning the whole Ervin family spruced up and went to church. Sam's father looked as he did every other day in his black suit with the cutaway tails, but the children had to clean up, dress up, and pass their mother's inspection before heading off to morning services. The First Presbyterian

Church in Morganton had a well-to-do congregation that included bankers, lawyers, and many of the town's merchants. Sam's father served as an elder for over a third of a century, and the rest of the family was active as well.[34]

As in most southern churches, a male minister conducted the service and an all-male session determined policy, but it was the women who ran the church. In a society that limited public roles for women, the church provided opportunities for expression, leadership, and the pursuit of issues that mattered to them. The Ervins' church hosted several very active missionary societies that reflected the deep paternalism rooted in both Christian doctrine and southern society. Women raised funds and volunteered to bring salvation and uplift to the "foreigners," the "Negroes in the South," the mountain people, the Indians, and the "fatherless ones" at the Barium Springs Orphanage. There was even some outreach to "the Colored Women's Conference" for joint projects in the region. Mother Ervin served as the treasurer of the Ladies' Aid Society for some time at the turn of the century, but as her daughter Catharine later recorded in her booklet "The History of Women's Work," published in the 1930s, the fact that all the Society's records "are in the handwriting of Mr. Ervin may be an indication of the status of women at that time."[35]

During one particularly hot summer, Miss Laura convinced her husband that his regular black suit was far too warm for the season and that she was going to purchase a fashionable grey Palm Beach suit for him to wear. Soon it arrived and she persuaded him to wear it that Sunday to church. As the service began the whole family sat in their normal pew, the fourth from the front, but their father's space was empty. Not until the congregation stood for the first hymn did he sneak down to his seat, and he slipped out just as they stood to sing the last hymn. When the family arrived home, Samuel Sr. was seated in the swing on the front porch, wearing his old Prince Albert suit. "I have never felt so conspicuous in my entire life," he snapped. "I don't know which of you boys can wear that suit, but I will never wear it again." And he never did.[36]

Sam Jr. described his boyhood as "a carefree time, a very happy time." He spent his days doing chores, playing baseball, swimming with friends in the nearby Catawba River, playing hide-and-seek in the Presbyterian Church, and reading books on the front porch in summer or by the fireplace in winter. "Those were great days, really," Ervin recalled. "You had time to live."[37]

Those who knew Sam as a boy described him as being somewhat shy but good-natured and a bit of a prankster. Jean remembered that "even at a very young age Sam saw the funny side of things and knew what would provoke laughter in his contemporaries." Gladys Tillet, who grew up playing with the Ervin children in Morganton, recalled: "He was the sort of person you liked

A summer outing in 1916. Sam is lying under the running board looking up at Margaret Bell, who is perched on the rear fender. Two of his sisters are in the picture: Catharine is sitting behind the wheel and Laura is behind the front hood. Sam Ervin Library and Museum, Western Piedmont Community College, Morganton, North Carolina.

very much because he had those qualities of a young person coming along. He was always serious but humorous. He was a very well-mannered person, very devoted to his mother. I think of him as always in a good humor."[38]

Sam also had a reputation for being able to close out the world around him when he was engaged in one of his own projects, be it reading, writing, or drawing. He spent a lot of time alone, so engrossed in his own work that friends, family, and servants could come into the room, even clean around his feet, and he would not notice. As a child he drew and cut out a whole baseball team of rabbits in full uniform. He made detailed paper soldiers for reenacting the Civil War and a whole flotilla of little ships with sailors to play out adventures on the high seas. Sam was also an avid reader. He even read books while walking his little sister Eunice to school. She complained that it took forever because her brother would get so engrossed in his reading that he would just stop and stand with his head in the book until she nudged him forward. She claimed that on several occasions she had to stop him from walking into the street in front of wagons or carriages.[39]

In both appearance and temperament Sam resembled his grandfather more than his father. John Witherspoon Ervin was tall, lean, sensitive, and scholarly, while Samuel Ervin Sr. was of average height, very formal, and more practically oriented. Although Sam was only five when his grandfather died, the old man nevertheless had a profound impact on the boy. He spent hours tutoring his grandson and taught him to read by the age of four. "I don't remember so much his teaching," Sam recalled, "but when I didn't learn right quick he'd thump me on the head with his finger and say, 'Mighty thick, mighty thick.' "[40] A more important legacy, however, was the connection his paternal grandfather provided to the Ervin family's past—back through Reconstruction, the Civil War, the American Revolution, to the misty legends of his Scotch-Irish ancestors.

Sam Ervin loved history. As a boy he absorbed the stories passed down to him from his grandfather and father. In school he excelled in the study of history and in college he won awards for essays he published about his family's heritage. As an adult, one of the senator's favorite distractions from his work in Washington was visiting Civil War battlefields. In retirement, Ervin dedicated hours to genealogy and studying Ervin family history. Writing during the height of Watergate, Paul Clancy, Ervin's first biographer, suggested that "the study of family history is not just a hobby with men like Ervin. It is more like a passion. It places them in time. It gives them a fix on themselves in man's long journey through history and whispers to them that theirs is a noble tradition."[41]

For southerners, especially of Ervin's generation, the obsession with history was especially profound. Having inherited from their fathers and grandfathers the sting of defeat in the Civil War and the humiliation of occupation during Reconstruction, the southern men of the twentieth century then endured a lifetime of condemnation from the rest of the nation for their rigidly segregated society. Eventually they, too, faced defeat as the civil rights revolution overwhelmed their defenses, reformed their society, and dismissed them as mere racists. As the scholar Fred Hobson has explained, this unique historical experience has created in southerners a need to "tell about the South," in order "to explain, to justify, to defend, or to affirm" themselves and their southernness. Some followed the lead of William Faulkner into literature; others turned to scholarship, like W. J. Cash, who analyzed "the mind of the South"; still others wrote polemics or poetry. Sam Ervin studied history, especially the themes of patriotic duty, Presbyterianism, and the principled defense of constitutional law that dominated his family's self-perception and tradition.[42]

Sam was descended from Scottish Presbyterians who left Scotland in the late seventeenth century, settled in Northern Ireland for a generation, and then migrated to Williamsburg County, South Carolina, in 1732. Having been persecuted for their religion and mistreated by the English crown, these Scotch-Irish settlers prided themselves on their independence of mind and stubborn adherence to principle. The Presbyterian faith, with its love of book learning, its deference to bedrock doctrines, its commitment to paternalism, and its strong individualism, had a profound impact on Senator Ervin's worldview, and even his personality. "It's like the old Scotch Presbyterian used to pray," the senator later explained. " 'Lord, grant me to be right, for as thou well knowest, right or wrong, I never change my mind.' "[43]

The men of the Ervin family, including Sam's great-great-grandfather Colonel John Ervin, fought with General Francis Marion's brigade against the British during the American Revolution. After the war Colonel Ervin built a successful plantation along the Pee Dee River and was listed in the census of 1790 as the owner of twenty-nine slaves. The colonel married well, taking for his bride Jane Witherspoon, a relative of Dr. John Witherspoon who was president of Princeton University and a signer of the Declaration of Independence. Colonel John Ervin's Bible was passed from generation to generation and became one of Sam Ervin's most treasured possessions. The words the colonel wrote in the back had special meaning to Sam. He copied them carefully and knew them by heart:

> Nowe, my children—I Adjure you. Hold to your Hearts always, your Grand & Glorious Heritage. Your forbears have Laid downe requisite Precepts for you to follow. May they be a Stimulus to laudable Ambition so you will make Worthy contributions to your Country, be a faithful Servant to your Church & add Renown & Splendour to the History of the Irvine Family.[44]

The Ervin clan continued to thrive in the antebellum years of the Old South. Colonel John Ervin and his wife had several children, including James Robert Ervin, who practiced law in Cheraw, South Carolina. James followed his father's admonition to be faithful to the church, serve his country, and bring renown to the family name. He remained an active Presbyterian, became a leader of the Union Party that opposed John C. Calhoun's doctrine of nullification in the 1830s, and became a well-respected lawyer in his community. James's son, John Witherspoon Ervin, Sam's grandfather, was born in Cheraw and became a successful newspaper publisher and teacher. Then came the Civil War, forcing Witherspoon and the rest of the Ervin family to abandon their unionism and enlist in the Confederate cause.[45]

The Civil War and Reconstruction brought pain and poverty to the members of the Ervin family who once counted themselves as proud members of the South's aristocracy. Witherspoon served in the home guard and fought in one of the last skirmishes of the war at Dingle's Mill, South Carolina. His youngest son, Samuel, the senator's father, was only ten years old but still found his way onto the battlefield. When a Union general passed through town burning the courthouse and the school buildings, the Confederate soldiers hid in the woods to avoid capture. Samuel managed to sneak out to the woods and bring his father and the other men some lunch by pretending to be picking berries. When he reached the Confederate soldiers he imitated a man's voice and said, "Surrender, you rebels." They pulled their pistols on him but laughed when they saw who he was. Ultimately the Yankees left South Carolina, Cheraw, and the Ervins desolate. Three of Witherspoon's sons had been wounded in the war. His income disappeared with the collapse of the state's economy. The few students who returned to school after the war had no money to pay for his teaching, so they offered to trade personal items such as family watches and other treasures, which Witherspoon could not bring himself to accept. He managed to scrape by for a few years by selling articles, poems, and stories to newspapers, tutoring, and winning a few cash awards from literary contests, but the family endured severe poverty.[46]

Witherspoon never recovered from the shock of defeat and the destruction of his former life. Reconstruction turned his world upside down. He had owned two slaves in 1860, but after the war the "Negroes" were voting, holding political office, and refusing to show him the social respect to which he had become accustomed. Yankee soldiers insulted Witherspoon's sensibilities by occupying the South "like a conquered province" and by protecting the former slaves while punishing the landowning elite. Frustrated, embittered, and exhausted, Witherspoon left South Carolina to accept a teaching position in Morganton. He moved his family to the little village near the North Carolina mountains in 1874. Near the end of his life, about the time he was teaching his grandson Sam how to read, Witherspoon slipped into insanity. He spent his last years muttering about the rape of the South and writing romantic poetry filled with nostalgia for the lost cause of the Confederacy. The conclusion to his poem "The Burial of Stonewall Jackson" seems to have been as much his own eulogy as it was a remembrance of the fallen Confederate general:

> Now rests thy cold form, where the mountains around
> Encircle like guardsmen that thrice hallowed ground
> Where the hopes of a people that fought to be free
> Are buried in silence and sadness with thee.[47]

Samuel Sr. shared his father's views of Yankee imperialism and Negro inferiority, but he responded to the crises of Reconstruction and poverty in a

Senator Ervin's grandfather, John Witherspoon Ervin (1823–1902). Sam Ervin Library and Museum, Western Piedmont Community College, Morganton, North Carolina.

very different manner. If the father's story resembled Margaret Mitchell's *Gone with the Wind*, the son's life seems more like a southern version of a Horatio Alger novel in which a boy's luck, pluck, and virtue took him from rags to riches. Samuel was a hardscrabble kid who grew up during the Civil War having to fish and hunt to put food on the table. After the war, although he was only eleven, he hired himself out to pick cotton with the former slaves. He worked from early morning until sunset when he carried the heavy satchel on his back to the barn so the landowner could weigh the cotton and give him a half cent a pound. Years later he told the story to his daughter Jean: "On Saturday I'd go home and give the money to my mother. I loved my mother. That is what distressed me about poverty."[48]

The rage toward Reconstruction burned just as hot in Samuel as it had in Witherspoon, but the boy found a way to harness the energy. He secretly started a book about his experiences during Reconstruction but never tried to publish it. Years later when his surprised children heard about the manuscript and asked what had happened to it, he explained: "I had a wife and children to [support] so I threw myself into the practice of my profession which I've enjoyed and I threw the book into the fire."[49]

Samuel Sr. also found an outlet in the Democratic Party, which he and many other southern men saw as the best vehicle to battle the impact of Reconstruction. He ran for office only once, barely losing the contest for the Democratic nomination for district judge, but he remained passionately active in local and state politics. His children joked that before the fire was lit in the morning, their father kept warm from the heat he generated while reading the newspapers. He frequently wrote letters to the editor under the pen name "LEX," the Latin word for law. He traveled around the county to inspire the electorate on behalf of the Democratic cause during elections, and he sometimes took his children along with him. According to their memories, their father's rhetoric followed the high road: the vindictive Yankees misused federal power to subjugate the South and now the Democrats must ensure limited government, states' rights, and constitutional protection of individual liberties. It was a conservative civil libertarian philosophy that Sam Jr. would inherit.[50]

But not all Democrats were as high-minded as the Ervins. In the heated political culture of the 1890s, the Democrats castigated the Republicans as vindictive carpetbaggers, traitorous scallywags, and ignorant Negroes. Since Burke County had a significant number of Republicans, many of them freedmen, local Democrats thought nothing of corrupting the process just a bit to ensure that proper southerners stayed in power. One infamous ex-Confederate Democrat named Captain Joe Mills controlled the voting box in a section of Burke County known as Brindletown. On election morning the captain always appeared on the scene with a brace of pistols and a few kegs of mountain dew, and proclaimed that everybody could vote to suit themselves because that was their privilege, but that nobody could drink any liquor at Brindletown that day unless he voted Democratic. It was a standing joke in the county that the Brindletown box always contained just one Republican vote, allowed, according to Captain Mills, for the appearance of a fair election.[51]

Things took a more violent turn in the white supremacy election of 1898. Red Shirt Brigades, a Klan-like vigilante group of Democrats, intimidated African Americans from voting across the state. In the most notorious event of that election, Red Shirts killed approximately sixty black citizens during a coup d'état in the so-called Wilmington Race Riot. In Morganton, Red Shirts gathered at several of the polling places. Shortly after the polls opened, a group of African American men came to vote carrying sticks and clubs. According to the Ervin family's oral tradition, Samuel Ervin went up to the leader of the group and told him that there was a man at the polls who had vowed to kill before he would let a Negro vote. "It is not I," he said, "but I know who it is." The African Americans stayed there all day, but they did not try to vote. The election of 1898 marked the turning point in the disenfranchisement of black North Carolinians, a process considered "progressive" by the white Democratic Party that ruled the state for the next half-century.[52]

Samuel Ervin Sr. was clearly a product of the Old South, but he was also a champion of the New South. The railroads that connected Morganton to the rest of the Piedmont after the Civil War brought new economic opportunities, and Sam's father did what he could to expand them. He served as a director of the Alpine Cotton Mills and as a member of the board of a local bank. He also became the assistant division counsel for Southern Railways, one of his most profitable ventures. Perhaps Ervin's most important contribution to the coming of the New South in Morganton was his effort to establish a modern graded school. Around the turn of the century North Carolinians built thousands of new public schools and filled them with professionally trained teachers whose job was to help the next generation transition from a plantation to a commercial economy. The apostles of the New South saw the classroom as a platform to preach the benefits of the modern world of industry and as a training ground for the habits of wage labor. They also hoped to use the graded schools as a means to discipline the children of both races into the emerging system of Jim Crow segregation. When the Morganton public school opened in 1903, Samuel Ervin Sr. became the first chairman of the board of education, and Sam Jr. enrolled in the first grade.[53]

The extensive curriculum Sam faced in his first year of school disproves the old myth that the early public schools taught only the "three Rs"—reading, writing, and arithmetic. Sam's elementary school teachers taught lessons on language, drawing, history, physiology, and geography. They also put a heavy emphasis on moral and religious training. By the time Sam reached the ninth grade he had learned hundreds of Bible stories in school. Religion came easily to him, as did history and literature. It was math that gave him trouble, and sometimes science. He also had a problem with talking too much during class, for which he was punished by having to stay after school and memorize poetry verses. In later life, the senator joked that his ability to recall poetry so easily was due to his frequent detentions. In more serious moments, however, he attributed his love of poetry and literature to his older sister Catharine, whose lovely reading of verse inspired him as child.[54]

Sam always had a quick wit and a keen sense of humor, which his teachers did not always appreciate. In high school the students were required to answer the morning roll call by reciting a passage from Scripture. One day Sam answered by quoting Psalms 119, verses 99–100: "I have more understanding than all my teachers." His classmates exploded in laughter, but the teacher was not amused and kept him after school. When Sam protested that he had quoted the Bible accurately, she responded that he was not being punished because of the verse, but because he had not quoted it with the proper reverence.[55]

For some reason that even Sam could not understand, he spent much of his teenage years dreaming of going to sea. As graduation drew closer, he approached his father about the possibility of going to the Naval Academy in

Annapolis. It must have been hard for Samuel Ervin to hear that his second eldest son did not wish to follow in his footsteps and study law. Edward, the oldest son, was too ill with complications from asthma to attend college. Joe, the next in line behind Sam, seemed interested in the law but his osteomyelitis remained a serious challenge. Whatever his feelings, Samuel Sr. gave his son the money to enroll in the Naval Academy Preparatory School in the spring of his final year of high school, which in 1913 ran though the eleventh grade. Sam went to Annapolis, but after several weeks of study he failed the math entrance examination. Disappointed, he returned to his classes in Morganton. The day after graduation he signed up for a job on a road construction crew. Working ten hours a day behind a mule in the Piedmont sun was a long way from the ocean breezes for which he had hoped. So Sam pursued his second educational option, the one that had long seemed to be his most likely destiny, and applied to the University of North Carolina. After a long, hot summer of labor he walked down to the Morganton railway station and boarded the train to Chapel Hill.[56]

A young man coming to the University of North Carolina in 1913 entered a world set apart. Chapel Hill was an isolated academic outpost in the middle of the rural Piedmont. The railroad line ended at University Station, a cluster of four or five buildings in the middle of nowhere, and then students rode a spur track to Carrboro before walking the final mile to Chapel Hill. The central thoroughfare, Franklin Street, had a small business district surrounded by stately homes set back behind ancient trees. The campus began across the street, but magnificent oaks and poplars blocked the view of the academic buildings. Brick sidewalks carried the students into the center of campus, a quadrangle of dormitories and classrooms set around the traditional symbol of the university, the "Old Well." Everywhere long stone walls surrounded gracious green lawns. In this place of intentional seclusion, a garden of trees and flowers, stone and brick, North Carolina crafted its chosen youth.[57]

At the opening ceremonies on College Night the students gathered in Gerrard Hall for their orientation into college life. Upperclassmen led in the cheering of college yells and singing of college songs. Student leaders took turns imploring the newcomers to join various clubs, societies, and fraternities. Ervin found himself surrounded by other boys like himself, bright, enthusiastic, and from the so-called better families of North Carolina. The university was still small in 1913; his class was the largest yet, 278 of a total student population of 850. It was a tradition that every student had to know the first names of all his classmates by Christmas. Academic life began when the new students visited the home of the professor who would serve as their academic adviser. These occasions served the dual purposes of inspiring and challenging the freshmen. It was a big jump from recitations in the classrooms of the local graded schools to formal conversations in the parlors of nationally recognized scholars. Indeed, the message of those first few days was very intimidating: study hard, for not everyone is going to make it at Carolina—only 57 percent from Ervin's class would graduate—and participate in college life as well. While all Carolina graduates would join the ranks of the well-connected, only a few would gain admission to the inner circle of potential state leaders.[58]

Ervin was a serious student who worked hard for his academic success. He earned As or Bs in most of his classes, except for Latin, German, and physics, which he barely passed. Given his experience at Annapolis, he committed himself to making an A on every math exam he took at Chapel Hill. Ervin also built a distinguished record of student leadership. He avoided the elite private fraternities, but joined the Dialectic Literary Society, the Sigma Upsilon literary fraternity, the Phi Delta Phi legal fraternity, and the International Polity Club. He also served as an assistant editor of the university magazine, vice president of his academic class, and vice president of his law class. During his senior year his classmates elected him as class historian and as permanent class president. They also awarded him the senior superlatives of "Best Egg" and "Most Popular," but his unofficial nickname was "Tobacco Sam" for his reputation as a champion tobacco spitter.[59]

For a while Ervin flirted with becoming an English or history professor, but in the end he was drawn to the study of law. He stayed at the university for four years, during which time he completed a bachelor of arts degree and the first year of law school. He loved Chapel Hill, and by all accounts the university community embraced him as well. According to his senior yearbook: "Everything he meets, responds, and at once a sympathetic friendship ensues. Like Midas, he has that magic touch which makes everyone he meets his friend; and consequently he is liked by all."[60] Ervin later told his sister Jean that there was no aspect of the rest of his life that did not have some connection with either the friends he made at Chapel Hill or the studies he pursued there.[61]

Ervin studied with some of the most respected members of the Carolina faculty, and they had a permanent impact on his developing worldview. Like most students, he had come to Carolina with a mix of ideas, beliefs, and prejudices, some inherited from his family and others formed from his boyhood experiences in Morganton. But these intellectual bits and pieces were not yet organized into a coherent philosophy. The professors at Chapel Hill helped Ervin clarify his ideas and give them expression. They also served as role models for the gentlemanly values of the time.

Years later, Senator Ervin returned to Chapel Hill and spoke about some of

Ervin, on left, and friends enjoy a smoke while studying together at Chapel Hill in 1915.
Sam Ervin Library and Museum, Western Piedmont Community College,
Morganton, North Carolina.

his favorite professors. His comments reflect both his high regard for their teaching and the impact they had on his life:

> George Howe and Wilbur Royster were unable to make a Latin scholar of me. They nevertheless stand out in my recollection, Howe as a man of gentility and Royster as a man of intellectual integrity.

> Collier Cobb was an authority in geology. While I have forgotten much of what he taught about the earth's structure, I remember and strive to practice daily the truth he exemplified so well, i.e., that a good sense of humor can convert our leaden hours into golden moments.

> Charles Lee Raper did not belong to the devastating school of economists who promise an "abundance for all by robbing selected Peter to pay collec-

Ervin's graduation picture and cartoon in the Yackety Yack, *1917. The cartoon makes fun of Sam's reputation as a tobacco chewer. Sam Ervin Library and Museum, Western Piedmont Community College, Morganton, North Carolina.*

tive Paul." On the contrary, he preached the economic truths that earth yields nothing to man except the products of his own labor.

Horace Williams undertook to persuade those who sat at his feet to employ their minds to test the soundness of all ideas, and to be willing to follow the truth they discovered by so doing, wherever it led them.

By revealing to me some of the beauty and wisdom in literature, Greenlaw, Booker, Hanford, and Forrester indelibly implanted in my mind this exhortation: Make books your friends, for by so doing you can summon to your fireside the choice spirits of all the ages.

Bacot, Hamilton, Wagstaff, and Pierson taught me that history affords the best guidance to those who engage in public affairs. . . . As my preceptor in North Carolina History, Hamilton convinced me that our state is the habitat of gallant souls; and as my preceptor in constitutional history, he persuaded me that one cannot understand the institutions of today unless he understands the events of yesterday which brought them into being.[62]

Two of those historians had special significance to Ervin. The first, J. G. De Roulhac Hamilton, reinforced the racial and civil libertarian views of Sam's father. Hamilton was the preeminent North Carolina historian of his generation and belonged to the southern apologist school that justified the vigilante violence of the Ku Klux Klan and the Red Shirts as legitimate responses to Reconstruction. He argued that the vindictive Yankee occupation of the South, and the vile Reconstruction Acts—which disenfranchised former Confederate leaders and enfranchised the former slaves—represented an insult to the good white people of the South who had no choice but to resist such oppression with any means necessary. Hamilton vigorously supported white supremacy and the Anglo-Saxon institutions of government that protected it. Ironically, Hamilton also taught that North Carolina enjoyed a reputation as one of the most liberty-loving states in the Union, at least for the white men who mattered. Indeed, to Hamilton, the very act of disenfranchising Negroes, whom he considered illiterate and uncivilized, was proof of the progressive spirit of North Carolina. He taught that the white supremacy campaigns sprang from the same libertarian tradition that had earlier inspired the state to refuse to ratify the U.S. Constitution until a Bill of Rights was promised to protect individual freedoms. This race-based libertarian interpretation of North Carolina history inspired young Sam and helped to shape his emerging worldview. Years later, Senator Ervin distanced himself from Hamilton's racist language, but he defended his former professor's interpretation of Reconstruction long after the historical profession dismissed it as errant and racist.[63]

The second historian, Daniel Huger Bacot, provided Ervin with one of his favorite memories of Chapel Hill. One Halloween night, some of Bacot's students led a cow into the lecture room and tied her to the corner of the professor's desk. Word of the prank traveled across the campus and the next morning Ervin and all his fellow students arrived early to watch the famously dour professor's reaction. Bacot entered the classroom, glanced over at the cow, and calmly remarked: "Young Gentlemen, I'm delighted to observe that the intellectual strength of my audience has increased so much since my last lecture." He proceeded to teach the class for an hour without another mention of the cow standing beside him quietly chewing her cud.[64]

No one at the university had a greater impact on Ervin than President Edward Kidder Graham. Tall, handsome, and dynamic, Graham exemplified everything for which the university stood—honor, idealism, and service, or in the words of the school motto, "*Lux Libertas*," Light and Liberty. Contemporaries described him as looking somewhat like Emerson or a younger version of the president of the United States at the time, Woodrow Wilson. A more recent account of Graham suggested that he had a "sort of spiritual power coming out of him so strongly that it could project itself through faded photos sixty years later with unmistakable authority."[65] President Graham frequently addressed the student body during the required morning chapel services. His dramatic speeches on democracy and freedom resonated with the tenor of the times as the Great War raged in Europe and anxious Americans debated whether they would someday be called upon to join the fight.[66]

One particular chapel talk resonated with Ervin and his friends for the rest of their lives. Graham was discussing the great moments in the development of constitutional government. He reviewed the Magna Carta, the Petition of Right, the Declaration of Independence, and the Bill of Rights. But the students became restless, having heard it all before, and began to shuffle in their seats. Graham suddenly stopped talking, freezing the startled students in his outraged stare. Then, with icy clarity he declared: "Young gentlemen, these are not empty phrases. Cut them and they bleed with the blood of those who fashioned them and those who have nurtured them through the succeeding generations."[67]

In the spring of 1917 Ervin was finishing his last semester at Chapel Hill when President Wilson declared war on Germany to make the world "safe for democracy." Graham addressed the student body the following day, suggesting that the war was a crusade larger than either the American or French Revolutions. According to Graham, it would lead to "permanent peace" and world unity: "Our larger task is peace; our immediate task is war!"[68] Carolina students enlisted by the hundreds. Sam's father suggested that he finish school and wait until he was called up, but a month before his graduation Sam enrolled in officer training school at Fort Oglethorpe, Georgia. The approximately 250 Carolina men in the camp took great pride in the fact that they outnumbered the contingents from all the other southern schools. They organized a UNC Oglethorpe Club, gave speeches about their "spirit of service to humanity, to Uncle Sam, and to democracy," and sang "I am a Tar Heel Bred" at night in answer to songs from the other college boys. Meanwhile, back in Chapel Hill, the university awarded Ervin and sixty-four of his classmates their diplomas in absentia, their empty seats draped in red, white, and blue American flags.[69]

After training at Fort Oglethorpe for several months, Ervin was commissioned as a second lieutenant and joined Company I, the 28th Infantry, First Division in France. In February 1918 the First Division, under the command of General John J. Pershing, took control of forward trenches across from the German lines near the village of Seicheprey. These were the first American troops assigned to the front lines in the war. Ervin commanded a platoon assigned to some of the worst conditions along the line. Day after day they hunkered down in deep trenches filled with water, vermin, mud, and snow. Ervin's feet froze to the bottom of his shoes, thawed out, cracked, bled, and froze again. Gas bombs exploded overhead, causing a mad scramble of men trying to put on gas masks before a mere whiff of the green vapor led to a most gruesome death. There was no place to lie down and sleep in the wet holes in the frozen ground. The men's spirits sank. The reality of trench warfare was a long way from the speeches and songs back home. To make matters worse, Ervin came down with the flu. It was no ordinary influenza but the so-called "Spanish flu" of 1918 that spread into one of the worst pandemics in modern history. Back in Chapel Hill, Edward Kidder Graham caught the same flu and died later that year.[70]

Ervin was only twenty-one years old and an inexperienced officer. He struggled to lead his men in the only way he knew how, by working harder, staying awake longer, and pushing himself further than anyone else. He made arrangements for a few of his men to take turns sleeping in a dry dugout a few hundred feet down the line, but he stayed at his post in order to set a good example. Then it all fell apart. One of the men Ervin had sent to get a good night's rest in the dugout became confused in the dark of the night. When a sentry challenged him, the soldier, who was not an American and had only a basic understanding of the English language, forgot the password and started speak-

Ervin in World War I uniform before leaving for Europe in 1917. Sam Ervin Library and Museum, Western Piedmont Community College, Morganton, North Carolina.

ing in his native tongue. The sentry thought the soldier was speaking German and shot him to death.[71]

Ervin heard the gunshots and mistakenly thought that an enemy attack had begun. He panicked, firing a signal flare to order a defensive artillery barrage. It took only a few minutes for Ervin to discover that there was no German attack, and that he had been partially responsible for the death of one of his own men. Exhausted and still sick, he put one of his noncommissioned soldiers in charge of the platoon, went to the dugout, and fell into a troubled sleep. The next morning the Army relieved Ervin of his command and reassigned him to a secretarial post away from the front. Even worse, Ervin discovered that he might be court-martialed for abandoning his post in the face of the enemy. Tested by war, Sam Ervin had failed. He begged his superiors to let him return to the front to prove himself, but they refused. Finally he negotiated a deal with his commanding officer, Colonel H. E. Ely. Ervin agreed to resign his commission as a Second Lieutenant and accept an honorable discharge for inefficiency and then reenlist as a private in his old platoon.[72]

Ervin felt a shame so deep that he decided not to tell anyone back home what had happened. He only told his family that he had been transferred to a desk job and had reenlisted as a private in order to get the chance to fight the enemy face to face, which was technically true. He did not, however, tell them about his failure of leadership or the possible court-martial. Ervin kept this secret for most of the rest of his life. He repeated the same incomplete story to reporters and to his first biographer, and even included it in his official Senate record. When the truth slipped out in 1976, two years after he retired from the Senate, Ervin finally admitted his deception and set the record straight in his autobiography.[73]

It is difficult to understand why Ervin was so ashamed for so long, especially given what happened a few days later when he returned to the front. Perhaps his desperate sense of embarrassment and a burning need to redeem himself help to explain the heroism he displayed over the next several months. Only two days after returning to his old outfit as a private, Ervin "went over the top" in the battle of Cantigny, the first battle fought by Americans in World War I. He was assigned to a "carrying party" moving ammunition and barbed wire from the rear into the heart of the battle. During several trips back and forth Ervin came under intense enemy fire. At one point German artillery shells rained down so heavily that he had to take cover in a hole with several engineers who were trying to set up barbed wire fences. An American was hit just a few feet away and Ervin crawled forward to try to help him. A shell flew over his head and landed in the hole he had just left, killing all the engineers.[74]

As Ervin turned back toward his own lines, machine gun fire sprayed through the field of tall grass he was crossing. Down below him he saw an injured German soldier with a broken arm. Ervin tried to make a splint for the wounded man, but as he knelt down an enemy bullet pierced his foot. His boot quickly filled with blood, and the German shouted, "Wir sind verdammte Schweine" (we are damn swine) in apology. Ervin hobbled back to an aid station, where he later learned that the Americans had successfully defended the town of Cantigny from the German counterattack. After the war the Army awarded Ervin the Silver Star for his "courage and perseverance" under fire.[75]

Ervin spent several weeks in the hospital before returning to his company. His timing could not have been worse. Just days later the First Division of the 28th Infantry Division led the charge in the horrific battle of the Soissons. It was a turning point in the war, stopping the last German offensive, but victory came at a terrible price. On 18 July 1918, Ervin's company entered the battle with about 180 men. Five days later only 38 remained alive and unwounded.[76]

During the initial American attack, Ervin's platoon leader was killed when a shell landed behind him, igniting the signal flares in his pack. The man was cut into pieces by the exploding rockets. Private Ervin was given command of the platoon and led them forward into battle. After fighting through a swamp in which Ervin lost both his leggings, the platoon fell under heavy fire from a German machine gun nest that was threatening to mow down the American troops up and down the line. Ervin hit the ground and waited, but no one else was in a position to take out the German gun. He called for volunteers and led the attack himself.[77]

Ervin and four other men jumped up and ran straight toward the machine gun in a 100-yard suicide sprint. First one of his men was hit, then a second. Both men died instantly. Ervin fired his automatic rifle, killing one of the Germans. Seconds later he felt a weight hit his upper leg as he was smashed into the ground just short of the machine gun. Shell fragments had cut through his ammunition case and tore deep into his bone. The two remaining men reached the embankment and killed the gunners. They rushed back to Ervin, bandaged his wounds as best they could, and tried to carry him back to their platoon. But realizing that the three of them would be a clear target, Ervin ordered the men to go on. He crawled into an abandoned trench just before a French tank rolled over the top of the ditch. Just seconds later a shell hit and destroyed the tank.[78]

Ervin worked his way along the trench toward an American platoon that had just taken out another German position. Leaning on his rifle for support he limped up to the officer in charge. For a second neither man recognized the other, but Ervin had stumbled upon one of his classmates from Chapel Hill,

Samuel I. Parker. The two organized the fortification before Parker ordered Ervin back to the rear. Weakened from loss of blood, he only hobbled a little way before falling into a trench next to several corpses. Unable to go on, he drifted into unconsciousness. The next day a French civilian found Ervin and helped him back to a farm house, where he received some basic medical attention and drank a great deal of wine. For Ervin, the war was over. After several terribly painful days, an ambulance took him to a hospital where doctors removed the shell fragment from his bone marrow. He spent months moving from one hospital to another fighting a series of infections in his leg.[79]

Back in Morganton his family was in a state of panic. They had followed Sam's movements as best they could by reading the *New York Times* each morning and marking his battalion's position with pins on a large map. The only information they could get about him came when the post office delivered one of his infrequent letters. At first his notes were reassuring and filled with the patriotism of a new recruit: "I am . . . forgetting the little bit of law I once knew and shall have to begin all over, when Pershing and I have taught Kaiser Bill that the world doesn't desire to be 'civilized.' "[80] But soon after the battle of Cantigny they received a letter with a different tone. In a note to his mother on Mother's Day Ervin wrote: "The events of the past twelve months have given me a far deeper insight into the true significance of things than I ever possessed before. And my hope and prayer is that I may be spared to come back in honor and safety in order that I may repay a small part of the great debt that I owe to you."[81]

After the battle of Soissons the family learned of Sam's injury, but for months the letters they sent to the hospital were returned with a note saying the recipient could not be found. Finally, word came in February 1919 that he had been moved to another medical facility and would soon be shipped home to the States. "He is not bedfast but is able to be up and around, and is as well as could be expected under the conditions," the letter explained. The words were not very reassuring to his worried mother and father.[82]

Ervin returned to Morganton a few months later. His youngest sister, Jean, ran all the way from her fourth grade classroom to welcome her big brother home. She remembers him climbing stiffly out of the car dressed in his military uniform. He walked with a limp and seemed much thinner than she remembered. He let her play with the heavy helmet he carried under his arm and she found an old piece of dried chocolate smashed up under the leather band. When the family explained how worried they had been when their letters were returned, Ervin joked: "I knew where I was all the time."[83]

But his behavior over the next few months suggested that he had been, and still was, more lost than he would admit. Ervin was no longer as sure of himself

Ervin's mother standing on the front porch during World War I under a flag with one star signifying that one son, Sam, is serving in the military. Courtesy of Jean Ervin, Picture Burke Photographic Collection, Burke County Library.

and his place in the world as he had been back in Chapel Hill before the war. Jean noticed that her brother smoked a lot, at least two packs of cigarettes a day. She caught glimpses of him up late at night, unable to sleep. He seemed nervous and fidgety. He would not talk about the war and only answered his father's frequent questions with vague responses. Thus everyone in Morganton was very surprised when years later, in 1932, the testimony of his former classmate and fellow soldier Samuel Parker convinced the War Department to award Ervin the Distinguished Service Cross for his heroic conduct at Soissons. The official recommendation came from General Hanson E. Ely, who fourteen years earlier had been the colonel who dismissed Lieutenant Ervin and then allowed him to reenlist as a private. Of course no one but Ervin understood the significance of that secret fact. All anyone in Morganton knew right after the war was that "Little Sam" was home safe, but that he needed some time to find himself again.[84]

CHAPTER TWO

JUST A COUNTRY LAWYER

During the Watergate hearings of 1973, when Republican senator Edward Gurney, the most pro-Nixon member of the committee, complained about Ervin's "harassment" of a witness, Senator Ervin paused for a moment and then, in his most pronounced good-ol'-boy southern accent, replied: "Well, I'm sorry that my distinguished friend from Florida doesn't approve of my method of examining the witness. I'm just an old country lawyer and I don't know the finer ways to do it. I just have to do it my way." The audience burst into laughter and applauded, just as Ervin knew they would.[1]

Not long afterward Senator Howard Baker, a Republican from Tennessee, responded to yet another of Ervin's country lawyer lines by kidding his colleague about his supposedly humble legal background. Baker reminded the audience that the chairman of the committee had graduated from Harvard Law School with honors. Ervin defended himself with a story: "I had a friend introduce me to a North Carolina audience. He said he understood I was a graduate of Harvard Law School, but thank God no one would ever suspect it."[2]

Indeed, Sam Ervin had been a country lawyer, and he also attended Harvard, although if it had not been for his older sister Catharine he might have never earned his law degree. As a young man Ervin respected his father, idolized his mother, and cared deeply for all nine of his sisters and brothers, but he seemed to hold a special spot in his heart for Catharine, or "Cat" as she was called at home. Cat had helped him write his first letter to his father, and she was the one who inspired his love of poetry by reading verse to him in his childhood. After the war, when Ervin temporarily lost his footing and struggled to get his life back on track, it was Cat who made the suggestion that helped him find the path back to physical and mental health—she urged him to go to law school.[3]

Everyone else in the family seemed to think that Little Sam should start practicing law with his father right away. Sam Sr. actually invited his son to join his law practice just one day after he returned from France. He had already finished the equivalent of one year of law school before the war, and all he needed to become a lawyer was to pass the bar exam. Ervin returned to Chapel Hill in the summer of 1919 for a legal refresher course and he passed the bar on the first try later that year. But Catharine sensed that her brother was not ready to settle down yet. She thought that he needed a little more time before diving into the family business. So one day when they were alone in the living room of the old house she challenged him to consider getting away for a while. "Why don't you go to Harvard?" she suggested. Ervin was taken by surprise. "What for?" he asked. "Because it's the best law school in the country," Cat insisted. "Because it will help you grow. Because it will be worthwhile for its own sake."[4] The idea intrigued Ervin. Some of his former classmates from Chapel Hill were already making plans to study at Harvard. They included one of his best friends, Floyd Crouse, who later served with Ervin in the state legislature; Thomas Wolfe, the famous author from Asheville, who was neither close to Ervin nor often in agreement with him; and Albert Coates, who became Ervin's lifelong friend and a Chapel Hill legend as the founder and director of the UNC Institute of Government. Ervin could take some time, study, lose himself in the things he loved the most—books, ideas, libraries, and, most important, the law.[5]

But there was one problem. Sam had met Margaret Bell before the war, in 1916, when she visited her uncle in Morganton. At that time Margaret was sixteen years old, four years younger than Sam, and lived in Concord, North Carolina. Sam was walking down the street when she passed by in an open car. He recalled being smitten immediately. They talked at a party a few days later and began to date during his senior year at Chapel Hill. Sam had planned to take her to his commencement ball when the war intervened. He wrote her often from France and they resumed dating as soon as he returned home. Sam knew he wanted to marry her, but she was still attending Converse College in South Carolina and he did not have enough money to support her in Boston.[6]

After talking it over with Margaret, he decided to attend Harvard for only one year and then propose to her when he returned. He did not need a law degree, having already passed the bar exam, so he went to Boston and enrolled in all the best classes, those usually taken by students in their third year. But

Margaret Bell, later Mrs. Sam Ervin, at age seventeen. Sam Ervin Library and Museum, Western Piedmont Community College, Morganton, North Carolina.

Sam discovered that he loved his studies almost as much as he loved Margaret. After getting her assurance that she would not commit to any of his rivals for yet another year, Sam returned to Harvard and took the second-year classes. The following year Sam managed to get Margaret's permission to finish his degree at Harvard, so he completed the first-year courses and passed his final examinations in 1922.[7]

Years later, in 1954, Erwin Griswold, the dean of Harvard Law School, read in a *New York Times* story that the new senator from North Carolina claimed that he did not know many of his classmates at Harvard because they had traveled through the law school in one direction while he had traveled through it in another. At first Griswold refused to believe the story, but after checking the records himself the dean confirmed that Ervin was indeed the only man in the history of Harvard Law School to go through it backward. For the next twenty years Senator Ervin's critics joked that his view of the Constitution was as backward as his legal education.[8]

Not much is known about Ervin's years at Harvard. He studied very hard and did not go out often, except to an occasional dance sponsored by The Southern Club of Harvard, to which he belonged. He spent most of his free time with fellow southerners, a small minority of Confederate sympathizers surrounded by Unionist Yankees. They took most of their meals together with other law students in Memorial Hall. One of Ervin's favorite stories from Harvard concerned a Massachusetts classmate who brought a guest to lunch one day. The law student explained to his guest that Memorial Hall had been built to honor the Harvard men who had died in the Civil War. One of the southerners at the table corrected him: "You're wrong," he said. "It's a monument to the accuracy of Southern marksmanship."[9]

In the early 1920s Harvard was generally considered to offer the best legal education in the country. The weighty ambiance of the law school was made famous by one of Ervin's professors, Edward "Bull" Warren, who would open the first day of his class by instructing his students to look first at their classmate on the right, and then at their classmate on the left. "One of the three of you won't be back because of poor grades," he would warn. Ervin remembered that some of his fellow veterans from World War I, men who had faced enemy gunfire without flinching, would retreat from the classroom before facing Warren's harsh sarcasm if they did not know the correct answer to a question. On one occasion Professor Warren interrogated a student by repeating the facts of a case, summarizing the court's rulings, and then asking the terrified student if the ruling was correct. "I can conceive of the court making that ruling," the student answered. Warren presented the student with two more cases and each time the student stammered, "I can conceive of the court making that ruling." Finally Warren snapped, "You have conceived three times and have not given birth to a single thought!"[10]

In spite of the hard work, or maybe because of it, Ervin enjoyed his time in law school and profited from it greatly. The long hours of solitude served as a balm for his troubled spirit. He emerged from Harvard healed from his wounds of war, both physically and emotionally. Ervin also regained his intellectual footing. Before the war he had woven together a life philosophy from the reinforcing threads of his inherited identity, boyhood experiences, and the education and socialization he received at Chapel Hill. But the war challenged his naive idealism, leaving him shaken and unsure. At Harvard his legal training provided Ervin with more than just a mastery of case law; it gave him an opportunity to rebuild and expand his frayed worldview.

The Harvard law professors introduced Ervin to a more coherent legal theory, one that reinforced his political, religious, and cultural presumptions. They insisted that the law was certain, that legal truth was obtainable, and that only errant lawyers and activist judges could destroy its clarity. Ervin embraced their teachings, which he summarized by quoting the aphorism of Justice Oliver Wendell Holmes: "The life of the law has not been logic; it has been experience." In other words, the law has not been based on the weak rationalizations of men and women who cannot help but to fall victim to their own flawed biases. Instead, lawyers and judges have followed the legal precedents and sound judicial rulings of the past upon which good government and justice have historically depended. Such a legal philosophy fit perfectly with Ervin's conservative worldview. And, more important, it allowed him to live in a clean world of abstraction and theory instead of the messy world of flawed humanity and confused realities.[11]

Harvard also had a profound impact on Ervin's libertarian principles. He already had strong opinions about the importance of protecting individual freedom from overzealous government, at least from a southern perspective. First his father and then the professors at Chapel Hill had made sure that he understood the lessons of Reconstruction when the federal government supposedly destroyed the white man's civil liberties through occupation and suppression. But in law school Ervin studied with renowned civil libertarians such as Roscoe Pound and Zechariah Chafe Jr. Both men wrote and taught in response to the many repressions of freedom that occurred in the United States during World War I and the 1920s, including the sedition laws, the Red Scare, the Palmer raids, and the Sacco and Vanzetti trial. Ervin read Pound's *The Development of Constitutional Guarantees of Liberty*, and later Chafe's classic

The Freedom of Speech. These law professors reintroduced him to the writings of the founding fathers and had him study the great libertarian justices of the Supreme Court and influential contemporary judges such as Learned Hand. By the time Ervin left Harvard, he had expanded his view of civil liberties and formed a systematic legal and constitutional ideology that would guide him throughout the rest of his life.[12]

Ervin returned home to Morganton in 1922. There was much to do. First he set up his law practice. He moved his books into a room that his father built onto his own little law office right across the street from the Burke County Courthouse. His father did not approve of Sam's installation of a telephone, a contraption that the elder Ervin did not trust and seldom used. Next came his political duty. While Ervin was still finishing up at Harvard the Burke County Democratic Party had nominated him to run for the state legislature, without his knowledge or permission. He accepted the challenge and began a canvass of his district to try to reverse the Republican victories of recent years. That November he won by a comfortable margin.[13]

Of course, Ervin also had some unfinished business with Margaret Bell. He went down to Concord with a five-pound Whitman's Sampler and a book of Kipling's poetry to propose to his one and only sweetheart. Margaret did not give Sam a clear yes or no answer. Instead, she suggested a private arrangement by which they would continue to date with the understanding that they would probably get married someday. Margaret had started teaching school and she was just not yet ready to move to Morganton and settle into being a full-time wife. He agreed—he did not have much choice—and for the next two years he rode the train back and forth to Concord until she accepted his proposal.[14]

In June 1924, they had a large wedding in the Concord Presbyterian Church. Over three hundred people attended, but Ervin's father stayed home in Morganton. He did not like weddings, or funerals, and would attend neither. After a brief honeymoon in Yellowstone National Park—they traveled on the train with free tickets provided by Southern Railways, one of Sam Sr.'s biggest clients —Sam and Margaret settled into their life in Morganton. Sam's father gave the couple the deed to the lot next to the Ervin homestead and the newlyweds built a comfortable one-story brick house that would be their home for the next sixty years.[15]

Ervin's law practice grew quickly, in part because of his father's caseload and in part because of his own initiative. Dick Michaux, Morganton's sheriff and one of Ervin's close friends, referred many of the folks he arrested to Little Sam for legal advice. Ervin defended everyone from moonshiners to petty thieves. He lost his first case, which concerned a lien placed on stacks of fodder in a corn field. His client was so poor that Ervin even paid the court costs for him. But soon he was winning more cases than he lost. Two years later, just after he got married in 1924, he had gained so many clients that on one occasion the Superior Court had to suspend its docket for a few days because Ervin was out of town on business.[16]

The two Ervins practiced law with distinctly different styles. Sam Sr. belonged to the old school of southern lawyers who argued cases with an eloquence and style aimed at impressing the jury as much as convincing it. Sam Jr. represented a new generation that was generally better trained than their predecessors and less dependent on colorful oratory. The elder Ervin won cases by overwhelming his opponents with his diligent preparation and knowledge of the law. His son excelled at legal argumentation. In the courtroom, like a man wielding a rapier instead of a broadsword, he liked to prick his opponents into confusion. As one newspaper explained: "He could raise a question with damaging implications before the half-dozen opposing attorneys could leap to their feet to voice an objection."[17]

The father and son had very different personalities as well. Sam Sr. did not laugh readily or share his son's warmth and sense of humor. Little Sam was fun-loving and, as one of his contemporaries suggested, "as easy as an old shoe."[18] Even as a young man, he liked to embellish his arguments with homespun stories. Sometimes his quick mind would get ahead of his words and he stumbled over his sentences. But instead of being a handicap, this awkwardness gave him a humble and unpretentious appearance that tended to endear him to people. Sam's father once confided to one of his daughters, "I have the respect of people; my son has their love."[19]

As different as they were, the elder Ervin clearly helped to shape Sam's views about the role of a lawyer. Little Sam held a deep respect for his father's professional integrity and work ethic. When they first began to practice law together, Sam Sr. advised his son that most lawsuits were not won in the courtroom but by careful preparatory work before the trial began. He insisted that they research every detail of a case before preparing the legal strategy, or as he liked to say: "Salt down the facts; the law will keep."[20] He also encouraged Sam to read the old standard law books, such as William Blackstone's *Commentaries on the Laws of England*. Senator Ervin later suspected that he was one of the few lawyers of his generation who read this work in its entirety. Both men agreed with Alexis de Tocqueville's observation that "the lawyer who knows law, serves his clients loyally, and maintains his own integrity can justly claim to be a member of 'the only aristocracy' which has a rightful place in a democracy."[21]

But Sam Ervin was no elitist. He was a true country lawyer. He represented all kinds of clients—rich and poor, black and white—in all kinds of cases, in all kinds of courts, all across western North Carolina. Ervin practiced law before the era of the legal specialist. One of his fellow lawyers later explained that "to make a living practicing law in those days in a small town you took what came in and made a specialty of the client's particular problem by going to the books and probing for an answer."[22] Being a country lawyer also meant a lot of travel. Ervin and the other attorneys would move from courthouse to courthouse, sometimes staying in the same hotel or boarding house for days at a time. They would match wits during the day and share dinner, drinks, and stories at night. Ervin had a reputation for being very partisan during a trial but, as one of his former adversaries remembered, "after it was [over], things quieted down, everything was all right again."[23]

Many of the cracker-barrel stories that Senator Ervin shared during his political career came from his days as a traveling country lawyer. One of his favorites was about an old mountain woman who came into his law office in Morganton to ask for some legal advice. He did some quick research, gave his advice, and asked that she pay a fee of five dollars. The woman turned to leave and said, "I ain't a-going to pay it." Ervin pointed out that she had asked for his legal advice and that he had given it to her. But the mountain woman retorted, "Yeah, but I ain't a-gonna take it," and walked out.[24]

Ervin also liked to tell the story about two neighbors down home in North Carolina who owned adjoining farms and had a dispute over a boundary line. One farmer told the other, "If you do not concede that the boundary line between your farm and mine runs where I say it runs, I am going to sue you in the superior court." The other farmer said, "That's all right; I'll be there when the case is tried." The first farmer retorted: "If I don't win that case in superior court, I will appeal it to the Supreme Court of North Carolina." But his neighbor answered, "That will be all right; I will be there when the appeal is heard." Then the would-be plaintiff said, "And if I don't win in the Supreme Court of North Carolina I will appeal it up to the Supreme Court of the United States." The prospective defendant said, "That will be all right; I'll be there when that appeal is heard, too." Exasperated, the first farmer yelled, "And if I don't win in the Supreme Court of the U.S. I'll take it right straight to hell." His neighbor calmly answered, "I'll not be there, but my lawyer will."[25]

A lot of Ervin's stories came from humorous moments in the courtroom. He remembered one occasion when a Burke County resident named Joshua Hawkins was charged with operating an illegal distillery. When the judge called his case, he noted Mr. Hawkins's first name and in an attempt to add a little levity to the hearing asked, "Are you the Joshua the Bible tells us about who made the sun stand still in Jericho?" "No, Your Honor," Hawkins responded. "I'm the Joshua who's accused of making the moonshine in Burke."[26]

Some of Ervin's own quick comebacks became famous around the Burke County courthouse. During a trial he asked a stubborn witness a question and demanded: "Answer it yes or no." Not hearing any response, he thundered, "Answer the question!" "I did," grunted the mountaineer; "I nodded my head." Ervin, who had looked away for a second, snapped: "Yes, I heard it rattle, but I couldn't tell if it moved up and down or sideways."[27] Fellow attorney J. Braxton Craven Jr. recalled another example of Ervin's sharp wit. Craven was opposing him in a trial and sat silently as Ervin carried a witness through a series of questions. When Craven rose and began to cross-examine the witness with the same line of questioning, he was surprised when Ervin rose to object. He was so dismayed that he broke courtroom etiquette and addressed Ervin directly rather than speaking to the court. "My questions are not different than yours," he complained. "There is one difference," Ervin shot back. "You didn't object, and I do."[28]

One of Ervin's most awkward moments came during a legal dispute over Clara Fleming's will. Fleming, an elderly African American woman, had just passed away and some disappointed members of her family were contesting her will on the grounds that she had not been mentally capable when she wrote it. Ervin decided to call Betty Powell, his family's former cook, as a character witness. Since Powell had known the deceased, and since she was one of the most respected members of the black community, Ervin called her to testify that the old woman had been of sound mind. When Powell took the stand Ervin followed proper courtroom procedure and asked, "Will you please tell his honor and the jury what your name is?" Powell, looking disgusted, answered, "Look here, Mr. Sam, don't be asking me no fool questions like that. You know my name as well as you do your own."[29]

Of course, not all of Ervin's experiences in the courtroom were so humorous. There was a serious side to the law, sometimes deadly serious. Ervin hated murder cases. He disliked defending accused murderers because of the pressure to save a life, and he disliked prosecuting accused murderers because of his discomfort with taking a life. To his regret, Ervin participated in the only two capital murder cases in Burke County during his lifetime that led to the defendants being put to death.

In 1926 Arthur Montague, a black construction worker from Georgia, broke into the infirmary of the North Carolina School for the Deaf in Morganton and raped a twelve-year-old white girl. The court appointed Sam and his father to assist several other local attorneys in defending Montague. It was an open and shut case and the jury sentenced Montague to death. Racial tension filled the town and the courthouse. One juror later reported that during their deliberations, when one person jokingly asked if there was any chance of a hung jury, another juror responded, "If we go out there and say not guilty, we'll be a hung jury."[30] Although his client's guilt was obvious, Ervin appealed the case to the State Supreme Court just to be sure that everything had been done that could be done, for which he received a good deal of criticism back home in Morganton. He paid the expenses for the appeal out of his own pocket. The sentence was upheld and Montague went to the electric chair.[31]

A second murder case involved a black man named LeRoy Jackson who broke into the house of an elderly white couple to steal their valuables and ended up killing the husband. Escaping to his home, Jackson tried to burn the property he had stolen in order to conceal his guilt, but a metal rosary survived the fire and tied him to the crime. The court retained Ervin to assist with the prosecution and he successfully got a guilty verdict and a death sentence. This case, too, was appealed to the North Carolina Supreme Court, where it was also upheld. Chief Justice Walter P. Stacy, who wrote the court's opinion, later told Ervin that the Jackson case was the most thoroughly prepared and prosecuted murder case he had ever dealt with during his long service on the state's highest court.[32]

Being involved in murder cases could lead a lawyer into dangerous situations, and Ervin experienced one particularly scary incident after being assigned to help the prosecutor send a mountaineer named Beau Franklin to the penitentiary on a manslaughter charge. Several years later Ervin was driving by himself along an isolated country road near the mountain community of Jonas Ridge when he came on Franklin standing next to the road, waving at him to stop. Beau, who had just recently been released from prison, had a reputation as a very dangerous good ol' boy, especially when he had been drinking. Ervin pulled over, and Franklin asked him to come down to his house so that he could show him something. Ervin followed him to the back of the house where Franklin showed a very relieved Ervin a litter of fox cubs he had just found in the woods. A few years later Franklin was again charged with murder and asked Ervin to defend him. Protesting that he was innocent Franklin pleaded, "You sent me to prison last time; I want you to keep me out this time." Ervin won the case on a hung jury and Franklin went free. Later Ervin heard that on his deathbed Franklin had confessed to killing the man.[33]

While Ervin spent long hours at his office and countless days away from home, Margaret went about her traditional duties running the house and raising their growing family. Samuel Ervin III was born a little over a year after they were married, Leslie came along four years later in 1930, and Laura arrived in 1934. When Margaret and Sam were first married she had thought that he was more worldly than he turned out to be. She had expected that they would go out more and have more fun. But Margaret soon discovered that Sam was a homebody. He worked very hard and retained his amazing powers of concentration from childhood. Even children playing in the same room would not distract him. Early on Margaret began to suspect that he would accomplish great things, and she determined to support him no matter where it would lead them. Eunice, one of Sam's sisters, thought that Margaret was one of the most remarkable people she had ever met. Years later in a television interview Eunice remembered that Margaret "was the epitome of the southern normal," adding with a smile, "and she didn't mind it a bit, you know." Jean, the youngest of Sam's siblings, came to believe that Sam and Margaret's marriage was probably the happiest she had ever known. "I never heard either of them speak a cross or unkind [word] to each other," she recalled.[34]

An indispensable part of the Ervins' household was their cook, Essie Tate. They hired her the year after their marriage and built a room with an attached bathroom for her to live in downstairs. Just as his parents had depended on Polly and Betty Powell to help raise their children, Sam and Margaret relied on Essie's essential help in their home. They thought of her as a member of the family. She served the Ervins for thirty-seven years, and when she passed away in the early 1960s the senator and his whole family traveled back to Morganton for the funeral, where they were invited to sit with the Tate family. In later years, Ervin often cited his close relationship with Essie, and Polly and Betty before her, in his defense against charges that he was a racist. Perhaps in the mid-twentieth century, when white North Carolinians could still deceive themselves that their black neighbors were content with the racial status quo, this paternalistic defense would have been more convincing than it seems today.[35]

But by the 1920s things were changing in Morganton, and not just in race relations. Even Sam Ervin could not help but notice the growing challenges to the traditional life he and Margaret were building. Substantial shifts in the old way of life had already begun. The historical trends of agribusiness, industrialization, and urbanization that swept across the South in the early twentieth century came to Morganton just as Ervin assumed his role as a new member of the town's ruling class.

Burke County experienced several significant population shifts between 1920 and 1930. While the country remained predominantly rural, a new trend of families moving from the countryside into the town had begun. The mechanization and modernization of farming methods changed the nature of agriculture, leading successful large landowners to diversify by investing in new industrial enterprises while putting increased strains on small farmers and agricultural workers. In the 1920s more than 3,000 tenant farmers fought against the odds of falling prices and growing debt in Burke County, but their numbers decreased every year. Meanwhile, Morganton doubled in size in just ten years, growing to more than 6,000 residents in the 1920s. This growth put strains on the town's infrastructure as roads had to be built and new services such as electricity and sewers had to be expanded. The road in front of the Ervins' house was paved in 1924, the year they moved in, but not all services reached Morganton's citizens evenly. The sewer system did not reach the black sections of town for another thirty years. In spite of Ervin's insistence that there was no black discontent in Morganton, African Americans were voting with their feet and leaving the city at an unprecedented rate. The nonwhite population of the town dropped by 6 percent during the 1920s, down to 16.9 percent from a high of around 30 percent before the Civil War.[36]

The trend toward the industrialization of Burke County expanded rapidly in the 1920s. In 1923 Duke Power Company completed three dams on the Catawba and Linville Rivers to create Lake James, named after company pioneer James B. Duke, just outside of Morganton. The large lake, which covered 6,500 acres with 152 miles of shoreline, provided recreational opportunities as well as hydroelectric power. This new power source, coupled with improved rail service provided by the Southern Railway, stimulated the manufacturing sector. Existing textile and apparel factories expanded while new factories opened their doors. Likewise, the furniture industry grew as both the Drexel and Table Rock Furniture companies expanded their operations. To meet the financial needs of the growing economy, the First National Bank of Morganton constructed a new and larger facility in 1923, and five years later a second bank, Morganton Industrial, opened to fill the growing demand for installment loans.[37]

Economic growth brought social changes as well, not all of which were welcomed by the more "respectable" citizens of Morganton. More industry and more jobs attracted more people, many of them transients and others unfamiliar with traditional customs. Local residents complained about the breakdown in civility and manners. As Susan Graham Erwin remembered, in the old days "good manners were important. Girls were taught to be ladies and boys to be gentlemen, and both sexes were taught to be modestly and neatly dressed."[38] In "polite society" people did not discuss certain topics and accepted their prescribed roles. But with Burke's transformation from an agricultural to a manufacturing region, she lamented that "the manners, customs, and ethics of that earlier and more gracious time had long since vanished and could never come again."[39]

The leading citizens of Morganton responded to these economic and social challenges in various ways. The public schools represented one tool to control the changing population through a curriculum designed to discipline and bring "progressive civilization" to an increasingly unruly populace. The town's government also passed new ordinances to cope with new challenges. It became illegal for any young person under the age of seventeen to buy or light a cigarette in public, and one had to be twenty years old to enter or play in any of the pool rooms around town. The speed limit remained at 10 miles per hour in town, but if a car encountered a person riding a horse or driving a team of horses, the law mandated that the car turn out of the way to the right and "pass without interference."[40]

The town elite tried to reinforce traditional social norms through symbolic cultural events as well. Morganton erected a new Civil War statue on the courthouse square in 1918—a Confederate private standing on guard (appropriately facing north). They also held a parade on Confederate Memorial Day every year. An equally popular event was a pageant portraying the history of Burke County called "The Birthright." Sponsored by the Morganton High School, and held outdoors to accommodate the large crowd, the original play included the defeat of the "fierce Cherokee" and their "dreadful massacres of white people," the lament of the old happy slaves, songs such as "Old Black Joe" and "Gwine Back to Dixie," and a reenactment of the rise of the "great Ku Klux Klan," which created "a veritable Empire of the South to protect the Southern country." Several members of the Ervin family participated in the pageant, and Sam served as one of its historical advisers.[41]

The changes sweeping over Morganton in the 1920s, as well as the other towns in the North Carolina Piedmont, consolidated the power of the local elites. There is significant debate among scholars over the best way to characterize this group, but whether they are labeled an "oligarchy," "hegemony," "court house ring," or just simply "the leading citizens," it is clear that during the 1920s the real power over most North Carolinians' daily lives lay in the hands of a small group of local, upper-class, business-oriented men. Perhaps historian Jasper Barry Shannon best described them as the "banker-merchant-farmer-lawyer-doctor-governing class."[42]

These men shared a vision of conservative modernization based on white supremacy, minimal government, social hierarchy, low wages, and anti-unionism. In spite of the growing contradictions inherent in their ideology—

such as preserving social inequality while championing equal opportunity—or maybe because of these contradictions, the New South elites dedicated themselves to defeat any and all challenges to the political status quo. But as long as they remained securely in control, these Christian gentlemen felt a moral obligation to take care of their citizens. Historian William Chafe has described their philosophy as a "progressive mystique." The essential element of this ideological self-perception was paternalism, or governing those under one's care in a manner similar to the way in which a traditional father cares for this children—firmly but lovingly. Chafe suggested that to maintain their power these Tar Heel elites combined their paternalism with a strict code of gentlemanly civility in all social interactions, and with token gifts of privilege or opportunity to appease occasional dissatisfaction from below.[43]

A similar political culture dominated politics at the state level. The most famous description of North Carolina in the first half of the twentieth century was coined by V. O. Key, who called the state a "Progressive Plutocracy." Key observed that the state enjoyed "a reputation for progressive outlook and action in many phases of life, especially industrial development, education, and race relations."[44] But Key also described the state's dominant leadership as a plutocracy of businessmen and their lawyers who maintained strict control over the state's government. Following their victory in 1898, the Democrats dominated this plutocracy and ruled the state for the next seventy years, most of Sam Ervin's lifetime. Within this one-party rule a series of coalitions, or political machines, competed for supremacy, but all these coalitions existed well within the Progressive Plutocracy model. According to Key, "the effectiveness of the oligarchy's control [was] achieved through the elevation to office of persons (chiefly lawyers) fundamentally in harmony with its viewpoint."[45]

In the early 1920s Sam Ervin was one of the young lawyers being groomed to join North Carolina's Progressive Plutocracy. Indeed, he had quickly assumed his place as a new member of Morganton's ruling class soon after returning from Harvard. Along with the status that came from his growing law practice, and belonging to an established family, he earned a reputation as a community leader by becoming a member of almost every civil organization in Morganton. To say that Ervin was "a joiner" is an understatement. During the 1920s he belonged to the Scottish Rite Masons, Odd Fellows, Knights of Pythias, Patriotic Order Sons of America, Kiwanis, and the American Legion, for which he was a founding member. He also served the community as a member of the Board of Trustees of the Morganton Graded Schools, an elder of the First Presbyterian Church (where he also taught Sunday School), an officer in the National Guard, and a member of the North Carolina legislature.[46]

Volunteering for community service was one thing, but running for elected office was something entirely different, something Ervin did not like. His early encounters with politics were not all that positive. When the Democratic Party nominated him for the state legislature in 1922, he accepted the responsibility as his civic duty. For the same reason he agreed to run again in 1924, 1925, and 1930, before demanding that they leave him alone and get someone else to represent them in Raleigh. The only time Ervin ever sought elective office himself was in 1926 when he ran for district solicitor, a position more often called district prosecutor. It was also the only time he ever lost an election. While he carried his own county easily, he lost the election in nearby Caldwell County because of what most observers agreed was ballot tampering. His father was so mad that he threatened to shoot or sue every "crook" in the county, but Sam held his father back, suggesting that it was just not important enough to get in a fight over.[47]

Ervin did not enjoy his time in the state legislature all that much, either. The sessions were tedious and he found little joy in arguing about restricting fishing net sizes or regulating the sale of calves for veal. The important decisions were made by committee chairmen who all belonged to the political machine of Senator Furnifold Simmons, who had run the state for almost thirty years. Simmons came from down east and his power lay with the agricultural interests of the state. Ervin represented the Piedmont and its growing industrial sector and therefore had little impact or power in the legislature. For the most part he followed the advice given to him by Morganton's hometown philosopher, Lum Garrison: "When you go to the legislature, pass no more laws, and 'peal half of those we've already got."[48] The legislative sessions only lasted a few months each year, and Ervin did not see his position in the North Carolina House as nearly important as his legal career. Nonetheless, he took his responsibility of representing his constituents seriously and had some minor successes. Some of the first bills he proposed assisted two of Morganton's most important institutions—the North Carolina School for the Deaf and the Broughton Hospital for the mentally insane.[49]

Ervin also pushed for a bond to increase funding for an African American school district in Morganton. This act of paternalism became his primary defense against those who would attack his record on civil rights in the future. He never understood why civil rights activists would not accept that such benevolent actions toward blacks did not constitute a sufficient answer to the problem of race relations. Indeed, most of his record as a legislator demonstrates Ervin's genuine sense of paternalistic responsibility for those weaker members of society under his care. He believed it was his duty to care for the poor, minorities, women, working people, and the deaf or mentally ill. He did not consider that the system should be changed to empower those groups to help themselves.[50]

The political calm of the North Carolina legislature ended abruptly in 1925. Fundamentalist Christians, infuriated by the inclusion of Darwin's theory of evolution in two North Carolina textbooks, demanded that the General Assembly ban any reference to Darwin in all public educational materials. The issue had been simmering for years. Fundamentalists were motivated not only by their fury against Darwin's scientific notions, which seemed to contradict the biblical account of creation, but by a host of satanic "isms" that they felt threatened their traditional values, including alcoholism, communism, unionism, relativism, and Catholicism. Evolution became the symbolic target for all of the modern world's challenges. When David Scott Poole, an evangelical Presbyterian and newspaperman from Hoke County, proposed a bill to prohibit the teaching of evolution in the public schools and colleges of the state, evangelical preachers and their passionate followers descended on Raleigh. The old capital had not seen such a sensational event for decades. Politicians quickly fell into warring camps, with fundamentalists agreeing with Poole that "the religion of the Lord Jesus Christ is on trial" and modernists supporting the president of the University of North Carolina, Harry Woodburn Chase, who countered that the Poole bill represented "tyranny over the mind."[51] A full-blown culture war broke out. In the words of one anti-evolution politician, "the professors are lined up against the folks."[52]

Ervin did not have to think long about where he belonged in this fight. He was a graduate of Chapel Hill, an up-and-coming member of the Progressive Plutocracy, and a descendent of fiercely independent Scotsmen who prided themselves on their defense of individual freedom. Ervin was also influenced by his recent membership in the Freemasons, who, as the senator later explained, were "dedicated to the principle that the minds and spirits of men by right ought to be free from civil and ecclesiastical tyranny."[53] In addition, while the Ervins were active Presbyterians, they were more conservative than reactionary, and they had not supported the other cultural crusade of the early twentieth century either—Prohibition. When North Carolina debated whether to become the first state to outlaw the sale of alcohol by popular vote in 1908, Sam Sr. wrote stinging letters against the referendum to area newspapers. In 1923, Ervin voted against the Turlington Act, which made it illegal for anyone to make, buy, sell, or transport liquor under any circumstances in the state. The bill passed 107–3, proving in Ervin's words "that it was morally respectable for politicians to drink wet as long as they voted dry."[54] After the Prohibition measure passed, the elder Ervin continued to ferment wine in his basement (he claimed it was only to supply the communion wine for the First Presbyterian Church, but most churches had changed to grape juice by that time). In 1925, Sam Sr. became very agitated about the Poole bill and again expressed his opinion in the press. He wrote a letter to the editor of the *Raleigh Times* belittling the preachers who believed that acceptance of the theory of evolution would destroy Christianity.[55]

Although a young legislator, only twenty-eight years old, with little seniority and even less enthusiasm for public speaking, Sam Ervin rose quickly to oppose the Poole bill on the floor of the General Assembly. In an early demonstration of his talent for using humor as a political weapon, Ervin suggested that if the supporters of the Poole bill had been sitting in the Spanish legislature when Columbus undertook to make his first voyage of discovery to America, they would have proposed legislation to prohibit his sailing for fear he might fall off the edge of the earth. Ervin concluded that the bill would serve no good purpose except to absolve the monkeys "from all responsibility for the conduct of the human race in general and that of the North Carolina Legislature in particular."[56] After a long and very contentious debate, the legislature defeated the Poole bill by a vote of 67–46, and North Carolina was spared the humiliation that its neighboring state endured later that year when the infamous Scopes "monkey trial" took place in Dayton, Tennessee.[57]

Ervin's speech against the Poole bill added to his reputation as a promising young leader in the western part of the state. His successful legal practice, his membership in all the right organizations, his service in the legislature, and his willingness to take a stand against the Poole bill had impressed many across North Carolina.[58] But Ervin's most significant service to the Progressive Plutocracy in the 1920s came after the sensational murder of Gladys Kincaid in 1927.

Gladys was a fifteen-year-old white girl who lived with her family on the outskirts of Morganton. She worked in the Garrou Knitting Mill and walked home around 5:30 every evening. One Tuesday afternoon a neighbor noticed a black man walking up the street with a large pipe in his hand just several minutes before Gladys passed by. Mrs. Whisenant mentioned to her son that the pipe must be for chasing away wild dogs. When Gladys did not return home at the normal time her worried mother sent family members out to search the neighborhood. They heard a groan coming from behind a clump of bushes just off the road where they found her lying unconscious. Gladys had been attacked and her skull crushed. The bloody pipe lay just a few feet away. She died later that night without regaining consciousness.[59]

Neighbors immediately identified the person Mrs. Whisenant had seen carrying the pipe as a black construction worker from Asheville named Broadus Miller. Miller had been renting a room just up the street for the past couple of weeks while working on a temporary building job. In his room they found a raincoat with fresh blood stains. From that moment on there was little doubt, at least in the minds of Morganton's white citizenry, that Miller had killed Gladys and had run into the countryside to try to save his life. While no one will ever know exactly what happened between Broadus Miller and Gladys Kincaid that evening that led to her death, the local paper filled in the blanks the next morning on the front page: "The story is the blood-curdling one of a pretty young girl the victim of a black brute, who in overcoming her resistance fatally wounded her before he was able to accomplish his fiendish purpose."[60]

A massive manhunt began immediately. Hundreds of men, some deputized by the sheriff, others acting as vigilantes, searched the countryside. For several days a series of clues excited the community. First they found Miller's discarded clothing, then occasional sightings of a lone black man in the woods raised hopes they would find the killer. Jean Ervin remembered that she and other neighborhood children were not allowed to play outside for days.[61] Eventually the trail went cold, fear and frustration grew, and the manhunt began to spiral out of control. The *Raleigh News and Observer* reported that at one point more than 1,000 armed men lined a stretch of road outside of Morganton and that altogether more than 2,000 had joined the search. Packs of hunting dogs led the searchers in different directions across the mountains while the *Morganton News-Herald* inspired them on with its overheated rhetoric: "a pretty, innocent young girl, just blossoming into her teens, the victim of a savage-minded, unspeakably brutal black beast."[62] Speculation that Miller would be lynched spread throughout Morganton and across the state.

Wanting to prevent a total breakdown of law and order, and hoping to protect North Carolina's progressive image, Governor A. W. McLean sent one of his trusted aides to Morganton. As soon as State Pardon Commissioner Edwin B. Bridges arrived in town, he met with Sheriff J. J. Hallyburton and a man referred to in official documents as "the attorney of the sheriff"—Sam Ervin. Commissioner Bridges explained that it was up to the three of them to prevent Miller from becoming a victim of mob rule. They devised a plan to place two "high-powered cars" in the mountain area where Miller was thought to be hiding so that if found he could be taken away before he was lynched.[63]

The following morning, Sunday, 3 July, a report reached Morganton that someone had broken into a restaurant near Linville Falls and stolen some food. Suspecting that the robber might be Miller, Ervin and the other two officials jumped in one of the cars and raced up the mountain. Before they arrived, almost a hundred other searchers converged upon the area of the robbery. A former policeman from Morganton, Commodore Burleson, spotted Miller in the woods and the two men exchanged six or seven shots before Miller was hit. According to witnesses, Miller died immediately. Burleson and the others put Miller's body in a car and sped toward Morganton, passing Ervin, the sheriff, and the commissioner going the other direction.

Just after noon, as the citizens of Morganton headed home from church, the car from Linville Falls drove into downtown with Miller's feet sticking out the window. The men in the car shouted, "Here's your Nigger, come and look at him!"[64] With a crowd gathering, several men dragged Miller's body out of the car into the courthouse where they laid it in a hallway just outside the sheriff's office for viewing. By the time the car carrying Ervin arrived at the courthouse, the crowd had grown to several thousand and angry voices were shouting that the corpse should be brought outside. Commissioner Bridges, Sheriff Hallyburton, and Ervin met with Commodore Burleson to review the events of the shooting, but the crowd became increasingly restive. Some members of the crowd suggested that the body be hung from a nearby tree, while others demanded that it be dragged through town behind one of their cars. Fearing a riot, Ervin and the others decided to put the corpse on a board and take it outside where the crowd could view it one at a time by passing down a roped-off path. Burleson stood over the dead man displaying his gun and posing for pictures all afternoon until everyone who wanted had a chance to see the body. That night Ervin and the others secretly whisked Miller's body out of town for a secret burial to prevent its mutilation.[65]

The near lynching of Broadus Miller's body became a minor scandal in North Carolina. Several newspapers criticized the commissioner and sheriff for giving in to the crowd's demand to drag the body outside for public display and enable what one editorial called "a carnival of community hate."[66] Ervin's name did not appear in any of these negative stories, although the *Morganton News-Herald* and Commissioner Bridges's official report both credited him with playing a major role in helping to defuse a dangerous situation.[67] For a few weeks Morganton's better citizens defended the moderate reputation of their town against the condemnation of the better citizens of self-proclaimed more moderate North Carolina towns, but the war of words soon subsided and the incident was pushed to the back of the state's memory, as are so many other embarrassing moments of history. Once again, however, Sam Ervin had risen to the occasion and helped North Carolina maintain its shaky progressive reputation.[68]

The presidential election the following year created a political rift in North

Carolina's Democratic Party. For thirty years the Democrats had controlled the government in the Tar Heel State, although the Republicans remained a significant minority. But in 1928 the national Democratic Party nominated Al Smith for president. The urbane governor of New York was both a Roman Catholic and a critic of Prohibition. Facing Smith on the November ballot was Republican Herbert Hoover, a Protestant and a supporter of Prohibition. The campaign rekindled the cultural politics of 1925. The most powerful politician in the state, Senator Furnifold Simmons, who had run the dominant Democratic political organization since 1898, could not accept Smith's candidacy and threw his support to Hoover. Other Democrats remained loyal to their party and its candidate. Sam Ervin and his father strongly supported Al Smith and condemned the anti-Catholicism that swept across the state. The senior Ervin once again fired off letters to local newspapers, while Little Sam claimed to be the first North Carolinian to shake Smith's hand when he got off the train on his first campaign swing through the state.[69]

The presidential election of 1928 did not go the way they had hoped, but the resulting power shift within the state Democratic Party definitely swung in Ervin's direction. Hoover won the White House and easily carried North Carolina that November, making him the only Republican to win a statewide election there between 1896 and 1972. But Furnifold Simmons's betrayal of his party's presidential standard-bearer caused a backlash that ended his control of the state Democratic Party. The leadership shifted to newly elected Governor O. Max Gardner, a millionaire textile owner from the southern Piedmont town of Shelby. He and his successors in the governor's mansion—J. C. B. Ehringhaus (1933–37), Clyde R. Hoey (1937–41), J. Melville Broughton (1941–45), and R. Gregg Cherry (1945–49)—emerged as the dominant force in state politics for the next two decades and became known as the Shelby Dynasty. Ervin knew these men. He had practiced law with them, introduced them at the local Kiwanis and Knights of Pythias meetings, and ran their campaigns in Burke County. Like Ervin, they represented a new generation of politicians who were mostly from the industrializing Piedmont section of the state. These newest members of the Progressive Plutocracy spent less time recalling the travails of Reconstruction and more time praising the opportunities of the New South. They reformed state government agencies with an emphasis on efficiency, accepted the New Deal (conditionally), cleaned up local and state election procedures, and took their paternalistic responsibilities seriously. And while they toned down the racial rhetoric of their predecessors, they did not abandon white supremacy, a probusiness agenda, or anti-unionism. It was on this last point that they would need Sam Ervin's help to put down the most significant challenge to their control of the state in the first half of the twentieth century.[70]

During the Great Depression of the 1930s a labor crisis in the mill villages led to the general textile strike of 1934. The strike itself has been well documented in the historical record, and the fact that Ervin served in the National Guard that helped to defeat the uprising is also well known if seldom remembered. But what has not heretofore been revealed is the important role that Ervin played during the most critical moments of the strike in North Carolina, and in the cover-up that took place afterward.[71]

Even before the stock market crash of 1929, North Carolina's economy was struggling. Several major industries, especially textiles, had already experienced downturns in the late 1920s, but the Great Depression hit the mills hard, causing the owners to lay off some workers and to push those who remained even harder. Longer hours, lower wages, and the stretch-out system—which forced the mill hands to pick up ever-increasing work loads—bred resentment and multiplied grievances. As the owner's paternalism failed to relieve the suffering of the workers and their families in the mill villages, labor unions began to successfully organize some of the mills. Early strikes broke out in several North Carolina towns such as Gastonia and Marion, but the mill owners were able to crush these local uprisings through a combination of intimidation and violence.[72] In September of 1934, however, the United Textile Workers Union called for a national textile strike and hundreds of thousands of southern mill workers joined the picket lines. The textile owners panicked. As mills closed down all across the Piedmont they sent terrified telegrams to Governor Ehringhaus demanding protection from the "anarchists, communists, brigands and union leaders," who threatened to overturn their control of the cotton mill world. When it became clear that local officials could not handle the crisis, the governor called out the National Guard.[73]

Sam Ervin was the captain and commanding officer of Company B, 105th Engineers, the Morganton unit of the National Guard. On Saturday, 15 September 1934, the Company was ordered to strike duty in the Gastonia area. Because so many of the soldiers in the North Carolina Guard were also boys who worked in the local mills, the state officers wisely assigned companies to serve in areas away from home to reduce the risk of defections or conflicting loyalties. On Monday, the commanding officer in Gastonia, Major Paul R. Younts, ordered Ervin and his men to prepare to take up positions outside the Knit Products Company Mill in the nearby town of Belmont. Having heard of threats that "blood would be shed" if the Guard moved into Belmont, Younts and Ervin met with several self-proclaimed strike leaders later that afternoon.

They informed the strikers that the Guard's purpose was "to prevent violence and protect life and property." They promised to "protect the right of the strikers to picket peaceably," but added that soldiers would also "protect the right to work of those who desired to work." In effect, these orders meant that the real purpose of the National Guard was to keep the mills open, thus defeating the strike.[74]

Very early the next morning, 18 September, Ervin led his men to the mill, where they ran barbed wire between the strikers and the street that led to the mill. The crowd swelled to several thousand by 7:00 A.M., the time that the owners had announced they would reopen. The strikers overflowed their designated area and filled the street, making it impossible for anyone to enter the mill. Throughout the morning, cars carrying would-be workers tried to break through the mob, only to be chased away by angry strikers. Ervin thought that he saw several men in the crowd with bulges in their pockets, which he assumed to be concealed handguns. He heard people yelling, "Get the damn scab," "Get that yellow son of a bitch," and other language that he described as "filthy in the extreme."[75] Several cars were overturned and their occupants roughed up before being run out of the area.

Major Younts, Ervin, and other officials at the mill decided that the only way to reopen the factory would be to put the willing workers, or "scabs" as the strikers called them, on large delivery trucks guarded by the local police and provided by the mill owners. Around 1 P.M. the local sheriff drove up in his car and attempted to open a path to the mill. The crowd seized and attempted to overturn the vehicle before the Highway Patrol sent a rescue team to save the sheriff and escort him to safety. The strikers' direct attack on an officer of the law provoked Major Younts to order the National Guard to clear the street. A detachment of soldiers with fixed bayonets drove the mob to the other side of the barbed wire. Having opened the entrance to the factory, the trucks rolled in and the mill began operating again by mid-afternoon. The crowd remained just on the other side of the barbed wire throughout the day, threatening the troops and even passing out business cards from Bentley's Funeral Home to the soldiers suggesting that they might need the address before they left town.[76]

That night around 9:00 the strikers suddenly threw a volley of rocks at the mill, shattering a number of windows. Some of the rocks hit the soldiers as well. At practically the same moment a soldier ran over to Ervin, who was the officer on duty, to report that a shot had been fired at a sentry guarding the rear of the mill. Whether or not a gun had actually been discharged has never been confirmed, but Ervin responded to what he perceived to be a credible report of a gunshot by approaching the strikers and ordering that they disperse immediately. The strikers held their ground. Ervin thought that he saw members of the crowd holding pistols and knives. Fearing that a riot might break out at any second, he ordered the soldiers to clear the entire area around the mill. On Ervin's orders the National Guard advanced on the strikers. The crowd resisted by pushing, shoving, and throwing rocks. The soldiers drove forward and moved the workers backward by pricking them with their bayonets. Ervin ran down the line warning his men to watch out for weapons, but there were no reports of guns or knives being used against the troops.[77]

As the Guard forced the strikers to retreat, Ervin heard that one of the workers had been seriously injured. He rushed over to the mill houses across the street from the factory, where a trail of blood led into a small room in which Ernest Riley lay bleeding to death from a bayonet wound. It was not clear why Riley had been attacked since he did not seem to have been on the picket line nor in the immediate area in front of the troops. Several witnesses in the crowd said he had been stabbed by an angry soldier who chased him up to the porch of the house, but there were conflicting accounts of what had actually happened. Numerous strikers were stabbed by bayonets that night, but only a dozen or so required medical attention and only Riley died of his wounds.[78]

The general textile strike continued for another week before union leaders called off the picket lines, but the violence at Belmont marked the climax of the uprising in North Carolina. The National Guard held a private inquest into Riley's killing seven days after his death in which Ervin and several other officers testified. None of the strikers or civilian witnesses were invited to tell what they had seen. The inquiry concluded that a riotous mob had initiated the violence and that the officers and soldiers had all acted properly. The National Guard claimed that it could not determine which soldier had bayoneted Riley due to poor lighting in the area and because it could not find even one of their soldiers who could identify him. In spite of repeated demands by furious strikers, union leaders, and even a few local government officials, the Guard refused to investigate further. Ervin, the officer on duty, was officially cleared of any wrongdoing and his name was kept out of the press and subsequent historical accounts.[79]

But Ervin must have been troubled by the cover-up because he lobbied his commanding officers to allow an open investigation. He even spoke personally to Governor Ehringhaus, urging that the state cooperate fully with any legal proceeding. Soon thereafter the governor and Guard officials did make public statements about their willingness to allow all military personnel to testify if a trial were held, but they also continued to claim that they did not know which guardsman had stabbed Riley.[80]

These statements were lies. Ervin had written to his commander "in strictest confidence" explaining that he had "talked to the boy most concerned" and that the guardsman was willing to go to trial if necessary.[81] Ervin argued that if the matter were not resolved in court "the public would finally come to the conclusion that we have something to hide."[82] Clearly, Ervin believed that he and his men had done nothing wrong that night in Belmont and he wanted the chance to debate those who thought they had. But the state continued to stonewall and no one, including Ervin, ever revealed the name of the soldier or any other information they knew about the incident. No one was ever brought to trial for Riley's death. In a manner similar to the Broadus Miller affair seven years earlier, and other embarrassing challenges to the Progressive Plutocracy in the early twentieth century, the story of the strike of 1934 in general, and the violence at Belmont in particular, was relegated to the shadows of North Carolina history.[83]

Ervin reimmersed himself in his law practice in Morganton and never spoke about all that happened in Belmont. He was thirty-eight years old and a very busy lawyer. The Depression took its toll on the Ervin family's finances, his income fell to half of what it had been before the stock market crash, and he worked harder than ever to make enough money to keep the books balanced. Margaret and Essie Tate supplemented Ervin's diminished income with a chicken coop and a garden. His father, now almost eighty years old, continued to practice law but took on far fewer cases. Age had accomplished what neither Yankee soldiers, Reconstruction, nor countless opposing attorneys had been able to do—slow down Samuel Ervin Sr. Thus his son had to carry almost all of the family practice on his shoulders. At the same time his civic responsibilities increased again. As the Shelby group solidified its control over the Democratic Party, and therefore the state, Ervin became an increasingly visible member of its western wing. With more status came more statewide responsibilities. The North Carolina Bar elected Ervin as their vice president, the University of North Carolina put him on its board of trustees, and the governors whose campaigns he managed in Burke County offered him rewards such as general counsel of the North Carolina Highway Commission and as an associate member of the North Carolina Industrial Commission, both of which he turned down.[84]

The one appointment Ervin really wanted was to the North Carolina Superior Court. Most lawyers dream of becoming judges someday and Ervin was no exception. But most Superior Court judges are elected to the bench, and that presented a couple of problems. First, Ervin's one and only run for elective office—to become a district prosecutor in 1926—had been both unsuccessful and unpleasant. Second, the man holding the Superior Court judgeship in his

Sam Ervin in his hometown law office, 1944. Photograph by Gordon Ryders. A copy is in the Sam Ervin Library and Museum, Western Piedmont Community College, Morganton, North Carolina. Copyright Daily News L.P. Courtesy of the New York Daily News.

district was a personal friend and another member of the Shelby Dynasty, making it impossible for Ervin to challenge him in an election. Ervin's only hope was that the governor would award him one of the special traveling Superior Court positions that are filled through appointment instead of by election. But his polite inquiries through various friends to Governor Ehringhaus had been unsuccessful.[85]

Ervin's first chance to sit on the bench came in 1935, but it was not what he had expected or wanted. During the Depression the judicial system in Burke County had trouble keeping up with the growing number of petty criminal cases. The County Commissioners responded by forming a new Criminal Court to handle misdemeanors and they asked Ervin to become its magistrate. For the next two years he presided over the court, which met on Tuesday mornings in the old courthouse across the street from his law office. The responsibility was not so great as to prevent him from continuing his own law practice but it did bring some added income. He presided over all sorts of cases—assault, robbery, public drunkenness, disorderly conduct, and the like.[86]

Judge Ervin quickly impressed his colleagues with his mastery of criminal law and procedures, but the characteristic for which he was most remembered was compassion. One morning the sheriff brought a ragged stranger to the Criminal Court. His clothes were ripped, his hair unkempt, he needed a shave, and he was shaking from the effects of alcohol. He had been arrested while trying to hitchhike a ride to Asheville where he hoped to be admitted to the Veterans Administration Hospital. Ervin questioned the man and discovered that he had fought in World War I but had been down on his luck for the past few years. He instructed an officer of the court to take the man across the street to a barbershop for a haircut and shave, and then to a local doctor's office for a sedative to calm his nerves. Ervin asked that both charges be made to his own account. Then he handed the officer a five dollar bill and told him to walk the man to the bus station, buy him a ticket to Asheville, and give him whatever change was left over. In Burke County's Criminal Court the law was still personal enough to allow such acts of kindness. Ervin's paternalism was sincere. He was, first and foremost, a gentleman.[87]

When Ervin first went to the bench his father implored him to never forget that he, too, had once been a lawyer and to always be patient with the attorneys who came before him, especially when he thought they were wrong. Years later, Senator Ervin remember his father's advice: "The first quality of a judge should be that he was a gentleman and to treat everybody with consideration, lawyers and parties and witnesses and jurors and everybody else. Try to make them as comfortable as possible."[88] He also remembered what he had been taught at

Harvard, that he should preside with the cold neutrality of an impartial judge. These behaviors are all part of that nebulous characteristic called judicial temperament. Judge James Braxton Craven Jr., who practiced law in front of Judge Ervin, later praised him by paraphrasing Justice Potter Stewart's comment about obscenity: "I can't define judicial temperament, but I know it when I see it."[89] Craven believed that Senator Ervin's eventual national fame did not come from his ability as a legislator, or his ol' country lawyer stories, but from the judicial temperament he displayed as the "Commanding Magistrate" of Watergate.[90]

Ervin believed that becoming a judge was a special calling, a position of power that required the highest level of personal integrity. Given the seriousness and responsibilities of a position on the bench, he thought that a magistrate must adhere to the highest principles of honor and fairness. He often quoted these verses from one of his favorite poets, Walter Malone:

Dost thou not tremble to assume thy seat,
And judge thy fellow travelers to the tomb?
Dost thou not falter as thy lips repeat
The Comrade's downfall, thy Companion's doom?[91]

In 1937 Ervin finally got the job he wanted. He had been very active supporting Clyde Hoey's successful campaign for governor in the fall of the previous year. Hoey was the son-in-law of former Governor O. Max Gardner, who began the Shelby Dynasty, and he was a good friend of Sam's father. Hoey's first appointment as governor was to name Ervin as a special Superior Court judge. Ervin got the call on Saturday, was sworn in Monday morning in the Burke County Courthouse, and left immediately for Charlotte where he took his place on the bench of the Superior Court of Mecklenburg County. There was no period of transition, no training session, no orientation. The lawyers on the docket that day had been preparing their legal briefs for weeks, but Ervin heard the case for the first time that afternoon. He had to grasp the intricacies of the trial immediately, master the legal and procedural issues, and rule appropriately at once. Such a challenge would have intimidated many novice judges. Judge Ervin handled it with ease.[92]

For the next seven years Ervin traveled the state as a special Superior Court judge. Because he did not have his own district, he had to spend around forty weeks a year holding court in over fifty different counties. Most of his assignments were in larger cities such as Greensboro, Winston-Salem, Durham, and Charlotte, but he also held court down east along the coast and up west through the mountains. The assignment was perfect for an aspiring politician who wanted to make connections all over the state, but Ervin had no political aspirations, except perhaps the long shot of getting a seat on the State Supreme Court—a possibility his hometown newspaper had already boasted might happen someday. He often heard cases four or five days a week, sometimes as many as thirty-five a day, before returning to his hotel at night to study the law books and prepare for the next day. On Friday afternoon he got in his car and traveled back to Morganton for the weekend. The work was intellectually challenging and physically exhausting. Sometimes the nights could be lonely. But by all accounts, Sam Ervin was one of the best judges North Carolina had seen for a long while.[93]

Young lawyers and critical reporters are some of a judge's harshest critics. In Rockingham County a recent law school graduate named Susie Sharp had developed a very low opinion of the overall quality of the trial judges who had come to preside over their Superior Court sessions. Sharp and her friend, Jule McMichael, made a sport out of bemoaning the ignorance of the judiciary. Then Judge Ervin came to town. By the end of his first week of court, Sharp's friend turned to her and gushed: "Susie, Judge Ervin knows everything; he's unbelievable; he's too good to be true!"[94] Sharp, who went on to become the first woman to serve on the North Carolina Supreme Court, and the first woman elected as a chief justice of any state's Supreme Court, remained an enthusiastic admirer of Ervin for the rest of her life. She later wrote, "Every lawyer with an important case wants a competent judge, one who can be counted on not to commit reversible error." Sam Ervin, she insisted, was that kind of judge.[95] Reporters almost unanimously agreed with Sharp's assessment. Newspaper stories noted his "brilliant career" and "impressive reputation." The Kinston Free Press took the unusual step of printing the rave reviews local court officials and attorneys gave to Judge Ervin when he visited their district. "He seems to know how to use mercy without wasting it," they observed. "His personality is attractive. He has a sense of humor. He makes friends easily."[96]

Indeed, Ervin did bring his usual joviality to the court. He liked to tell the story of an old justice of the peace who became exasperated by the tactics of a young lawyer trying his first case. The young lawyer kept rising and exclaiming: "I object. You are not proceeding according to the law." Finally the old magistrate could stand it no longer. He shouted: "Young man, quit jumping up and saying, 'I object. You are not proceeding according to the law.' I'll have you to understand I am running this court, and the law hasn't got a damn thing to do with it."[97]

Judge Ervin's own reaction to a strong-willed lawyer demonstrates his very different approach to running a court. After Ervin ruled on a case and returned to his chambers, the sheriff came in and said: "Your Honor, the defense attorney's out on the street and he's cussin' you out real good. Do you want him brought in and cited for contempt?" Ervin asked, "How long has he been out there?" "About ten minutes," answered the sheriff. "Well, let him be," said Ervin. "It's the privilege of a lawyer to cuss out the court for a reasonable length of time after he loses a case. He's still got some cussin' time coming to him."[98]

Yet, in spite of the levity, the accolades, and his love of the law, being a circuit judge took its toll on Ervin. The constant parade of sin and sadness that passed in front of him day after day disturbed his soul and weakened his body. He began smoking a lot more cigarettes, almost two packs a day, just as he had right after the war. He gained ten pounds in just a couple of years. It was also during this time that his friends first noticed the involuntary twitching of his eyebrows that became so famous to the rest of the country during Watergate. He suffered a series of treatable but troubling medical problems, including sinus infections, digestive disorders, and finally, in 1942, a bleeding ulcer. Factors beyond the courtroom weighed heavily on Ervin as well. His older brother, Ed, who suffered his whole life with debilitating asthma, passed away in 1932. His beloved sister Catharine died in 1940 after a long and painful battle with Hodgkin's disease. His children had grown up while he was away at court, and his oldest, Sam III, was approaching draft age and would probably be called up to serve in the Second World War soon. And there were the pesky neighbors and friends who looked up to Ervin and sought out his advice on all sorts of personal, political, and legal matters. No matter how exhausted he was, nor how late in the evening, he was too polite to turn them away.[99]

In December 1943, Sam's younger brother Joe came up to Morganton to talk with him. Joe had graduated from Chapel Hill, married a popular Morganton girl, and become a successful lawyer in Charlotte. After sitting on the front porch exchanging small talk for a while, Joe told Sam that he was thinking of running for the U.S. Congress. "Should I do it?" he asked. Without hesitation Sam told him no. "Why not?" Joe demanded. "Because you work too hard. Because you are inflexible. Because you can't compromise," Sam answered. Joe was getting angry and accused Sam of having exactly the same traits. But Sam held his ground, pointing out that at least he was not thinking of running for Congress. "You're on the court," Joe snapped. "It's the same thing." Sam paused for a second and answered, "No, I'm not. I just resigned."[100] His official resignation took effect on 30 December 1943. Once again, Sam wanted to be just a country lawyer.

Ervin settled back into his law practice in the spring of 1944. His reputation and many connections across the state brought him a lot of work. He also took on a profitable contract with the Southern Railway and spent more time than ever before drafting contracts and corporate charters, but he liked trial work the best. Other lawyers invited him to join their most important cases, and at one point he had been retained in litigation pending in nine different Superior Courts and the Federal District Court all at the same time.[101] In spite of his heavy workload, Ervin quit smoking and read a series of self-improvement books to help him better manage his lifestyle. His favorite was Dale Carnegie's *How to Stop Worrying and Start Living*. He stopped teaching Sunday school at the Presbyterian Church and tried to cut back on his civic duties, although by his own count he still belonged to seventeen different clubs and organizations.[102]

Life, however, did not allow Ervin the respite he desired. His father died in 1944 at the age of eighty-nine. Though expected, the loss still hit hard. The *Morganton News-Herald* printed a long obituary recalling the old man's distinctive dress and distinguished legal career. He was, the paper concluded, a "noble patriarch." That same year Sam III joined the army and Joe won his seat in Congress. Still, Ervin was back in Morganton, back in court, and back in his semi-mythical South of moonlight, magnolias, and moonshine.[103]

On Christmas Day 1945, the Ervins gathered together in Morganton for a traditional holiday dinner. The war had ended and the family was in good spirits. When the telephone in the hallway rang, just as they were sitting down to eat, no one had cause for alarm. Essie Tate came in to tell Ervin that the call was for him. It was Assistant Attorney General Lamar Caudle, an old family friend, calling from Washington, D.C. The news he shared shot through the heart of the whole family—Joe had committed suicide.[104]

Since taking his seat in Congress earlier that year, Joe Ervin had experienced a series of setbacks. The House of Representatives did not move as fast or as efficiently as Joe had expected when he arrived in Washington. He was a very junior congressman and his bills were bottled up in committee. One initiative Joe cared about deeply involved a technical proposal to protect the government against frivolous lawsuits from service personnel just leaving active duty. The comptroller general's office helped Joe draft the bill, and the committee to which he presented it responded with enthusiasm. But when he learned that lobbyists had killed the bill before it even came up for a vote, Joe was outraged. "Here is a thing that everyone admits is wrong and improper and indecent," he snapped to a friend. "Why can't we correct it?"[105] In typical Ervin style, Joe responded to adversity by working harder. He put in long days, labored through the weekends, and worked during holidays. Friends on Capitol Hill took him aside and begged him to slow down and take a few breaks, but he responded, "I just haven't the time."[106]

Just a few months before Christmas Joe seemed to be taking stock of his situation. "I believe you would like to know that I have decided to sweep my own doorstep for awhile and quit trying to help solve too many other problems," he wrote to his worried brother.[107] He even considered leaving Congress when his term expired. Then, on a wintery day, Joe slipped on a patch of ice and reinjured his bad leg. The osteomyelitis had never healed, and though he walked with a slight limp he did not let people know the extent of his agony. The only known treatment at the time consisted of implanting live maggots into the bone to eat away at the diseased marrow. Joe received treatment at Walter Reed Hospital but decided his leg would not allow him to travel home for the holidays. He convinced his wife to go back to Morganton since her elderly parents were expecting her home for Christmas.[108]

Lamar Caudle called Joe on Christmas Day when he did not show up at their house for dinner as planned. There was no answer. He hurried over to Joe's house to find a note stuck in the door warning to be careful as the house was filled with gas. Caudle called the police and they found Joe's body lying over two chairs in front of the stove. He had a pistol in one hand and a knife in the other, just in case the gas did not work. He left a love letter to his wife, thanking her for all the happiness but offering no explanation. Sam concluded that his brother's osteomyelitis had returned and he just could not face it again.[109]

Ervin took care of the funeral, answered all the condolence letters, and tried to return to work, but the Democrats were in trouble and they needed Ervin to bail them out. After not being able to agree on a replacement to finish out the second year of Joe's term, they called to ask if Sam would take the position. He said no, but the calls kept coming. One afternoon his eighty-year-old mother came across the street to talk to her son. "Go ahead and run," she told him, "because I want people to find out I have one son who can stand up and face life." Ervin replied softly to his mother's uncharacteristically harsh comment, "You have to remember I've never been confronted by the discouragement Joe's had."[110] Ervin thought it over for a few more days before finally agreeing to finish Joe's term, but only under one condition—that they understood he would not seek reelection.[111]

Sam Ervin was elected to Congress without opposition in January 1946 and remained in Washington until the following January. It was not a particularly fulfilling year for him, and he did not leave much of a mark on Congress. His longest speech on the floor of the House of Representatives lasted four and a half minutes. In it he attacked a bill placing limitations on the military draft at the end of World War II as "a draft law under which no one could be drafted."[112] As one might expect, he found a mountain anecdote to belittle the bill. It was the first story he told in the U.S. Congress. Ervin explained that it was the tradition back home in North Carolina for country folk to gather annually in church cemeteries to remove the briars and weeds from around their relatives' graves. One day a "colored boy" named George who had been hired to help them was pulling up some weeds when, according to Ervin:

> All at once he broke into laughter, such as might reasonably be provoked by the act of a solemn body like this passing a draftless draft law. I said, "George, what are you laughing about?" He says, "Boss, don't you see that joke that is written on the tombstone?" I said, "No George. What is it?" I got down and read it. In addition to the name and the date of death of the deceased, there were these words, "Not Dead, but sleeping." I said, "George, what's so funny about that?" He said, "Boss, he ain't fooling nobody but himself."[113]

The joke was funny, and effective, but the needless emphasis on race reflected the insensitivity that was common back in 1946. The story falls under the category of "nigra jokes" that Ervin and many of his white contemporaries, from both the South and the North, shared with one another. Ervin intended no racial slight; that just came with the joke. In later years, when he came to understand that others saw an inherent racism in these "nigra stories," he stopped telling them in public and removed the "colored boy" line from this one. It was just one of the many changes Ervin faced as he tried to negotiate the rapidly transforming world around him.[114]

Ervin built a consistently conservative record during his one year in Congress. He voted against federal housing programs and against demobilizing the military too quickly right after the war. He also opposed the extension of government price controls, suggesting that one of his constituents summed up the public's confusion perfectly when he asked that price controls be continued on the things he bought but removed from the things he sold.[115] Ervin voted for funding the House Committee on Un-American Activities, which he later regretted. Years later Ervin remembered only one vote he cast during his year in the House "of which I am heartily ashamed." In 1946 he supported President Harry Truman's bill allowing him to draft railroad workers if they went on strike. Ervin, among many members, realized the next day that the law violated the Thirteenth Amendment's prohibition of involuntary servitude. For Ervin there were two lessons to be learned from his mistake: first, no legislature should ever pass any bill quickly and especially not during a time of hysteria; and second, no one should ever weaken the filibuster in the Senate, which in this case allowed Senator Robert Taft of Ohio to stand alone and prevent the passage of an unconstitutional bill.[116]

Perhaps the dominant theme of Ervin's short stint in the House was his opposition to organized labor. Indeed, his anti-union sentiments may rival his stand against civil rights as the most consistent aspect of his entire political career. He railed against United Mine Workers chief John L. Lewis and the "paralyzing coal strike" and called on the government "to seize the mines and take what steps may be necessary" to solve the ongoing problems.[117] He also criticized the Wagner Act, which the Roosevelt administration pushed through Congress soon after the strike of 1934 to protect the rights of workers to unionize. Ervin thought that the Wagner Act was an unwise piece of legislation because it did not require strikers to negotiate on the demand of their employers or force them to allow non-strikers to cross picket lines. To Ervin, the National Labor Relations Board (NLRB), which the Wagner Act established to adjudicate laborers' complaints, was unconstitutional because it took away the right of every American, and every factory owner, to a trial by jury. It also gave judicial and regulatory power to the executive branch of the government, with which he disagreed. Ervin applied the same reasoning in his opposition to the Equal Employment Opportunity Commission (EEOC).[118]

In 1946 the Washington establishment took little note of these constitutional arguments by a lame-duck freshman congressman, but industrialists back home heard them loud and clear and renewed their lobbying for him to stay in Congress. Ervin remained steadfast, however; he would not run for reelection. In a letter to Charles A. Cannon of Cannon Mills, he explained that he really missed practicing law and that he was worried about his finances. "I have three children to educate," Ervin wrote, "and know that I cannot do so upon the congressional salary." As soon as he finished out Joe's term in January 1947, Ervin headed back to Morganton, assuming he would never have to live in Washington again.[119]

Ervin settled back into his one-story brick house, set up shop in the old law office he had shared with his father across the street from the Burke County Courthouse, and once again enjoyed watching the sun set behind Table Rock Mountain. At the end of a long day filled with what he liked to do best—practice law—he could sit on the porch, talk with family and friends, sip some whiskey and ginger ale, and then retreat into his study to read or do a little research on the Ervin family's history. In spite of all that happened over the last few years, he was a happy man.

But Morganton was not the same town he had known as a child, nor even as a young man back in the 1920s. The pace of change all across the state of North Carolina escalated again after World War II. Military spending during the war jump-started industrial production and spurred more capital-intensive businesses in heavy manufacturing, communications, and technology. Transportation improvements and a rising standard of living greatly increased tourism in the Tar Heel State, especially down at the beach and up along the new Blue Ridge Parkway that ran across the upper tip of Burke County.[120]

The African American struggle for freedom had never been dormant in the state, but it was reinvigorated after the war. The year Ervin returned home from Washington, a black World War II veteran from North Carolina named Charlie Hauser refused to give up his seat on a bus traveling not far from Morganton. After the local authorities threw him in jail, he posted bail, got on another bus, and sat right back in the exact same spot. He was just one of many black Tar Heels demanding equal treatment before the law. In spite of Morganton's modest efforts to meet the Supreme Court's fifty-year-old mandate of providing separate but equal public facilities for both races, the town's leaders had not yet provided their one and only black school with adequate facilities. The civil rights revolution even began to reach into Ervin's personal life. The new minister at the Presbyterian Church publicly supported some of the movement's goals, and Sam III came back from the war with new ideas about racial justice. Not only did Sam III's two sisters agree with him, but they were talking about enrolling in coeducational colleges, thus breaking the traditional mold Ervin women had followed for generations of attending all-women schools. One of his daughters, Leslie, eventually went on to become a lawyer, a decision Ervin did not encourage but would not prevent.[121]

Ervin did not oppose all these changes. Indeed, he embraced the economic transformations and even opened his mind, just a little, to consider the social challenges to the status quo. He had never thought that blacks, or women for that matter, should be denied equal opportunities in life; he just believed they should have separate ones. He had pushed for greater funding for Morganton's black school when he was in the state legislature, and he had given fair treatment to the women lawyers who appeared before him in court. He repeatedly recommended Susie Sharp for judicial positions, including the U.S. Supreme Court. Ervin had always provided the best legal services he could to all his clients, no matter if they were black or white, rich or poor, male or female. To his mind that was what being a good man and a responsible leader meant in North Carolina. But changing the political structure to allow some of these groups to have actual power—now that was something else altogether.

In this time of economic and social transformation the state needed good leaders, and in 1947 the Shelby Dynasty needed Sam Ervin. At first Governor R. Gregg Cherry asked him to serve as the chairman of the North Carolina State Board of Elections, but he refused. Then the governor appointed Ervin to a special commission to update the state's court system, which he could not resist. The commission's roster read like a "who's who" of the best legal minds in the state. At the first meeting they voted unanimously to make Ervin their chairman. Educational leaders in the Piedmont asked him to serve as their lobbyist in Raleigh, which he also agreed to do. "Education is to the soul of the child what sculpture is to the block of marble," he wrote the legislators. But when the governor called in January 1948, Ervin knew what he was going to ask, and he did not know how he was going to answer.[122]

Governor Cherry wanted to appoint Ervin to the North Carolina Supreme Court. Several years earlier he would have jumped at the chance to get on the state's highest court. Now he was not so sure. Accepting the position would mean moving to Raleigh and taking a significant cut in pay, from the more than $30,000 he made as an attorney to the $8,000 he would earn as an associate justice. Certainly it was a privilege and an honor, but was it his duty? He stayed up all night thinking about it. The next day he called the governor and declined. But once again the phone started ringing. Fellow attorneys encouraged him and local bar associations endorsed him. Ervin told them all he would rather stay in Morganton and practice law. "There is more fun in going up to the plate than in umpiring," he insisted.[123] But it did not take much to change Ervin's mind, and when the governor's office called back he accepted. The public response was overwhelmingly positive. One newspaper observed, "The new justice bears a name that long has stood for leadership in North Carolina and for achievement in legal circles." A friend concluded, "The man and the position are well met."[124]

On Justice Ervin's first day on the Supreme Court, Chief Justice Walter P. Stacy explained the unofficial rules of their private conferences. After hearing public arguments in a case the justices always asked the newest member to express his views first so that he would not feel any pressure to conform to the opinions of the more senior members. Stacy also told Ervin that the court followed another important rule: "Nothing which is said in this conference is ever revealed by any member of the conference, and nothing that anyone says is ever made public in any way."[125] The chief justice explained that the reason for the rule was not only to protect confidentiality but to ensure a vigorous and open debate: "If you have a good thought or some sound view about the case that is discussed, it will be very helpful; and if you have a fool thought, you don't have to worry about its consequences because it will not be attributed to you outside." "And," he added, "if you have such a fool thought there is nothing better to do than voice it in the presence of friends so they can swat it if it deserves to be swatted."[126] The best advice of the day, however, came from Justice A. A. F. Seawell, who, as the second most junior member of the court, had moved over one chair to give Ervin his former place on the far left of the bench. Seawell leaned over to Ervin and whispered, "You've got the best seat on the court. You can look out the window, and watch the squirrels running up and down the trees on the Capitol grounds, and ignore the nuts who argue cases before us."[127]

Justice Ervin delighted both lawyers and reporters alike with his clear opinions and keen sense of humor. Another distinguished jurist from North Carolina, Justice J. Braxton Craven Jr., concluded that Ervin's opinions were incomparably superior to the others written at that time. "The truth is that judges write poorly," Craven explained. "We have a pretty good excuse: We have to be precise and the discipline of precision does not make for poetry." The result is a style of writing that Craven called "tedious Gothic." "Mr. Justice Ervin was never cryptic, never inscrutable," Craven recalled, "but neither did he bore the reader to tears."[128] Ervin took pride in writing opinions in clear, unambiguous language based on carefully researched precedents, but he liked to have some fun as well. After Ervin had been on the court for a few years, a friend and fellow attorney wrote to him: "No sooner do I read in one case about the notes of Gabriel's horn trembling into silence than I read in another case about some judge murdering the King's, the Queen's, and everybody else's English with that linguistic monstrosity 'and/or.' . . . Keep at it! You relieve the tedium and dullness of the law."[129]

Quotations from Justice Ervin's opinions remain popular among North Carolina lawyers and judges, who cite them both to spice up their legal arguments and to give them more status and authority. Justice Craven's wife, also an attorney, once told him, "When I run across an Ervin opinion I can quit looking."[130] In the 1980s former governor and associate justice Dan K. Moore discovered one of Ervin's opinions that clarified certain rules of evidence so definitively that it had been cited in 178 other cases.[131] Bruce Tindall gathered some of the best lines from Ervin's opinions as part of a collection titled "Down Home Truths from Senator Sam Ervin," including the following:

Truth does not come to all witnesses in a naked simplicity. It is likely to come to the biased or interested witness as the image of a rod comes to the beholder through the water, bent or distorted by his bias or interest.

State v. Hart, 1954

Whether a statute produces a just or an unjust result is a matter for legislators and not for judges.

Deaton v. Deaton, 1953

The case illustrates anew the oft recurring truth that procedural mishaps befall litigants who shadow box with unrealities in their pleadings.

Wilkens v. Finance Co., 1953

Judges are not required by law to be more ignorant than all other men.

State v. Scoggin, 1952

Courts should not sustain legislative acts which sacrifice the constitutional rights of the individual to what is called social progress.

In re Housing Authority, 1952

The very sordidness of the evidence strongly tempts us to say that justice and law are not always synonymous and to vote for an affirmance of the judgement of death on the theory that justice has triumphed, however much law may have suffered. But the certainty that justice cannot long outlive law gives us pause.

State v. Bridges, 1949

What may be the ultimate fate of the prisoner in this case is of relatively minor importance in the sum total of things. In any event, his role on life's stage, like ours, soon ends. But what happens to the law is of gravest moment.

State v. Bridges, 1949[132]

When Justice Ervin served on the North Carolina Supreme Court, it had a reputation for being very efficient and very conservative, especially when it came to reaffirming precedents and supporting business. The justices turned out their decisions in about six weeks, while most of the other states' highest courts took six months to a year. The justices also produced few rulings that upset the status quo. Many of the court's decisions came down as unanimous, but that fact masked the intensity of the internal debates within the private conferences. Discussions could be very heated before a majority of justices decided the case and the minority agreed to put aside their dissenting views for the sake of legal clarity. Ervin fit in well on the court, although some observers described him as a "conservative libertarian," meaning that he leaned more toward limiting government power and protecting constitutional rights than did some of the other justices.[133]

Ervin demonstrated his libertarian streak in one of his most famous opinions, *State v. Palmer* (1949). Jim Palmer was a black man sent to death row for a brutal murder. When the case reached the Supreme Court, Ervin found that some of the state's evidence had been improperly submitted and the rest of the case against Palmer was extremely weak. He wrote: "The State's evidence may beget suspicion in imaginative minds. But when it is laid side by side with law and logic, it does not rise to the dignity of proof." Ervin then quoted the passionate prosecutor Delphidius from ancient Rome: " 'Oh, illustrious Caesar! If it is sufficient to deny, what hereafter will become of the guilty?' to which Julian replied, 'If it suffices to accuse, what will become of the innocent?' "[134] Ervin never forgot what Jim Palmer told the newspaper reporter who informed him of the court's ruling and asked how it felt to be freed: "Boss, we never get off death's row. We are on death's row from the day we are born to the day we die."[135]

In 1952 Tar Heel politics threatened to disturb Ervin's secluded life on the court. His friends from Burke County sponsored an Ervin for Governor rally in the state capitol during the same weekend that the Democrats were holding their annual Jefferson-Jackson dinner, the party's most important political gathering of the year. There had been a flurry of talk about Morganton's favorite son making a bid for the governor's mansion for several weeks, most of it coming from the western Piedmont. When newspapers asked Justice Ervin about the movement to draft him as a candidate, he pleaded "not guilty of being an accessory before the fact," but he did not nip it in the bud as he claimed later in life. Indeed, he spent considerable time during the weekend at the impromptu Ervin Campaign Headquarters in the Hotel Sir Walter posing for pictures and entertaining guests. But when his old classmate and good friend William Umstead announced that he was entering the race, Ervin promptly withdrew his name from consideration. Umstead won the election that November.[136]

Ervin's brief flirtation with running for governor seems out of character. His political career had never once progressed through democratic elections but had always advanced through appointments from his friends in the Progressive Plutocracy. It is unlikely he would have actually given up his seat on the court and jumped into a political campaign with uncertain results. Perhaps Ervin let his friends from back home push him along for a while until he came to his senses. It would not be the first time, nor the last, that he enjoyed being the center of attention. Whatever his motivation in 1952, it was the only time Ervin gave any hint of wanting to leave the court.[137]

One of Ervin's predecessors, Justice Willis J. Brogden, observed that the North Carolina Supreme Court was an institution where the justices were placed in a mausoleum while they still lived and hanged in effigy after they died. Ervin did not seem to mind the cloistered life at all. He enjoyed wrestling with legal abstractions on the high court much more than he had liked dispensing personal justice in the Superior Court. His health was good and his spirits high. He was the youngest member on the court when he arrived, only fifty-one years old, and he could anticipate a long career within its stately pillars and marble walls. Eventually Ervin even found a way for the family to move back to Morganton. He wrote his opinions in his study at home and sent them off via the mail. He only traveled down to Raleigh to hear arguments and participate in conferences. The trip back home only took a few hours. He could hop in his car and enjoy the drive through the rolling hills of the Carolina Piedmont, past Chapel Hill, past the county courthouses where he and his father had practiced law together, past old towns filled with old friends, until he saw the Blue Ridge Mountains rise in the distance and knew he was home. Justice Sam Ervin had found his niche in the world, and he planned to stay there for the rest of his life.[138]

CHAPTER THREE

SENATOR SAM

On 12 May 1954, North Carolina's senior senator died quietly at his desk in the Senate Office Building. The stroke that took Clyde R. Hoey's life left the state without an effective voice in the Senate at a time when it desperately needed strong leadership.[1] Just five days after Hoey's death, the U.S. Supreme Court knocked out the legal props supporting the South's entire system of racial segregation when it handed down its historic decision in *Brown v. Board of Education*. A unanimous Court declared that "in the field of public education the doctrine of 'separate but equal' has no place. Separate educational facilities are inherently unequal."[2] Governor William B. Umstead, himself nearly incapacitated by a heart attack the preceding year, turned to an old friend and college classmate to defend the state at this critical juncture. Umstead appointed Judge Sam Ervin to the United States Senate.

Few senators have entered the national arena as unexpectedly, or as dramatically, as did Sam Ervin. Within a few months of his surprising appointment, Ervin found himself embroiled in two of the most significant episodes of recent American history—the debate over the Supreme Court's desegregation ruling and the censure of Senator Joseph McCarthy. These two events thrust the new senator into the national spotlight, where his powerful opposition to *Brown* and courageous stand against McCarthy earned him the admiration of the inner circle of the Senate's leaders. In the Senate, collegial respect often translates into power, and Ervin quickly established himself as a force to be reckoned with in the two areas that would dominate his entire political career —civil rights and civil liberties.

Many of Ervin's admirers in North Carolina have played down the senator's record on civil rights. They have insisted that he opposed civil rights legislation not because he was a racist, but because he was a genuine civil libertarian. Ervin, they have argued, feared that in the process of protecting the civil rights of African Americans the federal government threatened the constitutionally protected individual liberties of all Americans. Today, most Tar Heels affectionately remember their "Senator Sam" as the heroic champion of civil liberties, not the staunch opponent of civil rights.[3]

But such contentions ignore and distort the reality that racial issues dominated most of Ervin's attention during his two decades in the Senate. His skillful legal opposition to the *Brown* decision, and to every civil rights bill from 1954 to 1974, earned him a reputation in the South as a brilliant constitutional scholar and in other sections of the country as a racist southern obstructionist. Indeed, he played such an important role in the political struggle over civil rights that if Watergate had never occurred, Sam Ervin's most significant historical legacy would have been his constitutional defense of racial segregation.

Ervin might never have become a senator if the *Brown* decision had not inflamed the tinderbox of racial hatred and fear that had long been smoldering just below the surface of North Carolina's political culture. The Court's desegregation ruling in May 1954 ignited a firestorm of protest among white Carolinians.[4] Cries of defiance competed with, and sometimes overwhelmed, the traditional voices of moderation on which the state's reputation as the most progressive southern state had rested.[5] Although Governor Umstead reminded his fellow Tar Heels, "The Supreme Court of the United States has spoken. . . . This is now the latest interpretation of the Fourteenth Amendment," he also stated that he was "terribly disappointed" and took immediate steps to circumvent the decision.[6] Racist appeals dangerously heated the state's political climate. The Ku Klux Klan, which had been declining in the state prior to *Brown*, came alive and launched a petition drive under the name "North Carolinians for Preservation of the White Race, Inc."[7] Thousands of angry white citizens signed the petitions, which threatened: "If the Supreme Court forces the whites to go to school with the Negroes against their will, this will be discrimination, and they should expect retaliation in kind."[8]

It was in this context that Governor Umstead faced the thorny challenge of appointing someone to fill Clyde Hoey's vacant seat in the U.S. Senate. It is clear that the *Brown* decision played a significant part in the selection process. Several of the state's newspapers had suggested that Irving Carlyle, a popular lawyer and political ally of the governor, would be Umstead's likely choice. But before the governor made his decision, Carlyle gave a speech at the Democratic state convention in which he concluded with some impromptu comments about *Brown*. Speaking from notes hastily scribbled on a scrap of paper, he stated: "The Supreme Court of the United States has spoken. As good citizens we have no choice but to obey the law as laid down by the Court. To do otherwise is to cost us our respect for law and order. And if we lose that in these critical times, we will have lost the quality which is the source of our strength as a state and as a nation."[9] His plea for compliance was not well received.[10] When Umstead named Ervin, and not Carlyle, many concluded that Carlyle had disqualified himself by suggesting a moderate response to *Brown*.[11]

A few newspapers had mentioned Judge Ervin as one among many possible candidates to replace Hoey, but none had portrayed him as a leading contender. However, several of Ervin's and Umstead's mutual friends worked behind the scenes to orchestrate Ervin's appointment. Soon after Hoey's death they asked Ervin about his interest in becoming a senator. The judge responded that he had no " 'hankering' for the job," but assured them he would accept the nomination if Umstead offered it. His friends then urged the governor to select Ervin by arguing: "His appointment would receive almost unanimous approval and that at this time would do much to allay the fears which have resulted from the recent Supreme Court decision."[12]

Ervin, too, was thinking about *Brown* and the growing agitation in Washington for civil rights. In a letter to one of his supporters he confided that he "entertained neither illusions nor delusions about Washington, whose chief activity is selling North Carolina and the rest of the South down the river." Ervin continued, "Whoever goes to the Senate will be charged with direct responsibility for assisting in ending this political trend."[13]

To be sure, *Brown* and the maintenance of racial segregation was not the only issue on the governor's mind. Umstead also had political reasons for choosing Judge Ervin as the state's next senator. The governor felt a great deal of pressure to select someone who would be able to win the special election scheduled for that November and then win reelection in 1956 when Hoey's term expired.[14] The people of North Carolina had been represented by eight different senators in the past ten years, and Umstead realized that the state needed a senator who would bring stability and unite the warring factions of the Democratic Party.[15]

In Judge Ervin, Umstead found the perfect choice. Cloistered in the marble hallways of the State Supreme Court for six years, Ervin had avoided the party's recent internecine battles. Having previously served as a traveling Special Superior Court judge, Ervin had become friends with the courthouse gang in many of the state's one hundred counties. And as a member of North Carolina's Progressive Plutocracy, he claimed to be "acquainted with virtually all the lawyers in the state."[16]

In addition, the governor had held Ervin in high regard since their days at Chapel Hill. As a freshman in 1913, Ervin had attended a Bible study group that Bill Umstead, a sophomore, led every Sunday morning in the Old East Dormitory. When Umstead asked Ervin to lead a prayer, the embarrassed freshman could only offer: "Lord, help us. Amen." Later that day, when Ervin apologized that he was not accustomed to praying in public, Umstead assured him: "I've heard preachers pray for hours about our needs. You covered them fully in less than half a dozen words."[17] They became friends and stayed in touch over the years.

Governor Umstead soon learned that other North Carolinians thought highly of Sam Ervin as well. When organized delegations started lobbying the governor to send their favorite candidate to the Senate, Umstead would read a list of names under consideration and ask them to pick a second choice. Almost every group chose Judge Ervin.[18] Thus, by appointing Ervin, Umstead presented his party with a future candidate who not only appeared willing to fight *Brown* and defend North Carolina's traditional system of race relations, but also possessed the classic winning political combination of no enemies, no political baggage, and many influential friends.[19]

Judge Ervin was in Raleigh, participating in the North Carolina Supreme Court's final conference before its summer adjournment, when the new chief justice, Maurice V. Barnhill, signaled him into his office. After closing all the doors to ensure their privacy, Barnhill whispered to Ervin that the governor wanted to meet with him, probably to discuss the Senate vacancy. The chief justice told his startled colleague that "the situation in Washington is deplorable" and that he hoped Ervin would accept the appointment if offered.[20]

Later that afternoon, the old college friends sat on the secluded side porch of the governor's mansion and discussed the possibility of Ervin going to the Senate. According to Ervin, when Umstead asked if he would accept, he expressed his sincere hope that the governor would choose someone else. "My first love is law—not politics," Ervin insisted. "However, I would accept appointment to the Senate as a duty."[21] The only promise Ervin remembers that the governor asked of him was that he would seek reelection.[22] The day after their meeting, Umstead announced that Sam Ervin would be North Carolina's next senator.

Ervin's decision to accept the appointment is somewhat surprising given his negative comments about his previous experience in Washington and his frequent references to how much he enjoyed living in North Carolina and working on the court. Ervin's explanation that he felt a patriotic duty to respond to the call of his state and his country is plausible but incomplete. While it is true that Ervin was a humble man, he was also ambitious and susceptible to the praise and prodding of others, as demonstrated by his flirtation with a run for governor in 1952. No doubt his old friend Bill Umstead knew how to play on his sense of duty while sitting on the porch of the governor's mansion that afternoon. But it is also likely that Ervin harbored the same sense of destiny, or what Presbyterians call predestination, that has propelled so many reluctant souls forward at times of great opportunity and challenge.

The press, though surprised by Umstead's choice, expressed nearly unanimous support. The *Durham Morning Herald* praised Ervin's "vigorous and well balanced intellect," and the *Asheville Citizen-Times* called him "a man of demonstrated ability, integrity and intelligence."[23] But while newspaper reporters agreed on Ervin's intellectual merits, they had a harder time characterizing his political philosophy. Several newspapers described him as a "moderate" after he told reporters on the day of his appointment: "I believe in clinging to the tried and true landmarks of the past, but I am willing to test the soundness of new ideas."[24] Other newspapers, relying on an unnamed friend's description, labeled him a "conservative-liberal."[25] The *Raleigh News and Observer* confessed, "We are not quite sure what a conservative-liberal is," but speculated that in 1956 Ervin might be popular enough to become the first of five appointed North Carolina senators to win reelection in his own right.[26] The only critical comments came from Raleigh's African American newspaper, the *Carolinian*, which worried that "our next senator may follow the tradition of opposing civil rights."[27]

Sam Ervin, born the year of *Plessy v. Ferguson*, 1896, became a U.S. Senator less than a month after the *Brown* decision, on 11 June 1954. That morning, he arrived in Washington, D.C., on a train with two special Pullman cars filled with family and friends. On one car hung a banner proclaiming, "Sam J. Ervin, Jr., U.S. Senator, Burke County." Later that day, Ervin was officially sworn in by Vice President Richard Nixon.[28]

Miss Margaret stood quietly by her husband's side during most of that hectic first day in Washington, but she excused herself for a few minutes to sit in on the sensational Army-McCarthy hearings being conducted just around the corner from the reception. The cavernous Senate Caucus Room, with its marble columns and high decorated ceilings, could barely contain the throng of spectators and reporters who crowded around the central table where the junior senator from Wisconsin sat badgering a witness. It had been four years since Joe McCarthy had burst upon the national scene by charging that Secre-

Ervin and his family arriving at the Union Station train platform in Washington, D.C., in 1954. From left, his daughters Laura and Leslie, the senator, Mrs. Ervin, daughter-in-law Betty, and Sam J. Ervin III. Ervin Family Papers, 4498, Southern Historical Collection, Wilson Library, University of North Carolina at Chapel Hill. Copyright AP/World Wide Photos. Courtesy of AP Images.

tary of State Dean Acheson knowingly employed 205 Communists in the State Department. In spite of his failure to produce even one actual Communist from his fictitious list, McCarthy had become a formidable figure in the Senate, especially after his intervention in the reelection bid of his leading critic, Senator Millard Tydings of Maryland, resulted in Tydings's resounding defeat. Now at the height of his power, McCarthy was taking on the Army, and Mrs. Ervin sat in disbelief as the man who was now her husband's colleague twisted facts, bullied witnesses, and impudently bellowed out "point of order, point of order" when his opponents tried to speak.[29]

Shaken by what she had seen, Miss Margaret implored her husband to avoid Joe McCarthy.[30] This was advice that Sam Ervin intended to heed. More imme-

*Senator Ervin reenacts his oath-taking with then Vice President Richard Nixon on
11 June 1954. North Carolina's senior senator, Alton A. Lennon, is standing in the middle.
Copyright AP/World Wide Photos. Courtesy of AP Images.*

diate concerns than McCarthyism dominated the new senator's time, such as
learning Senate protocol, setting up his office, and, more significant, helping
his state circumvent the Supreme Court's desegregation ruling. On hearing
that he had been assigned to the Government Operations Committee, Ervin
joked with reporters that he would certainly not volunteer to serve on McCarthy's infamous Permanent Investigations Subcommittee: "I doubt if even my
sweet disposition would last very long there."[31]

Ervin formed a negative opinion of Senator McCarthy rather quickly during
his first few weeks in Washington. Distanced from the intensity of McCarthyism
by his cloistered existence in the North Carolina Supreme Court, Ervin had
actually felt a vague sense of support for America's leading Communist-hunter.
Like most southern conservatives, Ervin had feared that Communists were
infiltrating the federal government, and in casual conversations he had defended McCarthy.[32] But after leaving his sheltered life on the court, Ervin began
to change his mind. On 9 June, just after his appointment, Ervin criticized
McCarthy's one-man subcommittee hearings. A few days later he ducked a

direct question about McCarthy by explaining that as a judge he had been accustomed to basing his opinions on precedent, and he just could not find a precedent for Senator McCarthy. But by the end of his first month in Washington, having observed firsthand the ungentlemanly tactics McCarthy employed, Ervin was urging voters "to get rid of" McCarthy by electing a Democratic majority to the Senate, which would immediately remove the Wisconsin Republican from his subcommittee chairmanship.[33]

In spite of his growing dislike of McCarthy, Ervin did not want to cross swords with the dangerous senator, and it soon began to appear as though he would not have to. The Army-McCarthy hearings, which ended the week after Ervin's arrival, marked the high water mark for both Senator McCarthy and the tide of anticommunist hysteria that bore his name. McCarthy had miscalculated badly when he accused the Army of harboring Communists within its ranks. After considerable waffling, the Army fought back. The televised hearings left most of the twenty million Americans who tuned in with the same conclusion that Mrs. Ervin had drawn—that McCarthy was more of a bully than a hero. With McCarthy's public support diminishing, the Senate leadership finally found the courage to try to tie down the loose cannon that had been rolling dangerously across its deck for the past four years.

On 2 August 1954, the Senate took its first step toward censuring McCarthy by forming a special committee to investigate his official behavior. Lyndon Johnson, the Senate minority leader, had the responsibility of picking three Democrats who, along with three Republicans, would face the unenviable task of sitting in judgment of Senator McCarthy. Lady Bird Johnson remembered that her husband viewed the committee selection as "a very serious thing that had to be done. . . . I never saw him try harder to create a committee that would be above reproach, of balanced Democrats and conservatives and somebody deeply rooted and versed in the Constitution."[34]

Johnson's search for Democrats who had the prestige, and courage, to take on "Tail Gunner Joe" did not go well. All his first-round candidates turned him down. The conservative leaders of the southern bloc, Walter George and Richard Russell, both of Georgia, refused to serve. Likewise, all the Catholic senators—one of whom he wanted on the committee to deflect the inevitable charges of anti-Catholicism that would come from McCarthy's Catholic supporters—all found excuses to evade the assignment.[35] Finally, Colorado's Edwin C. Johnson, a universally respected senior member of the Senate, agreed to lead the Democratic contingent, with one stipulation; he insisted that the other two Democrats be lawyers, preferably with judicial experience, since he had no legal training and wanted the committee to operate in a judicial, jurylike manner.

This selection process was supposed to be conducted in utmost secrecy, but rumors began to circulate around Washington that Lyndon Johnson might be considering the new senator from North Carolina for the committee.[36] Ervin confided to a reporter, "I pray the good Lord no such calamity will befall me. I can imagine no worse misfortune," and he quickly began to search for reasons why he should not be chosen.[37] Seizing on his earlier criticisms of McCarthy, Ervin suggested that if he served on the six-man censure committee McCarthy "could have me disqualified" for "prior judgment." Ervin also argued that "men ought to be appointed who have been here a long time and acquired prestige. I'm just the lowest down senator in seniority. . . . It's not the obligation of a poor little country fellow who just got here."[38]

But Lyndon Johnson needed senators with judicial experience, and he summoned Ervin to his office. When Ervin walked through the door, he found the minority leader surrounded by a group of the Senate's most revered Democrats, including Earle Clements of Kentucky, Walter George, and Ed Johnson. LBJ explained his predicament and told Ervin that Mississippi's John Stennis, also a former judge, had agreed to serve with Ed Johnson on the committee. Then the persuasive Texan asked Ervin if there was any reason why he should not be the third Democrat on the committee. Ervin reviewed his litany of excuses, stressing his prior statements against McCarthy. At first, Johnson seemed nervous about Ervin's comments tainting the committee and undermining the Senate's attempt to discipline McCarthy. But Walter George intervened, assuring Ervin that his statements had been relatively mild and asking him if, as a former judge, he could dismiss his predilections and base his decisions solely on the evidence presented. Here was Ervin's chance to escape, but his sense of duty and honesty would not allow him to take it. After a long pause, he assured his colleagues that he could judge McCarthy fairly and that he would consent to serve on the committee.[39] The next day when his colleagues offered their congratulations and sympathy, Ervin thanked them for the orchids but suggested that they might have to send a wreath later.[40]

When Vice President Nixon announced the makeup of the Senate's special committee, the public reaction was less than pleasing to Johnson and the Senate leadership. Like the Democratic representatives, the three Republicans assigned to the committee—Utah's Arthur V. Watkins as the chairman, plus Frank Carlson of Kansas and South Dakota's Francis Case—were not the renowned solons most reporters had expected. A popular joke at the time suggested that the Senate was throwing the lion into a den of lambs.[41] Johnson's aide, George E. Reedy, reported to his boss that while much of the press corps remained skeptical, "there is general agreement that the Democratic side is stronger than the Republican side, and most of the press boys are impressed by Ed Johnson and John Stennis."[42] Ervin, of course, was an unknown. Luckily for the committee, McCarthy's immediate charge that Ervin and several other committee members were prejudiced against him did not appear credible to the press.[43] The statements of confidence coming from Johnson and other Senate insiders convinced most reporters to temper their misgivings and give the committee a chance to prove itself.[44]

The Watkins Committee impressed its critics by maintaining a strict judicial atmosphere, even in the face of McCarthy's repeated attempts to disrupt the hearings. Watkins's goal was to get his committee "off the front pages and back among the obituaries," and one reporter observed that "the difference between the Army-McCarthy hearings and the Watkins Committee hearings was like that between a Hollywood premiere and a coroner's inquest."[45] Following the advice of his committee members, Watkins ruled that the proceedings would not be televised, and he wielded the gavel with calm authority. At one point McCarthy became so frustrated after Watkins ruled his histrionics out of order that he told reporters it was "the most unheard of thing I ever heard of."[46]

Senator Ervin remained fairly quiet during the proceedings, only engaging in one brief debate with McCarthy over his method of cross-examining General Ralph Zwicker during the Army-McCarthy hearings. Ervin especially questioned the appropriateness of McCarthy's statement "Don't be coy with me, General." Ervin explained: "Now I rather admire that, in a way. Personally, I would never have been bold enough to have made that observation on a cross-examination of anybody in the military service, unless perhaps it were a WAVE or a WAC, and I then would have been bold enough to do so only under romantic circumstances, where I was surrounded with soft music, moonlight, and roses; and I am satisfied I never would have been bold enough to give that admonition to either a general or a top sergeant." After a few minutes of discussion, McCarthy snapped: "That was my system of cross-examination. You might use different language, Senator Ervin, when you have an evasive answer. That was my system of trying to pull teeth. I finally pulled some of them and got some of the information." Sensing that McCarthy was about to launch an all-out attack, Ervin simply responded, "That is all," and ended the debate.[47]

Ervin's more significant contribution to the Watkins Committee occurred behind the scenes. When the senators began to consider how to go about the delicate business of censuring one of the most powerful and feared politicians in America, Ervin and Stennis recommended that the committee accept the wisdom of an old southern legal maxim: "Salt down the facts, the law can wait." They advised the committee to follow a conservative strategy of keeping the focus on the evidence of McCarthy's misconduct and away from debates over politics, legal precedents, policy, or the Communist threat. They also persuaded their colleagues to limit the actual charges against McCarthy to a few solid cases. The committee's final report, which recommended censuring McCarthy on two counts of disorderly behavior, reflected the southerners' wise counsel.[48]

As soon as the report was released, McCarthy lashed out at the Watkins Committee. In addition to repeating his accusation that several of the senators had been biased from the start, he also charged that the members of the committee had served as the "unwitting handmaidens, involuntary agents, and attorneys in fact of the Communist Party."[49] Ed Johnson quickly denied that he had entertained any prejudice against McCarthy when the hearings began and observed that in his long career he had been called many things but that this was the first time he had ever been called a "handmaiden" of anybody or anything.[50]

Ervin responded to McCarthy's attack during an appearance on "Meet the Press." Miss Margaret had now become so offended by McCarthy's ungentle-manly and distinctively unsouthern attacks on her husband that she relieved him of his promise to avoid a direct fight with McCarthy, and for the first time since taking his seat on the committee Ervin let his disdain for McCarthy show.[51] Objecting to McCarthy's "unwitting handmaiden" charge, Ervin suggested that if McCarthy did not believe that accusation to be true, then he had "attempted to assassinate the character of these senators and ought to be expelled from membership in the Senate for moral incapacity." If he did believe the charge to be true, then Ervin concluded that "McCarthy was suffering from mental delusions of gigantic proportions and ought to be expelled from the Senate for mental incapacity."[52]

The Senate met in an extraordinary special session a few days later to debate McCarthy's censure. Actually, the decision to discipline him had already been made by the inner circle of the Senate's leaders from both parties when they had formed the Watkins Committee. Therefore, the floor debate was more political theater—the ritualistic working out of public postures and symbolic arguments—than an effort to determine McCarthy's guilt or innocence. Still, a cloud of fear and apprehension seemed to engulf the proceedings. The Army-McCarthy hearings had broken McCarthy's spell over the public, but Mc-Carthyism was far from dead. Mail poured into Washington from across the country.[53] An organization calling itself "The Committee of One Hundred Americans for The Sole Purpose of Liquidating Traitors" threatened several senators by warning them: "You will censure Sen. McCarthy but we assure you that we will have enough courage to blow up the Senate to pieces. . . . So, vote for censure and be prepared to die."[54]

On the third day of the historic debate Ervin was writing out some notes for a speech he planned to give the following day when he received word that Watkins had postponed his own speech and the Senate was ready to hear him right away. Gathering his note cards and yellow legal pads, Ervin came forward to make one of the first and most dramatic speeches of his career. Speaking extemporaneously to a Senate chamber uncharacteristically full—due to the absence of any competing Senate business during the special session—the freshman senator from North Carolina took on Joe McCarthy.

Having watched McCarthy shrewdly turn the righteous anger of his adversaries against them in previous debates, Ervin chose a different weapon for his attack—humor. When Ervin had asked a member of his staff, Harry Gatton, if he had any suggestions for his upcoming speech against McCarthy, Gatton reminded the senator how his humorous stories had a way of pricking inflated egos and deflating overblown arguments. As Ervin delivered his speech to the packed Senate chamber, he inserted several of his favorite mountain tales at strategic points in his argument.

Commenting on McCarthy's characterization of the members of the Watkins Committee as "unwitting handmaidens" of Communism, Ervin told the story about a young lawyer who went to an old lawyer for some advice: "The old lawyer said, 'If the evidence is against you, talk about the law. If the law is against you, talk about the evidence.' The young lawyer said, 'But what do you do when both the evidence and the law are against you?' 'In that event,' said the old lawyer, 'give somebody hell. That will distract the attention of the Judge and jury from the weakness of your case.'" Ervin suggested that "this is precisely what Senator McCarthy is doing in his response to the report of the Select Committee."[55]

To defend himself against the charge of prior prejudice, Ervin attacked McCarthy's practice of taking statements out of context. Again, Ervin had just the right yarn to make his point, this one concerning a North Carolina preacher from the 1880s:

At that time the women had a habit of wearing their hair in top-knots. This preacher deplored that habit. As a consequence, he preached a rip-snorting sermon one Sunday on the text "Top Knot Come Down." At the conclusion of his sermon an irate woman, wearing a very pronounced top-knot, told the preacher that no such text could be found in the Bible. The preacher thereupon opened the Scriptures to the 17th verse of the 24th chapter of Matthew and pointed out these words: "Let him which is on the house-top not come down to take anything out from this house." Any practitioner of the McCarthy technique of taking things out of context can readily find the text "top not come down" in this verse.[56]

By the end of his speech Ervin had the Senate eating out of his hands. But he had saved his best story for last.

Many years ago there was a custom in a section of my country, known as the South Mountains, to hold religious meetings at which the oldest members of the congregation were called upon to stand up and publicly testify to their religious experiences. On one occasion they were holding such a meeting in one of the churches, and old Uncle Ephraim Swink, a South Mountaineer whose body was all bent and distorted with arthritis, was present. All the older members of the congregation except Uncle Ephraim arose and gave testimony to their religious experiences. Uncle Ephraim kept his seat. Thereupon, the moderator said, "Brother Ephraim, suppose you tell us what the Lord has done for you." Uncle Ephraim arose, with his bent and distorted body, and said, "Brother, he has mighty nigh ruint me." This is just about what Senator McCarthy has done to the Senate.[57]

The Senate erupted in laughter. Ervin, suddenly turning serious, warned that while the Senate was trying the issue of whether McCarthy's behavior deserved condemnation, the American people were trying another issue—whether the Senate would remain intimidated by McCarthy. Ervin concluded: "Does the Senate of the United States have enough manhood to stand up to Senator McCarthy? The honor of the Senate is in our keeping. I pray that Senators will not soil it by permitting Senator McCarthy to go unwhipped of senatorial justice."

Ervin received a great deal of praise for his speech, both at the time and in the years since. Lyndon Johnson told him, "You showed you don't scare easily."[58] Senator Thomas Hennings of Missouri confided to Ervin that he had been "deeply affected" by his performance.[59] To be sure, not all of the reaction was positive. One California woman wrote, "What a big windbag you turned out to be," and a frustrated Kentuckian addressed him as "Dear First Term Fathead." Other critics called him a "filthy little crackpot," a "RED worm," an "egg head," a "moron," and worse.[60] But in North Carolina local politicians reported to Ervin that the response to his speech had been overwhelmingly positive, and the state's newspapers praised their senator for his "courage,

"OH, EVERYBODY TALKIN' 'BOUT HE'VEN AIN'T GOIN' THERE"

Press reaction to Ervin's role in bringing down Senator Joe McCarthy was overwhelmingly positive, as illustrated by this cartoon by Hugh Haynie in the Greensboro Daily News, *1954. A copy is in the Sam Ervin Library and Museum, Western Piedmont Community College, Morganton, North Carolina. Courtesy of the* Greensboro Daily News.

eloquence and rare good humor."[61] The *Asheville Citizen* concluded: "Somebody had to say it right-out and plain. The Judge did. Bully for him!"[62]

Ervin's speech against McCarthy has taken on mythic proportions in North Carolina. Even before he became a national folk hero during the Watergate scandal, every summation of Ervin's career—ranging from full biographies to banquet toasts—has exaggerated the significance of Ervin's speech and overstated his "key role" in bringing down Joe McCarthy.[63] Ervin's speech did not significantly affect the outcome of the McCarthy episode. Not one major historical work on the McCarthy affair describes Ervin's role as central, and most fail to even mention his remarks to the Senate. Actually, the senator's legal advice to the Watkins Committee, and his defense of the constitutionality of the committee's recommendations in a brief comment late in the debate, were more important than his celebrated speech.[64] But even these contributions are not enough to earn Senator Ervin more than a passing mention as a supporting character in the historic McCarthy drama.

Ervin's stand against McCarthy tells us more about the senator's integrity and moral philosophy than about his place in American history. He opposed McCarthy not only because the Wisconsin senator threatened individual liberty, but also because he had not behaved like a gentleman. McCarthy had not played by the rules of the senatorial club and he had to be punished. But unlike most of his colleagues, Ervin did not believe that McCarthy's transgressions deserved retaliation in kind. After the Senate voted 67–22 to condemn McCarthy on 2 December 1954, he became the most despised man in Congress. He was privately snubbed and publicly humiliated. Whenever he rose to address the Senate, his colleagues would rudely shuffle papers or talk loudly as though he were not there. Ervin never took part in these attacks. On the contrary, he treated McCarthy with courtesy and kindness.[65] When McCarthy died in 1957, his wife requested that Ervin be among the Senate's official representatives at the funeral, but he came down with the flu and could not attend.[66]

Soon after the McCarthy affair came to a close in December 1954, Ervin headed back to Morganton for a much-needed rest. Asked by a reporter what he planned to do during the Christmas recess, Ervin's eyes lit up as they always did when he was about to tell a joke and he recited this child's poem:

I wish I was a little rock
A-sitting on a hill
A-doing nothing all day long
But just a-sitting still.

Then, Ervin paused and emphasized, "Not sitting 'at' a still!"[67]

But Ervin found that he had little time to rest. While he had been busy fighting Joe McCarthy, his fellow segregationists had been scrambling to find a defense against the *Brown* decision. The Supreme Court had stated unequivocally that racial segregation in public schools was unconstitutional, but many southerners hoped that the Court's implementation ruling, which was expected in the spring of 1955, would allow enough time for local school boards to develop methods to circumvent the desegregation order. Segregationists throughout the South came up with elaborate schemes to evade *Brown*, ranging from localized gradualism to statewide defiance.[68] Ervin supported their efforts, but the senator publicly urged his fellow southerners to take a "wait and see attitude," while he privately worked to develop legal and constitutional arguments to fight against the Supreme Court's intervention in southern race relations.[69]

In May 1955 the Supreme Court issued its enforcement decree, known as *Brown II*. In apparent concession to the South, the Court left implementation of its desegregation decision in the hands of southern federal jurists with the vague admonition to proceed "with all deliberate speed." The waiting was over and the white South sprang into action.[70]

The real battle against *Brown* was not fought in the Senate but in the federal courts and state governments south of the Mason-Dixon line. In these arenas, Sam Ervin and his senatorial colleagues had less of a role to play than the judges and state politicians back home. Judge John J. Parker, a friend of Ervin's and a fellow alumnus of Chapel Hill, stepped forward soon after *Brown II* to offer what would become the South's most effective legal strategy for maintaining racially segregated schools. Parker, a justice on the Fourth District Court of Appeals, offered an interpretation of *Brown* in *Briggs v. Elliot*, the first of the five desegregation cases consolidated under the single title *Brown v. Board of Education* to be retried. To the delight of white southerners, Parker explained that *Brown* "does not require integration. It merely forbids discrimination. It does not forbid such discrimination as occurs as the result of voluntary action. It merely forbids the use of government power to enforce segregation."[71]

The "*Briggs* Dictum," as it came to be known, provided a legal rationale to delay school integration. It implied that no effort had to be made to integrate public education; all the states had to do to comply with *Brown* was create "freedom of choice" plans by which each child could decide where he or she wished to attend classes. In fact, these plans denied any real choice to African Americans by including exhaustive administrative procedures and almost unlimited appeals. Sam Ervin and other segregationist politicians quickly embraced Parker's opinion as the authoritative interpretation of the Court's desegregation ruling. Most, but not all, of the federal jurists in the South also followed Parker's lead in circumventing the implications of *Brown*.[72]

Southern state governments reacted to *Brown II* almost as quickly as the federal courts in the South in their response to Virginia senator Harry F. Byrd's call for "massive resistance." With white citizens councils stirring up racial animosity, some states threatened to close their schools before they would allow white pupils to sit next to blacks. Several state officials even dredged up the old theory of interposition and declared *Brown* to be unconstitutional and therefore null and void within their state's boundaries.

In spite of North Carolina's reputation as a progressive southern state, its response to *Brown* differed little from that of its sister states from the old Confederacy. The North Carolina legislature approved the Pearsall Plan, which turned over control of the public schools to the local school boards and enabled them to institute freedom of choice schemes.[73] Ervin publicly supported the Pearsall Plan, staying in close contact with the governor's office during its development and implementation.[74]

In the Tar Heel State, economic reprisals and incidents of violence discouraged many African American families from attempting to send their children to the better-funded white schools. But some parents refused to be intimidated. In Old Fort, not far from Morganton, black families who tried to enroll their boys and girls in the all-white school faced a hostile crowd at the school door. A few days later, several whites attacked one of the African American men who organized the parents, beating him severely.[75] In another North Carolina mountain town, Bryson City, several whites circulated a rumor that the community's most respected white supremacist had given a gun to a local eccentric and would post him at the school the day the parents planned to talk with the school principal. The parents went to the school anyway and courageously proceeded with their meeting, even after seeing the supposed assailant standing by the front door. No shooting occurred, but a few days later one of the parents was fired from his job—a clear message that economic pressure would accompany the threats of violence.[76] North Carolina's version of massive resistance was so successful that Ervin could predict that racial segregation in the public schools "will be changed very slowly by the Supreme Court's latest decision."[77]

With the courts and state governments working in tandem to circumvent *Brown*, the southern senators' primary role became that of a cheerleading squad—to excite the crowd and whip up support. Numerous empirical studies have concluded that most Americans are only vaguely familiar with the actions of the Supreme Court.[78] Citizens may hold general opinions approving or disapproving of the direction the Court has moved on certain issues, but they seldom have more than a vague awareness of the Court's actual decisions. Political leaders, therefore, play a crucial role in shaping the public's opinion of the Supreme Court. Senators and other elected officials serve as judicial interpreters: they inform their constituents when significant rulings have been made and suggest how they should respond. The ability of politicians to control public opinion should not be overstated, but their power to manipulate the public's reaction to Supreme Court decisions such as *Brown* cannot be denied. According to one legal scholar, "There seems to be little question that if the sustained reaction of southern political leaders to *Brown* had been different than it was, so too would have been the response of their constituents."[79]

Ervin played the role of cheerleader well. He had dedicated his first press conference, given just a few days after his appointment to the Senate, to an attack on *Brown* and the Supreme Court. His comments were forceful, articulate, and based on legal principles. Few of his criticisms were original, but the press reported them in detail and with respect, probably because they came from a former North Carolina Supreme Court justice capable of stating his opinions in well-developed legal arguments.[80] Over the next few years, as massive resistance spread across the South, Ervin's sophisticated opposition to the *Brown* decision earned him a reputation as one of Jim Crow's most articulate defenders.

Yet despite his sustained attack on the Supreme Court, Ervin's response to *Brown* placed him in the moderate camp of southern leaders. Ervin embodied what historian William Chafe has called North Carolina's "progressive mystique," and he faithfully followed the etiquette of "civility."[81] The senator eschewed the overt racist rhetoric that many of his fellow colleagues shouted so venomously. Senator James O. Eastland of Mississippi, one of the South's shrillest spokesmen for white supremacy, insisted that the Court "had responded to a radical, pro-communist political movement," and he instructed his constituents: "You are not required to obey any court which passes out such a ruling. In fact, you are obligated to defy it."[82] In Georgia, the successful candidate for governor warned that "the meddlers, demagogues, race baiters and Communists are determined to destroy every vestige of states' rights," and he vowed to stop them, "come hell or high water."[83] In contrast, Ervin never condoned law-breaking of any kind. Nor did he ever utter a directly racist comment in public. Sam Ervin saw himself as a gentleman and a lawyer, and he explained his objections to *Brown*, as well as to all the civil rights legislation of the next twenty years, in polite legal argumentation based on constitutional principles.

During the civil rights battles, Senator Ervin presented a less strident and more thoughtful image than many of his southern contemporaries. Undated photograph from Sam J. Ervin Papers, Subgroup A: Senate Papers, 3847A, Southern Historical Collection, University of North Carolina at Chapel Hill.

Ervin's reputation as the Senate's leading constitutional authority, which served him so well during the Watergate scandal, rested primarily on his performances as the South's constitutional expert during debates over civil rights. Many of the legal arguments Ervin developed during these debates became intertwined with the central tenets of his constitutional philosophy and shaped every aspect of his political career. The *Brown* decision presented Ervin with his first opportunity to advance the constitutional themes and tactics he would depend upon in most of his battles against civil rights and the Supreme Court over the next two decades.

Ervin built his case against *Brown* on four major premises. First, he echoed the states' rights philosophy that had once again become the South's defensive battle cry.[84] Second, Ervin argued that "the Constitution ought to be interpreted according to the principles of constitutional law and nothing else whatever on the face of the earth."[85] When several of Ervin's constituents urged him to accept *Brown* because it was morally correct, he answered: "Our views diverge because you think that the Constitution ought to be interpreted to conform to the precepts of religion while I think it ought to be interpreted to conform with the principles of Constitutional law."[86] Third, Ervin charged that in *Brown* the Supreme Court "exercised a power denied to it by the Constitution itself—the power to amend the Constitution."[87] He believed that because the Court had expanded the meaning of the Fourteenth Amendment beyond the original intent of its authors—by applying the "equal protection" clause to the racial makeup of public schools—it had "usurped" the power of Congress and the states to change the Constitution, and was therefore guilty of judicial activism.[88]

Ervin's fourth and most important argument against *Brown* rested on the legal doctrine of *stare decisis*, which holds that when a principle of law has been settled by a series of decisions, it is binding on the Court and should be followed in all similar cases. He insisted that in *Brown* the Court had overturned established precedents and had threatened the stability of the law by "casting on the scrapheap of history the sound decisions made by the able Judges who sat upon the Supreme Court from the days of John Marshall through the days of Charles Evans Hughes."[89] He even asked, tongue-in-cheek, if the words inscribed on the Supreme Court building should be changed from "Equal Justice Under Law" to "Justice According to the Personal Notions of the Temporary Occupants of This Building."[90]

All four of these arguments reflect the conservatism of Ervin's constitutional philosophy. He believed that the original intent of the framers of the Constitution and its amendments could be readily discerned and that the

Supreme Court was forever bound to abide by it. He viewed any reversal, reinterpretation, or expansion of a constitutional provision by the Court to be a "usurpation of power" and a rejection of "established legal precedents and rules." Thus, Ervin's philosophy preserved the status quo and guaranteed the power of the southern states to deny African Americans their civil rights without fear that the U.S. Supreme Court would interfere.

Many historians have agreed with Numan Bartley, who dismissed such constitutional arguments as mere "legal sophistries that served as cloaks for white supremacy."[91] Yet Ervin was not alone in advancing these constitutional positions.[92] After 1954, legal scholars engaged in a vigorous debate over many of the points the former judge raised.[93] Furthermore, Ervin had built his judicial philosophy on the respected tenets of what Morton J. Horwitz has called the tradition of "liberal jurisprudence," and his conservative view of the Supreme Court has been shared by many well-known scholars and politicians.[94]

Still, there is a persuasive counterargument to each of the charges Ervin leveled at *Brown*. First, though the Constitution does reserve some powers to the states, these powers do not include the right of a state to violate the equal protection clause of the Fourteenth Amendment. Second, Ervin's contention that the Court's decisions should be based solely on "the principles of constitutional law" suggests a naive interpretation of judicial behavior. The rulings of any court always reflect the religious, cultural, and scientific values of the judges who decide them.[95] Ervin's third charge, that the Court "usurped" the power of the Congress and the states to amend the Constitution, runs contrary to the basic principle of judicial review. Since the days of Chief Justice John Marshall, the Court had established its power to interpret the meaning of the Constitution and determine the constitutionality of actions of both the state and federal governments.[96]

As to Ervin's fourth argument, which is the foundation upon which his other legal points rest, if all justices followed his strict understanding of *stare decisis*, no decisions would ever be overturned and the law would become static. Of course, courts must follow precedents or the judicial system would fall into anarchy. However, in *Hertz v. Woodman* (1909) the Supreme Court explained: "The rule of *stare decisis*, though one tending to consistency and uniformity of decision, is not inflexible. Whether it shall be followed or departed from is a question entirely within the discretion of the Court, which is again called upon to consider a question once decided."[97]

Some scholars have argued that Ervin contradicted himself on this point. In a 1956 article defending *Brown*, Harvard Law School Professor Charles Fairman pointed out that while Ervin served on the North Carolina Supreme

Court he had defended the practice of overruling precedents in the light of further study or a change in circumstances.[98] He quoted one of Ervin's opinions in which he had argued: "There is no virtue in sinning against light or in persisting in palpable error, for nothing is settled until it is settled right."[99]

Ervin responded to Fairman's accusation by insisting that his statement had been taken out of context and bore no more resemblance to the Supreme Court's action in *Brown* than "my homely face bears to the beauteous countenance of Miss America."[100] He admitted overturning a prior ruling in the North Carolina case, but insisted that he had not reversed a legal principle based on a series of decisions as the rule of *stare decisis* requires. Instead, he had only reversed a single case "much weakened as an authoritative precedent by a dissenting opinion of acknowledged power and force of reason."[101] Technically, Ervin was correct: a single case does not establish a precedent. But Professor Fairman had successfully demonstrated that even the conservative Judge Ervin occasionally found a legitimate reason for overturning prior decisions and reinterpreting the law.[102]

In truth, Sam Ervin's response to the Supreme Court's desegregation decision was not so much a legal critique as a political strategy. In the furious battle over *Brown*, most of the Court's advocates, and opponents, found the legal subtleties of the debate confusing and irrelevant. What did matter, to both sides, was that a former North Carolina Supreme Court justice with a Harvard law degree advanced the argument that the South had legitimate legal reasons to resist the racial integration of its public schools.

The significance of Ervin's crusade against *Brown* rested not only on what he said but also on how he said it. Much as he had in his Senate speech attacking Joe McCarthy, Ervin decorated his technical legal arguments against *Brown* with colorful mountain anecdotes and wrapped his defense of Jim Crow in lofty philosophical principles. The senator also knew how to play to the crowd, writing different types of speeches for different types of audiences. Ervin's clever rhetorical strategy is apparent in two speeches he delivered against *Brown* the year after the Court issued its desegregation decision, one in Richmond, Virginia, the other in New York City.[103]

In March 1955 Ervin spoke to the annual Democratic Jefferson-Jackson Dinner in Richmond. His address, entitled "Our Heritage: A Blessing and an Obligation," was primarily an assault on *Brown*, but he told his audience that he would "forego discussion of the transient issues of the hour . . . to consider the fundamental principles which must be preserved if the America we know and love is to endure."[104] To explain these principles, he quoted Woodrow Wilson: "Liberty has never come from the government. Liberty has always come from the subjects of it. The history of liberty is a history of resistance. The history of liberty is a history of limitations of governmental power, not the increase of it."[105] Ervin suggested that the Supreme Court's recent actions represented a dangerous "usurpation of power"—just the kind of increase in the government's power Woodrow Wilson had warned against. As usual, his speech was devoid of sexual innuendo, Communist conspiracies, or any of the other blatant fear-mongering tactics popular in the South at the time. Instead, he reassured his audience that their fight against *Brown* was within the American tradition of fighting tyranny and preserving liberty.

Of course, Ervin always had a few stories from down home to share with his audience. On this occasion, he recited a tale tinged with racial overtones but stopped short of an overtly racist attack:

> My diplomatic colored friend, Jock Fleming, went automobile riding with two companions. The automobile was undoubtedly full of gasoline. Its occupants were allegedly full of moonshine. The automobile left the road and turned over, causing substantial injuries to Jock's two companions. Jock was unhurt. After extricating Jock's two companions from the wreckage and sending them to the hospital for medical attention, Morganton's Chief of Police, Fons Duckworth, undertook to ascertain by inquiry of Jock who was driving the automobile at the time of the accident. He received this reply from Jock: "For God, white folks, for God, I don't know. The last thing I remember all three of us were riding on the back seat."[106]

Ervin suggested that Jock's answer reminded him of the Eisenhower administration in Washington, since it appeared that everybody was riding in the back seat and no one was steering the country in any direction.

Ervin told a lot of stories, many of which did not involve African Americans, but his choice of this particular story for this particular occasion demonstrates the subtle manner in which he could identify with his audience's racism without abandoning his role as the gentlemanly constitutional scholar. Imagine the white crowd's delight as he mimicked Jock's accent and exaggerated his deferential reply to the white chief of police. Imagine, too, the feelings of the black waiters in Richmond's Hotel John Marshall who probably clenched their teeth, and perhaps their fists, as they stood silently in the back of the dining room.[107]

The following month, Ervin addressed the Harvard Law School Association of New York City. This was a different kind of occasion, and it called for a different kind of speech. The senator wisely replaced the story of Jock Fleming's automobile accident with a few anecdotes unblemished by racial humor. Ervin titled this address "Alexander Hamilton's Phantom." He explained that in 1787, Hamilton had rejected the need for tighter controls on the Supreme Court in the Constitution because "the supposed danger of judiciary encroachment . . . is, in reality, a phantom."[108] Hamilton had reasoned that the men chosen to sit on the Court would be highly qualified and would realize the need for judicial restraint. The errors of the present Court, though, Ervin said, showed that Hamilton's phantom had become a reality.

"Alexander Hamilton's Phantom" was well received in the South. Southern law journals reprinted it, newspapers quoted it, and Ervin sent thousands of copies to his friends and constituents.[109] The speech found its way to an odd assortment of audiences: it was passed out at a luncheon club in Birmingham, Alabama; circulated at the Rotary Club of Hampton, Virginia; distributed to the Episcopal clergy in Atlanta, Georgia; and carried door to door in several small towns in Tennessee.[110] In North Carolina, some newspapers observed with pride that their senator had achieved a national reputation, and one bragged that he did not behave like a "sourhead southerner" or a "bigot" but spoke like "an experienced jurist with a Harvard education."[111] Only the *Asheville Citizen* expressed any concern. The paper, located near Ervin's home in the mountains where for generations Jeffersonian ideas had been treated with reverence and Hamiltonian concepts considered blasphemous, wondered "how in tarnation a good Burke County boy got caught quoting A. Hamilton in broad daylight."[112]

Both of Ervin's speeches against *Brown* not only exhibited the senator's trademark constitutional argumentation and folksy oratory, but also demonstrated his consistent practice of sticking to the rhetorical high road. Instead of attacking his opponents' intended results—such as allowing black children the same educational opportunities white children enjoyed—Ervin defended constitutional principles he believed his opponents were threatening. By packaging his case against *Brown* in time-honored American principles, subtle racism, folksy anecdotes, and constitutional wrapping, Ervin attempted to bring some much-needed respectability to the southern defense of racial segregation.[113]

As Ervin stumped the South attacking the Supreme Court, some of Dixie's other senators decided that a more unified effort was needed. In 1956, South Carolina's Strom Thurmond and Virginia's Harry Byrd instigated a movement among the South's representatives in Congress to issue a "Southern Manifesto" against the Supreme Court's desegregation decision. They circulated a bold statement that not only attacked *Brown* as unconstitutional, but also endorsed massive resistance and interposition as legitimate strategies. After southern moderates balked at signing such a radical document, the leader of the southern caucus, Walter George, assigned a committee of three senators with recognized legal talent to redraft the document and tone down the rhetoric. The committee included Richard Russell as the chairman, John Stennis, and Sam Ervin.[114]

Ervin later claimed that he had played a major role in writing the Manifesto, helping to consolidate it into a single statement after each of the three senators had written his own draft. He also took credit for toning down the bellicosity and building up the legal arguments. Ervin told his constituents that his goal was "to draft the declaration to serve as a lamp of moderation in these crucial days."[115] But the senator's moderation had limits, and he warned of "the dangers that lie ahead if agitators from the outside continue to stir up this issue."[116]

On 12 March 1956, Walter George defiantly read the Southern Manifesto to the Senate. The revised version did not endorse interposition or specifically mention massive resistance, but it did call on all southerners "to resist forced integration with any lawful means."[117] Even with its most strident phrases removed, the Manifesto remained a dramatic call to arms, or as one constitutional scholar described it, "a calculated declaration of political war against the Court's decision."[118] One hundred and one of the South's 128 national representatives signed the document, and its release evoked expressions of support throughout Dixie.

The Southern Manifesto had a significant impact on North Carolina's elections that year. All but three of North Carolina's representatives had signed the statement, and two of those three lost in the Democratic primary, with their refusal to support the Manifesto clearly contributing to their defeat.[119] Ervin, whose participation in writing the document was well known in his home state, carried every one of the state's one hundred counties in the primary. That November Ervin became the first appointed senator in North Carolina's history to win reelection in his own right. He never had to worry about reelection again.[120]

Sam Ervin's short first term as a U.S. senator foreshadowed the principal themes and contradictions of the rest of his political career. His stand against Joe McCarthy had demonstrated his commitment to defend civil liberties and the integrity of the Senate from the excesses of a powerful politician who had manipulated anticommunism into self-aggrandizement. His opposition to the *Brown* decision illustrated his commitment to defend Jim Crow segregation and the southern way of life from the rulings of a revitalized Supreme Court that finally put the law on the side of the African American struggle for freedom.

Ironically, it was not his role as a defender of civil liberties during the McCarthy affair—which has often been overstated—but his opposition to civil rights after the *Brown* decision—which has often been overlooked—that propelled Ervin to a position of power in the Senate. In 1956, the same year that his southern colleagues selected Ervin to help write the Southern Manifesto, they orchestrated his appointment to the powerful Judiciary Committee. James Eastland of Mississippi, the committee chairman, also assigned the North Carolinian to the recently formed Subcommittee on Constitutional Rights, where any future civil rights bill would begin its laborious journey through the legislative process. By placing Ervin on these strategic committees, the southern bloc positioned the ex-judge where his legal skills could do the most damage to any new civil rights challenges. Within the year, they would realize just how shrewd their assignment had been.

THE SOFT SOUTHERN STRATEGY

When Sam Ervin attended his first Senate Judiciary Committee meeting in 1956, the Congress had not passed a civil rights bill since Reconstruction. At the close of the legislative session the preceding year, an exasperated Roy Wilkins, the executive director of the National Association for the Advancement of Colored People (NAACP), complained: "More than one hundred civil rights bills were introduced during the session by members of both parties. [Yet] not one of these bills was voted upon. Not one was even brought to the floor for debate. Not a single federal civil rights bill as such has been enacted by Congress for more than three-quarters of a century!"[1]

Most of the blame—or, from Sam Ervin's perspective, the credit—for Congress's inactivity in the field of civil rights belonged to the southern bloc in the Senate. Because of their seniority, the southern Democrats had gained a stranglehold over the Senate's leadership and committee system. In 1956, no fewer than twenty-one of the Senate's committees and subcommittees were chaired by southern segregationists.[2] Of these, the Judiciary Committee was the South's most important stronghold. Time after time, southerners killed civil rights bills by having them assigned to the Judiciary Committee, where they experienced superfluous amendments, endless hearings, canceled meetings, and other stalling tactics. So effective was this strategy that the Judiciary Committee became known as "the civil rights graveyard."[3]

But by 1956, both the leadership and the strategy of the infamous southern bloc was in transition. The old guard, led by Georgia's senior senator, Walter George, was passing the reins of power to a new generation of segregationists.

A meeting of the Southern Caucus, which held significant power in the U.S. Senate in the 1950s and early 1960s. Ervin is seated second from left. Photograph taken in 1963. Sam Ervin Library and Museum, Western Piedmont Community College, Morganton, North Carolina.

Traditionally, historians have focused on four southern senators who assumed special leadership roles. Richard Russell of Georgia replaced Walter George as the southern bloc's strategic general. Russell, a bachelor, was rumored to spend all his evening hours memorizing minuscule points of parliamentary procedure to thwart civil rights legislation on the Senate floor. Virginia's Harry Byrd gained fame for his masterminding of the South's massive resistance to racial integration. As one scholar concluded, Byrd, "more than any other single individual, determined the shape and style of the movement as it evolved in the decade after 1954."[4] Perhaps the most outspoken senatorial defender of segregation was Strom Thurmond of South Carolina, the presidential candidate for the States Rights Party in 1948. Mississippi's James Eastland, who chaired the Senate Judiciary Committee, became the fourth powerful voice in the southern bloc. Eastland was the chief spokesman for the Deep South and the primary source of the conspiracy theory that the civil rights movement operated under the influence of the Communist Party.[5]

In the mid-1950s, Sam Ervin emerged as a fifth member of this elite group of southern senatorial leaders. From his position on the Judiciary Committee and its Subcommittee on Constitutional Rights, Ervin crafted a new legal-constitutional strategy that became the primary weapon in the southern bloc's arsenal against civil rights legislation. By the end of the decade, North Carolina's ol' country lawyer had become Jim Crow's leading defense attorney in the U.S. Senate.

Reporters labeled Ervin's new constitutional strategy to defeat civil rights bills the "soft southern approach."[6] Ervin replaced the traditional, angry, racist rhetoric of the past with a polite, legalistic approach that proved much more effective. Dismissed by some scholars as mere "legal sophistry," the soft southern strategy has received far less attention than the more openly racist approaches practiced by such outspoken segregationists as Byrd, Thurmond, and Eastland.[7] Many civil rights activists, however, believed Ervin's legal strategy to be a far greater threat to their movement, and the NAACP repeatedly warned its lobbyist on Capitol Hill to build a strong legal case because "Senator Ervin . . . will be using his remarkable talents to build a negative record."[8]

We underestimate the complexity of the South's response to the Second Reconstruction, and overlook the intricacies of southern racist thought, when we portray all opponents of civil rights as ignorant and irrational demagogues. To be sure, many were. But some of the white defenders of the segregated South developed shrewd and coherent political philosophies to maintain segregation. Sam Ervin's soft southern strategy represented one of the most insidious and effective examples of the white South's response to the African American struggle for freedom.[9]

In 1956, the political context that had allowed the southern Democrats in the Senate to block every civil rights bill since 1875 changed abruptly. Several factors combined to create a new political environment that brought hope to African Americans and fear to southern segregationists. First, black activism had been increasing on several fronts. The NAACP and the Leadership Conference on Civil Rights (LCCR) had intensified their lobbying efforts on Capitol Hill and, encouraged by the *Brown* decision, showed a renewed determination to force Congress to act.[10] These organizations were reinforced by a new wave of direct action protests by African Americans in the South, best exemplified by the drive to integrate the bus system of Montgomery, Alabama, in 1955.

Second, an increasing number of white liberals and intellectuals recognized the need for significant advances in civil rights.[11] A mixture of disdain for racial discrimination, a concern for the image of the United States in the Cold War battle for world opinion, and a desire to remove the barriers that racial politics put in the way of their own political agenda inspired many white reformers to enlist in the crusade for civil rights. Liberals in both political parties had begun a serious push for a major civil rights bill in the spring of 1956, but had, once again, met with frustration.[12]

Then, in November, a number of African Americans did something that shook the political landscape and sent tremors of fear through both the South and the Democratic Party—they voted Republican. Civil rights leaders such as Roy Wilkins and Clarence Mitchell, executive director of the LCCR, had been warning the Democrats for several years that black voters would not tolerate their party's support of southern obstructionism much longer. Encouraged by a steady expansion in black voter registration, these leaders canvassed the country before the 1956 presidential election and challenged African Americans to reconsider which party had done more for them recently. Mitchell reminded black audiences that if the Republicans gained control of Congress, they "would automatically eliminate 21 southern chairmen from the key committee posts they now hold."[13] In the middle of the campaign, Mitchell's wife, Juanita, announced she was switching her support to Eisenhower.[14] Brightly colored posters appeared in black neighborhoods in several northern cities that read: "When you feed the head of a dog you nourish the whole body. Remember when you vote for a Democratic Senator, Representative or Alderman in New York, Chicago, Detroit—or anywhere—you vote to make EAST-LAND and the Southern race-baiters chairmen of the important committees in Congress."[15]

Unprecedented numbers of African Americans voted in the 1956 presidential election with a surprising percentage casting their ballots for Eisenhower.[16] There was an 18 percent increase over 1952 in the vote for Eisenhower in predominantly black districts.[17] Not since 1936 had there been such a discernible change in black voting patterns. The Democrats lost twenty-five of the country's largest thirty-six cities, including traditional Democratic strongholds such as Baltimore, Chicago, Memphis, and Jersey City.[18] *Newsweek* observed: "Everywhere, the consensus is the same: The days when the Democrats could count on getting 80 percent of the Negro vote are over. They'll have to fight for that vote now."[19] *Time* reported that the election "encouraged Republicans to try even harder for the Negro's vote" and "convinced Northern and Western Democrats that they must start paying more than lip service to civil rights."[20] A majority in both the House and the Senate, and in both political parties, suddenly seemed anxious to pass a civil rights bill.[21]

The new momentum for civil rights legislation posed a tremendous challenge to Ervin and the southern bloc in the Senate. Traditionally, the southern Democrats could rely on the help of conservative Republicans—as well as moderate Democrats who did not wish to see their party torn apart by racial politics—to stand aside while the South's obstructionists bottled up civil rights bills in committee. But after the 1956 election, both Republicans and non-southern Democrats stood to gain politically by supporting a civil rights bill. If the Eisenhower administration produced legislation moderate enough to gain widespread support, the southerners would be left standing alone, an isolated minority unable to kill the bill in committee. Then, Ervin's colleagues might have to fall back on their ultimate weapon, the filibuster, in what might be a failed effort to stop the legislation.

Choosing to filibuster in 1957 could be terribly costly to the southern bloc. In the past, simply threatening to filibuster had been so effective that the actual talkathon seldom occurred. A southern filibuster had an aura of invincibility about it. It evoked images of all-night sessions, hour after hour filled with ugly racist rhetoric, week after week in which no other business could be brought before the Senate. But if they resorted to the filibuster in 1957, when, in the changed political climate, a coalition of Republicans and non-southern Democrats might gain the two-thirds vote necessary for cloture, the South would stand considerably weakened before future civil rights measures that promised to be even stronger.[22]

To the southerners' regret, the Eisenhower administration sent a civil rights package to Congress that was moderate, sensible, and potentially effective. The legislation contained four parts. Title I created a civil rights commission authorized to investigate and report violations of civil rights laws. Title II expanded the Justice Department's small Civil Rights Section into a full division with its own assistant attorney general and significant increases in its staff and resources. Neither of these proposals was particularly controversial. Far more threatening to the South were the other two sections of the bill that greatly expanded the powers of the attorney general to act in civil rights cases. Title III empowered the attorney general to initiate suits on behalf of the victims of many types of racial discrimination, and Title IV enhanced his power to seek injunctions to protect the right to vote.

Especially troubling to Ervin and his colleagues was the civil rights bill's emphasis on protecting the franchise, not because it was drastic but because it put them on the defensive. For constitutional purists like Sam Ervin it was very difficult to argue against guaranteeing any citizen's right to vote, even if that person was, as Ervin pronounced it, a "Nigra."[23] How could Ervin, whose rhetoric was filled with references to individual rights, oppose a measure to protect the most basic right of every American—to cast a ballot in a free election?[24]

THE SOFT SOUTHERN STRATEGY

Dixie's old strategy appeared to be out of date. The segregationists' traditional weapons of race baiting, burying the bill in committee, and threatening to filibuster seemed far less threatening in the new political climate created by the independence of the African American vote in 1956. The southern bloc had to scramble to find a new means of defeating the civil rights bill of 1957, and Sam Ervin's recent committee assignments put him right in the middle of their effort to develop that new strategy.

As expected, the Senate assigned the bill to the Judiciary Committee in January 1957, and Eastland immediately sent it to the Subcommittee on Constitutional Rights. Senator Thomas Hennings, the liberal Democrat from Missouri who chaired the subcommittee, hoped to conduct quick hearings and return the bill to the full committee with a favorable recommendation. Senator Ervin had other plans. The North Carolinian wrote to the governors of every southern state asking if they, or their representatives, wished to testify against the civil rights bill.[25] He then demanded that the subcommittee postpone its hearings so that the governors' schedules could be accommodated. The southern foot-dragging had begun. To many observers, it looked as though the segregationists would rely on their traditional strategy after all.[26]

On the first day of the hearings, Attorney General Herbert Brownell appeared before the subcommittee to defend the administration's civil rights bill. Across the table, behind a pile of law books and legal notes, sat Sam Ervin, who planned to cross-examine the attorney general on every title and every clause of the proposed legislation. The jousting match between the administration's and the segregationists' legal champions lasted three days, and it attracted an exceptional amount of media attention. Reporters flocked to the dramatic subcommittee hearings, attracted by the political theater as much as by the content of the debate.

Just as he had after the *Brown* ruling, Ervin won over many reporters by his polite demeanor and folksy anecdotes. Typical of the favorable coverage was a story in the *Baltimore Sun* that reported, "Holding the bridge for the South is a handsome, amiable, small-town North Carolina lawyer . . . who possesses a talent for extended discussion that has civil rights proponents quivering."[27] Many of the witty jabs Ervin and Brownell threw at each other during the next few days found their way into the newspapers. At one point, Ervin illustrated his complaint that the scope of the bill was too broad by telling the story of a Presbyterian and a Methodist who were arguing over predestination: "The Methodist said he'd just as soon not be a Presbyterian and be predestined to go to hell." And the Presbyterian came right back and said that was better than to be a Methodist and not know where in the hell you're going. Whereupon the

Methodist brother knocked the Presbyterian brother down. "Now, Mr. Brownell," Ervin asked, "don't you agree that under this bill that would be a federal crime?" The attorney general, a Methodist, careful not to get into a religious argument with Ervin, a Presbyterian, thought it over for a second before kidding: "Senator, I just can't imagine a Methodist doing anything like that." "This," explained Ervin in his most exaggerated southern drawl, "was a North Carolina Methodist," causing Brownell, the subcommittee, and the press to break into laughter.[28]

Not all of the Ervin-Brownell contest was so light-hearted. Beneath both men's civil demeanor simmered intense emotions that occasionally boiled into the open.[29] Ervin's deep commitment to defending the South from outside attacks against its social system of race relations drove him to work exceptionally hard during the hearings. Sometimes the strain showed. In response to Brownell's accusation that North Carolina had turned African Americans away from the polls, Ervin unwisely snapped: "I have never heard of a single individual, until this morning, that has ever been denied his right to register and vote on account of his race or color."[30] As Raleigh's African American newspaper observed, "Either Senator Ervin is an inveterate liar or he is grossly ignorant of what is going on in North Carolina."[31]

Brownell, too, found himself under extraordinary pressure—not all of it coming from the hearings. During and soon after his appearance before the subcommittee, the attorney general's children received obscene mail, his wife got threatening phone calls, his family members across the country were followed by private detectives hoping to dig up embarrassing revelations, and he awoke one morning just in time to chase away several men who were dumping kerosene on his house in an attempt to burn it to the ground.[32]

It was only a matter of time until Brownell snapped under this extreme pressure. The moment came when the direction of Ervin's questioning suggested that the administration might rely on Title III to send federal troops into the South to enforce court-ordered school desegregation. Brownell exploded in anger, denouncing the implication that the president of the United States would act "recklessly and unconstitutionally." Red-faced and furious, Brownell declared: "I personally cannot sit by and allow any such implication to show in the record. This has gone far enough!"[33] The attorney general emphatically insisted that no one in the administration had any intention of calling up the militia to enforce school desegregation—a comment that would come back to haunt him after Eisenhower sent troops into Little Rock for that very purpose later in the year.[34]

As the hearings wore on, the press corps began to detect the outline of the

South's new strategy to defeat the civil rights bill. Reporters noted how Ervin was "putting the south's best foot forward" and "supplying a new twist to an old argument." They observed that the North Carolinian had "abandoned the emotionalism of other days and fought Attorney General Brownell's right to vote proposals with adroit legal points," which "raised a cloud of legal doubt" over the constitutionality of the bill. As he had during his opposition to the *Brown* decision, Sam Ervin brought a new legal-constitutional dimension to the South's fight to preserve the racial status quo. One journalist who watched the ex-judge question the attorney general on the legal nuances of the bill summed up Ervin's strategy: "Speak softly, but carry a law book."[35]

In many ways, the soft southern approach Ervin developed during the hearings to fight civil rights on the national level resembled the tactics North Carolina employed on the local level. The Tar Heel State's deceptively moderate response to the civil rights movement favored gradualism over confrontation, and was so successful that in 1976 Jack Bass and Walter DeVries characterized North Carolina as "perhaps the least changed of the old confederate states."[36] William Chafe's case study of Greensboro, North Carolina, demonstrates how this strategy actually operated. He describes how white North Carolinians relied on their "progressive mystique" of paternalism and civility to rationalize and maintain the state's unjust system of race relations.[37] During the hearings, Ervin mixed his conservative constitutional theory with his home state's progressive mystique to create his soft southern strategy against civil rights.

Ervin's intricate cross-examination of Brownell proved to be very profitable for the southern bloc. Several of the legal issues he focused upon became the primary targets in the segregationists' attack on the legislation. First, the senator discovered a technicality within the bill that he argued the administration had inserted so the president could send federal troops into the South to force racial integration. This accusation was an emotional time bomb that would eventually destroy a key provision of the proposed legislation.[38] In making the charge, Ervin evoked emotions that came from deep within the southern psyche; he played on the region's historical nightmares of Reconstruction—the "Tragic Era"—when federal bayonets forced the mixing of the races after the Civil War.[39]

A second legal issue Ervin developed during the subcommittee hearings involved the new powers the bill would grant the attorney general—especially the authority to initiate suits and injunction proceedings. Civil rights advocates had become justifiably frustrated with the snail-like pace of the legal system in the South. Many doubted that Jim Crow would ever be dismantled by individual suits brought by the actual victims of racial discrimination. By empowering the attorney general to initiate legal suits and request that federal judges issue injunctions barring further discrimination, the bill provided the federal government with powerful new tools to combat segregation. Ervin saw it differently. He contended that these powers would lead to "lawsuits as numberless as the sand" and would "establish government by injunction in the place of government by law in the civil-rights field."[40] He objected to the discretionary power the attorney general would have to single out some suspected lawbreakers while ignoring others. Ervin insisted that "the proposed law would constitute a political weapon of the first magnitude which any Attorney General, who happens to be a pragmatic politician, could pervert from its avowed purposes to curry favor with some groups or to browbeat State officials into submission to his will."[41] He warned: "This is a despotic power which no good Attorney General ought to want, and no bad Attorney General ought to have."[42]

But Ervin's most controversial and potentially damaging legal criticism of the legislation was his insistence that it denied southerners their constitutional right to a trial by jury. Under Title IV, the attorney general could seek a federal court injunction ordering a southern election official to register African Americans to vote. If an African American later claimed he or she had still not been allowed to vote, Ervin pointed out that then a judge could punish the white registrar for contempt of court—without witnesses, without a hearing, and without a jury trial. Title III depended on the same injunction procedure to achieve other civil rights goals, including school desegregation, also without jury trials. Saying that it was "a tragic error to protect the civil rights of one group through a process which denies a liberty equally precious, that of trial by jury," he offered an amendment to guarantee jury trials.[43]

The jury trial issue was classic Ervin, and it demonstrates the two ways in which his soft southern strategy helped the white South deny civil rights. First, Ervin's legal arguments added a constitutional veneer of respectability to the southern defense of racial discrimination. Ervin did not challenge the goal of the civil rights bill—to allow African Americans to vote—but he defended a constitutional principle that he insisted the proposal endangered, the right to a jury trial. It was never the ends of civil rights legislation but always the means that he attacked. Second, Ervin tried to unearth a constitutional threat within the bill that would scare wavering senators away from supporting it, or at least toward amending it. If Ervin could convince enough moderates that a civil rights bill should be altered to protect the constitutional rights of all Americans, he could weaken it to the point that it no longer offered any real help to African Americans.

Ervin called the civil rights bill of 1957 both unwise and unconstitutional. He charged that in spite of the attorney general's assurances that the administration's plan represented "a moderate approach," it was actually "as drastic and indefensible a legislative proposal as was ever submitted to any legislative body in this country."[44] In typical Ervin hyperbole, he compared the defenders of the bill to Job because, like the biblical character, "they multiply words without knowledge."[45] If they would examine the measure as closely as he had, Ervin insisted, they, too, would hesitate to approve this "Pandora's box containing so many legal miseries," especially the denial of the precious constitutional right to a trial by jury.[46] Ervin explained that he and his southern colleagues had to reject the legislation because of their obligation "to preserve the American constitutional and legal systems for all Americans of all races and all generations."[47] "We cannot increase the rights of one group by destroying the rights of all groups," he concluded.[48]

Many civil rights proponents responded angrily to Ervin's soft southern strategy. They objected to his constitutional attack on the civil rights bill in general, and to his jury trial amendment in particular. Roy Wilkins of the NAACP observed with frustration: "The southern state and regional governments which have shamelessly flouted the 14th and 15th amendments to the Constitution, . . . which have encouraged and defended the registrars in the flouting, and which have come to power at home and in Washington by reason of this flouting, have now the unmitigated gall to advance the transparently spurious claim that the proposed bill would violate a constitutional right."[49] Those who supported the civil rights bill correctly pointed out that the constitutional guarantee of a trial by jury applied only to criminal indictments, and had never covered the kind of civil actions contemplated by the bill.[50]

The NAACP also set out to discredit Senator Ervin's motives. It circulated a pamphlet revealing that as a member of the North Carolina Supreme Court, Judge Ervin had concurred in four cases in which the court upheld a contempt citation without a jury trial. All four cases limited picketing by union workers during strikes at textile mills in North Carolina. The NAACP suggested that Ervin's newfound concern for the right to a trial by jury in contempt cases stemmed more from his support of "the program of 'massive resistance' " than from his respect for constitutional rights.[51]

Ervin defended himself by insisting that the function of a judge is different from that of a legislator. "When I was a judge I went by the law as it was established," Ervin explained. "I didn't try to substitute my personal notions for law." Then, taking another jab at the U.S. Supreme Court, Ervin added, "If all judges followed my example this country would be in a much better fix today."[52]

Still, the NAACP had shown that the genesis of Sam Ervin's concern for the lack of jury trials in civil contempt hearings coincided with his interest in defeating civil rights bills in the Senate. As the author of the NAACP broadside explained: "If the Southern opponents of civil rights were the least bit sincere in their attacks on the use of injunctions and contempt in civil rights cases, they would long ago have directed their attention to conditions in their home states. Instead, they have waited until it has been proposed to use these processes in a constructive manner to protect civil rights. Now they purport to see defects in these time-tested legal procedures that never occurred to them before."[53]

The liberals also charged that Ervin and his southern colleagues wanted to guarantee jury trials because they knew that an all-white southern jury would never convict a white registrar for denying an African American the right to vote.[54] Joseph Rauh Jr., the national chairman of Americans for Democratic Action (ADA), called Ervin's jury trial question "a sham issue" and suggested that the southerners were "asking for jury trials because Southern white juries can be counted on NOT to do justice." Rauh explained that Ervin and his friends "know they can't defeat this legislation head-on, so they seek to gut the bill by requiring a jury trial before the court can issue an injunction."[55] Ervin struck back hard, insisting that "any intimation from any source that juries in North Carolina will not return honest verdicts is absolutely without foundation."[56] "This is a mass indictment on a whole people and a whole section of the country," Ervin declared. "It is not supported by fact."[57]

Soon after Ervin made his impassioned defense of southern juries, an incident in Montgomery, Alabama, demonstrated the hollowness of his argument. On 30 May 1957, an all-white jury heard the closing statements in the trial of two young white men accused of bombing a black church. This violent act was only one of many that followed the end of Martin Luther King Jr.'s successful boycott of the segregated bus system in Montgomery. White supremacists had bombed four black churches, the homes of two ministers supporting integration, and a black taxi cab stand with its accompanying private residence. The attorneys for the two white defendants told the white jurors that their verdict would "determine our very civilization and our way of life" and that a finding of not guilty would "go down in history as saying to the Negroes that 'you shall not pass.'" They pleaded for the jury to remember that "every white man, every white woman, and every white child in the South is looking to you to preserve our sacred traditions." After only an hour and a half of deliberations, the jury's verdict of not guilty brought an outburst of applause from the packed courtroom.[58]

In spite of the civil rights advocates' success at demonstrating the flaws in

Ervin's constitutional arguments, his sermons in support of guaranteeing jury trials continued to win converts. Moderates inside and outside the South came forward to confess that they, too, believed in protecting the right to a jury. Dr. Charles Alan Wright, a professor of law at the University of Texas, was one of several legal scholars who came out in support of the jury trial amendment. Dr. Wright admitted to Ervin that in spite of his "enthusiastic support" for the *Brown* decision and President Eisenhower's civil rights program, "I cannot escape the deep conviction that you are entirely right in your stand as to jury trials."[59] Virginius Dabney, a prominent southern liberal and editor of the *Richmond Times-Dispatch*, wrote that the denial of jury trials in civil rights cases "should frighten and dismay the whole country."[60] The ACLU's national committee, which lobbied for the bill, discovered that its membership was almost evenly split on the issue.[61] The labor movement, which had long suffered from court injunctions against striking workers, was also divided over jury trials in contempt proceedings. John L. Lewis, head of the United Mine Workers—who had once been fined by a judge for defying an injunction during a strike—wrote Ervin in support of the amendment, calling jury trials "a reasonable protection to all citizens."[62] Even Minnesota's Hubert H. Humphrey, perhaps the most eloquent champion of civil rights in the Senate, struggled privately with the question of jury trials in contempt cases. He later admitted: "I had mixed emotions really. This was a terribly difficult issue for me because my Populist background always emphasized the importance of jury trial. My father talked to me about things like that."[63]

As the public debate over jury trials raged, Ervin and his fellow segregationists continued to drag their feet in the Senate committees. The Subcommittee on Constitutional Rights did not report the civil rights bill to the Judiciary Committee until 19 March, after Ervin had exhausted fifty-one witnesses in thirteen days of public hearings—a feat that produced a subcommittee record of 899 printed pages. At that point, James Eastland, the chairman of the Judiciary Committee, took over the southern stall. He scheduled only one committee meeting a week, none lasting more than a half hour. When the committee convened, Eastland consistently overlooked the liberals' attempts to gain the floor. Instead, he recognized Ervin, who lectured his fellow senators about the constitutional dangers in the bill until Eastland accepted a motion to adjourn. On 3 June, Eastland allowed a vote to be taken on Ervin's trial-by-jury amendment, which passed by a vote of 7–3.[64] With the segregationists firmly in control of the bill in the Judiciary Committee, the liberals began to despair of ever dislodging it from Eastland and Ervin's clutches.[65]

Then, on 20 June 1957, the civil rights advocates made a bold move to rescue their bill from strangulation in the Judiciary Committee. Fourteen senators joined Thomas Hennings of Missouri in sponsoring a clever parliamentary tactic to place the House version of the bill, which had passed the lower chamber two nights before, directly on the Senate's calendar—thus bypassing the Judiciary Committee.[66] Their success at marshalling enough votes to achieve this victory demonstrated the growing strength of the pro–civil rights coalition. It also signaled the beginning of the most important round of the 1957 civil rights fight—the debate in the full Senate.[67]

Thus far, most observers had identified Ervin as the leader of the southern forces. But before the floor fight commenced the North Carolinian yielded command of the southern bloc to Richard Russell. Ervin's talent was legal argumentation and constitutional theorizing, not political maneuvering or backroom deal-making. One North Carolina columnist summed up the conventional wisdom on Ervin's political skills when he observed: "Senator Ervin, as his best friends point out, is relatively inexperienced in politics; he may even be innocent in politics."[68] Russell, however, was a political horsetrader and a master parliamentarian. The two men made a great team—Russell controlled the political maneuvers, Ervin provided the legal ammunition. As one newspaper suggested, if Russell was "the South's skilled generalissimo," then Ervin was "his intellectual chief of staff."[69]

Though Russell was the floor commander, the segregationists continued to rely on Ervin's soft strategy when the full Senate took up the civil rights bill in July. The southern bloc assigned the same team that had written the Southern Manifesto—Russell, Ervin, and Stennis—to spearhead its attack on the civil rights bill during the opening hours of the floor debate.[70] Each of their speeches reflected the style and substance of the soft southern approach.[71] One reporter observed that the southerners forsook the old "blood-and-thunder oratory" of days gone by and "spoke more in sorrow than in anger."[72] Sherman Adams, Eisenhower's closest adviser, later recalled: "The administration expected a filibuster and other evasive tactics, but the [southern] Democrats surprised us by launching a head-on attack on the merits of the bill itself."[73]

Russell led off the segregationists' assault by repeating Ervin's earlier charge that the bill would allow the Eisenhower administration to send troops into the South. He denounced the bill as "cunningly designed to vest in the Attorney General unprecedented power to bring to bear the whole might of the Federal Government, including the armed forces if necessary, to force a commingling of white and Negro children in . . . the South."[74] Building on Ervin's argument, Russell implied that the president had been misled by his attorney general and the civil rights advocates into believing that the bill was a modest protection of

THE SOFT SOUTHERN STRATEGY

The three emerging leaders of the southern bloc in the U.S. Senate meet to discuss strategy. From left, Richard Russell, John Stennis, and Sam Ervin. Photograph in Life, *30 July 1957. A copy is in the Sam Ervin Library and Museum, Western Piedmont Community College, Morganton, North Carolina. Hank Waller, photographer / Time & Life Pictures / Courtesy of Getty Images.*

voting rights when, in fact, Title III represented a radical extension of federal power into every aspect of southern life. Eisenhower seemed to reinforce Russell's accusation with his admission the following day at a press conference: "I was reading part of that bill this morning and there were certain phrases I didn't understand."[75] After conferring with his advisers and meeting with Russell, the president agreed to drop his support for Title III. His action was motivated by political expediency—sacrificing the bill's most objectionable proposal to gain more support for the remaining sections—and by his personal belief that the only truly legitimate goal of a civil rights bill should be to guarantee the right to vote.[76] Without the president's backing, the liberals could not protect Title III, and the Senate voted to delete it from the bill. Ervin's exhaustive cross-examination during the subcommittee hearings had provided the rhetorical bayonet Russell used to cut out the heart of the 1957 civil rights bill.[77]

The southerners' next goal was to eviscerate the bill by adding a jury trial amendment similar to the one Ervin had sponsored in the Judiciary Committee. The central theme of both Stennis's and Ervin's opening speeches, as well as those of almost every other southern senator during the next few weeks, was the danger the bill posed to the constitutional right to trial by jury. Once again, Ervin's soft southern approach proved effective. Several newspapers reversed their earlier editorial positions and announced that they now accepted Ervin's jury trial arguments. The *Washington Star* explained: "We do not believe Senator Ervin is seeing monsters under the bed, or indulging in mere oratorical rhetoric, when he says that if the Federal Courts are given the power to suppress crime by injunction, . . . without juries, in the field of civil rights, . . . there is no valid reason to suppose that on some other day, some other well intentioned administration, headed by a President who wants to accomplish what seems to be a morally desirable and politically helpful end, will not resort to the same subtle evasion of a basic principle of free government."[78]

The jury trial issue had so weakened support for the bill that the civil rights advocates struggled to patch together a compromise. In private negotiations, Lyndon Johnson, the Senate majority leader, orchestrated a deal that guaranteed jury trials in criminal contempt cases dealing with voting rights, but not in civil cases in which the penalty was less than three hundred dollars or forty-five days in jail.[79] In spite of a solo filibuster by Strom Thurmond, the longest ever conducted by a single senator (twenty-four hours and eighteen minutes), the Senate narrowly approved the amendment on 1 August, and six days later the senators passed the severely weakened civil rights bill by a vote of 72–18. All 18 "no" votes were cast by the South's die-hard segregationists.

This editorial cartoon by Hugh Haynie from the Greensboro Daily News, *5 June 1957,
satirizes Ervin's soft southern approach to defeating the civil rights bill of 1957.
Courtesy of the* Greensboro Daily News.

Most of the civil rights advocates in the Eisenhower administration shared Deputy Attorney General William Rogers's assessment that adding the new jury trial amendment to the bill was like "giving a policeman a gun without bullets."[80] The president confided to his cabinet that he considered the jury trial amendment to be "one of the most serious political defeats of the past four years" and later complained to Republican legislative leaders: "I cannot understand how eighteen Southern Senators can bamboozle the entire Senate."[81]

Ervin considered the South's campaign to weaken the Civil Rights Act of 1957 to be "a legislative victory of the greatest magnitude," and he expressed pride in the role he played in shaping the South's strategy. Ervin boasted to a friend, "I think I can justly claim a substantial degree of credit for the decision of the Southern Senators to pursue [their moderate] course of action,"[82] and he bragged to a constituent that he had "probably spent more time than any other single member of Congress in an effort to defeat the Civil Rights Bill or to render it less obnoxious."[83] Others agreed with Ervin's self-assessment. In his typical back-slapping style, Lyndon Johnson wrote Ervin: "Your brilliant legal analysis captured the attention of the nation. Without it, the debate could have become a shambles and the country should always be grateful to you."[84] National publications such as the *New Republic* pointed out how "the southern strategy enabled Sam Ervin to make a reputation as a shrewd analyst," and several noted his leadership role during the debate.[85] In North Carolina, the *Winston-Salem Journal* expressed delight at "hearing about 'the right to trial by jury' rather than worn-out assertions of white supremacy" during the debate, and it gave credit for the "somewhat higher plane" of the South's fight against civil rights to their Senator Sam, "whose quick legal mind is better suited to the job than the rantings of the old-fashioned demagogue."[86]

Of course, the soft southern strategy was not the only reason for the South's success in watering down the bill. Richard Russell's skillful command of the southern forces and Lyndon Johnson's shrewd political compromises have long been recognized as central elements in the familiar story of the civil rights battle of 1957. But it was Sam Ervin who developed the legal arguments that gutted the civil rights bill, earning him the reputation as the South's number one constitutional defender and establishing him as a member of the elite group that governed the southern bloc in the Senate.[87]

In truth, Ervin and his segregationist colleagues had only gained a partial victory in 1957. The southerners' claim that they had successfully whittled down the civil rights bill to the point that, as Mississippi governor James Coleman said, "it was a fairly harmless proposition," could be matched by the claim of civil rights advocates that they had achieved the symbolic victory of enacting the first civil rights law since Reconstruction.[88] Although Roy Wilkins described the bill as "a bitter disappointment," he and the NAACP still defended the legislation as "constituting a start toward our goal, and a start is better than standing still."[89] Martin Luther King Jr. expressed the hope of many African Americans when he predicted that "the full effect of the Civil Rights Bill will depend in large degree upon the program of a sustained mass movement on the part of Negroes."[90] King's remark proved to be prophetic.

The battle over civil rights shifted from Washington, D.C., to Little Rock, Arkansas, in September 1957. When a federal court ordered the schools in Little Rock to begin desegregating their classrooms, Governor Orval Faubus mobilized the National Guard—ostensibly to prevent violence, but actually to stop integration. Faced with this direct challenge to federal authority, President Eisenhower reluctantly sent in troops to enforce the rule of law and protect the nine black students who had enrolled in Little Rock's Central High School.

Senator Ervin quickly added his voice to the chorus of angry southerners supporting Faubus and condemning Eisenhower. "September 24, 1957, was another tragic day for Constitutional government in America," Ervin said. "On that day the President of the United States ordered federal troops to invade a sovereign State for the purpose of enforcing the Judicial usurpation of May 17, 1954 [the *Brown* decision], at the point of a bayonet."[91] Ervin also needled the administration in his weekly newspaper column by recalling Attorney General Brownell's emotional testimony earlier that year when he had angrily denied Ervin's implication that the civil rights bill might lead the president to send troops into the South to enforce integration. Ervin wrote, "I would now like to ask Mr. Brownell whether or not my line of questioning was in order and whether or not the implication contained therein is not a fact, a tragic fact."[92]

Ervin continued to harass the administration about the Little Rock incident for several months. He demanded that the Army reveal the actual cost of its military operation in Arkansas.[93] The Army refused, explaining that "it would be incompatible with the public interest to disclose the contents of this document."[94] Evidently the Democrats in Little Rock appreciated Ervin's defense of their governor's actions because they chose him as the keynote speaker for their annual Jefferson-Jackson banquet the following spring. Developing a theme he would return to years later during Watergate, Ervin attacked what he termed Eisenhower's misuse of executive power, reminding his audience that "the powers of the President of the United States are limited. Indeed, he has no power whatever except those vested in him by the Constitution, and those granted him by Congress."[95] The segregationists listening to the senator's speech must have been pleased when he concluded: "Operation Little Rock ought to give pause to those people who seek at all hazards to convert the public schools of the South from educational institutions into sociological laboratories for experiments in race relations."[96]

The Little Rock crisis was only one of many incidents of white backlash that occurred in the mid-1950s. All across the South the gathering clouds of massive resistance threatened to blot out the few rays of hope for real progress in civil rights. In North Carolina, petitions circulated in several Tar Heel counties that threatened the safety of the NAACP's representatives if they did not leave town, and Governor Luther Hodges failed by only twelve votes to pass legislation aimed at driving the NAACP out of the state.[97] In Yancey County, the school board refused to allow black students to attend the all-white modern school building, even after the public safety commission condemned the dilapidated one-room "Negro school." The board choose instead to bus them to a segregated school in Asheville, forty miles away.[98] In Charlotte, the court sent two black boys to jail for kissing a white girl. The authorities refused to release them, even after they had served their full terms, explaining that the boys' families were too poor to provide what the officials deemed to be "a good home situation."[99]

It was worse in the Deep South. In Lowndes County, Mississippi, where only 52 of a possible 9,299 black voters were registered, African Americans received anonymous threatening letters: "Last warning. If you are tired of living, vote and die."[100] In another Mississippi county, the number of black voters dropped from 485 to none after white supremacists murdered one African American leader and wounded another with shotgun blasts. No one was brought to trial.[101] Racial violence increased throughout Dixie. The Justice Department reported in 1958 that during Eisenhower's first four years in the White House there were six racially motivated killings in the South; twenty-nine other shootings; forty-four beatings; five stabbings; forty-one bombings of homes, churches, and schools; and seven burnings of similar buildings.[102]

The violence and massive resistance in the South clearly demonstrated the need for effective federal legislation, but neither party showed any real interest in another civil rights bill.[103] Eisenhower's new attorney general, William Rogers, suggested that "the best interest of the country" would be served by a "rest" from civil rights.[104] Over the next few years, the Eisenhower administration provided so little support to the NAACP's proposals that Roy Wilkins charged the Republicans of "running out on the civil rights issue."[105] The Democrats also backed away from supporting any additional legislation. When Lyndon Johnson and his party did take tentative steps to initiate a weak civil rights bill, Wilkins characterized their proposal as "a sugar-coated pacifier" and described their actions as mere "shadow-boxing."[106] The politicians on both sides of the aisle were so unsupportive between 1957 and 1959 that Wilkins later recalled that "most days it felt as if I were wading through mud."[107]

Once again, the importance of the black vote pushed politicians from both parties into action. In the midterm elections of 1958, a number of Republican senators who had been lukewarm toward civil rights lost their reelection bids to Democratic and Republican newcomers who campaigned on strong civil rights platforms.[108] Roy Wilkins told the NAACP that "the chances of a new federal civil rights act were heightened by the election of liberals . . . to both major parties in Congress," and Senator Paul Douglass, a liberal Democrat from Illinois, claimed the election results gave Congress "a national mandate" to pass a substantial civil rights bill.[109] The approach of what appeared to be a competitive contest for the presidency in 1960 also brought pressure on both parties to strengthen their record on civil rights.[110]

The Civil Rights Commission added to the momentum for congressional action when it issued its first official report in September 1959. The report detailed how white southerners continued to bar African Americans from voting booths and public schools, and it recommended new legislation to strengthen the inadequate Civil Rights Act of 1957.[111] The southern segregationists tried to deflate the mounting pressure for civil rights by attacking the commission—Sam Ervin labeled the commission's report "unconstitutional and unwise"—but the momentum was so great that columnist Russell Baker observed: "The chief question before the present Congress is not whether civil rights legislation will be passed but how strong a bill it will be."[112]

In many ways, the story of how Congress passed the Civil Rights Act of 1960 appears to be a rerun of 1957. The similarities exist because Sam Ervin and the southern bloc once again followed the soft southern strategy.[113] As had been the case in 1957, Ervin played the starring role in what one senator called the South's "teeth pulling and stalling operation."[114] Ervin politely challenged subcommittee quorums, called numerous witnesses, cross-examined Attorney General Rogers in excruciating detail, and whittled away hours reciting poetry, quoting scripture, and telling mountain stories.[115] At one point in the hearings a frustrated Thomas Hennings pleaded: "I've learned Aesop's fables by heart. I've heard the Senator extol the virtues of Nicodemus. I'm quite sure he was a great man. But he's been dead many years and it's time to take up the present."[116] One civil rights lobbyist reported hearing Senator Hennings complain to a friend: "I just told [Wisconsin senator] Alex Wiley if he'd stop laughing at Senator Ervin's jokes, we might be able to get this bill out of the subcommittee."[117]

The effectiveness of the soft southern strategy depended upon Ervin's finding a constitutional rationale for defeating or weakening civil rights bills. In 1960, the senator's primary legal objection to the proposed legislation concerned what he considered its violation of the due process clause of the Fifth Amendment. The central provision on the 1960 legislation allowed for federal "referees" to oversee voting rights challenges by African Americans.[118] Ervin complained that the court-appointed referees, whom he labeled "carpetbaggers," would be empowered to hold hearing "in camera," thus denying the local registrar accused of discrimination the right to defend himself or herself, the right to legal counsel, or even the right to know that a hearing had been scheduled.[119]

Liberal proponents of the referee plan believed that Ervin was trying to pull a legal stunt similar to the one he had gotten away with in 1957 with the jury trial issue. They argued that if the referee's hearings were opened, and turned into contested judicial contests, African Americans would be discouraged from even trying to register to vote. They also suggested that since the results of the closed hearings could be appealed through the judicial system, the bill did protect due process.[120] But Ervin insisted that the closed hearing violated the Fifth Amendment's guarantee of due process of law, and the senator attacked what he saw as the liberals' presumption that "every member of the Caucasian race who happens to reside below the Mason-Dixon line is a dishonorable character" and not worthy of "the same constitutional protection commonly accorded murderers, thieves, dope-smugglers, and kidnappers."[121]

But in a notable departure from the storyline of 1957, the segregationists had to support Ervin's soft southern approach with an old-fashioned southern filibuster in 1960. In a move to strengthen the very limited civil rights package pending before the Senate, liberals tried to add amendments to include the original Title III provision that had been cut from the 1957 bill, appropriate federal funds to assist school systems trying to integrate racially, add a congressional endorsement of the *Brown* decision, and grant the Department of Health, Education, and Welfare the authority to aid directly school systems wishing to comply with the Supreme Court's desegregation ruling. To counter the liberals' strengthening amendments, Richard Russell divided his colleagues into teams of three and began a filibuster designed to wear down the civil rights proponents and ensure a more moderate bill. Reflecting the influence of the soft southern strategy, most of the southerners avoided inflammatory racial rhetoric, choosing instead to expound on their legal and philosophical objections to the bill.[122] The filibuster wore on for weeks and brought the business of the Senate to a complete standstill.[123]

Sam Ervin used his first turn at the microphone to lecture his colleagues on the unconstitutional nature of civil rights bills and the dangerous judicial activism of the Supreme Court under Chief Justice Earl Warren. The old judge droned on for an hour or so, occasionally raising his voice to override the sound of snoring coming from the Senate cloakroom where army cots had been set up for the senators on call. Soon after one o'clock in the morning, James Eastland, who sat at his desk puffing a cigar, broke in to say that Ervin "is making a great speech—I think senators ought to hear it," and he asked for a quorum call. From cots and sofas scattered throughout the Capitol building, the senators scurried into the chamber, half asleep, in various stages of formal and informal dress, until the quorum had been met. Then Ervin picked up his lecture where he left off and continued until 3:00 A.M., when he surrendered the floor to one of his colleagues.[124] Several day later, at 1:39 in the afternoon of 4 March 1960, Ervin was back on the floor telling one of his favorite stories when the Senate officially set a new endurance record—it had been in continuous session for fifty-four hours and eleven minutes, longer than ever before in its 171-year history.[125]

The southern filibuster had the desired effect. The liberals' repeated attempts at cloture failed, as did their efforts to strengthen the civil rights bill.[126] Lyndon Johnson, working behind the scenes as he had in 1957, again engineered a compromise that allowed both sides to claim a partial victory. The referee plan remained intact, but Title III and the liberals' other strengthening amendments never made it into the weak bill. Many observers agreed with Pennsylvania senator Joseph Clark, who said: "Surely in this battle on the Senate floor the roles of Grant and Lee have been reversed. The eighteen implacable defenders of the way of life of the Old South are entitled to congratulations from those of us they have so disastrously defeated."[127] Roy Wilkins agreed with Clark's assessment, confessing that the bill "falls far short of meeting the needs of the people" and describing the referee plan as constituting "an obstacle course which the disfranchised southern Negro voter will find not much easier to negotiate than the maze he currently faces."[128] The southern bloc had won again.

In the late 1960s, the historian I. A. Newby cautioned against dismissing the white defenders of the segregated South as "crackpots, bigots, or uneducated simpletons." Newby complained that scholars "too often ignore segregationists, or more accurately, too hurriedly dismiss them as nothing more than unreasoning demagogues. . . . As a result they misunderstand and underestimate their adversary."[129] In spite of the hundreds of articles and books that have been published on almost every aspect of the civil rights struggle, many historians still "misunderstand and underestimate" the southern defense of segregation.

Too often, the white segregationists whom scholars choose to include in their narrative histories, textbooks, and even class lectures are the most reactionary racists the South produced. Senators Strom Thurmond and James Eastland, Alabama's outspoken governor George Wallace, and Birmingham's infamous police commissioner Eugene "Bull" Connor are usually cast as the racist villains in most historical civil rights dramas. But are these outspoken segregationists the most significant defenders of Jim Crow, or simply the most colorful? Missing from the historical spotlight are southern leaders who may have been somewhat less sensational but who actually played a more important role in developing and carrying out the South's political strategy to maintain segregation.[130]

Sam Ervin is a case in point. In spite of his service as Jim Crow's primary constitutional champion and his authorship of the soft southern strategy, the senator is seldom mentioned as a leader in the South's crusade to defeat civil rights. Yet Ervin's mountain stories and constitutional arguments had proven to be a more formidable weapon than the racist tirades of Dixie's old-fashioned demagogues. After listening to one of Ervin's moonshiner tales during a civil rights debate, New York senator Jacob Javits remarked: "This is an illustration of why our problem is made more difficult. Those who oppose the bill, with very deep conviction, are very charming people and know such good stories."[131] Missouri senator Thomas Eagleton concluded that Ervin "did more harm, was more destructive of civil rights, than the ignoramuses and the jackasses like Eastland and [Theodore] Bilbo, because he did believe himself to be a constitutional expert and he could quote judicial decisions and oppose civil rights from a constitutional stance."[132]

Certainly Ervin and his legalistic strategy helped the southern bloc to achieve its primary goal in the 1950s—to maintain southern race relations by obstructing federal intervention in local affairs.[133] The segregationists in the Senate had prevented Congress from taking any action to support the *Brown* ruling, and they so weakened the Civil Rights Acts of 1957 and 1960 that neither posed a serious challenge to white supremacy. Thus, by 1960 less than 1 percent of African American students in the South attended integrated schools, and less than 30 percent of all eligible African Americans were registered to vote. As the decade came to a close, the southern senators could rejoice that Jim Crow was alive and well.[134]

But when they turned their attention from the past to the future, the segregationists' mood changed from contentment to concern. Many southern senators feared that in spite of their victories in the legislative battles of 1957 and 1960, they were still losing the war. The necessity of a filibuster in 1960 had forewarned of trouble ahead. In addition, the increasing importance of the black vote, the activism of the Supreme Court, and the possible commitment of future presidents to real progress in race relations all suggested that the new decade would bring even stronger challenges to segregation in the South. Senator Russell Long of Louisiana warned a crowd in New Orleans in 1960: "We have won most of the battles at the legislative level. We have never been out-talked or out-maneuvered. But I am frank to tell you that our situation is a lot worse than it was 12 years ago when I first went to the Senate. . . . I must honestly warn you that the situation in Washington is likely to get worse before it starts getting better."[135]

Long's warning was prophetic. Even as the southern bloc mounted its successful filibuster against the Civil Rights Act of 1960, black students in Ervin's home state set off a new wave of direct action protests that would soon overwhelm the senator and his soft southern strategy against civil rights. On the first day in February, four freshmen at North Carolina A&T staged a sit-in at a Woolworth's lunch counter in Greensboro. Within days the protest spread to Durham. By the end of the week the movement had expanded further—to Raleigh, Fayetteville, High Point, and Elizabeth City. By mid-summer, thousands of students had staged direct action protest in over one hundred cities across the South.[136] After the founding conference of the Student Nonviolent Coordinating Committee (SNCC) met in Raleigh later that year, its first chairman, Marion S. Barry Jr., wrote a letter to Ervin and every member of Congress saying: "What do we want? Our answer is firm and clear: We want all the rights, opportunities, and responsibilities enjoyed by any other American, no more and no less; and we want these things now!"[137]

CHAPTER FIVE

CLAGHORN'S HAMMURABI

One morning during the Democratic National Convention of 1960, Gladys Tillet decided to give Sam Ervin a piece of her mind. The two had been friends since their childhood in Morganton. Tillet, a former suffragist and a liberal delegate from North Carolina, supported the strong civil rights plank proposed by John F. Kennedy, the party's likely presidential nominee. Ervin did not, and he led the southern effort to dilute it in the platform committee. Failing there, Ervin took the segregationists' cause to the convention floor in a nationally televised speech. It was not one of his better performances, and the speech was not well received. The delegates overwhelmingly gave Kennedy the civil rights plank he wanted.[1]

The next morning, while sharing breakfast with Ervin at a hotel restaurant, Tillet could not resist telling her old friend just what she thought of his speech. "Sam," she said, "what you did last night did not help you and it did not help the South, and I just wish you hadn't made that speech. I really suffered sitting there listening to you. I know the plank ought to be in there, and I believe there must be something in you that can tell you it ought to be in there from the standpoint of human rights. I just can't sit down here without saying that." "Gladys, I had to do that," Ervin answered. "[The southerners] were all threatening to walk out and Kennedy would never have been nominated."[2]

The argument "I had to," or reluctant necessity, runs throughout Ervin's defense of his controversial stand against civil rights. In this case, Ervin excused himself by claiming political necessity. Far more often Ervin insisted that he had to fight civil rights forces in order to "preserve the Constitution." But the challenge Gladys Tillet put to Senator Ervin that morning cannot be so easily dismissed. She had touched upon one of the central questions of Ervin's career: How could such a reputed champion of constitutional rights for all Americans be such a consistent foe of civil rights for African Americans?[3]

The senator emphatically denied that there was a contradiction between his dedication to civil liberties and his opposition to civil rights. On the contrary, he maintained that he had to vote against every civil rights bill proposed between 1954 and 1974 because "civil rights are constitutional wrongs." He argued that civil rights legislation threatened freedom by stripping power from the states and centralizing it in the federal government, especially in the executive branch. Ervin also believed that civil rights bills "steal freedom from one man to confer it on another" by inevitably restricting the personal choices and property rights of white Americans in order to benefit black Americans. As Ervin explained, "It is not the 'civil rights' of some, but the civil liberty of all on which I take my stand."[4]

The senator's critics rejected these lofty philosophical explanations for his record on civil rights. Ervin, they said, was just a "Claghorn's Hammurabi." Like the fictional Senator Claghorn on the Fred Allen radio show in the 1930s—and the Warner Bros. cartoon rooster Foghorn Leghorn thirty years later—Ervin looked, acted, and sounded like an old-fashioned Dixie windbag. Like Hammurabi, the ancient Babylonian ruler, the senator provided a legal foundation, and his segregationist colleagues built a defense of their endangered civilization upon it. Many civil rights proponents also disputed Ervin's reputation as a constitutional scholar, describing him as "an overblown constitutional lawyer" and a "rational segregationist." Some simply dismissed him as a racist.[5]

Throughout his life the senator expressed deep anguish whenever anyone charged him with racism. During congressional hearings on immigration in 1965, Ervin suggested that Ethiopians had no right to be treated as favorably as immigrants from northern Europe. "I don't know of a single contribution that the Abyssinians [Ethiopians] have made," Ervin said. "Why should we put them on an equality with those countries that wrote our Constitution and gave us our common laws?" When a reporter concluded that Ervin opposed immigration reform because he held racist opinions about Africans, the senator called the newspaper and demanded an apology. George B. Autry, who served on Ervin's staff, recalled: "Those charges really hurt the Senator. He couldn't understand how people could say such a thing about him."[6] Ervin consistently disavowed any racist motivations in speeches he delivered against civil rights on the Senate floor. "My opposition does not arise out of any matter of race," he insisted. "All of my life I have been a friend to the Negro race. As a citizen, a lawyer and a judge, I have done everything within my power to see to it that all citizens enjoy equality before the law."[7]

But when Ervin had the opportunity to publicly disclaim the racist theory of white biological supremacy, he demurred. In 1963 an interviewer asked Ervin point blank: "Do you agree with [Mississippi governor Ross Barnett] that the Negro race is inferior to the white race?" Ervin answered with a story: "There was a man in my county one time who was talking about building fences. He said the best fence posts were made out of a locust tree. He said they would last two lifetimes. He said he had tried it. I have only lived one part of a lifetime, and I don't think you can measure the relative abilities of races in a generation."[8]

In contrast to the hesitancy he revealed in his statements on white supremacy, Ervin proudly enunciated his views on Jim Crow when he told *Look* magazine in 1956: "I believe in racial segregation as it exists in the South today." Since his childhood, he had lived in, and approved of, a racially divided world. Ervin did not endorse the extreme segregationist positions held by some of his southern senatorial colleagues. He stated publicly that he thought it was wrong to deny African Americans access to any professional or business opportunity open to whites. But Ervin did believe that in the area of social relations the races should remain separated. He insisted that segregation was not the product of racial prejudice, but the result of "a basic natural law, which decrees that like shall seek like. Whenever and wherever people are free to choose their own associates, they choose as their associates members of their own race."[9]

Ervin argued that "the relations between the white and Negro races in North Carolina [were] as harmonious as relations between any two races anywhere on the face of the earth."[10] The senator denied that black Tar Heels faced economic discrimination, citing as proof that "they operate banks, insurance companies, public transportation systems and other substantial business enterprises."[11] Ervin also claimed that most African Americans in his state supported the Jim Crow system. "The majority of Negroes, like the majority of whites, prefer to go to their own churches, their own social organizations and their own fraternal organizations," he explained. "I believe that they prefer to send their children to their own schools."[12]

If North Carolina enjoyed such harmonious race relations, why then was there such an active civil rights movement within Ervin's home state? The senator's answer echoed the comfortable rationalizations popular among white southerners. He suggested that "the present attack on racial segregation is spearheaded mainly by three groups: well meaning outsiders, whose unfamiliarity with the South causes them to 'darken counsel by works without knowledge'; political opportunists who hanker after votes; and Negro leaders who demand that all governmental powers be diverted from their proper functions to force the involuntary mixing of the races."[13]

Ervin seemed to lay most of the blame for the "needless agitation" that "threatens our national sanity" on the first group—the meddling outsiders. He described them as "bungling busybodies who have no personal contact with the conditions out of which the problem arises."[14] The senator cited one of his favorite mountain characters, Josh Billings, as having said, "It is better to be ignorant than to know what ain't so." Ervin suggested that while these northerners may not be ignorant they "'know what ain't so' as far as southern problems are concerned."[15]

It goes without saying that Ervin had grossly misrepresented the southern civil rights movement. The students from the Student Nonviolent Coordinating Committee (SNCC) who staged sit-ins across North Carolina, the young people from the Congress of Racial Equality (CORE) who rode the Greyhound buses on Freedom Rides through Raleigh and Charlotte, the activists from the Southern Christian Leadership Conference (SCLC) who organized nonviolent protests in cities throughout the South—none of these fit Ervin's description. Those Ervin saw as outside agitators leading a visionless band of lawless discontents were actually participants in indigenous movements working toward a clearly articulated goal: the total destruction of racial segregation.[16]

At the heart of the civil rights movement was the strategy of nonviolent civil disobedience. In most of the direct action protests of the early 1960s, civil rights activists behaved with conspicuous grace and dignity while steadily increasing their demands for racial equality. Eventually, they forced a crisis of what the Reverend Martin Luther King Jr. called "creative tension" in which the white authorities had either to negotiate or resort to violence. All too often the sit-ins, freedom rides, and voter registration drives exposed the ugly racism behind de jure segregation when they evoked violent reactions from the supposedly law-abiding white communities of the South.[17]

Ervin had misjudged the true nature of the civil rights movement, but he clearly understood the power of nonviolent civil disobedience. He feared that the moral outrage generated by television coverage of furious white mobs assaulting peaceful African American protesters would overwhelm his soft southern strategy to preserve Jim Crow. Ervin knew that the southern demagogues who whipped up racist emotions and incited violence undercut his legal strategy for defeating civil rights bills, and he attacked them as "the chief aids and abettors of those who would pass such bad legislation."[18]

Ervin consistently denounced racial violence. In 1961 Ervin was the first white southern politician to condemn the bloody attacks on the freedom riders.[19] Senator Philip Hart, a civil rights proponent from Michigan, wrote to his constituents in praise of Ervin's actions: "One of the fine events during these trying days was the quick response which Senator Ervin of North Carolina gave forcefully calling for a return to law and order and protection of the freedom riders. This is responsible southern leadership of which we can all be proud." In 1962 Ervin called Governor Ross Barnett's actions at Ole Miss "illegal" and "foolish," and in 1963 he labeled Alabama governor George Wallace's tactics at Tuscaloosa "unwise."[20] Ervin abhorred the racial hatred and violence, and he regretted the political backlash he knew such radical tactics would provoke.[21]

With incessant, mounting pressure, the civil rights movement shook the foundations of the southern white power structure in the early 1960s. The political tremors could be felt on Capitol Hill, where Ervin worried about how long he and his southern colleagues could stop the federal government from destroying Jim Crow. But in the absence of a national mandate for civil rights, or a real presidential commitment to end racial discrimination, the segregationists still held the upper hand in the Senate.

In 1962 Ervin and the southern bloc easily turned back the Kennedy administration's legislative proposal to abolish poll taxes and literacy tests. By the 1960s the poll tax had few defenders. Only five southern states—Alabama, Arkansas, Mississippi, Virginia, and Texas—still charged their citizens a fee to vote in federal elections. But when civil rights proponents and President Kennedy asked Congress to outlaw poll taxes by legislation, instead of by a constitutional amendment, the southern bloc once again unfurled its battle flags. The southerners could not tolerate any congressional tampering with state election laws for fear of setting a dangerous precedent. Ervin played his usual role of constitutional scholar during the debate, explaining that though he did not personally support poll taxes, he could not stand by and allow the Congress to rob the states of their constitutional power to determine voting qualifications within their own boundaries.[22] Against the wishes of the NAACP, Kennedy backed down and supported a bill sponsored by Senator Spessard Holland of Florida to abolish poll taxes through a constitutional amendment, which would require ratification from three-quarters of the state legislatures. Ironically, then, the ratification of the Twenty-fourth Amendment in January 1964 actually represented a political victory for the South.[23]

The Kennedy administration's attempt to outlaw literacy tests met with even greater resistance in Congress since many southern states depended upon these

CLAGHORN'S HAMMURABI

arbitrary devices to prevent African Americans from voting. The Justice Department sponsored a bill abolishing all literacy tests and mandating that anyone over the age of twenty-one who had completed the sixth grade would automatically qualify to vote. Again, it was Richard Russell who mobilized the southern caucus and sent his constitutional champion to oppose the legislation on the Senate floor. Ervin railed against the measure as unconstitutional because it eroded traditional state control of the electoral process, and as unnecessary because the federal government had all the laws it needed to protect the franchise.[24]

Ervin told the Senate that the administration's requests for additional legislation reminded him of the time John was courting Mary:

John and Mary were sitting on the bench one night. The moon was shining brightly. The odor of flowers permeated the atmosphere. . . . John said to Mary, "Mary, if you wasn't what you is, what would you like to be?" Mary said, "John, if I wasn't what I is, I would like to be an American Beauty rose." Then Mary turned the inquiry on John and asked, "John, if you wasn't what you is, what would you like to be?" John said, "Mary, if I wasn't what I is, I would like to be an octopus . . . [with] a thousand arms." Mary said, "John, if you was an octopus and you had a thousand arms, what would you do with them?" John said, "Mary, if I was an octopus and had a thousand arms, I would put every one of them around you." Mary said, "John, go on away. You ain't using the two arms that you already got."

Ervin suggested that the Justice Department should use the laws already on the books to protect the rights of African Americans instead of asking Congress to pass new, unconstitutional ones.[25]

Ervin had privately expressed another reason for his reluctance to abolish literacy tests during a similar debate in 1957. A constituent warned the senator that since the "colored" population had reached 73 percent where he lived in Northampton County, outlawing literacy tests meant "political suicide." Ervin responded, "I am also aware of the situation that exists in your county, as well as several other eastern counties relative to the percentage of Negro population as compared to the white population and I fully agree that we must insist upon educational requirements if we are to continue our form of government."[26]

Once again, the senator and his soft southern strategy helped to defeat an important civil rights bill. Ervin kept the anti–literacy test bill buried in his Constitutional Rights Subcommittee as long as possible—subjecting Attorney General Robert Kennedy to a grueling cross-examination—before helping to lead a southern filibuster on the Senate floor. The *Raleigh News and Observer* suggested that "Ervin is the ideal filibusterer. He is tireless, voluble and so amiable that the fiercest liberals have trouble disliking him. . . . He can tell stories by the dozen, quote scripture by the yard and talk about the Constitution, it seems, forever." *Time* magazine called Ervin "Sunny Sam" and reported, "When he bobs his greying head and puckers his face into a smile even his opponents have to grin back." Ervin's constitutional arguments were effective. Such notable political figures as former president Dwight Eisenhower and Republican senator John Sherman Cooper of Kentucky—an influential proponent of civil rights—announced that they had decided that anti–literacy test legislation was unconstitutional. After several weeks, and two unsuccessful cloture votes, the administration retreated and the bill died.[27]

That November, Ervin easily won reelection. The senator outpolled every other politician in every race on the state's ballot. Ervin completely ignored his Republican candidate and only spent the absurdly small sum of $1,241.03 on his campaign, far less than any of his senatorial colleagues. His consistent opposition to civil rights certainly contributed to his overwhelming victory, as did his successful soft southern strategy, which reflected his home state's preference for racial civility and paternalism over demagoguery and violence.[28] But the political environment in which Ervin and his constitutional strategy had enjoyed such success was changing, both in North Carolina and across the nation.

In spite of his electoral landslide, Senator Ervin could no longer count on the unqualified support of all Tar Heel Democrats for his uncompromising stand against civil rights. Ervin's feud with Terry Sanford, North Carolina's governor from 1961 to 1965, is a case in point. Ervin and Sanford not only belonged to competing wings of the state's Democratic party and had supported different Democratic presidential candidates in 1960—Ervin backed Lyndon Johnson and Sanford worked for Kennedy—but they also held very different visions of North Carolina's future. Ervin, a traditionalist, favored a continuation of the status quo, while Sanford, a modernizer, wanted gradual change in several areas, most notably race relations.[29] Unlike Ervin, Sanford rejected Jim Crow and supported some of Kennedy's more modest civil rights initiatives. Eventually, their disagreements became personal. Ervin secretly opposed Sanford's appointment to a federal job after his term as governor expired, advising the president that "politically, he is somewhat poverty-stricken."[30] For his part, Sanford called Ervin "a constitutional phony" behind his back.[31]

When Ervin returned to Washington in 1963, he found that the civil rights movement had further eroded the southern bloc's power on Capitol Hill. Across the South, outraged white mobs were increasingly responding to peaceful direct action protests with vicious lawlessness. In Mississippi white supremacists had committed over sixty-four acts of violence against African Americans, most of whom were simply attempting to register to vote. James Meredith's admission to the University of Mississippi in September 1962 had resulted in a race riot causing two deaths and over three hundred injuries. Even in North Carolina, which took pride in its moderate reputation, white violence was on the rise. In Siler City a white policeman shot and killed a young black man who the officer claimed had been drunk and attempted to run away. An autopsy revealed no alcohol in the dead man's body. In Edenton police arrested and then beat the NAACP's youth adviser after he and eight other young people attempted to picket a segregated movie theater. Everywhere, it seemed, direct action protests against racial segregation brought a violent reaction from the local whites, embarrassing Ervin and undercutting his soft southern strategy.[32]

Just as Ervin had feared, the Kennedy administration responded to the political pressure generated by the protests and violence by sending a new civil rights package to Congress in February 1963. Kennedy's proposals were mild and his message was partisan.[33] Civil rights advocates complained that Kennedy was simply trying to placate them and win some political points by sending up a sacrificial bill to be slaughtered on Capitol Hill.[34] The southerners were equally displeased. When asked about Kennedy's motives, Ervin suggested the president was just "hankering after votes," and Senator Russell Long of Louisiana observed, "This is one of those things where the decision was: 'Ask not what's good for your country, ask what's good at the next election.'" Throughout the spring and into the summer Ervin kept the bill bottled up in his Subcommittee on Constitutional Rights.[35]

To dramatize the desperate need for civil rights legislation, Martin Luther King Jr. and the civil rights movement began an assault in April against one of the pillars of the segregated South—Birmingham, Alabama. When the city's police commissioner, Bull Connor, unleashed the violent power of the police on a peaceful demonstration, television cameras brought vivid pictures of snarling police dogs, high-pressure water cannons, and club-wielding policemen attacking women and children into living rooms across America. A few days later, the bombing of King's hotel and his brother's home released the pent-up rage of young blacks, who rioted throughout the night and set fire to sections of the city.[36]

President Kennedy feared that the events in Birmingham foreshadowed even worse racial violence in the future, and the bloodshed forced him to reconsider his own moral commitment to civil rights. After long discussions with advisers, including his brother the attorney general, the president ordered the Justice Department to draft a new and extensive civil rights bill. Special Counsel Theodore Sorensen recalls that following Birmingham, President Kennedy "felt it was something which had to be done: that a national crisis required it." After attending a meeting with the president in June 1963, civil rights lawyer Joseph Rauh thought that for the first time Kennedy "was prepared if necessary to sacrifice everything for the fight. It was a moral issue." On 11 June 1963, George Wallace's dramatic but unsuccessful attempt to prevent the integration of the University of Alabama by standing in the schoolhouse door gave Kennedy an excellent opportunity to announce his new civil rights package. Historian Carl Brauer believes that Kennedy's eloquent speech that evening, committing himself and the presidency to the moral cause of civil rights, "marked the beginning of what can truly be called the Second Reconstruction, a coherent effort by all three branches of the government to secure blacks their full rights." Sam Ervin's fear that racial violence would undercut his ability to preserve Jim Crow had come to pass.[37]

The new civil rights bill of 1963 did not have easy sailing in Congress. It represented the strongest set of legislative proposals to fight racial segregation in almost 100 years. In addition to the measures he had asked for in February, Kennedy requested a ban on racial segregation in public facilities, new authority for the attorney general to initiate school desegregation proceedings, and more executive power to withhold federal expenditures as a tool to force desegregation. Liberal congressmen immediately offered amendments to make the bill even stronger. It was not at all clear that Congress would actually pass such a comprehensive bill into law. Much would depend on whether Minority Leader Everett Dirksen and the Republicans in the Senate would support the Democratic proposals in sufficient numbers to overcome the inevitable southern filibuster. But before this crucial turning point could be reached, Kennedy's bill had to run the usual southern gauntlet of hearings and stalling tactics in the Judiciary Committee.

As had Eisenhower's two attorneys general before him, Robert Kennedy came to Capitol Hill to defend a civil rights bill against Sam Ervin's legal attacks. On 7 July 1963, 350 spectators crowded into the Senate Office Building auditorium to hear Kennedy offer his opening statement to the Judiciary Committee. But before Kennedy could start, Ervin announced that he intended to make a few remarks first. "I'd have to talk very rapidly to finish it in an hour," Ervin warned. With that, the attorney general and his aides politely gathered up their charts and briefs and left the overcrowded hearing room to Ervin, who launched into a section-by-section attack on the whole civil rights package that lasted two full days.[38]

When Kennedy returned to the hearings, "The Sam and Bobby Show" became a media event. The attorney general was well prepared for the confrontation. Vice President Johnson had warned the administration that no matter how carefully they drafted the bill there was bound to be something in it that the southerners would use "to make us look silly," and the NAACP had cautioned Kennedy about Ervin's "remarkable talents."[39] In addition, the attorney general had testified in front of Ervin before, and he knew the senator's constitutional and rhetorical strategies well. So when the legal sparring began, Kennedy was able to match Ervin case for case and legal precedent for legal precedent. For weeks the two lawyers went at each other, Kennedy maintaining that the bill was "clearly constitutional," Ervin insisting that it was "clearly unconstitutional," and the press reporting the most significant and entertaining exchanges each day in the newspapers.[40]

In spite of their philosophical differences, Ervin thought highly of both John and Robert Kennedy. All three had worked together on the McClellan "Rackets Committee" in the 1950s. Bobby had served as the Senate committee's chief counsel, and after the hearings then-Senator Jack Kennedy had cosponsored with Ervin a major labor reform bill, the Landrum-Griffin Act, as well as an anti-bombing bill—an association that later hurt Kennedy politically with northern black voters.[41] Ervin had also supported the attorney general at his confirmation hearings in 1961. Countering criticism that Bobby was too youthful and inexperienced, Ervin recalled a debate in Asheville, North Carolina, between two candidates for the state legislature. When one attacked the other as being too young, he responded by pledging to the audience that "if you overlook my youth, I promise I'll never be so young again as long as I live."[42]

Ervin intended "The Sam and Bobby Show" to be a forum on the constitutionality of the bill. The senator objected to every title of the proposed legislation, but he especially disliked the section that would ban racial discrimination in places of public accommodation. Ervin insisted that the administration could not base its power to regulate public accommodations on the Fourteenth Amendment because it clearly did not pertain to anything more than state actions. When Kennedy finally admitted, "I think you made a very forceful argument on the question of the constitutionality of the legislation under the Fourteenth Amendment," Ervin had scored a point. "But," the attorney general continued, "it is quite clear that it is constitutional under the Commerce Clause."[43]

The senator snapped back, "It is quite clear to me . . . that the bill is unconstitutional," and he cited numerous cases in which the Supreme Court had ruled that Congress had no power to regulate any goods or activities that had not crossed state lines or had come to rest within a state. This time, however, it was Kennedy who scored the point. The attorney general correctly pointed out that each of the cases Ervin mentioned had been overturned by later decisions that expanded the meaning of the Commerce Clause.[44]

Whenever possible, Kennedy turned the discussion away from abstract legal theory to focus on the concrete realities of racial injustice in the South. Kennedy recounted compelling cases of discrimination and cited quantitative data to demonstrate the extent of the problem. Ervin tried to dismiss some of the most embarrassing statistics by telling one of his mountain anecdotes. "This story has no application to the Attorney General," Ervin began.

> Down in my country an old storekeeper had been selling groceries to a mountaineer on credit. The mountaineer came in to pay his grocery bill. The storekeeper told him the amount of the grocery bill, which exceeded considerably what the old mountaineer thought it would be. The old mountaineer complained that the bill was too large. The storekeeper got out his account books and laid them on the counter and said: "Here are the figures; you know figures don't lie." The old mountaineer said: "I know figures don't lie, but liars sure do figure."[45]

"Honest men also figure," Ervin continued. "I have lived in North Carolina all my life, and I know that some of the inferences you have drawn from your figures are not very accurate. In saying this, I do not challenge your good faith." Kennedy replied, "Senator, I am just giving the figures." "That is what the storekeeper was giving the old mountaineer," Ervin countered. "That is why it is so difficult even to proceed," Kennedy explained, "because if we are not going to recognize that there is a problem, if we are going to state that figures do not mean anything, that everything is fine, that we are making satisfactory progress, then we are not going to get any place. If we cannot recognize the fact that there is a problem, Senator, we are not going to get very far."[46]

Ervin's temper, which had been rising, now boiled over. Standing to defend his homeland he retorted: "Mr. Attorney General, I will maintain at any time, and in any place, under any conditions, that North Carolina is more like heaven than any other place on earth. Despite this, I will admit that we have many unsolved problems down there. But I think we could solve them much better if we did not get so much interference from up here on the banks of the Potomac." At this point Chairman James Eastland had to call for order.[47]

As hard as Ervin pushed Kennedy to defend the constitutionality of the civil rights bill, Kennedy pushed Ervin to respond to the actual problems of racial discrimination. Week after week, the attorney general kept probing Ervin's moral conscience and challenging his motives. "How are we to bring up our children, Senator, if there is not going to be some leadership and assistance from somebody such as yourself?" Kennedy asked. "I think you have a responsibility. But you are against every part of this section of the bill." And a minute later: "Senator, with the kind of prestige you have in the United States, you could make a major difference in ending these kinds of practices as well as bringing this country through a very difficult period of transition. That is all I ask of you, Senator." "The only thing you have a right to ask of me is that I stand and fight for the Constitution and for the basic rights of Americans," Ervin snapped. "That is what I'm doing now."[48]

Ervin's face was flushed and he again rose to his feet: "You are not correct in saying I have never spoken out against discrimination. All of my life I have fought against it. As a member of the North Carolina legislature many years ago, one of my first acts was to introduce a bill to authorize the issuance of bonds to defray the cost of construction of an adequate school for the Negro children of my hometown. As a member of the school board in my hometown, I fought for equal compensation for all teachers regardless of their respective races. As a member of the legislature of North Carolina, I have always fought for liberal appropriations for the adequate education of all of North Carolina's school children. As a citizen, lawyer and judge in North Carolina, I have always stood for the right of all men to stand equal before the law. As a citizen and a public official, I have always stood for the right of every qualified voter to register and vote. So you are not very just to me in saying I have not fought discrimination."[49]

The attorney general's probing had hit another of Ervin's emotional nerves, and, more important, revealed a weak spot in the senator's defense. Ervin's impassioned speech was theatrically effective but misleading. True to the paternalistic ethic of the genteel South, Sam Ervin had addressed some of the most grievous inequalities of the Jim Crow system. As a genuine southern gentleman he honestly cared about the well-being of all North Carolinians, white and black. But while Ervin had worked to improve the lives of individual African Americans within the system, he had never attempted to reform the system itself. He had proposed funding increases for black schools and teachers, but had never suggested restructuring North Carolina's educational budget or ending its inequitable race-based financial divisions. He had supported the right of African Americans to vote, but he had done nothing to change the state laws or combat the illegal practices that kept blacks off the ballot. He had offered free legal service and personal economic assistance to indigent black individuals in his community, but had never attacked the legal barriers to economic opportunity that prevented African Americans from helping themselves.

Ervin's paternalistic actions and his opposition to civil rights legislation were two parts of the same traditional southern system that maintained Jim Crow. Howard Lee, the first African American to be elected mayor in North Carolina in the twentieth century, explained: "Blacks tended to be rejected in the South as a race, as a whole, but accepted individually, and I always found that if that kind of system could continue then the power brokers could decide who would have certain privileges and who would not. . . . And it would be those privileges that would still give them a certain amount of power."[50]

Lee's description of the southern paternalistic system helps explain Ervin's absolute opposition to all civil rights legislation. The mayor believed that "Senator Sam's position [against civil rights] was based to a great extent on a very unique position that many power brokers took within North Carolina and throughout the South. And that position is that if laws are enacted which give freedom to the whole then there is no longer the opportunity to give and take privileges. . . . With the enactment of civil rights laws, this whole process, this whole system crumbled."[51]

After a successful run of over a month, "The Sam and Bobby Show" came to an end in September when Senator Eastland suspended the hearings until some unspecified date in the future. The legal confrontation had ended in a draw, but Kennedy had won the moral debate. Ervin could not admit to Robert Kennedy, and perhaps not even to himself, that the social and political structure of North Carolina exploited African Americans. To do so would have caused irreparable damage to his public defense of Jim Crow, as well as to his private moral universe. So, flushed out by the attorney general's gentle but poignant accusations, the senator had to abandon his constitutional cover and deliver impassioned speeches to defend his beloved North Carolina's poor civil rights record and his own questionable commitment to fighting racial discrimination.

Ervin's abstract constitutional arguments increasingly appeared outdated and irrelevant as events in 1963 pushed the country toward the high point of the Second Reconstruction. On 28 August more than 200,000 people marched on Washington to demand civil rights. But the optimism generated by Martin Luther King Jr.'s eloquent expression of his dream of racial harmony quickly dissipated a month later when a bomb exploded in a black Birmingham church, killing four African American girls sitting in their Sunday school class. The pressure for racial progress generated by 978 demonstrations in 209 cities over the summer had elicited many ugly incidents of white backlash, but none ripped at the nation's heart more than the deaths of these four children.[52] The bombing affected even die-hard segregationists. Arkansas senator J. William Fulbright secretly informed the White House that he was so distraught by the

The debate between Sam Ervin and Bobby Kennedy over civil rights began during hearings in 1962 and climaxed with "The Sam and Bobby Show" of 1963. Editorial cartoon by John Sink, Durham Morning Herald, 15 April 1962. Scrapbook (vol. 7) in Press Clipping files, Sam Ervin Papers, Subgroup A: Senate Papers, 3847A, Southern Historical Collection, University of North Carolina at Chapel Hill. Used by permission of the Durham Morning Herald.

girls' deaths that he would work behind the scenes to help pass some kind of a civil rights bill.[53] But the mood in the South remained tense. Many southern whites vented their anger at the president. In Mississippi, signs dotted the landscape which read, "K. O. the Kennedys."[54]

On 22 November President Kennedy was assassinated in Dallas. News of the tragedy reached Washington almost immediately. All business stopped as people gathered around television sets in their offices or huddled by their radios. Sam Ervin was terribly shaken. Emerging from his office, he looked ashen and very old. The senator leaned against the doorway and muttered, "A thing like this makes you sick."[55]

Standing before a joint session of Congress just five days after Kennedy's assassination, President Lyndon Johnson told the nation, "No memorial oration or eulogy could more eloquently honor President Kennedy's memory than the earliest possible passage of the civil rights bill for which he fought so long." That same day, the nation's leading civil rights spokespersons announced that they would gather around the late president's grave at Arlington National Cemetery to rededicate themselves to Kennedy's dream of "equal rights for all Americans whatever their race or color." The power of such emotional symbolism, coupled with LBJ's uncompromising commitment to pass the civil rights bill, created the political momentum necessary to dislodge the bill from the southerners' grasp in the Judiciary Committee. The segregationists immediately launched a filibuster, but they knew that they had little chance to defeat the bill. Richard Russell confessed that "under the existing circumstances, the odds in favor of this short-sighted and disastrous legislation are very great."[56]

Not that Sam Ervin gave up. He suggested that the civil rights bill was "as full of legal tricks as a mangy hound dog is of fleas," and he called it "a debasement of constitutional government and an exaltation of governmental tyranny." Ervin told stories, recited Shakespeare, discussed the importance of jury trials, and logged more filibustering hours than any other southern senator. He even wrote a personal letter setting out his constitutional objections to every member of the Senate that opened with the plea: "You love your country. I ask for its sake that you read the enclosed statement in its entirety."[57]

Ervin and the southern bloc stuck to the soft southern strategy in 1964. Some newspaper reporters complained that the segregationists had been so scholarly during the filibuster that they were finding it difficult to get anything sensational to put into their press releases. But the national media no longer found Ervin as entertaining as they once had. The *Los Angeles Times* ran a story on Ervin under the headline "Senator Not Always Humorous," and several other newspapers reported Clarence Mitchell's complaint that Ervin was wasting the country's time "telling jokes about Uncle Remus, Brer Rabbit or some other kind of folklore."[58]

Ervin's most significant contribution to the civil rights debate was his attempt to weaken the bill by protecting southerners accused of racial discrimination from double jeopardy. He offered an amendment to prevent the U.S. government from trying a defendant for violating a federal public accommodations law if that person had been acquitted in a sympathetic state court for the same offense. Civil rights proponents feared that adoption of Ervin's amendment would gut the bill. Once again, Ervin had found a constitutional principle upon which he could fight a civil rights bill. Support for Ervin's amendment was surprisingly strong, and it actually passed a roll call by one vote. A parliamentary technicality, however, prevented it from becoming part of the bill, and an eventual compromise worked out in a meeting of the Senate's leadership limited Ervin's amendment to a protection against double jeopardy on only federal statutes.[59]

On 10 June 1964, a coalition of Democrats and Republicans forced a cloture vote and won, defeating a southern filibuster for the first time in modern history. Richard Russell and the majority of the southern bloc were ready to admit defeat, but not Sam Ervin. Along with two of his colleagues, Strom Thurmond and Russell Long, Ervin declared that he planned to continue the fight, irritating Russell and the other southerners. In response, Majority Leader Mike Mansfield kept the Senate in session for thirteen straight hours, which resulted in thirty-four roll calls—the most ever taken in the Senate in a single day. Such pressure brought an end to Ervin's final resistance. A few weeks later, President Johnson signed the Civil Rights Act of 1964 into law, ending de jure racial segregation in the United States.[60]

The civil rights movement did not rest on its laurels. In the summer of 1964, young people bravely traveled the back roads of Mississippi encouraging African Americans to register and vote. "Freedom Summer" did not add many new names to the state's voter rolls, but the murder of three civil rights workers, one black and two white, focused the national spotlight on the racial terror in Mississippi and the need for federal legislation to extend the ballot. Fearing political retaliation from white southern voters, Lyndon Johnson initially showed little enthusiasm for sending a new civil rights bill to Congress. But that November, black voters gave Johnson a wake-up call by providing him with the margin of victory in four southern states—Arkansas, Florida, Virginia, and Tennessee. Then on "Bloody Sunday," 7 March 1965, six hundred peaceful protestors marching from Selma to Montgomery to demand black voting rights were severely beaten by state and local police on the Edmund Pettus Bridge. President Johnson responded to the horrific scenes of violence in Selma by submitting a powerful new voting rights bill to Congress and calling for its quick passage in a nationally televised speech before a joint session of Congress. Johnson concluded his impassioned address by pleading, "This cause must be our cause too. It is not just Negroes, but all of us, who must overcome the crippling legacy of bigotry and injustice. And," the president added, "we shall overcome."[61]

Johnson's voting rights package contained many of the proposals Ervin had helped to defeat in the past, plus a few new measures to guarantee the franchise. Most important, it sent federal officials into the South to register qualified voters, suspend literacy tests, and oversee any change in a state's electoral rules that might dissuade black voters. Any southern county or state that administered literacy tests and had more than 50 percent of its eligible citizens fail to register or vote in the presidential election of 1964 would fall under federal supervision. Liberals in Congress strengthened the bill by giving the attorney general the right to initiate suits against those states that still required a poll tax in local elections. There was considerable momentum in Congress to pass Johnson's voting rights bill quickly.[62]

Once again, white racist violence had undercut Ervin's soft southern strategy and created a political climate in which his legal objections seemed irrelevant to an outraged nation. The senator still went through the motions. He said that the voting rights bill "would make the constitutional angels weep," because it violated the constitutional mandate against *ex post facto* laws by punishing a state for acts that occurred in the past. He further argued that it constituted a bill of attainder because it deprived localities of their powers without a judicial trial.[63] But no one paid much attention. "Senator Ervin complains daily about his constitutional objections to the bill," one newspaper editor observed. "But he is out of fashion, both because there is defeatism among those who have campaigned alongside him and because there are many, including southerners, who acknowledge the need for some way of processing speedily the claims of those discriminated against at the polls." Those legal experts who took the time to consider the merit of Ervin's constitutional objections dismissed them as incorrect, outdated, and exaggerated. One scholar later concluded that Ervin's argument was "amazingly weak from a constitutional point of view . . . [and] would scarcely be made even by a law school neophyte—so contrary is it to all law on the subject."[64]

Ervin knew he was beaten. "Thou shalt not follow a multitude to do evil, Exodus, chapter 23, verse 2," he told the nearly empty Senate chamber. Then, a bit later, he pointed to Mike Mansfield and said: "I have nothing on my side but the right. I'm afraid my good friend has all the votes on his." The Voting Rights Act of 1965 passed through Congress with surprising ease. Proposed in March, the president signed it into law that August.[65]

Ervin was particularly miffed because thirty-four of North Carolina's one hundred counties fell under the new law's provisions. The Tar Heel State was associated with Georgia, Alabama, Mississippi, and the other recalcitrant states of the Deep South, tarnishing its reputation as progressive in the region. Ervin also resented the law's implication that registrars in his home state had discriminated against black voters. Instead, the senator laid the blame on African Americans themselves. "The disproportionately low registration and low voting of Negroes in North Carolina is due more to apathy, . . . to poor schooling and poor school attendance than to election officials' arbitrary denial of the right to register on account of race," he insisted.[66]

Subsequent events proved Ervin wrong. African Americans flocked to the polls after the Voting Rights Act removed the barriers that had prevented them from casting their ballots. By 1972 more than one million African Americans added their names to the registration lists in the states covered by the act, increasing the percentage of eligible black voters from about 29 percent to almost 57 percent. In North Carolina the gap between black and white registration narrowed to nearly 20 percent in just a year and a half.[67]

The passage of the Civil Rights Act of 1964 and the Voting Rights Act of 1965 marked a significant turning point in the history of the civil rights struggle. For decades the traditional legislative agenda for most civil rights activists had included two basic goals: ending Jim Crow segregation and guaranteeing African Americans the right to vote. Both had been accomplished by 1965. But the southern caucus was not yet ready to abandon its fight to maintain white supremacy. Even as Congress enacted Lyndon Johnson's civil rights bills in the mid-1960s, the segregationists in the Senate shifted the battle from a fight over legislation to a struggle over implementation.

Just a few minutes after cloture had been voted on the Civil Rights Act of 1964, Ervin initiated what proved to be a protracted debate over how the administration should enforce the bill's desegregation mandate by offering the first of a southern barrage of 119 weakening amendments. The senator's effort failed, but the Leadership Conference on Civil Rights (LCCR) warned that the Ervin amendment was a harbinger of a new and more dangerous southern resistance. "If we are to create a climate of compliance," the LCCR warned, "we must use the forces mustered to obtain passage of the bill to see that the law is observed and enforced."[68] The Johnson administration had similar concerns. One aide observed that the Civil Rights Act of 1964 "will convey important new enforcement authorities, but in and of itself it will do very little. The accomplishment will come in the enforcement. Accordingly, it is of the highest importance that the scheme of enforcement be carefully thought out."[69]

The Department of Health, Education, and Welfare (HEW) had the responsibility of implementing Title IV, which called for the desegregation of the South's public schools. HEW began its new assignment cautiously. In 1965 the department's first published guidelines required only that each southern school district submit a desegregation plan. All but seventy of the more than two thousand southern school districts did so. Most school administrators, however, interpreted the Civil Rights Act far differently than did the bureaucrats in HEW. The southerners understood that they could no longer deny

African American students admittance to the school they chose to attend. But they denied that the law forced them actually to integrate their dual school systems, as HEW seemed to imply.

The seventy recalcitrant counties, most of them in Georgia, refused to submit any desegregation plan or cooperate with HEW at all. To defend his home state's actions, Senator Herman Talmadge requested an evening appointment with President Johnson on 12 March 1965 at the White House. Talmadge took Sam Ervin along to help him plead his case. Evidently, they had little effect on their old friend, for the president continued to support HEW's request that all of Georgia's school districts file desegregation plans.[70]

Nevertheless, HEW's guidelines in 1965 failed to open many schoolhouse doors to African American children. Over 75 percent of southern school districts maintained their freedom of choice plans, which resulted in only a 2 percent increase in the number of black students attending desegregated schools. Baker County, Georgia, gained national attention by accepting only 22 of the 165 requests by African American children who wanted to attend previously all white schools. School officials cited "forged signatures," "too many children from the same family at one school," and vague "technical deficiencies" in denying these black students their choice.[71]

HEW responded to such southern intransigence by issuing strict new guidelines in 1966 that required outright integration. The federal department's new commissioner of education, Harold Howe, who had left the University of North Carolina to accept his post, explained that "a school district is held to have an affirmative duty to eliminate—in fact as well as in form—any racial characteristics of its system of Education."[72] Recent court rulings prevented HEW from rejecting the South's freedom-of-choice plans outright, but Attorney General Nicholas Katzenbach informed the president that the administration only had to tolerate the voluntary choice plans if "they actually result in Negro children moving to white schools": "The guidelines suggest, for the first time, some numerical standards of achievement."[73] As one aide concluded, after considering "every angle of this highly explosive issue," the administration turned away from its old policy of "paper compliance and tokenism" and adopted a new, tough, numerical "test of effectiveness."[74]

The southern caucus was outraged. Senators Russell, Stennis, and Ervin, the same team that had written the Southern Manifesto, sent a stinging letter to President Johnson, their former Senate colleague, "to protest vigorously the abuse of power involved in the bureaucratic imposition of the Guidelines" and to "earnestly beseech your personal intervention to right this wrong and have this order revoked."[75] In the Subcommittee on Constitutional Rights, Ervin thundered against the new commissioner of education, who had "zealously promulgated new rules and regulations which go far beyond the legislative power which Congress allocated to him."[76] To contest HEW's requirement that some students be bused to different schools to achieve the goal of "racial balance," the senator cited the language of the Civil Rights Act of 1964 itself: "Nothing herein shall empower any official or court of the United States to issue any order seeking to achieve a racial balance in any school by requiring the transportation of pupils or students from one school to another in order to achieve such racial balance."[77] To remind HEW of Congress's intent in passing the bill, Ervin quoted Vice President Hubert Humphrey, who as one of the bill's chief sponsors two years before had stated that "while the Constitution prohibits segregation, it does not require integration. The busing of children to achieve racial balance would be an act to effect the integration of schools. In fact, if the bill were to compel it, it would be a violation, because it would be handling the matter on the basis or race."[78]

Many of Ervin's arguments in 1966 foreshadowed his attacks on executive power during Watergate. The senator criticized what he considered to be the executive branch's unconstitutional assumption of Congress's sole authority to legislate, complaining that HEW should not have the power to set its own desegregation guidelines. He said that the new guidelines illustrated what James Madison meant in *The Federalist* when he wrote, "The accumulation of all powers, legislative, executive, and judiciary, in the same hands, whether one, a few, or many, and whether hereditary, self-appointed, or elective, may justly be pronounced the very definition of tyranny."[79] Ervin cited Justice Louis D. Brandeis, who once stated: "Experience teaches us to be most on our guard to protect liberty when the government's purposes are beneficent," and he threw in his favorite quote from Daniel Webster as well: "Good intentions will always be pleaded for every assumption of authority—it is hardly too strong to say that the Constitution was made to guard the people against the dangers of good intentions. There are men in all ages who mean to govern well, but they mean to govern. They promise to be good masters, but they mean to be masters."[80]

Ervin and the southerners gave great speeches, but President Johnson steadfastly backed HEW's insistence that the southern school districts fully comply with its 1966 guidelines. Furthermore, the administration threatened to cut off all federal funding to those southern school districts that did not begin to take genuine steps toward integration.[81] The new guidelines worked. The percentage of African American students attending school with white children in the South more than doubled that year, from 11.5 to 24.8 percent. By 1970 the figure had reached 89.7 percent.[82]

Though clearly on the defensive, Ervin and the southern bloc continued to explore various methods to undermine HEW's desegregation orders. Every time legislation concerning public education was introduced in the Senate, the southerners offered amendments to weaken HEW's authority, limit its enforcement powers, or prohibit outright the busing of students to achieve a racial balance. Their amendments were repeatedly beaten back.[83] With so little power left in Congress, the segregationists had to put their hope in the courts, where several suits challenging the right of the federal government to order school integration were pending. They would soon meet defeat there as well.[84]

Even as Ervin sought to undermine the implementation of existing civil rights laws, he had to fight against enactment of new legislative proposals. These bills reflected the expanded agenda of the civil rights movement after 1965. The violent riots that erupted in the Watts section of Los Angeles, just five days after Johnson signed the Voting Rights Act, demonstrated the federal government's failure to address the housing, education, and economic discrimination African Americans faced in the nation's urban centers. In 1965 the Johnson administration began to study legislative proposals aimed not only at ending de jure segregation in the South, but also toward eliminating de facto discrimination throughout the United States.[85]

The political climate, however, was changing. The winds that had turned so quickly against Ervin and his fellow southerners after Kennedy's assassination in 1963 slowly began to shift back in their favor following the long hot summers of rioting in 1965 and 1966. An emerging white backlash in the North strengthened the southern bloc's ability to resist President Johnson's new civil rights bills. By 1966 surveys revealed that 44 percent of whites outside the South thought that the administration had pushed integration too fast, up 8 percent from the preceding year. The polls reported a similar trend in northern opinion concerning school desegregation. While the number of white southerners who objected to sending their children to an integrated school had *decreased* from 86 percent to 64 percent over the past few years, the number of white northerners who would object had *risen* from 53 to 60 percent.[86]

Several factors contributed to the growth of this white backlash. Suburban whites' horror at the burning inner cities and the anarchy of the riots was undermining the administration's expansion of the civil rights agenda. Johnson's political advisers warned him that the rioters "will become identified with the civil rights movement and thereby compound the difficulty of those seeking long range solutions." Many middle-class whites also resented paying taxes for government programs that benefited someone other than themselves. One presidential aide worried that "the Great Society has become associated in the public mind with eliminating ghettos and generally pouring vast sums into the renovation of the poor and the Negro. The average American is tired of it."[87]

The cry of "Black power!" fueled white backlash as well. The revolutionary rhetoric of SNCC's Rap Brown and Stokely Carmichael especially troubled moderate white liberals, many of whom had played crucial roles in the civil rights victories of 1964 and 1965. At one stormy meeting of the Leadership Conference on Civil Rights, the AFL-CIO threatened to leave the organization if the radicals from SNCC and CORE were not expelled. The labor organization withdrew its demand only after moderate representatives from the NAACP and SCLC—who also feared SNCC's militants—promised "to simply isolate them."[88] The White House worried about the growing influence of the new breed of angry black leaders whom one presidential adviser described as "romantics who are ready to ride like Don Quixote against the windmills of racism at the drop of a cop."[89]

The content of the civil rights bills Johnson proposed after 1965 also exacerbated white backlash. Several of the president's domestic advisers believed that open housing legislation would do more to break down racial barriers and address the needs of African Americans living in the inner city than any other single measure.[90] But they also warned that "the housing issue may be the most controversial and explosive of all civil rights issues . . . [because] this would be the first attempt to secure legislation on a civil rights problem that exists in serious form in the North as well as the South."[91] Given the political climate outside the South, the president's aides worried that open housing legislation would be "extremely dangerous to pursue this year because of the political repercussions it is likely to have on a number of congressmen," and they predicted "we may be in for one hell of a fight."[92]

When Johnson sent his civil rights package up to Capitol Hill in 1966, Ervin observed: "It should be most interesting to watch the politics of the debate now that other than Southern oxen are being gored."[93] The senator eagerly anticipated the political discomfort of northern members of Congress who had supported civil rights bills in the past but now faced a rising white backlash among their constituents. Senator Philip Hart of Michigan, who introduced the president's bill, received 107 letters against open housing legislation and only one for it.[94] He warned his northern colleagues that in the past "fingers were pointed at the South. Now we're talking about our own neighborhoods. This is, therefore, a test of our own sincerity."[95] Congress did not pass the test. In 1966, and again in 1967, northern Republicans and many Democrats stood aside while Ervin and his southern colleagues turned back the president's civil rights bills.[96]

But how could northern politicians who had voted for the civil rights acts of 1964 and 1965 explain their sudden change of heart? Once again, Sam Ervin provided a respectable constitutional rationale for opposing civil rights.[97] The senator targeted the controversial open-housing proposals for his harshest criticism. According to Ervin, "Open-housing legislation is a gross intrusion on personal liberty and a dangerous grant of unrestrained powers in the name of civil rights." The bill threatened personal liberty because it was "a frontal assault on the right to own and use private property, the source of liberty, without which all other liberties succumb to tyranny." The bill represented "a dangerous grant of unrestrained power" because the Secretary of Housing and Urban Development (HUD) would receive the discretionary power to initiate, investigate, and punish property owners who HUD determined had discriminated against minorities. "I have searched my memory in vain to find another example of the unfettered power that would be given to a political appointee such as the Secretary of Housing and Urban Development," Ervin said. "This kind of power a good Secretary would not want and a poor one should not have. It raises Shakespeare's question, 'Upon what meat doth this our Caesar feed, that he is grown so great?' "[98]

In 1967 Senator Ervin played an important role in the confirmation fight over President Johnson's nomination of the first African American to sit on the Supreme Court, Thurgood Marshall. Ervin led the attack against Marshall in the Judiciary Committee. The senator refrained from commenting on Marshall's civil rights record, choosing instead to criticize his "judicial activism." Scrupulously avoiding any reference to his race, Ervin labeled Marshall "a constitutional iconoclast": "His words and deeds have convinced me that Judge Thurgood Marshall is a judicial activist, who cannot discharge the duties of a Supreme Court Justice with what Edmund Burke called 'the cold neutrality of an impartial judge,' and for this reason his elevation to the Supreme Court would not further constitutional government in our land." Ervin's criticism of Marshall earned a good deal of positive press coverage. Even newspapers that eventually supported Marshall's nomination, such as the *Omaha World-Herald*, thanked Ervin for raising the legitimate concern of judicial activism and complimented the senator because "in his lengthy pronouncements he did not make a single reference to the fact that Mr. Marshall is a Negro." But in spite of Ervin's objections, the Senate confirmed Marshall by an overwhelming margin.[99]

The senator had more success opposing LBJ's choice of Justice Abe Fortas to become the new chief justice in 1968 following the announcement of Earl Warren's retirement. Fortas had a solid record of supporting civil rights. To attack Fortas, Ervin resurrected the imagery of Alexander Hamilton's phantom from his famous speech in 1955 against the *Brown* ruling.[100] In spite of Hamilton's assurance that Supreme Court justices would be bound by legal precedents, Ervin concluded that "a study of the decisions of the court in which Mr. Fortas has joined indicates an easy willingness to depart from the words and history of the Constitution, and, if necessary . . . to cast into the judicial garbage can sound precedents of past courts."[101] Ervin helped to conduct a committee filibuster that held up Fortas's nomination in the Judiciary Committee for weeks, while some of the justice's other enemies dug up evidence of unethical behavior that eventually derailed his nomination and forced him off the Court.[102]

Given the revival of Ervin's soft southern strategy, the continuing urban riots, the growth of white backlash, and the Johnson administration's inability to pass a civil rights bill since 1965, few political observers expected Congress to enact strong civil rights legislation in 1968.[103] But that January the Senate began consideration of a civil rights package sent over from the House that included a mild open housing bill. Just a few months earlier an alliance of southern Democrats and Republicans had defeated a similar housing proposal in the Senate, and there was no indication that Senator Dirksen or his party had experienced a change of heart over the Christmas recess. As expected, the southerners began to filibuster against the housing measure as soon as debate began on 18 January. No one on Capitol Hill could have predicted that the Senate was just a few weeks away from approving landmark open-housing legislation.

Two other provisions from the House bill appeared to have a better chance to survive the Senate in 1968—reform of the selection process for federal and state juries and strengthening of the federal government's protection of civil rights workers. Ervin, who led the southern opposition in 1968, accepted a reasonable compromise on jury selection, but offered a substitute amendment that sought to weaken the protection for civil rights workers by simultaneously circumscribing and expanding the bill's coverage.[104] The Ervin amendment limited the scope of the legislation by changing its constitutional basis from the broad sweep of the Fourteenth Amendment to what he believed to be the more restricted scope of the Commerce Clause. But Ervin's amendment also expanded the bill's coverage by omitting the phrase "because of his race, color, religion, or national origin." By dropping any reference to race, the Ervin amendment would extend the federal government's protection to all Americans—black or white—who faced violent attempts to prevent them from exercising their constitutional rights. Desirable as this might seem, the LCCR warned "it could be too much of a good thing," since the much broader coverage would render the bill unenforceable.[105]

Behind the scenes, the Senate leadership tried to reach a compromise between Ervin and the civil rights proponents. Sensing victory, and confident that without Dirksen's support the liberals could not muster enough votes for cloture on the housing bill, Ervin stubbornly refused to cooperate and the negotiations collapsed. But Ervin had made a serious political mistake. If the southerners had compromised at this point they could have contained their losses to the mild bills designed to reform jury selection and protect civil rights workers. Instead, Ervin's intransigence antagonized moderate senators and gave the disorganized liberals time to rebuild their coalition.[106] Ervin's political blunder by itself does not explain the passage of the landmark Civil Rights Act of 1968. As one reporter concluded, "an incredible combination of circumstances —grave mistakes by southern Democrats, sheer luck on the part of Senate liberals and dogged determination by a small band of senators who refused to surrender on open-housing" all contributed to the bill's enactment.[107] On 6 February the Senate rejected the Ervin amendment by a larger margin than expected. Just moments later, Senators Walter F. Mondale of Minnesota and Edward F. Brooke of Massachusetts proposed their own amendment—a bold, far-reaching open-housing bill. Encouraged by this show of strength, the Johnson administration and the civil rights lobby set out to put together a strong but reasonable housing measure that could attract enough votes to overcome the southerners' filibuster. The turning point came when Senator Dirksen performed an amazing flip-flop and announced that he, too, wanted to enact open-housing legislation.[108] After accepting several amendments, including Ervin's controversial Indian Bill of Rights that extended several constitutional freedoms to Native Americans, the Senate voted to approve one of the most significant and surprising civil rights bills in American history.[109]

Even in defeat, Ervin found an opportunity to joke with his colleagues. He told the Senate that the housing bill reminded him of a story. "A man was visiting in a distant city and received a telegram from the undertaker reading as follows: 'Your mother-in-law died today. Shall we cremate or bury?' The man wired back—'Take no chances. Cremate and bury.'" Ervin suggested the open housing bill "both cremates and buries one of the most precious rights of all Americans—the right to private property."[110]

The story of the Civil Rights Act of 1968 demonstrates more than just Ervin's lack of political acumen or his wealth of entertaining stories. A close analysis of the substitute amendment the senator offered to weaken the bill raises serious questions about the consistency of his constitutional philosophy.

His attempt to limit the scope of the bill by basing it on the Interstate Commerce Clause, and his effort to expand the bill by dropping any reference to "race, color, religion or national origin," both contradicted constitutional positions he had espoused just a few years earlier.

In 1963 Ervin had written that "the interstate commerce clause is a dubious peg" on which to hang civil rights legislation.[111] At that time the senator was engaged in a debate with Attorney General Robert Kennedy over the civil rights bill of 1963, which included a section outlawing racial discrimination in public accommodations. During "The Sam and Bobby Show," Ervin insisted that the administration's use of the Commerce Clause to justify civil rights action by the federal government was "clearly unconstitutional."[112] The following year Ervin wrote: "Once we begin using the commerce clause to affect matters that have no rational connection with the free flow of goods, then we have fatally dropped the bar to government tyranny that was the purpose of the original framers of the Constitution, who were so careful to construct safeguards against an all-encompassing federal government."[113] Yet in 1968 Ervin's own substitute amendment proposed changing the constitutional rationale for the federal government's protection of civil rights workers from the Fourteenth Amendment to the Commerce Clause. Why? The senator believed that the Supreme Court had been wrong to expand the federal government's power over commerce, and he hoped that some day a more conservative Court might agree with him. If such a reversal occurred, and the Ervin amendment passed, only acts of violence against civil rights workers occurring on interstate highways would be covered; activities on rural farm roads would not. As one of Johnson's aides suggested, Ervin insisted upon reference to the Commerce Clause "obviously with the intent of restricting the coverage of the legislation."[114]

An even greater inconsistency can be found in the senator's explanation for why his amendment dropped any reference to the race of the victim. Ervin's substitute retained all the protections offered to persons exercising their constitutional rights, but omitted the phrase "because of his race, color, religion, or national origin." This deletion would expand the coverage of the bill as to make it unenforceable.[115] But Ervin offered a very different rationale for his amendment when he introduced it to the Senate in 1968. Although he expressed his reluctance to have the federal government enter into the field of law enforcement against the crimes of violence enumerated in the civil rights bill, Ervin told the Senate, "If we are going into that field, we ought to get into it with a law that applies alike to all men, under all circumstances, not have one murder punished as a federal crime because of the race of the accused or the race of the victim and another exempt from punishment because in that case the race of the accused and the victim is the same." Ervin concluded: "It will be a sad day in America when we start passing special criminal laws for some people, and then exempt from those laws other people who commit exactly the same acts, solely on the basis of race, color, religion, or national origin, of the accused or the alleged victims of the accused."[116] In short, the senator was arguing that it was wrong to write laws that discriminated against any citizen because of his or her race.

Sam Ervin—the die-hard segregationist who opposed the *Brown* decision, wrote the Southern Manifesto, and defended North Carolina's Jim Crow laws— insisted in 1968 that the law should be color-blind. The senator was embracing the basic principle of the *Brown* ruling, which he had castigated and ridiculed for over a decade. How could such an amazing reversal be explained?

Senator Ervin never announced his change of opinion to the press, nor did he explain it on the floor of the Senate. Even many of his closest friends did not know the extent of his rethinking of *Brown* until they read his explanation in his autobiography published in 1984, ten years after his retirement. But there, in the clearest possible language, he confessed: "My original opinion respecting the decision in the *Brown* case, which was based on my intellectual acceptance of the constitutionality of the separate but equal doctrine, was wrong."[117]

According to Ervin, after his work on the Southern Manifesto he "gave priority of study and thought to the Constitution in general, and the three Civil War Amendments and their history in particular, and relevant Supreme Court decisions." As a result he "gradually became inseparably wedded to certain abiding convictions." First, he came to believe that "the Constitution is, indeed, color-blind as the first Justice John Marshall Harlan maintained in his dissent in *Plessy v. Ferguson*." Second, he decided "that as amended by the Thirteenth, Fourteenth, and Fifteenth Amendments, the Constitution makes all persons in our land free and equal before the law, and forbids the government at any level to use the race of any·of them as a criteria for the bestowal of any legal right or the imposition of any legal responsibility." Thus, Ervin deemed *Brown* to be "a sound decision," and he accepted its mandate for a color-blind society.[118]

How like Sam Ervin, the Claghorn's Hammurabi, to explain his reversal on *Brown* as a change of mind rather than a change of heart. But ideology is not the wellspring of all human motivation. Not even Sam Ervin, who seemed so withdrawn in his abstract world of legal theory, could have been solely motivated by constitutional principles alone.

Perhaps Ervin grew. Maybe the repeated attacks against his character pierced his thick legal skin and stung the sensitive man who hid inside. Maybe the personal stories of racial discrimination, violence, and poverty he heard during all those hours of testimony began to tug at his conscience. Maybe the overwhelming moral imperative illustrated so valiantly by civil rights marchers in Birmingham, Selma, and elsewhere stirred his sense of justice. Maybe the disturbing and often heated arguments with his own children, who supported civil rights, had unsettled him. Senator Ervin, the deeply private southern gentlemen, never said.

Neither did Ervin ever explain exactly when he changed his mind about *Brown*. The earliest indication that he was rethinking the desegregation decision came in 1956 when Ervin praised the *Briggs* dictum written by his old friend Judge John J. Parker. When the *Briggs* case was remanded to the District Court, Parker wrote that the *Brown* ruling "does not require integration. It merely forbids discrimination."[119] According to Judge Parker, all that the Supreme Court had ordered was for state governments to end their race-based, or color-conscious, school assignments. Seizing on the *Briggs* dictum, southern school districts turned the color-blind intent of *Brown* on its head by passing freedom-of-choice plans to slow school desegregation.

By 1963 Ervin had developed Parker's logic into a powerful weapon against any government desegregation program. During his confrontation with Bobby Kennedy, Ervin asked the attorney general, "Do you not agree with me that denying a school child the right to attend his neighborhood school and transferring him by bus or otherwise to another community for the purpose of racially mixing the school in that other community is a violation of the Fourteenth Amendment as interpreted in *Brown versus Board of Education*?"[120]

After a few minutes of squirming and protesting, Kennedy admitted, "You can make an argument along those lines." But when Ervin paused for a second during his subsequent lecture on Judge Parker's interpretation of the color-blind principle of *Brown*, Kennedy interrupted to ask: "Would you say, Senator, that the procedures or practices which are followed in southern communities, where an individual is not permitted to attend his neighborhood school, but is taken maybe ten, fifteen, or twenty miles so that he attends a segregated school; is that a violation of the rights of an individual?" "I'm asking you another question," Ervin protested, and the audience laughed. A few minutes later, Ervin conceded that the southern practice also violated the Supreme Court's ruling.[121]

As the Kennedy and Johnson administrations slowly shifted from color-blind to color-conscious approaches to fight racial discrimination in the 1960s, Ervin gradually stopped defending de jure segregation and began endorsing a color-blind society. For example, in 1966 HEW's tough new guidelines called for school districts and hospitals to take "affirmative actions" to achieve a "racial balance" by placing students and patients on the basis of their race.[122] Ervin responded by attacking HEW for violating the *Brown* decision. "Current HEW policies require assignment of school desks and hospital beds according to race," Ervin complained. "Such requirements will lead to every American being officially identified according to his race, creed, or national origin. This can only bring divisiveness to our people. These are not the proper policies of a government which is supposed to be color-blind."[123]

Though it is unclear exactly why or when Senator Ervin decided to abandon his opposition to the Court's desegregation ruling, the strategic implications of his latent endorsement of *Brown* cannot be ignored. In the 1960s Ervin increasingly evoked the color-blind principle of *Brown* to fight the new color-conscious principle behind affirmative action programs. The more civil rights proponents embraced effective tools such as busing and quotas to reach numerical goals of racial balance in schools, housing, and employment, the more they fell into the moral paradox of advocating preferential racial discrimination in order to achieve racial nondiscrimination. For Ervin to take advantage of this contradiction between means and ends in the emerging liberal consensus on civil rights, he had to abandon his former belief in racial segregation and accept the conviction that no government should discriminate, for any reason, against any citizen on the basis of his or her race. Thus, by 1968, defending *Brown* and the doctrine of a color-blind society had become an integral part of Ervin's revitalized soft southern strategy.

Sam Ervin's famed constitutional opposition to civil rights was never as consistent as he and his apologists claimed. During the 1960s the senator subtly shifted constitutional positions, misapplied legal principles, built his arguments on outdated Supreme Court cases, and, most significant, reversed himself on *Brown*. Of course, some of his constitutional objections did raise substantial concerns, especially when he argued for legislative resistance to executive lawmaking. The most consistent aspect of Ervin's record on civil rights, however, was not his constitutional philosophy but his steadfast opposition to every judicial, legislative, and executive action designed to empower African Americans. North Carolina's country lawyer not only wanted to preserve the Constitution, he also wanted to preserve Jim Crow. His constitutional arguments represented the best legal case he could build to defend his guilty client.

CHAPTER SIX

CONSERVATIVE CIVIL LIBERTARIAN

From the day he arrived in Washington, D.C., Sam Ervin seemed to fit the popular stereotype of an old-fashioned, conservative southern senator. He certainly looked the part with his thick mane of white hair, full jowls, and bushy eyebrows, and he sounded right as well with an accent that echoed the distinctive mountain tones of the western Carolinas. Ervin's high-profile defense of racial segregation added to his southern senatorial credentials, as did his penchant for quoting the Bible, reciting romantic poetry, and telling cracker-barrel stories.

Ervin fit this stereotype so well that it became an increasingly popular way for the national media to portray the senator, especially during his frequent battles against civil rights legislation. In the early 1960s, as the political tide began to turn against the southern segregationists, national newspaper reporters often characterized Ervin as just another Dixie windbag whose exceptional talents were wasted defending Jim Crow. "There is a matter of sadness and regret here," wrote a Washington correspondent who covered Ervin's well-publicized civil rights debates with Robert Kennedy in 1963. "The best minds of the South—Ervin of North Carolina, Russell of Georgia, Stennis of Mississippi, and Hill of Alabama—all caught in the hold of history and the politics of local passions. The hearings are a great show. But tragedy is at the heart of them—and not only the tragedy of the Negro."[1]

Even Washington insiders occasionally described Ervin as just another one-dimensional Senator Claghorn. In April 1961, Joseph L. Rauh Jr., vice chairman of the Americans for Democratic Action (ADA) and a prominent civil rights advocate, attacked Ervin and his southern colleagues for not living up to their responsibility to protect civil liberties. "What if the best brains in the South were put to work in trying to make civil liberties work instead of fighting it?" he asked an audience at the Duke University Law School. Citing Ervin's exceptional ability to defeat or weaken civil rights legislation, Rauh concluded that the senator was "a great man whose mind is in chains."[2]

But Sam Ervin cannot be so easily dismissed. Newspaper reporters in North Carolina who had followed Ervin's career closely since 1954 described him as "a complex man," "more complicated than his enemies and most of his friends realize," "easily misunderstood," and ideologically unclassifiable.[3] Joe Rauh certainly would not have criticized Ervin for failing to defend civil liberties had he read a few Tar Heel newspapers before he addressed the Duke law students. The North Carolina press reported that Ervin protested the deportation of a Guatemalan immigrant who was denied the right to counsel, defended the separation of church and state, proposed legislation to protect the rights of the mentally ill, discussed his upcoming hearings on government wiretapping, expressed his concern for the constitutional rights of Native Americans, and cosponsored legislation to provide public defenders for federal court defendants unable to pay attorney's fees—all during the same week that Rauh disparaged his record as a civil libertarian.[4]

Just a few months before Rauh's speech, Ervin had inherited the chairmanship of the Subcommittee on Constitutional Rights, which had jurisdiction not only over civil rights but also over civil liberties. This assignment marked a turning point in the senator's career. After almost a decade of inactivity on civil liberties, Ervin suddenly sprang into action. The new chairman surprised his critics by pushing forward on the subcommittee's entire civil liberties agenda and even expanding it. Ironically, at the same time that Ervin was solidifying his reputation as a Claghorn's Hammurabi because of his opposition to civil rights, he began to establish himself as the Senate's foremost champion of civil liberties.

To be fair to Rauh and Ervin's other critics, the senator had not demonstrated much concern for civil liberties during the six years between his courageous stand against Joe McCarthy in 1954 and his appointment as chairman of the Subcommittee on Constitutional Rights in 1961. His outspoken opposition to the Supreme Court's desegregation rulings after 1954 and his ongoing battles against civil rights legislation consumed his time and energy. But Ervin's preoccupation with civil rights does not adequately explain his inconsistent record on civil liberties in the 1950s. The two are inextricably linked because his

In the 1960s Senator Ervin's national public image improved as his reputation for defending civil liberties grew. Here he is pictured with Lori Wagner, the 1966 March of Dimes Poster Girl. Sam Ervin Library and Museum, Western Piedmont Community College, Morganton, North Carolina.

uncompromising opposition to the first profoundly weakened his commit-ment to the second.

Nowhere is this clearer than in Ervin's battles against the Supreme Court. Soon after Earl Warren became chief justice in 1953, he led the Court into a series of decisions that profoundly affected social and political life in the United States and greatly expanded civil rights and civil liberties. The first of these rulings, *Brown v. Board of Education*, infuriated southern segregationists by sweeping away the legal basis for racial discrimination. Over the next few years Ervin and his colleagues in the southern caucus attacked the Warren Court mercilessly, but as a minority in the Senate they could not muster enough support to mount a successful assault. That changed, however, when the Court handed down a number of controversial opinions in 1956 and 1957 that upheld the due process and free speech claims of alleged Communists.[5]

In 1956 the Supreme Court began to issue a series of rulings known collec-tively as the Cold War Cases. These decisions diminished the impact of the government's anticommunist laws and practices that had been spawned by the excesses of McCarthyism. In *Pennsylvania v. Nelson* the Court curbed state sedition laws by ruling that such legislation was the sole domain of Congress, not the states, causing an outcry from champions of states' rights. Just over a year later, on 3 June 1957, the justices delivered a ruling that resulted in a federal defendant receiving permission to examine an FBI report that formed the basis of the case against him. *Jencks v. United States* aroused alarm that criminals and subversives could now look through secret FBI files. No sooner had conserva-tives begun to protest the *Jencks* decision than the Court handed down rulings on the constitutional rights of accused Communists in four more cases all announced on 17 June 1957—thereafter known to dedicated anticommunists as "Red Monday." In *Yates v. United States* the Court severely restricted the scope of the Smith Act, in *Watkins v. United States* and *Sweezy v. New Hampshire* it limited the power of legislative investigative committees to compel the testi-mony of suspected Communists, and in *Service v. Dulles* a unanimous Court overturned the secretary of state's improper discharge of a foreign service official.[6]

By expanding the civil liberties of accused Communists, the Warren Court incensed the far right of the Republican Party, which now joined Ervin and the southern Democrats in denouncing the judicial activism of the justices. One of the most vehement Republican attacks on the Court came from Senator Wil-liam E. Jenner of Indiana. In a speech from the Senate floor, Jenner sounded much like a southern segregationist when he charged that "the Supreme Court has dealt a succession of blows at key points of the legislative structure erected by Congress for the protection of the internal security of the United States. . . . The Court has become, for all practical purposes, a legislative arm of the Government."[7]

In spite of the reputation Sam Ervin had earned during the McCarthy era as a moderate defender of civil liberties, he quickly joined those conservatives criticizing the Cold War Cases. Only days after Red Monday, Ervin shared his opinion that "these decisions are encouraging to communists and I will do what I can to avoid their consequences." Ervin employed the same rhetoric he had developed as a weapon against *Brown* in his new assault on the justices. "The Court has shown an increasing tendency to lay aside its judicial knitting and arrogate to itself the power to make rather that interpret law," he maintained, and its rulings "serve to further illustrate the dangers that lurk in the actions of the Supreme Court which tend to reduce the states to meaningless zeros in the body politic." The senator was also quick to perceive how *Nelson*, the first Cold War Case in 1956, might convince Republican conservatives to join the southerners in their Court bashing. "I think those of us who have been in the minority on this matter will now pick up considerable support from others following this ruling," he predicted.[8]

The controversy over the Warren Court's commitment to civil liberties grew even more contentious just seven days after Red Monday when the justices relaxed censorship of some sexually explicit materials. In the first of a series of obscenity cases, *Roth v. United States*, the Court ruled for the first time that literature with strong sexual content was not necessarily obscene if it possessed some "socially redeemable" quality.[9] Conservatives like Ervin could not believe that the Supreme Court would hold that a state or local government was constitutionally powerless to enact laws prohibiting the selling of what it considered pornography. When the Court later overruled New York State's censorship of the film *Lady Chatterley's Lover*, an incensed Ervin complained that "the right of freedom of speech is not absolute and I do not believe that it contemplates that people can preach the practice of adultery."[10]

The Court further incurred the wrath of Ervin and his fellow conservatives by expanding the rights of the accused in *Mallory v. United States*. Andrew Mallory was a mentally impaired black man who had raped a young white girl. After his arrest police questioned him for almost seven hours until he confessed to the crime. There was never any question about Mallory's guilt, but the Court unanimously ruled that his confession could not be admitted as evidence because an inordinate time had elapsed between arrest and arraignment, raising suspicions about how the police had secured Mallory's supposedly voluntary confession. Mallory was set free.[11]

The critics of the Court immediately added *Mallory* to their list of judicial aberrations. "The Supreme Court—which has recently handed down decisions to give greater protection to Communists and criminals—has now issued an edict which will give greater protection to such heinous criminals as rapists and murderers," Strom Thurmond told the Senate. "The choice we face in this country today is judicial limitation or judicial tyranny. Congress must take action to limit the power of the Court."[12] Subtle and not so subtle racial overtones connecting black men to rape and crime filled the Senate chamber. "How many more eight-year-old girls will be raped in 1957 because the Supreme Court was so zealous a protector of Andrew Mallory's rights?" asked Senator Jenner.[13] Sam Ervin added, "I believe that in recent years enough has been done for those who murder, rape, and rob; and that it is about time for Congress to do something for those who do not wish to be murdered, or raped, or robbed."[14]

This thunder on the right grew into a powerful anti-Court coalition. Southern segregationists resentful of desegregation rulings, national security alarmists angered by the Cold War Cases, and traditional conservatives fearful of an increase in pornography and crime joined together to mount a vigorous legislative attack aimed at imposing stringent curbs on the Court's powers. Some congressmen wanted to reverse specific aspects of the unpopular rulings, leaving the Court's authority untouched. But a more serious effort to hamstring the Court was launched by Senator Jenner, who proposed a general limitation of the Supreme Court's power. The Jenner bill would remove the Court's jurisdiction over actions by congressional committees and over state and federal authorities administering anti-subversive programs.[15]

Senator Ervin initially seemed ambivalent toward the Jenner bill, in spite of the fact that many distinguished legal scholars condemned the measure. Even some conservatives who had previously joined Jenner in criticizing the Court backed away from endorsing his proposal. Almost every member of the Duke and University of North Carolina law schools, including his old friend Daniel H. Pollitt, wrote to Ervin urging him to vote against the bill.[16] Some defended the Court's controversial rulings on due process, the freedom of expression, and the rights of the accused because these decisions protected basic civil liberties. Others considered Jenner's proposal to be a draconian measure posing a serious threat to the integrity of the Supreme Court. But Senator Ervin refused to take a definitive stand: "There are some provisions in this bill that I favor and some that I am against." But he added, "I do feel that there is need of this type of legislation to curb the recent actions of the Supreme Court."[17]

When the Jenner bill reached the Senate Judiciary Committee in 1958, Ervin worked behind the scenes to strip the measure of its most objectionable provisions. He voted for most of the amendments offered by Senator John Marshall Butler of Maryland designed to soothe the misgivings of some conservatives that the bill was too radical. But even a few of Butler's amendments were too harsh for Ervin to stomach.[18] As one journalist noted, Ervin was "conservative rather than reactionary" and he seemed an uncomfortable ally of the far right.[19] Nonetheless, Ervin threw his support behind the Jenner-Butler bill that emerged from committee. Although more moderate than the original, it still represented a dramatic reduction of the Supreme Court's jurisdiction. Retired circuit judge Learned Hand, perhaps the most respected conservative critic of the Warren Court, warned that if the new bill was enacted it "would be detrimental to the best interests of the United States."[20]

Ervin's anger at the Court had overcome his concern for civil liberties. In May he struggled to defend his support of the Jenner-Butler bill during a television interview:

I don't like to put restraints on courts. Fundamentally, I don't like to put restraints on anything. . . . But there are some objections to any kind of law of this nature. But, on the other hand, to my mind there's a very much more fundamental objection. I mean, a more serious question is this: If judges are going to make laws, if judges are going to destroy the states, if judges are going to ignore the fundamentals of our constitutional system and attempt to limit the power of Congress to discharge its constitutional duties, then we are in danger of being ruled by a judicial oligarchy. I think that danger is a much more transcendent danger than these other things. We may have to put some restraints on judges if judges are not going to put restraints on themselves.[21]

The debate in the Senate pitted liberals, who praised the justices for championing civil liberties, against conservatives, who castigated the Court for exceeding its proper bounds. Senator Thomas Hennings Jr. of Missouri, a liberal who chaired the Subcommittee on Constitutional Rights, led the opposition to the Jenner-Butler bill. He warned that this "irresponsible" measure "could deprive many American citizens of their constitutional rights" and be "the first step toward destroying the governmental concept of separation of powers."[22] Ervin, however, maintained that it was the Court that threatened constitutional government by destroying the power of the states and encroaching on the legislative power of Congress. "I respect our democratic institutions," he insisted, "but I am compelled to speak out against what I am convinced is usurpation of power whether it be in the judicial, legislative, or executive branches."[23]

By the time the bill reached the Senate floor, Ervin had become a true believer. After heated debate, the Jenner-Butler bill failed by a vote of 49–41, with Ervin and the southern bloc supporting the losing cause. Undaunted, Ervin helped to lead the fight the next day to pass an even more chilling curb of the Court. Brought over from the House of Representatives, H.R. 3—nicknamed the "States Rights Bill"—would have reversed recent Court interpretations by declaring that federal laws preempted state legislation only if specifically stated by Congress, or if the federal and state laws were in direct conflict. The Senate rejected the bill by just one vote. Ervin, who had originally hedged his support of the Jenner bill, emerged from the congressional debate as a leader of the movement to limit the Court.[24]

At first glance it appears that Ervin joined the Court-curbing coalition because his concern for civil liberties was less important than his hostility to judicial activism, but several of Ervin's liberal senatorial foes detected a different dynamic behind the furor over the Court—the continuing opposition to the school desegregation ruling. Senator Paul Douglas of Illinois explained, "This is all part of a 'reverse the Court' campaign which stems largely, although not entirely, from the earlier decision in the Brown case." Recalling the recent racial turmoil in Little Rock, Arkansas, and the segregationist governor who had defied the Supreme Court's desegregation order, Douglas added, "I think we must choose on whose side we stand. Do we stand on the side of Governor Faubus, or do we stand on the side of the Supreme Court?"[25]

Even more direct was Congressman Barratt O'Hara, also from Illinois, who attacked the motivation of those who attempted to resurrect H.R. 3 the following year. "Everyone knows that the real issue here is civil rights," he told the members of the House. "My colleagues from the South, gallantly fighting on the last foothold of what they know is a lost battlefield, have wrapped themselves in the brilliant robes of the dear old doctrine of Federal preemption as they battle to the last drop of devotion for the continuance of the social order in which they believe and by which they have lived." O'Hara perceptively made the connection between the southerners' strategy to pass H.R. 3 and the soft southern strategy Ervin had perfected to weaken the civil rights bill in 1957. "Their strategy is superb. But they are not fooling themselves. They know that, no matter what label they give it, this is the civil rights battle of 1959 and that the strategy they are using is patterned exactly on that of the civil rights battle in the 85th Congress when trial by jury was the battle cry."[26]

Whether Sam Ervin was primarily motivated by his opposition to judicial activism, to civil rights, or to both, his efforts to curb the Supreme Court raise serious questions about his commitment to civil liberties in the 1950s. Ervin not only resisted the justices' attempts to guarantee the constitutional rights of African Americans, alleged Communists, producers of controversial literature, and criminal suspects, but he also failed to initiate or support any legislative protections for these unpopular groups. Such a record challenges the popular portrait of Senator Ervin as a consistent, lifelong champion of the constitutional rights of all Americans.[27]

Yet Ervin's civil libertarian impulses had not been entirely dormant in the 1950s. The senator demonstrated considerable moderation in 1957 when the Senate considered limiting the scope of the Court's *Jencks* decision with specific legislation. In *Jencks* the Court held that defendants in criminal cases have the right to examine FBI reports of witnesses who testify against them. Surprisingly, in light of his anti-Court rhetoric, Ervin argued that in this particular case the justices ruled correctly because "a fundamental principle of evidence holds that a defendant has the right to try to contradict the testimony and supporting evidence of witnesses against him." A more moderate bill, limited to clarifying the procedures under which FBI files must be produced, passed the Senate with Ervin's support.[28]

Ervin also spoke out in defense of freedom of the press and in opposition to excessive government secrecy in the 1950s. He consistently criticized the tendency of both congressional committees and executive officials to withhold information from the public by going into executive sessions or hiding behind the cry of national security. Speaking before the North Carolina Press Association in 1955, Ervin quoted James Madison: "A popular government without popular information or the means of acquiring it is but the prologue to a farce, or tragedy, or perhaps both."[29] Ervin strongly disapproved of the Eisenhower administration's reliance on "executive privilege" to keep information from Congress, and in 1958 he supported the unsuccessful congressional efforts to pass a Freedom of Information Act.[30]

But these few actions represented the exception and not the rule. More often than not Ervin could be found on the side of those fighting against the extension of both civil rights and civil liberties in the 1950s. He never missed a meeting of the Subcommittee on Constitutional Rights scheduled to debate civil rights, but he seldom was present at its hearings to discuss civil liberties. Instead it was Thomas Hennings, the subcommittee's liberal chairman, who provided the impetus for its quiet hearings on topics such as "Freedom of Information and Secrecy in Government," "Secrecy in Science," and "Wiretapping, Eavesdropping, and the Bill of Rights," none of which Ervin attended.[31]

On 13 September 1960, Thomas Hennings died at his home in Washington, D.C. Frequently ill, the fifty-seven-year-old senator had been inactive since May when surgery left him unable to work on Capitol Hill. The *New York Times* observed that "the loss will be especially significant on the conservative-dominated Judiciary Committee . . . where Senator Hennings fought an uphill battle for civil rights and other legislation."[32] Liberals were especially worried about who would replace Hennings as chairman of the critically important Constitutional Rights Subcommittee. According to the strict rules of the Senate's seniority system, one of three conservative southerners would take over Hennings's leadership of the subcommittee: Olin Johnston of South Carolina, John McClellan of Arkansas, or Sam Ervin. As Clarence Mitchell, the executive director of the Leadership Conference on Civil Rights (LCCR), lamented at a meeting just before the presidential election of 1960, "You guess which one of them will be the best man to have in charge of implementing the civil rights pledges made in party platforms."[33] As it turned out, Ervin succeeded Hennings.

For the second time, the death of a senator had profoundly reshaped Sam Ervin's political career. Just as Clyde Hoey's stroke in 1954 had led to Ervin's unexpected appointment to the Senate, Thomas Hennings's death in 1960 had suddenly propelled Ervin to the chairmanship of an important subcommittee with enormous potential for doing both mischief and good. Almost all civil rights bills had to pass through the Subcommittee on Constitutional Rights, giving Ervin an excellent opportunity to impede their progress. But when he took over Hennings's subcommittee he also inherited the former chairman's active civil libertarian agenda.[34] The subcommittee's broad mandate "to examine, investigate, and make a complete study of any and all matters pertaining to constitutional rights" gave Ervin considerable leeway to launch hearings on almost any other legal or constitutional issue as well.[35] One reporter suggested that the senator "resembled a youngster in a candy store who couldn't make up his mind what he wanted because there was so much to choose from."[36] Now Ervin had both the opportunity and the power to pursue his own interests in civil liberties.

Ervin assumed control of the subcommittee in January 1961. He immediately sought to soothe liberal fears by promising not to bottle up civil rights bills. "We will have adequate hearings on civil rights bills or any other bills that are referred to us," he pledged. But at the first closed-door meeting of the subcommittee's members, Ervin stressed their "grave obligation to hold back unsound legislation," and Senator McClellan sarcastically wondered aloud about a bill that would provide civil rights for southern white people. In response to questions from his liberal colleagues, Ervin also expressed his commitment to continue all the subcommittee's ongoing civil liberties investigations. Two of the most significant studies focused on groups whose constitutional rights had long been neglected by their government—the mentally ill and members of the Armed Services.[37]

Many mental patients unknowingly surrendered their legal rights when they passed through a hospital door. During its preliminary study, the subcommittee learned of a twenty-three-year-old woman in New Jersey who had voluntarily entered a mental hospital after suffering a nervous breakdown. Her doctors eventually decided she had recuperated, but, following standard procedure, they released her to the custody of her father. The father wanted nothing to do with his daughter and recommitted her against her will. Every time the doctors let her go, the father sent her right back. Unable to regain control over her own life, she reached a point of exasperation and shouted that she wanted her freedom, only to be strapped to a bed by an orderly.[38]

The subcommittee also heard the story of a respected businessman in Washington, D.C., who had been arrested on the minor charge of overdrawing his bank account by a sum of $100. Because the defendant had once been a patient in a mental hospital, the municipal judge at the arraignment immediately committed him to a hospital to determine his mental competency to stand trial. The hospital certified that the defendant was mentally competent, but added that his crime may have been related to his mental illness. When the businessman returned to court, he wisely accepted the advice of his lawyer and sought to enter a guilty plea. Since he had no prior record, it seemed likely that he would be put on probation or given a suspended sentence. But over the defendant's objections, and in spite of the hospital's recommendation, the judge ruled that the businessman was mentally incapable of participating in the proceedings and refused to accept his plea of not guilty. Ironically, during the trial the prosecution argued that the businessman was *not guilty* by reason of insanity, while the defense insisted that the defendant was *guilty*, fully competent, and deserving of the usual light sentence. In the end, the judge found the businessman not guilty by reason of insanity and committed him, against his will, to a local mental hospital where he remained for over a year.[39]

Incidents such as these produced concern that persons suspected of being mentally ill were sometimes denied due process of law in commitment procedures, during criminal trials, and in the review of their cases. Some patients had been committed to institutions based upon statements from persons who barely knew them, while others claimed that they had been hospitalized only because they preferred to act or dress in a manner that others found objectionable. Few had any legal recourse to challenge the evidence or the procedures that had deprived them of their liberty. Once committed, many lost the right to vote, to buy and sell property, or to retain custody of their children. Far too often they did not even have the right to receive treatment so that they could return to society. Responding to these reports, Senator Hennings, just a few months before his death, had ordered his subcommittee staff to prepare for hearings on what he called the "legal no-man's land" of the practices governing the mentally ill.[40]

Ervin enthusiastically continued the investigation. As a lawyer and judge in Morganton, he had become familiar with the legal problems of the mentally ill. He himself had presided over many commitment proceedings, and the state-run Broughton Hospital for the mentally handicapped was one of Morganton's largest enterprises. Ervin once recalled the story of a motorist whose car blew a tire on a highway just across the fence from the mental hospital. Not particularly adept at changing a tire, he struggled with the jack while several mental patients looked on. One of the inmates offered to explain how the jack worked. When the startled motorist glanced over in disbelief, the patient snapped, "Look, I may be nuts, but I'm not stupid."[41]

After conducting a successful run of hearings in March 1961, Ervin sponsored a new mental health bill for the District of Columbia that he hoped would also serve as model legislation for the fifty states. The measure encouraged voluntary hospitalization, reformed commitment procedures, and established a patient's "bill of rights" that included the right to treatment and to periodic review.[42] In spite of overwhelming support—it won the praise of every member of the subcommittee and passed the Senate by a vote of 72–1—it took three years for it to reach the president's desk. Lyndon Johnson signed Ervin's mental health bill into law on 15 September 1964, calling it "a victory for civil liberties."[43]

It took Ervin even longer to pass legislation reforming the military justice system. Under Hennings's leadership, the subcommittee had begun an investigation into the legal rights of servicemen and women. Cases of commanding officers unfairly influencing disciplinary hearings, defendants not being allowed proper legal representation during court-martial, and soldiers receiving less-than-honorable discharges without the protection of due process of law infuriated Ervin, who pushed ahead with hearings.[44]

The subcommittee learned that even minor blemishes on a service record could cast a shadow over a veteran for the rest of her or his life. One marine who had been charged with rape at the Cherry Point base in North Carolina was cleared of all charges during his court-martial. In spite of the fact that the court had completely exonerated him, the Marines still discharged him "under honorable conditions" instead of the normal "honorable discharge" most veterans receive. The ex-marine left the state fearing that this miscarriage of justice might haunt him sometime in the future. He moved to the Midwest and secured a good job as a pilot for a major airline. But when his employers discovered his tainted discharge, they fired him.[45]

This marine's story was one of hundreds that convinced Ervin to sponsor a comprehensive military law reform bill designed, in Ervin's words, "to extend to servicemen the same rights they are defending."[46] The Military Justice Act guaranteed all soldiers legally trained counsel whenever they were involved in courts-martial or in administrative procedures involving discharge under other than honorable conditions. The legislation also suspended the practice of allowing commanding officers virtually complete authority to choose court-martial personnel, ensured that an experienced and impartial law officer presided over major disciplinary actions, and protected the right of the accused to confront and cross-examine witnesses. It took seven years, but Ervin finally pushed his Military Justice Act through Congress in 1968.[47]

Like the mentally ill and military personnel, Native Americans living on reservations did not benefit from the constitutional and legal protections enjoyed by most Americans. As separate political communities, Indian tribes retained the primary power to administer criminal and civil law within their reservations. But because these Indian governments existed before the Constitution was written, the Native Americans living under their jurisdiction were not protected by the Bill of Rights. The Indians on these reservations could not claim such basic rights as the freedom of speech, the freedom of religion, or the right to be free from unnecessary searches and seizures. To make matters worse, a complex and sometimes contradictory series of treaties, laws, and policies over the past two hundred years had left the 280,000 Native Americans living on reservations in a legal nightmare in which federal, state, and tribal governments all had control over various aspects of their lives.[48]

Sam Ervin was no stranger to the problems of the Indians. More Native Americans lived in North Carolina than in any other state east of the Mississippi River. The majority belonged to one of the two largest tribes in the state, the Lumbees and the Eastern Cherokees. The Lumbee Indians made up approximately one-third of the population of Robeson County in eastern North Carolina. One Lumbee, Helen Maynor Scheirbeck, served on Ervin's subcommittee staff. The Eastern Band of the Cherokee lived on the Qualla Boundary in the mountains of western North Carolina. Their ancestors had escaped the Trail of Tears—the terrible forced migration of the rest of their tribe to Oklahoma between 1835 and 1838. Ervin had visited their communities, knew their history, and understood the legal difficulties under which they lived. In 1960 the Cherokees had adopted Ervin as an honorary villager for "as long as the green grass grows and the rivers flow," and they named him "SA MI TSA EQUA NI KE KA NA WA OE SDI GO SI SCI" which, roughly translated, means "lawgiver" in Cherokee.[49]

On a day in which civil rights speeches filled the Senate chamber in 1961, Ervin rose to announce that his Subcommittee on Constitutional Rights would conduct an investigation of the constitutional rights of Native Americans. He proudly claimed to be conducting "the first congressional inquiry into this most important and all too long neglected area of law."[50] Over the next six years the subcommittee held hearings in Washington, D.C., Arizona, California, Colorado, New Mexico, and North and South Dakota. Ervin and his staff interviewed hundreds of witnesses, including representatives from Indian tribes, national Native American associations, and the Bureau of Indian Affairs.[51]

As was his usual practice, Ervin provided some poignant anecdotes to strengthen his arguments and enliven his hearings. The senator recounted the story of General Benjamin Lincoln's peace negotiations with the Creek Indians. One of the Creek chiefs asked the general to sit down beside him on a log. After a few minutes, the chief asked the general to move a little further down the log. A few minutes later, the Indian again asked the general to move. This request was repeated until the general got to the end of the log. The chief again demanded, "Move further," to which the general replied, "I can move no further." "Just so it is with us," said the chief. "You moved us back to the waters, and now ask us to move further."[52]

Ervin also repeated the joke about the Indian who went to New York City from his reservation for a business meeting. While strolling along one of the busy thoroughfares, he was approached by a native New Yorker, who inquired, "And how do you like our city?" "Fine," replied the Indian, "and how do you like our country?"[53]

The subcommittee's investigation convinced Ervin to draft legislative proposals "to provide our Indian citizens with the rights and protections conferred on other Americans."[54] One of Ervin's bills submitted these tribes to the same constitutional limitations imposed on federal and state governments. Another bill directed the secretary of the interior to develop a model code of justice for Indian courts; the extant code had not been revised for over forty years. Perhaps the most popular of the senator's proposals among Native Americans was his bill preventing a state from assuming jurisdiction over criminal or civil cases involving Indians on reservations until it obtained the consent of the affected tribes. First introduced in 1964, these bills underwent several revisions before merging into a single legislative package that Ervin labeled "the Indian Bill of Rights."[55]

The Senate was deep into its debate over Lyndon Johnson's civil rights proposals in 1967 when Ervin tried a novel approach to getting his Indian Bill of Rights through Congress—he attached his bills designed to grant Native Americans their constitutional rights to the administration's legislation designed to give African Americans their civil rights. During hearings in the Senate Judiciary Committee, Ervin offered two amendments to the pending civil rights measures. The first greatly expanded the scope of an administration bill aimed at protecting civil rights workers; the second was the Indian Bill of Rights.[56]

Liberals suspected that Ervin and his southern colleagues were up to their old tricks. In 1964 the segregationists had unsuccessfully attempted to kill civil rights legislation by expanding its coverage to include sex discrimination. Now it appeared that Ervin was trying a similar strategy in 1967. Indeed, there is little doubt that Ervin did conspire to defeat the bill protecting civil rights workers by broadening its coverage to the point of absurdity with his first amendment. In this context, his second amendment, the Indian Bill of Rights, appeared to be just another ruse by the wily old senator from North Carolina. The Judiciary Committee voted to remove both of Ervin's amendments.[57] "I thought that I had finally found a civil rights bill that I could support," Ervin said, but "it is my intention to see that if there is no Indian bill, there will be no civil rights bill."[58] Responding to the liberals' distrust of his intentions, Ervin suggested: "If all things were possible in Congress, and if a southerner offered a measure assuring everyone passage to heaven regardless of his sins, there would still be some who would condemn the bill and would think they had to vote against it."[59]

President Johnson's civil rights proposals did not survive the session, but the Senate did approve the Indian Bill of Rights by a unanimous voice vote when Ervin offered it as a separate bill just before adjournment. On the advice of his staff, the president urged Congress "to enact it this session," but the bill died in the House of Representatives when the Committee on Interior and Insular Affairs refused to hold hearings on it.[60] In part, the committee was responding to pressure from tribal chiefs who did not welcome the restrictions Ervin's bill placed on the power of their tribal courts, as well as to the Pueblos in New Mexico who objected to the bill's reliance on the concept of individual rights, which was alien to their communal culture. Ervin would have to find a way to bypass the House committee if he wanted to secure enactment of his proposal.[61]

The following year Ervin outsmarted his opponents in what may have been the shrewdest political move of his career. In the midst of the heated debate over the open housing bill in the spring of 1968, Ervin startled his colleagues by offering the Indian Bill of Rights as an amendment after the civil rights bill had reached the Senate floor. The House had already approved the open housing bill. If the Senate passed the Indian Bill of Rights as an amendment to this bill, which had already cleared the House, it would bypass the House Committee on Interior and Insular Affairs and would only have to survive the House-Senate conference.[62]

It was a brilliant parliamentary maneuver, and it left the Senate in disarray. Fearing that Ervin intended to scuttle the open housing bill, Senator Mike Mansfield immediately jumped to his feet to argue that the amendment was not germane to the civil rights bill under consideration. His Montana colleague, Lee Metcalf, who was presiding over the Senate, ruled in Mansfield's favor. Ervin countered by insisting that an amendment to confer legal rights on red men was germane to a bill to give legal rights to black men. Declaring that "the ruling of the Chair scalps the Indians," Ervin demanded an official roll-call vote on his amendment.[63]

Ervin had pushed the liberals into a corner. As Senator Clinton P. Anderson of New Mexico later inquired, "How can one vote against civil rights for Indians?"[64] Clarence Mitchell of the LCCR, who watched Ervin's political moves from the Senate gallery, believed the Indian Bill of Rights was a trap, but he publicly insisted that his associates endorse it "as a gesture of fairness to a long deprived part of the population."[65] With the support of many liberals, the Senate overturned the chairman's ruling by a vote of 54–28 and then passed Ervin's amendment by a vote of 81–0. It survived the conference committee, and on 11 April 1968 the Indian Bill of Rights became law.

Arthur Lazarus Jr., the chairman of the American Bar Association Committee on Indian Affairs, put the enactment of the Indian Bill of Rights into historic perspective when he observed: "One hundred years after adoption of the fourteenth amendment, forty-four years after all native-born American Indians were declared to be citizens of the United States, and eleven years after the Constitution followed the flag overseas, the Bill of Rights finally came to Indian reservations."[66] The Cherokee expressed their gratitude to Ervin by presenting him with two gifts—a beautifully carved and painted wooden gavel, and a blowgun that they thought he might put to good use in the Senate. Ervin used the gavel to open the Watergate hearings in 1973. There are no reports of his using the blowgun—although it must have been a temptation.[67]

Ervin's civil libertarian agenda had expanded at a rapid pace, and with unusual success, since he had taken over the chairmanship of the Subcommittee on Constitutional Rights in 1961. By 1968 he had clearly outgrown Joe Rauh's questionable characterization as "a great man whose mind is in chains." Even the national news media that once dismissed him as just another Senator Claghorn because of his opposition to civil rights began to portray him as "one of the Senate's most effective modern-day guardians of civil liberties."[68]

In each of his legislative successes, Ervin had extended the constitutional protections of the Bill of Rights to groups who had been overlooked or pushed aside by the federal government. In 1967, Senator Richard Russell praised Ervin as "a constitutional scholar and a champion of constitutional principles." He had sought "without consideration for political gain," Russell explained, "to ensure that the rights of such forgotten minorities as the serviceman, the American Indian and the mentally ill are not infringed upon."[69]

One "forgotten minority" conspicuously absent from this list were African Americans. Neither Russell nor Ervin saw any contradiction between Ervin's emerging reputation as a civil libertarian and his adamant opposition to civil rights. "I see my attitudes toward these things as part of the same pattern," Ervin explained to a reporter. "One condition of freedom is as much absence of regimentation of the individual as possible. The stronger the government is, the less freedom the individual has." Ervin believed that the centralization of power inherent in civil rights legislation threatened "the right of the individual to govern himself" in the same way that the unchecked power of mental hospitals, military courts, and tribal governments threatened the individual rights of the mentally ill, military service personnel, and Native Americans. The common thread running through his subcommittee hearings on each of these issues, Ervin suggested, was his concern for protecting individual liberty against unbridled government power.[70]

This limited government theme complemented the deeply conservative nature of his political ideology. Defending the rights of individual members of neglected groups did not make Sam Ervin a liberal. To the contrary, it reinforced his conservatism. He was not pushing to create new protections for neglected or oppressed groups but trying to extend established rights to individuals who had been denied traditional constitutional protections. His libertarian impulse was more paternalistic than reformist. But a southern paternalist had two related responsibilities: to protect those within the system and to defend the system itself. It is that second, defensive, responsibility that helps to explain why Ervin not only fought against civil rights but also resisted two other groups seeking change in American society—unions and women.

Ervin had always opposed unions, dating back to his actions during the textile strike of 1934 and his probusiness leanings as a lawyer and judge. In the

Senate he became one of labor's staunchest foes and industry's best friends. In the late 1950s he played a leading role in the Senate's probe of labor racketeering. His aggressive questioning of Teamsters president James Hoffa during the hearings of the so-called Rackets Committee earned him accolades from business interests and, ironically, an alliance with his Senate colleague John Kennedy and his younger brother Robert, who served as counsel to the committee.[71] The resulting Kennedy-Ervin bill of 1958 to regulate the internal affairs of labor unions became the basis of later legislation, although Ervin did not like the end result since he felt that subsequent amendments "mummicked" it all up.[72] In the 1960s and 1970s he repeatedly attacked the National Labor Relations Board (NLRB) and filibustered against repeal of a key anti-labor provision of the Taft-Hartley Act in 1965 and 1966.[73]

The most controversial anti-labor action of Ervin's career involved his appearance before the Supreme Court in *National Labor Relations Board v. Darlington Manufacturing Company* in 1964. The NLRB had found the South Carolina-based Darlington Company guilty of shutting down one of its textile mills to avoid unionization. Darlington appealed the ruling to the Supreme Court, and Ervin accepted the textile company's invitation to argue one aspect of its case before the justices. Many observers thought Ervin's actions represented a conflict of interest since he was serving in the Senate and should not become personally involved with a legal matter on which he might have to cast a vote in the future. His critics also wondered why he took on this case since it was the first time he had represented any client in any court since closing down his law practice when he became a senator. Ervin countered that there was no conflict of interest because his view of the Constitution would lead him to the same position as a senator or as a lawyer. In spite of numerous objections, Ervin did argue his part of the case before the Supreme Court, which he won.[74]

What only Ervin knew at the time, however, was that back during his brief tenure as a member of the House of Representatives in 1946 he had faced a similar conflict of interest. A local manufacturing firm wanted to retain Ervin as its lawyer in a possible hearing before the NLRB, and Ervin wrote to his friend, Assistant Attorney General Lamar Caudle, asking for advice as to whether or not it would be ethical. Caudle responded that the law "prohibits a Member of Congress" from "agreeing to receive any compensation whatever for services rendered in relation to ... any matter ... in which the United States is interested," adding, "I went into the subject thoroughly and can arrive at no other conclusion."[75] Thus he advised Ervin to wait until his term expired in January 1947 before taking on the client. Ervin retained the letter among his personal papers, but he appears to have ignored its advice when he jumped into the Darlington case in 1964 and received payment for his legal services. It is interesting to note, however, that in the three other Supreme Court cases after *Darlington* in which he appeared while serving as a senator he did not accept any payment.[76]

When questioned about the amount of his fee in the Darlington case, Ervin responded with a story about a lawyer back home in North Carolina who would not tell his colleagues what he had been paid for an insanity case he had won. When two of his attorney friends pushed him to tell them the size of the fee, the lawyer asked if they could keep a secret. They quickly assured him that they could. "Well, so can I," the lawyer snapped.[77] Although Ervin was repeatedly pressed to reveal what the Darlington Company paid him, he always refused and cited the right to privacy as his defense. Documents released after his death, however, reveal that the textile company paid him $50,000, which would indeed have raised eyebrows at the time since his salary as a senator was only $30,000. Though it would be rash to conclude that Ervin did anything unethical in taking the Darlington case or by accepting the large fee, it was certainly unwise since it left him open to the charge that he was unduly biased in favor of the textile industry—which he was.[78]

In a similar manner Ervin went to unprecedented lengths to defeat the equal rights amendment (ERA). The amendment's primary clause, which stated that "equality of rights under the law shall not be denied or abridged by the United States or by any State on account of sex," became the central goal of the women's rights movement from the 1960s through the 1980s. No politician did more than Sam Ervin to defeat the ERA. He spoke against it for many years and in 1972 led the unsuccessful opposition at both the committee level and on the Senate floor when Congress passed the amendment. Failing there, Ervin worked closely with conservative activist Phyllis Schlafly to craft the anti-ERA strategy that eventually killed the amendment before it could be ratified by the required number of states.[79]

As always, Ervin explained his opposition to the ERA in legal and constitutional terms. First, he argued that it was unnecessary because of the protections already afforded to women by the Fourteenth Amendment and by the growing number of state and local antidiscriminatory measures. Second, he deemed it unwise because it would greatly expand federal government power and would give the federal courts final say over all state laws covering everything from marriage and divorce to child support, wills, and domestic relations. He claimed that such an extension of government power would lead to "ridiculous possibilities," including a new wedding oath—"with this ring—and with the permission of the Federal Government—I thee wed."[80]

But there was much more to Ervin's attack on the ERA. "I'm trying to protect women from their fool friends and from themselves," he explained.[81] Ervin warned that by ignoring the "physiological and functional differences" between men and women, the amendment would lead to unisex bathrooms, male and female prisoners sharing jail cells, the end of statutory rape protection for young girls, and, worst of all, "sending the daughters of America into combat to be slaughtered or maimed by the bayonets, napalm, the poison gas and the shells of the enemy." He concluded that "the amendment would destroy the social fabric of America."[82]

Unlike his soft southern strategy against civil rights, in which he avoided dubious scare tactics in favor of respectable legal argumentation, Ervin frequently employed sensational rhetoric against the ERA. His exaggerated charges did not carry much weight on the Senate floor, and legal scholars pointed out that he was ignoring the overwhelming legal evidence against them, but they did play well in local church meetings and anti-ERA rallies across the country. The fact that a senator had suggested that these horrible scenarios might actually come true lent them credibility in the anti-ratification debates in the fifty states. "I feel so important," wrote an anti-ERA activist from Florida, "when I speak and say this is the latest from Sen. Ervin's office."[83]

Women's rights activists dismissed Ervin as nothing more than a male chauvinist pig, but once again the senator's motives cannot be so easily explained. He did not discriminate against the women around him in his daily life. North Carolina Supreme Court Justice Susie Sharp defended Ervin by pointing out that he was one of the few politicians on Capitol Hill to have a woman serve as his administrative assistant. Sharp also insisted that he worked harder than anyone she knew to put a woman on the U.S. Supreme Court. "He recommended me every time there was a vacancy," she recalled, "in spite of my efforts to stop him."[84] Miss Margaret shared her husband's traditional views on the place of women in society, but at least one of Ervin's sisters and both of his daughters disagreed with him on the ERA and were not shy about saying so. When his daughter Leslie decided to attend law school the senator supported her, even though he was not enthusiastic about her choice. Why Ervin chose to fight the ERA so vociferously, and why he dedicated so much of his time and energy to defeating the amendment in the middle of his busiest years in the Senate—just as his battles with Richard Nixon were all coming to a head— remain hotly debated questions. But to Ervin it was not complicated at all. He was just preserving the Constitution.[85]

Civil rights activists, union organizers, and feminists represented three groups who faced discrimination, struggled on an uneven playing field for

Senator Ervin accompanies the North Carolina representative in the Cherry Blossom Festival, April 1962. Sam Ervin Library and Museum, Western Piedmont Community College, Morganton, North Carolina.

equal opportunities, and turned to the government for help. Ervin opposed them all. When they accused him of being racist, probusiness, and sexist, he answered that they just did not understand. The senator claimed that it was not the ends but the means of their movements that he disliked, although he did seem especially critical of the goals of the women's movement. To Ervin, the government should never be used to help some groups succeed by limiting the freedom of the individual. As long as Ervin, and his supporters, could cling to this rational explanation of his behavior they did not have to confront the irrational feelings and values that lay deeper inside the man.

Ervin cherished the traditional life he had experienced as a child growing up in North Carolina. He believed that his forefathers had founded a society of order and a government of balance and that both should be maintained and defended. He followed the gentlemen's rules of the old days and he claimed not to understand why anyone would want to change them. The concept of group rights made no sense to him. He passionately believed in individualism. Thus, by protecting individual freedom he considered himself to be a true liberal, of the nineteenth-century variety anyway, which in the context of the later twentieth century made him very conservative since he was, quite literally, conserving the world as it was. The reporters in the 1960s who complained that "it is not easy to put a label on Sam Ervin" should have considered "conservative southern libertarian," with an emphasis on "conservative."[86]

The argument that Ervin was a consistent civil libertarian would eventually become the orthodox interpretation of the senator's complex political career. Ervin's many supporters back home in North Carolina, members of the press, and even his early biographers all accepted, in varying degrees, the theory that both his defense of civil liberties and his attacks on civil rights reflected his unwavering opposition to any government interference with individual rights. "Senator Ervin thinks the Constitution should be taken like mountain whiskey," John Herbers of the *New York Times* wrote, "undiluted and untaxed."[87] Thus one mythology began to replace another: Sam Ervin the tragic southern segregationist became Sam Ervin the heroic civil libertarian.

But Ervin cannot be reduced to the static simplicity of either of these characterizations. Just as the first stereotype of a one-dimensional southern obstructionist was shattered by Ervin's renewed concern for civil liberties after 1961, the second stereotype of a consistent civil libertarian cannot withstand the evidence of his inconsistent record in the 1950s and his opposition to civil rights, labor unions, and the ERA. Both conceptions fall short because they overstate Ervin's dedication to unchanging principles and fail to account for the development of his political philosophy. It was not Ervin's vaunted constitutional consistency, but the evolution of his constitutional ideology in reaction to changing conditions and new challenges that best explains his record on both civil rights and civil liberties.

Ervin's concern for civil liberties had ebbed and flowed with the tide of racial politics in the 1950s. For a brief time he had been able to navigate his own course through the turbulent waters of the 1960s, lending credence to his reputation as a steadfast defender of constitutional rights. But as the decade progressed, Ervin would be pulled ever deeper into the contradictions of his libertarian philosophy by ominous currents beyond his control.

CHAPTER SEVEN

PRIVACY AND THE FALSE PROPHETS

An enthusiastic crowd had gathered in Washington, D.C., to hear the Bible-quoting senator from North Carolina preach a political sermon to the "People's Forum on Privacy." Sam Ervin took his text for the evening from the Book of Ezekiel in the Old Testament. "The Lord tells Ezekiel to go out and warn the people against the false prophets of Israel," Ervin explained, "men who saw 'delusive visions' and practiced 'lying divinations.' These men pretended to have divine powers to bring about miracles and they misled the people. Ezekiel tells us that these foolish prophets followed only their own spirit and saw nothing; that they were 'like foxes among the ruins.' "[1]

"There are abroad in our land today false prophets," Ervin warned his audience. "They hold that man's very nature can be changed and that he can be coerced to conform his thoughts and attitudes to the standards which are thought socially or politically desirable." According to Ervin, these "twentieth-century soothsayers" believed that "government can exercise a degree of control and intimidation over those it governs which will produce a high degree of political stability." "As in the Scriptures," Ervin cautioned, "it is easy to be lured by their glittering wares and the golden promises of instant social good. . . . [But] the gospel they declaim would lead to a repression over men's minds. . . . They have forgotten that the most precious freedom secured to the individual by our Constitution is the privacy of the mind, the freedom of his thought, and the sanctity of his conscience."[2]

The senator never mentioned anyone by name, but the identity of the false prophets was, to borrow one of Ervin's favorite expressions, "as clear as the noonday sun in a cloudless sky." Ervin's speech was an attack on the rapidly increasing government programs in the executive branch that threatened individual privacy, the federal bureaucrats who ran them, and their present boss— President Richard Nixon. The year was 1971, and Ervin was engaged in an escalating conflict with the Nixon administration over a series of civil liberties issues. The political battle lines were well defined. On one side was the Nixon administration, with its tough law-and-order programs, concerns for national security, and claims of inherent executive powers. On the other side was Sam Ervin, the Senate's popular country lawyer, constitutional champion, and, according to Tom Wicker of the *New York Times*, "eloquent defender of American civil liberties."[3] Watergate was but a year away.

A decade earlier, when the senator took over the Subcommittee on Constitutional Rights in 1961, no such clarity existed. Ervin had no rhetorical device, such as his allusion to the false prophets, around which he could build a coherent expression of his ideology, and there was no single convenient target, such as Richard Nixon, upon whom he could focus his attack. Ervin's dedication to civil liberties was considered suspect and his civil libertarian philosophy obscure. In contrast to his sweeping critique of the Nixon administration's civil liberties record in the 1970s, the senator's agenda for the Constitutional Rights Subcommittee in the early 1960s remained fairly limited. For the most part, Ervin seemed content to focus the subcommittee's work on the reasonably safe goal of extending constitutional rights to previously neglected groups such as the mentally ill, military personnel, and Native Americans.[4]

But as the decade progressed, Ervin became embroiled in several controversial civil liberties battles not of his own making. First, the senator's ongoing interest in criminal justice led him into the contentious national debates over the rights of criminal defendants, wiretapping, and bail reform. Second, Ervin was pulled into the fight over mandatory school prayer and the separation of church and state. And third, a subcommittee investigation introduced Ervin to the false prophets lurking in the executive branch and their new information-gathering programs that threatened the privacy rights of both the government's employees and average American citizens.

This unexpected agenda led the conservative senator into new and personally challenging political terrain. He found himself traveling in liberal circles and working with surprising allies, including the ACLU, the AFL-CIO, and even some civil rights organizations. Ervin also encountered contradictions in his political philosophy, forcing him to clarify some of his ideas and amend others. But by 1968 he had forged a powerful new civil libertarian worldview built around the central tenet of every individual's right to privacy.

"As a lawyer, legislator, and judge," Ervin wrote in his autobiography, "I entertained the abiding conviction that the administration of criminal justice is the most sacred obligation of government." Consequently, Ervin became an active participant in the many controversial criminal justice debates that thundered through Congress during his twenty years in Washington. By the end of his career, the national media generally portrayed Ervin as a consistent civil libertarian—an interpretation obviously enhanced by the senator's performance in the Watergate hearings. But during the previous decade, his criminal justice record had been so complex and contradictory that the press corps had found it very difficult to explain his actions. Ervin joined conservatives in attacking the Supreme Court for coddling criminals and in supporting the extension of government wiretapping. Ervin sided with liberals, however, when he sponsored legislation such as the Criminal Justice Act of 1964 and the Bail Reform Act of 1966, both of which extended the rights of the accused. Like most of his fellow reporters, Lloyd Preslar of the *Winston-Salem Journal* was so perplexed by the senator's paradoxical behavior that he could only conclude that "it isn't easy to put a label on Sam Ervin."[5]

Beginning in 1958, Ervin offered a bill in every session of Congress to overturn the Supreme Court's ruling in *Mallory*, which threw out the confession of a rapist because of a lengthy delay in his arraignment.[6] Ervin thought that the Court had "magnified the rights of criminals out of all proper proportion, while the right of society to protection has been ignored."[7] When police in Philadelphia arrested Andrew Mallory in 1960 for committing another rape, an angry Ervin demanded that "the rising tide of crime . . . points to the need for a change in the Mallory Rule on the admissibility of voluntary confessions."[8]

But the Court was headed in a different direction. In *Escobedo v. Illinois* (1964) and *Miranda v. Arizona* (1966) the justices put further limitations on the police by requiring that before suspects can be questioned they must be informed of their right to remain silent, warned that anything they say may be used against them in court, and reminded that they have a right to the presence of a court-appointed attorney.[9] Ervin was irate at the Supreme Court's rulings, telling the Senate about a trial judge who, because of *Miranda*, was compelled to overturn the conviction of a mother who had beaten her child to death. "Don't thank me," said the judge, "thank the Supreme Court."[10] Believing that "public safety had been relegated to the back row of the courtroom," Ervin unsuccessfully proposed a constitutional amendment to reverse *Miranda* and allow all voluntary confessions to be admissible in court.[11]

In spite of Ervin's distrust of many other forms of government power, he maintained "an abiding confidence" in the police.[12] Ervin publicly criticized those who "give the impression that the most undesirable people in the United States today are the officers of the law," and he ridiculed the idea "that society does not need more protection against criminals but that criminals need protection from the officers."[13] During Thurgood Marshall's confirmation hearings in 1967, Marshall defended the *Miranda* decision by recalling that he once represented an Oklahoma man who "voluntarily confessed" after he was beaten up for six days. Ervin simply dismissed the idea of police brutality. "All this we hear about police brutality just isn't true," he snapped. "The brutality is usually on the other foot."[14]

Perhaps Ervin's naive faith in the police contributed to his support of government wiretapping on the state level. He wanted to enact legislation granting state and local police more power to conduct electronic eavesdropping "in virtually all cases," provided they got a court order first.[15] But soon after Ervin held brief hearings on wiretapping in 1961, liberal senators on his subcommittee such as Edward V. Long of Missouri complained that in Ervin's zest to expand state wiretapping powers he had not held sufficient hearings nor followed the subcommittee's rules of procedure. Long successfully delayed, and eventually killed, Ervin's push to extend the legal ability of state authorities to eavesdrop on private conversations.[16]

Ervin's position on federal wiretapping was far more complex. True to his southern states' rights philosophy, the senator opposed the Kennedy administration's proposals to widen the federal government's authority to intercept electronic communications—even while he supported the same power being granted to the states.[17] Ervin broke from his conservative allies who wanted more federal wiretapping to crack down on crime, and he joined Edward Long and other liberals who described Attorney General Robert Kennedy's bill as "dangerous."[18] Yet Ervin did believe that properly gained evidence from wiretaps conducted under a court order should be admissible as evidence. "Congress should attempt to find a middle ground," Ervin argued, "which would make reasonably certain that officers would not use wiretapping indiscriminately to invade the privacy of citizens, and at the same time should not disable the government by forbidding the use of wiretapped information in serious offenses. I believe we can find a middle way."[19]

As pressure mounted in the late 1960s to give the government more weapons in the escalating war against crime, Ervin's middle way became less and less tenable. Liberals opposed wiretapping as a step toward a police state, while conservatives supported it as a necessary tool for regaining law and order. The Johnson administration engaged in a spirited internal debate over government wiretapping before the president decided to ask for legislation to protect privacy and place stringent controls on electronic eavesdropping.[20] Ervin strongly supported Johnson's position. But the political appeal of getting tough on crime was too great. Over the president's objections, Congress added features to the Omnibus Crime Control and Safe Streets Act of 1968 authorizing federal and state law enforcement officials to conduct wiretaps in a wide variety of cases.[21] Ervin backed away from his earlier statements against wiretapping and voted for the legislation, leaving Long and the liberals alone and unsupported in their futile attempts to modify the bill. Ervin's biographers have all suggested that as a civil libertarian the senator generally opposed federal wiretapping. But in 1968 when his "middle ground" disappeared, Ervin moved to the right and on four separate occasions voted in favor of a sweeping extension of the government's power to tap its citizens' phones. It was a move he would later regret.[22]

Ervin's acceptance of wiretapping, like his opposition to *Miranda*, supported his conservative credentials, but his simultaneous efforts to reform the criminal justice system appeared downright liberal. When he became the chairman of the Subcommittee on Constitutional Rights in 1961, Ervin inherited ongoing investigations into "Police Detention Prior to Commitment and Arraignment" and "The Fourth Amendment and Modern Methods of Crime Prevention." The senator also solicited the opinions of judges, lawyers, law professors, officials of the Justice Department, and his own staff concerning additional problems existing in criminal justice. The responses helped him to set a reform agenda for his subcommittee that stood in stark contrast to his reputation as a tough-on-crime conservative.[23]

In 1966 Ervin sponsored four bills designed to correct several long-standing inequities in court procedures to which the federal government was a party. The first of these reforms required the government to file suits against private parties within specified periods of time. Ervin thought it wrong that citizens wanting to sue the government had to meet strict timelines but the government was free to sue at any time it wished. The second proposal authorized the government to pay court costs when it lost a lawsuit. Up until the enactment of this legislation, the government had never paid the court costs when it lost, but always collected the costs when it won. The other two bills broadened the government's authority to settle certain types of cases out of court, saving citizens with a claim against the government, and the taxpayers, both time and money. "These bills are not flashy or dramatic," one White House aide wrote to the president, "but they are significant."[24] Another staff member concluded, "These bills are good bills, sound and enlightened bills which enhance both

PRIVACY AND THE FALSE PROPHETS

government fairness and efficiency in its civil litigation. The administration should be proud to claim them as their own."[25]

Another of Ervin's reform efforts concerned the government's dismal record of providing legal aid to poor defendants accused of federal crimes. Every attorney general since 1937 had asked for legislation providing compensation for federal public defenders to ensure that indigent defendants received a fair trial. Every year nearly 10,000 persons—30 percent of all defendants in criminal cases—received court-appointed attorneys.[26] But these lawyers were paid little if anything for their services, and their clients often received less than adequate counsel. In 1963 President Kennedy made indigent legal aid one of his legislative priorities in his State of the Union address. That same day, Ervin introduced his own bill to provide for compensated counsel in federal courts.[27]

The senator's experiences as a trial lawyer and judge had persuaded him of the need for such a law. Ervin remembered one particular case from his days as a young attorney when he served as the appointed counsel for a poor defendant in a capital case. He lost the trial and received $12.50 for his services. But in order to file an appeal for his client, Ervin had to pay $84 of his own money for a transcript of the court record. To add insult to injury, a local newspaper, unaware that Ervin had been appointed to the case, accused him of filing the appeal only because of the fee he would earn. It is not surprising that one of the first bills Ervin sponsored as a North Carolina state legislator authorized the state to pay for the trial transcripts of indigent defendants.[28]

Several decades later, Senator Ervin led the Constitutional Rights Subcommittee through an extensive study of the legal aid available to poor defendants in federal courts. He summarized the subcommittee's findings in a 1963 issue of the *American Bar Association Journal*: "If 'equal justice under the law' is to be more than a hollow phrase, then indigent defendants must be afforded adequate counsel. . . . The wealthy defendant need never fear an inadequate defense. It is now up to Congress to eliminate that fear for the indigent."[29] The following year Ervin combined the key features of his bill with a similar administration bill and pushed the legislative package through Congress. The Criminal Justice Act of 1964 extended the Sixth Amendment right to counsel to all Americans—even those who could not afford to pay for it.[30]

Ervin believed that the poor had also been denied the Eighth Amendment's protection against excessive bail. He was not alone. In the early 1960s a substantial movement to reform bail practices in the United States began in New York City when the Vera Foundation launched an experiment called the Manhattan Bail Project. Appalled by the number of poor defendants who spent months in jail because they could not afford bail, the founders of the Manhattan Bail Project worked to convince judges that most defendants, regardless of their economic status, could be released on their own recognizance and trusted to return for their day in court. Of the 2,195 defendants released at the urging of the Vera Foundation, only fifteen failed to appear for trial—a default rate far better than for those who had been released on monetary bail. The Manhattan Bail Project was so successful that cities across the country started their own bail reform programs and Attorney General Robert Kennedy agreed to sponsor a National Conference on Bail and Criminal Justice in 1964. On the eve of the National Bail Conference, Ervin introduced a series of bills designed to reform bail practices in the federal courts.[31]

During hearings Ervin held on his bills in 1964, the attorney general testified that judges needlessly held thousands of persons in jail because "they can't pay for their freedom."[32] Kennedy told Ervin's subcommittee about Daniel Walker of Glen Cove, New York, who was arrested on suspicion of robbery and spent fifty-five days in jail because he could not afford the bondman's fees. During his incarceration he lost his job, his car, and his credit rating. He was later found to be the victim of mistaken identity and released. Kennedy also shared the story of a Los Angeles man detained in jail before trial for a minor crime because he could not pay his bail. He was in jail for 207 days before being acquitted. The attorney general claimed that these were but a few examples of how the bail system hurt the poor.

As Kennedy rose to leave at the end of his testimony, he paused and looked at Ervin with a grin. It had only been a year since he had appeared in the same room for "The Sam and Bobby Show," in which the two men had engaged in contentious debates over civil rights. "Could I also make a personal remark?" Kennedy asked. "I appreciate being here with you, Senator Ervin, and all of us being on the same side of this matter." Ervin chuckled in agreement.[33]

The senator's hearings convinced him that isolated reforms of the existing bail system would be insufficient and he proposed a new omnibus bail reform bill to the Senate. Based on the right of all Americans to be considered innocent until proven guilty, the act required that a person charged with a noncapital federal crime be released from custody while awaiting trial on his or her personal recognizance. The only grounds for a judge's not releasing defendants was a reasonable fear that they would not appear for trial.[34] The Johnson administration enthusiastically supported Ervin's Bail Reform bill. With the president's endorsement it passed the Senate by a voice vote and the House by a roll call vote of 319–14. Johnson's staff urged him to stage an elaborate White House signing ceremony for the bill. "It has received favorable editorial comment in leading newspapers," one aide explained, "and is a very popular measure with the Congress, judges, lawyers and professors, as well as law enforcement officials throughout the nation—and with liberals."[35] President Johnson agreed, scribbling the words "get every liberal" at the bottom. On a pleasant June afternoon in 1966 more than 300 members of Congress and invited guests, a good number of them liberals, heard the president single out the conservative senator from North Carolina for his work in guiding the Bail Reform Act of 1966 through Congress. It may have been the most important legislative achievement of Sam Ervin's career.[36]

Ironically, Ervin received this presidential praise for protecting the rights of the accused after having just completed two weeks battling Johnson's civil rights proposals in the Constitutional Rights Subcommittee. The *Raleigh News and Observer* ran an editorial puzzling over "the droll double life of Sen. Sam Ervin," and the *Winston-Salem Journal* awarded Ervin a special "Jekyll and Hyde Award" that year. Reporters often noted that Ervin's concern for the legal rights of the poor not only seemed to contradict his opposition to civil rights, but also his tough talk against *Miranda* and his acquiescence in wiretapping. In the criminal justice debates of the 1960s the senator appeared to be a bleeding-heart liberal one minute and an anticrime conservative the next.[37]

Despite these apparent contradictions, Ervin's growing civil libertarian record did contain several consistent themes. At the heart of his divergent criminal justice positions was the concept of balance. According to Ervin, government "must strike a balance between the right of society to security and the right of the individual to fairness."[38] In support of his position he quoted Justice Benjamin Cardozo: "Justice, though due to the accused, is due to the accuser also. The concept of fairness must not be strained till it is narrowed to a filament. We are to keep the balance true."[39] Thus Ervin thought that the government's failure to provide public defenders and fair bail for the poor tilted the scales of justice too far toward the interests of the public, while the *Mallory* and *Miranda* rulings tipped them too far toward the interests of the accused. Other themes running throughout Ervin's battles for civil liberties included his preference for states' rights over federal authority—best illustrated in his support of state wiretapping—and his general resistance to any increase in the power of the executive branch of government. Of course he remained a constant critic of the Supreme Court.[40]

Throughout the 1960s Ervin maintained his conviction that the Warren Court's judicial activism threatened to destroy the Constitution, individual freedom, and perhaps the republic itself. The senator believed that the Court was usurping the legislative powers of Congress, and he condemned what he considered its lack of reverence for long-established precedents. Ervin told the press: "I am inclined to think that the precedent to which some Members of the Supreme Court are most faithful is the precedent set by Josh Billings' mule, which didn't kick according to no rule."[41] The Warren Court offended Ervin's conservative sensibilities on a wide variety of issues. A partial list would include Supreme Court rulings that further limited state censorship of pornography; invalidated state poll taxes; extended a suspect's right to counsel to include police lineups; ordered the reapportionment of congressional districts on the principle of one man, one vote; protected the NAACP from harassment by southern state governments; upheld open occupancy laws; and outlawed mandatory school prayers.[42]

Ervin criticized the Supreme Court on the Senate floor, in the press, through law review articles, and in speeches across the country, but in 1966 he was presented with a unique and unexpected opportunity to give the justices a piece of his mind. That February, the Federal Bar Association of the District of Columbia invited Ervin to be the master of ceremonies at a luncheon in honor of Johnson's new attorney general, Nicholas Katzenbach, and deputy attorney general, Ramsey Clark. Upon his arrival, Ervin discovered to his delight that Chief Justice Earl Warren would be sitting next to him and all but one of the other justices would be in attendance. Here was a rare chance to confront the justices face to face. Ervin later wrote that at that wonderful moment he recalled the words of the old hymn: "This is the day I long have sought, and wept because I found it not."[43]

Rising to begin his remarks, Ervin told the story of a young lawyer in North Carolina who attended an evangelical service and was unexpectedly called on to pray. His prayer came straight from his lawyer's heart: "Stir up much strife among thy people, Lord, lest thy servant perish." With a devilish gleam in his eye, Ervin added that the Supreme Court had proven the truth of the famous hymn line "The Lord moves in mysterious ways His wonders to perform," because its rulings had stirred up so much strife and caused so much litigation that it had served as the Almighty's answer to the young lawyer's prayer.[44]

Ervin could not resist telling the justices a story to illustrate how his home state was responding to their controversial rulings on school prayer. A teacher in North Carolina had recently learned that the Supreme Court now forbade prayer in the schools. A few days later she arrived at her classroom early to find a group of boys huddled together down on their knees. "What are you doing?" she demanded. "Shooting craps," one of the boys answered. "That's all right," she responded. "I was afraid you were praying."[45]

Ervin's joke on school prayer probably gave the justices one of their few opportunities to laugh at an issue that had generated a great deal of ill will. Ever since 1962, when the Court ruled in *Engel v. Vitale* that state-sponsored prayer in the public schools violated the First Amendment's "establishment of religion" clause, defenders of school prayer had attacked the justices with a vengeance. The Court received more negative mail in the weeks after the *Engel* decision than ever before in its history. In subsequent rulings, *Abington Township Pa. v. Schempp* and *Murray v. Curlett*, both decided on 17 June 1963, the Court ruled that actions such as reading from the Bible and reciting the Lord's Prayer in classrooms were also unconstitutional.[46] The rhetoric on Capitol Hill was intense. Congressman John Rooney of New York warned that the rulings "could put the United States schools on the same basis as Russian schools," and Representative Frank Becker, also of New York, called the decisions "the most tragic in the history of the United States."[47] As might have been expected, the most extreme response came from southern politicians still furious at the Court for *Brown*. "They put the Negroes in the schools, and now they've driven God out," cried Congressman George W. Andrews of Alabama.[48]

Ervin, too, belittled the Court's decision. The day after the justices announced their ruling in *Engel*, Ervin told the Senate that the Court had held in substance "that God is unconstitutional and for this reason the public schools must be segregated against Him." Though far less strident than many of his southern colleagues, Ervin unequivocally stated that the justices had made a mistake. "The First Amendment was intended to establish freedom *of* religion," the senator insisted. "It was not intended to establish freedom *from* religion." "For more than 175 years the country has placed a practical construction on the First Amendment that non-sectarian prayers and simple reading of the Bible does not conflict with the establishment of religion clause," he explained. "If children of parents who object are not compelled to attend, I don't see anything wrong."[49]

Ervin's defense of school prayer seemed to run counter to his often-stated commitment to what Thomas Jefferson called "the wall of separation" between church and state. Ervin liked to quote the famous biblical verse from the Book of Matthew, "Render, therefore, unto Caesar the things that are Caesar's, and to God the things that are God's," and he often stated his belief that government had no business interfering in the exclusive domain of the church.

Until the debate over school prayer, Ervin's actions had supported his words. Since the 1950s, Ervin had served as one of the leading congressional opponents of any government aid to church-related schools. He fought against a series of federal laws that authorized federal grants and loans to parochial schools and sectarian colleges and universities, including the Higher Education Facilities

Act of 1963, the Elementary and Secondary Education Act of 1965, and the Higher Education Act of 1965. Ervin declared that the United States was mistakenly "rendering to God the things that are Caesar's by giving federal money to religious institutions." He unsuccessfully offered amendments to exclude church-related institutions from these federal appropriations, and he sponsored bills to obtain judicial review of the constitutionality of these expenditures by granting individual taxpayers standing to sue in federal courts. On several occasions Ervin's judicial review bills passed the Senate but died in the House, victims of heavy lobbying by the Kennedy and Johnson administrations.[50]

Ervin believed the church should stay out of Caesar's domain as well. "Political liberty cannot exist where the state is controlled by any religious institution," he argued.[51] In a 1960 edition of the *Presbyterian Survey*, Ervin, himself a Presbyterian elder, wrote against official church bodies or local churches taking public stands on political issues. He encouraged individual churchmen to participate in political affairs, but insisted that if a church body advised the government on how it should manage its affairs that body would "violate the fundamental American doctrine of the separation of church and state."[52] Ervin frequently criticized church groups that supported civil rights, and he publicly denounced Protestants who urged voters in 1960 not to elect John Kennedy because of his Catholic faith.[53] "If we are to preserve religious liberty, or indeed, any kind of liberty," Ervin insisted, "we must keep the state's hands out of religion and religion's hands off the state."[54]

The storm of controversy stirred up by the Supreme Court's school prayer rulings reached full strength in 1966. In March of that year Senate Minority Leader Everett Dirksen introduced a resolution calling for a constitutional amendment to permit voluntary prayer in the public schools. Dirksen's amendment earned widespread support, eventually attracting forty-eight co-sponsors. When a reporter asked Dirksen if he thought his prayer amendment could actually be adopted, the senator snapped, "Hell, yes."[55]

Dirksen's proposal spawned fear on Capitol Hill. Senators who opposed the amendment because of their commitment to the separation of church and state dreaded having to cast a public vote against school prayer. Even some conservative southerners privately expressed their discomfort with Dirksen's amendment. Senator Richard Russell confided to a friend, "While I intend to vote for this resolution if it ever reaches the floor of the Senate, I am not as excited about it as some people and I declined to become a co-sponsor."[56] But Dirksen muscled his resolution onto the Senate calendar in September 1966, forcing the first vote taken in Congress on a school prayer bill since the controversy began. Like it or not, each senator had to take a public stand on school prayer.

As the date for the floor debate drew near, Ervin's position remained unclear. The senator's personal desire to protect Christian prayer in the schools and his frustration at the Supreme Court's judicial activism pushed him toward supporting the Dirksen resolution. Yet he feared that it violated the First Amendment and endangered religious freedom. Even members of his own staff did not know how he was going to vote. Would Ervin follow his cultural and religious instincts and support it, or be true to his constitutional instincts and oppose it?[57]

Ervin's decision, and his subsequent actions, have taken on mythic proportions. The story recounted most often, in a wide variety of sources, suggests that Ervin did not make up his mind until the night before the Senate debate was scheduled to begin. That evening, he confided to a member of his staff that he could not bring himself to support the Dirksen amendment because of the harm he believed it would render to the Constitution. The next morning, 20 September 1966, Ervin and George Autry, his chief aide on the Constitutional Rights Subcommittee, carried a Bible and a stack of notes and law books four or five feet high over to his desk on the Senate floor, where Ervin spoke extemporaneously for an hour and a half against the resolution. According to these legendary accounts, the chamber slowly filled with senators who came to hear the old constitutionalist defend the First Amendment. In what is often described as "perhaps his best Senate speech," Ervin is portrayed as having "singlehandedly caused the thing to be defeated" by convincing enough wavering senators to vote against it.[58] One of Ervin's biographers wrote that in a rare moment of political honesty, Senator William Fulbright of Arkansas came up to Ervin after his speech and confessed that he had intended to follow the line of least resistance and support Dirksen's resolution, but, he admitted, "after listening to your speech, I couldn't vote for [it]."[59] The following day the Senate voted 49–37 for the school prayer amendment, but that was nine votes short of the two-thirds majority needed to amend the Constitution. Many of Ervin's friends and several of his biographers have suggested that the senator's last-minute decision to protect the wall of separation between church and state, and his moving Senate speech, saved the day.[60]

As dramatic and appealing as these accounts might be, they do not stand up to scrutiny. Ervin himself provided the most accurate account of his role in defeating the Dirksen amendment. In his autobiography Ervin helps to separate fact from fiction by explaining that the senators who opposed the school prayer amendment held a legislative strategy session prior to the Senate debate at which they selected him as their chief spokesman. Ervin remembered that they chose him for two reasons: "First, they deemed it advisable for a Senator from

Ervin may have been a Bible-quoting conservative, but his dedication to the separation of church and state eventually led him to oppose mandatory prayer in the public schools. Here he appears with the Reverend Billy Graham at a prayer breakfast in 1959. Sam Ervin Library and Museum, Western Piedmont Community College, Morganton, North Carolina.

the so-called Bible Belt of the South to lead the attack on the amendment; and second, they knew I had studied in detail the history of the First Amendment and the Supreme Court cases construing it."[61] Ervin also carefully avoided claiming too much responsibility for the final outcome. He correctly observed that "William Fulbright, of Arkansas, Ralph W. Yarborough, of Texas, and I were the only Senators from the eleven Southern states who voted in the negative," thus dismissing the notion that his speech had changed many votes.[62] Actually, with a few notable exceptions, the battle lines over the school prayer amendment did not differ significantly from the political alignments found on the other controversial social issues of the 1960s such as social welfare and civil rights legislation.[63]

Stripping the exaggerations away from the story of Ervin's opposition to the school prayer amendment does not lessen either the eloquence of his speech nor the significance of his heroic stand. It may well have been the most moving speech of his Senate career. It certainly was the most personal. Rejecting the prepared text offered to him by George Autry, Ervin crafted a remarkable

"Watch it! Ervin's reaching for his Bible . . ."

Editorial cartoon by Robert Graysmith, San Francisco Chronicle, 12 August 1973. Copyright 1973 Chronicle Publishing Company. Courtesy of the San Francisco Chronicle.

speech from the notes and books stacked on his desk. Ervin spoke about his own faith in God, quoting the book of Psalms: "The heavens declare the glory of God; and the firmament showth his handiwork." The senator explained the awe with which he observed "the order and regularity of the process of life and nature as the tide ebbs and flows, and the harvest succeeds the seedtime, and as the heavenly bodies move in their orbits without mishap in conformity with natural laws." He expressed his reverence toward the capacities of humankind as well, which can "obey conscience, exercise reason, study holy writings, and aspire to righteous conduct in obedience to spiritual laws." "On the basis of these things," Ervin concluded, "I affirm with complete conviction that the universe and man are not the haphazard products of blind atoms wandering aimlessly about in chaos, but, on the contrary, are the creations of God, the Maker of the universe and man."[64]

"I revere religion," Ervin insisted, but he told the Senate that he felt compelled to oppose the Dirksen amendment in order to "protect and preserve the right of freedom of religion for all men." The senator offered two reasons for his change of heart. First, he was convinced that the Court had not prohibited voluntary prayer but only state-prescribed prayers in the schools. Second, he believed the proposed amendment would turn the schools into religious battlefields by granting "every school board in the country the power to pass a law providing for the establishment of religion. . . . A Protestant board could establish a Protestant religion. A Catholic board could establish a Catholic service. A Jewish board could set up a Jewish religion." Once he was convinced that the Court had ruled correctly, he felt bound to fight against the Dirksen amendment. "I am afflicted by a Scotch-Irish conscience which will not let me follow after the multitude," Ervin confessed. "It would be very easy from a political point of view to be for this amendment. But it would be the annihilation of the First Amendment's protection of religion."[65]

Ervin concluded his address by pleading with his colleagues to defeat the school prayer amendment. "For God's sake," Ervin shouted, "if you want to amend the Constitution, let us draw an amendment which will give equality of religious freedom to every human being in the United States. . . . Let us preserve for all Americans of all generations the right to bow their knees and lift their voices to their own God in their own way. We can do this by standing by the First Amendment as it has been written and interpreted. I close with a prayer that the Senate will do exactly this and no more."[66]

Ervin's opposition to the Dirksen amendment was an act of political courage. Public opinion in the South against the *Engel* and *Schempp* school prayer rulings was nearly as hostile as it had been to the *Brown* desegregation decision. Many southern states simply ignored the Supreme Court's ban on required school prayer; Mississippi mandated daily Bible reading in its schools for more than a decade after *Schempp*.[67] Politicians across the South competed with one another to offer the most fervent and pious defense of prayer in the school. In North Carolina the pressure on Ervin to vote for the Dirksen amendment was intense. In 1966 the Tar Heel State was the most homogeneously Protestant state in the country and one of the most enthusiastic centers of the Bible Belt. Ervin's mail in support of the school prayer amendment greatly outnumbered the few letters he received opposing it. B. Everett Jordan, the state's other senator, was an enthusiastic cosponsor of the Dirksen amendment. But none of these political factors deterred Ervin from taking the stand he believed to be right. Still, just to be on the safe side, the senator did take the precaution of sending a copy of his speech to every preacher in North Carolina.[68]

Ervin's opposition to mandatory school prayer did not cost him as much political support as might have been expected. It may even have helped him.

North Carolina newspapers responded to Ervin's speech with rave reviews. The *Charlotte Observer* entitled its editorial "Amen, Senator," and Lloyd Preslar of the *Winston-Salem Journal* acclaimed Ervin as "the brave civil libertarian, the unyielding defender of the Bill of Rights, the spokesman for those in the Senate who would not bow to expediency." The praise for Ervin's speech did not stop at the state's borders. The *Richmond News Leader* observed, "It required political courage of the highest order for Senator Ervin to take the lead in defeating [Dirksen's] plan." The *Washington Post* called Ervin "an authentic hero."[69]

It is rare to find a senator or member of Congress willing to place philosophical consistency over political expediency. It is even more unusual to find a politician who will let his constitutional ideology override his cultural instincts when the two are in conflict. Sam Ervin's switch from a critic to a defender of the Supreme Court's ban on required school prayer demonstrated that his constitutional beliefs did serve as more than a mere rationalization of his conservative goals.[70]

Ervin's changing position on school prayer also revealed that his constitutional philosophy was not a static but a dynamic ideology. Because the senator's constitutional principles not only reflected but also interacted with his personal beliefs and experiences, his ideology changed over time. It responded to many influences, including the increasing momentum of the civil rights movement, the new political agenda he inherited as the chairman of the Subcommittee on Constitutional Rights, the emerging racial, class, and gender challenges to the status quo in North Carolina, and the senator's own self-esteem and internal psychological dynamics. Ervin's opposition to civil rights remained unshaken, but his surprising reversal on school prayer—along with his recent concern for the constitutional rights of neglected groups and his advocacy for indigent defendants' legal rights—demonstrated Ervin's growing commitment to an emerging civil libertarian ideology.[71]

By the mid-1960s Ervin's efforts to defend civil liberties rivaled his attacks on civil rights for the majority of his time and energy. In addition to the episodes discussed above, Ervin surprised his colleagues by opposing several legislative proposals he considered to be threats to individual liberty. The senator took on the owners of big league sporting teams who wanted an exemption from the antitrust laws because he thought the exemption robbed players of their right to work for whom they wanted. He also criticized a congressional drive to deny participants in both federal and state prisoner work release programs from receiving their social security and workman's compensation benefits. Ervin fought the proposal because he believed it discriminated against the inmates and would hamper attempts to rehabilitate them.[72]

The senator also found time to support several additional bills to protect civil liberties. He cosponsored the Freedom of Information Act of 1966, designed to open government records to the public, and he assigned his subcommittee to monitor its implementation. He also fought to secure enactment of the Narcotic Addict Rehabilitation Act of 1966, which defined drug addiction as a medical problem that required treatment along with punishment.[73] Ervin had become one of the hardest-working civil libertarians on Capitol Hill. One reporter suggested that the senator had "been busier than a horse fly in a corral" trying to keep up with his ever-expanding agenda.[74]

Various elements of Ervin's civil libertarian ideology emerged as he jumped from issue to issue, but these philosophical trends eventually coalesced into a single, powerful theme during his escalating battles to protect the rights of government employees. In 1964 the Subcommittee on Constitutional Rights began to receive numerous complaints from federal government workers and job applicants who felt their privacy had been invaded. The subcommittee's subsequent investigation revealed shocking abuses of the information-gathering power of the federal government, and it launched Ervin upon a new campaign to protect the constitutional right to privacy.

Many federal employees objected to voluntary questionnaires circulated by the Civil Service Commission asking them to identify their race, religion, and national origin. Some of the workers thought the questionnaire violated civil service rules prohibiting the listing of an employee's nationality or religion. Others feared that their job or chance for employment might be endangered if they identified themselves as members of a certain race or religious faith. A few federal employees expressed anger at the pressure they felt to complete the supposedly voluntary forms. One government department posted lists of those who had not returned the questionnaires and stated it was "essential" for them to do so. Another agency harassed its workers with a series of follow-up letters that did not stop until the employee answered the government's questions.[75]

Government workers also complained about their encounters with embarrassing psychological and personality tests. One woman who applied for a job in the Foreign Service was required to answer 570 questions on sex, religion, and her personal habits. The government asked her, among other things, to indicate whether she was troubled by "deciding whether I'm really in love," "being too inhibited in sex matters," and "differing from my family in religious matters." She also had to respond to true and false questions such as "Christ performed miracles," "Many of my dreams are about sex," and "Once in a while I think of things too bad to talk about." Another applicant told of his experience of being strapped to a polygraph machine and asked: "Have you ever engaged in sexual activities with an animal? When was the first time you had relations with your wife? Did you have relations with her before you were married? How many times?" The subcommittee received reports that some government agencies even asked job applicants about bed wetting, the color of their bowel movements, the age at which they began menstruation, and their attraction to members of the same sex. Senator Ervin termed these questions "shocking" and launched a full investigation to determine the scope of the practice. How, he asked, could the government justify "such an invasion of privacy?"[76]

The subcommittee's investigation led to sensational hearings in 1965 and 1966 that revealed even more examples of government intrusion into its employees' personal affairs. The Treasury Department drafted a memorandum encouraging its executives to participant in after-hours programs to promote the civil rights objectives of the Johnson administration. Ervin was especially upset by reports that several agencies had put pressure upon their employees to attend lectures and sensitivity sessions on the rights and wrongs of race relations. These events were "voluntary" but attendance would be taken. A new "Code of Ethics Questionnaire" in the Internal Revenue Service required government workers to reveal details about their personal finances, including a list of their creditors, types of indebtedness, property, and other assets. The Department of Agriculture required similar financial disclosures from more than 21,000 of its employees. Even its raisin inspectors and file clerks had to comply. The Army was charged with coercing its soldiers into buying savings bonds and making charitable contributions. Some servicemen complained of being threatened with reassignment to Vietnam if they failed to cooperate.[77]

The hearings produced lively debate between Ervin and representatives from the Johnson administration, especially Civil Service Commission Chairman John Macy. Macy admitted that there had been some regrettable errors and misapplications of the administration's information-gathering systems, but he offered an articulate defense of the government's need to collect data about its employees. He claimed that the controversial questions cited from personality tests had been taken out of context, and that it was not the answer to any specific question but the overall pattern of responses that indicated the mental health of the applicant. Macy explained that only those workers being considered for high security assignments or suspected of suffering from mental problems were asked to take the tests. He also argued that information concerning race, religion, and national origin was needed to comply with civil rights legislation, and that the financial disclosure forms helped to prevent unethical behavior and conflicts of interest. Macy suggested that the government needed "more, not less" information on its employees, but he promised that the administration would continue to seek "the full observance of all employee rights, including the valued right to privacy."[78]

Ervin was not convinced. "Forms and practices such as these . . . are appropriate to totalitarian countries and Gestapo states. They have no place in a free society of men," he snapped. "Big Brother now knows the race, ancestry and sex life of his employees. He knows their assets and creditors, and even the cash surrender value of their life insurance, and the contents of their safe deposit boxes. The federal service has analyzed, systematized, categorized and computerized. I think it is time we humanize it and returned to constitutional concepts."[79] Ervin sponsored a Bill of Rights for federal employees that would prohibit government agencies from requiring their workers or job applicants to answer certain personal questions or to take part in or contribute to activities not directly related to their work. The proposal would set up a Board of Employees' Rights to handle complaints and authorize government workers to take their grievances to federal court even before exhausting administrative remedies.[80]

Ervin's bill became the centerpiece of his new crusade for privacy. Of course, the senator had taken public stands in defense of the right to privacy before, most notably during his opposition to Senator McCarthy's witch hunts. But his hearings on the federal government's invasions into its workers' privacy seemed to introduce Ervin to a new way of conceptualizing his rejuvenated civil libertarian agenda. With increasing frequency the right to privacy served as the central theme of Ervin's emerging civil libertarian philosophy and the focus of his subcommittee's investigations.

While Ervin continued his efforts to pass the Bill of Rights for government employees, he turned his attention toward two related privacy issues—the government's growing number of computerized data banks and the controversial new census questionnaires. The senator first began to fear that the government's use of computers threatened the right to privacy in 1965 when he helped to defeat the Department of Health, Education, and Welfare's proposal to create a computerized National Data Center. Even after their victory, Ervin and the staff of the Constitutional Rights Subcommittee continued to collect evidence suggesting that the privacy of every American was endangered by the government's rapidly expanding computer technology.[81]

One day in 1967, the seventy-year-old senator marched downtown to an IBM computer center to confront the machines himself. On the basis of his firsthand experience, Ervin concluded that the computer was a technological wonder with great potential for helping humanity. He even joked that "computers are so wonderful that I once considered introducing an amendment to allow a computer to be elected president. But, I found that while it can make logical conclusions from information fed in to it, it cannot draw illogical deductions from logical facts. For this reason, a computer could never be elected president and I didn't introduce my proposed amendment." Ervin's admiration for computer technology continued even after a Social Security computer erroneously sent him a check for $754.25 in lump sum death benefits a few years later.[82] But the senator did worry about the power computers gave to an increasingly centralized federal government. "We have nothing to fear from the computer as a machine," Ervin explained. "Alone it does not threaten individual privacy. The threat to privacy comes from men." Because of his concern that the men and women who operated the government's computers did not have adequate supervision or restrictions, Ervin added government computers, data banks, and dossiers to the growing list of topics to be investigated by the Subcommittee on Constitutional Rights, and he planned to hold public hearings in the near future.[83]

Letters also began to flood the subcommittee's offices complaining about new privacy-invading government questionnaires. As computer technology spread throughout the executive branch, making it easier for officials to store and manipulate information, the government's desire to gather data of all kinds increased dramatically. Surveys of the attitudes of the elderly, the finances of hunters, the destinations of vacationers, the reactions of shark attack victims, and a plethora of other amazing topics arrived in citizens' mail boxes every day. The subcommittee learned that between 1965 and 1968 the Census Bureau alone had conducted eighty-seven surveys for twenty-four other agencies that included approximately six million people.[84]

These burdensome questionnaires often carried implicit threats of penalty if they were not promptly returned. If the recipients of one study did not respond to the questionnaire before the predetermined deadline, they received a second form by certified mail, then a phone call, and finally a visit from a Census Bureau employee. Of further concern to many of the people who wrote Ervin were press reports suggesting that the decennial census of 1970 would not only carry a penalty of a $100 fine or imprisonment for thirty days for failure to participate, but would invade individual privacy of Americans at an unprecedented level. The Census Bureau confirmed that it planned to select millions of Americans at random to answer additional mandatory questions about their personal lives. Ervin thought that the proliferation of such government studies and questionnaires represented further proof of the need for Congress to legislate a balance between the individual's desire to keep silent and the government's quest for data. He promised to add hearings on the upcoming census to his rapidly expanding campaign to protect the constitutional right to privacy.[85]

There is some irony in the fact that Ervin, the Senate's foremost champion of a strict construction of the Constitution, became one of its most distinguished advocates of the constitutional right to privacy. The founding fathers had not actually written a right to privacy into the Constitution. Ervin, however, agreed with those legal scholars who argued that the implication was clearly there, located in the Bill of Rights and the Fourteenth Amendment. The senator concurred with Supreme Court Justice Louis Brandeis, who characterized "the right to be left alone" by the government as "the most comprehensive of rights and the right most valued by civilized men." Ervin frequently quoted Brandeis's statement that "any act or policy or program of government which deprives a person of his freedom; any use of power which attempts to make him conform his intellectual and political views and actions to the prevailing opinion of the day is an act which deprives him of his privacy and infringes on those rights secured by the First Amendment."[86]

Senator Ervin later claimed that the origins of his concern for the right to privacy sprang from his family's roots in the foothills of the Blue Ridge Mountains. His father had been outraged by the high-handed practices of the federal revenuers who roamed the North Carolina countryside looking for moonshiners. "My father always deplored officers going in and searching private dwelling places without any warrant," Ervin recalled. "He made it clear in no uncertain terms that he didn't think actions of that kind had any place in a free society. So I attribute my becoming interested in things like this to my father's very pronounced feelings."[87]

Ervin's attraction to the concept of privacy may also have been fueled by his distrust of what he considered to be the "false prophets of the behavioral sciences." The senator disparaged the "sociological follies" behind the egalitarian programs of the 1960s, and he belittled the "pseudo-scientific instruments such as personality tests and lie detectors" that government bureaucrats relied upon in what he considered to be their vain attempts to probe the mysterious inner workings of the human soul. Ervin suggested that "the whole process smacks of twentieth-century witchcraft."[88]

Ervin's commitment to privacy rights can be traced to other sources as well. His interest in privacy reflected his desire to protect personal idiosyncrasies and individual differences in an increasingly homogeneous world, or, as Ervin himself put it, the right "to have and hold and even enjoy our anxieties, allergies and our aspirin tablets."[89] The right to privacy also dovetailed nicely with Ervin's reverence for the southern constitutional tradition that denounced any federal government intrusion into a citizen's life. In his definitive study *Privacy and Freedom*, Alan Westin identifies three of the ideas celebrated in the South's constitutional tradition—individualism, the right to a private associational life, and civil liberty based upon a belief in limited government power—as the basic privacy-supporting values in American society.[90]

All these factors undoubtedly played a role in forming Ervin's growing interest in the right to privacy, but one additional influence must also be taken into account—his opposition to civil rights. Some of the first citizen complaints that attracted Ervin to the issue of privacy involved the new questionnaires asking government workers to identify their race. Ervin learned of this practice soon after the heated political battle over the Civil Rights Act of 1964, and he held his hearings on government employees' right to privacy at the same time that he was fighting against HEW's controversial school desegregation guidelines that required school districts to meet numerical standards of racial balance after 1965.

Ervin seized upon the Civil Service Commission's new minority group status questionnaires as yet more proof of the Johnson administration's plan to establish racial quotas. Commission chairman John Macy explained during his testimony that the questionnaires' only purpose was to detect agencies where employment discrimination existed, and he insisted that the suggestion of racial quotas was not only untrue but "unthinkable." Ervin, however, maintained that the questionnaires—like the racial "indoctrination" lectures, sensitivity training sessions, and required off-duty activities in support of the administration's civil rights goals—represented preferential treatment of African Americans and an unconstitutional extension of governmental power. In a return to the soft southern strategy against civil rights, which he first developed in 1957, Ervin did not publicly attack these practices because they promoted racial justice, but because they endangered another constitutional right: government workers' right to privacy.[91]

It was not the first time the right to privacy had served as a weapon in the South's defense against civil rights. During debates over the Civil Rights Act of 1960, the southern bloc argued that the constitutional right to privacy prevented the federal government from interfering with an individual's prerogative to discriminate in his or her selection of marital partners, family members, or friends. According to Senator Russell Long of Louisiana, the right to privacy "includes the right to join private clubs which admit as members only persons of one's own race, the right to send one's children to private schools which admit as students only persons of one's own race, and the right to instruct and urge one's children with whom to associate."[92] In 1965 Senator Allen Ellender of Louisiana posited that the right of privacy precluded HEW from interpreting the Civil Rights Act of 1964 as a mandate to force racial integration of public schools: "The far-reaching implications of such an interpretation are indeed frightening. Federal power can be used in this manner to coerce private clubs, any fraternal organization, any religious or social organization—and gradually creep into one's own home."[93] In this context it is difficult not to conclude that Ervin's new interest in the right to privacy was, in part, related to his ongoing defense of the racial status quo in North Carolina.

Both the national and North Carolina press corps questioned Ervin's motivations for choosing to fight against government intrusions into government workers' privacy. Responding to the controversy over the minority identification questionnaires, John Cramer of the *Washington Daily News* wondered, "How much of the resentment springs from race bias on the part of the protesters, from an honest conviction that the Equal Employment Opportunity drive in Government is evolving into a program of discrimination-in-reverse, or from a belief that the questionnaire involves an unwarranted invasion of privacy?" He observed that Ervin had publicly emphasized the latter point, but even reporters in the senator's home state suggested that he had been "attracted to his crusade by a fear that the Civil Service Commission was moving toward the establishment of a quota system for the employment of Negroes."[94]

As in most aspects of Ervin's career, race played a significant role in shaping his beliefs and behavior. It is impossible to determine the extent to which his racial prejudice generated his interest in the right to privacy, yet it would be naive to dismiss its influence altogether. Ervin built his emerging civil libertarian ideology upon a constitutional philosophy that had been designed by generations of southerners to rationalize and defend Jim Crow. As the concept of privacy became the primary expression of his civil libertarian ideology, the senator made sure that it harmonized with his opposition to civil rights.

Ervin's new crusade for privacy may have grown out of the South's conservative antigovernment tradition, but it earned accolades from both sides of the political spectrum. Conservatives, who had long considered Ervin their constitutional champion, interpreted his attacks on Big Brother as attacks on big government, and they understood his civil liberty rhetoric as shorthand for opposing welfare, labor unions, and civil rights. Liberals, who had long distrusted Ervin, began to offer their grudging respect for his surprising, if somewhat confusing, civil libertarian record. Many of Ervin's old ideas about the rights of individuals against government power began to take on a new relevance for liberals in an age of huge bureaucracies, electronic surveillance, and computers.[95]

But they also understood that the senator was no born-again liberal. Though the *New Republic* praised Ervin's commitment to protecting civil liberties against abuses of power by the central government, the magazine also noted that "if a threat to individual liberty doesn't come from Washington, Ervin seems unable to get terribly excited about it."[96] Ervin frustrated these liberal civil libertarians by continuing to condemn *Miranda*, turning a blind eye to invasions of privacy coming from state governments, and resisting all civil rights proposals.[97] Lawrence Speiser of the ACLU concluded: "When he's good, he's very, very good and when he is bad, he's horrid."[98]

Yet on the issue of a constitutional right to privacy, Ervin and the liberals saw eye to eye. Liberal civil libertarians heartily supported the senator's expanding privacy agenda and enthusiastically endorsed the centerpiece of his legislative offensive, his Bill of Rights for government employees. The senator worked side by side with lobbyists from the ADA, the ACLU, the AFL-CIO, and even a few civil rights organizations to secure passage of his bill, and he easily convinced liberal senators such as George McGovern and Philip Hart to cosponsor the legislation.[99]

The only major obstacle to the enactment of Ervin's employee Bill of Rights was the last minute pressure brought to bear by the CIA, which demanded that because of national security concerns it should be exempt from the legislation's restrictions. An angry Ervin blasted the agency in a sharply worded Senate speech for suggesting that any government agency should be beyond the scope of constitutional protections of the right to privacy. "Apparently what they want is to stand above the Law," Ervin shouted. But the power of the CIA was too great, and Ervin had to accept an amendment limiting the bill's application to the intelligence agencies.[100]

In September 1967, the amended Employee's Bill of Rights passed the Senate by an overwhelming margin, but it ran into trouble in the House of Representatives, where hearings were not scheduled until the following year. When the House Subcommittee on Manpower and Civil Service took up Ervin's proposal in June 1968, the Johnson administration set out to defeat it. Civil Service Commissioner John Macy led the administration's attack by complaining that it would limit the effectiveness of the executive branch and needlessly challenge its autonomy. He was supported by representatives from the Department of Defense and the Justice Department who again argued that national security might be endangered by even the limited restrictions Ervin's bill would place on the intelligence agencies. Ervin went over to the other chamber to testify in behalf of his proposal, lashing out at his opponents: "The order has gone out to kill S. 1035, and we can only marvel at the equanimity with which the Administration's troops have carried out their orders. . . . They have obediently marched up Capitol Hill and back down, leaving, I fear, a wake of half-truths, misconceptions, and innuendos about this employee rights legislation." Despite his effort, the bill died in the subcommittee, but Ervin promised to rejoin the battle during the next congressional session.[101]

The irony that the conservative senior senator from North Carolina would lead the fight to protect privacy rights, while bashing the FBI and CIA from the Senate floor, delighted Ervin's new civil libertarian friends. "You were superb," wrote Lawrence Speiser of the ACLU. "Yesterday was my birthday. I can't think of a better present than to have you so vigorously attacking the concept that any government agency should be exempt from the requirements of the Constitution." The reaction from Ervin's old conservative allies was far less kind. One right-wing newsletter criticized Ervin for protecting "homosexuals, anarchists, revolutionaries, and degenerates in government." "The Subcommittee on Constitutional Rights has been called the ACLU's channel in the Congress," an editorial warned, "and its chairman, Sam J. Ervin, Jr., is so obsessively engrossed in his reputation as a constitutional rights lawyer that he is a pushover for practically anything politically worded the right way."[102]

As these reactions from both the left and the right suggest, Sam Ervin had changed. The same senator who criticized the Supreme Court for protecting the rights of alleged subversives in the Cold War Cases in 1956 condemned the CIA for endangering the privacy rights of their employees and hiding behind the smokescreen of national security in 1967. In 1955 Ervin had called for the repeal of a New York law preventing employers from asking job applicants to list the name under which they were born. If the applicant's original name had a foreign sound, Ervin explained, "that might lead to employing some good American in his place."[103] But eleven years later, in 1966, Ervin led the fight to protect government workers from questionnaires requiring them to identify their race, religion, and national origin. Ervin had not completely abandoned his conservative roots, as his acquiescence to wiretapping, opposition to civil rights, and repeated attempts to restrict the Supreme Court attest. But over the course of a decade, Ervin crafted an expanded civil libertarian philosophy, far different from the one he had espoused in the 1950s. At the heart of this new philosophy was his commitment to the constitutional right to privacy.

Throughout the 1960s most of Ervin's efforts to protect civil liberties had earned the blessings of a sympathetic majority within the Kennedy and Johnson administrations. But his bill to protect the privacy rights of government employees, as well as his new investigations into the government's computerized data banks and census questionnaires, antagonized an executive branch wary of any congressional challenge to its prerogatives. These skirmishes would be but the first in a long series of clashes between the senator and the White House over issues relating to privacy and presidential power. The following year would bring more hearings in the Constitutional Rights Subcommittee that challenged the government's power to collect data on its employees and citizens. It would also bring a new president to Washington with revolutionary ideas about constitutional rights and the powers of his office. Sam Ervin's commitment to the right to privacy had put him on a collision course with Richard Nixon.

CHAPTER EIGHT

A TIME OF DOUBT AND FEAR

Sam Ervin would have been only a minor figure in the history of the United States had it not been for Richard Nixon. Ervin did play an important supporting role in the congressional struggle over civil rights legislation, and he certainly deserves recognition for his protection of civil liberties in the 1960s. But Ervin never stood at center stage until he helped to bring an end to the Nixon presidency. The Watergate scandal was clearly the defining event of Ervin's career and guaranteed his place in history.

The battle between Sam Ervin and Richard Nixon, however, did not begin with Watergate. Disagreements over civil liberties, civil rights, and the constitutional separation of powers arose almost immediately after Nixon took office and developed into three distinct, but interrelated, political confrontations. Each of the ensuing clashes is significant in itself, but taken together they suggest a pattern of escalating conflict between Ervin and Nixon that began during the first few days of the president's administration.

Ervin had never held a high opinion of Nixon. In 1946, when Ervin took his brother's seat in the House of Representatives for one year, his office was located close to that of Jerry Voorhis. Though the conservative North Carolinian did not agree with many of the liberal Californian's opinions, he regarded Voorhis as a dedicated congressman and a friend. Ervin was appalled during the midterm election that November when Nixon defeated Voorhis by characterizing him as a Communist sympathizer. Nixon's red-baiting campaign against Helen Gahagan Douglas during his successful run for the Senate in 1950 and his alliance with Senator Joe McCarthy served to further Ervin's suspicions. Ervin's distrust of Nixon was shared by more than a few of his colleagues in the southern bloc of the Senate. Richard Russell once confided to a friend that "Mr. Nixon, if he ever assumes the Presidency, would be the worst President imaginable."[1]

Throughout the 1950s and 1960s, Ervin and Nixon had surprisingly few dealings with one another. During Nixon's two terms as Dwight Eisenhower's vice president, Senator Ervin tended to agree with Nixon's opposition to Communism, but to disagree with his support of civil rights. As a loyal Democrat, Ervin supported the candidacy of John Kennedy during the presidential election of 1960, yet he did not take a particularly aggressive stand against Nixon during the campaign. Nixon's shift toward more conservative stances on civil rights and other domestic issues during the 1960s actually brought the two politicians closer together by the end of the decade. Ervin, however, maintained his long-held skepticism concerning Nixon's personal integrity and commitment to constitutional rights.[2]

Both Ervin and Nixon ran for office in 1968. Ervin campaigned for a third term in the Senate, while Nixon launched his second attempt to capture the White House. It was a turbulent election conducted in a country reeling from race riots, escalating crime, political assassinations, and the seemingly endless war in Vietnam. Pain and fear cut deep into the American political culture. After Nixon defeated several Republican challengers to earn the nomination of his party, he faced two strong opponents—the Democratic candidate, Hubert H. Humphrey, and the candidate of the American Independent Party, George Wallace. Ervin, too, encountered a very serious threat to his political future in 1968. But the real challenge to his reelection bid came not from either Nixon's rejuvenated Republicans or George Wallace's angry insurgents but from within his own party.[3]

In the fall of 1967, Terry Sanford launched an unofficial campaign to defeat Sam Ervin in the Democratic primary. The senator and the popular former governor represented two different political organizations within North Carolina's Democratic Party. Ervin came from the more traditional wing that resisted any alteration in southern racial, economic, or social relations. His faction enjoyed the support of established North Carolina industries such as textiles, furniture, and agriculture. Sanford was allied with the modernizers in the Democratic Party who favored moderate reform of the state's social and economic relations in order to advance the growth of new business opportunities in technology, finance, and manufacturing. One newspaper summed up the difference between the two camps by suggesting that the philosophy of the Ervin group "tends to be one of resistance to change," while the approach of the Sanford organization "is one of innovation," especially in such matters as "race relations, fighting poverty, and educational advances."[4] Both groups, however, remained within the moderately conservative middle of the South's rightward-leaning political culture.

The two factions had been feuding for several years, and so had their nominal leaders. The dispute had grown to such proportions by 1966 that Senator B. Everett Jordan of North Carolina felt compelled to warn the Johnson White House about the rift, including that "Governor Sanford said some awful mean things about Ervin in times past." That same year Ervin supported an administration effort to award Sanford a foreign ambassadorship. The senator told a presidential aide that given Sanford's threats to run against him, "it would get Sanford out of the State and get him far away." The ambassadorship did not materialize, but Sanford's run to unseat Ervin very nearly did.[5]

The first direct shot in the long-awaited duel came in October 1967, when Sanford conducted a poll asking voters whom they would choose in a head-to-head primary contest between himself and Ervin. The results were not encouraging. The poll indicated that he trailed Ervin by fifteen to twenty points. But Sanford decided to see if a little campaigning would boost his support. He spent the next few months discussing the pros and cons of a primary challenge on television shows and in newspaper interviews, and he sent out over 200,000 letters to targeted constituents. Ervin's staff countered with a letter-writing campaign of their own that put Democratic leaders throughout the state on the spot by asking for early pledges of active support.[6]

For several months talk of the impending showdown filled North Carolina's newspapers and airwaves. Political pundits speculated that the contest would pit Sanford's "organizational ability and flair for political innovation" against Ervin's powerful "anti–civil rights record" and aptitude for exploiting the "popular issues of 'law and order.'" But almost every discussion of a possible Ervin-Sanford contest suggested that "the bugaboo of race" would transform the primary into a mean-spirited campaign. "If [Sanford] does decide to run," one editorial predicted, "you can look forward to the most gripping Senate race in North Carolina since Frank Graham and Willis Smith rattled the timbers fifteen years ago." Memories of that primary contest, often described as "the dirtiest statewide political campaign in recent history," terrified many of the Democratic faithful. Sanford, too, worried about the probability of what he called a "drastically divisive" campaign, and he confided to his aides that the race issue was "certainly the issue that can win for Ervin."[7]

In spite of new poll results in February 1968 showing the potential candidates running neck and neck, Sanford decided not to enter the primary. "As I saw it, it would have been close at best," Sanford explained. "The results were highly doubtful. . . . When you're likely to just stir up a fight in the face of an uncertain outcome, then you have an obligation to your party and your state." Sanford shared his thinking during an interview conducted several years later:

> I concluded that I could beat him probably. But I concluded that if I did beat him it would have divided the state so badly that the candidate for governor, Bob Scott, would have been defeated, and I probably would have been defeated in the general election, too, and it just wasn't worth it. . . . It would have been the worst campaign, the toughest campaign that North Carolina would have had in my memory, and I just didn't think it was worth it.[8]

Whether Sanford could have actually defeated Ervin is debatable, but David Cooper of the *Winston-Salem Journal* seemed to express the conventional wisdom of the time when he wrote: "In the minds of many state Democrats, Ervin . . . has built an anti–civil rights record that would make him almost unbeatable in a contest against any North Carolina political figure." Still, Sanford's decision not to run spared Ervin the only real political threat he ever faced in his long career.[9]

Sanford believed that his threat to run against Ervin in 1968 had a moderating effect on the senator. "I think I did Senator Ervin a lot of good," Sanford claimed. "I think he has come on with some much more progressive attitudes that he started developing in the heat of that little short campaign. There's nothing like knowing if you don't shape up somebody might run against you." A close look at Ervin's campaign, however, suggests that, rather than shift to the left, the senator instead moved further to the right, closer to Richard Nixon.[10]

Ervin staked out very conservative positions on two of the most divisive issues of the 1968 election—civil rights and crime. Ervin's adamant opposition to civil rights was nothing new, but when Senator Russell fell ill during the civil rights debate on the open housing bill in the spring of 1968, Ervin assumed the leadership of the remnants of the once mighty southern caucus. Ervin's new role, and the resulting increase in media attention, reinforced his reputation as a racial conservative during the formative stages of the campaign.[11]

Ervin's tougher stance against crime could be seen in his willingness to drop his civil libertarian objections to the expansion of federal wiretapping in the Safe Streets and Crime Prevention Act of 1968, and by his renewed attempts to overturn the Supreme Court rulings in *Mallory* and *Miranda* by congressional action.[12] When the crime bill reached the Senate Judiciary Committee in 1968, Ervin successfully offered two amendments to deny the federal courts jurisdiction over voluntary confessions and eyewitness testimony. A third Ervin amendment would have prohibited the Supreme Court from reviewing an individual's conviction in a state court on a writ of habeas corpus.[13]

The full Senate eventually removed Ervin's drastic court-curbing measures from Title II of the bill, but not before Ervin wrote to every member of the Senate urging them to support his proposals. To bolster his argument, Ervin cited a recent statement from Nixon's presidential campaign entitled "Toward Freedom From Fear," which attacked the Court's coddling of criminals and supported current efforts to restrict the Supreme Court. Carl T. Curtis, a Republican senator from Nebraska, could not resist needling his old friend during an election year. "I am delighted that you are on the Nixon band-wagon," he wrote. Ervin quickly responded, "I would rather look at Title II with the happy thought that Mr. Nixon is joining the *Ervin* bandwagon, begun two years ago, to rectify the *Miranda* decision."[14]

It is hard to know whether Ervin or Nixon had boarded the anticrime bandwagon first. Both politicians had been early and loud critics of the Warren Court's rulings extending the civil liberties of alleged criminals, both had consistently attacked the rising crime rate, race riots, and anti-war demonstrations as threats to traditional American values, and both had made the restoration of law and order a central theme of their 1968 campaigns. In spite of the fact that Ervin was a Democrat and Nixon a Republican, the two candidates held almost identical opinions about the need for the federal government to get tougher on crime.

Ervin and Nixon appeared to agree on almost everything else in 1968 as well. Indeed, Ervin seemed more in harmony with Nixon than with the Democratic nominee, Hubert Humphrey. From Vietnam to defense spending, from civil rights to reducing the size of government, Sam Ervin and Richard Nixon saw eye to eye. To be sure, some differences did exist; for instance, Nixon supported the equal rights amendment (ERA) while Ervin opposed it. But on the vast majority of issues, the two conservatives staked out common ground. Nixon even endorsed Ervin's Bill of Rights for government workers, promising that "an important task of the new administration will be to assure the protection of the constitutional rights of federal employees."[15]

Nixon, who eight years earlier barely lost the presidency to John Kennedy, this time finished on top by a slim margin. In a tight three-way race, Nixon defeated Humphrey and Wallace but received only 43 percent of the popular vote. Ervin, who felt confident of his own reelection as soon as Sanford withdrew from the primary, had publicly endorsed Humphrey, calling him "the greatest friend the farmers of this nation have ever had." Few other Tar Heel Democrats risked openly supporting the Minnesotan, a leading champion of civil rights, and even Ervin conceded that "there is dissatisfaction within the Democratic Party of North Carolina." But Ervin defended both Humphrey and his party by insisting, "No organization is perfect. The only perfect person I know is my wife and she made a foolish mistake when she married me." Not surprisingly, Ervin's endorsement did Humphrey little good in North Carolina, where he lost to Nixon by a wide margin and only barely finished ahead of Wallace.[16]

Ervin, however, cruised to an easy victory. He garnered a 61 percent majority in his rout of his Republican rival, and he attracted more votes than any other candidate for any other office on the state's ballot. Ervin received nearly double the ballots cast for Humphrey. The North Carolina returns revealed not only the strength but also the conservative character of Ervin's victory. The vast majority of Humphrey voters, mostly loyal Democrats, also chose Ervin, with the exception of African Americans, who tended to split their otherwise straight Democratic ticket to reject the senator and his negative record on civil rights. Ervin attracted about one-third of the Nixon voters in North Carolina, and three-quarters of the Wallace voters, to earn his landslide victory. One study concluded: "Ervin was the shining light of North Carolina Democrats in 1968 for his ability to hold Humphrey voters, bring Wallace voters back to support other Democratic candidates, and cut the party's losses to the Republican presidential candidate."[17]

At first glance it might appear that the concurrence of conservative opinion between Ervin and Nixon carried over into the president's first term. In spite of Nixon's later attempts to paint Ervin as an intensely partisan politician during Watergate, the Democratic senator voted with the Republican president's position over 60 percent of the time during Nixon's first four years in the White House, making him one of the most independent Democrats in Congress. Ervin only supported the presidential programs of his friend and fellow Democrat Lyndon Johnson 41 percent of the time. But the apparent harmony between Ervin and Nixon is deceiving. As the cool winds of political reality began to dissipate the rhetorical hot air of the campaign, significant differences between the tactics, priorities, and constitutional philosophies of the two men became increasingly obvious.[18]

The first conflict between Ervin and Nixon stemmed from the new president's desire to crack down on crime in the District of Columbia. During the campaign, Nixon had labeled Washington "the crime capital of the world" and promised quick action to combat the rapid breakdown of law and order in the nation's capital. Major crime in Washington had increased by 25 percent in 1968, with the biggest jumps in rape (53 percent) and robbery (45 percent).

Senator Ervin, upper middle of photograph, looks on as President Nixon delivers a State of the Union address (n.d.). Sam Ervin Library and Museum, Western Piedmont Community College, Morganton, North Carolina.

Responding to intense pressure to convert his campaign rhetoric into action, Nixon sent a note to his chief domestic aide, John Ehrlichman, the day after arriving in the White House: "It is of the highest priority to do something meaningful on DC crime *now*. Talk to [Attorney General John] Mitchell—give me a timetable for action."[19]

Several days later Nixon issued his "Message on Crime in the District of Columbia," which included a recommendation that Congress enact legislation permitting "temporary pretrial detention" of criminal suspects whose "pretrial release presents a clear danger to the community." Nixon's proposal represented a direct attack on Ervin's Bail Reform Act of 1966. The ensuing battle quickly escalated into an all-out war over constitutional rights, civil liberties, and the right to privacy that raged through all six years of the Nixon administration.[20]

It took several more months for the administration to formulate its anti-crime program, but in July 1969 Nixon sent several legislative proposals up to Capitol Hill. The centerpiece of the president's "war on crime" was the District of Columbia crime bill. Attorney General Mitchell hailed the D.C. crime bill as "a model anticrime program" that he hoped would be copied by all fifty states.

As it progressed through the legislative process, the bill picked up more and more provisions, most of them proposed by the Justice Department.[21] When the omnibus crime bill, as it came to be known, emerged from committee in the summer of 1970, it contained many reasonable proposals, such as hiring a thousand more policeman, ten more judges, and forty more prosecutors for Washington. It also recommended a reorganization of the District's court system to achieve greater efficiency. But the bill included draconian measures to make jury trials optional for juveniles, increase police wiretapping powers, allow preventive detention of "hard-core criminals," and authorize "no-knock" searches by police.[22] In spite of his own tough-on-crime reputation, Ervin led the fight in the Senate to dilute what he called Nixon's "ominous" crime measure, which was "as full of unconstitutional provisions, unjust provisions, and unwise provisions as a mangy hound dog is with fleas"—a metaphor he borrowed from his fight against the 1964 Civil Rights Act. Ervin further characterized the measure as "a garbage pail of some of the most repressive, nearsighted, intolerant, unfair, and vindictive legislation that the Senate has ever been presented." He denounced Nixon's anticrime proposals during two sets of hearings before the Subcommittee on Constitutional Rights, and he played a major role in stripping the bill of many of its most objectionable provisions during debates on the Senate floor. But two of the president's ideas—preventive detention and no-knock police searches—caused protracted debates in Congress that highlighted the emerging rift between Ervin and the Nixon administration.[23]

Nixon's proposal to allow preventive detention brought into public view a criminal justice debate that had been simmering behind the scenes for several years: Should a judge have the power to deny bail to an accused perpetrator of a non-capital offense who may pose a danger to the community if released while awaiting trial? Nixon and Attorney General Mitchell argued that crime rates were being increased by "dangerous hard-core recidivists" who were arrested for one crime, released on bail, and then committed more crimes before they had been brought to trial for their first offense. Citing compelling anecdotal evidence—such as the story of a bank robber who missed his first court date because he was busy robbing another bank—the administration argued that "there is no real alternative to detention of such persons if the community is to receive the protection it deserves."[24] Opponents of preventive detention worried that it would lead to the kind of "upside-down Wonderland justice" the White Queen dispensed in Lewis Carroll's *Through the Looking-Glass*. The Queen told Alice: "There's the King's Messenger. He's in prison now, being punished: and the trial doesn't even begin till next Wednesday: and of course the crime comes last of all." "Suppose he never commits the crime?" asked Alice. "That would be all the better, wouldn't it?" the Queen responded. Alice thought, "There's a mistake somewhere."[25]

Ervin, too, thought that there was a mistake somewhere, and he believed it stemmed from the Nixon administration's lack of respect for the Constitution. He complained that locking people up because they *might* commit a crime violated the Eighth Amendment's protection against excessive bail and the Fifth Amendment's due process clause, not to mention the traditional presumption that a defendant is innocent until proven guilty. The senator believed that the way to solve the problem of accused criminals committing more crimes while out on bail was to shorten the length of time between arrest and trial. "For the life of me," Ervin explained, "I cannot understand why any Department of Justice would rather have preventive detention, which holds vital provisions of the Constitution in utter contempt, than speedy trial, which seeks to enforce fundamental constitutional rights."[26]

Ervin also argued that while preventive detention would have a detrimental effect on the rights of all Americans, it would have almost no effect on the rising crime rate. He cited statistics from a recently released study by the National Bureau of Standards that found, much to the White House's chagrin, that only 5 percent of those defendants eligible for preventive detention under the president's bill were rearrested for dangerous or violent crimes during the period of their release. Thus, Ervin could assert that even the administration's own study implied that twenty persons would have to be detained in hope of preventing a violent crime by just one of them.[27]

But Ervin's primary objection remained that preventive detention was "inconsistent with a free society." In his opening statement before the Constitutional Rights Subcommittee, the senator declared:

> If America is to remain a free society, it will have to take certain risks: One is the risk that a person admitted to bail may flee before trial. Another is the risk that a person admitted to bail may commit a crime while free on bail.
>
> In my judgment, it is better for our country to take these risks and remain a free society than it is for it to adopt a tyrannical practice of imprisoning men for crimes which they have not committed and may never commit merely because some court may peer into the future and surmise that they may commit crimes if allowed freedom prior to trial and conviction.[28]

Like Nixon's preventive detention proposal, the president's request that Congress allow police to conduct no-knock searches spawned an intense debate on Capitol Hill. The administration wanted to authorize police in the

District of Columbia, and narcotics agents throughout the country, to enter private dwellings without first knocking and identifying themselves. In arguing for no-knock entry, advocates emphasized that without the element of surprise criminals too often managed to escape or to dispose of certain kinds of drug and gambling evidence before the police could seize it. The Nixon administration suggested that under its proposal a judge would usually order a no-knock warrant in advance, but in some special circumstances law enforcement officers would be able to decide on the spot to forgo the normal warning before launching a raid. Proponents of the legislation conceded that it raised constitutional concerns, but as Nebraska Republican Roman Hruska, who introduced the measure in the Senate, explained, "We are grappling for survival in the battle against crime."[29]

Ervin believed that Nixon's no-knock proposals would nullify the Fourth Amendment's protection against unreasonable searches and seizures, and repudiate the ancient principle of the common law which held that every man's home is his castle. He warned that the administration and its supporters in Congress were "so zealous in their efforts to enforce the law that they would emulate the example set by Samson in his blindness and destroy the pillars upon which the temple of justice itself rests." Moreover, he predicted that not only criminals but also innocent men and women, and even law enforcement officials themselves, would be harmed when police burst into private premises without identifying themselves and encounter confused residents likely to resist the unknown intruders with violent force.[30]

Ervin attracted more national press coverage during his outspoken opposition to preventive detention and no-knock police raids than ever before in his career. The vast majority of this media attention was positive. Ervin's rhetorical flourishes—such as denouncing the president's anticrime package as "a blueprint for a police state," or suggesting that it should be "confined forever in some special branch of the Smithsonian Institute designed to house legal curiosities"—helped to make him one of the media's favorite southern senators. "Everyone's done their piece on Ervin," Paul Clancy, the Washington correspondent for the Charlotte Observer, explained. During and soon after Ervin's fight against the D.C. crime bill, stories about North Carolina's pugnacious senior senator began to appear in magazines such as Harper's, the New Republic, the New York Times Magazine, Progressive, and even Playboy.[31]

All of this favorable media attention contributed to Ervin's improving national public image. Having already earned grudging respect as a constitutional scholar and born-again civil libertarian, the senator began to become something of a hero to liberals around the country who enjoyed his lively attacks on the Nixon administration. NBC anchorman David Brinkley reminded his television audience that "in past years, when Sam Ervin quoted the Constitution on civil rights and racial questions, the same people who now admire him were dismissing him as just one more southern segregationist trying to use the Constitution to support his views. He got a lot of mail in those days accusing him of being a racist. Now he gets a lot of mail calling him the liberals' hero." Brinkley astutely concluded that while "it must be an interesting and enlightening experience for Senator Ervin, . . . he's old enough and politician enough to know that in this country, that is how it works."[32]

Ervin's entertaining opposition to Nixon's crime bill may have won him liberal accolades, but he lost the legislative battle against preventive detention and no-knock searches. Politicians who had whipped the public's fear of crime into a frenzy during the last election now found themselves to be victims of their own exaggerations. They had no choice but to respond to the political pressure they had created. Although the Senate had originally removed the preventive detention and no-knock provisions in its version of the bill, the House reinserted both measures and the Senate-House Conference agreed to keep both in the final draft. The revised omnibus District of Columbia crime bill passed both houses of Congress in July 1970, giving Nixon the tough law and order image he desired.[33]

Time proved Ervin's predictions about the D.C. crime bill to be true. Lawlessness in the nation's capital continued to increase, but within a few years preventive detention and no-knock police raids had begun to fade away. These new practices had become more trouble than benefit to police in the District, who eventually withdrew their support of both. Preventive detention remained in the criminal code, in spite of what one study called its "virtual non-use." But after several tragic no-knock raids resulted in the deaths of police and innocent citizens across the country, and after the Watergate scandal created a different atmosphere on Capitol Hill, Ervin managed to convince Congress to repeal the no-knock authorization in 1974.[34]

The historical significance of the D.C. crime bill was not its effect on crime, which was nil, but the suspicion it raised in the mind of Ervin and others about Nixon. As the *New York Times'* Tom Wicker later observed, "The legislation gave the administration an early but lasting reputation—not just with Sam Ervin— for putting anticrime expediency above the protections of the Constitution." It was, Ervin said in a number of his speeches, "a time of doubt and fear."[35]

Nixon's crime bill was only one of a series of actions taken by the new administration that offended Ervin's civil libertarian sensibilities. Just a few months after Nixon's inauguration in 1969, the senator learned that officials in

A TIME OF DOUBT AND FEAR

the Treasury Department had begun checking library lending lists to discover which books certain "suspicious" Americans had checked out.[36] Soon thereafter he discovered a Secret Service program that tried to predict who might harm public officials by asking all government employees to report anyone who insisted on personally contacting high government officials or who attempted to embarrass the president—a description that would fit Ervin and most Democratic congressmen.[37] The senator also learned that the Department of Health, Education, and Welfare (HEW) had started a blacklist of U.S. scientists whom the agency would not hire because of their opposition to the Vietnam War, and there were rumors that the Post Office Department was opening and reading the overseas mail of American citizens.[38] In each case, Ervin responded with a vigorous protest and demanded a full report. Seldom did he receive a satisfactory answer.

The senator's public attacks on the administration's frequent invasions of privacy concerned some of Nixon's top aides, especially Tom Charles Huston, a right-wing ideologue who wanted to increase dramatically the administration's domestic surveillance of its political opponents.[39] Huston wrote to White House Chief of Staff H. R. Haldeman complaining:

> It appears the standard pattern is developing: the Washington *Post* drums up a story, Sam Ervin gets outraged, and the Administration acts like a kid caught with his hand in the cookie jar. [Press Secretary Ron] Ziegler's response to press inquiries implied: (1) some local, zealous agents were operating on their own; (2) we didn't know anything about it; and (3) it is being stopped, implying we shouldn't have been doing it to start with.[40]

Huston not only considered the government intrusions Ervin protested against to be "perfectly legitimate," but he took the fact that they had been discovered as "another example of inadequate coordination within the intelligence community."[41] So Huston began to work on a plan to shore up the administration's domestic intelligence capability, the first step in a chain of events that was to lead to Watergate.[42]

While Huston wanted to improve the White House's ability to gather domestic intelligence on its political enemies, other presidential aides recommended strategies to strike back against what they considered Nixon's greatest foe—the press. One of the president's advisers, Patrick Buchanan, presented Nixon with a proposal to unleash Vice President Spiro Agnew on the network news organizations through a series of public attacks. Buchanan even supplied a draft of a vitriolic press-bashing speech for Agnew to deliver that threatened television stations with revocation of their federal licenses if they continued their critical coverage. Nixon agreed with Buchanan's ideas and liked the strident speech, commenting to an aide, "This really flicks the scab off, doesn't it?"[43]

Buchanan's recommendations fit right in with the president's own desire to strike back against what he perceived to be a hostile, biased, and liberal press. Nixon often scrawled angry personal notes instructing his staff to "hit," "fight," "knock," or "cut" reporters who had criticized him. "An *absolute* freeze on him," Nixon wrote about correspondent Sander Vanocur. "*Anyone* who violates [it] will be fired."[44]

At the president's urging, the White House embarked on a campaign of press intimidation that was unprecedented in its intensity and sophistication. The administration unleashed a barrage of lawsuits, subpoenas, tax audits, FBI investigations, private insults, and public attacks on the media. Though other presidents had attempted to counter what they thought to be unfair news coverage, one writer has maintained: "Richard Nixon was different. His efforts to cow his critics in the Fourth Estate were more deliberate, systematic, and exhaustive. And he was peerless in his hatred." Nixon's anti-press campaign was partially successful in chilling dissent, at least in the most popular source of news for most Americans, network television evening news programs. It did not, however, intimidate Senator Ervin.[45]

Ervin had long been an uncompromising champion of a free press. As early as January 1955, less than a year after arriving in Washington, the senator began to attack both the executive and legislative branches of the government for suppressing the news and withholding information from reporters. In the late 1950s and early 1960s, he consistently criticized presidents from both parties for excessive government secrecy. In 1965 he expanded his agenda by leading the Subcommittee on Constitutional Rights through public hearings on the conflict between protecting a defendant's right to a fair trial and guaranteeing the news media's right to free speech.

Ervin and his subcommittee also began to look into the rapidly expanding practice of judges ordering reporters to reveal their confidential sources during grand jury investigations and criminal trials. This practice reached epidemic proportions after 1968. Federal and state prosecutors, defense attorneys, and even the Justice Department served hundreds of subpoenas on newspaper reporters and radio and television stations in the first two years of the Nixon administration.[46]

Ervin's concern about the president's reaction to this trend, and his uneasiness with Nixon's emerging assault on the news media, spurred him to call for hearings on freedom of the press in 1971. He initially disagreed with witnesses who recommended that Congress pass a shield bill to prevent the government from forcing reporters to reveal their confidential sources. He preferred to let the Supreme Court resolve the conflict between First Amendment interests and the interests of justice in its pending *Caldwell* case. But after 29 June 1972, when the Court ruled in *Caldwell* that reporters did not have a First Amendment right to protect their sources against a subpoena, the senator proposed his own "newsmen's privilege" measure. Nixon, however, endorsed the *Caldwell* decision and opposed Ervin's shield bill.[47]

Questions about the president's commitment to freedom of the press increased over the next few months. Complaints from media representatives about the administration's unprecedented attacks became more frequent and more intense. *Newsweek* even went so far as to state that the recent clashes between the administration and the media were "without precedent in the history of the United States." Ervin joined the battle with a series of speeches in which he ran through his own litany of charges against the president.[48] He especially criticized the White House for misusing the Federal Communications Commission and its "fairness doctrine" to exercise "a not very subtle form of censorship" on radio and television stations.[49] He also vigorously condemned the administration's attempt to prevent the *New York Times* and the *Washington Post* from publishing the Pentagon Papers, which contained classified information concerning the Vietnam War. When the Supreme Court ruled against the president in *New York Times v. United States*, Ervin praised the justices for reaffirming "the belief of our Founding Fathers that a press free from governmental control is essential to a free society."[50]

These and other examples of the Nixon administration's campaign to intimidate the press troubled Ervin, but no incident disturbed him more than the White House harassment of CBS correspondent Daniel Schorr. One morning in August 1971, Schorr discovered an FBI agent in the studio probing into his personal life. When Schorr asked why he was being investigated, the agent only mumbled something about a routine background check and the possibility of a government job. Over the next few days the FBI talked to Schorr's bosses at CBS, his neighbors, and even members of his family. The questioning always concerned Schorr's patriotism and the kinds of people with whom he associated. No post ever materialized. Schorr could not believe that the Nixon administration would offer him a post since he knew that his critical reporting had earned him the enmity of the White House staff. Two of Nixon's closest advisers, H. R. Haldeman and John Ehrlichman, regularly referred to him as Daniel P. Schorr, although his middle initial was L. When Dan Rather, a friend of Schorr's at CBS, asked about the practice, Ehrlichman explained that the P. stood for "Prick."[51]

Ervin began an inquiry into the Schorr case in December 1971. In spite of several months of probing, and several days of public hearings, neither Ervin nor Schorr could find out why the newsman had been investigated by the FBI. The White House refused to cooperate with the hearings, only issuing a statement explaining that Schorr had been considered for a possible position in the environmental field. But when Ervin suggested that the testimony of the presidential aides responsible for this job search could quickly put to rest "the suspicion of many Americans that government appears anxious to use its power to control the press for its own purposes," the White House responded by trying to "turn the hearings off." After that effort failed, presidential counsel John Dean advised the White House staff to stonewall: "We have already responded to Ervin on this matter, but obviously he was not, and probably never will be, satisfied." Dean warned that supplying the senator with any further information would "only open an issue that does not need to be reopened." It was not until Ervin's Watergate investigation that he finally learned that it was the president himself who had ordered that Schorr be harassed. Nixon had become so angry over Schorr's critical reporting of a presidential statement that he snapped to Haldeman, "I want an FBI check on that bastard. And no stalling this time."[52]

The Schorr incident convinced Ervin that the president held no respect for freedom of the press. "The actions of the present administration appear to go beyond simple reactions to incidents of irresponsible or biased reporting, to efforts at wholesale intimidation of the press and broadcast media," Ervin concluded. Nixon, however, remained unconcerned, confiding to John Dean, "One hell of a lot of people don't give one God damn about this issue of suppression of the press."[53]

Ervin's condemnation of the president's campaign against the press is just one example of his escalating struggle with Nixon over civil liberties. Ervin and the staff of the Subcommittee on Constitutional Rights had become so overwhelmed with their investigations into the administration's draconian anti-crime proposals, repeated invasions of privacy, and disregard for the freedom of the press that they began to lose control over their own agenda. The senator did follow through with his plans to hold hearings on the Census and Federal Questionnaires in the spring of 1969, and his staff continued their investigation into government computers and data banks, but these initiatives were quickly overshadowed by the administration's repeated affronts to the right to privacy. Ervin also pushed for enactment of his Government Employees Bill of Rights, but, in spite of Nixon's promises during the campaign to support the measure, the White House lobbied against it and the legislation died, again in a House subcommittee. By the end of Nixon's first term, Ervin's decade-long crusade in the Senate as a champion of civil liberties had retreated into an embattled defense against the administration's numerous attacks on the Bill of Rights, the right to privacy, and freedom of the press.

Debates over civil liberties represented only one of the political battlefields in which Sam Ervin and Richard Nixon clashed during the early years of the president's administration. Their disagreement over the equal rights amendment added to the senator's distrust of the president. On one level there should have been no confusion about where the two men stood on this issue. Nixon had supported the amendment as vice president in the 1950s and had pledged to support it again during the election of 1968. Ervin had always spoken against what he called "the so-called Equal Rights Amendment" and led the handful of conservative senators who opposed it in the early 1970s. But it was not the fact that they disagreed about the ERA that bothered Ervin as much as the fact that Nixon was so inconsistent on where he stood as the proposed amendment approached passage in Congress.[54]

In spite of Nixon's history of speaking out in support of the ERA, members of his administration began to have concerns about the political fallout that might come if the amendment actually became law and voters gave the president the praise or the blame, depending on their opinions about women's rights. A debate raged inside the White House between those who urged Nixon to come out squarely in favor, and those who warned him to back off and waffle. One aide worried, "If the President in any way appeared to be explicitly withdrawing his support of the Equal Rights Amendment he would be far more vulnerable to partisan attack."[55] Another pointed out that if the ERA lost in the Senate, then the Democrats would argue that "when the going got rough, the President was willing to kill the Amendment through the efforts of the Southern Conservatives, specifically Senator Ervin. Thus, to the hypocrisy argument will be added a classic Southern Conservative vs. Liberal positioning."[56] Nixon's more conservative advisers warned him that the progress he had made in attracting southern voters might be lost if they thought he was supporting the "feminists." Finally, John Dean and John Ehrlichman recommended that the president take both sides. "While it is felt that you should take no action that would unduly stimulate passage," they argued, "it would seem desirable that you reaffirm your prior position of support. In this way, if the Amendment does pass, you will be accorded some credit for its enactment. Likewise, if it fail[s] to pass by reason of a crippling amendment or otherwise, such failure will not be attributed to you."[57]

Ervin hated such political waffling, and he knew exactly what Nixon and everyone else should do about the ERA—defeat it. Once again, the old North Carolinian mixed his inherited cultural conservatism with his strict constitutional constructionism. Working closely with Phyllis Schlafly, the conservative activist who spearheaded the movement to kill the ERA, Ervin gave speeches, wrote letters, offered amendments, and did all that he could to stop its passage in the Senate. He warned that the ERA would destroy the social fabric of America. During the final debate in the Senate he quoted the Bible, recited poetry, told some mountain stories, and lectured his colleagues on constitutional law, but it did no good. The ERA passed the Senate 84–8. In the long run, however, Ervin did help to kill the amendment. Many of the arguments he advanced during the floor debate found their way into anti-ERA propaganda, even though many of his more sensational charges—such as saying the amendment would mandate unisex bathrooms—were gross exaggerations.[58]

Ervin's growing distrust of Nixon was aggravated further by their disagreements over civil rights policy. In spite of the fact that both men had staked out similar positions during their 1968 campaigns against the quickening pace of school desegregation, against busing to achieve racial balance in the schools, and against the activist Supreme Court, Nixon's subsequent actions quickly disillusioned Ervin. The senator's hope that he would finally be able to look to the White House as an ally against civil rights was soon dashed by Nixon's policies.

Both Ervin and Nixon had reached out to angry white voters in 1968. Ervin, predictably, was emphatic and uncompromising in his opposition to the entire civil rights agenda, but Nixon was a bit more clever. He followed a "Southern Strategy" designed to attract the support of frustrated white southern Democrats. During a September campaign stop in Charlotte, Nixon endorsed the *Brown* ruling and the goal of desegregation, but then attacked virtually every effort of the federal government to achieve it. Nixon criticized HEW's practice of cutting off aid to schools that refused to integrate, labeled the practice of busing to achieve racial balance "useless," and promised that he would appoint only conservatives to the Supreme Court. Nixon's Southern Strategy successfully undercut support for George Wallace in the states of the upper South, such as North Carolina, and helped propel him into the White House.[59]

At first it appeared to Ervin that the newly elected president would honor his campaign rhetoric. Within a few days of taking office, the administration announced that it would grant an extension to five southern school districts that had failed to desegregate. In July, the White House abandoned the long-standing and effective policy of enforcing school integration through HEW funding cuts, and began to rely on lawsuits initiated by the Justice Department to bring pressure on noncomplying schools. This new policy conveniently shifted the anger of southern segregationists away from the Nixon administration and focused it instead on the federal courts. That August, for the first time in the modern civil rights era, lawyers from the Justice Department opposed their former NAACP allies and joined southern school officials to ask a federal court for a delay of a school desegregation deadline. Civil rights advocates were outraged. The Leadership Conference on Civil Rights (LCCR) warned that "the opponents of integrated schools are on the move again." The mood in the white South was markedly more upbeat. A headline in the *Miami Herald* proclaimed, "They're Whistlin' for Nixon in Dixie."[60]

One of the most heated civil rights debate in 1969 concerned the fate of the Voting Rights Act of 1965. This legislation, which the chairman of the U.S. Commission on Civil Rights had heralded as "the most effective civil rights measure ever enacted," was due to expire in August 1970. Civil rights advocates urged Congress simply to extend the act for an additional five years. Ervin, though, saw no good reason to continue a law which he perceived as "politically motivated and unconstitutional legislation designed to impose upon one section of the country onerous terms applicable to no other part." The Nixon administration took a middle position, recommending that the act—which had previously governed only the southern states with a history of racial discrimination—be nationalized. The Justice Department did not have the staff necessary to enforce a national voting rights act, so many civil rights advocates viewed the administration's proposal as a poorly disguised retreat.[61]

Ervin and the Nixon administration shared similar objectives in the debate over the future of the voting rights bill. The senator quietly informed the White House that while he hoped he did not have to vote in favor of their proposal, he would support it over any attempt to extend the present law. Working in tandem, the Nixon administration and Ervin tried, but failed, to weaken significantly the Voting Rights Act of 1970. After two sets of hearings before Ervin's Subcommittee on Constitutional Rights, and a protracted floor debate in which the Senate defeated a series of Ervin's amendments, Congress hammered out a compromise that retained the most significant aspects of the original legislation. Though he did not welcome defeat, Ervin must have appreciated the support of a more cooperative White House during the struggle.[62]

Ervin was even more satisfied with Nixon's attempts to rein in the Supreme Court. As candidates, both had criticized the liberal Warren Court for its judicial activism, aggressive promotion of desegregation, and alleged coddling of criminals. Nixon's choice of Warren E. Burger to be the next chief justice pleased Ervin, who wrote a friend that given Burger's record of acting more like a judge than a legislator, "the new Chief Justice will do what he can to reconvert the Supreme Court into a judicial body." The senator also supported Nixon's controversial Supreme Court nominations of two southerners, Clement F. Haynsworth Jr. and G. Harrold Carswell. Civil rights groups, labor unions, and their liberal allies blocked the nominations, but Ervin, like many in the South, appreciated Nixon's efforts. "There is reason to hope that the personnel of the Supreme Court is changing," Ervin wrote a colleague, "and that once again the Court may be controlled by judges who are willing to attribute to the words of the Constitution their obvious meaning."[63]

But the Supreme Court disappointed Ervin and Nixon by refusing the administration's request to delay school integration. A unanimous Court, including Chief Justice Burger, rejected Nixon's attempt to stall desegregation in thirty-three Mississippi school districts, and ordered an immediate end to the racially divided schools. In *Alexander v. Holmes County Board of Education*, the justices stated that the maintenance of segregated schools under "freedom of choice plans," or the pretense of "all deliberate speed," was no longer acceptable. The time for desegregation was "now."[64] Faced with this uncompromising judicial mandate, the Nixon administration set itself to integrating the southern school systems. Historians disagree over whether the lion's share of credit— or from Ervin's perspective, blame—should go to the courts, to the federal bureaucracy, or to President Nixon, but the statistics clearly show that the greatest progress toward desegregating the schools of the South occurred during Nixon's first term in office. The number of African American children attending all-black schools in the South fell from 68 percent in 1968 to 8 percent in 1972. Ervin and his southern colleagues had finally lost their long battle to delay racial integration. Ironically, their defeat came during the administration of the first president in a decade who held some sympathy for their cause.[65]

The Supreme Court handed Senator Ervin and President Nixon a second setback when, on 20 April 1971, it sanctioned busing to achieve school desegregation in *Swann v. Charlotte Mecklenburg Board of Education*. Ervin had entered an amicus curiae brief for the Classroom Teachers Association of the Charlotte-Mecklenburg Schools, and he was granted the opportunity to appear before the Court during the oral arguments. Ervin insisted that the color-blind logic of *Brown*—which he had only recently come to accept—forbade any government to bus students on the basis of their race. Nixon's Justice Department had also submitted a brief to the Court, but Ervin found it very unsatisfactory. "It is a weasel-worded brief," he wrote a constituent, "calculated to conceal rather than reveal any forthright position on the part of the Department of Justice. It did take a very weak stand against a quota system for assigning children to public schools on the basis of race, but said 'nary a mumbling word' against busing."[66]

Even before *Swann*, the Nixon administration's lack of support for Ervin's anti-busing initiatives in Congress had frustrated the senator. "During the year 1970, we have had eight votes in the U.S. Senate to find out whether the Nixon administration means what it says when it comes to neighborhood schools . . . [and] busing," Ervin complained. "But on each occasion the Nixon administration appeared to be on both sides of the question, and when it came to the votes Nixon was silent as a tomb on the subject." The senator repeatedly tried to shame the president into standing behind his promise to oppose busing by recalling the campaign speech Nixon had made in Charlotte during the election, but it did little good. "If there has ever been hypocrisy practiced on any issue," Ervin told a television interviewer, "it has been that of the Nixon Administration on the school issue."[67]

Even within the administration, some of Nixon's closest aides feared that their contradictory stand on busing was hurting him politically. Haldeman confided to Ehrlichman that "the fundamental problem with our position on busing is that it is not clearly perceived. . . . Nowhere is the gap between rhetoric and performance any clearer than in this area, and I would submit this one really fuels the credibility issue." Sensing the opportunity that was being lost by not taking advantage of such a hot issue, Haldeman argued that the administration's goal should be to "get our position clearly understood nationally" and then "exploit the hell out of it in key areas."[68]

While the Nixon administration struggled to clarify its position, Ervin's anti-busing crusade was gaining momentum. The senator garnered more support on the busing issue than he had during any civil rights fight for years. There appeared to be two reasons for the renewed popularity of his stand. First, the logic of Ervin's anti-busing argument was internally consistent. The senator had conveniently accepted the color-blind principle of *Brown* just in time to wield it as a weapon against the new color-conscious remedies to racial discrimination, such as busing, being proposed by civil rights advocates. Ervin could attack the busing of school children on the basis of their race as a violation of the antidiscriminatory *Brown* ruling, while chiding his opponents for contradicting themselves. He dusted off one of his favorite Aesop's fables to illustrate his point:

A man had lost his way in a wood one winter's night. As he was roaming about, a satyr came up to him and finding that he had lost his way, promised to give him a lodging for the night. As he went along to the satyr's cell, the man raised both his hands to his mouth, and kept blowing at them. "What do you do that for?" said the satyr. "My hands are numb with the cold," said the man, "and my breath warms them." After this they arrived at the satyr's home, and soon the satyr put a smoking dish of porridge before him. But when the man raised his spoon to his mouth, he began blowing upon it. "And what do you do that for?" asked the satyr. "The porridge is too hot and my breath will cool it," replied the man. "Out you go," said the satyr. "I will have naught to do with a man who can blow hot and cold with the same breath."

Ervin promptly added that civil rights advocates who contended on the one hand that the Constitution forbids discriminating against students on account of their race in assigning pupils to schools, but argued on the other hand that the Constitution obligates consideration of each student's race in order to bus them to schools to achieve a predetermined racial mix, were blowing hot and cold with the same breath.[69]

The fact that school desegregation was no longer just a southern problem provided the second reason Ervin enjoyed more support during the busing debates of the 1970s. As federal judges began to order northern school districts to develop desegregation plans, worried voters pressured their senators to protect them against busing. Ervin was quick to exploit this opportunity. He issued a warning to parents outside the South: "If you don't mind your child being bused for miles and miles in the busiest traffic of the day, then you don't have to worry about this problem. But if you believe, as I do, that the Federal Courts have no right to herd our children around like cattle, then you had better let your representative know how you feel, because it is going to happen where you live next."[70]

Some northern politicians who had been long-time supporters of civil rights abandoned their previous pro-busing positions and agreed with Ervin that court-ordered busing exceeded constitutional requirements. Senator Robert Griffin, a Republican from Michigan, even sponsored his own amendment to end busing just one year after delivering a speech on the Senate floor opposing one of Ervin's anti-busing amendments. When Ervin asked his colleague if he had at last seen the light, Griffin reportedly answered: "Yes, now that they've gored my ox just like you said they were going to."[71]

This shift in the political wind was not lost on the Nixon administration, especially after the 1972 presidential primary season commenced and George Wallace exploited the busing issue to win the Florida Democratic primary on 14 March 1972. Two days later, the president went on national television to propose that Congress adopt a moratorium on school busing. Nixon's moratorium notion, though, did not win the approval of either the Democratic-controlled Congress or the exasperated senior senator from North Carolina. Ervin attacked the administration's moratorium idea on the Senate floor, charging that it would only "continue the status quo" since it would apply only to future busing and not nullify the busing already begun in the South. "If it [busing] is wrong, it ought to be uprooted forever and thrown on the scrap heap of history," he shouted. "It ought to be ended once and forever."[72]

Ervin was even more outraged by Nixon's proposals to expand minority business opportunities. One of the most complex civil rights debates of Nixon's first term concerned whether or not the Equal Employment Opportunity Commission (EEOC) should be granted greater enforcement powers. Since the agency had been created in 1964, civil rights advocates had lobbied Congress to give the EEOC the ability to issue cease-and-desist orders to employers who failed to comply with federal equal opportunity standards. The White House disagreed, and so did Ervin. The thought of giving another agency in the executive branch quasi-judicial powers was anathema to the senator, given his understanding of the separation of powers doctrine. In true Ervin hyperbole, he described it as "a proposal to give to five bureaucrats, who are elected by nobody to do anything and who are responsible to nobody on the face of the earth, powers greater than those that the courts and the laws of the United States impose on the office of President." In 1971 Ervin and Senator James B. Allen of Alabama led a filibuster that blocked Senate passage of a bill based on the cease-and-desist model. But in the spring of 1972, the Nixon administration crafted a compromise measure that would enhance the EEOC's ability to take offending businesses to court. Once again, Ervin found himself in opposition to a civil rights proposal from Nixon.[73]

The debate over the EEOC in 1972 did little to enhance Ervin's reputation as a congressional leader. With the deaths of Richard Russell, who had masterfully commanded the Senate's southern bloc, and Everett Dirksen, who had skillfully played the role of the Senate's conservative power broker, it fell to Ervin to direct the attack against a stronger EEOC. He tried every trick in his old soft southern strategy book, but to no avail. The senator did not have enough votes to thwart the will of the majority, and he did not have the political skills of his predecessors. Hugh Davis Graham, who studied the congressional debates over the EEOC in detail, concluded: "The North Carolinian fired his blunderbuss early, often, and usually ineffectively. He tended to rush forward amendments that had not been thought through, amendments whose supporters had not been courted and counted in advance." According to Graham, Ervin "squandered his opportunities in the showdown on the Senate floor in 1972," which resulted in another civil rights victory for Nixon.[74]

The centerpiece of Nixon's program to promote economic justice for African Americans was the Philadelphia Plan—named after the city in which it was first implemented in September 1969. This plan required all federal contractors in the Philadelphia area to meet specific goals for hiring minority workers before bidding on any government project. The Philadelphia Plan represented a bold affirmative action program that stood in stark contrast to Nixon's Southern Strategy and early attempts to slow the pace of school desegregation. Bewildered civil rights supporters, as well as southern obstructionists such as Ervin, wondered why the Nixon White House would push forward such a progressive civil rights program. The president's defenders have suggested that it was consistent with his conservative belief that black capitalism held the best hope for achieving racial justice. Nixon's critics have pointed to the obvious political advantage the plan offered to split the liberal coalition by pitting the self-interest of African Americans against that of labor unions. As the president confided to his aides, "Make civil rights people take a stand—for labor or for [civil rights]." Or maybe Ehrlichman came closest to the truth when he explained to the president that "some non-conservative initiatives [have been] deliberately designed to furnish some zigs to go with our conservative zags."[75]

Whatever Nixon's motivation, Ervin had no intentions of letting the Philadelphia Plan go unchallenged. He quickly organized hearings to dissect the plan in his Separation of Powers Subcommittee. Throughout the two-day hearings in October 1969, the senator contended that the plan set unlawful racial "quotas," while administration officials maintained that it only required "a good faith effort" to meet minority hiring "goals." Ervin relentlessly criticized the distinction between a quota and a goal, suggesting that in actual practice they amounted to the same thing. The president's spokesmen countered that some numerical goals were needed in an affirmative action program to measure progress toward overcoming blatant racial discrimination. Ervin retorted that if they were correct, then it seemed to him that affirmative action meant nothing more than "reverse discrimination."[76]

Ervin contended, however, that the real issue behind the debate over the Philadelphia Plan was not civil rights, but the administration's violation of the separation of powers doctrine. According to Ervin, the Philadelphia Plan was "an invalid attempt by the secretary of labor to engage in legislation—not merely in an area where Congress has not spoken, but in an area where Congress has specifically prohibited the action which the Secretary desires to take." Ervin quoted the language of Title VII of the Civil Rights Act of 1964 that "nothing contained in this title shall be interpreted to require" employment on account of "race, color, religion, sex or national origin." "That says as plain as any language can that no person on account of race is to be given preferential treatment," Ervin argued. Since the administration had created the Philadelphia Plan, which obviously did grant such preferential treatment to blacks, the senator concluded that it represented "a blatant case of usurpation of the legislative function by the executive branch of the Government."[77]

Ervin's arguments helped convince the majority of his colleagues to view the issue as a contest between the legislative authority of Congress and an overreaching executive branch. In December 1969, the Senate passed a rider to a minor appropriations bill that cut off funding to any executive action that the comptroller general—who reported to Congress, not the president—held to be in violation of any federal statute. Comptroller General Elmer Staats had already ruled that the Philadelphia Plan violated the Civil Rights Act of 1964. Nixon's aides advised him that many in the House also saw the issue more as a question of separations of powers than of civil rights, and Attorney General Mitchell admitted that the rider did raise "grave constitutional questions." Unwilling to see his prized affirmative action program stripped of its funding, the president ordered an all-out lobbying effort. Intense White House pressure defeated the rider in the House, and it did not survive the conference committee. The Philadelphia Plan went forward, leaving a frustrated Ervin stewing in defeat.[78]

The separation of powers issue that had surfaced during the debate over the Philadelphia Plan, and to a lesser degree during the fight over granting the EEOC cease-and-desist power, quickly expanded into one of the most important themes in the escalating conflict between Ervin and Nixon. Just as disagreements over civil liberties and civil rights had driven a wedge between these two conservatives after the 1968 election, a series of constitutional battles over the separation of powers contributed to the growing rift as well.

It is tempting to dismiss Ervin's interest in the separation of powers doctrine as just another product of his soft southern strategy against civil rights. Certainly his argument that the liberals' plan to give the EEOC quasi-judicial powers violated the constitutional checks and balances system and his insistence that the Philadelphia Plan represented an illegitimate attempt by the executive branch to usurp the legislative power of Congress were reminiscent of the equally abstract and legalistic arguments he proposed against every civil rights bill introduced since 1957.

Yet to dismiss the senator's separation of powers rhetoric as nothing more than an insincere ploy to defeat civil rights legislation would be a mistake. Ervin's traditional southern constitutional philosophy—a product of the racist ideology of the white South that had dominated the region's thought for over two centuries—did indeed function to retard racial justice by limiting the power of the federal government. But there was more than racism behind Ervin's constitutional philosophy. He believed that three essential concepts in the American scheme of government kept its citizens free: constitutionalism, meaning that government activity must be limited to only what the law allows; federalism, which disperses power between the state and federal governments; and the separation of powers doctrine, which divides the federal government's powers among the judicial, executive, and legislative branches. To Ervin's way of thinking, these constitutional principles mandated a very small and very restricted government. Such a theory of limited government not only worked against an activist civil rights agenda, but could also operate to protect individual civil liberties against government tyranny, or to check judicial and presidential abuses of power.[79]

A careful review of Ervin's career, however, does suggest that his concern for preserving the separation of powers doctrine correlated most often to his concern for preserving the South's racial status quo. In 1956, immediately after helping to draft the Southern Manifesto against the Supreme Court's *Brown* ruling, Ervin called for a congressional investigation of judicial and executive encroachments on the power of the legislative branch. At a press conference to promote this investigation, Ervin not only complained about the Court's desegregation ruling, but also cited a recent incident where a confused administration representative admitted in a Senate hearing that he could recall no legal basis for the Civil Aeronautics Administration's new policy of withholding federal aid to airports with segregated facilities. Ervin argued that "it has reached the point where lawyers in the executive branch openly admit they have no law for some of their actions."[80] In 1957, when President Eisenhower sent federal troops to enforce the Court's desegregation order in Little Rock, Arkansas, Ervin bemoaned the "tragic day for constitutional government," when "the President of the United States ordered troops to invade a supposedly sovereign state to enforce the judicial usurpation by the use of bayonets." The Eisenhower administration further angered the senator when it refused to turn over information he requested about the Little Rock operation because "it would be incompatible with the public interest to disclose the contents of this document." The following year Ervin told a crowd in the Arkansas capital, "I have been appalled by a practice which the present administration adopted during the Army-McCarthy hearings and has pursued ever since, . . . of withholding from the American people information concerning what the executive branch of the government is doing." The senator began to participate in subcommittee hearings on executive privilege a few months later. Not all of Ervin's complaints about the executive branch's withholding of information related to civil rights. For instance, he denounced the Eisenhower administration's "tendency to cover up" executive agreements it feared might be unpopular. But the vast majority of the cases in which the senator raised the question of separation of powers in the 1950s concerned judicial or executive efforts to combat racial discrimination.[81]

Ervin's practice of couching civil rights debates in the rhetoric of executive or judicial usurpation of the legislative power of Congress continued throughout the 1960s. In 1962 Ervin questioned President Kennedy's authority to issue an executive order banning discrimination in federal housing because "such an order would simply constitute legislation." "Under the Constitution," Ervin explained, "all of the legislative power of the Federal government is vested in the Congress. None of it is vested in the President." In 1964 he denounced the Civil Rights Act as "the baldest attempt in the legislative annals of our country to transfer from the Congress to the President the law-making power of the Federal Government." In 1966 he vigorously protested "the abuse of power involved in the bureaucratic imposition of the [HEW] guidelines" to eliminate racial imbalance in the public schools. Of course, not a year went by in which Ervin did not condemn Supreme Court rulings designed to protect the rights of African Americans as outrageous examples of "judicial activism."[82]

From time to time, Ervin would repeat his suggestion that Congress should conduct a formal study of the separation of powers question. In 1966 he finally got his chance. Senate Minority Leader Everett Dirksen was worried about congressional power being diminished by an activist Supreme Court that had overstepped its bounds, especially when it ruled against school prayer, and by an ever-expanding executive branch that seemed to trespass into Congress's legislative domain almost daily. With Ervin's help, Dirksen convinced the Senate Judiciary Committee to create a new Subcommittee on Separation of Powers to "search for legislative proposals, where necessary, to restore the three branches to their proper Constitutional roles, and preclude encroachments by one branch upon the process and functions of another." The Senate leadership named Ervin as the chairman of the new subcommittee.[83]

Few of Washington's political pundits thought that the Subcommittee on Separation of Powers would amount to much. Several dismissed it as just another forum in which southern segregationists and conservative Republicans could bash the Supreme Court. For the most part, the subcommittee's early investigations into constitutional questions about the balance of federal power gained little notice on Capitol Hill or in the press. "At that time we just couldn't interest anybody in those issues," former chief counsel Paul L. Woodward remembered. But in a rare example of accurate journalistic prophesy, James K. Batten of the *Charlotte Observer* predicted that Senator Ervin "may be shaping history without fanfare." "American political history has been shaped more than once by events which began unobtrusively, without notice or fanfare," Batten observed. "The study may come to nothing, of course. But in this capital, where competition for power goes to the heart of the governing process, this is the sort of thing that could become very big indeed."[84]

By the time Nixon had been elected president, the Separation of Powers Subcommittee had already held public hearings on the role of the Supreme Court, as well as on the proper procedures for calling constitutional conventions. Ervin had also launched subcommittee investigations into constitutional questions such as whether presidents could sign executive agreements with foreign countries without congressional consent; the extent to which a president could impound funds appropriated by Congress; whether the National Labor Relations Board and other executive agencies had overstepped their statutory authority; and what should be done about the increasingly common practice of administrative departments justifying their withholding of information from Congress with a claim of "executive privilege." Each of these long-simmering separation of powers issues predated the Nixon administration, but they boiled over soon after Nixon entered the White House.[85]

Disagreements over the Philadelphia Plan initiated the debate between Ervin and the Nixon administration over the proper balance of power between the executive and legislative branches, but their first real showdown over a purely separation of powers issue came in December 1970, when the president attempted to pocket veto an act of Congress. The Family Practice of Medicine Act passed both the House and the Senate by overwhelming majorities and was presented to the president on 14 December. The Constitution allows a president ten days either to sign a bill or veto it. If Congress has adjourned, however, a president may pocket veto the measure since there would be no one on Capitol Hill to receive his veto and objections. On 22 December Congress went home for Christmas, but it followed the traditional practice of granting unanimous consent for the Secretary of the Senate to receive messages from the president during the recess. Ignoring Congress's preparations, Nixon declared that the Senate had "adjourned" when the ten-day signing period expired on

24 December, and that he would therefore exercise his right to pocket veto the bill. No president had ever done this before.[86]

When Congress returned from its Christmas vacation, Ervin held a press conference to explain why Nixon's action was unprecedented and unconstitutional. A group of perplexed reporters listened as the Senate's leading constitutional scholar patiently reviewed the subtleties of the issue. Ervin concluded his legal lecture by declaring that since the president could not pocket veto the Family Practice Act during a congressional recess, and since he had not signed it, the measure had actually become law. Ervin's conclusion was meaningless except as a clever debating strategy. Even if the majority of Ervin's colleagues would agree with his interpretation and declared the bill to be in force, Nixon could simply refuse to spend the money and thus compel a constitutional showdown with Congress. In 1970, few legislators were ready for such a direct confrontation.[87]

Ervin would not let the pocket veto issue fade away. He held hearings on the matter in January 1971, and drafted the Pocket Veto Act that defined "adjournment" to mean an adjournment *sine die*, at the end of a congressional session, and not during a weekend or a brief recess. Ervin's proposal did not pass, and the Family Practice Act died. Nixon had won round one. Ervin, however, sent the White House a message from the Senate floor: "There is no doubt in my mind that President Nixon violated the doctrine of separation of powers." And Ervin had a message for his colleagues as well: "I think this controversy boils down to a very simple question. Will the Congress demand that the Executive Branch of government respect its rights, duties, and obligations as set out by the Constitution?"[88]

Another separation of powers battle between Ervin and Nixon concerned the practice of impoundment, a term referring to a president's refusal to disburse funds appropriated by Congress. Impoundment was not a new concept. Ever since Thomas Jefferson declined to spend money that Congress had set aside for gunboats in 1803, presidents had occasionally delayed or deferred dispensing funds that Congress had authorized for a specific purpose. Under Nixon, however, impoundment grew to immense proportions. The Subcommittee on Separation of Powers began studying impoundment in 1968, but when Ervin discovered that the Nixon administration had impounded approximately $11.1 billion—a sum far greater than that withheld by any of Nixon's predecessors—he scheduled public hearings in March 1971.[89]

Ervin worried not only about the unprecedented amount of the Nixon administration's impoundments, but also about the type of programs the president targeted. Nixon did not limit his impoundments to military expenditures, where he could justify his actions as falling under his authority as the Commander in Chief, or to specific cases where unforeseen circumstances clearly suggested that a congressional mandate be reconsidered. Instead, Nixon employed impoundment as a tool to reject the expressed will of Congress. Such a "policy impoundment," as Hubert Humphrey called it, threatened to overturn the constitutional balance of power by circumventing Congress's power of the purse. Ervin protested that "under the present impoundment practice, the President has an item veto over acts of Congress. There is not a word in the Constitution giving such a power." Ervin further explained that "by impounding appropriated funds, the President is able to modify, reshape, or nullify completely laws passed by the Congress, thus making policy through Executive power, an exercise of his office which, as any elementary student of Government knows, flies directly in the face of constitutional principles."[90]

Ervin's hearings ended inconclusively, and Nixon went right on impounding funds. The president's impoundments would eventually exceed $15 billion and affect more than one hundred different programs. Ervin fought back by introducing the Impoundment Procedures Act, which required the president not only to inform Congress each time he failed to spend appropriated funds, but also to stop any such impoundment at the end of sixty days unless Congress specifically approved his decision. The measure passed the Senate but died in the House. Not yet ready to accept defeat, Ervin reintroduced his anti-impoundment proposal and continued his subcommittee's investigation with an eye toward reopening his hearings in the near future.[91]

A third item on Ervin's agenda for the Separation of Powers Subcommittee concerned executive privilege—the president's right to withhold information from Congress. Like impoundment, executive privilege had a long, turbulent history filled with presidential claims and congressional complaints. At the inception of the Subcommittee on Separation of Powers in 1967, Ervin had included the subject of executive privilege among the long list of constitutional questions he proposed to study. But widespread frustration within Congress at its inability to secure vital information from the Nixon administration prompted Ervin to call for public hearings in July 1971. The senator's timing was excellent. The controversy surrounding the administration's efforts to suppress publication of the Pentagon Papers broke just before Ervin opened the hearings, helping to highlight the issue of government secrecy and sharpen the focus on executive privilege.[92]

The hearings revealed the difficulty of defining exactly what constituted executive privilege. The Nixon administration had set out its policy on releasing information to Congress in a memorandum from the president dated 24 March 1969. Nixon expressed his desire to comply to the fullest extent possible with congressional requests, and he promised that executive privilege would only be exercised "in the most compelling circumstances and after a rigorous inquiry into the actual need for its exercise." The memorandum further stated that executive privilege would only be claimed "with specific Presidential approval." Two years later, during Ervin's hearings in 1971, administration representatives testified that, true to the spirit of his official policy, Nixon had evoked executive privilege on only a handful of occasions. Ervin, however, cited numerous cases in which the administration had not made a formal claim of executive privilege, but still prevented Congress from receiving the information it sought. Ervin, therefore, defined executive privilege far more broadly than did the Nixon administration: "As I use the term, it refers to the Executive branch's denial of any kind of information to any person, be he a member of the Congress or of the taxpaying public."[93]

Ervin seemed to follow a carrot-and-stick strategy to force concessions from the Nixon administration. Ervin offered a carrot when he conceded that the president must be able to withhold information that "would impede the performance of his constitutional responsibilities," and the senator expressed his hope that a thorough study of executive privilege "will afford the Executive and the Legislative Branches an opportunity to come together and find some common ground that will more clearly define the powers, duties, and prerogatives of the two branches in this sensitive area." But Ervin also threatened to wield a stick when he supported a bill sponsored by Senator J. William Fulbright of Arkansas that would require any federal official withholding information from Congress to produce a formal statement claiming executive privilege signed by the president. Ervin hinted at the dangers that lay ahead if the Nixon administration did not work toward a reasonable compromise with Congress on executive privilege by recalling Woodrow Wilson's observation that "warfare between the Legislative and Executive Branches can be fatal."[94]

The first serious skirmishes in what would indeed become an all-out war over executive privilege broke out early in 1972. Ervin warned the president's men that he had "had it" with their use of executive privilege when they refused to cooperate with his investigation into the Daniel Schorr incident that January. Ervin even threatened to subpoena any member of the president's staff who refused to appear before his subcommittee. Nixon called Ervin's bluff, however, and the aides did not testify. But a few months later it was Ervin who held the stronger hand. That April, the senator threatened to block the confirmation of Richard Kleindienst to replace John Mitchell as attorney general unless the White House reversed its claim of executive privilege and al-lowed Peter Flanigan, a presidential aide, to testify on the role Kleindienst had played in the International Telephone and Telegraph Corporation (ITT) affair. Allegations that the Justice Department had dropped antitrust charges against ITT in exchange for a $400,000 donation to the Republican Party had led to a congressional investigation, and Ervin wanted to ask Flanigan what he knew about it. According to notes of a White House meeting taken by Ehrlichman, Mitchell warned the president that "Ervin won't quit til [he] gets Fl[anigan,]" and he cautioned that to "fight it out" meant "probably forever." This time the president capitulated. But Ervin knew better than to read too much into his victory. He later explained that it was only because "we had a club to hold over the Administration's head" that Nixon retreated in the Flanigan case. Executive privilege remained a contested battleground.[95]

To Ervin, executive privilege represented yet another example of presiden-tial aggrandizement at the expense of Congress. Like the Philadelphia Plan, the misuse of the pocket veto, and impoundment, executive privilege demon-strated how "the increased power of the Executive branch has enabled it to make crucial decisions absent any system of formal 'accountability' for the exercise of such powers beyond the presidential election every four years." Ervin believed that "because the President had been able to act through Execu-tive orders without the inconvenience and restraint of congressional authori-zation or delegation of power, there had been a very serious erosion of the principle of the separation of government power."[96]

As the end of Nixon's first term approached, the pace of the expanding confrontation between Ervin and Nixon over the balance of power between the legislative and executive branches seemed to be escalating. The senator had set an agenda for his Separation of Powers Subcommittee before Nixon entered the White House, but the president's aggressive actions not only accelerated his timetable but also dramatized his issues by providing flesh-and-blood exam-ples to what had been dry and skeletal constitutional debates. Just as Nixon's threats to civil liberties had begun to set the agenda for Ervin's Subcommittee on Constitutional Rights, the president's expansion of executive power was forcing the senator to adjust his plans for the Subcommittee on Separation of Powers. Ervin was increasingly finding himself on the defensive.

In July 1971, the president presented Congress with a new challenge to its legislative authority when he issued an executive order expanding the activities of the Subversive Activities Control Board (SACB). As a congressman, Nixon had helped to create the Communist-hunting panel back in 1950 during the height of the McCarthy hysteria. In recent years the board had done very little,

'OPEN UP—IN THE NAME OF THE SENATE!'

During the Nixon administration Senator Ervin led the congressional counteroffensive against the expanding power of the executive branch. Editorial cartoon by Gibson M. Crockett, Washington Star-News, *1973. A copy is in the Sam Ervin Library and Museum, Western Piedmont Community College, Morganton, North Carolina. Copyright 1973, 1974, 1975* The Washington Post. *Reprinted with permission.*

and Wisconsin's William Proxmire had been leading a handful of senators who wanted to cut off its funding. Ervin was not among them. Presidential aide Tom Charles Huston, however, saw an opportunity to "regain the initiative on the issue of student violence" by reinvigorating the SACB and granting it broad new investigatory powers. The president agreed and quietly issued his executive order on 2 July.[97]

Congress learned about Nixon's new plans for the SACB when the board's chairman casually revealed the executive order during hearings before the Senate Appropriations Committee. The committee quickly invited Assistant Attorney General Robert Mardian to explain how the president could give the SACB powers Congress had never intended it to have. Mardian told the senators that the president had relied upon his "inherent" constitutional powers in reshaping the SACB. Committee member Roman Hruska, who also sat on Ervin's two subcommittees, whispered to his aide, "When Sam hears that he'll hit the ceiling." He did. Ervin complained: "We hear 'inherent power' all the time these days. 'Inherent power' is just the modern equivalent of the divine right of kings." After hastily convening hearings before the Separation of Powers Subcommittee, the senator proposed legislation to restrict the activities of the SACB.[98]

The Nixon administration had initiated yet another clash with Ervin in June 1971, when the Justice Department launched an attack on the "Speech or Debate" immunity of members of Congress. While the Supreme Court was trying to decide whether or not to allow the publication of the Pentagon Papers, Senator Mike Gravel of Alaska began to read excerpts from the controversial document aloud in a late night meeting of a Senate subcommittee. The Justice Department retaliated by subpoenaing one of Gravel's congressional aides in order to question him on how the senator acquired a copy of the supposedly top-secret papers. Ervin rushed to Gravel's aid, not so much to defend him personally but to protect the independence of Congress. Ervin characterized the administration's subpoena as "a direct and broadscale attack on the rights of all Senators, and upon the constitutional guarantees which have been established to protect the Congress from harassment by a vindictive Executive." Gravel sued to stop the subpoena, and the case reached the Supreme Court in 1972. Ervin represented the Senate during oral arguments. When the justices disagreed with Ervin and ruled that the Constitution did not immunize a legislator from proceedings involving possible crimes committed by a third party, Ervin blasted the decision as "a clear and present threat to the continued independence of Congress." He also began to draft a bill to reverse the Court's decision.[99]

By the end of Nixon's first term, Ervin had proposed legislation to counter every one of the president's challenges to congressional authority. There was a bill to prevent presidential abuse of the pocket veto, another to stop impoundment, a third dealing with executive privilege, a fourth designed to kill the SACB, and a fifth aimed at preserving congressional immunity. The senator's counteroffensive included foreign as well as domestic issues. Ervin believed that the congressional role in international affairs had been eroded by the White House's increased reliance on executive agreements—which Congress did not even have the power to review—in the place of formal treaties—which the Senate had to ratify. So, in 1972, he held hearings before the Separation of Powers Subcommittee on executive agreements, and offered a bill to reverse this trend as well.[100] By 1972 Ervin had become the recognized expert in Congress on all matters relating to what Arthur Schlesinger Jr. called Nixon's "imperial presidency." As Schlesinger concluded the following year, "The main author of the comprehensive congressional attack on presidential supremacy was, well before Watergate, Senator Sam Ervin of North Carolina."[101]

It was at this crucial moment in the struggle between Ervin and Nixon that fate intervened. Senator Allen Ellender of Louisiana suffered a heart attack and died on 27 July 1972. For the third time, the death of a senator had profoundly altered the course of Ervin's career. Just as Clyde Hoey's stroke in 1954 had led to Ervin's unexpected appointment to the Senate, and Thomas Hennings's untimely death in 1960 had suddenly propelled Ervin to the chairmanship of the Subcommittee on Constitutional Rights, Ellender's fatal heart attack set off a chain reaction of committee reassignments that led to Ervin's assuming the chair of the Government Operations Committee. It was Ervin's first opportunity at the helm of a full Senate committee. Never before had he wielded so much power.[102]

The Government Operations Committee had responsibility for the very issues that had generated many of the recent clashes between Ervin and Nixon. The Washington Post observed, "Senator Ervin's accession to this post is an unusually apt merger of personal concerns and committee jurisdiction. The senator from North Carolina, with his unique grasp of the Constitution, his country-lawyer eloquence, and his talented staff, has established himself as a champion of congressional prerogatives, a kind of de facto solicitor general for the legislative branch." Ervin could easily carry his agenda from the subcommittees on Constitutional Rights and Separation of Powers over to the Government Operations Committee, where he now had more power to push his bills though Congress. Within weeks he had scheduled new sets of hearings for early in 1973 on impoundment and executive privilege. The Post aptly concluded that the senator, "with his long list of grievances and proposed remedies, is now in the catbird seat."[103]

As the president considered the upcoming congressional term, he, too, began to prepare for a possible confrontation with Congress over the separation of powers. During meetings in the Oval Office, Nixon warned his aides that he would probably have to veto "15 bad bills," including congressional limits on "executive privilege" and "impoundment." The president suggested that his opponents would try to "wrap their cause in false clothing—attract support by framing a *false* issue—the Congress versus the President." Nixon believed that the American people were indifferent to such constitutional questions, but that they did care about the "same issues as in the campaign," such as "higher taxes" and "no inflation." "We must explain the *true* issues, put vetoes in [a] correct, simple, understandable context," Nixon told his staff, by attacking the Democrats' equation of "higher spending = higher prices + taxes."[104]

The president's men were soon carrying out their public relations offensive. Ehrlichman disseminated the new White House spin on all separation of powers issues throughout the White House, and he employed it himself during a press conference in which he skillfully shifted a question concerning impoundment into a discussion of avoiding taxes and balancing the budget. Ehrlichman also worked the president's line of defense into a letter he sent to Senator Charles Percy of Illinois: "I personally deplore efforts on the part of a few individuals in the Congress and in the press to drive a wedge between the Legislative and Executive branches of Government. I don't think that it is dictated by the issues which confront the country, nor by the natural desires of a majority of those in either branch. On the contrary, I think if jealousy of prerogatives and territorial imperative are permitted to enter into deliberation on the issues, we will get a bad result for the country."[105]

It was a clever strategy, and it might well have succeeded, had it not been for Watergate. Ervin's sensational Watergate hearings in the summer of 1973 put an end to Nixon's hope of avoiding a confrontation with Congress over the separation of powers. Instead, the hearings alerted the sleeping giant on Capitol Hill to the dangers of Nixon's imperial presidency. Slowly, with awkward, lumbering motions, Congress began to reassert itself. A year later Nixon resigned, and the national press heralded Sam Ervin as "the last of the founding fathers."[106]

Watergate did not occur in a historical vacuum. The specific context in which the Watergate hearings evolved had been shaped by three interrelated conflicts between Sam Ervin and the president that had begun soon after Richard Nixon entered the White House. Ervin's increasing concern for the administration's repeated threats to civil liberties, his growing distrust of the president's inconsistent civil rights policy, and his escalating opposition to Nixon's imperial presidency helped to determine the meaning and outcome of the Watergate scandal.

In hindsight, however, one of the early skirmishes between the senator and the Nixon administration is particularly important. No single episode foreshadowed Watergate more than the senator's investigation and hearings into the military's domestic intelligence system in 1970 and 1971. Sam Ervin's road to Watergate cannot be properly understood without a careful analysis of this pivotal event.

CHAPTER NINE

REHEARSAL FOR WATERGATE

"For the past four years, the U.S. Army has been closely watching civilian political activity within the United States." So charged Christopher H. Pyle, a former intelligence officer, in the January 1970 *Washington Monthly*. Pyle's account of Army spies snooping on law-abiding citizens and recording their actions in secret government computers sent a shudder through the nation's press. Images from George Orwell's *1984* of Big Brother and the thought police filled the newspapers. Public alarm prompted Senator Ervin's Subcommittee on Constitutional Rights to investigate. For more than a year, Ervin struggled against an Army cover-up to get to the bottom of the surveillance system. At last, frustrated by misleading statements, claims of inherent executive powers, and refusals to disclose information on the basis of national security interests, he called for public hearings to examine "the dangers the Army's program presents to the principles of the Constitution."[1]

Although he did not know it at the time, Senator Ervin had started down the road to Watergate. Of all the battles between Ervin and Nixon during the president's first term, this episode stands out as being especially significant. It was during the subcommittee's investigation of Army surveillance in 1970 that Ervin first encountered the actual issues that would lead him into the Watergate affair in 1973. The two incidents are strikingly similar. Ervin not only asked the same questions during both investigations, but he also followed the same strategies to get the answers. The Nixon administration learned from its experience in the Army spy scandal as well. During Watergate the president would call on many of the same staff members to repeat the same tactics they had developed three years earlier during the Army cover-up. Ironically, it was at the same time that Ervin began his investigation into the administration's domestic surveillance practices that Richard Nixon and his men began their own political espionage that put them, too, on the road to Watergate.

Ervin's Subcommittee on Constitutional Rights had been warning the country about the danger government computers and data banks posed to individual civil liberties since the mid-1960s, but it had not been able to produce enough public indignation to push the senator's legislative agenda through Congress. Then, one winter morning in 1969, Christopher Pyle walked into the subcommittee offices and told the surprised staff that the Army was spying on ordinary American citizens and storing illegal dossiers on their domestic political activity in its secret computers. Here was the break Ervin and his staff had been waiting for—a sensational example of the danger government surveillance and computers systems posed to the constitutional right to privacy. A few weeks later, Pyle's exposé in the *Washington Monthly* brought more media attention to the privacy issue than Ervin and his staff had been able to generate in years.

According to Pyle, the U.S. Army Intelligence Command for the Continental United States ("CONUS intelligence") included more than one thousand undercover agents operating in a nationwide system with more than three hundred offices. Agents sent their reports through a national teletype network to Fort Holabird, Maryland, where the Army kept its central computer. A staff of Army analysts filed these reports into a data bank that Pyle claimed "included descriptions of lawful political activities of civilians wholly unassociated with the military." Various publications came from this computer, including a booklet nicknamed the "Blacklist" that CONUS sent to commanding officers around the country to assist them in identifying "people who might cause trouble for the Army."[2]

Pyle reported that the military had greatly expanded the program far beyond its original purpose. He believed that the Pentagon activated the system in 1965 in order to gather logistical information for the Army's use during civil disturbances. But the increasing number of riots in the late 1960s and the military's insatiable desire for intelligence resulted in Army agents spying on all types of political activity. "Today, the Army maintains files on the membership, ideology, programs, and practices of virtually every activist political group in the country," Pyle charged, ". . . including such nonviolent groups as the Southern Christian Leadership Conference, Clergy and Laymen United Against the War in Vietnam, the American Civil Liberties Union, Women Strike for Peace, and the National Association for the Advancement of Colored People."[3]

Pyle's predictions for the future were equally alarming. "If the Army's fascination with the collection of domestic intelligence continues to grow as it has in the recent past," he cautioned, "the Intelligence Command could use military funds to develop one of the largest domestic intelligence operations outside the Communist world." Pyle's greatest fear, however, stemmed from the traditional American suspicion of unchecked power. He pointed out that neither Congress nor the courts had provided sufficient checks on the CONUS system. In several cases, intelligence officers had even kept the Army's civilian leaders in the dark. This lack of oversight led Pyle to warn that someday unscrupulous men might gain control of the government's growing domestic surveillance system and use it as "a weapon to be wielded against their personal and political foes"—a prophetic remark.[4]

Although Pyle succeeded in bringing the secret CONUS program to the public's attention, he left many apprehensive Americans wanting to know more, including Sam Ervin.[5] The senator joined more than a dozen other congressmen from both political parties in ordering the Army to issue "an immediate explanation." From the floor of the Senate Ervin declared, "Clearly, the Army has no business operating data banks for surveillance of private citizens; nor do they have any business in domestic politics." He went on to question the constitutionality of an "ever-curious" executive branch secretly watching and maintaining files on law-abiding Americans. He called the Army's surveillance program "a violation of the First Amendment rights of our entire nation."[6]

Instead of answering Ervin's concerns, the Army chose to cover up. Army General Counsel Robert E. Jordan III froze all responses to congressional inquiries. Agents received orders to gather only "essential elements of information" and not to discuss the CONUS operation with any civilian. Behind the scenes, intelligence officers at Fort Holabird removed from the files the embarrassing items to which Pyle had referred in his article. Officers also telephoned agents across the country telling them to hide, but not destroy, incriminating files until the controversy blew over. To organize its response to the crisis, the Pentagon formed a "task group" that met in the "Domestic War Room" deep in the basement of the Pentagon. As one member of the group later recalled: "[We] proceeded from the start to deny any and all charges, factual or otherwise."[7]

The military intelligence bureaucracy fought back tenaciously against members of Congress, reporters, or any other American citizen who wanted to know more about the Army's highly questionable domestic surveillance system. In the name of defending democracy and freedom, the officers in charge of the secret national security program acted in a manner more consistent with totalitarian regimes. In order to cover up the excesses of their domestic spying, CONUS commanders throughout the country began to replace all their newer agents with older career soldiers to prevent more disclosures. Intelligence units received orders "to just hide it, get it out of the way, this will all blow over." At some bases they destroyed the data but kept the "input" (the computer keypunch cards), or copied the information onto microfilm before destroying it. As one clerk later recalled, "The order didn't say to destroy the information, just destroy the Compendium [a computer data bank]." Typical were the actions of the officers in the 116th Military Intelligence Group at Fort McNair in Washington, D.C., who classified all their files and threatened that anyone disclosing anything about their domestic surveillance would be court-martialed or prosecuted in civilian court "for violation of national security."[8]

The Army supplemented its cover-up by employing a public relations strategy of justifications, limited confessions, and promises to sin no more. First, the Army defended the CONUS system by claiming to need information on potential civil disorders so that it could protect its facilities and carry out its responsibility to back up local authorities during domestic riots. Then General Counsel Jordan wrote to Ervin admitting that in the past the Army had operated a computer data bank "with names and descriptions of individuals who might be involved in civil disturbance situations," a polite way to describe the "blacklist." But Jordan assured the senator that after a recent review the Army had determined this information to be beyond its "mission requirements," and he declared that "all copies of the identification list have been ordered withdrawn and destroyed." He also guaranteed that "no computer data bank on civil disturbance information is being maintained." Apparently, Jordan hoped that by terminating CONUS's most objectionable practices, and presenting a more contrite attitude, he could appease the Army's congressional critics while reserving the Army's autonomy over its domestic intelligence system.[9]

At first, the Army's outrageous cover-up succeeded. As fresh news events crowded into the public's attention during the spring of 1970, and other issues demanded more of Congress's time, the pressure on the Army faded. Nixon's invasion of Cambodia, the massive protests against this extension of the Vietnam War, and the shootings at Kent State pushed the Army scandal off the newspapers' front pages. Eventually, only Ervin and the staff of his Subcommittee on Constitutional Rights, which now included Christopher Pyle as a special consultant, were pursuing the issue of the Army's domestic spying. In a manner that anticipated the Watergate story, a cover-up based on justifications, limited confessions, and solemn promises almost succeeded in killing any interest in the scandal. But as would also happen with Watergate, a few investigative reporters kept digging for new leads, and Ervin persisted in his conservative crusade to protect the constitutional right to privacy from what he considered to be the ever-growing danger of an activist federal government.

As he continued his battle against the Army's cover-up, Ervin began to grow suspicious about the actions and motives of the Nixon administration itself. The senator had not seen a direct connection between the Nixon White House and the Army's intelligence abuses when Pyle first broke the story in January 1970. It seemed clear that the military intelligence apparatus had grown out of control during the Johnson years, and there seemed no reason to suppose that the present Republican administration had anything to fear from a full disclosure of the facts. The first hint that the Nixon administration might be more directly involved came when Robert Jordan vaguely implied in his February letter to Congress that the Army might transfer the responsibility for gathering intelligence on civil disturbances to the Justice Department. Ervin was frustrated in his attempts to learn more about the proposal. The administration's lack of cooperation troubled him, especially in light of the president's recent moves against individual rights in so many other areas.[10]

Ervin's apprehension increased in April when key officials in the White House told the *New York Times* that the president, fearing the rising tide of bombings and violent anti-war demonstrations, wanted to expand the Justice Department's domestic surveillance responsibilities. The plan included stepping up the use of informers, undercover agents, and wiretaps in order to monitor militant left-wing groups and individuals. There was little doubt that real danger did exist. The American Insurance Association reported in May 1970 that riots and civil disorders in 1969 resulted in more than $31 million worth of property damage in the United States. A survey conducted by the FBI of 776 bombing and arson attacks during the period from 1 September 1968 to 15 March 1970 revealed total property damages of nearly $24 million. Eleven deaths were directly attributable to these incidents, six of them being self-inflicted through premature or accidental explosion. In a single two-week period in March 1970, the New York City Police Department recorded more than 2,200 separate bomb scares. The Nixon administration cited these and other troubling statistics to argue that the government must increase its ability to keep track of dangerous radicals and subversives. One Nixon aide dismissed the concern Ervin and others had been raising about the threat to civil liberties posed by domestic spying as a "hangup in the question of snooping," and he argued that "the greatest safeguard to the rights of individuals is to have good information on what the [radical fringes] are doing."[11]

Attorney General John Mitchell provided the legal basis for the increased domestic surveillance soon afterward. According to his spokesman, the administration had the right to collect and store information on civilian political activity because of "the inherent powers of the federal government to protect the internal security of the nation. We feel that's our job." Thus, the administration claimed a virtually unchecked power—not subject to congressional oversight—to carry out unlimited domestic surveillance on anyone it wished.[12]

On 23 June Ervin received even more bad news when the Army announced its new policies on domestic surveillance. At first glance the document seemed encouraging, but on further inspection the exceptions, qualifications, and loopholes led Ervin to conclude that the lack of clear criteria in the policy "could lead the average citizen—which I consider myself—to wonder just how much of a change it represents in government policy."[13] Ervin did find one very significant change in the Army's letter: it had indeed transferred a major section of the conus program to the Justice Department. The new statement of policy explained, "The Department of the Army relies upon the Department of Justice at the national level to furnish civil disturbance threat information required to support planning throughout the Army for military civil disturbance needs." To Ervin, this move represented a serious threat to civil liberties, especially in light of the Nixon administration's recent statements proposing an escalation of domestic surveillance. The senator did not object to the Justice Department carrying out its responsibility to keep tabs on suspected criminals. What concerned Ervin was his growing suspicion that this administration might not be content to operate within legal limits and constitutional constraints. Ervin responded to the Army's letter by expanding his committee's investigation to include all of the Justice Department's intelligence-related programs. He soon discovered that the attorney general was even less cooperative than the officials in the Defense Department had been.[14]

Ervin had no idea how close he was to stumbling onto the formative stages of the Watergate scandal. Behind the scenes the Nixon administration had already begun its unprecedented illegal efforts to turn the government's various espionage agencies into weapons the president could wield against those he perceived to be his enemies. In February 1970, just a few weeks after Ervin had begun his investigation into the Army's domestic intelligence system, Tom Charles Huston proposed a secret plan to Nixon that appears to represent a turning point in the administration's undercover activities.

Frustrated by the unwillingness of the fbi, cia, military intelligence, and other government agencies to expand their domestic spying as fast as the administration desired, Huston urged the president to centralize the command of all domestic intelligence activities into one secret interagency office in the White House. The ambitious aide wanted to wrestle control of the government's domestic surveillance apparatus away from what he considered to be overcautious bureaucrats and put it in the hands of Nixon's own men who would be more responsive to the president's wishes. Huston suggested that the administration could then launch a series of highly sensitive and controversial actions such as opening the sealed mail of American citizens, increasing undercover campus agents, more secret wiretaps, surreptitious entry of private dwellings, and expanding the Army's domestic counterintelligence mission— though even Huston worried about the domestic use of military intelligence agents. Basically, what came to be known as the Huston Plan proposed that the White House coordinate a covert operation by the entire government intelligence community to stifle dissent and stop protest by any means necessary, legal or not.[15]

On 5 June 1970, Nixon called the heads of the major intelligence agencies to the Oval Office and urged them to cooperate in developing the new domestic intelligence campaign Huston had suggested. Over the next few weeks Huston and representatives from each of the intelligence branches hammered out the details at the CIA's headquarters in Langley, Virginia, where they could maintain maximum secrecy. Huston presented their formal report to the president on 25 June. Nixon approved the plan, but instead of signing his own name the president wisely instructed Huston to issue the new directives under his own signature—thus protecting himself from any embarrassment should the illegal document ever become public. The official memorandum of 23 July carried only Huston's name, but CIA Director Richard Helms later observed that the whole scheme was "basically Richard Nixon's doing, and he called it the Huston Plan."[16]

Just a few days later Nixon changed his mind. FBI director J. Edgar Hoover had been leery of the Huston Plan from its inception, correctly assuming that it represented the president's desire to push him aside and gain control of the Bureau. Hoover surprised Nixon by strenuously objecting to the illegal surveillance, wiretapping, and letter-opening practices mentioned in the plan. He also argued that it was unconstitutional for military intelligence operatives to spy on domestic political activity. Fearing Hoover's power, and knowing that the wily FBI director could easily destroy the whole operation by leaking it to the press or to Congress, Nixon rescinded the Huston Plan on 28 July 1970.[17]

But the story does not end there. The administration officially abandoned the plan but then unofficially implemented many of its measures in various forms over the next few years. William Sullivan, a high-ranking FBI official who worked closely with Huston, later asserted that revoking the Huston Plan not only resulted in the creation of the secret White House Special Investigative

Unit—nicknamed "the Plumbers"—but to many other unauthorized activities as well. Although Huston later denied that his proposals led to Watergate, he admitted that if Hoover had gone along with his plan the administration would never have had to do its own "black-bag jobs." For instance, Nixon was to claim that he created the Plumbers unit only to plug leaks of information from his administration to the press, but, in fact, it carried out break-ins and wiretaps similar to those Huston had encouraged. Eventually, of course, members of the Plumbers unit would be arrested during their fateful attempt to bug the Democratic National Committee headquarters in the Watergate office building in June 1972.[18]

It is certainly ironic that during the same months in the spring of 1970 that Ervin began trying to restrict the administration's domestic spying, Huston and Nixon began trying to expand it. Of course at that time Ervin could not have imagined the scope of the Huston Plan nor the depth of the president's growing paranoia toward his critics. But he had begun to suspect that the Nixon administration's lack of support for his investigation into the Army's CONUS system was somehow connected to its own domestic surveillance plans. What had started as a conflict between Ervin and the Army over the CONUS intelligence system was about to escalate into an all-out battle for public opinion between Ervin and the Nixon White House over the government's constitutional power to spy on the American people.[19]

Sam Ervin marched into the Senate on 29 July 1970, prepared to renew and expand his crusade against the Army's domestic intelligence system. Rising to address his colleagues, Ervin reviewed the events of the past few months—the shocking revelations of the military's domestic spying, the dishonesty of government officials, and the Defense Department's cover-up and half-hearted reforms—and he blasted the Army for maintaining "a deterrent power over the individual rights of American citizens." But the senator aimed his verbal assault not only at the Pentagon but toward the White House as well. His speech linked the military's domestic spying with other surveillance practices in the Nixon administration. He charged that the Army's intelligence data-banks "appeared to be part of a vast network of intelligence-oriented systems which are being developed willy-nilly throughout the land, . . . [representing] a potential for political control and intimidation which is alien to a society of free men."[20]

To combat this danger Ervin announced that his Subcommittee on Constitutional Rights would hold hearings on "Federal Data Banks, Computers, and the Bill of Rights." The senator planned to include the sensational issue of military domestic spying in his larger crusade for privacy and use the hearings as a means of generating public pressure against both the Army and the president. Ervin elaborated in his autobiography: "Some of the evils I opposed were substantially alleviated when they were exposed to public view in committee hearings and on the Senate floor. After all, sunlight is a powerful purifier."[21]

After his announcement, both Ervin and the Nixon administration followed new tactics to gain the best possible position in the upcoming hearings. Ervin and his allies faced the struggle of prying information out of an uncooperative executive branch while trying to rouse public indignation against the administration's domestic spying. The president's men countered by maintaining their cover-up while launching a publicity campaign of their own. Because Ervin's hearings would take the form of a political drama performed before the national media, the primary goal of both strategies became winning the battle for public opinion.

Not everyone agrees that Ervin deliberately attempted to manipulate public opinion through his committee hearings. Some of Ervin's admirers argue that he was innocent of the ways of the press. Former staff member Rufus Edmisten maintains that "not one time in his career did he ever say 'have you contacted the press?' or 'have you got it arranged?' That meant little to him, he didn't care. . . . He knew of course that what went on in those hearings had to get out some way, but he left that totally to us and never mentioned it." His old-fashioned political style also convinced many of Ervin's fans that he cared little about media attention. They point out that even though he knew that success on modern-day television news programs depended on tightly packaged arguments and a slick stage presence, Ervin stubbornly held to an antiquated rhetorical style.[22]

But the contention that Ervin ignored the power of the press rests too heavily on the popular stereotype of the senator as a simple country lawyer—a stereotype he enjoyed and cultivated.[23] His long, rambling stories may not have fit into a thirty-second spot on the nightly news, but his folksy and sincere image played well in committee hearings when contrasted with the behavior of the well-rehearsed bureaucrats who defended the administration. Lawrence Baskir, who worked closely with Ervin as chief counsel to the Subcommittee on Constitutional Rights during the Army investigation, stated the issue clearly: "A person like Ervin is either naive . . . and eventually lucky that fate and time make it all work very well, or he is so subtle and so sophisticated that it looks like it is all happening without him." Baskir sheds some light on this question by placing the senator in the role that most of his staff have suggested is the best way to understand him: "Ervin knew how to appeal to the jury. He was a trial lawyer, you understand. But [as a senator] the jury had now become 99 other members and the whole country, or the press corps, and he knew how to play to them."[24]

Sam Ervin may have been described as a "country lawyer" and a "good ol' boy," but to southerners these labels suggest political acumen, not naivete. Ervin was well aware that he would have to attract and sustain the press's attention if he wanted to focus sunlight on the Nixon administration. His actions before and during the hearings were carefully planned to manipulate public opinion, and he cleverly kept the sensational issue of the Army's domestic spying at the center of his larger crusade to persuade the Nixon administration to respect the right of privacy.

Ervin's frequent appearances in the media led the press to portray him as the leader of the political coalition opposing the Army's domestic spying. Once reporters discovered—or rediscovered—that Ervin's folksy sayings made good copy, they increasingly turned to him as the chief spokesman for those who criticized the administration's domestic political surveillance. In addition, Ervin's definition of the issue as a matter of privacy seemed to offer the best explanation for what was holding the various factions of the coalition together.

Here is a vivid example of the old truism that "politics makes strange bedfellows." Ervin, the conservative southerner, was joined by opponents of the Vietnam War, liberal congressmen, investigative reporters, and Democrats in general looking for an opportunity to give President Nixon a political black eye. But Ervin's most unusual partner was the American Civil Liberties Union. Senator Ervin and the ACLU had been on opposite sides of the political battlefield for over a decade. They had sparred over civil rights legislation, the *Miranda* ruling, the legitimacy of opposition to the draft, and a host of other issues. But the military's domestic intelligence system provided a common enemy that brought Ervin and the ACLU together on libertarian ground.

The ACLU provided valuable assistance to Ervin in his effort to frame a constitutional argument against the Army's domestic spying. Earlier in the year the ACLU convinced Arlo Tatum, who had learned from Pyle's article that CONUS agents had watched and recorded his peaceful political speech in Oklahoma, to become the chief plaintiff in its suit against Secretary of Defense Melvin Laird and others. Besides wanting to prove that the Army spies had exceeded their legally prescribed limits, Tatum and the ACLU hoped to establish that the very existence of a military domestic intelligence system violated the First Amendment because of the "chilling effect" it had on legal political activity. They argued that if citizens knew the Army was recording their actions in a government data bank they might be deterred from exercising their constitutional rights.[25]

The ACLU filed suit in Federal District Court in Washington, D.C., in April 1970. Suspecting that the Army's cover-up might lead to the destruction of evidence, and seeing an opportunity to force the CONUS system into the open, the ACLU lawyers requested a preliminary injunction ordering the Army to stop its destruction of the domestic intelligence files and deliver them to the court. The Army countered by asking that the case be dismissed because there was no evidence of anyone's constitutional rights being violated. The judge in the case, George L. Hart Jr., a graduate of Virginia Military Institute and a troop commander in World War II, showed little patience with the ACLU's arguments and refused its request. When the ACLU lawyer asked to present a witness who had infiltrated a church youth group as a spy for the Army, the judge refused to hear testimony and scoffed: "Did they have a sign saying No Military Personnel Admitted?" After a brief hearing, he rejected the legitimacy of the chilling effect doctrine and dismissed the case. The ACLU announced it would appeal.[26]

Ervin regarded the ACLU's fight in the courts as an important accompaniment to his investigation of the Army's political surveillance. Though he hoped his upcoming hearings would embarrass the Army into curtailing its domestic spying, he realized that the pressure of public opinion was only of temporary value. The ACLU's suit, on the other hand, might end the Army's domestic surveillance by culminating in a Supreme Court decision declaring the surveillance unconstitutional. But the path through the federal judiciary would be long and slow. In the winter of 1970–71, Ervin's public hearings offered the quickest way to halt the Army's spying.

As the date for the hearings approached, the furor over the Army's domestic spying had become so great that even President Nixon felt compelled to offer a public denial. He issued a statement claiming he "totally, completely and unequivocally opposes spying by the military on American political officials." Press secretary Ron Ziegler added, "It is absolutely not going on in any way at this time." He assured the country that the president did not condone domestic spying and did not think it should be done in the future. Behind the scenes, however, Nixon had a markedly different response. Upon reading of one former military operative's confessions the next morning in his news summary, he wrote a curt note to Chief of Staff H. R. Haldeman: "I thought this was handled! Let him have it."[27]

The Nixon administration had no intention of surrendering the battlefield of public opinion to Ervin, and it fought back with its own public relations counteroffensive. But unlike Ervin, who stressed First Amendment freedoms to build support, the president's men appealed to those conservatives who cared more about protecting law and order from Communism than preserving civil liberties for hippies and radicals. The senator's attacks on the Army for violating constitutional rights were answered by the urgent claim that the nation was in grave danger from internal subversion and needed to build up its national security.

The White House had been employing the national security argument as a justification for strengthening the government's domestic surveillance powers since Nixon's first year in office. It was the rationale that Nixon had used to defend his "law and order" program, including the D.C. crime bill, and that Attorney General Mitchell had employed to sustain his claim that he possessed an inherent power to wiretap anyone he deemed a threat to the nation's safety. The national security argument also had become the primary justification for the administration's effort to consolidate the government's intelligence agencies. Mitchell had promised to build a network of computer link-ups between all the federal and state law enforcement agencies in the country, and he had created several new agencies in 1970 to achieve his goal. Later, during Watergate, Nixon would attempt to hide his administration's abuse of its surveillance powers under this same national security blanket.[28]

The administration supported its public relations campaign with several concrete actions in January 1971. Any Cold War patriot who feared that the administration would cut back its domestic surveillance activities because of the embarrassment it suffered over the Army's spy scandal must have taken heart at the Justice Department's announcement that it was expanding its Internal Security Division. The new head of the agency, Robert Mardian, praised by the right wing as a "hard-liner," announced he would move decisively to counter "New Left subversion." John Mitchell also reinforced the administration's continuing commitment to national security by rejuvenating the moribund Subversive Activities Control Board and naming two new organizations to its list of suspected Communist fronts. That same month, the Justice Department charged Father Daniel Berrigan and several nuns with conspiring to blow up the steam pipes below the White House and kidnap Secretary of State Henry Kissinger. The indictment, which resulted from FBI wiretaps, was heralded by the White House as proof of the left wing's dangerous activities and as a vindication of domestic surveillance practices.[29]

Law and order advocates around the country echoed the administration's cry for national security and defended the Army's domestic intelligence operation as an absolute necessity in the war to protect freedom. "The United States is engaged in a global struggle," wrote James Burnham in the *National Review*, "with decisive victory or even more decisive defeat at stake. This struggle, not some possible conflict that might start at some moment of the future, is our century's World War III." Francis J. McNamara, past staff director of the House Committee on Un-American Activities, echoed the theme of immediate danger in *Human Events*: "Subversive elements dedicated to disrupting and destroying this nation are continually recruiting and training new members. The orderly participant in one demonstration can be a violent provoker in another one tomorrow." McNamara argued that since the Army might be called into a riot situation, "it has a continuing obligation to gather as much information as possible on actual and potential provocateurs." *Army* magazine summed up the military's position: "When called on to preserve peace you must know who threatens it."[30]

The administration accompanied its national security rhetoric with specific moves designed to convince the public that the Army's domestic spying had been brought under control. On 23 December 1970, Secretary of Defense Laird announced a major reorganization of the intelligence system: "I want to be certain that Department of Defense intelligence and counter-intelligence activities are completely consistent with constitutional rights, all other legal provisions, and national security." Laird announced, among other changes, that in the future all intelligence agencies would report directly to him, and he assigned Assistant Secretary of Defense Robert F. Froehlke to review all relevant policies. Laird also explained that henceforth Froehlke and Chief Counsel J. Fred Buzhardt would serve as the Defense Department's primary spokesmen on the issue of domestic intelligence.[31]

Laird's announcement appeared to represent a serious attempt by the administration to protect civil liberties, but he had actually taken a step away from a real reform of military domestic intelligence. His reorganization weakened the position of Robert Jordan and the other civilian officials in the Army who had been struggling to restrict domestic surveillance since they discovered it growing out of control during the last years of the Johnson administration. By letting Froehlke and Buzhardt speak for the Defense Department, Laird also reduced the role Jordan and his fellow reformers played in directing the military's defense against Ervin's investigation. The overall effect of the reorganization was to centralize the control of the military's intelligence system in the hands of Nixon's appointees in Laird's office.[32]

Ervin returned to the floor of the Senate on 8 February for his last attempt to influence public opinion before the hearings. He again defined the basic issue in the hearings as one of privacy and explained that the subcommittee would "look to the way the power of government will be exercised over the individual in decades to come." To set the tone for what he hoped would be a serious drama of revelation, the senator employed his most emphatic rhetorical style. In language surely aimed at the press corps he warned that "unless we take command now of the new technology [for political surveillance] . . . 'liberty' will sound only as a word in our history books, the lamented dream of our Founding Fathers."[33]

Back in January 1970, when Christopher Pyle first revealed the military's CONUS system, Ervin had thought it would be just one more battle in his conservative crusade for civil liberties. He had hoped that the Army spy scandal would be the sensational issue he needed to draw the public's attention to the government's ongoing threat to the right to privacy. But after the Army's initial cover-up, the Defense and Justice Department's extended cover-ups, and then the administration's full-scale public relations campaign, Ervin's investigation had become much more significant—it had escalated into a direct confrontation between the senator and the White House. Almost accidentally, Sam Ervin, the conservative southern segregationist and hawk on Vietnam, had become the chief spokesman for the liberal coalition opposed to Nixon's burgeoning domestic surveillance systems. North Carolina's ol' country lawyer was poised to open public hearings that would challenge the executive branch's domestic intelligence policies for the first time since the Cold War began.[34]

Ervin had wisely chosen the Old Senate Caucus Chamber as the arena for his confrontation with the administration. It was a room filled with history. The Teapot Dome inquiry, the Army-McCarthy hearings, and other scandalous dramas of the past had been acted out there. Its Corinthian pillars, high chandeliers, and marble walls provided just the backdrop Ervin wanted for his investigation of the military's domestic spying. The senator would return to this same setting two years later to stage his Watergate investigation.[35]

Since early in the morning of 23 February 1971, television crews had been setting up their equipment and reporters had been jockeying for places at the press table. By ten o'clock the room was ablaze in white light and spectators filled the public gallery. Sam Ervin's hearings on "Federal Data Banks, Computers and the Bill of Rights" promised to be good political theater. The senator had challenged the Nixon administration to a public debate over one of the central questions of the American political experience—how to balance the constitutional rights of the individual with the national security needs of the state.

When Ervin entered the chamber that morning and took his seat at the committee table, reporters clicked on their tape recorders and the television cameras zoomed in. Sitting there in the blinding light Ervin must have felt a sense of victory. Finally he had attracted the media attention he had lacked during all his previous hearings on the right to privacy. Finally his warnings about the danger of unchecked executive power would be heard by a national audience. Some observers detected a triumphant gleam in the senator's eye.[36]

One of the traditional high points of a congressional hearing is the chairman's opening statement, and Ervin was well aware of the significance of the moment. Since his priority for the hearings was to highlight the issue of privacy, he began by attacking the government's expanding "information power" that threatened civil liberties. "These hearings were called," he declared, "because Americans in every walk of life are concerned about the growth of government and private records on individuals. . . . They are concerned that they are constantly being intimidated, coerced, or pressured into revealing information to the wrong people, for the wrong purpose, at the wrong time."[37]

Then, playing to the crowd and the cameras, Ervin lifted a heavy, leather-bound Bible and explained: "This particular family Bible weighs eleven pounds. Contrast it to this piece of microfilm, two by two inches, which contains on it 1,245 pages of a Bible, with all 773,346 words of it. This means a reproduction of 62,500 to one." Ervin paused briefly before continuing. "Someone remarked that this meant the Constitution could be reduced to the size of a pinhead. I said I thought maybe that was what they had done with it in the Executive Branch because some of those officials could not see it with their naked eyes." The audience laughed, the senator smiled, and the television cameras captured it all.[38]

Having established privacy as his main theme, Ervin went on to define the major issues of the hearings. He condemned the government's increasing desire to computerize its files without providing adequate safeguards, warned of the inadequacy of congressional controls over those computer banks, and attacked "the curtains of secrecy and evasion" behind which the executive branch hid information from the Congress and the American people. Referring directly to the Army's domestic spying, he delivered the most frequently quoted line from the hearings: "When people fear surveillance, whether it exists or not, when they grow afraid to speak their minds and hearts freely to their government or to anyone else, then we shall cease to be a free society."[39]

When Ervin chose to fight the Army's domestic surveillance system by holding public hearings, he was drawing a powerful weapon from the congressional arsenal, but it depended upon the cooperation of the news media for its effectiveness. If issues raised in hearings were sensational enough to sustain media interest, then the subcommittee's power would be enhanced tremendously. But if hearings failed to catch the public's attention, they would often fall short. The Army-McCarthy and Watergate hearings are outstanding examples of how collaboration between a congressional committee and the media can shape public opinion. As these examples suggest, public hearings are strongest when they uncover corruption or expose wrongdoing. Ervin intended his hearings on "Federal Data Banks, Computers, and the Bill of Rights" to offer the same kind of dramatic revelations.[40]

To Ervin's delight, journalists filled the newspapers and airwaves with reports taken from the hearings of the military's domestic surveillance abuses. He had scheduled several days for Christopher Pyle and other intelligence officers to share their stories. While many of the specific episodes had been reported in the months leading up to the hearings, the former agents' testimony made a compelling case for an intelligence system running wild. In Colorado Springs, the Army infiltrated a church youth group because its leader had once attended a peaceful protest against the Vietnam War. In Kansas City, Army agents requested that the local high schools and colleges supply the names of students who were considered "potential trouble makers" and "too far left or too far right in their political leanings." It appeared that classroom statements by students and teachers were filed in police and Army data banks. Among the "dangerous" individuals in the CONUS files were Coretta Scott King, State Representative Julian Bond of Georgia, folk singer Arlo Guthrie, and two former military officers who had opposed the Vietnam War.[41]

Some of the Keystone Kops surveillance was almost as humorous as it was unsettling. One agent reported that he had been assigned to keep an eye on Martin Luther King's funeral for signs of violence and Communist infiltration. He was also instructed to photograph the dignitaries in attendance and dutifully file the pictures at Fort Holabird. When Mrs. King made a speech recalling that her husband "had a dream," an Army analyst asked the reporting agent to find out to which dream she was referring. Other revelations, however, were more disturbing. Plainclothes military intelligence agents worked undercover at both the Democratic and Republican National Conventions in 1968 and sent secret reports back to Fort Holabird. The Army had also spied on elected officials, "targeting" for surveillance critics of the Vietnam War such as Senator Adlai Stevenson III and Congressman Abner Mikva, both of Illinois. Judge Otto Kerner, the former Illinois governor and chairman of the Kerner Commission that investigated the race riots of the 1960s, became a subject for military surveillance after the commission report had concluded that there was no Communist conspiracy behind the urban violence in the 1960s. It became increasingly clear that the Army was guilty of practicing purely political surveillance on American citizens whose actions and statements could in no way be construed as likely to incite a riot or endanger national security.[42]

"THAT'S NAVAL INTELLIGENCE, SENATOR. ARMY INTELLIGENCE IS UP THERE."

Editorial cartoon by Bill Mauldin, Chicago Sun-Times, 1970. A copy is in the Sam Ervin Library and Museum, Western Piedmont Community College, Morganton, North Carolina. Copyright 1971 Bill Mauldin. Courtesy of the Mauldin Estate.

The ranking Republican on the subcommittee, Senator Roman L. Hruska from Nebraska, led the administration's defense during the hearings. After listening to several days of testimony detailing the Army's misuse of its computer-based surveillance system, Senator Hruska interrupted to ask, "But is this so new? When printing was invented, it was thought to be a radical new propaganda device. But it hasn't been such a terrible step forward in the development of civilization. The same might be said for computerized data banks.... I think on balance they may be very beneficial." Hruska argued that the administration's computer systems were both well-managed and necessary. He referred to "increases in skyjackings," "organized crime," and "the recent rash of dynamiting," and he chided Ervin and the subcommittee by concluding, "I know you wouldn't want to impair the ability nor the efficiency and effectiveness of anyone who wants to investigate a dynamiting."[43]

The battle lines of the debate became clear as Hruska and Ervin sparred over the issues for the next half an hour. Hruska argued that increased threats to national security mandated the computerized surveillance, and he proposed that Americans trust the self-restraint of the executive branch. Ervin countered that the government's recording of citizens' political statements in computers had a chilling effect on their exercising their First Amendment rights, and he insisted that recent surveillance abuses proved that the executive branch could not be trusted to police itself. It was the classic debate between national security and civil liberties, between the needs of the state and the rights of the individual.

The following week an unknown terrorist detonated a bomb in the rotunda of the Capitol building. No one was hurt and the damage was minimal, but when the hearings resumed on 2 March 1971, the day after the explosion, the atmosphere in the Old Senate Caucus Room was quite different. Extremely tight security greeted the spectators as they entered the hearing room. Capitol police inspected briefcases and double-checked press passes.[44]

Senator Hruska took full advantage of the new climate in his opening remarks. "I am somewhat disturbed by the imbalance of the testimony presented last week," Hruska complained, "and the interpretation which has been placed upon it by certain segments of the media and of the public.... I support the Chairman and others in the notion that there must be proper safeguards, but the people must receive every protection possible against those elements who consider even the United States Capitol Building as a legitimate object of their violence." Hruska argued that no one would ever know how many potential dangers were deterred by the Army's surveillance, and he reminded the audience that "burning buildings, bomb explosions, and mob violence also have their own chilling effect."[45]

The Nebraska senator concluded his remarks by recognizing for the first time what had long been an obvious element in the hearings, partisan politics. He pointed out that it was the Johnson administration that had initiated the growth in the military's domestic spying, and he subtly reminded the subcommittee that the initiative for increasing domestic intelligence had come from the Democrats' own Kerner Commission. Responding to Hruska's statement, Democratic senator Birch Bayh of Indiana, who was attending the hearings for the first time, stated: "I think this issue has to be taken out of the political arena. It is a matter that ought to be carefully studied regardless of one's political affiliation." But Ervin's investigation of the Army's domestic spying had included some partisan motivations from the start. Chief of Staff Baskir later explained: "As many blows as we could take against the administration in the context of everything else we were doing was ok [to Ervin]. After all, we were Democrats. . . . [But] there was quite a bit of discomfort in the early part of the investigation as we started taking shots at the administration . . . when they would protest 'We didn't do this, it was the Democrats who did it.' "[46]

Senator Ervin probably did not harbor much concern about his hearings embarrassing the Democratic Party or damaging the legacy of the Johnson administration. He certainly had not refrained from attacking President Johnson in the 1960s when they disagreed over civil liberties, Medicare, consumer protection, and especially civil rights. These hearings were neither the first nor the last time that Ervin would take both the Republicans and his fellow Democrats to task for endangering the right of privacy. To Ervin, some issues were more important than partisan politics.[47]

Luckily for Ervin and the Democrats, the Nixon administration had adopted the Army's program as its own. As Baskir explained, "Even though they were not responsible for the program, they took responsibility for it. They defended it, they justified it, they tried to cover it up, and it was not too long before it was their program and not just an inherited program. . . . They wanted to do a whole lot more."[48] As Nixon's law and order and national security agendas emerged during his first term, Ervin found more and more issues that united his partisan impulses with his philosophical crusade for privacy. The Army spy scandal had become one of those issues. Senator Hruska and the administration could claim that Ervin was only playing partisan politics, and they could suggest that the Army's intelligence abuses were all caused by the Democrats, but they knew better.

Undeterred by Hruska's criticisms, Ervin continued the hearings, making headlines that afternoon by blasting the Army for maintaining an "illegal" surveillance system that threatened ordinary citizens' First Amendment rights.

Ervin also rejected the idea that the executive branch had learned its lesson and could now be trusted to respect civil liberties. If anything, he thought that the Nixon administration had demonstrated a consistent lack of respect for the Constitution. Even after the bombing, Ervin refused to accept the arguments that Americans should surrender their basic constitutional rights or alter the traditional balance of power between Congress and the president in exchange for the government's dubious promise of greater security.[49]

Across town, the Defense Department's Task Force continued to operate in the basement of the Pentagon. More than thirty agents were monitoring the hearings and preparing the Army's defense. The Task Force was disturbed by all of the public exposure, but one statement in Christopher Pyle's testimony caused special alarm. In a brief comment, overlooked by most observers, Pyle had mentioned the Van Deman files.

When Col. Ralph H. Van Deman retired from his job as the Army's chief intelligence officer in 1929, he began collecting information on supposed subversives in the United States. With the help of a large network of supporters, and with the unofficial assistance of his friends in the government, he amassed more than 120,000 files before his death in 1952. The files had been lurking behind the scenes in Washington politics for years. Rumors suggested that they had been consulted by Senator Joseph McCarthy and by the House Committee on Un-American Activities. These dossiers may also have been the source for the information Richard Nixon used to red-bait Jerry Voorhis during his campaign for the House in 1946.[50] Pyle had come across some evidence indicating that these folders had become part of the Army's intelligence collection at Fort Holabird. During his testimony he said, "I think that it would be very interesting for this subcommittee to find out what happened to Colonel Van Deman's files."[51]

The possible exposure of the Van Deman files called for quick action by the Pentagon Task Force. The Army had indeed received the files, in 1968, and it wished to avoid the embarrassment of having to admit it before Ervin's subcommittee. Fred Buzhardt, now the Nixon administration lawyer in charge of the Army's defense, arranged for the dossiers to be transferred to Senator James O. Eastland's Subcommittee on Internal Security. Eastland was also the chairman of the Judiciary Committee, the parent committee over Ervin's Subcommittee on Constitutional Rights. By sending the files to Eastland, Buzhardt accomplished two goals: First, if he was asked about the files during his appearance before Ervin's subcommittee, he could deny that the Army had them; second, he could also send a subtle reminder to Ervin that Eastland was not entirely supportive of his attack on the government's internal security establishment. On the morning that Buzhardt and Assistant Secretary of Defense Robert Froehlke arrived to testify before Ervin's subcommittee, the trucks carrying the Van Deman files were being unloaded at Eastland's office.[52]

Froehlke began his testimony by asking if he could read his prepared statement in its entirety. It was eighty-four pages long. Reading the complete text would discourage questions by the senators and kill the theatrical atmosphere Ervin needed to sustain the media's interest. But without hesitation Ervin granted Froehlke's request, and the assistant secretary began a two and a half hour recitation. Ervin the judge had won out over Ervin the showman. Two years later, the senator followed the same practice when he allowed all the witnesses in the Watergate hearings to read their full statements, no matter how long. "We will play by the rules," the senator said privately, "even if they don't."[53]

In his statement Froehlke admitted that the Army had let its program grow out of control. He confirmed the accusation that files had been kept on both Senator Stevenson and Representative Mikva, and he verified most of the other agents' testimony as well. The only major charge he denied was that the Army had spied on the Democratic and Republican conventions in 1968, but he did not directly refute the evidence demonstrating the presence of undercover military agents.[54]

Froehlke suggested that the "culprit" behind the unprecedented growth of domestic military surveillance was the Civil Disturbance and Information Collection Plan issued in May of 1968 by the Johnson administration.[55] This plan implied that "external subversive forces" were behind most domestic protests. It also warned that "a true insurgency" might take place if the media and "dangerous subversive elements" like the NAACP, the ACLU, and student anti-war protesters were not watched carefully. Froehlke pointed out that the plan had been rescinded on 9 June 1970. Ervin interrupted to wonder how Froehlke could talk about the plan in public since the Defense Department had refused his requests to have it declassified. It was declassified by the end of the day.[56]

The long-awaited confrontation between Ervin and the Army took place that afternoon. The senator began his cross-examination by questioning Froehlke and Buzhardt on the legality of the Army's domestic surveillance. Ervin, playing his ol' country lawyer role, tried to maneuver the slick bureaucrats into a corner. He presented example after example from the former agents' previous testimony which implied that domestic military intelligence had a chilling effect on constitutional rights. Froehlke and Buzhardt were forced to hide behind the basic thesis of their defense: "We don't think there

REHEARSAL FOR WATERGATE

was any violation of the First Amendment. . . . We maintain that there was no illegal activity. We maintain there was [only] inappropriate activity."[57]

No matter how hard the senator pushed he could not get the Pentagon's representatives to concede that the CONUS program inhibited civilians' constitutional rights. The following exchange is typical:

ERVIN: For example, do you think it was legal and constitutional activity for Army intelligence agents . . . in large numbers to attend a student rally [outside Fort Carson, Colorado] and have five or six helicopters flying overhead taking photographs, do you think that is something that is sanctioned by the First Amendment?

FROEHLKE: I don't think it makes much sense from the management point of view.

BUZHARDT: . . . I will say in general that direct agent observation, merely watching somebody, does not appear to me to violate any constitutional rights of the individual observed.

ERVIN: Doesn't it have a tendency to deter a person from exercising his constitutional right to participate?

BUZHARDT: Mr. Chairman, I would not be prepared to say that it did unless there was some specific evidence that someone was deterred. If it was unknown, then the man would not know it, so it could hardly deter his activities.

ERVIN: They would know there were five helicopters flying above them, wouldn't they?

BUZHARDT: As I said, I don't know in that particular case precisely.

ERVIN: I will be perfectly frank. If I had five helicopters flying over my head and I had gone out to make a speech on a subject . . . I think it would deter my freedom of speech very much for the Army to have five helicopters flying over my head and to have 53 agents, law enforcement officers, and press there watching me talk to a crowd of people that didn't number more than 70, when you count only the demonstrators.

FROEHLKE: If the facts are as you allege, I think we will all agree at the very minimum that it was inappropriate.

Both sides clung stubbornly to their arguments, but by the end of the afternoon Ervin appeared to have won the debate. Although Froehlke and Buzhardt never conceded that the Army's domestic spying was illegal or unconstitutional, Ervin had backed them into a defensive position. His vivid examples, such as his reference to the helicopters at the Fort Carson rally, tended to discredit their argument that military domestic intelligence did not deter the exercise of constitutional rights. The reaction of the press also indicated that Ervin had prevailed. The *Washington Post* titled its front-page story "Ervin Views Army Spying as Illegal" and editorialized that the hearings represented "a fine example of how useful a Congressional investigating body can be in exposing and exploring a public problem."[58]

Ervin wanted to take advantage of the press coverage that the Army spy scandal had generated to lead the committee into a public survey of the administration's other data banks and computer systems. His primary goal for the hearings had always been to use the sensational military spying case to draw attention to his larger crusade for privacy. Spokesmen from HEW, the Transportation Department, and other administrative agencies discussed their computerized files before the subcommittee during the week that followed the Army's appearance.

But Ervin was most anxious to learn about the data banks in the Justice Department. The Nixon administration had dodged most of the senator's inquiries thus far, and he had experienced great difficulty finding out what the White House meant when it announced that the Department of Defense's responsibility for domestic surveillance had been transferred to the Internal Security Division of the Department of Justice. Ervin wanted to know if the attorney general had established any controls over his intelligence computers in order to protect the right of privacy. He also wanted to challenge the constitutionality of the administration's swelling domestic intelligence system. The legal battle between Senator Ervin and President Nixon's Department of Justice promised to be as explosive as his confrontation with the Department of Defense had been.

On Tuesday afternoon, 9 March, Assistant Attorney General William H. Rehnquist presented the Justice Department's prepared statement. Once again, reporters filled the press tables and spectators crowded into the public gallery. Like the Pentagon's spokesmen the week before, Rehnquist received Ervin's permission to read his entire statement to the subcommittee. After a brief review of the legal basis upon which the administration based its investigative power, Rehnquist explained that "the responsibility of the executive branch for the execution of the law extends not merely to the prosecution of crime, but to the prevention of it." He admitted that isolated examples of the abuse of government power had occurred, but he reminded the subcommittee that "the courts have been reluctant, and properly so, to enter upon the supervision of the Executive's information-gathering activities." Echoing the Army's argument, Rehnquist stated that though these abuses were regrettable, they did not represent an infringement of any individual's constitutional rights. Still, he pledged that the Justice Department would take all appropriate steps to prevent any further mistakes from occurring. Rehnquist concluded by promising that "self-discipline on the part of the Executive branch [would] provide an answer to virtually all of the legitimate complaints against excesses of information gathering."[59]

Senator Ervin did not like what he heard. The old southern constitutionalist could find little comfort in the suggestion that executive self-discipline was sufficient to prevent abuses of government power. Even more disturbing to the senator was Rehnquist's reiteration of the argument that the Army's domestic surveillance did not represent a violation of constitutional rights. Since one of Ervin's primary goals for the hearings was to prove that some types of government surveillance resulted in a chilling effect that was unconstitutional, he could not let Rehnquist's statement go unchallenged.

Ervin's first question to Rehnquist drove right to the heart of the issue: "Do you feel that there are any serious constitutional problems with respect to collecting data on or keeping under surveillance persons who are merely exercising their right of peaceful assembly or petition to redress grievance?" Rehnquist shot back: "My answer to your question is, no, Mr. Chairman," and the debate was underway. But just as Ervin began to build his case, he was called to the floor of the Senate for a vote. The confrontation was rescheduled for the following Wednesday, 17 March.[60]

When Ervin and Rehnquist once again faced each other across the witness table, the senator immediately refocused the discussion on the chilling effect doctrine. Ervin asked: "Do you not concede that government could very effectively stifle the exercise of the First Amendment freedoms by placing people who exercise those freedoms under surveillance?" Rehnquist answered that though it was possible that the Army's domestic surveillance might have had such a collateral effect, the knowledge of that program in the 1960s had not deterred 200,000 people from coming to Washington to protest against the Vietnam War. Ervin countered with his own favorite example, the episode at Fort Carson, and for the second time in the hearings he conjured up the image of military helicopters intimidating peaceful demonstrators by hovering over their heads. Again he asked if that was not a violation of constitutional rights, and again Rehnquist replied that it was not.[61]

The legal debate went back and forth with Ervin growing more and more agitated. Finally, his eyebrows twitching and his face contorted in an angry scowl, the senator demanded: "Well, it is certainly to be deplored in a free society to have people spied on, isn't it?" Rehnquist, much more in control of his emotions, answered: "I fully agree. But Senator, if one were to say that any sort of governmental conduct that might remotely have a chilling effect, if one might use that word, on associational activities is a violation of the Constitution, we would tremendously expand that doctrine beyond its present state of development."[62]

Rehnquist had struck the main chord of the debate. Ervin and his allies wanted to establish the legitimacy of the chilling effect doctrine and apply it as a constitutional check against government surveillance; the Nixon administration did not. No matter how well Ervin's hearings illuminated danger to the Constitution inherent in government domestic surveillance, the administration's spokesmen could claim that the courts had not yet declared that the mere gathering of information, no matter how aggressive, was a violation of the First Amendment. Although Ervin continued to badger Rehnquist for over an hour, the debate had passed its peak. The issue of whether the administration's domestic surveillance practices were constitutional would not be resolved in Ervin's hearings but in the courts, where *Laird v. Tatum* was still pending. Ervin and the Nixon administration had reached a stalemate.

Once again, the press sided with Ervin in his confrontation with the administration. The *Washington Post* chided Rehnquist for his lack of cooperation and agreed with Ervin that executive self-discipline was not a sufficient protection against possible abuses of privacy. Other newspapers were even more critical. Tom Wicker of the *New York Times* said Rehnquist's self-discipline argument was similar to "asking a goat to guard a cabbage patch," and other editorialists described it as "audacious" and "ludicrous." The *Albany Times-Union* called Rehnquist's statement that government surveillance of law-abiding citizens was not prohibited by the Constitution "an insult to the millions of Americans who are listed in the dossiers of federal agencies."[63]

But even as Ervin won another round in the battle for public opinion, he lost his fight to continue the hearings. When he adjourned the subcommittee after the Justice Department's testimony that Wednesday afternoon, he still hoped to coerce Defense Department officials into returning for a second showdown, this time with the actual generals who had overseen the domestic intelligence accompanying them. He was also considering recalling the Justice Department's spokesmen. But he had run out of time. A host of other issues demanded his attention, and the press was losing interest. Ervin encountered other complications as well. Froehlke and Buzhardt stubbornly refused to allow the generals to testify, and they became increasingly uncooperative as the threat of their reappearing before the subcommittee diminished with each passing week. Furthermore, to reconvene the hearings without new sensational

stories of government abuses would accomplish little, and no such information had surfaced. Thus, Ervin's hearings, which had opened with much fanfare, ended without a dramatic closing scene.[64]

Although this indecisive ending made it difficult for the news media to offer
an overall summary of the hearings, several magazines and newspapers did run
wrap-ups over the next few weeks. As had been the case throughout Ervin's
investigation, the reaction in the press was positive. *Time*'s response was typical, suggesting that though the hearings produced no clear-cut plans for re-
medial legislation, "they did accomplish the aim of the subcommittee chairman, North Carolina Senator Sam J. Ervin, by dramatizing the difficulty of
preserving privacy in a world drifting toward 1984."[65] But the liberal journals
that had supported Ervin's crusade against the Army's domestic spying from
the start expressed disappointment that more had not been accomplished. The
New Republic complained that in spite of the many questions that had not been
answered, "the story has faded away." Likewise, the *Progressive* lamented that
the hearings "provided a depressing demonstration of how difficult it is, even
in a relatively open society, to impose restraints on a government contemptu-
ous of the rights of its citizens."[66]

Voices inside the subcommittee echoed the frustrations expressed in the
liberal journals. Christopher Pyle believed that the Army had won the confrontation because Froehlke still claimed that under certain circumstances the
military might once again conduct domestic intelligence.[67] "The hearings," he
said, "began with a bang and ended with a fizzle." Another staff member
criticized Ervin for being too easy on the Army: "Ervin hasn't kept the Army's
feet to the fire enough. Sure he held hearings and issued reports but he didn't
really force the issue. He could have but he didn't." Apparently Senator Edward
Kennedy agreed with this assessment of Ervin's performance, because he attempted, unsuccessfully, to wrest control of the hearings away from Ervin and
continue them in his own Administration Practices Subcommittee.[68]

Conservatives, too, complained about the hearings, but for the opposite
reason; they thought Ervin had pushed his investigation too far. *Human Affairs*
began its editorial by praising Ervin: "It is impossible not to share Sen. Sam
Ervin's concern over the proliferation of anti-privacy devices, data-banks,
computer-dictated credit ratings, Big Brother surveillance of ordinary citizens,
and so on." But the magazine then explained why the senator was wrong:
"What too many critics of these distasteful activities overlook is the fact that
this country is facing at least a para-revolutionary situation, and that we need
to know more about the backgrounds and activities of the activists."[69] Once
again, conservatives justified domestic surveillance by stressing the need for

national security. One of Ervin's constituents echoed the administration's arguments in a letter she sent him: "If one has nothing to hide, why object to the files? We need someone to find out what is going on in our country. It seems that those who would destroy our freedom must not have their rights denied in any way. But those of us who have worked hard for our living and tried to serve our country have no rights at all. Let's root out our enemies of our Democracy, wherever and whoever they may be."[70]

While liberals criticized Ervin for not going far enough and conservatives criticized him for going too far, the majority of Americans appeared to support the senator. The praise heaped on Ervin and his hearings in the mainstream media was one indication of his broad base of support. Ervin's staff estimated that 95 percent of the editorials written about the hearings were favorable. The public also demonstrated its approval by sending thousands of letters to the subcommittee from across the country commending the senator for his investigation. In spite of the fact that he had failed to get through prohibitive legislation, or establish the chilling effect doctrine, Ervin had succeeded in raising the public's concern about the threat unrestricted government surveillance posed to the right of privacy.[71]

Once born, the issue of government surveillance took on a life of its own. Less than a week after Ervin adjourned his hearings, two startling events coincided to set off another furious debate between the administration and its critics. First, on 21 March, several members of the House and Senate charged that the Justice Department had tapped their office telephones. These accusations could not be substantiated, but some congressmen, including House Majority Leader Hale Boggs of Louisiana, blamed the FBI and called for Hoover's resignation.[72] Then, a few days later, several newspapers mysteriously received copies of classified FBI files in the mail. A secret organization, calling itself "The Citizens Commission to Investigate the FBI," had broken into the Bureau's offices in Media, Pennsylvania, on 8 March and stolen the embarrassing documents from the FBI's confidential files. Attorney General Mitchell warned that publishing the Media papers would endanger national security, but once in print all that the documents endangered was the FBI's credibility.[73]

The stolen papers revealed for the first time the FBI's widespread domestic intelligence practices aimed at containing dissent within the United States. The Bureau had gone far beyond the Army's mere political spying; it had created disruption programs to thwart the legal political activities of various domestic organizations for at least fifteen years.[74] The vast majority of the FBI's targets were liberal. According to one analysis of the Media documents, only two of the political surveillance cases involved right-wing groups, ten concerned immigrants, and over two hundred dealt with left or liberal groups.[75] Though some of the FBI's projects seemed perfectly legitimate—for example, the infiltration of violence-prone organizations such as the Black Panthers—others appeared to amount to nothing more than political harassment of the government's critics, especially opponents of the war in Vietnam.[76]

Now that yet another government agency, the FBI, had been caught spying on the legal political activities of American citizens, debates over the proper balance between individual freedom and national security filled the newspapers. Many of the questions Ervin had raised about the Army's domestic intelligence were now being asked about the FBI in particular and the Nixon administration in general. The danger of unrestricted domestic surveillance, which Ervin's hearings first brought to the public's attention, had become one of the most important continuing issues on the national agenda during the spring of 1971, more than a year before the Watergate break-in.

Ervin received numerous invitations to lead a full congressional investigation of the FBI. Several senators and staff members on Ervin's Subcommittee on Constitutional Rights urged him to expand the earlier hearings to include the Bureau's political surveillance.[77] The Washington Post went even further when it joined the New York Times and several members of Congress in calling for a select Senate committee to discover the extent to which the FBI was "invading the privacy of Americans for the sake of protecting them from themselves." The Post suggested that "the outstanding senator to head a thoroughgoing investigation of the FBI—of the whole range of domestic intelligence and criminal investigating activity by the federal government—is, in our judgment, Sam Ervin of North Carolina. Tough, fair-minded and with a profound commitment to American constitutional liberties, Senator Ervin has pioneered in the study of incursions into privacy. It would offer reassurance to the whole country if he would now indicate a willingness to take on this difficult and important assignment."[78]

But Ervin demurred. He resisted efforts within his subcommittee to launch a full probe of the FBI, and he expressed no interest in heading a special congressional investigation. Ervin did write Attorney General Mitchell to request "documents involving surveillance guidelines, criteria for intelligence gathering and specific information on FBI activities in this field," but his effort was half-hearted and soon abandoned. It was one thing to challenge the domestic surveillance practices of the Army, which had no business spying on the political activity of American citizens, but quite another thing to question the FBI, which carried the primary responsibility for protecting the United States from the Communist threat.[79]

Ervin admitted that the FBI "may need some ethical refurbishing," but he explained that "the Bureau had been given legal responsibilities for investigating a great range of federal criminal laws, many of them vaguely worded. These include all of our espionage and security laws. . . . The investigative power of the Federal law enforcement officers should perhaps be better defined in writing, [but] that is not the same as saying that they have been acting illegally."[80]

Ervin and his apologists provided other excuses for his decision to stay out of the FBI scandal. Among them is their insistence that the senator was so over-committed to his other projects, such as his participation in the Supreme Court's *Swann v. Charlotte Mecklenburg* busing case and his upcoming hearings on the president's controversial practice of impounding funds, that he simply could not find the time to launch a new major investigation in the spring of 1971. Also, some members of his staff claimed that Ervin feared antagonizing Judiciary Committee chairman James Eastland, who might cut off Ervin's civil libertarian crusades in his Constitutional Rights Subcommittee.[81]

But there is another, simpler possibility. Perhaps Ervin's civil libertarianism had its limits. It may be that the senator's Cold War sensibilities, his long-held respect for the Bureau, and his personal admiration for J. Edgar Hoover kept him from attacking the FBI for its obvious civil liberties abuses. Whatever the reason, Ervin did not join the public fray over the FBI's political spying.[82]

He did, however, remain active in the fight to prove the legitimacy of the chilling effect doctrine. Robbed of his public platform by the abrupt end to the hearings, Ervin continued to present his case through a series of speeches he delivered in the summer of 1971.[83] "The Administration officials argue that there is no proof of the 'chilling effect' of these [surveillance] programs on First Amendment freedoms," he explained. "That is the most self-serving argument possible. How do you prove that people have been intimidated? You cannot, until it is too late."[84]

The senator told his audiences that the chilling effect was clearly demonstrated by a letter he had received during his hearings that spring. The author of the letter described how after the Kent State shootings in 1970 he had written Nixon to complain about the president's lack of compassion. The only response he received was a few mimeographed pages defending the war in Vietnam. In anger he had scribbled some rude notes in the margin of the copied pages, stuffed the whole thing in an envelope, addressed it to the White House, and stamped it. But then he paused: "Frankly, I wondered if it would be wise, if it would be prudent, if it would be safe to send it. I am a writer, Senator, and I wondered if sending my critical comments might not land me on some list or other that could be used against me in the future. Whether or not I did send the letter is really not the point. Surely that moment when I paused with that envelope in my hand must rank as one of the small deaths of the American spirit." Ervin concluded his speeches by suggesting that "this letter is the best answer I can give to the executive branch in response to their arguments about the constitutionality of Army surveillance over law-abiding Americans."[85]

Because Ervin still believed that the most promising means of preventing abuses of the government's domestic intelligence systems was to win a decision in the Supreme Court, he began to shift his efforts away from trying to renew the hearings and toward assisting the ACLU with the *Laird v. Tatum* case. So convinced was Ervin of the need for the Court to find the Army's domestic surveillance unconstitutional that he took time out of his busy schedule in the spring of 1972 to deliver an amicus brief to the justices calling the military's domestic spying a "cancer on the body politic."[86]

Ervin was shocked when the Supreme Court threw out *Laird v. Tatum* that June. The justices ruled that a supposed chilling effect did not demonstrate a justifiable claim to invoke the Court's jurisdiction. They did not decide whether the Army's domestic spying actually caused a chilling effect, nor whether that chilling effect was unconstitutional. The Court only ruled that a citizen could not sue the government on the basis of the abstract chilling effect doctrine alone. Thus, the Burger Court invoked the doctrine of "standing to sue" to avoid having to weigh the constitutional claims of the victims of Army surveillance against the Nixon administration's defense of national security.[87]

The closeness of the vote, 5–4, especially angered Ervin. He assumed that because the newest justice on the Supreme Court had been so closely associated with the administration's position he would recuse himself. But the deciding vote was cast by William Rehnquist, whom Nixon had appointed to the Court only a few months earlier. Ervin and the ACLU complained bitterly that Rehnquist should not have participated in *Laird v. Tatum* since he had served as the Justice Department's lawyer and chief spokesman during the hearings the year before.[88] Actually, the ACLU had considered filing a formal disqualification motion before the Court heard the case but had decided against it, having accepted Ervin's advice that Rehnquist surely would admit his prejudgment and refuse to participate.[89] Instead, Rehnquist stretched the bounds of judicial ethics to prevent the establishment of the chilling effect doctrine.[90]

The day after the Court's decision, Ervin introduced a bill to prohibit military surveillance of civilians. If the Supreme Court was not going to prevent a recurrence of the Army's domestic spying, then Ervin would try to stop it with legislation. But in the summer of 1972 the senator could find neither the time nor the support to enact his bill. He was preoccupied with so many other battles against the Nixon administration that holding new hearings was out of the question. Furthermore, Senators Hruska and Thurmond still vehemently opposed his proposals. Then came Watergate, and Ervin could not return to the issue of military surveillance for more than a year.[91]

Not long before Ervin retired from the Senate in 1974, he tried one last time to enact a law preventing the military from spying on the political activities of American citizens. On 9–10 April, he held new hearings and tried to stage a rerun of his drama from 1971. He even revealed a few new abuses of the Army's intelligence system. But the Defense Department had kept its intelligence system under fairly tight control and the media paid little attention to the hearings. Ervin had broad support for his legislation—thirty-four senators cosponsored it—but a block of conservative senators prevented the bill from advancing past the Judiciary Committee.[92] When Ervin left the Senate, the only safeguard against a recurrence of the Army's political spying remained the assurance of the administration that it could be trusted—a safeguard that had been discredited by the Watergate affair.[93]

Senator Ervin had begun his political campaign against what historian Arthur Schlesinger Jr. called Nixon's "imperial presidency" long before the Watergate scandal broke in 1972. Ervin's consistent defense of the right to privacy, along with his desire to preserve the separation of powers and prevent the expansion of civil rights, led him to oppose many of Richard Nixon's actions from the beginning of the president's first term. But of all those earlier skirmishes, none resembles Watergate as much as the senator's public hearings on the Army's domestic intelligence system in the spring of 1971. The events surrounding those hearings foreshadowed the story of Watergate in numerous ways. By the time Ervin decided to call for hearings in June 1970, the Army's cover-up had already introduced many of the strategies that would be repeated in 1973; indeed, as the hearings approached, the Pentagon's cover-up previewed Watergate even more. The Nixon administration developed a whole battery of new weapons to withhold information from the committee and prevent certain witnesses from testifying. These tactics were coordinated by the Defense Department's chief counsel, Fred Buzhardt, who repeated them when he directed the White House's Watergate legal defense two years later.

Another important similarity between the two incidents involves the battle for public opinion. During both sets of hearings Ervin played the part of a liberty-loving country lawyer who championed the constitutional rights of the individual, while the White House raised the cry of national security. In both cases the media sided with Ervin by providing valuable investigative reporting, giving his hearings plenty of coverage and supporting his arguments in editorials. During his investigation of the Army's domestic surveillance, Ervin built the coalition of supporters who would rally around him during Watergate.

It is also significant that accompanying court cases played a major role in both investigations. In 1971, *Laird v. Tatum* provided Ervin with important new information and the assistance of the ACLU. In 1973, the trial of the Watergate burglars produced significant new leads and the special prosecutor appointed by the Justice Department became a useful ally. When both sets of hearings ended inconclusively, the major issues in each—the chilling effect in 1971 and the surrender of the White House tapes in 1973—were resolved by the Supreme Court.

The actual committee hearings are strikingly similar as well. Most of the basic elements in the Watergate drama were present during Ervin's hearings on military intelligence. Both hearings were highly theatrical, both revealed shocking abuses of the nation's domestic surveillance apparatus, both produced evidence of the administration's political dirty tricks and blacklisting, and both revolved around the same central question: How can a democratic nation successfully balance its need for national security with its commitment to civil liberties? Many of the arguments and strategies Ervin and the Nixon administration developed during their debate in 1971 were repeated two years later, often by the same people.

So when the Senate called on Ervin to chair its special Watergate Committee in 1973, he had a good idea of what was to come in the months ahead. Ervin's crusade against the Army's domestic intelligence system had served as a rehearsal for Watergate.

CHAPTER TEN

TRUTH AND HONOR

In January 1973, Senator Ervin was snowbound at home in Morganton when Majority Leader Mike Mansfield called to ask him to head the Senate's investigation and public hearings into the Watergate affair. Neither Ervin nor anyone else was surprised. The Senate had been discussing the possibility of a select Watergate committee for several months, and Ervin had been considered the primary candidate to serve as its chair. Ervin's age and his reputation as the Senate's leading constitutional scholar helped him project the sense of judiciousness and authority the Democrats wanted. But it is not true, as some journalists suggested, that he was selected from "central casting" only because he fit the role of a "Wise Old Judge." Nor is it true, as Richard Nixon and his apologists have charged, that the Democrats chose Ervin as a partisan headhunter to lead a political witch hunt against the president. Rather, the Senate turned to Ervin because he had been crusading in Washington for more than fifteen years against the problems highlighted by the Watergate scandal, and because he had been on a collision course with Nixon from the first weeks of the president's administration.[1]

Since his appointment to the Senate in 1954, Ervin had frequently donned the mantle of the righteous defender of the pure Constitution against those who would pervert its ageless principles for temporary political gain. Ervin's courageous stand against Senator Joe McCarthy during his first year in Washington quickly established him as the next in a long line of respected southern constitutionalists. But over the course of the next decade, North Carolina's ol' country lawyer also employed his legal abilities to defend Jim Crow segregation and, in spite of the reputation he earned during the McCarthy episode, to oppose the Supreme Court's extension of constitutional protections to suspected Communists and accused criminals. A careful analysis of Ervin's constitutional rhetoric and political behavior in the 1950s reveals more contradiction than consistency.

Senator Ervin's political ideology underwent a significant evolution during the 1960s, however, when he assumed the chair of the Subcommittee on Constitutional Rights in 1961. Ervin inherited a civil liberties agenda, and an aggressive staff, that reinvigorated his dormant interest in protecting constitutional freedoms. The senator's renewed commitment to civil liberties coincided with a major shift in his position on civil rights as well. As African Americans and their allies began to pursue color-conscious governmental remedies to racial discrimination, Ervin reversed his position on *Brown* and became a born-again believer in its theory of a color-blind society. Ervin's radical change of direction not only provided him with a new weapon to wield against school busing and affirmative action programs, it also served to harmonize his constitutional philosophy concerning civil liberties and civil rights. By 1968, Ervin had constructed a more consistent worldview around the central idea that the growth of government power, in almost every area, must be checked to protect individual freedoms.

Then came Richard Nixon. During the president's first term, Ervin and Nixon repeatedly clashed over civil liberties, civil rights, and the separation of powers. Although he could not have known it at the time, the senator had started down the road to Watergate. From his two favorite subcommittees, Constitutional Rights and Separation of Powers, Ervin led the congressional counterattack against Nixon's imperial presidency. Following his extensive investigation of the Army's domestic spying program in 1970–71, Ervin held hearings to challenge Nixon's impoundment of funds, doctrine of executive privilege, restriction of newspersons' privileges, strengthening of the Subversive Activities Control Board, and other executive actions based on the president's claim of "inherent Constitutional powers." Watergate was the logical culmination of this progression.

Perhaps the metaphor of a road to Watergate is too teleological for historians. It is always dangerous for scholars, who know the outcome of a series of events, to find antecedents or to read motives and patterns back into the past. Ervin himself warned during the Watergate hearings that "most of us human beings are like lightning bugs who carry our lights behind us. We see better in retrospect than in prospect." Sam Ervin and his staff, though, clearly believed that the Watergate hearings represented the climax of their campaign against

Nixon's disregard for the Constitution. Rufus Edmisten, chief of staff of both the Separation of Powers Subcommittee and later the Watergate Committee, referred to those years as "the academic period": "We harkened back quite often [during Watergate] to all those experiences in the subcommittee hearings over the years. They were just a warm-up to Watergate." Lawrence Baskir, the chief of staff of the Subcommittee on Constitutional Rights, recalled: "I had very much, at that time, the realization that this was not an issue by issue thing; that this was now evolving into a full-fledged, progressive, and increasing campaign against the administration."[2]

Retracing Ervin's road to Watergate strengthens the traditional interpretation of Richard Nixon's place in history. Stanley Kutler summarized the orthodox assessment of the Nixon presidency when he wrote that "no 'fair' history of the Nixon era can overlook the centrality of Watergate." Revisionist historians, however, led by the ex-president himself, have urged scholars to deemphasize what John Mitchell called the "White House horrors" and refocus their attention on what they consider to be the more significant foreign and domestic accomplishments of the Nixon administration. Joan Hoff has argued that Richard Nixon is more than Watergate and Watergate is more than Richard Nixon. Some revisionists have even gone so far as to dismiss Watergate as, in the words of Patrick Buchanan, "Mickey Mouse misdemeanors." But Ervin's five-year, continuous, escalating struggle against Richard Nixon supports the traditional view that, as J. Anthony Lukas has written, Watergate "runs like a fault in the marble, through [Nixon's] entire administration, weakening and ultimately bringing down the entire edifice."[3]

Sam Ervin's personal opinion of Watergate was complex. Depending on the senator's mood, his audience, and the context of recent events, he might suggest that the scandal resulted from the moral flaws of Richard Nixon, from the "Gestapo mentality" of unlimited executive power within the White House, from Congress's timidity in enforcing constitutional checks and balances, from the systemic threat to liberty posed by the steady growth of the federal government, or from all of the above. He seldom offered a concise explanation. As one reporter warned, "It will be found rather a mistake to ask Ervin to summarize Watergate in a paragraph, since the first stopping place in his answer lies about an hour forward."[4]

Watergate dominated Ervin's last two years in the Senate, but he never had any intention of writing anything more about the scandal than the brief personal statement he attached to the Senate Committee's final report. That changed, however, when he read Nixon's memoirs in 1978. He was incensed by the former president's vindictive attacks and outright misrepresentations of the plain facts of Watergate. As he later explained, Nixon's autobiography "convinced me that I owed my country and history the obligation to set down on paper the truth respecting Watergate."[5] Although he had been retired for several years, Ervin set himself to writing a book to correct the historical record. The result, *The Whole Truth: The Watergate Conspiracy*, published in 1980, picks up where this book leaves off. It is a careful overview of the general Watergate story and a detailed explanation of the role Ervin and the Senate committee played in resolving the scandal. While a multitude of scholarly monographs and firsthand accounts of Watergate have appeared over the past four decades, Ervin's book has stood the test of time and remains one of the best single volumes on the scandal available today.[6]

According to Ervin, Watergate was the result of two successive conspiracies. The first conspiracy had a lawful objective, to reelect President Nixon in 1972, but turned to illegal means to achieve its ends. Members of the Committee to Reelect the President (CRP, but nicknamed CREEP by its detractors), under the direction of John Mitchell, carried out numerous unethical activities, including the following: hiring saboteurs to practice "dirty tricks" aimed at destroying the reputations of potential Democratic nominees; collecting large secret cash contributions and laundering them through Mexican banks; creating a private "enemies list" of people who had criticized the president or opposed his policies; misusing government agencies to harass the people on that list; and forming a clandestine unit, the Plumbers, to carry out illegal political surveillance. It was members of the Plumbers unit who broke into Daniel Ellsberg's psychiatrist's office. The president's men despised Ellsberg for releasing the classified Pentagon Papers, which undercut Nixon's Vietnam policy, and the Plumbers tried unsuccessfully to find some embarrassing information to get back at him. But it was another break-in for which they will always be remembered. In the early morning of 17 June 1972, the Washington, D.C., police caught several members of the Plumbers unit bugging the headquarters of the Democratic National Committee in the Watergate complex.

The second conspiracy sprung from the immediate efforts by some of the president's closest advisers to cover up the improper acts of the first conspiracy. Publicly, the president's men dismissed Watergate as nothing more than a "third-rate burglary." They promised that the trial of the seven Watergate burglars in Judge John J. Sirica's courtroom later that year would put an end to the scandal. Behind the scenes, however, they undertook a massive scheme to impede the investigation into Watergate by withholding evidence, misusing government agencies to obstruct justice, paying hush money to keep the original burglars quiet, and lying to government officials and the American people.

The cover-up successfully kept the scandal contained until after Nixon won reelection by a landslide in November 1972.

But Watergate did not go away. Two reporters for the *Washington Post*, Bob Woodward and Carl Bernstein, worked throughout the late summer and fall of 1972 to uncover remarkable new leads that tied the original burglars back to CRP and even to the White House itself. At the same time several members of Congress began preliminary investigations into Watergate. Senator Mike Mansfield, the Senate majority leader, grew increasingly worried about the serious implications of the *Post*'s revelations and about the political turmoil that could result from run-away congressional investigations. Fearing that neither the Senate Judiciary Committee nor the Government Operations Committee could conduct fair and efficient hearings into Watergate because of their size, and because of the presidential aspirations held by some of their members, he decided to form a special Senate committee to investigate the suspicious events surrounding the campaign activities of 1972. Mansfield conferred with Ervin about his plans to propose a select Senate committee, but he wanted to delay the start of its investigation until after the trial of the seven original Watergate defendants was completed.[7]

In January 1973, the Democratic Caucus approved Mansfield's proposal and unanimously supported his choice of Ervin to serve as chair. Several days later, when Senator Ervin finally escaped the icy roads of western North Carolina and returned to Washington, Mansfield gave him three reasons why they wanted him to head the proposed Senate special committee. First, Ervin had more judicial experience than any other senator; second, nobody could possibly accuse him of harboring presidential aspirations; and third, he was the most nonpartisan Democrat in the Senate. Mansfield later stated publicly that "Senator Ervin was the only man we could have picked on either side of the aisle who'd have had the respect of the Senate as a whole."[8]

The White House, however, suspected another reason for Ervin's choice. As presidential counsel John Dean later explained, "The White House and Sam Ervin had already crossed swords if you will on some other issues that were very fundamental to Sam Ervin and they had to do with separation of powers and his perception of what the President could and could not do. . . . So this was just another in a series of potential fights with Sam Ervin. It was assumed right off the bat he would be hostile or very aggressive politically."[9] The *New York Times* shared Dean's interpretation: "In the running tug-of-war between Congress and the White House in 1973, Senator Ervin seems to be holding the rope at the east end of Pennsylvania Avenue on virtually every issue."[10] Perhaps

Senator Hubert Humphrey summed it up best when he concluded that "Ervin is the right man at the right time in the right place."[11]

The Watergate criminal trial began in U.S. District Judge John J. Sirica's courtroom on 8 January 1973. Within several days the five burglars pleaded guilty and on 30 January the jury found the other two defendants, James McCord and Gordon Liddy, guilty as well. But shortly after reading the verdict Judge Sirica expressed his suspicion that the full story of Watergate had not yet been revealed and he urged the Senate to empower its committee to "get to the bottom of what had happened." Mansfield quickly brought his proposal forward to the full Senate on 7 February. The bill called for the creation of a special committee of seven senators, four Democrats and three Republicans, to be officially titled the Select Committee on Presidential Campaign Activities. Most people, however, simply referred to it as either the Watergate Committee or the Ervin Committee. The Senate passed the bill unanimously and Chairman Ervin and Vice Chairman Howard Baker, a Republican from Tennessee, immediately went to work assembling their staff. At its high point the committee employed almost one hundred staffers, including twenty-five lawyers and twenty investigators. By early March the Ervin Committee was operational and its investigation had begun. The senator hoped to begin public hearings in May.[12]

A worried President Nixon immediately ordered his staff to develop a strategy to discredit the Watergate Committee in general and Ervin in particular. During the weekend of 10 February his most trusted aides, including H. R. Haldeman, John Ehrlichman, and John Dean, met at Haldeman's California villa, Rancho La Costa, to work out their game plan. The La Costa proposals recommended that the White House take a public posture of full cooperation but privately attempt to hinder the investigation by withholding information and, if necessary, evoking executive privilege. The strategy called for a public relations effort to make the committee appear partisan. As John Dean later explained, "The ultimate goal would be to discredit the hearings."[13]

The White House even tried to enlist North Carolina Republicans in a campaign to smear Sam Ervin. Haldeman made at least two attempts to get local party officials to "dig up something to discredit Ervin and blast him with it."[14] When a reporter asked the senator about these inquiries into his past, Ervin explained that he was not worried because all the indiscretions he had committed in the past were barred by the statute of limitations and he had lost his capacity to commit further such indiscretions in the future. Republican congressman Charles R. Jonas Jr., who had managed Nixon's presidential campaigns in North Carolina in 1968 and 1972, told the *Charlotte Observer* that while he had not been asked by anyone to dig up any dirt on Senator Ervin, he considered it to be "an impossible task." Jonas added that in his opinion, Ervin "has a record of impeccable honesty and integrity. If I had to depend on any one person in the Senate to proceed fairly and in a way that would protect the innocent, it would be Senator Ervin."[15] Undeterred, the White House sent Vice President Spiro T. Agnew on a media blitz to attack Ervin as senile and the Watergate Committee as a partisan effort to embarrass the president. Secretary of Agriculture Earl Butz was dispatched to Charlotte, where he belittled Senator Ervin as a senile publicity seeker and compared the committee investigation to a political inquisition.[16] North Carolina's newly elected Republican senator, Jesse Helms, later joined the attack by implying that his colleague was conducting partisan hearings and harassing witnesses.[17] But not all Republican senators would whistle to the president's tune. The conservative Arizona Republican Barry Goldwater expressed his complete faith in Ervin: "I'd trust him with my wife's back teeth."[18] When some White House aides tried to convince reporters that behind Ervin's "sweet little ole country bumpkin" façade was a partisan Democrat out to "get the President," Hugh Sidey, a columnist for *Time*, suggested a very different conclusion. "He is not after anybody," Sidey wrote. "He is after something bigger—truth and honor."[19]

The Watergate cover-up ultimately depended on the seven original defendants keeping quiet. Although the White House paid them off with large cash bribes and promised them clemency, John Dean became increasingly anxious. On 21 March 1973, he tried to describe the danger to President Nixon: "We have a cancer—within—close to the presidency, that's growing."[20] Nixon already understood the problem. He knew that if the burglars or any of his other aides involved in the conspiracy began to talk, then the cover-up might topple like a row of dominoes, or as he graphically described it to Dean, "Sloan starts pissing on Magruder and then Magruder starts pissing on who, even Haldeman!"[21] Yet Nixon remained confident that the cover-up would hold and that he would win the battle of public opinion. As he explained to Dean, if the cover-up blows, "it will be a crisis among the intellectual types, the assholes, you know, the soft heads. Average people won't think it is much of a crisis unless it affects them."[22]

On 23 March Judge Sirica cracked the cover-up wide open when he publicly read a letter he had received from James McCord, one of the seven burglars. The letter alleged that the truth about Watergate remained hidden because of a massive White House conspiracy. McCord feared that the president planned to blame the CIA, which had formerly employed McCord, for the Watergate break-in. His loyalty to that agency, combined with a latent sense of honesty and perhaps guilt, seemed to have compelled his action. This bombshell initiated a new wave of suspicions and questions. The cover-up was falling apart. Events tumbled after each other in a confusing landslide during the month of April, culminating in the forced resignations of Dean, Haldeman, Ehrlichman, and Attorney General Richard Kleindienst. In a televised speech to the American people, President Nixon admitted that the scandal reached further into the White House than he had previously acknowledged. He accepted full responsibility for the mistakes of his subordinates but insisted that he had no personal involvement in the matter.[23]

As the Ervin hearings approached, Nixon tried to prevent his present and former aides from testifying by threatening a claim of executive privilege that would stop the committee from questioning them. When legal experts from across the political spectrum ridiculed the notion that a president could evoke executive privilege to stop an investigation into possible criminal actions, Nixon fell back to suggesting that he might allow either written or private questioning of his aides but that he would not abide their public testimony. A constitutional crisis loomed—what if the legislative branch subpoenaed the aides and the executive branch refused? Ervin, realizing that the time for a showdown with Nixon had finally arrived, called a press conference.[24]

The senator took on the president in front of a rack of microphones and in the glaring light of the television cameras. Paul Clancy, then a reporter for the *Charlotte Observer*, described the scene: "It was like nothing I've ever seen before on Capitol Hill. There were reporters and photographers everywhere in the cavernous Senate Caucus Room, almost literally hanging from the ornate chandeliers. There was one guy shooting film from a 20-foot ladder."[25] Ervin delivered a history lecture on executive privilege for over half an hour. He appeared comfortable in front of the cameras and even seemed to be enjoying himself. It was a virtuoso performance. "Divine right went out with the American Revolution and doesn't belong to White House aides," Ervin said. "What meat do they eat that makes them grow so great?" "I am not going to let anybody come down by night like Nicodemus and whisper something in my ear that no one else can hear. That is not Executive privilege. It is Executive poppycock." Ervin concluded by threatening to have the aides arrested if the president did not allow them to testify publicly and under oath before the Senate committee.[26]

By the time the cameras clicked off, a star was born. "Senator Sam" was on his way to becoming a folk hero. *Time* magazine put him on its cover, causing Miss Margaret to confide to a friend that it was all "so embarrassing."[27] *Time* opened its story with the kind of prose that would dominate both the print media and the airwaves for the rest of the summer: "The jowls jiggled. The eyebrows rolled up and down in waves. The forehead seemed sieged by spasms. Yet the lips continuously courted a smile, suggesting an inner bemusement. The words tumbled out disarmingly, softened by the gentle Southern tones and the folksy idiom. But they conveyed a sense of moral outrage."[28] *Time*'s congressional reporter, Neil MacNeil, recalled how Ervin had been called "the last of the founding fathers," and he concluded that it was a fair description. "For more than a dozen years, he has chaired hearing after hearing on constitutional rights and the erosion of the separation of powers," MacNeil explained. "Those hearings were conducted in all but empty committee rooms. . . . Now Congress has at long last taken alarm. It has decided that it needs a constitutionalist—a man of great legal knowledge and judicial temperament—and in discovering that fact, it has discovered Sam Ervin."[29] Of course it was not Congress that had suddenly discovered Ervin but the national press. The "Sam Ervin Show" had begun.[30]

The president eventually backed down from his claims of executive privilege, and the committee scheduled many of his closest aides to appear in the upcoming hearings. For several weeks the White House and the prospective witnesses struggled for credibility by issuing press releases and allowing leaks of their planned testimony. The resulting media build-up created a national television audience waiting eagerly for the Watergate spectacle to begin. On the day before the hearings began, Ervin delivered a speech at Bowdoin College in Maine. A faculty member approached Ervin and asked, "Senator, we all look for a great deal from you tomorrow; it must be a tremendous weight." With no arrogance whatsoever, Ervin looked at the young man and said: "Son, all my life I've been preparing for this moment. I am ready."[31]

Ervin opened the hearings on 17 May 1973, exactly eleven months after the break-in at the Watergate building. Ervin took his seat at the same table in the Senate Caucus Room where he had held the military surveillance hearings two years before, and where so many of the most famous investigations in American history had taken place. Ervin had also served on the committee that censured Joe McCarthy in the same marble-columned chamber at the start of his Senate career nineteen years earlier. The room was overflowing with spectators and reporters, as it would be every day of the hearings, with several rows of people standing in the back. Even a few celebrities showed up, such as Dick Cavett, Norman Mailer, and Lorne Greene, attracted to the television lights like moths to a lantern. Wearing his blue suit with the light blue shirt, which he had been told flattered him on television, Ervin called the hearings to order with his colorful Cherokee gavel. His opening remarks did not disappoint the audience. "We are beginning these hearings today in an atmosphere of the utmost gravity," Ervin drawled. "The questions which have been raised in the wake of the June 17 break-in strike at the very undergirding of our democracy."[32]

The committee presented itself as a combination of fact-finding mission and educational forum. As Vice Chairman Howard Baker explained, "The goal of the committee is to try and string together the subject matter and to present a coherent story and to produce a mosaic from all this that will identify faces, things, and places."[33] Ervin planned to follow a building block strategy during the public hearings. Stage one would set the scene by examining the events surrounding the break-in. The second stage would move into the testimony of the accusers, especially John Dean, who was now cooperating with the committee. In the third and final stage Ervin hoped to catch the big fish—Mitchell, Ehrlichman, and Haldeman.

The first stage of the hearings got off to a slow start, with only two witnesses having box office appeal—James McCord, now a convicted burglar, and Nixon's chief fund-raiser, Maurice Stans. McCord intrigued the audience by describing the cloak-and-dagger telephone calls and secret meetings through which the White House promised him clemency, hush money, and eventually a new job if he kept quiet. He also stated his belief that the president was aware of all these activities. As proof, he quoted his contact, John Caulfield—who had worked in John Dean's office—as telling him that Nixon "had been told of the forthcoming meeting with me and would immediately be told of the results of the meeting. I may have a message to you at our next meeting from the president himself."[34]

The testimony of Maurice Stans concerning the finances of Nixon's reelection campaign presented Ervin with a golden opportunity to apply his down-to-earth charm against the smooth sophistication of the president's men. During Ervin's questioning Stans tried to explain how he had destroyed most of the records of campaign contributions immediately after it was discovered that some of this money had been given to the Watergate burglars. He insisted that it "was very simple for the reason . . ."—at which point Ervin interrupted him in mid-sentence: "It's too simple for me to understand, really." Stans regained his composure and continued, "Mr. Chairman, for the reason that we were seeking to protect the privacy, the confidentiality, of the contributions on behalf of the contributors." With a smile Sam Ervin summed it up: "In other words, you decided that the right of the contributors to have their contributions concealed was superior to the right of the American citizens to know who was making contributions to influence the election of the President of the United States." The audience chuckled as the senator's eyebrows jumped up and down his forehead.[35]

The committee's second, accusatory, stage began with the testimony of the former deputy director of CRP, Jeb Stuart Magruder. Magruder took the stand on 14 June, explaining in detail the whole story of the break-in and cover-up operations. His testimony implicated almost all the major figures in the administration except Nixon himself. Magruder said that as far as he knew the president had not personally ordered the break-ins or participated in the cover-up. Instead, he identified John Mitchell as the top man behind the espionage operations and John Dean as the mastermind of the cover-up. Thus Magruder prepared the way for the committee's questioning of Mitchell in the third section of the hearing. But, more immediately, he set the stage for the committee's long-awaited star witness—John Dean.

The former presidential counsel had jumped from the White House ship before Nixon could throw him overboard. Dean realized that he was being set up as the scapegoat for the cover-up and cut a deal with the Ervin Committee to testify under a grant of partial immunity.[36] Owing to an upcoming state visit by Soviet leader Leonid Brezhnev, the Ervin Committee postponed its questioning of Dean for a full week. During this recess both the White House and Dean released secret documents to the press in order to buttress their respective positions for what promised to be the biggest confrontation of the Watergate hearings. From these leaks the public gained a fairly good idea of what Dean would tell the senators: he would implicate the president himself in the cover-up. The main question, therefore, was no longer what Dean would say, but whether or not he would be convincing. Being aware that nothing he said, no matter how true, would be believed unless he appeared trustworthy, Dean rehearsed his testimony carefully. Every detail was studied so that he could convince the public of his credibility. Dean knew his performance had to be perfect because he was pitting his word against the word of the president of the United States.

Dean's much anticipated testimony began on 25 June. Replacing his usual sporty clothes and contact lenses for a conservative suit and horn-rimmed glasses, the president's former counsel took up the entire first day reading from a 234-page prepared script. He charged that Nixon had participated in the cover-up since at least 15 September 1972, which implied that the president had lied repeatedly to the American people. He also described the paranoid atmosphere in the White House and explained that the Watergate affair was "an inevitable outgrowth of a climate of excessive concern over the political impact of demonstrations, excessive concern over leaks, [and] an insatiable appetite for political intelligence . . . regardless of the law."[37] Dean introduced the public to sensational aspects of the Watergate story they had never heard before, including the secret Huston Plan, which Ervin had almost stumbled upon in his hearings on military surveillance, the full purpose of the Plumbers unit, and the Nixon administration's secret enemies list. Dean's recall of specific, damning details was especially effective in shocking the audience, such as when he explained that the enemies list not only included the names of Democratic politicians and critical reporters but also prominent actors such as Tony Randall, Paul Newman, and Julie Andrews. Dean also detailed the White House's La Costa strategy to withhold evidence, deceive the public, and destroy the credibility of the Ervin Committee.[38]

Dean defended his story during four days of intense questioning by Ervin and the other committee members. He seldom appeared rattled or unsure of his memory. At one point, however, it appeared as though a major error in his testimony might destroy his credibility. Senator Edward Gurney of Florida, the most pro-Nixon member of the committee, pointed out that an important meeting Dean had located at the Mayflower Hotel actually occurred at the Statler Hilton. How could Dean expect people to trust his memory of the many detailed conversations with the president if he could not even remember the name of a major hotel? But after he returned from the next break Dean explained that his error was understandable because, as he had just been reminded, the coffee shop at the Statler Hilton was called the Mayflower Room. The audience broke into applause. Ironically, the tip had come from Daniel Schorr, the CBS reporter who was on Nixon's enemy's list.[39]

Dean's testimony before the Ervin Committee represented an important turning point in the Watergate story. His description of the "siege mentality" in the White House, and his detailed accounts of dirty tricks, enemy lists, public deceptions, and all the other unsavory activities began to expand the meaning of the scandal. Instead of a third-rate burglary that was covered up by some of the president's men, "Watergate" began to stand for a whole host of illegal and immoral acts. Furthermore, Dean had impugned the president's personal credibility and directly implicated him in the cover-up. Senator Baker best summed up the changing focus of the hearings when he coined the phrase that would be repeated endlessly during the next few months. "The net sum of your testimony is fairly mind-boggling," he told Dean. "It occurs to me at this point, . . . the central question is simply put: What did the President know and when did he know it?"[40]

When the hearings began Senator Ervin shared the belief of most Americans that the president had no prior knowledge of the break-in and had not participated directly in the cover-up. Instead, he anticipated that the committee would discover that some of Nixon's overzealous aides had run out of control in their efforts to reelect and then defend their president. Although he had a low regard for Nixon as a person, and even less respect for his attempts to build an imperial presidency, Ervin had a hard time accepting the notion that any president of the United States would actually stoop as low as the testimony at first suggested. But the longer the hearings progressed, the more Ervin's suspicions grew. Nixon's claims of executive privilege and his refusal to cooperate with the committee did not seem to be the actions of a man who thought the evidence would exonerate him. Ervin tried to maintain a public face of impartiality, but in private he doubted that Nixon was completely innocent. As he confided to a friend, "It has been my experience that the madam of a whorehouse is very seldom a virgin."[41] The events of the next few weeks would make it even harder for Ervin to believe in Nixon's innocence and to maintain his own judicial temperament.[42]

Following Dean's testimony, Ervin led the committee into the third stage of its hearings, in which he hoped to pin down the most important of the president's men—Mitchell, Haldeman, and Ehrlichman. Mitchell came first and presented the best defense he could for both himself and the president. His bellicose attitude, incomplete answers, and obvious contempt for the committee provided a stark contrast to Dean's revealing testimony. Ervin pointedly asked Mitchell the central questions: "Did you at any time tell the President anything you knew about the White House horrors?" "Did the President at any time ask you what you knew about Watergate?" Mitchell responded to both questions with a simple "No." "Well," Ervin snapped, "if the cat hadn't had any more curiosity than that he would still be enjoying his nine lives, all of them."[43]

As the senators continued questioning Mitchell, polls reported a deterioration in the president's standing. According to a Harris survey, 65 percent of Americans suspected that Nixon was withholding important evidence and, for the first time, more people thought that the president had prior knowledge of the break-in than those who believed his claim that he had known nothing about it.[44] As Mitchell's testimony evolved into a charade of evasion and contradiction, the public climate continued to turn against Nixon. Across the country cars sported new bumper stickers reading "Honk if you think he's guilty," and comedians increasingly joked about the president's declining popularity. African American comic Dick Gregory even bragged about sending Nixon a telegram thanking him for not having any blacks in his administration.[45] Many observers believed that Nixon would soon be forced to take some action to counter his fall in public opinion. What no one expected was the surprising testimony of Alexander Butterfield.

On Friday, 13 July, an assistant counselor for the Ervin Committee was running Butterfield, a former deputy assistant to the president, through some routine preliminary questions in the basement of the Dirksen Office Building across the street from the Senate hearings. Acting on an impulse the staffer asked, "Do you know of any basis for the implication in Dean's testimony that conversations in the President's office are recorded?" After a brief pause, Butterfield answered in a troubled voice, "I was hoping you fellows wouldn't ask me about that." The following Monday morning Ervin inserted Butterfield's name onto the witness list. When the committee reconvened after lunch Butterfield slipped into the witness chair. Minority counsel Fred Thompson (who would later become an actor as well as a Republican senator from Tennessee) asked Butterfield the fateful question: "Are you aware of any listening devices in the Oval Office of the President?" Butterfield answered, "I was aware of listening devices, yes sir." The room instantly fell quiet. The reporters in the press section put out their cigarettes and picked up their pencils as Butterfield explained that for the past two years every conversation in the Oval Office had been secretly taped. It was the most dramatic moment of the hearings. The revelation of the secret tapes changed the whole dynamic of Watergate. Dean's charges and Nixon's denials could be checked against irrefutable evidence. The answer to Baker's famous question could now be discovered by merely pushing the play button on a tape recorder.[46]

The following day Ervin announced the committee's unanimous request that the president turn over the tapes. Special Prosecutor Archibald Cox, who had been conducting a criminal investigation into Watergate since May, issued a similar request. Nixon, who was recovering in the hospital from pneumonia, ordered that all information about the tapes be withheld. The country waited in suspense as a second constitutional crisis began to build. On 23 July Nixon made it official. Claiming executive privilege, separation of powers, and national security, he refused to release the tapes: "The tapes are entirely consistent with what I know to be the truth and what I have stated to be the truth. However, . . . they contain comments that persons with different perspectives and motivations would inevitably interpret in different ways."[47] The Ervin Committee responded with a unanimous decision to subpoena the tapes, this time registering their votes dramatically by raising their hands at the beginning of the next morning's televised session. Cox also subpoenaed the tapes. The president again refused, thus sending the issue to the courts. The legal battle over the tapes would rage for many months to come. What Ervin and Cox suspected, the president already knew—if the tapes were released his presidency was over.[48]

The battle for the tapes overshadowed the testimony of Ehrlichman and

Haldeman, but their appearances before the committee still attracted a considerable amount of attention. Ehrlichman's testimony was especially noteworthy. It provided several spectacular moments, including a memorable slip from Hawaii Democrat Daniel Inouye: sitting in front of what he had assumed was a dead microphone, the senator could be heard muttering "What a liar" on national television. But the highlight of Ehrlichman's testimony came during his confrontation with Ervin, who was outraged by Ehrlichman's contention that presidential power was absolute. Ehrlichman maintained that while Nixon did not authorize the break-in of Ellsberg's psychiatrist's office, the president did have the inherent right to do so, as well as to take any other action he deemed necessary to protect national security. Ervin was incensed. "Foreign intelligence activities had nothing to do with the opinion of Ellsberg's psychiatrist about his intellectual or emotional or psychological state," Ervin snapped. When Ehrlichman's lawyer interrupted to ask, "How do you know that, Mr. Chairman?" Ervin retorted, "Because I can understand the English language. It's my mother tongue," and the audience broke into laughter.

But not all Americans reacted to Ervin's aggressive questioning of Ehrlichman with the same enthusiasm. Polls suggested that while a majority of the public, 62 percent, approved of the Ervin Committee's investigation, a growing minority, 29 percent, expressed criticism of what they perceived to be its anti-Nixon bias. As one man wrote to Senator Ervin, "Your questioning of Mr. John Ehrlichman proved that you are more interested in making a case against the President than you are in getting at the truth." Other letter writers were less kind. One critic concluded, "Mista Sambo, in my personal opinion you are a senile despicable old goat!" Another wrote, "I hope you and your whole stupid committee gets what that other tyrant, Martin Luther King got, and soon."[49] Ervin received several death threats, as did other members of the committee, but he refused a police escort except to help him walk into and out of the crowded caucus room, and on a few occasions to accompany him on the five-minute walk to his apartment. As an old-fashioned Presbyterian with a faith in predestination, Ervin figured that when his time was up, it was up.[50]

The senator's Watergate fame brought many inconveniences. Telephone calls from strangers came at all hours of the day and night. One persistent caller from Kentucky phoned every evening to tell Ervin what God had revealed directly to him that day about Watergate. The senator finally told the caller that he should not call again because unless God spoke directly to Ervin, the Almighty's revelations were secondhand or hearsay evidence and could not be admitted in the hearings. When the man called again that night with a new

Senator Ervin listens intently, and apparently disapprovingly, during the Watergate hearings, 1973. Seated to his right are Howard Baker and Fred Thompson. Sam Ervin Library and Museum, Western Piedmont Community College, Morganton, North Carolina.

message from God, Miss Margaret took the call, listened politely, hung up, and then ordered an unlisted phone number the next day.[51]

With the end of Ehrlichman's testimony the Ervin Committee concluded all three stages in the first phase of its investigation. Between 17 May and 7 August the senators had heard from thirty-three witnesses. Despite the best efforts by Mitchell, Ehrlichman, and Haldeman to discredit Dean's charges, pressure continued to grow on the president to respond to the accusations himself, or at least to release the tapes. On 15 August Nixon went before a nationwide television audience for his long-awaited response. He did not deal with the various charges in detail but urged the audience to put Watergate behind them. "After twelve weeks and two million words of televised testimony," Nixon argued, "we have reached a point at which a continued, backward-looking obsession with Watergate is causing this nation to neglect matters of far greater importance to all of the American people." He also explained that he could not turn over the tapes without compromising "the confidentiality of the office of the President." Nixon concluded, "I ask for your help to ensure that those who would exploit Watergate in order to keep us from doing what we were elected to do will not succeed."[52]

Ervin was not ready to quit just yet. "We're not going to continue the investigation until the last lingering echo of Gabriel's horn trembles into ultimate silence," Ervin told a crowd back in North Carolina, "but we are going to continue until we get the truth."[53] He resumed the hearings later that month in order to continue the dirty tricks and campaign financing sections of his inquiry, but by then the committee had passed its zenith and would no longer be at the center of Watergate. Although Ervin did not know it at the time, his hearings had already completed their most important task. By serving as the central forum for the public to learn about the Watergate scandal, and by allowing the American people to hear the testimony and weigh the evidence for themselves, the hearings had led to an important shift in public opinion. When the hearings began in May, the president stood under a shadow of suspicion concerning the Watergate break-in and cover-up, but when the hearings ended in August, Nixon stood under public indictment for all the White House misdeeds, not to mention possible legal indictment as well. Perhaps historian Theodore H. White best summed up the committee's significance when he suggested that the Ervin hearings delivered an "extraordinary exercise in American public education, never matched in history."[54]

The Ervin hearings continued to wear on week after week through the early fall, but when they produced no new sensational revelations the major networks took them off the air in late September. Ervin pushed on until November before wrapping up his public sessions and instructing the staff to begin to write its final report, which Ervin released on 12 July 1974. Meanwhile, other actors took center stage, especially Archibald Cox, the special prosecutor whom Nixon ordered to be fired in what became known as "the Saturday Night Massacre," and Cox's replacement, Leon Jaworski, who continued the battle for the tapes. In the end, Butterfield's disclosure led to the downfall of Richard Nixon. On 24 July 1974, the Supreme Court ruled unanimously that the president had to surrender the final tapes to the Special Prosecutor and to the House Judiciary Committee, which was already preparing to recommend impeachment. Nixon's own recorded words proved that he had personally obstructed justice and repeatedly lied to the courts, the Congress, and the American people. He resigned in disgrace on 9 August 1974, and Watergate passed from the realm of politics to the debates of history.

During the Watergate hearings Ervin had been thinking about his own future as well. His seniority and newfound fame brought him more political power than he had ever enjoyed before, and he had a full agenda of issues he wanted to pursue. But he would be seventy-eight years old when he stood for reelection in 1974. Could he ask the voters to trust that he would remain healthy and vigorous through the end of another six-year term? Miss Margaret did not hide her desire to return home to Morganton, but as always it would be her husband's decision. Just before Christmas in 1973 Ervin announced that he was giving Miss Margaret the present she most desired and would retire when his term expired in January 1975. His explanation to the press corps was classic Ervin: "Since time takes a constant accelerating toll of those of us who live many years, it is simply not reasonable for me to assume that my eye will remain undimmed and my natural force stay unabated for so long a time."[55]

Ervin's last year in the Senate was one of the most productive of his career. As the chairman of the Government Operations Committee he wielded significant power to push his agenda through Congress. He managed to pass three major pieces of legislation to rein in the imperial presidency. First, the Congressional Budget and Impoundment Control Act restricted sharply a president's ability to refuse to spend, or "impound," money the Congress had voted to spend. It also created the Congressional Office of the Budget and vigorously overhauled the entire federal government's budget process with an eye toward reinvigorating the role of Congress. Second, Ervin stopped Nixon from gaining control over his presidential tapes and documents. Nixon had made a deal with the head of the General Services Administration to keep all the tapes and, if he wished, destroy them. Ervin's bill annulled the deal and required the National Archives to retain and protect all the president's official materials. And third, the Federal Election Campaign Act of 1974 included several provisions recommended by the Ervin Committee after its investigation into Watergate, most importantly to create a National Election Commission to enforce new campaign contribution limits and to require that most political contributions be made public. Although the senator had reservations about some of the measures inserted into the final bill, especially those endorsing public financing of elections, he eventually supported the full package of reforms.[56]

Ervin also completed two bits of unfinished business from his long-running crusade to protect civil liberties. The Speedy Trial Act came out of Ervin's criticism of Nixon's draconian anticrime package from the president's first term. Ervin had argued that the real answer to the supposed problem of accused criminals committing further crimes while out on bail was not Nixon's preventive detention scheme but a reinforcement of the Sixth Amendment's guarantee of a speedy trial. This law helped achieve that goal by requiring courts to meet certain deadlines in the trial process. Ervin's second victory for civil liberties was especially sweet. In his last week in Congress he had the satisfaction of seeing the Privacy Act passed into law. This major legislative triumph permitted citizens for the first time to inspect information about themselves contained in agency files and databases. It also allowed them to challenge, correct, or amend that material. The law had several weaknesses, including exemptions for the CIA, FBI, and certain other government records, and it did not contain any specific provisions to protect the privacy of federal employees. But the Privacy Act represented the fulfillment of Ervin's long attempt to protect individuals from excessive government snooping. After the law's enactment, three of its Senate cosponsors, Edmund Muskie, Charles Percy, and Abraham Ribicoff, issued a joint statement: "This legislation would not have become public law without the extraordinary dedication, ability, and leadership of Senator Sam J. Ervin, Jr. of North Carolina. . . . For two decades, Senator Ervin was regarded by his colleagues in the Senate as a guardian and forceful exponent of the constitutional rights of our Nations's citizens. The hearings, reports, and legislation produced by the Subcommittee on Constitutional Rights . . . laid the groundwork for this first major privacy legislation."[57]

In spite of his new popularity among liberals, Ervin remained a conservative obstructionist to the very end. He led two successful filibusters, one to prevent ratification of the genocide treaty and another to stop the creation of the Consumer Protection Agency. Ervin also tried to prevent the unionization of hospitals by arguing that the separation of church and state should prevent the National Labor Relations Board from regulating church-affiliated medical facilities. His amendment, which would have exempted one-third of all the hospitals in the country, failed to pass the Senate. He provided one of only eleven votes against the first major housing bill since 1968, and he registered the only negative vote against a bill to allow the federal government to subsidize railroad pensions. Even during his last year in the Senate, Ervin remained in close touch with Phyllis Schlafly and other ERA opponents who were fighting ratification of the amendment in the states. He also held hearings against busing to achieve racial balance, which led to the addition of an anti-busing provision into the omnibus Education Amendments of 1974. "During the 19 years I have served in the U.S. Senate, I can think of no group of people who stood in greater need of relief from Government tyranny," Ervin concluded, "than the thousands of innocent, little schoolchildren who are being bused to schools many miles away from their neighborhoods in order to satisfy the social theories of Federal bureaucrats."[58]

And then it all came to an abrupt end. In January 1975 the senator bid farewell to his colleagues, threw his suitcases in the car, and drove himself and Miss Margaret back to North Carolina. Ervin said that he was looking forward to retirement, but it was not a smooth transition. While he loved being back among his old friends and walking the old familiar streets of Morganton, it was not easy to give up the power and politics of the Senate that had consumed his life for the past twenty years. For a while he kept on top of Senate business, calling his former colleagues several times a week to express his opinion on this or that legislation. Eventually he let go of Washington and turned back to his old favorite activities—reading, writing, and practicing a little law. Six days a week he walked the mile down to his old office in the Ervin Building across from the Burke County Courthouse, just as his father had decades before.[59]

Ervin's favorite activity, especially in his first years of retirement, was public speaking. Basking in his post-Watergate fame he accepted invitations to lecture all over the country, eventually traveling to forty-six states. He talked to bar associations, college commencements, and Democratic political gatherings. The star appeal of "Senator Sam" still held its magic with audiences and especially with young people. In March 1975 Ervin spoke at the University of San Francisco to almost 5,000 people who paid two dollars each to hear him. Afterward he needed an escort to get through the crowd. Before he could escape into a limousine, a college-age woman forced her way up to him and pushed an autograph book into his hand. "I was a member of the Sam Ervin Fan club," she later explained. "I don't know why, but I saw him in those hearings and I fell in love with him. The way he talks, the way he acts, I think he's just so *neat!*" A young man with long hair, who had also obtained an autograph from Ervin, stammered, "Thanks a lot. I mean, thanks a whole lot. And I want you to know I think you're really a hell of a man, too."[60]

Ervin also enjoyed appearing on television. For awhile he did the circuit of talk shows and political discussions, granting interviews to everyone from William F. Buckley Jr. to Dinah Shore. He even showed up in some bicentennial history spots in 1976. His most famous TV appearance was a commercial for the American Express Card, which ran for several years and paid him a hefty fee. "You know," he later joked, "the government takes 53 and a half percent of every dollar I make. I knew the government needed the money so I figured I'd make some more from the commercial so I could pay my income tax." In truth Ervin was making a lot of money from his speaking and television appearances, more than double what he had earned during his last year in the Senate. Eventually the pace of the invitations slowed down at just about the same rate as Ervin's desire to accept them.[61]

The Ervins lived well and happy in their brick house in Morganton for over

Editorial cartoon by Gibson M. Crockett, Washington Star-News, *13 December 1974.*
A copy is in the Sam Ervin Library and Museum, Western Piedmont Community College,
Morganton, North Carolina. Copyright 1974, 1975 The Washington Post.
Reprinted with permission.

Sam Ervin enjoying a good laugh in retirement. Sam Ervin Library and Museum, Western Piedmont Community College, Morganton, North Carolina.

a decade until old age caught up with them. Senator Ervin passed away in April 1985, one year before Margaret. He was eighty-eight years old. His health had been in decline for several years and he finally gave in to respiratory failure brought on by a three-week bout with emphysema, gall bladder surgery, and kidney failure. The First Presbyterian Church could not possibly hold the crowd of former colleagues and well-wishers who came to the funeral to pay their last respects. Newspapers across the country ran articles remembering Ervin with headlines such as "A Most Unlikely Hero" and "Not Quite Just a Country Lawyer."[62]

Just as the press had struggled to make sense of the senator's contradictory career during Watergate, reporters had difficulty defining Sam Ervin's historical legacy at the time of his death. In 1973, at the height of Watergate, admirers such as James J. Kilpatrick praised Ervin as the last of the founding fathers. They applauded him for championing civil liberties and defending the Constitution. But Tom Wicker and other more critical observers urged Americans to remember "the Watergate chairman's old clothes," especially his controversial record on civil rights. After Ervin's passing in 1985 the same two interpretive

Senator Ervin and Miss Margaret. Photograph by Jeff Stark, Morganton News Herald, *14 April 1973. A copy is in the Sam Ervin Library and Museum, Western Piedmont Community College, Morganton, North Carolina. Courtesy of the* Morganton News Herald.

themes competed for prominence in accounts of his life. Ervin's supporters claimed that all his actions stemmed from the senator's reverence for the Constitution and opposition to any governmental interference with individual rights. Ervin's detractors viewed him as an inconsistent civil libertarian who used the Constitution as a convenient cloak to hide his racism and partisan self-interest. But neither of these interpretations can account for the complexities, inconsistencies, and changes within Ervin's constitutional ideology.[63]

Perhaps it was Ervin himself who hinted at a more revealing way of understanding his career when he told the story of a ninety-five-year-old man who was celebrating his birthday down home in North Carolina. When a reporter suggested, "Well, you have lived a long time and have seen many changes in your life," the old man responded, "Yes, and I have been against every one of them." Sam Ervin, too, was against change. The senator may not have been quite as consistent a constitutional scholar as his admirers remembered, but he was a consistent opponent of any change in the traditional mores of southern society, especially in race relations. Ervin's career was dedicated less to "Preserving the Constitution," as he suggested in the title of his autobiography, than to preserving the southern status quo.[64]

Ervin's political ideology both shaped and served this primary goal. The senator's dedication to the Constitution cannot be credited as the singular motivation for his civil liberties agenda, or reduced to a mere cloak for hiding his racial biases. It was much more than that. Ervin's constitutional philosophy provided him with a legal conceptualization of the world that he truly believed, and it gave him a language to rationalize and defend the southern way of life that he deeply valued.

The senator did not form his constitutional ideology in isolation but developed it within a specific sociopolitical context and political culture that depended for its very existence on the exploitation of African Americans. Since the privileged leaders of white North Carolina in the early twentieth century could not face this reality and maintain their self-image as Christian gentlemen who presided over the most moderate of southern states, they created what William Chafe has called a "progressive mystique" to rationalize their state's unjust system of race relations. This progressive mystique was built upon racism, civility, and paternalism. It stressed that the wealthy, white, male leaders of southern society not only had a civic duty to repel any challenge to the established social order, but a moral obligation to care for and protect those dependent groups under their authority, including poor whites, factory workers, southern women, and even African Americans. Ervin embodied his state's progressive mystique and he was a consummate practitioner of the etiquette of civility. Thus, as a representative of North Carolina in the United States Senate, he opposed civil rights with his soft southern strategy and respectable constitutional argumentation. But he also took his paternalistic responsibility seriously, eventually defending the civil liberties of all Americans from the intrusive power of the federal government.[65]

Ervin's political ideology also reflected a southern constitutional tradition that went back to the eighteenth century. Like Thomas Jefferson, whom Ervin so greatly admired, and countless other southern strict constructionists, the senator embraced a constitutional philosophy that defended local autonomy over race relations by limiting the power of the federal government. This historic distrust of centralized government power is the key to understanding his opposition to civil rights on the one hand and defense of civil liberties on the other. But it should not be forgotten that the virulent federalism of the southern delegation to the Constitutional Convention in 1787 had at its core the preservation of black chattel slavery, just as the strict constructionism and states' rights rhetoric of later generations of southerners served the cause of white supremacy.[66] In this light, James Kilpatrick's famous description of Sam Ervin as the last of the founding fathers suggests a historical analogy he doubtlessly did not intend. Kilpatrick meant to compliment Ervin for acting in the tradition of the brave patriots of the American revolution who fought to preserve individual freedoms against government tyranny. The senator deserves such accolades for his bold opposition to Joe McCarthy, his renewed protection of civil liberties and the right to privacy in the 1960s, and certainly for his willingness to fight the excesses of Richard Nixon's presidency both before and during Watergate. But, like the founding fathers who drafted the Constitution he so admired, Ervin's preoccupation with maintaining the racial status quo contributed to an overly limited view of government power. Like Jefferson, Ervin saw government more as a danger to be checked than as a tool to be used. As president, however, Jefferson came to realize what Ervin could never accept—that the federal government must sometimes apply its power to effect positive change.[67]

Here lies the critical flaw in Ervin's constitutional philosophy. In a time of uncertainty and peril, he reminded the nation that it must be ever vigilant against the concentration of centralized power in order to protect constitutional rights and individual freedoms, as indeed it should. Sam Ervin never acknowledged, however, that sometimes it is necessary to exercise governmental power in order to extend those same rights and freedoms to all Americans.

NOTES

With regard to citations from the Sam J. Ervin Jr. Papers at the Southern Historical Collection in the Wilson Library of the University of North Carolina at Chapel Hill, readers should be aware of the following details. The Ervin papers are divided into two collections, Senate Papers: Subgroup A and Personal Papers: Subgroup B. Citations from the Ervin papers in this book are from Subgroup A unless "B.," denoting the Personal Papers, is used as an identifier. Since the research for this book was completed, the Senate Papers: Subgroup A have been reprocessed. Researchers should consult the reprocessing guide at the Southern Historical Collection to find the new box locations for the material cited below.

PREFACE

1. H. G. Jones, "In Light of History: Edward Gibbon and Sir Walter Raleigh," for the Associated Press, draft, 22 February 1984, North Carolina Collection, Wilson Library, University of North Carolina at Chapel Hill.

2. Samuel J. Ervin Jr., *The Whole Truth: The Watergate Conspiracy* (New York: Random House, 1980); Samuel J. Ervin Jr., *Preserving the Constitution: The Autobiography of Senator Sam Ervin* (Charlottesville, Va.: Michie, 1984).

INTRODUCTION

1. U.S. Congress, Senate, Select Committee on Presidential Campaign Activities, *Presidential Campaign Activities of 1972*, 93rd Cong., 1st sess., 1973, 2343–44 (hereafter cited as Watergate Hearings).

2. Jack Aulis, "Most Newsmen Deny Senator Sam Is Senile," *Raleigh News and Observer*, 8 July 1973, North Carolina Collection Clipping File, North Carolina Collection, Wilson Library, University of North Carolina Library (hereafter cited as NCC Clipping File); Marshall Frady, "Sam Ervin, Saving the Republic, and Show Business," in *Southerners: A Journalist's Odyssey* (New York: New American Library, 1980), 107.

3. Watergate Hearings, 2344.

4. This description is based on a video recording of the hearings included in *Senator Sam*, producer David Royal, New Atlantic Productions, 1988. A copy of this videocassette can be found in the Sam J. Ervin Papers, Subgroup A: Senate Papers, 3847A, Southern Historical Collection, Wilson Library, University of North Carolina at Chapel Hill (hereafter cited as Ervin Papers); Watergate Hearings, 2630–31.

5. The president and Haldeman are cited in Stanley I. Kutler, ed., *Abuse of Power: The New Nixon Tapes* (New York: Simon and Schuster, 1997), 208; "Transcript of a Telephone Conversation Between The President and Charles W. Colson on March 21, 1973, from 7:35 to 8:24 P.M.," White House Tapes, Watergate Special Prosecution Force File Segment, Nixon Materials, National Archives II; "The Country Lawyer and Friends," *Time*, 6 August 1973. The president, Haig, and Kissinger are cited in Kutler, *Abuse of Power*, 628–29.

6. The hearings earned an average Nielsen rating of 8.2 compared to the competition's 7.4. See Gladys Engel Lang and Kurt Lang, *The Battle for Public Opinion: The President, The Press, and The Polls During Watergate* (New York: Columbia University Press, 1983), 62–63.

7. *Time*, 16 April 1973; *Newsweek*, 28 May 1973; " 'Country Lawyer' Has Himself a Fan Club," *Durham Morning Herald*, 5 July 1973, NCC Clipping File.

8. Mark Arnold, "Combining 'Con Law' and Corn Pone," *National Observer*, 17 February 1973, Sam J. Ervin Papers, Subgroup B: Private Papers, 3847B, Southern Historical Collection, Wilson Library, University of North Carolina at Chapel Hill (hereafter cited as Ervin Papers, B.), folder 1179; Watergate Hearings, 2630–31.

9. Arnold, "Combining 'Con Law' and Corn Pone"; Watergate Hearings, 2630–31.

10. Watergate Hearings, 2631.

11. Ibid., 2479.

12. James Naughton, "Constitutional Ervin," *New York Times Magazine*, 13 May 1973; Ira Berkow, "Sam Ervin: Duty Is The Sublimest Word," Newspaper Enterprise Association, 21 June 1973, Ervin Papers, B., folder 779; Maury Green, "Watergate Hearings: Round 1," *Los Angeles Times*, 18 May 1973; Lawrence Maddry, *Virginian-Pilot*, 17 May 1973, Ervin Papers, B., folder 1181; *Time*, 16 April 1973, cited in Sara Townsend, "Sam Ervin: Not Just a Pretty Face," unpublished manuscript, 9 December 1989, in the author's possession. Much of the following analysis of Watergate press coverage is based upon Townsend's manuscript.

13. Arnold, "Combining 'Con Law' and Corn Pone"; Paul Clancy, "The Sam Ervin Show Is Favorite of Media," *Charlotte Observer*, 8 April 1973; James M. McNaughton, "Constitutional Ervin," *New York Times Magazine*, 13 May 1973.

14. Mary McCarthy, *The Mask of State: Watergate Portraits* (New York: Harcourt Brace Jovanovich, 1973), 10.

15. James A. Wechsler, "That Man Ervin," *New York Post*, 5 April 1973; "Uncle Sam," *Nation*, 17 September 1973, 226. As one reporter concluded, Ervin's "long love affair with the original version of the Constitution, . . . his reputation for fairness and his experience as a justice of the North Carolina Supreme Court have cast him in a leading role in the Watergate morality play." See James Naughton, "Constitutional Ervin," *New York Times Magazine*, 13 May 1973.

16. The theme of Watergate as a classic tragedy can be found in textbooks, historical monographs, and film, although the interpretation of the story varies considerably. Perhaps the best example is Theodore H. White, *Breach of Faith: The Fall of Richard Nixon* (New York: Atheneum Publishers, 1975). Sam Ervin's book on Watergate, *The Whole Truth: The Watergate Conspiracy* (New York: Random House, 1980), contains elements of this interpretation as well. For a perceptive overview of Watergate in public memory see Michael Schudson, *Watergate in American Memory: How We Remember, Forget, and Reconstruct the Past* (New York: Basic Books, 1992).

17. See Alfred H. Kelly, "History as Theater," *Reviews in American History* (March 1976): 132–37. For examples of news articles on Ervin that raised questions while still contributing to the creation of the Ervin myth in 1973, see "Defying Nixon's Reach for Power," *Time*, 16 April 1973; "Why Ervin Heads the Senate Inquiry," *U.S. News and World Report*, 28 May 1973; Edwin M. Yoder, "The Gospel According to Sam," *Ideas: Newsday's Journal of Opinion*, 22 April 1973, Ervin Papers, B., folder 1181; "Discovering the Virtues of North Carolina's Sam Ervin," *Greensboro Daily News*, 16 May 1973, NCC Clipping File.

18. Tom Wicker, "The Watergate Committee Chairman's New Clothes," *Southern Voices* 1 (March–April 1974): 7–8.

19. James K. Batten, "Sam J. Ervin Just Won't Fit in a Mold—He's Still a Man to Reckon With," *Charlotte Observer*, 2 April 1967. On Ervin's contradictory record see Stephen Klitzman, "Sam Ervin: Principle Not Politics," in *Citizens Look at Congress* (Washington, D.C.: Ralph Nader Congress Project, 1972), 1; "It Isn't Easy to Put a Label on Sam Ervin," *Winston-Salem Journal*, 26 September 1965, Ervin Notebooks, s-11; Roy Parker Jr., "Ervin to Be Civil Rights Champion," *Winston-Salem Journal*, 15 February 1965, Ervin Newspaper Clipping Notebooks (hereafter cited as Ervin Notebooks), Ervin Papers, s-11; Philip Warden, "Ervin: Man of Paradoxes," *Chicago Tribune*, 23 August 1970; Richard Starnes, "Constitutionalist is consistently Inconsistent," *Washington Daily News*, 24 November 1969, Ervin Papers, box 470; Frank Kane, "Southerner Charms, Enrages Conservatives, Liberals Alike," *Toledo Blade*, 12 April 1970, Ervin Papers, box 470.

20. Ervin, *Preserving the Constitution: The Autobiography of Senator Sam Ervin* (Charlottesville, Va.: Michie, 1984), 72; Bruce Tindall, "Down Home Truths from Senator Sam Ervin," unpublished manuscript, 1974, North Carolina Collection, Wilson Library, University of North Carolina at Chapel Hill.

21. Starnes, "Constitutionalist is consistently Inconsistent"; Davis Merritt, "Ervin Turns Meat Grinder on Mitchell," *Charlotte Observer*, 6 February 1970, Ervin Papers, box 470. While most journalists and scholars concede the paradoxes of Ervin's career, they almost universally conclude that the senator can be explained by understanding the basic consistency of his constitutional philosophy. For a sampling of this orthodox view of Ervin see John Herbers, "Senator Ervin Thinks the Constitution Should be Taken Like Mountain Whiskey—Undiluted and Untaxed," *New York Times Magazine*, 15 November 1970; "Senator Ervin: Hard to Define, But Theme is Liberty," *Raleigh News and Observer*, 1 January 1971, Ervin Papers, box 470; Clifford Kenneth Van Sickle, "The Oral Communication of Senator Sam Ervin: A Study in Consistency" (Ph.D. dissertation, Michigan State University, 1976); Paul Clancy, *Just a Country Lawyer: A Biography of Senator Sam Ervin* (Bloomington: Indiana University Press, 1974); David Leon Chandler, *The Natural Superiority of Southern Politicians: A Revisionist History* (Garden City, N.Y.: Doubleday, 1977), 306–18; David Zarefsky, "Fulbright and Ervin: Two Senators with National Appeal," in Calvin Logue and Howard Dorgan, eds., *A New Diversity in Contemporary Southern Rhetoric* (Baton Rouge: Louisiana State University Press, 1987), 162–63. Examples of a more critical analysis of Ervin can be found in Stephen Klitzman, "Sam Ervin: Principle Not Politics," in *Citizens Look at Congress* (Washington, D.C.: Ralph Nader Congress Project, 1972), and Dick Dabney, *A Good Man: The Life of Sam J. Ervin* (Boston: Houghton Mifflin, 1976).

22. Klitzman, "Principle Not Politics," 1. Civil rights proponents such as J. Francis Pohlhaus, general counsel for the NAACP, Joseph Rauh Jr., general counsel for the Leadership Conference on Civil Rights, Martha McKay of the National Women's Political Caucus, and writer Robert Sherrill agreed that Ervin's reputation as a constitutional expert was "over-rated." Sherrill believed that the senator's view of the Constitution was "static, one-dimensional, and simple minded." See Klitzman, "Principle Not Politics," 34. One journalist recorded the following observation from an unnamed Ervin critic: "I get the feeling around here in talking to men who really are constitutional experts, like Prof. Paul

Freund at Harvard, that they're somewhat amused that Ervin sets himself up as an expert because he was a state supreme court justice." James K. Batten, "Sam J. Ervin Just Won't Fit the Mold—He's Still a Man to Reckon With," *Charlotte Observer*, 2 April 1967.

CHAPTER ONE

1. "Ervin Remains Calm," *Greensboro Daily News*, 6 June 1954, in Sam J. Ervin Papers, Subgroup A: Senate Papers, 3847A, Southern Historical Collection, Wilson Library, University of North Carolina at Chapel Hill (hereafter cited as Ervin Papers), box 470; Ervin to Dick Dabney, Corrections to Dabney manuscript (hereafter cited as Ervin Corrections to Dabney), Sam J. Ervin Papers, Subgroup B: Private Papers, 3847B, Southern Historical Collection, Wilson Library, University of North Carolina at Chapel Hill (hereafter cited as Ervin Papers, B.), folder 934; Dick Dabney, *A Good Man: The Life of Sam J. Ervin* (Boston: Houghton Mifflin, 1976), 13–14.

2. William D. Snider, "Ervin's Rise to National Eminence," *Greensboro Daily News*, 21 November 1971, Ervin Papers, Box 470; Sam Ervin, *Humor of a Country Lawyer* (Chapel Hill: University of North Carolina Press, 1983), 10.

3. J. Alexander Mull and Gordon Boger, *Recollections of the Catawba Valley* (Boone, N.C.: Appalachian Consortium Press, 1983), 51–55.

4. William S. Powell, *North Carolina: A History* (Chapel Hill: University of North Carolina Press, 1977), 164–65; Dwight Billings, *Planters and the Making of a "New South": Class, Politics, and Development in North Carolina, 1865–1900* (Chapel Hill: University of North Carolina Press, 1979); Gavin Wright, *Old South, New South: Revolutions in the Southern Economy since the Civil War* (New York: Basic Books, 1986).

5. On the transformation of race relations in North Carolina during the period of Ervin's pre-Senate life (1896–1954) see John Haley, *Charles N. Hunter and Race Relations in North Carolina* (Chapel Hill: University of North Carolina Press, 1987); Glenda Gilmore, *Gender and Jim Crow: Women and the Politics of White Supremacy in North Carolina, 1896–1920* (Chapel Hill: University of North Carolina Press, 1996).

6. Although the historiographical debate between those who stress the discontinuity of southern history versus those who argue for continuity has raged on for half a century, the generalizations in this paragraph are agreed upon by both sides. This study is more concerned with the evolution and implications of elite white racist ideologies during Ervin's life (all of which falls within the "New South" era and later) than with deciding whether or not that evolution continued or discontinued dominant antebellum thought. On discontinuity see C. Vann Woodward, *Origins of the New South, 1877–1913* (Baton Rouge: Louisiana State University Press, 1951). On continuity see Billings, *Planters and the Making of a "New South."* For a summary of the debate see Numan V. Bartley, "Another New South?" *Georgia Historical Quarterly* 65 (Summer 1981): 119–37.

7. Elizabeth Fox-Genovese, "The Anxiety of History: The Southern Confrontation with Modernity," *Southern Cultures* 1 (Inaugural Issue, 1993): 65–82.

8. Richard Starnes, "Constitutionalist is consistently Inconsistent," *Washington Daily News*, 24 November 1969, Ervin Papers, box 470; Ervin Corrections to Dabney, Ervin Papers, B., folder 1159.

9. Susan Graham Erwin, *The Village That Disappeared* (Charlotte: Laney-Smith, Inc., 1996), 33–34; Thomas H. Roberts and Joe B. Whitlow, "Morganton Plans for the Future"

(Chapel Hill: UNC–Chapel Hill, Department of City and Regional Planning, 1951), North Carolina Collection, Wilson Library, University of North Carolina at Chapel Hill (hereafter cited as NCC); Edward W. Phifer Jr., *Burke County: A Brief History* (Raleigh: North Carolina Department of Cultural Resources, Division of Archives and History, 1979).

10. Ervin to Robert Lawrence, 6 April 1940, Ervin Papers, B., folder 932.

11. Susan Graham Erwin married Joe Ervin (note the different spellings of their last names) but always used her maiden name in her writings. Erwin, *Village That Disappeared*, 65, 70–71, quote on page 70; Catharine Ervin, "History of Women's Work," published by the First Presbyterian Church, Morganton, NCC.

12. Erwin, *Village That Disappeared*, 34; W. C. Ervin, "Catawba Valley and Highlands," NCC; Phifer, *Burke County*, 17–21.

13. Ervin, "Frankie Silver," in "Burke County Courthouses and Related Matters," pamphlet (Morganton: Historic Burke Foundation, Inc., 1985), 27–31; Phifer, *Burke County*, 135–36.

14. Ibid., 136–37.

15. J. Alexander Mull and Gordon Boger, *Recollections of the Catawba Valley* (Boone, N.C.: Appalachian Consortium Press, 1983), 55.

16. Jean Conyers Ervin, interview by author, 17 March 2001, Morganton.

17. Sam J. Ervin III, interview by Hilary L. Arnold, Morganton, 24 February 1993, in the Southern Oral History Program Collection (4007), Southern Historical Collection, Wilson Library, University of North Carolina at Chapel Hill (hereafter cited as SOHP).

18. Editorial, "S. J. Ervin, Sr., Noble Patriarch," quoted in Samuel J. Ervin Jr., "The Ervin Family," unpublished manuscript, 1980, Family History Section, North Carolina Room, Burke County Library, Morganton.

19. Jean Conyers Ervin, interview by author, 17 March 2001, Morganton.

20. Sam Ervin, *Preserving the Constitution: The Autobiography of Sam Ervin* (Charlottesville, Va.: Michie, 1984), 3.

21. Ervin Corrections to Dabney, Ervin Papers, B., folder 1159.

22. S. J. Ervin to Laura [Ervin], 12 May 1898, in Ervin Family Papers, 4498, Southern Historical Collection, Wilson Library, University of North Carolina at Chapel Hill (hereafter cited as Ervin Family Papers), folder 288.

23. Laura Ervin to "Papa," 3 October 1900, Ervin Family Papers, folder 73.

24. Jean Conyers Ervin, interview by author, 17 March 2001, Morganton; Judge Samuel J. Ervin III, interview by Hilary Arnold, 24 February 1993, SOHP; Ervin, *Preserving the Constitution*, 3–4; Clancy, *Just a Country Lawyer*, 32.

25. Clancy, *Just a Country Lawyer*, 25.

26. Margaret Brown to Laura Ervin, 12 February 1974, Ervin Family Papers, folder 68; Editorial, "A Grand Matriarch of a Devoted Family," *Morganton News-Herald*, 18 June 1956.

27. Judge Sam Ervin III, interview by Hilary Arnold, 24 February 1993, SOHP; Jean Ervin interview, transcript, *Senator Sam* (film), New Atlantic Productions (hereafter cited as Jean Ervin interview, *Senator Sam*); Laura Ervin Smith interview, transcript, *Senator Sam* (film), New Atlantic Productions; Ervin, *Preserving the Constitution*, 5.

28. Obituary, *Charlotte News*, 15 June 1956, Ervin Papers, B., folder 1174. For information on the family tragedies, see Ervin Corrections to Dabney, Ervin Papers, B., folder 1159.

29. Descriptions of Fern Hill and the house come from Jean Conyers Ervin, *The Youngest of Ten: An Autobiography* (Chapel Hill: Professional Press, 1997), 33–38.

30. Jean Conyers Ervin, "The Sam Ervin I Know," speech given to the North Caroliniana Society, 20 June 1980, Chapel Hill, North Caroliniana Society Imprints, No. 4, 1980, 18; Clancy, *Just a Country Lawyer*, 36; Jean Conyers Ervin, interview by author, 17 March 2001, Morganton; Ervin Corrections to Dabney, Ervin Papers, B., folder 1159.

31. Jean Ervin, "Sam Ervin I Know," 18.

32. Jean Ervin, *Youngest of Ten*, 39; Jean Conyers Ervin, interview by author, 17 March 2001, Morganton; Sam Ervin to Dick Dabney, 16 December 1975, Ervin Papers, B., folder 1165.

33. Clancy, *Just a Country Lawyer*, 36; Ervin quote from Ervin Corrections to Dabney, Ervin Papers, B., folder 1161.

34. Mark Andrew Huddle, *Lift High the Cross: A Bicentennial History of the First Presbyterian Church, Morganton, North Carolina* (Morganton: First Presbyterian Church, 1997).

35. Catharine E. Ervin, "History of Women's Work" (Morganton: First Presbyterian Church, n.d. [1930s]), 15.

36. Jean Ervin interview, *Senator Sam*.

37. Sam Ervin, interview by Paul Clancy, Reel 1, side 2, "Mother," A-316 (hereafter cited as Clancy interviews), SOHP; Starnes, "Constitutionalist is consistently Inconsistent," *Washington Daily News*, 24 November 1969, Ervin Papers, Box 470; Clancy interviews, Reel 1, side 2.

38. Jean Ervin, "Sam Ervin I Know," 20; Jean Conyers Ervin, interview by author, 17 March 2001, Morganton; Clancy, *Just a Country Lawyer*, 41.

39. Clancy, *Just a Country Lawyer*, 40–41; Eunice Ervin interview, transcript, *Senator Sam* (film), New Atlantic Productions, 30 (hereafter cited as Eunice Ervin interview, *Senator Sam*).

40. Ervin Corrections to Dabney, Ervin Papers, B., folder 1159; Clancy interviews, Reel 1, side 2.

41. Clancy, *Just a Country Lawyer*, 18. For a few examples of Sam Ervin's historical writing see Sam Ervin, "A Colonial History of Rowan County, North Carolina," in *James Sprunt Historical Publications* 16, no. 1 (1917) (for which he won an award); Sam Ervin, "Entries in Colonel John Ervin's Bible," *South Carolina Historical Magazine* 79 (July 1978): 219–27; Sam Ervin, "The Ervin Family," unpublished manuscript, n.d., Family History Section, North Carolina Room, Burke County Library, Morganton (hereafter cited as "The Ervin Family").

42. Fred Hobson, *Tell About the South: The Southern Rage to Explain* (Baton Rouge: Louisiana State University Press, 1983), 3; William Faulkner, *Absalom, Absalom* (New York: Random House, 1936); W. J. Cash, *The Mind of the South* (New York: Alfred A. Knopf, 1941).

43. John B. Boles, "The Discovery of Southern Religious History," in John B. Boles and Evelyn Thomas Nolen, *Interpreting Southern History* (Baton Rouge: Louisiana State University Press, 1987); Edwin M. Yoder, "The Gospel According to Sam Ervin," *Ideas: Newsday's Journal of Opinion*, 22 April 1973; Sam Ervin, quoted in Henry Mitchell, "He's Still The Story-Telling Country Lawyer," *Washington Post*, 19 December 1982.

44. "Descendants of Ervins from John Knox," Ervin Family Papers, folder 120b; Colonel John Ervin quoted in Sam Ervin, "Entries in Colonel John Ervin's Bible," *South Carolina Historical Magazine* 79 (July 1978): 225.

45. Sam Ervin to Spencer Ervin, 16 May 1946, Ervin Papers, B., folder 2; Sam Ervin, "The Ervin Family."

46. Jean Ervin, "Notes of Interview with Father," 1942, unpublished manuscript, Ervin Family Papers, folder 133b; Sam Ervin, "The Ervin Family"; Clancy, *Just a Country Lawyer*, 19–20.

47. Sam Ervin, "The Ervin Family"; Sam Ervin, "John Witherspoon Ervin," *Historical and Genealogical Magazine* (South Carolina) 46 (July 1945), in Ervin Papers, B., folder 1317.

48. Sam Ervin, "John Witherspoon Ervin, of Manning S.C.," unpublished manuscript, Ervin Family Papers, folder 1315b; Jean Ervin, "Father's Boyhood Stories," unpublished manuscript, Ervin Family Papers, Folder 133b.

49. Eunice Ervin interview, *Senator Sam*, 19.

50. Jean Ervin, *Youngest of Ten*, 21–25; Ervin, *Preserving the Constitution*, 3–4.

51. Ervin to Robert Lawrence, 6 April 1940, Ervin Papers, B., folder 932.

52. Eunice Ervin interview, *Senator Sam*, 19. On the election of 1898 see David S. Cecelski and Timothy B. Tyson, eds., *Democracy Betrayed: The Wilmington Race Riot of 1898 and Its Legacy* (Chapel Hill: University of North Carolina Press, 1998).

53. Ervin, "Samuel James Ervin, and His Wife Laura Theresa Powe," unpublished manuscript, Burke County Library; Ervin, *Preserving the Constitution*, 4–5; Phifer, *Burke County*, 26–30; James L. Leloudis, *Schooling the New South: Pedagogy, Self, and Society in North Carolina, 1880–1920* (Chapel Hill: University of North Carolina Press, 1996), xii, 37.

54. "Annual Report of the Graded Schools of Morganton, N.C. 1906–07," NCC; Ervin, *Preserving the Constitution*, 4; Jean Ervin interview, *Senator Sam*.

55. Ervin, *Humor of a Country Lawyer*, 27.

56. Dabney, *Good Man*, 35–38; Ervin Corrections to Dabney, Ervin Papers, B., folder 1159.

57. Albert Coates, "The University of North Carolina at Chapel Hill: A Magic Gulf Stream in the Life of North Carolina," 1978, Ervin Papers, B., folder 862.

58. Coates, "A Magic Gulf Stream"; Dabney, *Good Man*, 41–42.

59. Ervin, *Preserving the Constitution*, 13–17; Ervin Corrections to Dabney, Ervin Papers, B., folder 1161; *The Yackety Yack* (the University of North Carolina Yearbook), 1917, 62, NCC.

60. *Yackety Yack*, 62.

61. Jean Ervin interview, *Senator Sam*, 20.

62. Ervin, "My Gratitude to the University at Chapel Hill," in Jean Conyers Ervin, "Sam Ervin I Know," 38–39.

63. Clancy, *Just a Country Lawyer*, 49–51; J. G. de Roulhac Hamilton, *Reconstruction in North Carolina* (Raleigh: Presses of Edwards and Broughton, 1906).

64. Ervin, *Humor of a Country Lawyer*, 29.

65. Dabney, *Good Man*, 44.

66. Ibid., 43–44.

67. There are no known copies of the text of the speech, but this account comes from

Ervin, *Preserving the Constitution*, 17. See also Albert Coates, "Three North Carolinians Who Have Stood Up to Be Counted for the Bill of Rights," NCC.

68. Clancy, *Just a Country Lawyer*, 57.

69. "Ervin Heads Reunion of 1917 Class," *Morganton News Herald*, 1 June 1967, Ervin Papers, B., folder 863; *Alumni Review* 5 (June 1917), Ervin Papers, B., folder 932; Clancy, *Just a Country Lawyer*, 57–58. See also R. Jackson Marshall III, *Memories of World War I: North Carolina Dough Boys on the Western Front* (Raleigh: North Carolina Division of Archives and History, 1998).

70. Dabney, *Good Man*, 67; Ervin Corrections to Dabney, Ervin Papers, B., folder 1159–60.

71. Ervin, *Preserving the Constitution*, 22; Dabney, *Good Man*, 68; Ervin Corrections to Dabney, folders 1159–60.

72. Ibid.

73. Ervin's secret was revealed by his friend Samuel I. Parker to Dick Dabney while the latter was conducting research for his biography *Good Man*. The full truth of the incident will not be known until Ervin's official military records in the National Archives are no longer sealed under confidentiality. Ervin refused to release them to Dabney. My reconstruction of the incident is based on Ervin, *Preserving the Constitution*, 22–23, Ervin Corrections to Dabney, Ervin Papers, B., folder 1160; and Dabney, *Good Man*, 68, 313–14. Examples of the incomplete version can be found in Clancy, *Just a Country Lawyer*, 64.

74. Dabney, *Good Man*, 71–72.

75. Clancy, *Just a Country Lawyer*, 67–68; Ervin, *Preserving the Constitution*, 23–24; the memo upon which the Army awarded Ervin his Silver Star can be found in Ervin Papers, B., folder 976.

76. Ervin, *Preserving the Constitution*, 24.

77. Fred Hardesty, "Little Known Stories About Well-Known People," *The State* (April 1967): 20; Beatrice Cobb, "Morganton Man Is Further Honored For Heroism," *Greensboro Daily News*, 25 May 1932, Ervin Papers, B., folder 1160; Ervin Corrections to Dabney, Ervin Papers, B., folder 1160.

78. Ibid.

79. Clancy, *Just a Country Lawyer*, 72–73.

80. Ervin to Mrs. J. M. Starrell, 24 January 1918, Ervin Papers, B., folder 288.

81. Ervin to "Mamma," 12 May 1918, Ervin Family Papers, folder 51.

82. Jean Ervin interview, *Senator Sam*, 22–25; Ervin to "Mamma," 13 June 1918 (copied by Jean Ervin, 1973), Ervin Family Papers, folder 51; Ervin to Mrs. John Starrell, 24 January 1918, Ervin Papers, B., folder 288; Lieutenant Col. Royal Reynolds to Ervin family, quoted in Clancy, *Just a Country Lawyer*, 76.

83. Jean Conyers Ervin, interview by author, 17 March 2001; Ervin quoted in Albert Coates, "Three North Carolinians Who Stood Up to Be Counted for the Bill of Rights," draft copy, Ervin Papers, B., folder 863.

84. Jean Conyers Ervin, interview by author, 17 March 2001, Morganton; Ervin, *Preserving the Constitution*, 24–26; Beatrice Cobb, "Morganton Man Is Further Honored For Heroism," *Greensboro Daily News*, 29 May 1932.

1. U.S. Congress, Senate, Select Committee on Presidential Campaign Activities, *Presidential Campaign Activities of 1972*, 93rd Cong., 1st sess., 1973, 767 (hereafter cited as Watergate Hearings).

2. Watergate Hearings, 2593–95. These and other key moments in the proceedings are described and analyzed in Paul Clancy, *Just a Country Lawyer: A Biography of Sam J. Ervin* (Bloomington: Indiana University Press, 1974), 263–92.

3. For information on Catharine Ellerbe Ervin see Jean Conyers Ervin, *The Youngest of Ten: An Autobiography* (Chapel Hill: Professional Press, 1997), 44–46.

4. Dick Dabney, *A Good Man: The Life of Senator Sam J. Ervin* (Boston: Houghton Mifflin, 1976), 82; Ervin to Dick Dabney, corrections to Dabney manuscript (hereafter cited as Ervin Corrections to Dabney), Sam J. Ervin Papers, Subgroup B: Private Papers, 3847B, Southern Historical Collection, Wilson Library, University of North Carolina at Chapel Hill, folder 1161 (hereafter cited as Ervin Papers, B.).

5. Dabney, *Good Man*, 82.

6. Eunice Ervin, interview, transcript, *Senator Sam* (film), New Atlantic Productions (hereafter cited as Eunice Ervin interview, *Senator Sam*), 48; Jean Ervin interview, transcript, *Senator Sam* (film), New Atlantic Productions (hereafter cited as Jean Ervin interview, *Senator Sam*), 30–31; Clancy, *Just a Country Lawyer*, 58.

7. Ervin, *Preserving the Constitution: The Autobiography of Sam Ervin* (Charlottesville, Va.: Michie, 1984), 29–30; Jean Ervin interview, *Senator Sam*, 28–29.

8. Ibid.

9. Ervin, *Humor of a Country Lawyer* (Chapel Hill: University of North Carolina Press, 1983), 33.

10. Ibid., 35–36.

11. Ervin's own conservative legal philosophy is clearly spelled out in *Preserving the Constitution*, 111–50. He quotes Holmes on page 140.

12. This interpretation of Harvard's impact on Ervin's civil libertarian views relies heavily on Clancy, *Just a Country Lawyer*, 80–84.

13. Ervin, interview by Paul Clancy, Tape 4, Side 1, Southern Oral History Program Collection (4007), Southern Historical Collection, Wilson Library, University of North Carolina at Chapel Hill (hereafter cited as SOHP); *Lincoln County News*, 10 November 1926, and *Morganton News-Herald*, 16 November 1922, clippings in Ervin Papers, B., Folder 932.

14. Clancy, *Just a Country Lawyer*, 87–88, 101.

15. Jean Ervin interview, *Senator Sam*, 31–32; Clancy, *Just a Country Lawyer*, 88–91; Dabney, *Good Man*, 89, 95–96.

16. Ervin Corrections to Dabney, Ervin Papers, B., Folder 1161; Clancy, *Just a Country Lawyer*, 101–3; Ervin, *Humor of a Country Lawyer*, 105–6.

17. "Old-School Lawyers Have Passed from Scene," *Morganton News-Herald*, 4 February 1958, Ervin Papers, B., folder 1174.

18. H. Clay Ferree, *Winston-Salem Journal and Sentinel*, 21 June 1945, Ervin Family Papers, Southern Historical Collection, folder 68. See also Judge Sam Ervin III, interview by Hilary Arnold, 24 February 1993, SOHP.

19. William Bobbitt described Ervin's courtroom mannerisms in Bobbitt interview,

transcript, *Senator Sam* (film), New Atlantic Productions (hereafter cited as Bobbitt interview), 4. Ervin's father is quoted in Clancy, *Just a Country Lawyer*, 102.

20. Ervin quotes his father in "The Role of the Lawyer in America," speech draft, n.d., Ervin Papers, B., folder 696, 13.

21. Ervin Corrections to Dabney, Ervin Papers, B., Folder 1159; Ervin, "Remarks at Law Day Observance, Wake Forest Law School, Winston-Salem, NC," Ervin Papers, B., Folder 226. On Tocqueville see Stephen J. Whitfield, "A Century and a Half of French Views of the United States," *Historian* 56 (Spring 1994): 532–35.

22. Frank Patton to Dick Dabney, 23 October 1975, Ervin Papers, B., Folder 1164. Ervin wrote, "In my judgement I have always been a country lawyer—a man who rendered legal services of all kinds to the people of a relative rural country." Ervin Corrections to Dabney, Ervin Papers, B., folder 1159.

23. Bobbitt interview, 3.

24. Bruce McGarrity Tindall, "Down Home Truths from Senator Sam Ervin," unpublished manuscript, Ervin Papers, B., folder 1171.

25. Ibid.

26. Ervin, *Humor of a Country Lawyer*, 95.

27. Arthur T. Abernethy, "Mostly Absurdities," n.d., in Ervin Papers, B., folder 936.

28. J. Braxton Craven Jr. to Dick Dabney, 24 October 1975, Ervin Papers, B., folder 1164.

29. Clancy, *Just a Country Lawyer*, 104.

30. Ibid., 113.

31. Ervin to Watt Espy Jr., 26 June 1975, Ervin Papers, B., folder 18.

32. Ibid.

33. Clancy, *Just a Country Lawyer*, 114–18, quote on 115.

34. Jean Ervin interview, *Senator Sam*, 31–34, quote on 32; Jean Conyers Ervin, interview by author, 17 March 2001, Morganton; Eunice Ervin interview, *Senator Sam*, 48; Clancy, *Just a Country Lawyer*, 89–91.

35. Ervin, "Eulogy for Essie Adeline Tate," draft, n.d., Ervin Papers, B., folder 642; Dabney, *Good Man*, 102, 199–200.

36. John L. Cheney Jr., ed., *North Carolina Government, 1585–1974: A Narrative & Statistical History* (Raleigh: North Carolina Department of the Secretary of State, 1981), 1075; Thomas H. Roberts and Joe B. Whitlow, "Morganton Plans for the Future" (Chapel Hill: UNC–Chapel Hill, Department of City and Regional Planning, 1951), North Carolina Collection, Wilson Library, University of North Carolina at Chapel Hill (hereafter cited as NCC), 3–5; Edward W. Phifer Jr., *Burke County: A Brief History* (Raleigh: North Carolina Department of Cultural Resources, Division of Archives and History, 1979), 139.

37. H. Eugene Willard, *Images of America: Morganton and Burke County* (Charleston, S.C.: Arcadia Publishing, 2001), 71–73; Phifer, *Burke County*, 81–93; Ervin, "The Story of the Bank," NCC Clipping File.

38. Susan Graham Erwin, *Village That Disappeared*, 63–64.

39. Ibid., 74.

40. "Rules and Regulations, Course of Study, The Graded Schools of Morganton," NCC; James L. Leloudis, *Schooling the New South: Pedagogy, Self, and Society in North Carolina, 1880–1920* (Chapel Hill: University of North Carolina Press, 1996), xii; "Ordinances, Ordained and Published by the Town of Morganton, 1915," NCC.

41. Gil Billings, "Statue of Confederate Soldier Rededication," pamphlet printed by the Burke County Historical Society, 12 September 1993; "The Birthright: A Pageant Portraying the History of Burke County," printed program, 15 May 1924. See also Susan Graham Erwin, *Village That Disappeared*, 74, for what seems to be a related description.

42. Jasper Barry Shannon, *Toward a New Politics in the South* (Knoxville: University of Tennessee Press, 1949), 50. For a discussion of the various theories of elite leadership in the emerging New South see Earl Black and Merle Black, *Politics and Society in the South* (Cambridge, Mass.: Harvard University Press, 1987), 24–34.

43. William H. Chafe, *Civilities and Civil Rights: Greensboro, North Carolina, and the Black Struggle for Freedom* (New York: Oxford University Press, 1980).

44. V. O. Key Jr., *Southern Politics in State and Nation* (New York: Alfred A. Knopf, 1949), 205–6.

45. Ibid., 211. For more on Key's analysis of North Carolina, see Thad L. Beyle, "The Paradox of North Carolina," in *Politics and Policy in North Carolina*, ed. Thad L. Beyle and Merle Black (New York: MSS Information Corporation, 1975), 1–12; Paul Luebke, *Tar Heel Politics, 2000* (Chapel Hill: University of North Carolina Press, 1998), 1–19; and Alexander Lamis, *Southern Politics in the 1990s* (Baton Rouge: Louisiana State University Press, 1999), x–xxi. The cohesion of these political organizations should not be exaggerated. They existed more as loose coalitions than as actual political machines. See Anthony J. Badger, *North Carolina and the New Deal* (Raleigh: North Carolina Department of Cultural Resources, Division of Archives and History, 1981), 7–12.

46. Ervin, draft of personal biographical entry, Ervin Papers, B., Folder 922; Ervin, "History of the American Legion of the Department of North Carolina: 1920–1921," unpublished manuscript, Ervin Papers, B., folder 617.

47. Clancy, *Just a Country Lawyer*, 106.

48. Ervin, *Humor of a Country Lawyer*, 120.

49. For Ervin's record in the legislature see Ervin Corrections to Dabney, Ervin Papers, B., Folder 1160; *Journal of the House of Representatives of the General Assembly of the State of North Carolina*, Sessions 1923, 1924, 1925, 1931, NCC; Clancy, *Just a Country Lawyer*, 87–91.

50. Ervin proposed educational bonds for several school districts in the Morganton area during his first session in the legislature, but it was not his first bill as he sometimes claimed. His initial proposed legislation called for the creation of a new division within the Department of Printing and Labor dedicated to the deaf, and for a "competent deaf man to take charge of such division." *Journal of the House of Representatives of the General Assembly of the State of North Carolina*, Session 1923, NCC.

51. Willard B. Gatewood Jr., "Professors, Fundamentalists, and the Legislature," in *The North Carolina Experience*, ed. Lindley S. Butler and Alan D. Watson (Chapel Hill: University of North Carolina Press, 1984), 356.

52. Ibid.

53. Ervin, "Church and State and Freemasonry," *Maine Mason* 2 (Spring 1974): 15, Ervin Papers, B., folder 677. See also Reynold S. Davenport, *Sam J. Ervin, Jr.: The Man and the Mason* (Raleigh: Grand Lodge of Ancient Free and Accepted Masons of North Carolina, 1985).

54. Ervin, *Preserving the Constitution*, 38.

55. Ervin Corrections to Dabney, Ervin Papers, B., folder 1159; Clancy, *Just a Country Lawyer*, 92.

56. There is no written record of the speech as no minutes were taken of the floor debate in the legislature. This quote is from Ervin's recollection as written in his autobiography, *Preserving the Constitution*, 40.

57. George B. Autry, "Sam Ervin: The Book By and About Him," *Duke Law Review* (December 1985): 1246; Willard B. Gatewood Jr., *Preachers, Pedagogues, and Politicians: The Evolution Controversy in North Carolina, 1920–1927* (Chapel Hill: University of North Carolina Press, 1966).

58. C. W. Tillett Jr., to Ervin, 20 February 1925, Ervin Papers, B., folder 1. Ervin's speech was noted in several of the major newspapers around the state. See "House Declines to Table Poole Evolution Bill," *Raleigh News and Observer*, n.d. (1925), Ervin Papers, B., folder 1173.

59. "Negro Attacks White Girl, Inflicting Wound Causing Her Death; Whole Community Aroused," *Morganton News-Herald*, 23 June 1927.

60. Ibid.

61. "Search for Negro Outlaw Renewed with New Enthusiasm as Trail Seems to Lead Nearer," *Morganton News-Herald*, 30 June 1927; Jean Conyers Ervin, interview by author, 17 March 2001, Morganton.

62. "Hunt in Vain for Broadus Miller," *Raleigh News and Observer*, 27 June 1927; "A Trying Week," *Morganton News-Herald*, 30 June 1927.

63. Edwin B. Bridges to Governor A. W. McLean, 5 July 1927, McLean Governor Papers, Correspondence, 500–526, North Carolina State Archives, North Carolina Division of Archives and History, Raleigh (hereafter cited as NCSA).

64. "Broadus Miller Meets His Doom in Gun Battle," *Raleigh News and Observer*, 4 July 1927.

65. Edwin B. Bridges to Governor A. W. McLean, 5 July 1927, McLean Governor Papers, Correspondence, 500–526, NCSA; "Broadus Miller Shot Down by Lone Pursuer," *Charlotte Observer*, 4 July 1927; "Long Hunt for Negro Outlaw Ended Sunday," *Morganton News-Herald*, 7 July 1927; "Broadus Miller Meets His Doom in Gun Battle," *Raleigh News and Observer*, 4 July 1927.

66. "Needless Atrocity," *Raleigh News and Observer*, 5 July 1927.

67. Edwin B. Bridges to Governor A. W. McLean, 5 July 1927, McLean Governor Papers, Correspondence, 500–526, NCSA; "Pardon Commissioner Says Slaying Necessary," *Morganton News-Herald*, 7 July 1927; "Long Hunt for Negro Outlaw Ended Sunday," *Morganton News-Herald*, 7 July 1927.

68. "Says Slaying Justified, McLean Pleased Broadus Miller Was Not Lynched," *Charlotte Observer*, 5 July 1927; "Report of Mob Violence Irks Burke Sheriff," *Charlotte Observer*, 6 July 1927; "Indignation," editorial, *Morganton News-Herald*, 7 July 1927. See also Bruce Edward Baker, "Lynching Ballads in North Carolina" (M.A. thesis, University of North Carolina at Chapel Hill, 1995), 44–55.

69. Ervin Corrections to Dabney, Ervin Papers, B., folder 1162; Clancy, *Just a Country Lawyer*, 107. For an insightful discussion of Tar Heel politics in a national context during the 1920s, see Glenda Gilmore, "False Friends and Avowed Enemies: Southern African Americans and Party Allegiances in the 1920s," in *Jumpin' Jim Crow*, ed. Jane Dailey, Glenda Gilmore, and Bryant Simon (Princeton: Princeton University Press, 2000), 219–38.

70. "Grand Lodge Knights of Pythias Holding Annual Convention Here," *Morganton*

News-Herald, 14 June 1924; Badger, *North Carolina and the New Deal*, 7–12; Luebke, *Tar Heel Politics, 2000*, 10–15.

71. Neither of Ervin's two biographers gives more than one sentence to his role in the strike of 1934 and I have found no other reference to it in any of the historical literature. See Dabney, *Good Man*, 115. The best source on the cotton textile towns and the strike of 1934 is Jacquelyn Dowd Hall, James Leloudis, Robert Korstad, Mary Murphy, Lu Ann Jones, and Christopher Daly, *Like a Family: The Making of a Southern Cotton Mill World* (New York: W. W. Norton, 1987), especially 325–54. For briefer overviews of the strike of 1934, see Douglass Carl Abrams, *Conservative Constraints: North Carolina and the New Deal* (Jackson: University Press of Mississippi, 1992), 35–54; Badger, *North Carolina and the New Deal*, 29–33.

72. John A. Salmond, *Gastonia 1929: The Story of the Loray Mill Strike* (Chapel Hill: University of North Carolina Press, 1995); John L. Bell Jr., *Hard Times: Beginnings of the Great Depression in North Carolina, 1929–1933* (Raleigh: North Carolina Department of Cultural Resources, Division of Archives and History, 1982), especially 31–40.

73. John Hanes to J. C. B. Ehringhaus, 6 September 1934, Governor J. C. B. Ehringhaus Papers, General Correspondence, box 139, folder "Strike Situation Correspondence," NCSA (hereafter cited as Ehringhaus Papers); "60,000 Textile Workers Idle in Carolinas," *Charlotte Observer*, 4 September 1934; "More Troops Called to N.C. Strike Front," *Charlotte Observer*, 11 September 1934.

74. There are many contradictory accounts of what happened in Belmont on 17 and 18 September 1934. My summary follows closely the testimony Sam Ervin gave to the National Guard's Court of Inquiry, a copy of which can be found in Ervin Papers, B., Folder 943 (hereafter cited as Ervin Testimony, Court of Inquiry), quotes found on page 7. Ervin's testimony does not agree with newspaper accounts that relied upon other witnesses. See "Strike Picket Dies of Bayonet Wounds," *Charlotte Observer*, 20 September 1934.

75. Ervin Testimony, Court of Inquiry, Ervin Papers, B., folder 943, 9.

76. Ibid., 10; Paul R. Younts to J. Van B. Metts, 28 September 1934, Adjutant General's Department Papers, General Correspondence, Box AG 113, Folder "Special Duty Textile Strike, 1934," NCSA (hereafter cited as Adjutant General's Papers).

77. Ibid., 11–12.

78. Ibid., 12–13; "Two Men are Badly Injured as Guardsmen Use Bayonets," *Charlotte Observer*, 19 September 1934; "Citizens Act to Keep Order in Strike Zone," *Charlotte Observer*, 20 September 1934.

79. "Court of Inquiry in Death of Ernest K. Riley," Ehringhaus Papers, Box 139, folder "Riley: Court of Inquiry," see especially 32–33; Ervin to Adjutant General J. Van B. Metts, 16 December 1934, Ehringhaus Papers, box 163, folder "Belmont"; Resolution, Central Labor Union of Salisbury and Vicinity, 10 December 1934; Ehringhaus Papers, box 103, folder "Belmont." For an example of how Ervin's name was left out of most official reports, see Memorandum, "Resume of Situation by Areas," 7, J. Vann B. Metts, 19 January 1935, Adjutant General's Papers, box 114, folder "Special Duty Textile Strike, 1934," NCSA.

80. J. Van B. Metts to W. H. Abernathy, 21 December 1934, Ehringhaus Papers, box 103, folder "Belmont"; J. C. B. Ehringhaus to J. H. Hill, 25 January 1935, Ehringhaus Papers, box 103, folder "Belmont."

81. Ervin to Adjutant General J. Van B. Metts, 16 December 1934, Ehringhaus Papers, box 163, folder "Belmont."

82. Ibid.

83. The strike of 1934 has been ignored in the standard North Carolina textbooks until recently. The most popular college text from the 1950s to the 1970s only mentions the strike in three brief sentences. See Hugh Talmage Lefler and Albert Ray Newsome, *North Carolina: The History of a Southern State* (Chapel Hill: University of North Carolina Press, 1973), 641. The strike is not mentioned at all in William S. Powell, *North Carolina Through Four Centuries* (Chapel Hill: University of North Carolina Press, 1989).

84. Income information found in Ervin Papers, B., box 87. "Ervin, with Open Mind, Girds for Congressional Assignment," *Charlotte Observer*, 13 June 1946. Ervin did not object to being labeled as a part of the Shelby Dynasty. See Ervin Corrections to Dabney, Ervin Papers, B., folder 1160.

85. Dabney, *Good Man*, 114; Clancy, *Just a Country Lawyer*, 121.

86. Ibid., Ervin Corrections to Dabney, Ervin Papers, B., folder 1160.

87. Gordon Boger, " 'Gentleman' Best Described Ervin," *Morganton News-Herald*, 25 April 1985.

88. Clancy, *Just a Country Lawyer*, 122.

89. Craven also wrote, "It is worth noting that Senator Ervin was introduced to his profession at the Harvard Law School by what Karl Llewellyn calls the strange ideas of Langdell. Certainly he must have been taught to admire what Pound called the Formal Style: that it is a good judge's business to steel himself against emotion, and against deflection by sense or sense of justice which may run counter to 'the law,' lest such should lead him to neglect his stern duty." James Braxton Craven Jr., to Richard Dabney, 24 October 1975, Ervin Papers, B., folder 1164.

90. Ibid. Braxton's letter is reproduced in Ervin, *Preserving the Constitution*, 382–85.

91. Walter Malone, "To a Judge," quoted in its entirety in Ervin, *Preserving the Constitution*, 45–46.

92. Clyde Hoey to Ervin, 21 July 1936, Ervin Papers, B., folder 1; "Governor Appoints Ervin," *Raleigh News and Observer*, 10 January 1937, NCCF; Dabney, *Good Man*, 119–20.

93. "Appointment of Judge Ervin Popular and Pleasing," *Morganton News-Herald*, 15 January 1937, Ervin Papers, B., folder 932. Ervin ruled on several historically significant cases during his seven years on the Superior Court, including two murder cases in which he sentenced the defendants to death and then required that the appointed counsels appeal his rulings. Both men were eventually executed. Ervin also had one of his opinions, *Williams v. North Carolina* (1947), appealed to the U.S. Supreme Court, where it was upheld by the majority but with stinging dissents by Justices William O. Douglas and Hugo L. Black. Ervin's service on the Superior Court is discussed more fully in Clancy, *Just a Country Lawyer*, 120–34; Dabney, *Good Man*, 119–29.

94. Susie Sharp to Richard Dabney, 7 November 1975, Ervin Papers, B., folder 1164.

95. Ibid. See also Suzie Sharp to Ervin, 27 June 1949, Ervin Papers, B., folder 982; [Judge Susie] Sharp and [Judge William H.] Bobbitt, interview, transcript, *Senator Sam* (film), Ervin Papers, B., 1–7.

96. "His Honor," *Kinston Free Press*, November 1938, Ervin Papers, B., folder 932; "Judge Ervin Re-appointed," n.d., Ervin Papers, B., folder 936. Ervin collected additional

newspaper clippings assessing his time as a Superior Court judge and published them in his autobiography. See Ervin, *Preserving the Constitution*, 377–81.

97. Clancy, *Just a Country Lawyer*, 121.

98. This story is attributed to Brooks Hays in a newspaper clipping by E. E. Edgar titled "Quick Reading," n.d., Ervin Papers, B., folder 1211.

99. Medical Report, Elbert Persons to Ervin, 27 December 1948, Ervin Papers, B., folder 982 (hereafter cited as Ervin Medical Report); Jean Ervin, *Youngest of Ten*, 46; Ervin Corrections to Dabney, Ervin Papers, B., folder 1160.

100. Dabney, *Good Man*, 128–29; Ervin Corrections to Dabney, Ervin Papers, B., folder 1160. Ervin explained his official reasons for resigning in Ervin to L. T. Harsell Jr., 10 February 1944, Ervin Papers, B., folder 1.

101. Ervin Corrections to Dabney, Ervin Papers, B., folders 1160, 1161.

102. Ibid., folder 1165; Ervin Medical Report, Ervin Papers, B., folder 982.

103. Editorial, *Morganton News-Herald*, 14 July 1944.

104. Dabney, *Good Man*, 135; Ervin Corrections to Dabney, Ervin Papers, B., folder 1165.

105. U.S. Comptroller General Lindsay Warren to Ervin, 29 December 1945, Ervin Papers, B., folder 907.

106. *Congressional Record*, 79th Cong., 2nd sess., 14 January 1946.

107. Joe Ervin to Sam Ervin, 26 October 1945, Ervin Papers, B., folder 904.

108. U.S. Comptroller General Lindsay Warren to Ervin, 29 December 1945, Ervin Papers, B., folder 907; "Rep. Joseph W. Ervin is Dead: Funeral Services Today," *Charlotte Observer*, 26 December 1945.

109. "Rep. Joseph W. Ervin is Dead: Funeral Services Today," *Charlotte Observer*, 26 December 1945; "Joe Ervin," *Charlotte Observer*, 27 December 1945; Clancy, *Just a Country Lawyer*, 135–37; Ervin, *Preserving the Constitution*, 47.

110. Dabney, *Good Man*, 136–37. Ervin Corrections to Dabney, Ervin Papers, B., folder 1160.

111. J. C. B. Ehringhaus to Ervin, 5 January 1946, Ervin Papers, B., folder 871; "Judge Sam Ervin's Nomination Solves Problem for Party," *Charlotte Observer*, 2 January 1946, NCC Clipping File.

112. "Lawmaker for Draft Extension," *Army and Navy Bulletin*, 20 April 1946, Ervin Papers, B., folder 872.

113. Clancy, *Just a Country Lawyer*, 140–41; Ervin, *Humor of a Country Lawyer*, 165.

114. For a revised version of the joke see Bill M. Wise, *The Wisdom of Sam Ervin* (New York: Ballantine Books, 1973), 7–8. Confirmation of the frequency of "Nigra jokes" is found in Senator Roman L. Hruska, interview by author, 26 June 1989, Omaha, Nebraska; B. B. Dougherty to Ervin, 24 January 1946, Ervin Papers, B., folder 871.

115. Ervin, "Should the OPA Be Revived?" reprint of speech, 10 July 1946, Ervin Papers, B., folder 872.

116. Ervin, "The Role of a Southern Senator," n.d., transcription, 12, Ervin Papers, B., folder 748.

117. Ervin, "Which Has More Vitality, John L. Lewis or the American Constitution?" reprint of speech, 8 May 1946, Ervin Papers, B., folder 872. It is interesting to note that the speech was reprinted in *Industrial News Review* 58 (June 1946).

118. Ervin to Charles A. Cannon, 11 January 1946, Ervin Papers, B., folder 871, "Non-Political Views of Our Labor Laws," *Charlotte Observer*, 10 May 1946, Ervin Papers, B., folder 872. For a full explanation of Ervin's views on labor see Ervin, *Preserving the Constitution*, 187–94.

119. Ervin to Charles A. Cannon, 19 January 1946, Ervin Papers, B., folder 871.

120. Thomas C. Parramore, *Express Lanes and Country Roads: The Way We Lived in North Carolina, 1920–1970* (Chapel Hill: University of North Carolina Press, 1983). On the impact of tourism in the mountains see Richard D. Starnes, *Creating the Land of the Sky: Tourism and Society in Western North Carolina* (Tuscaloosa: University of Alabama Press, 2005).

121. Nat Irvin, "Courage: Man is upfront about refusal to sit in back," *Winston-Salem Journal*, 19 October 1997; Jeffrey J. Crow, Paul D. Escott, and Flora J. Hatley, *A History of African Americans in North Carolina*, 2nd ed. (Raleigh: Office of Archives and History, North Carolina Department of Cultural Resources, 2002), 145–52; Rev. Joseph B. Clower Jr. to Joe Ervin, 7 June 1945, Ervin Papers, B., folder 904; Roberts and Whitlow, "Morganton Plans for the Future," NCC; Judge Sam Ervin III, interview by Hilary L. Arnold, 24 February 1993, SOHP, 15–16. Information on Ervin's daughters is found in Clancy, *Just a Country Lawyer*, 130; Dabney, *Good Man*, 61–63.

122. Ervin Corrections to Dabney, Ervin Papers, B., folder 1160; "Minutes of the Organization Meeting of the North Carolina Commission for the Improvement of the Administration of Justice," 24 July 1947, Ervin Papers, B., folder 863. Ervin's quote on education is from Ervin to Members of the General Assembly, 3 March 1947, Ervin Papers, B., folder 964.

123. Ervin quoted in H. G. Hedrick to Ervin, 20 August 1948, Ervin Papers, B., folder 981. For the story of his appointment and salary see Clancy, *Just a Country Lawyer*, 144; Ervin Corrections to Dabney, Ervin Papers, B., folder 1160; Ervin to C. David Swift, 2 February 1948, Ervin Papers, B., folder 978.

124. *Raleigh Times*, 5 February 1948, clipping in Ervin Papers, B., folder 979; I. G. Greer to Ervin, 4 February 1948, Ervin Papers, B., folder 979.

125. Quotations are taken from U.S. Senate, Committee on the Judiciary, Hearings before the Subcommittee on Constitutional Rights, *Privacy and the Rights of Federal Employees*, 89th Cong., 2nd sess., 1966, 240.

126. Ibid.

127. Ervin, *Preserving the Constitution*, 50.

128. J. Braxton Craven Jr. to Dick Dabney, 24 October 1975, Ervin Papers, B., folder 1164.

129. F. E. Winslow to Ervin, 23 April 1954, Ervin Papers, B., folder 981. See also "Conservative Libertarian," *Time*, 8 March 1971.

130. J. Braxton Craven Jr. to Dick Dabney, 24 October 1975, Ervin Papers, B., folder 1164.

131. Associate Justice Dan K. Moore, remarks to the North Caroliniana Society, 20 June 1980, in Jean Conyers Ervin, *The Sam Ervin I Know* (Chapel Hill: North Caroliniana Society, 1980), 10–11. Ervin's opinions also received national attention and praise. An associate solicitor of the Veterans Administration wrote: "The opinion by Justice Ervin . . . is undoubtedly the most complete and carefully prepared opinion on priority of liens and claims in

receiverships I have ever read." See C. P. Pate, Chief Attorney, Veterans Administration, to Ervin, 22 October 1952, Ervin Papers, B., folder 981. See also "Price Control Violation Raises Unique Question," clipping from *Judicial Highlights*, in Ervin Papers, B., folder 2.

132. Bruce McGarrity Tindall, "Down Home Truths from Senator Sam Ervin," unpublished manuscript, Ervin Papers, B., folder 1171, 3–6, 69.

133. Ervin, "A Congressional Salamagundi," an address to a meeting of the North Carolina Bar, 27 October 1966, reprinted in *North Carolina Bar* 13 (1966): 29; "Conservative Libertarian," *Time*, 8 March 1971; Emery B. Denny, "History of the Supreme Court of North Carolina—From January 1, 1919, until January 1, 1969," *North Carolina Reports* 274 (1968): 611–30.

134. Ervin, *Preserving the Constitution*, 54–55; Clancy, *Just a Country Lawyer*, 142–43.

135. Ervin to Adrian J. Newton, 29 October 1975, Ervin Papers, B., folder 1164; Ervin, *Preserving the Constitution*, 55.

136. "Ervin-for-Governor Movement Causes Speculation in Capital," *Charlotte Observer*, 12 February 1952, Ervin Papers, B., folder 936. Ervin told his first biographer that he discouraged the move to make him governor, but the evidence suggests that he let the momentum build for a few weeks. See "Ervin-for-Governor Session," *Raleigh News and Observer*, 4 February 1952, NCC Clipping File; "Ervin Boomed for Governor," *Asheville Citizen*, 30 January 1952, NCC Clipping File.

137. Ervin's son thought that he might have felt a little isolated during his first years on the Supreme Court, that in some ways he missed the contacts with people he had as a lawyer and as a trial judge. Judge Sam Ervin III, interview by Hilary L. Arnold, 24 February 1993, SOHP, 14. Others insisted that Justice Ervin was very content on the bench. Adrian Newton, a clerk at the Supreme Court remembered, "He [Ervin] enjoyed life to the fullest extent and you couldn't be around him a moment without he'd have you laughing. You could tell he was getting as much pleasure out of his stories as other people. I never saw him that I recall when he seemed to be blue or down and out in the slightest. He could always see the humorous side of things. He was a joy to have around." Quote in Clancy, *Just a Country Lawyer*, 147.

138. Brogden is quoted in Ervin, "McCarthyism," unpublished manuscript chapter, Ervin Papers, B., folder 779; "Under the Dome," *Raleigh News and Observer*, 31 January 1948, Ervin Papers, folder 982; Ervin Corrections to Dabney, Ervin Papers, B., folder 1161.

CHAPTER THREE

1. Alton Lennon, North Carolina's other senator, was a lame duck who had just been defeated in the Democratic primary by ex-Governor Kerr Scott. On Hoey's death see "Nation's Leaders Mourn Passing of Ex-Governor," *Asheville Citizen*, 13 May 1954; "Ex-Governor, 76, Succumbs at Office Desk," *Durham Morning Herald*, 13 May 1954; *Raleigh News and Observer*, 13 May 1954.

2. *Brown v. Board of Education, Topeka Kansas*, 347 U.S. 483 (1954). See Richard Kluger, *Simple Justice: The History of Brown v. Board of Education and Black America's Struggle for Equality* (New York: Knopf, 1976); J. Harvie Wilkinson III, *From Brown to Bakke: The Supreme Court and School Integration, 1954–1978* (New York: Oxford University Press, 1979); Raymond Wolters, *The Burden of Brown: Thirty Years of School Desegregation* (Knoxville: University of Tennessee Press, 1984).

3. Both of Ervin's previous biographers struggled briefly with the question of his opposition to civil rights before basically agreeing with the orthodox interpretation that he was a consistent constitutional scholar who acted as moderately as any white southerner could in the 1950s and 1960s. Paul R. Clancy, *Just a Country Lawyer: A Biography of Sam J. Ervin* (Bloomington: Indiana University Press, 1974); Dick Dabney, *A Good Man: The Life of Senator Sam Ervin* (Boston: Houghton Mifflin, 1976).

4. For some time before 1954, southern politicians had been anxious about the Supreme Court's shifting position on the constitutionality of de jure racial segregation. The Court, in a series of decisions, had chiseled away at the laws that protected the white race's privileged position. But southerners began to panic when the Court agreed to consider *Brown* in 1952. A year before his death, Senator Hoey had confided that he "hesitated to think what the result would be" if the Court forced the desegregation of North Carolina's schools. The state's attorney general predicted "calamitous results" and feared that "an adverse decision in these cases would bring about more difficulties and trouble in the South than anything that has happened since the Civil War." Attorney General Harry McMullan to Senator Clyde R. Hoey, 2 December 1953, William B. Umstead Papers, North Carolina State Archives, Raleigh (hereafter cited as Umstead Papers); I. Beverly Lake, "United States Supreme Court: Separation of Races in Public Schools," an unpublished legal brief prepared by the N.C. Dept. of Justice, undated, Umstead Papers. For the southern response to *Brown* see Numan Bartley, *The Rise of Massive Resistance: Race and Politics in the South During the 1950s* (Baton Rouge: Louisiana State University Press, 1969); Francis M. Wilhoit, *The Politics of Massive Resistance* (New York: George Braziller, 1973); Earl Black, *Southern Governors and Civil Rights: Racial Segregation as a Campaign Issue in the Second Reconstruction* (Cambridge, Mass.: Harvard University Press, 1976). For North Carolina's response see William Chafe, *Civilities and Civil Rights: Greensboro, North Carolina, and the Black Struggle for Freedom* (New York: Oxford University Press, 1980). For a competing analysis see Jonathan Houghton, "The Politics of Sly Resistance: North Carolina's Response to *Brown*," paper delivered at the Organization of American Historians Annual Meeting, 11 April 1991.

5. North Carolina's reputation as a "progressive" southern state is discussed in V. O. Key Jr., *Southern Politics in State and Nation* (New York: Alfred A. Knopf, 1949), 205–28; Thad L. Beyle, "The Paradox of North Carolina," and Merle Black, "North Carolina: The 'Best' American State," both in *Politics and Policy in North Carolina*, ed. Beyle and Black (New York: MSS Information Corporation, 1975), 1–11; Thomas C. Parramore, "Sit-Ins and Civil Rights," in *The North Carolina Experience*, ed. Lindley S. Butler and Alan D. Watson (Chapel Hill: University of North Carolina Press, 1984), 104; H. G. Jones, "North Carolina, 1946–1976: Where Historians Fear to Tread," in *Writing North Carolina History*, ed. Jeffrey J. Crow and Larry E. Tise (Chapel Hill: University of North Carolina Press, 1979), 214–19.

6. Umstead's remarks are discussed in Wilhoit, *Politics of Massive Resistance*, 31; Chafe, *Civilities and Civil Rights*, 65.

7. On the decline of the Klan, see Willard G. Cole, Editor, *News Reporter*, Whitesville, N.C., to William B. Umstead, 2 April 1953, Umstead Papers, box 47.

8. Petitions from "North Carolinians for Preservation of the White Race, Inc." were

sent to the governor from across the state between May and September of 1954; Umstead Papers, box 47.

9. "Democratic Party Platform, 1954," *North Carolina Manual, 1955* (Raleigh, 1955), 136–49; "Tar Heel of the Week: Irving E. Carlyle," *Raleigh News and Observer*, 15 October 1961.

10. There is some debate concerning the reaction to Carlyle's speech. See "Platform Flays GOP Rule," *Raleigh News and Observer*, 21 May 1954; "Tar Heel of the Week: Irving E. Carlyle," *Raleigh News and Observer*, 15 October 1961; and Chafe, *Civilities and Civil Rights*, 65–66n9, 365.

11. "Tar Heel of the Week: Irving E. Carlyle," *Raleigh News and Observer*, 15 October 1961; Clancy, *Just a Country Lawyer*, 152–53; Dabney, *Good Man*, 141. For a contrasting opinion of Carlyle's chances see Edward L. Rankin, interview by Jay Jenkins, August 1987, Southern Oral History Program Collection, Southern Historical Collection, Wilson Library, University of North Carolina at Chapel Hill (hereafter cited as SOHP).

12. H. L. Riddle Jr. to William B. Umstead, 21 May 1954, Umstead Papers, box 62.

13. Ervin to R. P. Reade, 20 May 1954, Umstead Papers, box 58.1. Ervin's statement supports V. O. Key's thesis that the primary role of a southern senator was to maintain the status quo in race relations by preventing national intervention in local affairs. See V. O. Key Jr., *Southern Politics*.

14. Umstead's last Senate appointment, Alton Lennon—whom he picked to fill the seat left vacant by the death of Willis Smith in 1953—had recently been defeated in the Democratic primary by one of Umstead's rivals, former governor Kerr Scott. Lennon lost the election in spite of his vigorous attempts to emulate the racist tactics that helped Smith beat out Frank Graham in the infamous 1950 Democratic primary. Lennon charged that Scott had attempted to end North Carolina's system of racial segregation when he served as governor. See "Lennon Declares Scott Opposed Segregation," *Greensboro Daily News*, 19 May 1954; "Senate Candidates Deplore Ruling," *Raleigh Carolinian*, 22 May 1954; "Ad Reprints Draw Heavy Protests," *Greensboro Daily News*, 28 May 1954; Chafe, *Civilities and Civil Rights*, 58. On the Graham-Smith election of 1950, see Julian M. Pleasants and Augustus M. Burns III, *Frank Porter Graham and the 1950 Senate Race in North Carolina* (Chapel Hill: University of North Carolina Press, 1990).

15. See Hugh Talmage Lefler and Albert Ray Newsome, *North Carolina: The History of a Southern State*, 3rd ed. (Chapel Hill: University of North Carolina Press, 1973); Paul Luebke, *Tar Heel Politics, 2000* (Chapel Hill: University of North Carolina Press, 1998).

16. Ervin, *Preserving the Constitution: The Autobiography of Senator Sam Ervin* (Charlottesville, Va.: Michie), 46.

17. Ibid., 63.

18. Ibid., 64; Clancy, *Just a Country Lawyer*, 152.

19. Ervin had been within the inner circle of North Carolina politics since returning to the state in 1923. His connections had helped him gain his judicial appointments. Ironically, Clyde Hoey, whom Ervin was soon to replace, had appointed him as a Superior Court judge in 1937 when Hoey served as North Carolina's governor. It is also significant that by sending Ervin to the Senate, Umstead created an empty seat on the state Supreme Court which he could also fill with a political supporter.

20. Ervin, *Preserving the Constitution*, 64–65; Clancy, *Just a Country Lawyer*, 153.

21. Ervin, *Preserving the Constitution*, 64.

22. Ibid.

23. "Governor Umstead Makes His Choice for the Senate," *Durham Morning Herald*, 7 June 1954; "Morganton Jurist Named by Umstead as Hoey Successor," *Asheville Citizen Times*, 6 June 1954.

24. "State Supreme Court Member Succeeds Hoey," *Durham Morning Herald*, 6 June 1954, in Sam J. Ervin Papers, Subgroup A: Senate Papers, 3847A, Southern Historical Collection, University of North Carolina at Chapel Hill (hereafter cited as Ervin Papers), box 469.

25. "Morganton Jurist Named by Umstead as Hoey Successor," *Asheville Citizen Times*, 6 June 1954, Ervin Papers, box 469.

26. "Let's Not Label Judge Ervin Yet," *Raleigh News and Observer*, 7 June 1954, Ervin Papers, box 469.

27. Editorial, *Raleigh Carolinian*, 12 June 1954.

28. "Beaming Ervin Climbs Aboard Washington Merry-Go-Round," *Charlotte Observer*, 12 June 1954, Ervin Papers, box 469; "Sam Ervin Takes Oath as Senator," *Raleigh News and Observer*, 12 June 1954, Ervin Papers, Ervin newspaper clippings notebooks, s-1 (hereafter cited as Ervin Notebooks).

29. "Beaming Ervin Climbs Aboard Merry-Go-Round," *Charlotte Observer*, 12 June 1954, Ervin Papers, box 469; Ervin, interview by Paul Clancy, tape 6, side 1, Ervin Papers. On the career of Joe McCarthy see Thomas C. Reeves, *The Life and Times of Joe McCarthy* (New York: Stein and Day, 1982); David M. Oshinsky, *A Conspiracy So Immense: The World of Joe McCarthy* (New York: Free Press, 1983); Richard H. Rovere, *Senator Joe McCarthy* (New York: Harcourt, Brace, 1959). Studies of McCarthyism and related topics include Thomas C. Reeves, ed., *McCarthyism*, 2nd ed. (Malabar, Fla.: Robert E Krieger Publishing Co., 1982); Michael Paul Rogin, *The Intellectuals and McCarthy: The Radical Specter* (Cambridge, Mass.: MIT Press, 1967); Robert Griffith, *The Politics of Fear: Joseph R. McCarthy and the Senate* (Lexington: University Press of Kentucky, 1970); Richard M. Fried, *Nightmare in Red: The McCarthy Era in Perspective* (New York: Oxford University Press, 1990).

30. Ervin, interview by Paul Clancy, tape 6, side 1, Ervin Papers.

31. "Sam Ervin Takes Oath as Senator," *Raleigh News and Observer*, 12 June 1954, Ervin Notebooks, s-1.

32. Ervin to Charles A. Cannon, 28 October 1954, Ervin Papers, box 2. Ervin often expressed strong anticommunist opinions: See Ervin to C. R. Wharton, 4 October 1954, Ervin Papers, box 1; Ervin to Henry Sloan, 18 October 1954, Ervin Papers, box 2.

33. "Ervin Statements on McCarthy Summarized," *Winston-Salem Journal*, 6 August 1954, Ervin Papers, box 469. Ervin's negative opinion of McCarthy is more obvious in his letters to constituents. See Ervin to W. C. Maxwell, 21 June 1954, Ervin Papers, box 1; Ervin to Mary Masland, 21 June 1954, Ervin Papers, box 1; Ervin to Eleanor Casey, 22 June 1954, Ervin Papers, box 1.

34. Quoted in Robert Dallek, *Lone Star Rising: Lyndon Johnson and His Times, 1908–1960* (New York: Oxford University Press, 1991), 456.

35. Democratic Policy Meeting Minutes, 5 August 1954, Box 364, Senate Papers, Lyndon

B. Johnson Presidential Library (LBJL). The best account of LBJ's problems in forming the committee is in Rowland Evans and Robert Novak, *Lyndon B. Johnson: The Exercise of Power* (New York: New American Library, 1966), 83–85.

36. The rumor of Ervin's possible appointment came from Vermont Republican senator George D. Aiken, who suggested Ervin had no real contest for his reelection in November and had a clean record on the issue of McCarthy. Bruce Jolly, *Greensboro Daily News*, 4 August 1954, Ervin Notebooks, s-1.

37. "Under the Dome," *Raleigh News and Observer*, 22 November 1954, Ervin Notebooks, s-1.

38. "Ervin Wants to Stay Off Committee," *Winston-Salem Journal*, 5 August 1954, Ervin Papers, box 469.

39. This account is based on the handwritten notes Ervin wrote in preparing his autobiography, as well as published accounts of the meeting. See Sam J. Ervin Papers, Subgroup B: Private Papers, 3847B, Southern Historical Collection, University of North Carolina at Chapel Hill (hereafter cited as Ervin Papers, B.), box 22; Evans and Novak, *Exercise of Power*, 84.

40. "'Calamity' Ervin Calls Appointment," *Winston-Salem Journal*, 6 August 1954, Ervin Papers, box 469.

41. Rovere, *Senator Joe McCarthy*, 223.

42. Memorandum, George E. Reedy to Lyndon B. Johnson, 5 August 1954, Senate Papers, box 374, folder McCarthy, LBJL.

43. "Ervin Asserts He Can Be Fair," *Raleigh News and Observer*, 8 September 1954, Ervin Notebooks, s-1. Walter Winchell had called Ervin a member of the "no-pro-Joe club" and attacked him for bias because of his earlier statements against McCarthy. His remarks were reported in the *New York Times*, 8 September 1954.

44. Typical of the press reaction was Walter S. White of the *New York Times*, who called the committee members "Senate types," men with the respect and trust of the inner councils of the Senate; *New York Times*, 6 August 1956, 6. When told of the Democratic members of the committee, Republican senator William Knowland of California said, "I would be perfectly willing to go before them on trial of my life." Minutes of Democratic Policy Committee Meeting, 5 August 1954, Senate Papers, box 364, LBJL. Johnson reiterated the judicial experience of his appointments in his comments. "Statement by Senate Dem. Leader," 5 August 1954, Senate Papers, box 374, LBJL.

45. Anthony Leviero, *New York Times*, 12 September 1954; quoted in Robert Griffith, *Politics of Fear*, 300.

46. *New York Times*, 31 August 1954, 8.

47. U.S. Congress, Senate, Select Committee to Study Censure Charges Against Senator Joseph R. McCarthy, Hearings, Part I, 83rd Cong., 2nd sess., 1954. Ervin intervened in the hearings several other times to inquire about classification of government documents and government secrecy, an issue that would later take on special significance to his career.

48. Arthur V. Watkins, *Enough Rope: The Inside Story of the Censure of Senator Joe McCarthy* (Englewood Cliffs, N.J.: Prentice-Hall, 1969), 34. The committee charged McCarthy with two counts of disorderly conduct: the first for contemptuously frustrating the Senate Rules Committee in its efforts to investigate accusations of financial misconduct on

his part, and the second for mistreating General Zwicker during the Army-McCarthy hearings. Some critics would later condemn the Senate for disciplining McCarthy for breaches of etiquette rather than for his real offenses to civil liberties.

49. McCarthy complained that the committee "imitated Communist methods—that it distorted, misrepresented and omitted in its effort to manufacture a plausible rationalization for advising the Senate to accede to the clamor for my scalp." *New York Times*, 16 November 1954, Ervin Notebooks, s-1; "Ervin Target of Hot Blast By McCarthy," *Charlotte Observer*, 27 October 1954, Ervin Notebooks, s-1; "McCarthy Accusation Denied by Ervin," *Hickory Daily Record*, 27 October 1954, Ervin Notebooks, s-1.

50. Johnson's remarks are reported in Ervin, *Preserving the Constitution*, 100. See also Edwin Johnson to Joseph McCarthy, 10 September 1954, Ervin Papers, B., box 7, McCarthy file.

51. Ervin, interview by Paul Clancy, tape 6, side 1, Ervin Papers.

52. Ervin's comments from "Meet The Press" are reported in *Congressional Quarterly Almanac*, 1954, 465. Several newspapers criticized Ervin and others for their virulent attacks on McCarthy, arguing that these senators were lowering the dignity of the Senate in the same manner as had McCarthy. See "Speaking of Censures," *Wall Street Journal*, 18 November 1954, Ervin Notebooks, s-1; "Important Issues Are Obscured by Emotional Debate on McCarthy," *Charlotte Observer*, 21 November 1954, Ervin Notebooks, s-1.

53. Ervin's mail ran approximately one half for censure and one half against. Ervin, *Preserving the Constitution*, 99; "Under the Dome," *Raleigh News and Observer*, 6 December 1954, Ervin Notebooks, s-1.

54. Committee of One Hundred Americans for the Sole Purpose of Liquidating Traitors to Thomas Hennings, postmarked "2 December 1954," Thomas Hennings MSS, folder 8454, Joint Collection University of Missouri Western Historical Manuscript Collection—Columbia and State Historical Society of Missouri Manuscripts, Columbia, Missouri (hereafter cited as Hennings Papers).

55. *Congressional Record*, 83rd Cong., 2nd sess., 1954, 14893.

56. Ibid. Also retold in Samuel J. Ervin Jr., *Humor of a Country Lawyer* (Chapel Hill: University of North Carolina Press, 1983), 162.

57. *Congressional Record*, 83rd Cong., 2nd sess., 1954, 14893; Ervin, *Humor of a Country Lawyer*, 162–63. Gatton especially recommended that Ervin tell this story.

58. Clancy, *Just a Country Lawyer*, 164.

59. Thomas C. Hennings Jr. to Ervin, 2 December 1954, Hennings Papers, folder 2215.

60. "Under the Dome," *Raleigh News and Observer*, 6 December 1954, Ervin Notebooks, s-1.

61. Representative L. H. Fountain wrote to Ervin that "compliments galore are being poured on you by the people of my district." Fountain to Ervin, 18 November 1954, Ervin Papers, box 2; "They Stood Up," *Greensboro Daily News*, 17 November 1954, Ervin Notebooks, s-1; "Senator Ervin Speaks Out Courageously," *Charlotte News*, 17 November 1954, Ervin Notebooks, s-1; "Crusader or Clown," *Wilmington Morning Star*, 17 November 1954, Ervin Notebooks, s-1.

62. "Judge Sam Ervin Had the Floor," *Asheville Citizen*, 17 November 1954, Ervin Notebooks, s-1. James B. McMillan wrote to Ervin that his remarks had "done more to reduce this character to his proper proportions than anything which has happened since

the McCarthy affair began." McMillan to Ervin, 16 November 1954, Ervin Papers, box 1. Frank Graham told Ervin: "Your voice and words came to us in our little apartment hotel on East 56th Street with reassuring power," and he expressed his "deep appreciation for your righteous indignation and homely wit, and your cutting through to open bare the fundamental issues involved in a struggle which tests the highest faith and traditions of the Senate and the American people." Graham to Ervin, 16 November 1954, Ervin Papers, box 1.

63. For example, see William McWhorter Cochrane, "A Third of a Century in Senate Cloakrooms," North Caroliniana Society Imprints, number 17, 1988, 7; Bill M. Wise, *The Wisdom of Sam Ervin* (New York: Ballantine Books, 1973), xxvi; Clancy, *Just a Country Lawyer*, 164.

64. When Ohio senator John W. Bricker argued that the committee's punishment of McCarthy was unjust because there existed no prior Senate rule defining "appropriate behavior," Ervin defended the committee, explaining: "The rule goes back to the beginning of our government. The Constitution of the United States in many provisions is self-executing. It requires no act of Congress to give them validity." *Congressional Record*, 83rd Cong., 2nd sess., 1954, 15998, 6324–25.

65. Ervin even gave McCarthy the benefit of the doubt about his repeatedly incorrect and slanderous statements. Ervin later recalled that on several occasions he stepped in to protect McCarthy by suggesting that perhaps his staff had misled him or provided incorrect information to him. Ervin, interview by Paul Clancy, tape 2, side 1, and tape 6, side 1.

66. Clancy, *Just a Country Lawyer*, 165; Ervin, *Preserving the Constitution*, 110.

67. "Ervin Heads Home, Happy over Censure," *Charlotte Observer*, 4 December 1954, Ervin Notebooks, s-1.

68. See Bartley, *Massive Resistance*; Wilhoit, *Politics of Massive Resistance*; Chafe, *Civilities and Civil Rights*.

69. *Washington Evening Star*, 10 June 1954, Ervin Notebooks, s-1.

70. Jack Bass, *Unlikely Heroes* (New York: Simon and Schuster, 1981); Jack Walter Peltason, *Fifty Eight Lonely Men: Southern Federal Judges and School Desegregation* (Urbana: University of Illinois Press, 1970).

71. *Briggs v. Elliot*, 132 F. Supp., 779. On Judge Parker see William C. Burris, *Duty and the Law: Judge John J. Parker and the Constitution* (Bessemer, Ala.: Colonial Press, 1987).

72. On "freedom of choice" plans, see Chafe, *Civilities and Civil Rights*; and Earl Black, *Southern Governors*. On the southern courts see Bass, *Unlikely Heroes*; and Peltason, *Fifty Eight Lonely Men*.

73. William Bagwell, *School Desegregation in the Carolinas: Two Case Studies* (Columbia: University of South Carolina Press, 1972); Peter H. Gerns, "Constitutional Law—Equal Protection—Use of Fee Simple Determinable to Enforce Racial Restriction Provisions," *North Carolina Law Review* 34 (December 1955); Robert H. Wettach, "North Carolina School Legislation—1956," *North Carolina Law Review* 35 (December 1956); Paul T. Ervin, "Civil Rights in North Carolina," *North Carolina Law Review* 42 (December 1963); Chafe, *Civilities and Civil Rights*, 72–82; Edward L. Rankin, interview by Jay Jenkins, August, 1987, SOHP.

74. For examples of Ervin's support of the Pearsall Plan see Ervin to Mrs. William W. Johnson, 14 February 1956, Ervin Papers, box 18; and Ervin to Mrs. John Bond, 17 January

1955, Ervin Papers, box 11; Ervin, "The Case for Segregation," *Look*, 3 April 1956, 32–33. For examples of Ervin's correspondence with officials in the North Carolina state government see Ervin to Attorney General Harry McMullan, 6 May 1955, Ervin Papers, box 7; Thomas J. Pearsall to Ervin, 26 March 1957, Ervin Papers, box 25. Also interesting is Ervin's frequent correspondence with the outspoken segregationist and government official I. Beverly Lake: see Lake to Ervin, 22 November 1954, and Ervin to Lake, 3 December 1954, Ervin Papers, box 4; Lake to Ervin, 10 February 1956, and Ervin to Lake, 14 February 1956, Ervin Papers, box 18.

75. Memo from Charles Davis and John Alexander, "Developments in the Old Fort Case," 14 February 1957, American Friends Service Committee Archives, Philadelphia (hereafter cited as AFSC Papers).

76. The parent fired from his job was rehired a few months afterward when his boss could not find anyone to do the work as well as his former employee. Memo from John Alexander, "Visit to Bryson City," 29 January 1957, AFSC Papers; Memo from John Alexander, "Information on the case of Rev. J. E. McDowell, Swain County, North Carolina," 29 January 1957, AFSC Papers.

77. "Ervin Sees Slow Change in N.C.," *Charlotte Observer*, 3 June 1955, Ervin Notebooks, s-3.

78. Thomas R. Marshall, *Public Opinion and the Supreme Court* (Boston: Unwin Hyman, 1989); Jesse H. Choper, *Judicial Review and the National Political Process: A Functional Reconsideration of the Role of the Supreme Court* (Chicago: University of Chicago Press, 1980); John H. Kessel, "Public Perceptions of the Supreme Court," in *The Impact of Supreme Court Decisions*, ed. Theodore L. Becker (New York: Oxford University Press, 1969), 193–205.

79. Choper, *Judicial Review*, 152.

80. "It's Nice to Hear N.C. Senators Speaking Out and Above a Whisper," *Raleigh Times*, 14 June 1954, Ervin Papers, box 469; "Ervin on Court Decision," *Greensboro Daily News*, 12 June 1954, Ervin Papers, box 469.

81. Chafe, *Civilities and Civil Rights*, 6–10.

82. Eastland is quoted in Fred Rodell, "The Pattern of Defiance," *Look*, 3 April 1956, 24.

83. Marvin Griffin, *New York Times*, 18 May 1954, quoted in Bartley, *Massive Resistance*, 68.

84. Ervin believed that the Court's ruling represented another encroachment by the federal government on the powers reserved to the states by the Tenth Amendment, and that the *Brown* decision threatened the states' right to manage their own systems of public education. Ervin also argued that when the states ratified the Fourteenth Amendment in 1868 the federal and state governments and the courts declared that each state reserved the right to control its own public schools, and there was no suggestion that the amendment required the states to maintain racially mixed schools.

85. Ervin to Ada M. Field, 23 February 1956, Ervin Papers, box 18.

86. Ervin to Lewis E. Everline, 15 March 1956, Ervin Papers, box 18; Ervin to Mary Frances Lacey, 15 June 1954, Ervin Papers, box 4; Ervin to Ada M. Field, 23 February 1956, Ervin Papers, box 18. Ervin also disagreed with the Court's inclusion of social science data in its interpretation and opinion. Ervin wrote a friend that "it is a fearful thing to contemplate the theory of the [*Brown*] opinion that the meaning of the Constitution

changes without action on the part of the States and Congress when new books are written on psychological subjects." Ervin contended that if a Court changed the interpretation of a constitutional provision because of "changes in public opinion or anything else" it would be guilty of "reckless disregard for its official oath and duty." To support his argument, Ervin cited the works of Thomas M. Cooley, whom he called "the greatest authority of all time on the American Constitution." Ervin to Ada M. Field, 23 February 1956, Ervin Papers, box 18.

87. Ervin to Ada M. Field, 23 February 1956, Ervin Papers, box 18.

88. Ervin argued that the authors of the Fourteenth Amendment did not intend to prohibit the states from segregating school children on the basis of race, and therefore the Court must honor those authors' original intent. If anyone wished to change the meaning of the Fourteenth Amendment, Ervin thought that they should follow the procedure spelled out in Article V of the Constitution, which calls for the approval of two-thirds of both houses of Congress and of three-fourths of the states. Ervin frequently quoted George Washington's farewell address to stress the danger implicit in the Court's usurpation of power. In 1796, Washington said that if the people ever wanted to change any part of the Constitution, they should follow the amendment process outlined in the Constitution itself. Then he warned: "But let there be no change by usurpation; for though this, in one instance, may be the instrument of good, it is the customary weapon by which free governments are destroyed." See Ervin, "Alexander Hamilton's Phantom," address before the Harvard Law School Association of New York City, 28 April 1955, reprinted in *Vital Speeches of the Day*, 15 October 1955, 22–26; Ervin, "The Power to Interpret is Not the Power to Amend," *U.S. News and World Report*, 11 May 1959, 120; Ervin to Emanuel Celler, 6 February 1957, Ervin Papers, box 26.

89. Ervin to Mary Frances Lacy, 15 June 1954, Ervin Papers, box 4.

90. Ervin, "Alexander Hamilton's Phantom," 22–26.

91. Bartley, *Massive Resistance*, 7. Francis M. Wilhoit argues: "The unscientific and extra-constitutional nature of the South's counterrevolutionary ideology proved to be a fatal flaw when the ideology was tested (and found wanting) in showdowns with the federal courts and other federal agencies." Wilhoit, *Politics of Massive Resistance*, 70, 215.

92. See James F. Byrnes, "The Supreme Court Must Be Curbed," *U.S. News and World Report*, 18 May 1956, 50; Strom Thurmond, "The Constitution and the Supreme Court," *Vital Speeches of the Day*, 15 October 1955, 29–32.

93. See George W. Stumberg, "Supporting the Opinion of the Supreme Court," and Eugene Cook, "Opposing the Opinion of the Supreme Court," in *American Bar Association Journal* (April 1956): 313–20; Fagan Dickson, "Equal Justice Under Law for All Citizens," and Sims Crownover, "A Deliberate and Dangerous Exercise of Power," *American Bar Association Journal* (August 1956): 727–32.

94. Morton J. Horwitz, "The Jurisprudence of *Brown* and the Dilemmas of Liberalism," in *Have We Overcome?: Race Relations since Brown*, ed. Michael V. Namorato (Jackson: University Press of Mississippi, 1979), 173–87. For scholars and politicians who agree with the basic tenets of Ervin's judicial philosophy, see Raoul Berger, *Government by Judiciary: The Transformation of the Fourteenth Amendment* (Cambridge, Mass.: Harvard University Press, 1977); Lino A. Graglia, *Disaster by Decree: The Supreme Court Decisions on Race and the Schools* (Ithaca, N.Y.: Cornell University Press, 1976); Thomas J. Higgins,

Judicial Review Unmasked (West Hanover, Mass.: Christopher Publishing House, 1981); Symposium, "Construing the Constitution," *University of California Davis Law Review* 19 (1985): 1–30; Edwin Meese, "The Attorney General's View of the Supreme Court: Toward a Jurisprudence of Original Intention," *Public Administration Review* 45 (1985): 701.

95. Since the rise of the Legal Realist School in the 1930s, the debate over unbiased judges and "neutral principles" has raged unabated. See Herbert Wechsler, "Toward Neutral Principles of Constitutional Law," *Harvard Law Review* 73 (November 1959); and rebuttals by Louis H. Pollak, "Racial Discrimination and Judicial Integrity: A Reply to Professor Wechsler," *University of Pennsylvania Law Review* 108 (November 1959); Arthur S. Miller, *Politics, Democracy, and the Supreme Court: Essays on the Frontier of Constitutional Theory* (Westport, Conn.: Greenwood Press, 1985); and Mark Tushnet, *Red, White, and Blue: A Critical Analysis of Constitutional Law* (Cambridge, Mass.: Harvard University Press, 1988). In addition, the Court did not base its ruling in *Brown* on sociological data alone, as Ervin and other southern critics charged, but on legal arguments and the precedents established by a series of preceding cases as well. On the legal precedents for *Brown*, see Edmond Cahn, "Jurisprudence," *New York University Law Review* 30 (January 1955): 150–69; and Charles L. Black Jr., "The Lawfulness of the Segregation Decision," *Yale Law Journal* 69 (January 1960): 421–30. For a legal discussion of *Brown*, see Kluger, *Simple Justice*; and Wolters, *Burden of Brown*.

96. Even if Ervin's argument concerning the primacy of original intent is granted, most scholars have agreed with the unanimous Court in *Brown* that the original intent of the framers of the Fourteenth Amendment "cannot be determined with any degree of certainty" and that the amendment did not directly address the question of racial segregation in the schools. See Alexander M. Bickel, "The Original Understanding of the Segregation Decision," *Harvard Law Review* 69 (November 1955): 1–65.

97. *Hertz v. Woodman*, 218 U.S. 205 (1909), cited in Fagan Dickson, "The Segregation Cases: Equal Justice Under Law for All Citizens," *American Bar Association Journal* 42 (August 1956): 732. The legal scholar Arthur S. Miller once explained: "Law, like society, changes and grows; it is a process, not a static system." Arthur S. Miller, *The Supreme Court: Myth and Reality* (Westport, Conn.: Greenwood Press, 1978), 102.

98. Charles Fairman, "The Attack on the Segregation Cases," *Harvard Law Review* 70 (November 1956): 83–94.

99. *State v. Ballance*, 229 N.C. 764, 51 S.E.2d 731, 733 (1949), repeating language in *Sidney Spitzer and Co. v. Comm'rs*, 188 N.C. 30, 32, 123 S.E. 636, 638 (1924).

100. Ervin to Emanuel Celler, 6 February 1957, Ervin Papers, box 26.

101. Ibid.

102. Fairman also demonstrated that South Carolina Governor and ex–Supreme Court Justice James Byrnes had voted to overrule a legal precedent in *Edwards v. California*, 314 U.S. 160 (1941). See Fairman, "The Attack on the Segregation Cases," *Harvard Law Review* 70 (November 1956): 92.

103. On Ervin's rhetoric style see David Zarefsky, "Two Senators with National Appeal: Fulbright and Ervin," in *A New Diversity in Contemporary Southern Rhetoric*, ed. Cal M. Logue (Baton Rouge: Louisiana State University Press, 1987); Waldo W. Braden, *Oral Tradition in the South* (Baton Rouge: Louisiana State University Press, 1983); Clifford

Kenneth Van Sickle, "The Oral Communication of Senator Sam Ervin: A Study in Consistency" (Ph.D. dissertation, Michigan State University, 1976).

104. Ervin, "Our Heritage: A Blessing and an Obligation," a speech delivered to the Jefferson-Jackson Day Dinner, Richmond, Virginia, 4 March 1955, Ervin Papers, box 453.

105. Ibid.

106. Ibid.

107. Quite a few of his favorite tales poked fun at poor whites or at fellow lawyers. The best collections of Ervin's stories are Ervin, *Humor of a Country Lawyer*, and Bruce Tindall, "Down Home Truths," unpublished manuscript, 1974, North Carolina Collection, Wilson Library, University of North Carolina at Chapel Hill.

108. Ervin, "Alexander Hamilton's Phantom," 22–26.

109. See *Texas State Bar Journal* 19 (February 1956): 535, Ervin Papers, box 469; *Shreveport* (Louisiana) *Times*, 19 June 1955, Ervin Notebooks, s-2; *Houston Chronicle*, 7 July 1956, Ervin Notebooks, s-2; J. L. Hamme to Ervin, 2 December 1955, Ervin Papers, box 11.

110. Hugh A. Locke to Ervin, 12 August 1955, Ervin Papers, box 11; Lucien H. Von Schilling to Ervin, 7 September 1955, Ervin Papers, box 11; Shepard Bryan to Ervin, 25 October 1955, Ervin Papers, box 11; W. T. Mallison to Ervin, 30 August 1955, Ervin Papers, box 11.

111. *Raleigh News and Observer*, 2 May 1955, Ervin Notebooks, s-2; *Charlotte Observer*, 6 May 1955, Ervin Notebooks, s-2; *Morganton News Herald*, 2 May 1955, Ervin Notebooks, s-2; *Greensboro Daily News*, 2 May 1955, Ervin Notebooks, s-2.

112. "Judge Sam and the Court," *Asheville Citizen*, 30 April 1955, Ervin Notebooks, s-2.

113. Ervin's legalistic defense of Jim Crow segregation attracted the attention of the national press which increasingly began to choose Ervin as its representative segregationist in articles dealing with the South and the Supreme Court. See Ervin, "The Case for Segregation," *Look*, 3 April 1956, 32–33; "The Race Issue," *U.S. News and World Report*, 18 November 1955, 30.

114. "Senator Sam Ervin Says," weekly newspaper column, 22 March 1956, Ervin Papers, box 449; "The Kurfees-Ervin Campaign," *Winston-Salem Journal*, 16 May 1956, Ervin Notebooks, s-4.

115. "Senator Sam Ervin Says"; "The Kurfees-Ervin Campaign," *Winston-Salem Journal*, 16 May 1956, Ervin Notebooks, s-3.

116. "Senator Sam Ervin Says."

117. *Congressional Record*, 84th Cong., 2nd sess., 12 March 1956, 3948–4004.

118. Alexander M. Bickel, *The Least Dangerous Branch: The Supreme Court at the Bar of Politics* (Indianapolis: Bobbs-Merrill, 1962), 256.

119. The fact that the Southern Manifesto had some effect on North Carolina's congressional elections is obvious, but Governor J. P. Coleman of Mississippi overstated the case when he interpreted the defeat of the two non-signers as a warning to all politicians "not to insult the South's convictions." Other factors played a role as well. See "The Race Issue and the Primary," *Winston-Salem Journal*, 29 May 1956, Ervin Notebooks, s-3; "N.C. Defeats Stir Capital," *Charlotte Observer*, 29 May 1956, Ervin Notebooks, s-3.

120. John L. Cheney Jr., ed., *North Carolina Government 1585–1979: A Narrative and Statistical History* (Raleigh: North Carolina Department of the Secretary of State, 1981).

Ervin won the special election of 1954 easily because the Republicans decided not to field an opponent. The closest thing to an election scare for Ervin came in 1968 when ex-Governor Terry Sanford hinted at challenging him in the Democratic primary. Sanford ultimately chose not to run, in part because he did not believe he could defeat Ervin.

CHAPTER FOUR

1. Roy Wilkins to Sam Ervin, 16 September 1955, box 388, folder 64, in Sam J. Ervin Papers, Subgroup A: Senate Papers, 3847A, Southern Historical Collection, Wilson Library, University of North Carolina at Chapel Hill (hereafter cited as Ervin Papers).

2. The southerners also controlled seven of the Senate's most important nine committees. C. Vann Woodward, "The Great Civil Rights Debate," *Commentary*, October 1957, 283.

3. This nickname was widely used; see UPI press release, "Civil Rights," 27 January 1962, box RO92, Russell Long Papers, Louisiana and Lower Mississippi Valley Collections, Louisiana State University Libraries, Louisiana State University (hereafter cited as Long Papers).

4. Francis M. Wilhoit, *The Politics of Massive Resistance* (New York: George Braziller, 1973), 76.

5. Wilhoit called these four senators the "tutelary geniuses," ibid., 76–85.

6. William S. White, "Rights Program Likely to Pass," *New York Times*, 25 March 1957.

7. Numan Bartley, *The Rise of Massive Resistance* (Baton Rouge: Louisiana State University Press, 1969), 7. Francis M. Wilhoit argues: "The unscientific and extra-constitutional nature of the South's counterrevolutionary ideology proved to be a fatal flaw when the ideology was tested (and found wanting) in showdowns with the federal courts and other federal agencies." Wilhoit, *Politics of Massive Resistance*, 70, 215.

8. NAACP Memorandum, 2 July 1964, box 68, folder "Civil Rights Act of 1964, general," NAACP Papers, series A, group III, Manuscript Division, Library of Congress (hereafter cited as NAACP Papers). Unless otherwise noted all citations from the NAACP Papers can be found in series A, group III.

9. The southern defense of segregation has been neglected in recent historiography. Most scholars who have addressed this topic focus on the most radical and racist white reactions. See Neil R. McMillen, *The Citizens' Council: Organized Resistance to the Second Reconstruction, 1954–64* (Urbana: University of Illinois Press, 1971); Bartley, *Rise of Massive Resistance*; and Wilhoit, *Politics of Massive Resistance*. These studies are extremely valuable, but the less radical, and more insidious, aspects of the southern reaction to the Second Reconstruction has not received sufficient attention. Pioneering studies of the South's legalistic strategy against civil rights—of which Ervin's soft southern strategy should be considered an integral part—include William Chafe, *Civilities and Civil Rights: Greensboro, North Carolina, and the Black Struggle for Freedom* (New York: Oxford University Press, 1980); Elizabeth Jacoway and David R. Colburn, *Southern Businessmen and Desegregation* (Baton Rouge: Louisiana State University Press, 1982); and Kermit L. Hall and James W. Ely Jr., eds., *An Uncertain Tradition: Constitutionalism and the History of the South* (Athens: University of Georgia Press, 1989).

10. Violence against African Americans in the South—such as the murders of George Lee, Lamar Smith, and Emmett Till—also motivated civil rights lobbyists to push more

aggressively for congressional action to protect the franchise. Steven Lawson, *Black Ballots: Voting Rights in the South*, Contemporary American History Series, ed. William E. Leuchtenburg (New York: Columbia University Press, 1976), 158–59.

11. For example, see Gunnar Myrdal, *An American Dilemma: The Negro Problem and Modern Democracy* (New York: Harper and Row, 1944); John Dollard, *Caste and Class in a Southern Town* (New Haven: Yale University Press, 1937); The President's Commission on Civil Rights, *To Secure These Rights* (New York: Simon and Schuster, 1947).

12. For more detailed accounts of the events of 1955–56, see Robert Frederick Burk, *The Eisenhower Administration and Black Civil Rights* (Knoxville: University of Tennessee Press, 1984), 12; Lawson, *Black Ballots*, 140–64; Richard Bolling, *House Out of Order* (New York: Dutton, 1965), 179; Denton L. Watson, *Lion in the Lobby: Clarence Mitchell, Jr.'s Struggle for the Passage of Civil Rights Laws* (New York: William Morrow, 1990), 319–56.

13. Watson, *Lion in the Lobby*, 352.

14. J. W. Anderson, *The Tangled Origins of the Civil Rights Bill of 1956–1957* (University: University of Alabama Press, 1964), 138.

15. A copy of this poster can be found in Bryce N. Harlow Papers, B. 8, Dwight D. Eisenhower Presidential Library (DDEL), Abilene, Kansas (hereafter cited as Harlow Papers).

16. The NAACP noted that black registration in the South had grown from 140,000 in 1940 to what they hoped would be close to 3 million in 1956; Watson, *Lion in the Lobby*, 348. In North Carolina black registration rose from 125,000 in 1955 to 145,000 in 1956, according to Roy Wilkins's testimony before the Senate Judiciary Committee in 1957; see "Roy Wilkins's Testimony," copied in Ervin Papers, box 388, folder 70. But discrimination remained the norm in North Carolina. In Mecklenburg County only 8,750 of 29,472 nonwhite residents over twenty-one years of age were registered; in Robeson County, only 4,000 of a possible 22,062 eligible nonwhite citizens were registered. See "Special Report," 7 June 1957, Southern Regional Council, in box 14, Richard Bolling Papers, Joint Collection, University of Missouri Western Historical Manuscript Collection and State Historical Society of Missouri Manuscripts, Columbia, Missouri (hereafter cited as Bolling Papers).

17. Watson, *Lion in the Lobby*, 355.

18. Anderson, *Tangled Origins*, 139; "For Whom Did Negroes Vote in 1956," *Congressional Quarterly Weekly*, 7 June 1957.

19. "6,000,000 Negro Votes," *Newsweek*, 9 April 1956, 35.

20. "The Congress, Ready for Civil Rights," *Time*, 24 December 1956, 11.

21. Richard Bolling argues that the 1956 presidential election returns meant that some kind of civil rights bill would have to be passed in 1957 because Lyndon Johnson and the moderate Democrats could not risk having their party seen as the one killing civil rights. Bolling, *House Out of Order*, 179, 182.

22. For a perceptive discussion of the southerners' filibuster problem in 1957, and an overall assessment of the politics of the Civil Rights Act of 1957, see George E. Reedy to Michael L. Gillette, 2 June 1957, George E. Reedy Oral History, Lyndon Baines Johnson Presidential Library (LBJL), Austin, Texas.

23. African Americans in North Carolina repeatedly complained about Ervin's manner of referring to them as "Nigras." See "Tar Heel Senator Says 'Nigras' doing Well," *Carolina Times* (Raleigh), 23 February 1957.

24. Liberals were aware of the difficulty that focusing the bill on voting rights would have upon the southerners. Richard Bolling later wrote: "Perhaps, I even speculated, the southern opposition in Congress to voting rights could be reduced to a beleaguered group of fanatics who would be placed in the unenviable position of opposing legislation to provide effective legal guarantees that all Americans . . . be allowed to register and vote." Bolling, *House Out of Order*, 176.

25. For example, see Ervin to Gov. James Folsom (Alabama), 5 February 1957, Ervin Papers, box 25, folder 190; Ervin to Gov. Luther H. Hodges (North Carolina), 31 January 1957, Ervin Papers, box 25, folder 190; Ervin to Gov. Orval Faubus (Arkansas), 31 January 1957, Ervin Papers, box 25, folder 190.

26. "Congress Plays Political Poker," *Washington Star*, 16 February 1957, Ervin Papers, box 469, folder 2b.

27. Thomas O'Neal, "Politics and People," *Baltimore Sun*, 20 May 1957, Ervin Papers, box 469, folder 2b.

28. See U.S. Congress, Senate, Hearings, Subcommittee on Constitutional Rights, 85th Cong., 1st sess., 14 February to 5 March 1957, 22; "Oh, Well, Maybe That's Different," *Winston-Salem Journal*, 15 February 1957, Ervin Newspaper Clippings Notebooks, Ervin Papers, s-5 (hereafter cited as Ervin Notebooks); Tom Wicker, "Ervin Raps Brownell on Civil Rights Plan," *Winston-Salem Journal*, 15 February 1957, Ervin Notebooks, s-5. At one point, Ervin complained that the attorney general's answers reminded him of the man in a carnival booth who sticks his head through a hole in the canvas so people can throw baseballs at him. "I am sure you would never be hit," Ervin insisted. Brownell calmly responded that it is difficult for an outfielder to catch a baseball when it is thrown in the direction of the catcher. Another of Brownell's answers led Ervin to complain that the witness "was squirrel hunting and I am looking for rabbits." "Racial Solution Held South's Aim," *New York Times*, 16 February 1957; "Ervin and Brownell Clash on Civil Rights," *Washington Star*, 15 February 1957, Ervin Notebooks, s-3.

29. At one point, Brownell responded to one of Ervin's many legal lectures by snapping: "I'd have to grade you a zero on that." Ervin, obviously miffed, retorted childishly: "If we're going in for grading, I'd say you were 99 and 99/100 wrong on that." "Racial Solution Held South's Aim," *New York Times*, 16 February 1957; "Zero for Mr. Brownell," *Charleston News and Courier*, 17 February 1957, Ervin Notebooks, s-3.

30. U.S. Congress, Senate, Hearings, Subcommittee on Constitutional Rights, 85th Cong., 1st sess., 14 February to 5 March 1957, 24.

31. Editorial, *Carolina Times* (Raleigh), 23 February 1957. Ervin's grueling schedule of ten to twelve hours a day had so weakened him that he suffered a kidney attack in early April. Ervin to W. Burford Lewallen, 22 February 1957, Ervin Papers, box 388, folder 71.

32. Herbert Brownell Oral History Interview, no. 5, interviewed by Ed Edwin, 12 April 1968, OH 157, Columbia University Oral History Project, DDEL, 251.

33. Ervin is often given credit for this revelation, but it was a staff attorney, Robert Young, who actually put the question to Brownell. Ervin immediately came to Young's defense when Brownell became angry. See U.S. Congress, Senate, Hearings, Subcommittee on Constitutional Rights, 85th Cong., 1st sess., 14 February to 5 March 1957, 214–20; "Brownell Ire Aroused by Questions," *Washington Post*, 17 February 1957; "Civil Rights

Questions Protested by Brownell," *Washington Star*, 17 February 1957, Ervin Notebooks, s-3; "Brownell Vexed by Rights Inquiry," *New York Times*, 17 February 1957.

34. An internal memo in the Eisenhower administration suggested: "Military force has not been and will not be necessary to enforce federal court decisions. To even suggest that the administration contemplates the use of troops to enforce civil rights decrees is pure demagoguery." Memo, Anne Whitman to Bryce Harlow, n.d., Bryce N. Harlow Papers, box 8, DDEL.

35. William S. White, "Rights Program Likely to Pass," *New York Times*, 25 March 1957; Robert C. Albright, "South on Civil Rights," *Washington Post*, 4 March 1957; "People of the Week," *U.S. News and World Report*, 5 April 1957, 16; "Congress Plays Political Poker," *Washington Star*, 16 February 1957, Ervin Papers, box 469, folder 2b.

36. Jack Bass and Walter DeVries, *The Transformation of Southern Politics: Social Change and Political Consequences since 1945* (New York: Basic Books, 1976), 218–47.

37. William Chafe, *Civilities and Civil Rights*, 2–10.

38. Ervin correctly argued that because the Civil Rights Act of 1957 was part of an amendment to the Enforcement Acts of 1870, empowering the president to use the armed forces during Reconstruction, it would allow future administrations to send troops into the South to enforce the civil rights covered by this proposed bill.

39. Woodward, "Great Civil Rights Debate," 287.

40. Sam Ervin and Olin Johnston, "Minority Report to Accompany S. 83," Subcommittee on Constitutional Rights, 85th Cong., 1st sess., 10 May 1957, Ervin Papers, box 388, folder 74, 2. Hereafter cited as Minority Report, 1957.

41. Ibid.

42. Ervin and Johnston, Minority Report, 1957, 4.

43. Sam Ervin, "A Tragic Error," *Atlanta Journal*, 15 March 1957, Ervin Notebooks, s-3. The jury trial issue had been raised before, but when Ervin adopted it as his principal objection to the civil rights bill it gained a new respectability. Congressman L. Mendel Rivers of Charleston, South Carolina, had mentioned the jury trial issue on the first day of the congressional debate over civil rights in 1956. See J. W. Anderson, *Eisenhower, Brownell, and the Congress: The Tangled Origins of the Civil Rights Bill of 1956–1957* (University: University of Alabama Press, 1964), 88. The *New York Times* wrote that the jury trial issue "is the brainchild of the astute Senator Ervin of North Carolina; and there is no doubt that it has specious appeal. But it is really a device to undermine one of the most important provisions of the pending bill." Editorial, *New York Times*, 7 June 1957.

44. Ervin and Johnston, Minority Report, 1957, 1. See also Ervin, "Current Civil Rights Proposals Will Only Heighten Race Tensions," *Atlanta Journal*, 15 March 1957, Ervin Notebooks, s-3.

45. Ervin and Johnston, Minority Report, 1957, 20.

46. Ibid., 29.

47. Ibid., 1.

48. Ervin, "A Tragic Error," *Atlanta Journal*, 15 March 1957, Ervin Notebooks, s-3.

49. Roy Wilkins, NAACP press release, 9 May 1957, NAACP Papers, box a73, folder "Press Releases, 56–57."

50. This is a key criticism of Ervin's jury trial argument. Even Ervin had to admit that

jury trials in civil cases had never been protected under the Constitution. See Frank W. McCulloch to Richard Bolling, 6 June 1957, Bolling Papers, box 14. On 27 July 1957, eleven law school deans and thirty-four law school professors issued a statement that the absence of a jury trial provision in the civil rights bill did not violate due process of law. See *Congressional Quarterly Almanac*, 85th Cong., 1st sess., 1957, 567. Ervin's primary antagonists on these legal issues were Senator Jacob Javits, Senator Paul Douglas, and Congressman Emanuel Celler. See Senator Jacob Javits, testimony before the Subcommittee on Constitutional Rights, U.S Congress, Senate, Hearings, Subcommittee on Constitutional Rights, 85th Cong., 1st sess., 14 February to 5 March 1957, 421–27; statement of Senator Paul Douglas, *Congressional Record*, 85th Cong., 1st sess., 8601–8614. Congressman Emanuel Celler debated Ervin on "The American Forum," Sunday, 9 June 1957, NBC, a transcript of which can be found in the Ervin Papers, box 388, folder 74.

51. J. Francis Pohlhaus, "Justice Samuel J. Ervin, Jr., and Contempt," NAACP Press Release, 2 April 1957, NAACP Papers, box a73, folder "Press Releases, 6–7."

52. "American Forum," 9 June 1957, NBC, Ervin Papers, box 388, folder 74. See also Ervin to James B. L. Rush, editorial page editor of the *Winston-Salem Journal*, 3 August 1957, Ervin Papers, box 26, folder 215.

53. J. Francis Pohlhaus to Roy Wilkins, 7 June 1957, NAACP Papers, box a72, folder "Clarence Mitchell."

54. "Bogus Jury Issue," *Washington Post*, 5 June 1957, Bolling Papers, box 14.

55. Tom Wicker, "South's Type of Justice Criticized," *Greensboro Daily News*, 30 March 1957, Ervin Notebooks, s-3.

56. Ibid.

57. Ervin to Ruth Sigmon, 12 July 1957, Ervin Papers, box 26, folder 208.

58. "2 in Montgomery Freed in Bombing," *New York Times*, 31 May 1957, Bolling Papers, box 14; "Pair Freed in Church Blast," *Nashville Tennessean*, 31 May 1957, in NAACP Papers, box a73, folder "Press Releases, sc-7." Liberals cited the Montgomery case as an example of why Ervin and his colleagues were insisting upon jury trials. See "Trial by Jury," *New Republic*, 10 June 1957, Bolling Papers, box 14. Southerners pointed to the Clinton, Tennessee, integration case to support their claims. See "The South," *Time*, 24 December 1956, 15.

59. Dr. Charles Alan Wright to Ervin, 21 May 1957, Ervin Papers, box 288, folder 71.

60. "South on Civil Rights," *Washington Post*, 4 March 1957, Ervin Papers, s-3.

61. Lawson, *Black Ballots*, 187.

62. John L. Lewis to Ervin, 1 August 1957, Ervin Papers, box 26, folder 215. On labor's response, see Lawson, *Black Ballots*, 191–92. Attorney General Brownell believed that the jury trial issue originated with the unions and the southerners picked it up from them: Brownell Oral History, Interview no. 5, by Ed Edwin, 12 April 1968, OH 157, Columbia University Oral History Project, DDEL.

63. Hubert Humphrey oral history interview, LBJ Oral History Collection, by Joe B. Frantz, 17 August 1971, LBJL. Other notable northern senators who eventually supported the jury trial amendment were John Kennedy and Paul Douglass. See Lawson, *Black Ballots*, 187, 192. Surprisingly, even Ervin's antagonist Joe Rauh later admitted, "I had some second thoughts about the jury trial amendment. . . . It had some civil liberties aspects to

it." Joseph L. Rauh Oral History Interview, by Charles T. Morrissey, 23 December 1965, John F. Kennedy Library (JFKL), Boston, Massachusetts.

64. "Jury Plan Wins Rights Bill Test," *New York Times*, 4 June 1957; "Eisenhower Civil Rights Bill is Amended," *New York Herald Tribune*, 4 June 1957, Ervin Notebooks, s-4.

65. Press Release, Thomas C. Hennings Jr., 20 June 1957, Hennings Papers, folder 461; Hennings to Paul Douglas, 16 July 1957, folder 462, Thomas C. Hennings Jr. Papers, Joint Collection, University of Missouri Western Historical Manuscript Collection—Columbia and State Historical Society of Missouri Manuscripts, Columbia, Missouri (hereafter cited as Hennings Papers).

66. William White, "Senators Devise New Rights Move," *New York Times*, 29 May 1957; William White, "Senate, 45 to 39, Sends Rights Bill Straight to Floor," *New York Times*, 21 June 1957; "Ervin Blasts Rights Hassle," *Charlotte Observer*, 25 June 1957, Ervin Notebooks, s-4; Thomas C. Hennings Jr., Press Release, 20 June 1957, Hennings Papers, folder 461; Hennings to Paul Douglas, 16 July 1957, Hennings Papers, folder 462.

67. The vote to avoid the Judiciary Committee was 45–39. William White, "Senate 45 to 39 Sends Rights Bill Straight to Floor," *New York Times*, 21 June 1957.

68. "Judge Sam in Richmond," *Raleigh News and Observer*, 10 May 1955, North Carolina Collection Clipping File, number 45, North Carolina Collection, Wilson Library, University of North Carolina at Chapel Hill (hereafter cited as NCC Clipping File).

69. "When Both Sides Are Right," *Greensboro Daily News*, 9 July 1957, Ervin Notebooks, s-4.

70. "Civil Rights Battle Opens in Senate," *Charlotte Observer*, 9 July 1957, Ervin Notebooks, s-4; Doris Fleeson, "Southerners Score in Civil Rights Debate," *Washington Star*, 10 July 1957, Ervin Notebooks, s-4; "Foes Lose One Bid to Delay Rights Bill," *Greensboro Daily News*, 10 July 1957, Ervin Notebooks, s-4.

71. While Russell, Stennis, and Ervin all followed the basic outline of Ervin's soft southern strategy, Russell continued to rely on more racist rhetoric than the others. Russell did support a soft southern strategy to defeat civil rights legislation, but only because he felt it would be the most effective weapon available. See Gilbert C. Fite, *Richard B. Russell, Jr.: Senator from Georgia* (Chapel Hill: University of North Carolina Press, 1991).

72. Tris Coffin, "How Lyndon Johnson Engineered Compromise on Civil Rights Bill," *New Leader*, 5 August 1957, 3, in H. Alexander Smith Papers, Seeley G. Mudd Manuscript Library, Princeton University (hereafter cited as Smith Papers).

73. Sherman Adams, *Firsthand Report: The Story of the Eisenhower Administration* (New York: Harper and Row, 1961), 340. *Congressional Quarterly Almanac* reported: "Senior southern senators, represented by Sen. Samuel J. Ervin Jr. (D.-N.C.), announced Aug. 28, when debating a compromise amendment to the bill, that there would be no southern filibuster because it obviously could not succeed and because such action might so anger the Senate as to promote demands for hardening the rules against filibusters." *Congressional Quarterly Almanac*, 85th Cong., 1st sess., 1957, 563.

74. *Congressional Record*, 85th Cong., 1st sess., 1957, 10771.

75. Quoted in Lawson, *Black Ballots*, 178; Burk, *Eisenhower Administration and Civil Rights*, 171.

76. "Rights Bill Debate Hints Compromise," *New York Herald Tribune*, 9 July 1957,

Ervin Notebooks, s-4. Eisenhower's motives are discussed in Burk, *Eisenhower Administration and Civil Rights*, 16, 87, 89, 110, 127, 131; Lawson, *Black Ballots*, 144.

77. Charles J. Bloch, "The Communist Platform of 1928 and the Law of the Land, 1958," *North Carolina Bar* 5 (November 1958). Bloch, in a speech to the North Carolina Bar, stated: "I know that more than any one man was Senator Ervin responsible for the exposure of the Brownell chicanery which lurked in the background of the 1957 Civil Rights Bill. He exposed one of its primary purposes—the use of federal troops to enforce judicial decrees."

78. "Swapping Civil Rights," *Washington Star*, 11 July 1957, Ervin Notebooks, s-4. Also editorializing in favor of a jury trial amendment were the *Washington Post*, 2 August 1957, and the *Raleigh News and Observer*, 3 August 1957, Ervin Notebooks, s-4.

79. On jury trials and the Johnson amendment see Carl A. Auerbach, "Jury Trials and Civil Rights," *New Leader*, 29 April 1957, 16–18; "Civil Rights—Backstage Drama," *Newsweek*, 12 August 1957, 25–26; Tris Coffin, "How Lyndon Johnson Engineered Compromise on Civil Rights Bill," *New Leader*, 5 August 1957, 3–4, Smith Papers.

80. Legislative Leadership Meeting, 6 August 1957, supplementary notes, Whitman files, box 2, DDEL.

81. Minutes of Cabinet Meeting, 2 August 1957, Whitman Files, box 9, DDEL; Adams, *Firsthand Report*, 342.

82. Ervin to Dr. T. Franklin Williams, 27 September 1957, Ervin Papers, box 26, folder 220.

83. Ervin to Robert D. Deziah, 16 September 1957, Ervin Papers, box 26, folder 220. In his autobiography, Ervin wrote: "I was usually asked by the other Southern Senators who shared my views to spearhead the opposition to [civil rights proposals] in the debate on them in the Senate. In so doing, I devised and followed a new strategy. I avoided all arguments having racial connotations, and focused what I said on the specific constitutional, legal, and pragmatic weaknesses of the proposals." Sam Ervin, *Preserving the Constitution: The Autobiography of Senator Sam Ervin* (Charlottesville, Va.: Michie, 1984), 154.

84. Lyndon Johnson to Ervin, 8 August 1957, Ervin Papers, box 26, folder 218; and LBJ-a, congressional file, box 43, folder "Ervin," LBJL.

85. *New Republic*, 29 July 1957, 2. Other publications that portrayed Ervin as a leader during the debate were "People of the Week," *U.S. News and World Report*, 5 April 1957, 16; Walter F. Murphy, "Some Strange New Converts to the Cause of Civil Rights," *Reporter*, 27 June 1957, 13; "The Civil Rights Bill: What It Is and Where It Stands," *Time*, 6 May 1957, 26; Telford Taylor, "Crux of the Civil Rights Debate," *New York Times Magazine*, 16 June 1957, 25.

86. "Civil Rights Debate," *Winston-Salem Journal*, 7 June 1957, Ervin Notebooks, s-4.

87. Tris Coffin, "How Lyndon Johnson Engineered Compromise on Civil Rights Bill," *New Leader*, 5 August 1957, Smith Papers; "Civil Rights—Backstage Drama," *Newsweek*, 12 August 1957. The *New Republic* pointed out how "the southern strategy enabled Sam Ervin to make a reputation as a shrewd analyst," *New Republic*, 29 July 1957, 2; Newspapers in North Carolina glowed with pride for their senator whom they credited for the "somewhat higher plane" of the South's resistance. See "The Civil Rights Debate," *Winston-Salem Journal*, 7 June 1957, Ervin Notebooks, s-4.

88. Though the southerners had stripped the bill of its most significant provisions, it

still gave birth to the Civil Rights Commission, which would play a crucial role in building the case against the segregated South in the future. In the 1960s, Senator Philip Hart would look back on the 1957 Civil Rights Act and suggest that it "may well prove to be the most significant step taken by the Congress," because the commission "reported the facts that pricked the conscience of America." Philip Hart Press Release, 1 April 1964, box 565, Philip Hart Papers, Michigan Historical Collection, Bentley Library, University of Michigan, Ann Arbor (hereafter cited as Hart Papers).

89. Memorandum, the Secretary to the Executive Staff, 7 August 1957, NAACP Papers, box a71, folder "civil rights gen., Aug. 57."

90. Martin Luther King Jr. to Richard Nixon, 30 August 1957, William Rogers Papers, box 50, file 7, DDEL. The African American community was split on whether or not to recommend that Eisenhower veto the enfeebled bill. A. Phillip Randolph, Asa T. Spaulding, and many other activists joined Carl Murphy of the *Afro-American* and James Hicks of the *Amsterdam News* in urging the president not to sign the bill. Memorandum, "Black Reaction," O.F.B. 430, 102-B-3, DDEL.

91. Ervin to Edmond W. Price, 25 September 1957, Ervin Papers, box 26, folder 220. See also Ervin, "Senator Sam Ervin Says," weekly newspaper column, 3 October 1957, Ervin Papers, box 387, folder 56; Ervin to Homer M. Adkins, 5 November 1957, Ervin Papers, box 26, folder 223.

92. Ervin, "Senator Sam Ervin Says," weekly newspaper column, 3 October 1957, Ervin Papers, box 387, folder 56.

93. Ervin to Wilber M. Brucker (Secretary of the Army), 19 November 1957, Ervin Papers, box 387, folder 56.

94. Wilber M. Brucker to Ervin, 4 October 1957, Ervin Papers, box 26, folder 220.

95. Ervin, draft of the Jefferson-Jackson Day Speech, Little Rock, Arkansas, 29 March 1958, Ervin Papers, box 26, folder 220. See also Ervin to Dr. T. Franklin Williams, 27 September 1957, Ervin Papers, box 26, folder 220.

96. Ervin, press release, "Excerpts from Jefferson-Jackson Day Speech at Little Rock, Arkansas, 29 March 1958," Ervin Papers, box 453, folder 46.

97. "Petition Circulated," *Monroe Enquirer*, 11 November 1957, NAACP Papers, box a279, folder "Reprisals, N.C."; North Carolina NAACP Press Release, 13 June 1957, NAACP Papers, box a279, folder "Reprisals, N.C."

98. Memorandum, to All Cooperating Agencies, from Paul Rilling, Southern Regional Council, 28 September 1959, NAACP Papers, box a105, folder "N.C." The black parents refused to subject their children to daily eighty-mile bus trips, and set up their own school in a local church while fighting the school board in court. In 1962, the school board erected a segregated two-room elementary school for its African American pupils. Memo, Bill Bagnell to Jean Fairfax, 27 February 1962, American Friends Service Committee (AFSC) Papers, AFSC Archives, The Friends Center, Philadelphia, Pennsylvania.

99. "Young Negro Boys Involved in 'Kissing Case' Start New Lives," *Kinston Daily Free-Press*, 13 February 1959, Ervin Notebooks, s-5. The NAACP eventually obtained the boys' release by helping to improve their families' homes. For a discussion of racial violence in North Carolina, see Michael Myerson, *Nothing Could Be Finer* (New York: International Publishers, 1978).

100. "A Report from the South on the Negro Voter," *Reporter*, 27 June 1957, 9–12.

101. Ibid. Neighboring Louisiana reported that its rural northern parishes lost 15,326 black voters between 1956 and 1959, while adding 10,880 new white voters to their rolls. Public Affairs Research Council of Louisiana, Inc., "PAR Analysis, no. 84," January 1960, Long Papers, box RO 92.

102. Burk, *Eisenhower Administration and Civil Rights*, 231; Bob Angers, "Interposition," *Franklin* (Louisiana) *Banner Tribune*, 17 November 1960, Long Papers, box RO 92.

103. Frustrated by the weakened Civil Rights Act of 1957, Roy Wilkins announced that the civil rights forces would begin pushing for a new bill immediately. NAACP Press Release, "NAACP to Press for New Civil Rights Measures," 13 December 1957, NAACP Papers, box a73, folder "Press Releases, 56–57." The 1957 civil rights bill proved to be so unworkable that the Justice Department brought only three suits under its provisions between 1957 and 1959. Part of the blame for the low number of suits rests with the Justice Department's overly cautious decision to win a few symbolic cases and not risk any precedent-setting losses. See Lawson, *Black Ballots*, 205–12.

104. Ibid.

105. NAACP Press Release, "GOP Runs Out on Civil Rights," 30 July 1959, NAACP Papers, box a73, folder "Press Releases, 58–59." Part of the Republicans' lack of enthusiasm no doubt came from the upheaval caused by the Little Rock episode and from political advisers who worried about white backlash. One Republican activist in Florida warned against isolating southern voters by strengthening the 1957 bill. "I really believe that we have a great chance of carrying the South," he explained, "if we don't disturb the people too much with impossible planks on civil rights." W. F. Parker to William P. Rogers, 18 July 1960, Rogers Papers, box 53, folder 5, DDEL.

106. NAACP Press Release, 22 January 1959, NAACP Papers, box 73, folder "Press Releases, 58–59"; NAACP Press Release, "Failure of Congress," 18 September 1959, NAACP Papers, box a73, folder "Press Releases, 58–59."

107. Roy Wilkins, *Standing Fast*, 261. For a review of congressional actions on civil rights between 1957 and 1960, see Daniel M. Berman, *A Bill Becomes a Law: Congress Enacts Civil Rights Legislation*, 2nd ed. (New York: Macmillan, 1966), 7–48.

108. Anthony Lewis, "Election Brightens Prospects for Civil Rights Action," *New York Times*, 9 November 1959; "Democrats Plan a Broad Program in New Congress," *New York Times*, 7 November 1959; Russell Baker, "Butler Declares Rights is '60 Issue," *New York Times*, 8 November 1959.

109. "Civil Rights Gains in Congress Seen," *New York Times*, 31 December 1959; "Senator Predicts Action on Rights," *New York Times*, 9 November 1959.

110. Anthony Lewis, "Election Brightens Prospects for Civil Rights Action," *New York Times*, 9 November 1959; Carl M. Brauer, *John F. Kennedy and the Second Reconstruction* (New York: Columbia University Press, 1977), 7–29.

111. United States Commission on Civil Rights, Report, 1959.

112. Ervin, "Statement of Senator Ervin on Report of the Commission on Civil Rights," press release, 8 September 1959, Ervin Papers, box 453, folder 64. "Southerners Assail Civil Rights Report," *Charlotte Observer*, 9 September 1959, Ervin Notebooks, s-5. Russell Baker, "Republicans Plan a Civil Rights Bill to Test New Rule," *New York Times*, 14 June 1959.

113. Ervin explained the soft southern strategy to his constituents in 1960: "The only way the argument against civil rights legislation can be effectively made is to carry on

debate on a high plane, thus affording the Senate and the country an opportunity to study the proposals." "Senator Sam J. Ervin Says," weekly newspaper column, 3 March 1960, Ervin Papers, box 450.

114. This description was attributed to Senator Kenneth B. Keating, Republican of New York, in "Dirksen Pledges Fight for Civil Rights Action," *Washington Evening Star*, 6 July 1959, Hennings Papers, folder 5233. Roy Wilkins and the officers of the LCCR complained to the Senate that "like a broken record the same theme had been played again and again. The Constitutional Rights Subcommittee had voted out a bill, albeit woefully inadequate, after extensive hearings, and thereupon the filibuster in the full Judiciary committee has been going strong." Roy Wilkins, Arnold Aronson, Patrick Murphy Malin, et al., to Senator Stuart Symington, 3 September 1959, box 17, Stuart Symington Papers, Joint Collection, University of Missouri Western Historical Manuscript Collection and State Historical Society of Missouri Manuscripts, Columbia, Missouri (hereafter cited as Symington Papers).

115. Don Oberdorfer, "South's Defense Attorney, Ervin Rights Fight 'Star,' " *Charlotte Observer*, 22 March 1959, Ervin Notebooks, s-5; Holmes Alexander praised Ervin's statesmanship and fearlessness, even though he disagreed with his constitutional position in "Thought v. Dogma: The Racial Problem," *Los Angeles Times*, 17 April 1959, Ervin Notebooks, s-5. Ervin not only dominated the Constitutional Rights Subcommittee and Judiciary Committee hearings, but also served as the South's primary defender in the Senate Rules Committee when civil rights proponents relied on a parliamentary maneuver to reassign the bill there in the hope that it might escape the southern stranglehold.

116. Drew Pearson, "Nicodemus Quoted on Civil Rights," *Washington Post*, 21 August 1959, Ervin Notebooks, s-5.

117. Paul R. Clancy, *Just a Country Lawyer: A Biography of Senator Sam Ervin* (Bloomington: Indiana University Press, 1974), 183.

118. Much of the debate over the Civil Rights Act of 1960 revolved around which of the two different approaches to protecting the franchise—labeled the "referee" and the "registrar" plans—would be more appropriate. Ervin objected to them both. For clarity, all such proposals will be referred to as the "referee plan" in this chapter. For a discussion of these alternatives see Berman, *A Bill Becomes a Law*, 44–46, 51–56.

119. Ervin to Governor John S. Battle, 1 February 1960, Ervin Papers, box 389, folder 95; "Ervin Pins 'Carpetbagger' Tag on Federal Vote Registrar Plan," *Washington Post*, 19 January 1960, Ervin Notebooks, s-5; "Senator Sam J. Ervin Says," weekly newspaper column, 28 January 1960, Ervin Papers, box 450; "Ervin Mans Front Line," *Winston-Salem Journal*, 17 February 1960, Ervin Notebooks, s-5; Russell Baker, "South Opens Fire on Referee Plan for Civil Rights," *New York Times*, 1 April 1960.

120. See Lawrence Walsh testimony, U.S. Senate, Committee on the Judiciary, *Hearings on HR 8601*, 86th Cong., 2nd sess., 1960, 23.

121. Russell Baker, "South Opens Fire on Referee Plan for Civil Rights," *New York Times*, 1 April 1960. Ervin also believed the bill to be unconstitutional because it vested a judicial power in the Civil Rights Commission, which is an executive branch agency. See Ervin to Governor John S. Battle, 1 February 1960, Ervin Papers, box 389, folder 95.

122. Most southern congressmen echoed Ervin's legal objections to the civil rights bill. See Russell Long, speech notes, Long Papers, RO 92. Congressman Edwin E. Willis's

rhetoric can be found in "Louisiana Congressman's View," *Shreveport Times*, 3 August 1960, Long Papers, box r-91.

123. Ervin played a greater role in the 1960 filibuster than he had in the 1957 debate. Some observers noted how Ervin took over much of the "leg work" from Richard Russell during the floor debate. See Lynn Nisbet, "Ervin Succeeds Russell," *Kinston Daily Free Press*, 9 April 1960, Ervin Notebooks, s-5; Al Perry, "Ervin Wields Power," *Twin City Sentinel*, 8 April 1960, Ervin Notebooks, s-5. On the filibuster see Burk, *Eisenhower Administration and Civil Rights*, 223; Berman, *A Bill Becomes A Law*, 82–88.

124. Don Oberdorfer, "The Night Sam Ervin Spoke Few Listened, Many Slept," *Charlotte Observer*, 3 March 1960. Other descriptions of Ervin's role in the filibuster include "Filibuster Boasts Light Moments Too," *Honolulu Sunday Advertiser*, 13 March 1960, Ervin Notebooks, s-5; "Under the Dome," Raleigh *News and Observer*, 14 March 1960, Ervin Notebooks, s-5; "Filibuster Unlikely over Civil Rights Bill," *Winston-Salem Journal*, 3 April 1960, Ervin Notebooks, s-5.

125. "Filibustering," *Newsweek*, 14 March 1960, 240.

126. "Republicans Lean to Cloture Move in Rights Debate," *New York Times*, 26 February 1960. Prior to 1960, eight attempts to evoke cloture against a southern filibuster preventing civil rights had been made in the twentieth century. None had succeeded.

127. Lawson, *Black Ballots*, 246.

128. NAACP Press Release, "Civil Rights Bill Fails to Meet Needs—Wilkins," NAACP Press Release, 14 April 1960, NAACP Papers, box a73, folder "Press Releases, 60–65."

129. I. A. Newby, *Jim Crow's Defense: Anti-Negro Thought in America, 1900 to 1930* (Baton Rouge: Louisiana State University Press, 1965), viii; I. A. Newby, *Challenge to the Court: Social Scientists and the Defense of Segregation, 1954–1966* (Baton Rouge: Louisiana State University Press, 1967), viii.

130. A survey of six popular college textbooks revealed that George Wallace received the most attention with twenty citations, followed by Strom Thurmond with eleven, Eugene "Bull" Connor and Orval Faubus with six each, and James Eastland and Jim Clark with three each. A review of several recent narrative histories of the civil rights era revealed a similar breakdown: George Wallace earned forty-nine citations; John Patterson, forty-four; Eugene "Bull" Connor, twenty-three; James Eastland, twenty-two; Strom Thurmond, ten; Herman Talmadge, Orval Faubus and Jim Clark, eight each; Richard Russell, five; Harry Byrd, four; John Stennis, two; and Sam Ervin, one. Textbooks included in the survey were Bernard Bailyn et al., *The Great Republic*, 3rd ed. (Lexington, Mass.: D. C. Heath, 1985); Paul S. Boyer et al., *The Enduring Vision* (Lexington, Mass.: D. C. Heath, 1990); Gary B. Nash et al., *The American People*, 2nd ed. (Grand Rapids, Mich: Harper and Row, 1990); George Tindall, *America: A Narrative History*, 2nd ed. (New York: W. W. Norton, 1988); Robert Kelley, *The Shaping of the American Past*, 3rd ed. (Englewood Cliffs, N.J.: Prentice-Hall, 1982); Thomas A. Bailey and David M. Kennedy, *The American Pageant*, 7th ed. (Lexington, Mass.: D. C. Heath, 1983). The four narrative histories surveyed were Steven F. Lawson, *Running for Freedom: Civil Rights and Black Politics in America since 1941* (New York: McGraw-Hill, 1991); Fred Powledge, *Free at Last?: The Civil Rights Movement and the People Who Made It* (Boston: Little, Brown, 1991); Taylor Branch, *Parting the Waters: America in the King Years, 1954–1963* (New York: Simon and Schuster, 1988); Harvard Sitkoff, *The Struggle for Black Equality, 1954–1980* (New York: Hill and Wang, 1981).

131. "Sunny Sam," *Time*, 1 June 1962, Ervin Notebooks, s-2.

132. Senator Thomas Eagleton, telephone interview by the author, 13 June 1989.

133. On the role of the southern senator, see V. O. Key, *Southern Politics in State and Nation* (New York: Alfred A. Knopf, 1949).

134. Donald R. Matthews and James W. Prothro, "Stateways Versus Folkways: Critical Factors in Southern Reactions to *Brown* versus *Board of Education*," in *Essays on the American Constitution*, ed. Gottfried Dietze (Englewood Cliffs, N.J.: Prentice-Hall, 1964), 143–45; David Garrow, *Protest at Selma* (New Haven: Yale University Press, 1978), 7, 11, 19.

135. Russell Long, untitled speech, delivered in New Orleans, 16 November 1960, reported in the *New Orleans Times-Picayune*, 17 November 1960, Long Papers, box RO 92.

136. NAACP Press Release, "Role of the NAACP in the Sit-ins," May 1960, NAACP Papers, box a290, folder "Sit-ins, NC"; Memorandum, Herbert L. Wright to Roy Wilkins, "Report on the Sit-ins," 2 March 1960, NAACP Papers, box a290, folder, "Sit-ins, NC"; Memorandum, Clarence Mitchell to Roy Wilkins, 18 April 1960, NAACP Papers, box a290, folder "Sit-ins, NC."

137. Marion S. Barry Jr. to Stuart Symington, 12 August 1960, Symington Papers, box 17.

CHAPTER FIVE

1. "Southern Forces Are Believed Outgunned for Battle over Civil Rights Plank," *New York Times*, 10 July 1960. The *Times* reported: "The principal southern spokesman will be Senator Sam J. Ervin . . . a shrewd and persuasive man." See also Claude Sitton, interview, transcript, *Senator Sam* (film), New Atlantic Productions (hereafter cited as Sitton Interview); "Strong Civil Rights Plank Drafted by Platform Committee," *Los Angeles Times*, 11 July 1960; "Platform OKd After Attack on Rights Plank," *Los Angeles Times*; "South Will Give Stand on Rights," *Charlotte Observer*, 11 July 1960; "With Calmness and Dignity the South Accepted Reality," *Charlotte Observer*, 14 July 1960, in Sam J. Ervin Papers, Subgroup A: Senate Papers, 3847A, Southern Historical Collection, Wilson Library, University of North Carolina at Chapel Hill, Newspaper Clippings Notebooks, s-5 (hereafter cited as Ervin Notebooks).

2. Paul R. Clancy, *Just a Country Lawyer: A Biography of Senator Sam Ervin* (Bloomington: Indiana University Press, 1974), 180.

3. This often repeated phrase became the title of Ervin's autobiography, Ervin, *Preserving the Constitution* (Charlottesville, Va.: Michie, 1984).

4. Ervin, *Preserving the Constitution*, 72, 163–85; Ervin to Basil L. Whitener, 14 April 1967, *Congressional Record*, 90th Cong., 1st sess., 1967, 9714. Ervin's remarks were also reported in David Leon Chandler, *The Natural Superiority of Southern Politicians: A Revisionist History* (Garden City, N.Y.: Doubleday, 1977), 316.

5. Stephen Klitzman, "Sam Ervin: Principle not Politics," in *Citizens Look at Congress*, Ralph Nader Congress Project, 1972, 1. Civil rights proponents such as J. Francis Pohlhaus, general counsel for the NAACP, Joseph Rauh Jr., general counsel for the LCCR, Martha McKay of the National Women's Political Caucus, and writer Robert Sherrill agreed that Ervin's reputation as a constitutional expert was "over-rated." Sherrill believed that the senator's view of the Constitution was "static, one-dimensional, and simple minded." See Klitzman, "Sam Ervin," 34.

6. Jack Claiborne, "Sam Ervin v. the 'Abyssinia Bloc,' " *Charlotte Observer*, 28 February

1965, Ervin Notebooks, s-11; James Robinson, "Sen. Sam Sings Praise of Irish," *Charlotte Observer*, 25 September 1965, Ervin Notebooks, s-11; Andrew Glass, "Ervin and Javits Clash," *Raleigh News and Observer*, 27 February 1965; George B. Autry, 11 April 1989, interview by the author. Ervin had made nativistic comments before. In 1955 he ridiculed a New York State law that made it illegal to ask a man what name he was born under. "If the original name had a foreign sound," Ervin said, "that might lead to employing some good American in his place." "Ervin Blasts Law 'Favoring' Foreign-Born," *Winston-Salem Journal*, 6 August 1955, Ervin Notebooks, s-2.

7. "Civil Rights Battle Opens in Senate," *Charlotte Observer*, 9 July 1957, Ervin Notebooks, s-4; Ervin to A. J. Walton, 23 May 1957, in Sam J. Ervin Papers, Subgroup A: Senate Papers, 3847A, Southern Historical Collection, Wilson Library, University of North Carolina at Chapel Hill, box 26, folder 203 (hereafter cited as Ervin Papers). During the debate over the Voting Rights Act of 1965, Ervin explained: "First, I should like to stress, as I have consistently done, that my objections to this bill relate solely to its inappropriateness and unconstitutionality—they have nothing whatever to do with considerations of race or color. I am confident in my own mind that no one desires more than I to see the last vestiges of racial discrimination eliminated and that no one abhors more than I the racial tension and violence that has erupted in many parts of the country and the atmosphere of lawlessness and intolerance that has engendered and encouraged such outbursts." Ervin, "New Version of Voting Rights Bill Manifestly Unconstitutional, Draft of Remarks to be Delivered to the Senate," n.d., 1965, Ervin Papers, box 391, folder 131.

8. Transcript, "Youth Wants to Know," n.d., 1963, Ervin Papers, box 390, folder 104. The author has found no statement by Ervin expressing his belief in biological white supremacy. However, circumstantial evidence suggests that, like most white men of his generation, Ervin held such beliefs. For instance, Ervin kept a subject folder containing racist propaganda and background materials against civil rights in his Senate office. The folder contains several pages of Ervin's handwritten notes, including the following quotations from Abraham Lincoln: "But Judge Douglas is especially horrified at the thought of the mixing of blood by white and black races. Agreed for once—a thousand times agreed. There are white men enough to marry all the white women, and black men enough to marry all the black women; and so let them be married." "Negro equality! Fudge! How long in the government of God, great enough to make and maintain this Universe, shall there continue knaves to send, and fools to gulp, so low a piece of demagogism as this." Ervin Papers, box 388, folder 64.

9. Ervin, "The Case for Segregation," *Look*, 3 April 1956, 32–33; "The Race Issue: South's Plans, How Negroes Will Meet Them," *U.S. and World Report*, 18 November 1955, 90.

10. Ibid., 95.

11. Ervin, "The Case for Segregation," *Look*, 3 April 1956, 32–33.

12. Ibid.

13. Ibid., 32.

14. Ervin to C. W. Houston, 18 September 1956, Ervin Papers, box 18, folder 292.

15. Ervin, "The Case for Segregation," *Look*, 3 April 1956, 37.

16. See Aldon D. Morris, *The Origins of the Civil Rights Movement: Black Communities Organizing for Change* (New York: Free Press, 1984).

17. On the civil rights movement and the strategy of nonviolent civil disobedience see

James W. Vander Zanden, "The Non-Violent Movement Against Segregation," *American Journal of Sociology* 68 (March 1963): 545–50; Stephen Lawson, *Running for Freedom: Civil Rights and Black Politics in America since 1941* (New York: McGraw-Hill, 1991), 67–68; David J. Garrow, *Bearing the Cross: Martin Luther King, Jr., and the Southern Christian Leadership Conference* (New York: William Morrow, 1986); Stephen B. Oates, *Let the Trumpet Sound: The Life of Martin Luther King Jr.* (New York: Harper and Row, 1982).

18. "Ervin Deplores Ala. Violence," *Winston-Salem Journal*, 22 May 1961, Ervin Notebooks, s-6.

19. "Alabama Asks U.S. Help as Violence Erupts," *New York Times*, 22 May 1961; "Alabama Rioting," *Washington Post*, 24 May 1961; Senator Philip Hart, "Report from Washington," 29 May 1961, Philip Hart Papers, Michigan Historical Collection, Bentley Library, University of Michigan, Ann Arbor, box 100, folder "Civil Rights: Freedom Riders, 1961" (hereafter cited as Hart Papers).

20. "Ervin Unquestioned Leader," *Raleigh News and Observer*, July 1963, Ervin Notebooks, s-8; "Senator Ervin Criticizes Gov. Wallace Tactics in School Dispute," *Wilmington Star*, 12 September 1963, Ervin Notebooks, s-8; Ervin form letter to constituents, October 1962, Ervin Papers, box 453, folder 114.

21. "Ervin Deplores Ala. Violence," *Winston-Salem Journal*, 22 May 1961, Ervin Notebooks, s-6; "Robert Kennedy Plea Fails to Sway Ervin on Rights," *Washington Star*, 11 September 1963, Ervin Notebooks, s-8.

22. Ervin appeared to be ambivalent about poll taxes. In an interview he expressed pride that North Carolina had abolished its poll tax some forty years earlier. But he added, "I think that anybody who is not willing to pay a dollar or a dollar and a half a year to support of the government, which protects his life and his liberty and his property, shouldn't—I'm not going to shed any tears over his failure to vote." Transcript, "Youth Wants to Know," n.d., 1963, Ervin Papers, box 390, folder 104.

23. For Ervin's opinions on the poll tax, see Transcript, "Youth Wants to Know," n.d., 1963, Ervin Papers, box 390, folder 104; *Congressional Quarterly Almanac* 18 (1962): 404–6; Roy Wilkins to Benjamin A. Smith, 23 March 1962, box a-69, folder "Civil Rights Leg., Congress," series A, group III, NAACP Papers, Manuscript Division, Library of Congress (hereafter cited as NAACP Papers).

24. "Remarks of Senator Sam J. Ervin, Jr. in the Senate on March 23, 1962," Ervin Papers, box 389, folder 99, 5. Ervin added that Kennedy's bill presented Congress "with the finest opportunity it has ever had to make an unmitigated ass of itself." See also Ervin, "Literacy Tests for Voters: A Case Study in Federalism," *Law and Contemporary Problems* 37 (Summer 1962): 481; Memorandum, Merrill to Ervin, 26 February 1962, Theodore Sorensen Papers, Subject files, box 30, John F. Kennedy Presidential Library (JFKL), Boston; "Ervin Attacks Constitutionality of Voter Qualification Bills," Ervin press release, 27 March 1962, box r-91, Russell Long Papers, Louisiana and Lower Mississippi Valley Collections, Louisiana State University (hereafter cited as Long Papers); Hearings before the Subcommittee on Constitutional Rights of the Senate Judiciary Committee, 87th Cong., 2nd sess., 1962, "Literacy Tests and Voter Requirements in Federal and State Elections"; "Southerners Criticize Kennedy's Rights Bill," *Winston-Salem Journal*, 2 January 1962, Ervin Notebooks, s-7; "Ervin Doubts Legality of Literacy Test Plan," *Washington Evening Star*, 27 January 1962, Ervin Notebooks, s-7.

25. "Remarks of Senator Sam J. Ervin, Jr. in the Senate on March 23, 1962," Ervin Papers, box 389, folder 99, 5.

26. Ervin to Morgan A. Coker, 22 August 1957, Ervin Papers, box 26, folder 219.

27. "Scripture Quoting Ervin Leads Fight," *Raleigh News and Observer*, 15 April 1962, Ervin Notebooks, s-7; "Sunny Sam," *Time*, 1 June 1962, 19–20; Carl M. Brauer, *John F. Kennedy and the Second Reconstruction*, Contemporary American History Series, ed. William E. Leuchtenburg (New York: Columbia University Press, 1977), 137. Ervin solicited opinions on the constitutionality of the bill from many law professors and all fifty state attorneys general. Approximately one-half agreed that the bill was unconstitutional. See "Bill on Literacy Divides Lawyers," *New York Times*, 19 March 1962; Douglass Maggs and Lawrence Wallace, "Congress and Literacy Tests," *Law and Contemporary Problems* 37 (Summer 1962): 523; Donald P. Kommers, "The Right to Vote and Its Implementation," *Notre Dame Lawyer* 39 (June 1964): 408.

28. Ervin's opponent in 1962, Claude E. Greene, a farmer and conservative Republican, attacked the senator as not being conservative enough on economic matters. See "GOP Farmer Takes on Ervin in Senate Race," *Charlotte Observer*, 28 October 1962, Ervin Notebooks, s-7; "Ervin Tops N.C. Ballot in Election," *Raleigh News and Observer*, 28 October 1962, Ervin Notebooks, s-7; "Ervin Apparently Ignores Existence of His Opponent," *Winston-Salem Journal*, 3 November 1962; "Senator Ervin Spent Little in Campaign," *Morganton News-Herald*, 18 December 1962. It is a mistake to conclude that the race issue alone explains Ervin's popularity, just as it is nonsense to rationalize Ervin's opposition to civil rights by suggesting that the political climate forced him to take a stand he would not have otherwise taken. Ervin embodied the class, race, and gender values of the dominant white culture in which he was raised. His constitutional philosophy, as well as his soft southern strategy, reflected the progressive mythology white North Carolinians held about themselves. See William Chafe, *Civilities and Civil Rights: Greensboro, North Carolina, and the Black Struggle for Freedom* (New York: Oxford University Press, 1982), 2–10; Klitzman, "Sam Ervin," 8–17.

29. Paul Luebke, *Tar Heel Politics: Myths and Realities* (Chapel Hill: University of North Carolina Press, 1990), 15–22.

30. Memorandum, Paul Popple to Walter Jenkins, Executive WE, WHCF, Lyndon B. Johnson Presidential Library (LBJL), Austin, Texas. Another memorandum to the president included the following remarks: "Senator Ervin stated that he did not like to exercise veto over an appointment. Senator Ervin then asked what the President was considering Governor Sanford for. I told him I didn't know for sure but possibly an Ambassadorship. He said he thought that would be fine and he would be good for it. Senator Ervin said it would get Sanford out of the State and get him far away. Senator Ervin said Governor Sanford had been saying he may run against him and he thought it would be good if he could get an appointment." Memorandum, Marvin [?] to the President, 16 July 1964, FO2, WHCF, LBJL.

31. Transcript, Terry Sanford Oral History Interview, 1 March 1973, by Joe B. Frantz, Tape 1, p. 17, LBJL. Sanford has denied that he held any personal dislike of Ervin, but circumstantial evidence suggests otherwise. A White House memorandum quotes B. Everett Jordan as saying: "Governor Sanford said some awful mean things about Ervin in times past." Memorandum, Marvin [?] to the President, 16 July 1964, FO2, WHCF, LBJL.

32. News Release, Voter Education Project, Atlanta, Georgia, 31 March 1963, Long Papers, box ro-92; "Bombed School Closed in Louisiana," *Washington Post*, 28 August 1963, Long Papers, box ro 92; "NAACP Intercedes in Killing by N.C Cop," NAACP press release, 27 July 1962, NAACP Papers, box a243, folder "N.C. Police Brutality"; Memorandum from Mr. Currant to Mr. Moon, 7 February 1962, NAACP Papers, box a243, folder "N.C. Police Brutality."

33. The bill included a new federal referee plan, judicial procedures to expedite voter registration, a four-year extension to the Civil Rights Commission, empowerment of the federal Office of Education to assist local communities attempting to desegregate, and reintroduced the anti–literacy test measure from the previous year. The bill did not include the old Title III or address economic discrimination.

34. Response to the bill was discussed on "Washington Report," CBS, 3 March 1963, Robert Kennedy Papers, Attorney General, Speeches, box 1, folder "CBS News, 3-3-63," JFKL.

35. Richard Bolling, *House Out of Order* (New York: E. P. Dutton, 1964), 190–94; Transcript, "Youth Wants to Know," n.d., 1963, Ervin Papers, box 390, folder 104; Transcript, "Reporters' Round-Up," Mutual Broadcasting System, 21 July 1963, Long Papers, box r-63. On Ervin's stalling tactics see Edward V. Long to Ervin, 22 June 1963, and Kenneth Keating to James O. Eastland, 3 April 1963, in Edward V. Long Papers, Box 204, folder 120B, Joint Collection, University of Missouri Western Historical Manuscript Collection—Columbia and State Historical Society of Missouri Manuscripts (hereafter cited as Edward Long Papers).

36. Events in Birmingham are described in Michael Droman, *We Shall Overcome* (New York: Dial Press, 1964); Harvard Sitkoff, *The Struggle for Black Equality* (New York: Hill and Wang, 1981), 127–58; Garrow, *Bearing the Cross*, 231–69; Lawson, *Black Ballots*, 279.

37. Theodore Sorensen interview, number 5, by Carl Kaysen, 3 May 1964, Oral History Project, JFKL, 133; Joseph L. Rauh Jr., interview by Charles T. Morrissey, 23 December 1965, Oral History Project, JFKL, 109; Brauer, *John F. Kennedy and the Second Reconstruction*, 260.

38. U.S. Senate, Judiciary Committee, *Hearings, Civil Rights—The President's Program, 1963*, 88th Cong., 1st sess., 1963, 23 (hereafter cited as Hearings, 1963); UPI Press Statement, 7 July 1963, Edward Long Papers, box 154, folder 120.

39. Dictaphone Recording, T. Sorensen and Lyndon B. Johnson, 3 June 1963, Sorensen Papers, Subject Files, box 3c, folder, "Civil Rights Leg. 1963," JFKL; Memorandum, Norbert A. Schlei to the Attorney General, 4 June 1963, Robert F. Kennedy Papers, Attorney General Files, General Correspondence, box 11, folder "Civil Rights Leg., 6-3-63," 4, JFKL. Memorandum, Joseph Rauh to Robert Kennedy, 2 July 1963, Robert F. Kennedy Papers, Attorney General Files, General Correspondence, box 11, folder "Civil Rights Leg., 6-3-63," 14. The legal history of the guidelines is discussed in J. R. Dunn, "Title VI, The Guidelines and School Desegregation in the South," *Virginia Law Review* 53 (January 1967): 42–88.

40. "Federal Control Over Marriages and Births?" *U.S. News and World Report*, 29 July 1963, 10; "Robert Kennedy Faces Rights Foes," *New York Times*, 21 July 1963; "Civil Rights," *Time*, 26 July 1963, 11–12; "Sam and Bobby Show Has Rerun," *Charlotte Observer*, 26 July 1963, Ervin Notebooks, s-9; "Bobby v. Senator," *San Francisco Chronicle*, 1 August 1963, Ervin Notebooks, s-9; "A Senator Tangles with a Kennedy," *Kansas City Star*, 3 August 1963,

Ervin Notebooks, s-9; "Senator Sam's Folksy Style Turns Hoots Into Laughs," *Charlotte Observer*, 1 August 1963, Ervin Notebooks, s-9; "Ervin Unquestioned Leader," *Raleigh News and Observer*, July 1963, Ervin Notebooks, s-9.

41. Memorandum, Marjorie McDenzie Lawson to John F. Kennedy, 27 December 1958, Pre-Presidential Papers, box 991, folder "Civil Rights—Civil Liberties," JFKL.

42. "Ervin's Humor Helps Bobby Get Approval," *Charlotte Observer*, 16 January 1961, Ervin Notebooks, s-6.

43. Hearings, 1963, 219; Jack Claiborne, "Ervin and Bobby Still Miles Apart," *Charlotte Observer*, 1 August 1963. Many of Ervin's constitutional objections to the civil rights bills of 1963 and 1964 were reruns of his earlier criticisms of previous civil rights bills. Ervin described the new powers the bills would grant to the attorney general as "discretionary" and "tyrannical," and he complained that the legislation would rob southerners of their right to a trial by jury. See Ervin, "The United States Congress and Civil Rights Legislation," *North Carolina Law Review* 42 (Fall 1963): 3–15; Ervin, "Political Rights as Abridged by Pending Legislative Proposals," *Federal Bar Journal* 24 (Winter 1964): 5–17; Robert H. Bork, "Civil Rights—A Challenge," *New Republic*, 31 August 1963, 21–24; Alexander M. Bickel, "Civil Rights and Congress," *New Republic*, 3 August 1963, 14–16; "Civil Rights Act of 1964," *Harvard Law Review* 78 (January 1965): 684–96; "Symposium on Civil Rights," *Federal Bar Journal* 24 (Winter 1964): 1–132.

44. Ervin's interpretation of the Interstate Commerce Clause was woefully outdated. The Supreme Court had dismissed such a narrow reading of the regulatory powers of the federal government in 1937 during the New Deal and had consistently reaffirmed the validity of an expanded interpretation of the Commerce Clause ever since. Norbert Schlei, one of Bobby Kennedy's closest advisers, later described the debate as "a lot of political smoke": "There is not a self-respecting lawyer who would have written you an opinion that the bill would be anything but constitutional right from the beginning. This was the kind of constitutional question that can be talked about in a political forum but is absolutely spurious as a legal issue." Norbert A. Schlei, interview by John Stewart, 20–21 February 1968, JFKL Oral History Project, 49–51. Alexander Bickel wrote: "This is now firmly established doctrine, regardless of how often Southern Senators deny it." Bickel, "Civil Rights and Congress," 14–16.

45. Hearings, 1963, 321–22.

46. Ibid., 322.

47. Ibid. This exchange from "The Sam and Bobby Show" is also discussed in Clancy, *Just a Country Lawyer*, 184–85.

48. Ibid., 416–17.

49. Ibid.

50. Howard Lee was the mayor of Chapel Hill. See Howard Lee interview, "Senator Sam," tape 4/5, 7–8 (hereafter cited as Lee Interview).

51. Lee Interview, 8.

52. Brauer, *John F. Kennedy and the Second Reconstruction*, 288; Memorandum, "After the March—The Immediate Task," Arnold Aronson to Cooperating Organizations, 30 August 1963, series D, Memos 63–66, Leadership Conference on Civil Rights Papers, Manuscript Division, Library of Congress, Washington, D.C. (hereafter cited as LCCR Papers); Memorandum, "The House Subcommittee Works in the Wake of the Birming-

ham Tragedy," Arnold Aronson to Cooperating Agencies, 20 September 1963, LCCR Papers, series D, Memos 63–66; Frank Sikora, *Until Justice Rolls Down: The Birmingham Church Bombing Case* (Tuscaloosa: University of Alabama Press, 1991).

53. Memorandum, Mike Manatos to Larry O'Brien, 1 October 1963, Lawrence F. O'Brien Staff Papers, box 18, folder "Fulbright #2," JFKL.

54. NAACP press release, "NAACP Calls for Removal of 'K. O. the Kennedys' Signs," NAACP Papers, box a177, folder "Kennedy, death of, 1963–4."

55. "Senator Sam Ervin: 'Thing Like This Makes You Sick,'" *Charlotte Observer*, 23 November 1963, Ervin Notebooks, s-9.

56. Lyndon B. Johnson, *Public Papers of the Presidents, 1963–64* (Washington, D.C.: U.S. Government Printing Office, 1965), 1, 8–10; "Statement by the Leadership Conference on Civil Rights," 27 November 1963, LCCR Papers, series D, memos 63–66. See also Memorandum, no. 15, from Arnold Aronson, 26 November 1963, LCCR Papers, series D, memos 63–66; NAACP press release, "News Media Seeks Views of Wilkins on Impact of Kennedy's Death," NAACP Papers, box a177, folder "Kennedy, death of, 63–63"; NAACP press release, "Civil Rights, 1963: A Summary," NAACP press release, 29 December 1963, NAACP Papers, box a73, folder "Press Releases, 60–63"; Memorandum, for Pierre Salinger, 8 January 1964, WHCF, ex FG 300/a, box 321, folder FG 400 11/22/64, LBJL; Brauer, *John F. Kennedy and the Second Reconstruction*, 314–15.

57. *Congressional Record*, 88th Cong., 1st sess., 1964, 15416–23; Ervin press release, "The Civil Rights Bill: A Bagful of Legal Tricks," 11 April 1964, Ervin Papers, box 453, folder 132; Ervin to Stuart Symington, 13 April 1964, box 18, Stuart Symington Papers, Joint Collection, University of Missouri Western Historical Manuscript Collection—Columbia and State Historical Society of Missouri Manuscripts, Columbia, Missouri; "Ervin Is Veteran in Rights Battle," *Raleigh News and Observer*, 5 March 1968, Ervin Notebooks, s-9; "Editor's Note, The Comments of Robert Bork and Philip B. Kurland," *Chicago Tribune*, 1 March 1964, Ervin Papers, box 390, folder 122.

58. Transcript, "Civil Rights Debate-Russell/McCarthy," CBS Radio, Washington, 1 May 1964, Audio Visual Series, 27, 9, Richard B. Russell Papers, Richard B. Russell Library, University of Georgia (hereafter cited as Russell Papers); "Senator is Not Always Humorous," *Los Angeles Times*, 13 March 1964; "Rights Bill Stranded in Senate for 10th Straight Day," *Washington Post*, 20 March 1964, Ervin Notebooks, s-10. Hubert Humphrey attacked Ervin during the filibuster debate by suggesting that Ervin was not against this bill, but any bill, since he used the same constitutional arguments in 1957 and 1960. See "Again the Filibusters," *New York Times Magazine*, 1 March 1964.

59. Ervin's amendment is discussed in Charles and Barbara Whalen, *The Longest Debate: A Legislative History of the 1964 Civil Rights Act* (Washington, D.C.: Seven Locks Press, 1985), 204–7; and Robert D. Loevy, *To End All Segregation: The Politics of the Passage of the Civil Rights Act of 1964* (Lanham, Md.: University Press of America, 1990), 287–88. The legislative history of the Civil Rights Act of 1964 is also described in Clifford M. Lytle, "The History of the Civil Rights Act of 1964," *Journal of Negro History* 51 (October 1966): 275–96; Hugh Davis Graham, *The Civil Rights Era: Origins and Development of National Policy* (New York: Oxford University Press, 1990), 125–52.

60. Whalen and Whalen, *Longest Debate*, 209; "Cloture Vote Made History in Senate," *Asheville Citizen*, 11 June 1964; Ervin Notebooks, s-10; Ervin, "Southern View: Legal Tests

Loom on Civil Rights," *Christian Science Monitor*, 18 June 1964; "They Went for Broke and Made It," *Charlotte Observer*, 20 June 1964, Ervin Notebooks, s-10; and *New York Times*, 11 June 1964.

61. *Public Papers, Johnson*, 1965, 1, 284. Mark Stern, *Calculating Vision: Kennedy, Johnson and Civil Rights* (New Brunswick, N.J.: Rutgers University Press, 1992), 210–26.

62. On the legislative history and political context of the Voting Rights Act of 1965, see Lawson, *Black Ballots*, 312–22; Garrow, *Bearing the Cross*, 357–430.

63. *Congressional Record*, 89th Cong., 1st sess., 1965, 9272; Ervin press releases, 26 May 1965, 8 April 1965, 29 April 1965, Ervin Papers, box 454, folders 176, 151, 154; "Doubters with Points," *Time*, 2 April 1965, 22–23; "Southerners Assail Voting Rights Bill," *Winston-Salem Journal*, 30 March 1965, Ervin Notebooks, s-11; "New Changes in Voting Bill Proposal," *Washington Post*, 31 March 1965, Ervin Notebooks, s-11; "Senator Ervin, Katzenbach Lock Horns over Provisions on Voting Measure," *Asheville Citizen*, 25 March 1965, Ervin Notebooks, s-11.

64. Lloyd Preslar, "Southern Rearguard Beset by Weariness," *Winston-Salem Journal*, 4 April 1965, Ervin Notebooks, s-11; Bernard Schwartz, *Statutory History of the United States: Civil Rights* (New York: McGraw-Hill, 1970), 2, 1469–72; Lawson, *Black Ballots*, 317. These and other scholars have pointed out that both of Ervin's charges against the bill were wrong. First, the *ex post facto* concept applied only to criminal, not civil cases. Second, the legislation was not a bill of attainder because the states could petition the judiciary if they wanted to escape coverage.

65. "Sen. Sam: Alone Against 'Multitude,'" *Charlotte Observer*, 15 May 1965, Ervin Notebooks, s-11.

66. Ervin press release, 29 April 1965, Ervin Papers, box 454, folder 154.

67. Sitkoff, *Struggle for Black Equality*, 197; Lawson, *Running for Freedom*, 115–16; Charles S. Bullock III and Charles M. Lamb, *Implementation of Civil Rights Policy* (Monterey, Calif.: Brooks/Cole, 1984), 42.

68. Memorandum, Arnold Aronson to Cooperating Agencies, 10 June 1964, LCCR Papers, series D, box 4, folder "Memos 1964"; Memorandum, Arnold Aronson to Cooperating Agencies, 19 June 1964, LCCR Papers, series D, box 4, folder "Memos 1964."

69. Memorandum, Phillip S. Hughes to Mr. White, 11 June 1964, Lee White Papers, box 6, LBJL.

70. "General Statement of Policies Under Title VI of the Civil Rights Act of 1964 Respecting Desegregation of Elementary and Secondary Schools," U.S. Department of Health, Education, and Welfare, 1965, Ervin Papers, box 387, folder 55; Memorandum, Nicholas Katzenbach to the President, March 1964, WHCF, HU, box 54, LBJL; Memorandum, Larry O'Brien to Jack Valenti, 9 March 1965, Manatos Papers, box 14, LBJL.

71. Memorandum, F. Peter Libassi to Harry McPherson, 23 March 1966, Douglass Cater Papers, box 14, LBJL; Memorandum, Douglass Cater to the President, 19 February 1966, Douglass Cater Papers, box 14, LBJL.

72. Harold Howe II, Address before the Mississippi State Advisory Committee, Civil Rights Commission, 16 April 1966, Jackson, Mississippi, Ervin Papers, box 387, folder 55.

73. Memorandum, Nicholas Katzenbach to the President, 10 February 1966, Douglass Cater Papers, box 14, LBJL. Several court cases had upheld freedom of choice plans, the most recent being *Kier v. County School Board of Augusta County*, Civil No. 65-c-5-H, W. D. VA, 5 January 1966.

74. "Revised Statement of Policies for School Desegregation Plans Under Title VI of the Civil Rights Act of 1964," March 1966, U.S. Department of Health, Education, and Welfare, Office of Education, Ervin Papers, box 367, folder 55; Memorandum, Douglass Cater to the President, 19 February 1966, Douglass Cater Papers, box 14, LBJL; Memorandum, Harold Howe II to the Secretary, 9 February 1966, Douglass Cater Papers, box 14, LBJL. The administration did not take such a provocative action lightly but spent considerable time weighing its options and their political ramifications. Attorney General Katzenbach urged the president, "It is better, I think, to move firmly now and attempt to get most of the painful steps behind us before 1968." He also warned "it will be politically painful, but less costly than carrying the problem forward through 1968 when, among other things, we will doubtless have increased civil rights pressures in the North." Memorandum, Nicholas Katzenbach to the President, 10 February 1966, Douglass Cater Papers, box 14, LBJL.

75. Richard Russell, John Stennis, Sam Ervin et al. to the President, 2 May 1966, WHCF, HU, box 50, LBJL.

76. Ervin press release, 31 March 1966, Ervin Papers, box 454, folder 221.

77. Ervin press release, 31 March 1966, Ervin Papers, box 454, folder 221.

78. "Opening Statement of U.S. Senator Sam J. Ervin Jr., Hearings before the Senate Subcommittee on Constitutional Rights on Civil Rights Legislation," 6 June 1966, Ervin Papers, box 391, folder 143.

79. Ervin press release, 31 March 1966, Ervin Papers, box 454, folder 221.

80. Address by Sam Ervin in accepting the George Washington Award from The Good Government Society, Washington, D.C., 1 May 1966, Ervin Papers, box 454, folder 228.

81. The Civil Rights Act of 1964 had granted the government the right to cut off federal money to school districts refusing to desegregate. But the enactment of the Elementary and Secondary Education Act of 1965 greatly increased federal aid to schools, providing HEW with the leverage it needed to back up its guidelines. See Bullock and Lamb, *Implementation of Civil Rights Policy*, 67–90.

82. Ibid., 65.

83. For example, in 1967 the southerners attempted to attach amendments to the Elementary and Secondary Education Act that would greatly reduce the government's ability to end dual school systems. See LCCR Memorandum, "Leadership Conference Statement on the Anniversary of the 1954 Supreme Court School Decision," 18 May 1967, LCCR Papers, series E, box 3, folder "Memos 1967."

84. Memorandum, Arnold Aronson to Participating Organizations, 7 December 1967, LCCR Papers, series E, 3. Several legal scholars have pointed to *United States v. Jefferson County Board of Education*, 372 F. 2d 836 (5th cir. 1966), as the crucial judicial transformation. See J. Harvie Wilkinson III, *From Brown to Bakke* (New York: Oxford University Press, 1979), 78–192; Jack Bass, *Taming the Storm: The Life and Times of Judge Frank M. Johnson, Jr.* (New York: Doubleday, 1993), 220–22. The Supreme Court rejected freedom of choice plans in *Green v. County School Board of New Kent County*, 391 U.S. 430 (1968). See Graham, *Civil Rights Era*, 372–75.

85. See *The Kerner Report* (New York: Bantam Books, 1968); Doris Kearns, *Lyndon Johnson and the American Dream* (New York: Harper and Row, 1976), 304–8; Sitkoff, *Struggle for Black Equality*, 199–223; James C. Harvey, *Black Civil Rights During the Johnson Administration* (Jackson: University Press of Mississippi, 1973).

86. Gallup Poll, 20 July 1966, McPherson Papers, box 22, folder "civil rights, 3," LBJL.

87. Memorandum, George E. Reedy to the President, 22 August 1965, McPherson Papers, box 21, LBJL. Another staffer worried that the Republicans would exploit white backlash as an issue to attract the suburban "swing vote" away from the Democrats in the presidential election of 1968. "We have a lot of feeling among members of Congress of too much bending over backwards to help Negroes. To a considerable extent, they think, the Negro is not meeting his responsibilities." Memorandum, Charles D. Roche to O'Brien, 11 March 1966, Charles D. Roche Papers, box 1, LBJL. Memorandum, Henry H. Wilson to the President, 10 December 1966, WHCF, WE, box 28 LBJL.

88. LCCR Memorandum to Jack Conway, 21 December 1966, LCCR Papers, series B, box "executive meetings, 1966–71."

89. Memorandum, McPherson to the President, 7 September 1966, McPherson Papers, box 22, folder "civil rights," 3, LBJL. After the southern bloc gathered enough northern votes to pass an amendment permitting racial segregation in hospitals, the LCCR worried that many senators had acted "in a spirit of retaliation against big city riots and the arrogant cries of 'black power.'" Luckily, the joint House-Senate conference committee threw the amendment out. Memorandum, "A Step Back from Civil Rights," LCCR memo 94, 4 October 1966, LCCR Papers, series d, folder "1966."

90. Memorandum, Joe Califano to the President, 25 October 1965, Legislative Background, Open Housing, box 1, folder "Open Housing—1965," LBJL.

91. Memorandum, Katzenbach to Califano, Lee White, and David L. Lawrence, 25 September 1965, Legislative Background, Open Housing, box 1, folder "Open Housing—1965," LBJL. Actually, the creation of the Equal Employment Opportunity Commission to fight job discrimination across the country in 1964 preceded open housing legislation and would have been the first civil rights bill to affect the North as well as the South in the modern civil rights era.

92. Charles D. Roche to O'Brien, 11 March 1966, Charles Roche Papers, box 1, LBJL.

93. Ervin to Whitney M. Young Jr., 29 June 1966, LCCR Papers, series G, folder 7.

94. Memorandum, Arnold Aronson to Cooperating Organizations, 15 June 1966, Series D4, folder 1960, LCCR Papers. The same memorandum reported that Ervin claimed to have received over 2,000 letters against open housing and only a half dozen or so for it.

95. "There Are Signs Southern Prophecy May Be Accurate," *Charlotte Observer*, 29 May 1966, Ervin Notebooks, s-12.

96. For descriptions of the political contests over the civil rights bill of 1966 and 1967, see Graham, *Civil Rights Era*, 255–70. In 1966 the Democratic Party lost forty-seven seats, almost all held by northerners who supported open housing. *Congressional Quarterly Almanac* 24 (1968): 153.

97. In addition to his constitutional arguments, Ervin suggested that the administration's proposals "must be counted among the sloppiest, vaguest, most ill-conceived and dangerous provisions ever to be seriously considered by the Senate—and I am well aware of the many sloppy, vague, and ill-conceived measures we have passed throughout the years." Ervin also tapped into white resentment against the riots by observing: "If Congress enacts this bill as presently drafted, if it capitulates again to the political pressure of unpeaceful demonstrators and to misplaced righteous indignation, we will be sharing in the demise of the Constitution. It is imperative that Congress rise above both the pressure

of demonstrators and the emotions aroused by extremists." Ervin, Opening Statement, Hearings before the Senate Judiciary Committee, Subcommittee on Constitutional Rights, Civil Rights Legislation, 6 June 1966, Ervin Papers, box 454, folder 234.

98. Ervin, draft of a speech to be delivered before the Senate, n.d., 1967, Ervin Papers, box 391, folder 148. The constitutionality of open-housing legislation is discussed in "Nondiscrimination in the Sale or Rental of Real Property: Comments on *Jones v. Alfred H. Mayer Co.* (688 Sup Ct. 2186) and Title III of the Civil Rights Act of 1968: A Symposium," *Vanderbilt Law Review* 22 (April 1969): 455–502. See especially Ervin's article "*Jones v. Alfred H. Mayer Co.* Judicial Activism Run Riot," *Vanderbilt Law Review* 22 (April 1969): 485–502.

99. Ervin press release, "The Thurgood Marshall Nomination," 30 August 1967, Ervin Papers, box 455, folder 311; "The High Court's Judicial Activists," *Omaha World-Herald*, 24 August 1967, Hruska Papers, box 126; "Wishful Thinking, Say We," editorial, *Omaha World Herald*, 24 August 1967, Hruska Papers, box 126. The vote for Marshall's confirmation was 69–11. Only the southern bloc voted against him, illustrating the obvious but unspoken role race played in the confirmation. See also Roman Hruska to Honorable Joseph Ach, 31 August 1967, Hruska Papers, box 126. Ervin had also held up the hearings on Marshall's appointment to the Court of Appeals in 1962 before voting against the nomination. On Marshall's confirmation fights see Carl T. Rowan, *Dream Makers, Dream Breakers: The World of Justice Thurgood Marshall* (Boston: Little, Brown, 1993), 272–309, especially 300–301; Michael D. Davis and Hunter R. Clark, *Thurgood Marshall: Warrior at the Bar, Rebel on the Bench* (New York: Birch Lane Press, 1992), 234–40, 263–76, especially 273–74.

100. Ervin, "Alexander Hamilton's Phantom," an address before the Harvard Law School Association of New York City, 28 April 1955, reprinted in *Vital Speeches of the Day*, 15 October 1955, 22–26.

101. Press Release, "Ervin Hits Judicial Activism of Justice Fortas," 21 August 1968, Ervin Papers, box 455, folder 377. See also Ervin, editorial in the *Washington Post*, 9 August 1968; "The Individual Views of Senator Ervin," a minority report accompanying U.S. Congress, Senate, Hearings before the Committee of the Judiciary on the Nominations of Abe Fortas and Homer Thornberry (Washington: Government Printing Office, 1968), also found in Ervin Papers, box 455, folder 377.

102. The Ervin-Fortas exchange is analyzed in detail in Bruce Allen Murphy, *Fortas: The Rise and Ruin of a Supreme Court Justice* (New York: William Morrow, 1988), 407–19. Murphy concluded that Fortas won most of his legal debates with Ervin during the confirmation hearings in 1968. See also Laura Kalman, *Abe Fortas: A Biography* (New Haven: Yale University Press, 1990), 333–56. Ervin, too, faced charges of an unethical conflict of interest because of his acceptance of a fee for his participation in *National Labor Relations Board v. Darlington Manufacturing Company et al.*, 380 U.S. 263 (1965). See Klitzman, "Sam Ervin," 22–24.

103. Senator Javits noted "the difficulty we have is that civil rights legislation has gotten out of fashion because it has merged with the urban crisis." Senator Hart said "Realism suggests that the odds are long with respect to housing." LCCR Memorandum, "Civil Rights Update," LCCR Papers, series E, box 3, folder "Memos 1968."

104. The LCCR identified Ervin as the "leader of the Southern opposition." Memorandum, Arnold Aronson to Participating Organizations, 28 February 1968, LCCR Papers,

series D, box 3, folder "Memos 1968." The *Congressional Quarterly* also named Ervin as the southern bloc's leader in the civil rights debate of 1968. *Congressional Quarterly Almanac* 24 (1968): 152. The compromise on jury selection had been worked out in 1967. See Justice Department Administrative History, Civil Rights Division, Vol. 7, Part 10, "Narrative History of Civil Rights Division." Ervin offered a similar version of this substitute amendment in 1967. For a careful analysis see Memorandum, Arnold Aronson to Participating Organizations, 23 October 1967, LCCR Papers, series E, box 3, folder "Memos 1967–73."

105. LCCR Memorandum, Arnold Aronson to Participating Organizations, 23 October 1967, LCCR Papers, series E, box 3, folder "Memos 1967–73." See also Memorandum, Stephen J. Pollak to the Deputy Attorney General, "Inadequacies of the bill urged by Senator Ervin," 25 January 1968, Warren Christopher Papers, box 9, LBJL; Memorandum, Larry Temple to the President, 22 January 1968, WHCF, LE HU2, WHCF, box 1, LBJL; "Javits Claims Ervin Bill Would Kill Rights Measure," *Fayetteville Observer*, 23 January 1968, Ervin Papers, box 469, folder 17.

106. See Memorandum, Mike Manatos to the President, 22 January 1968, LE HU2, WHCF, box 1, LBJL; John H. Averill, "Not the Session for Civil Rights, but . . . ," *Raleigh News and Observer*, 15 March 1968, Ervin Papers, box 469, folder 17.

107. John H. Averill, "Not the Session for Civil Rights, but . . . ," *Raleigh News and Observer*, 15 March 1968, Ervin Papers, box 469, folder 17. See also Graham, *Civil Rights Era*, 270–77.

108. Dirksen later explained that the devastating riots of 1967 had "put this matter in a whole new frame" for him, and he cited the need for returning Vietnam War veterans to obtain housing. But many observers noted other reasons for Dirksen's surprising about-face, including his fear of losing his grip on the Republicans in the Senate who had jumped out ahead of him on the open housing bill. See *Congressional Quarterly Almanac* 24 (1968): 160, 167; Edward L. Schapsmeier and Frederick H. Schapsmeier, *Dirksen of Illinois: Senatorial Statesman* (Urbana: University of Illinois Press, 1985), 186–89; Neil MacNeil, *Dirksen: Portrait of a Public Man* (New York: World Publishing Company, 1970), 320–28.

109. Many liberals believed Ervin's Indian Bill of Rights was only an attempt to dilute the civil rights bill, but the Johnson administration urged the amendment's adoption and it passed the Senate by a vote of 81–0. It prohibited tribal governments from violating specific constitutional rights of their members and prohibited states from assuming civil or criminal jurisdiction over Indian country without tribal consent. See *Congressional Quarterly Almanac* 24 (1968): 162. Clarence Mitchell thought the amendment "was a trap," but he supported it out of conviction. See Denton L. Watson, *Lion in the Lobby: Clarence Mitchell, Jr.'s Struggle for the Passage of Civil Rights Laws* (New York: William Morrow, 1990), 697.

110. *Congressional Record*, 90th Cong., 2nd sess., 1968, 4576.

111. Sam J. Ervin Jr., "The United States Congress and Civil Rights Legislation," *North Carolina Law Review* 42 (Fall 1963): 8.

112. Jack Claiborne, "Ervin and Bobby Still Miles Apart," *Charlotte Observer*, 1 August 1963, Ervin Notebooks, s-9. See also "Federal Control Over Marriages and Births?" *U.S. News and World Report*, 29 July 1963, 10.

113. Ervin, "Congress and Civil Rights Legislation," 7. See also Memorandum, n.d., 1964, NAACP Papers, box 68, folder "Civil Rights Act of 1964, Petitions of Congressmen."

114. Memorandum, Larry Temple to the President, 22 January 1968, LE HU2, WHCF, LBJL.

115. The head of Johnson's Civil Rights Division explained that "any violence motivated by an individual's employment by a business engaged in interstate commerce or because the victim was traveling in interstate commerce might be covered by the substitute bill." Memorandum, Stephen J. Pollak to the Deputy Attorney General, 25 January 1968, Warren Christopher Papers, box 9, LBJL, 3. Another Johnson aide advised, "If Ervin prevails, the bill would cover any assault or violence by one person on another in any public accommodation area. This would result in a broad extension of Federal jurisdiction in areas properly covered by local law enforcement at the present time." Memorandum, Larry Temple to the President, 22 January 1968, LE HU2, WHCF, LBJL.

116. *Congressional Record*, 90th Cong., 2nd sess., 1968, 397.

117. Ervin, *Preserving the Constitution*, 146.

118. Ibid., 141–50.

119. *Briggs v. Elliot* (132 F. Supp. 776).

120. Hearings, 1963, 302; James E. Clayton, "Sam and Bobby Show Enters Fourth Week," *Washington Post*, 9 August 1963.

121. Hearings, 1963, 302–3.

122. Memorandum, Harold Howe II to the Secretary, 9 February 1966, Douglass S. Cater Papers, box 14, LBJL.

123. Ervin, "Opening Statement Before the Senate Judiciary Subcommittee on Constitutional Rights," 6 June 1966, Ervin Papers, box 454, folder 234.

CHAPTER SIX

1. "Rights Bill: The Arguments in Congress," *New York Times*, 4 August 1963.

2. "Lawyers Criticized by ADA Speaker," *Charlotte Observer*, 17 April 1961, Sam Ervin Newspaper Clippings Notebooks, s-6, Sam J. Ervin Papers, Subgroup A: Senate Papers, 3847A, Southern Historical Collection, Wilson Library, University of North Carolina at Chapel Hill (hereafter cited as Ervin Notebooks).

3. Lloyd Preslar, "N.C. Delegation in Congress Took a Docile Course During Past Year," *Winston-Salem Journal*, 2 January 1966, Ervin Notebooks, s-12; James Batten, "Ervin, Liberals Couldn't Get Compromise in Bloom," *Charlotte Observer*, 11 February 1968, box 469, Sam J. Ervin Papers, Subgroup A: Senate Papers, 3847A, Southern Historical Collection, Wilson Library, University of North Carolina at Chapel Hill (hereafter cited as Ervin Papers); Lloyd Preslar, "It Isn't Easy to Put a Label on Sam Ervin," *Winston-Salem Journal*, 26 September 1965, Ervin Notebooks, s-11; Roy Parker Jr., "Ervin to Be Civil Rights Champion," *Winston-Salem Journal*, 15 February 1965, Ervin Notebooks, s-11; Richard Starnes, "Constitutionalist is consistently Inconsistent," *Washington Daily News*, 24 November 1969, Ervin Papers, Box 470.

4. "Ervin Protests Deportation Means," *Greensboro Daily News*, 7 April 1961, Ervin Notebooks, s-6; "Senator Ervin and Private School Aid," *Sampsonian*, 6 April 1961, Ervin Notebooks, s-6; "New Laws Planned for Mentally Ill," Wilmington *News*, 13 April 1961,

Ervin Notebooks, s-6; J. W. Davis, "Washington to Get Earful About the Electronic Ear," *Charlotte Observer*, 16 April 1961, Ervin Notebooks, s-6; "Sen. Ervin Gives Talk to Indians," *Greensboro Daily News*, 15 April 1961, Ervin Notebooks, s-6; Lloyd Preslar, "Ervin Asks for Public Defenders," *Winston-Salem Journal*, 18 April 1961, Ervin Notebooks, s-6.

5. *Brown v. Board of Education*, 347 U.S. 483 (1954). The most thorough account of the history of the *Brown* decision is Richard Kluger, *Simple Justice: The History of Brown v. Board of Education and Black America's Struggle for Freedom* (New York: Knopf, 1976).

6. *Pennsylvania v. Nelson*, 350 U.S. 497 (1956); *Jencks v. United States*, 353 U.S. 657 (1957); *Yates v. United States*, 354 U.S. 298 (1957); *Watkins v. United States*, 354 U.S. 178 (1957); *Sweezy v. New Hampshire*, 354 U.S. 234 (1957); *Service v. Dulles*, 354 U.S. 363 (1957).

7. Walter F. Murphy, *Congress and the Court: A Case Study in the American Political Process* (Chicago: University of Chicago Press, 1962), 154–55. For further discussion of the struggle between congressional conservatives and the Warren Court, see John R. Schmidhauser and Larry L. Berg, *The Supreme Court and Congress: Conflict and Interaction, 1945–68* (New York: Free Press, 1972); and Herman Pritchett, *Congress Versus the Supreme Court: 1957–1960* (Minneapolis: University of Minnesota Press, 1961). Pritchett argues that Red Monday became the catalyst for forming the coalition between conservative Republicans and conservative Democrats.

8. Ervin to Ernest Shupstik, 27 June 1957, Ervin Papers, box 26, folder 205; Ervin to Chauncey M. Depuy, 12 April 1956, Ervin Papers, box 18, folder 298; Ervin, "Senator Sam Ervin Says," weekly newspaper column, no. 67, 19 April 1956, Ervin Papers, box 449 (hereafter cited as "Senator Sam Ervin Says").

9. *Roth v. United States*, 354 U.S. 476 (1957).

10. "Ervin Attacks, Javits Defends High Court," *Winston-Salem Journal*, 13 July 1959. *Kingsley International Pictures v. New York State Board of Regents* 360 U.S. 684 (1959) dealt with a film portrayal of *Lady Chatterley's Lover* which portrayed adultery in a flattering light. Of course Ervin was begging the question since in *Roth* the Court clearly explained that sexually explicit material with some "socially redeemable" quality was not protected by constitutional guarantees of free speech and free press, but by the freedom of expression clause. For more on Ervin's views on censorship and pornography, see Ervin, *Preserving the Constitution: The Autobiography of Senator Sam Ervin* (Charlottesville, Va.: Michie, 1984), 127.

11. *Mallory v. United States*, 354 U.S. 449 (1957).

12. *Congressional Record*, 85th Cong., 1st sess., 27 June 1957, 10471.

13. *Congressional Record*, 85th Cong., 1st sess., 26 July 1957, 12808.

14. *Congressional Record*, 85th Cong., 2nd sess., 19 August 1958, 18481; Ervin, "In Defense of Law Enforcement Before the U.S. Senate," *Police Chief* 25 (October 1958): 24–30, Ervin Papers, box 453, folder 52; UPI Press Release summarizing the debate between Ervin and Hennings over *Mallory*, 19 August 1958, Thomas Hennings Jr., Manuscript Collection, folder 5157-B, Joint Collections, University of Missouri Western Historical Manuscript Collection—Columbia and State Historical Society of Missouri Manuscripts (hereafter cited as Hennings Papers).

15. William E. Jenner to Ervin, 2 August 1957, Ervin Papers, box 25, folder 188. Introduced 26 July 1957, the Jenner Bill sought to withdraw five areas of controversy from the Supreme Court's appellate jurisdiction: admissions to the practice of law in the state

courts; any function or practice of any congressional committee or subcommittee, the jurisdiction of any such committee, or any action or proceeding against a witness charged with contempt of Congress; administration by the executive branch of its employee loyalty-security program; any statute or executive regulation of any state the general purpose of which is to control subversive activities within the state; and rules, by-laws, and regulation of school boards or similar educational bodies concerning subversive activities among teachers.

16. Henry P. Brandis Jr., et al., to Ervin, 3 June 1958, Ervin Papers, Box 35, folder 201; Bernard Fensterwald to Ervin, 21 February 1958, Ervin Papers, box 35, folder 201.

17. Ervin to D. M. Swayngim, 14 March 1958, Ervin Papers, box 35, folder 201.

18. Ervin refused to support Butler's amendment reversing *Cole v. Young* by extending summary dismissal legislation to all federal jobs. "Senator Sam Ervin Says," 8 May 1958, no. 174, Ervin Papers, box 449. Ervin's moderating role in the Judiciary Committee is described in Murphy, *Congress and the Courts*, 165–66. Butler's amendments changed the character of the bill by withdrawing all but one of the appellate limitations originally proposed by Jenner. The new bill still forbade the Court to rule on admission to the practice of law in the states, and it provided other kinds of provisions to counter the Court's recent controversial decisions. See Murphy, *Congress and the Courts*, 32; and "Ten Votes for Wrecking," *Washington Post*, 2 May 1958.

19. William S. White described Ervin as "conservative rather than reactionary on most questions" and wrote that "he is conceded even by his liberal critics to be on the whole a lawyer of distinction and tolerance." See William S. White, "Legislation on Supreme Court," *Washington Star*, 25 April 1958, Hennings Papers, folder 472.

20. Learned Hand to Thomas Hennings, cited in Press Release, Thomas Hennings, 7 May 1958, Hennings Papers, folder 472.

21. "Supreme Court: Decision Time," WTOP Radio and Television, 29 May 1958, Ervin Papers, box 35, folder 21.

22. Bob Barnard, "Two High Court Curbs Supported by Ervin," *Winston-Salem Journal*, 22 April 1958, Ervin Notebooks, s-4; "Irresponsible Attack," *East St. Louis Journal*, 4 May 1958, Hennings Papers, folder 472; "Out Comes the Butler Bill," *New York Times*, 2 May 1958.

23. Ervin, "Senator Sam Ervin Says," no. 174, 8 May 1958, Ervin Papers, box 449.

24. H.R. 3 passed the House on 17 July and was offered as an amendment to a pending bill in the Senate on 20 August 1958. According to Don Oberdorfer of the *Charlotte Observer*, Ervin led the bill's proponents during the frantic two-day debate. See Don Oberdorfer, "States' Rights Bill Rejected in Close Vote," *Charlotte Observer*, 22 August 1958, Ervin Notebooks, s-4. For a full account and analysis of these congressional debates, see Murphy, *Congress and the Court*, 210–17; C. Pritchett, *Congress Versus the Supreme Court*, 117–33.

25. *Congressional Record*, 85th Cong., 2nd sess., 20 August 1958, 18693. Jacob Javits also politely suggested this interpretation during a radio debate with Ervin on the Westinghouse American Forum on the Air. See "Ervin Attacks, Javits Defends High Court," *Winston-Salem Journal*, 13 July 1959, Ervin Notebooks, s-5. Even newspapers in North Carolina shared this interpretation. Bob Barnard of the *Winston-Salem Journal* wrote: "The southerners in particular, it is generally agreed, want a chance to enlarge the debate

into a full-scale assault on the Supreme Court for its school desegregation rulings." Bob Barnard, "Two High Court Curbs Supported by Ervin," *Winston-Salem Journal*, 22 April 1958, Ervin Notebooks, s-4. C. Herman Pritchett, a student of the Jenner bill, has written: "To a very considerable degree the legislative opposition to the Court's security decisions was recruited from among southern members of Congress whose main concern was retaliation for the Court's segregation ruling." Pritchett, *Congress Versus the Supreme Court*, 120.

26. *Congressional Record*, 86th Cong., 1st sess., 23 June 1959, 10579. See also Pritchett, *Congress Versus the Supreme Court*, 83. On Ervin's soft southern strategy, see chapter 2.

27. The popular portrait of Ervin as a consistent champion of civil liberties can be found in George B. Autry, "Sam Ervin: The Book By and About Him," *Duke Law Journal* 1985 (December 1985): 1246–48; Ervin, *Preserving the Constitution*; Dick Dabney, *A Good Man: The Life of Sam J. Ervin* (Boston: Houghton Mifflin, 1976); and to a lesser degree Paul Clancy, *Just a Country Lawyer: A Biography of Senator Sam Ervin* (Bloomington: Indiana University Press, 1974).

28. "Ervin Fights Bill Aimed at FBI Evidence," *Asheville Citizen*, 5 June 1957, Ervin Notebooks, s-4. One historian believes that Ervin's support of a moderate Jencks bill in 1957 resulted from a deal between the segregationists and Senator Joseph O'Mahoney, who sponsored the important compromise on jury trials in the 1957 civil rights bill. See Walter F. Murphy, *Congress and the Court*, 145–46, 166.

29. "Secrecy: Farce or Tragedy," *Greensboro Daily News*, 24 January 1955, Ervin Notebooks, s-1; Arthur Johnsey, "Sen. Ervin Scores News Suppression," *Greensboro Daily News*, 21 January 1955, Ervin Notebooks, s-1; Al G. Dickson, "Ervin Spells Out Press Freedom," *Wilmington Star-News*, 23 January 1955, Ervin Notebooks, s-1.

30. "Government Secrecy Denounced," *Washington Evening Star*, 13 April 1956, Ervin Notebooks, s-3. On Ervin's support of the Freedom of Information Act, see Ervin to H. Galt Braxton, 15 April 1958, Ervin Papers, box 34, folder 187; Ervin, "H.R. 2767 and S. 921: Government Secrecy," Speech on the Senate Floor, 16 April 1958, Ervin Papers, box 453, folder 57.

31. The southern caucus assigned Ervin to the subcommittee in 1956 so that he could serve as their constitutional champion in civil rights debates (see chapter 3). But Thomas Hennings had also made it into an important vehicle for pushing his own civil liberties agenda. Ervin had a poor attendance record at the subcommittee's hearings on matters other than civil rights. See the following hearings, none of which Ervin attended: U.S. Congress, Senate, Committee on the Judiciary, Hearings before the Subcommittee on Constitutional Rights, *Freedom of Information and Secrecy in Government*, 85th Cong., 2nd sess., 1958; U.S. Congress, Senate, Committee on the Judiciary, Hearings before the Subcommittee on Constitutional Rights, *Secrecy and Science*, 86th Cong., 1st sess., 1959; U.S. Congress, Senate, Committee on the Judiciary, Hearings before the Subcommittee on Constitutional Rights, *Wiretapping, Eavesdropping, and the Bill of Rights*, 85th Cong., 2nd sess., 1959–60, Parts 1–5. Ervin did attend one day of hearings each during the following: U.S. Congress, Senate, Committee on the Judiciary, Hearings before the Subcommittee on Constitutional Rights, *The Right to Travel*, 85th Cong., 1st sess., 1957; U.S. Congress, Senate, Committee on the Judiciary, Hearings before the Subcommittee on Constitutional Rights, *Secrecy in Government*, 85th Cong., 2nd sess., 1958.

32. "Hennings is Dead; Missouri Senator," *New York Times*, 14 September 1960.

33. Denton L. Watson, *Lion in the Lobby: Clarence Mitchell, Jr.'s Struggle for the Passage of Civil Rights Laws* (New York: William Morrow, 1990), 433.

34. Hennings listed his 1959 agenda for the subcommittee as "Rights of persons subject to U.S. Military Jurisdiction; passports and the right to travel; police detention prior to commitment and arraignment; freedom of information and secrecy in government; the Fourth Amendment and modern methods of crime detention; fair hearing procedures for federal employment applicants; police methods and constitutional rights—in movies, radio and television programs." "Plans and Programs, Senate Judiciary Subcommittee on Constitutional Rights for period: 1 February 1959 through 31 January 1960," Hennings Papers, folder 5223. Hennings later added executive privilege and the rights of the mentally ill to his list of priorities.

35. Thomas Hennings, draft of resolution, n.d., 1955, Hennings Papers, folder 2041.

36. Stanley Moore, "For Senator Work Piles Up," *Morganton News Herald*, 1 May 1961, Ervin Notebooks, s-6.

37. Don Oberdorfer, "Ervin Promises Adequate Hearings on Civil Rights Bills," *Charlotte Observer*, 5 February 1961, Ervin Notebooks, s-6; Ervin, Press Release, 3 February 1961, Ervin Papers, box 405, folder 408; Minutes, "First Organizational Meeting of the Senate Constitutional Rights Subcommittee," 8 March 1961, Ervin Papers, box 405, folder 408.

38. "Senator Ervin Calls for Legal Protection of Mentally Ill," *Wilmington News*, 31 March 1961, Ervin Notebooks, s-6; Kay Ray, "A Model Law on Mental Illness," *Wilmington Morning Star*, 28 April 1961, Ervin Notebooks, s-6.

39. U.S. Congress, Senate, Committee on the Judiciary, Hearings before the Subcommittee on Constitutional Rights, *Constitutional Rights of the Mentally Ill*, 87th Cong., 1st sess., 1961, Parts 1 and 2 (hereafter cited as Rights of the Mentally Ill Hearings, 1961); Statement of the American Civil Liberties Union, Ervin Papers, box 408, folder 451.

40. Thomas Hennings, Press Release, 21 July 1960, Hennings Papers, folder 497. For a discussion of the legal aspects of the bill, especially the right to treatment, see "The Mentally Ill and the Right to Treatment—a Symposium," *University of Chicago Law Review* 36 (1969): 742–801; Morton Birnbaum, "The Right to Treatment," *American Bar Association Journal* 46 (May 1960): 499–505; "Editorial: A New Right," *American Bar Association Journal* 46 (May 1960): 516–17.

41. Ervin, "Senator Sam Ervin Says," no. 434, 5 June 1963, Ervin Papers, box 450; Ervin, "Judging Insanity," *Washington Post*, 4 June 1961.

42. Constitutional Rights of the Mentally Ill Hearings, 1961. See also U.S. Congress, Senate, Committee on the Judiciary, Hearings before the Subcommittee on Constitutional Rights, *To Protect the Constitutional Rights of the Mentally Ill*, 88th Cong., 1st sess., 1963; Charles G. Brooks, "D.C. Methods on Mentally Ill Are Attacked," *Washington Star*, 28 March 1961, Ervin Notebooks, s-6; Lloyd Preslar, "Hearings on Rights of Mentally Ill Set," *Winston-Salem Journal*, 24 March 1961, Ervin Notebooks, s-6; "Mental Health Law Hearings Are Begun," *Washington Post*, 27 June 1962; "Doctors, Lawyers, and Commitment," *Chicago Tribune*, 21 August 1962; Ervin, "Senator Sam Ervin Says," no. 391, 4 July 1962, Ervin Papers, box 450. The District of Columbia Mental Health Bill, which became law in 1964, served as the model for the ten states that approved substantial changes in their

mental health laws between 1964 and 1968. The law also served as the basis for Judge David L. Bazelon's opinion in *Rouse v. Cameron*, 373 F.2d 541 (DC 1966), announcing a statutory "right to treatment" in the District of Colombia and suggesting a constitutional right to treatment as well. See Phillip J. Cooper, *Hard Judicial Choices: Federal District Court Judges and State and Local Officials* (New York: Oxford University Press, 1988), 139–44.

43. "Ervin Hails Law for Mentally Ill," *Washington Post*, 17 September 1964; Lyndon B. Johnson to Ervin, 15 September 1964, WHCF, LE/HE, box 59, Lyndon Baines Johnson Presidential Library (LBJL). Ervin reopened hearings on the rights of the mentally ill five years later to determine the success of the District of Columbia legislation and explore additional issues. See U.S. Congress, Senate, Committee on the Judiciary, Hearings before the Subcommittee on Constitutional Rights, *Constitutional Rights of the Mentally Ill*, 91st Cong., 1st and 2nd sess., 1969–70.

44. Jerry Landauer, "Probe Begun on Rights of Servicemen," *Washington Post*, 17 November 1961; "'Court Sway' in Military is Attacked," *Charlotte Observer*, 29 December 1961, Ervin Notebooks, s-6; Ervin, "Senator Sam Ervin Says," no. 370, 8 February 1962, Ervin Papers, box 450; "Probers to Check Complaints by GIs," *Dallas News*, 5 July 1962, Ervin Notebooks, s-8; "Military Court Probe Set at Europe Bases," *Washington Post*, 5 July 1962; U.S. Congress, Senate, Committee on the Judiciary, Joint Hearings before the Subcommittee on Constitutional Rights and a Special Subcommittee of the Committee on Armed Services, *Constitutional Rights of Military Personnel*, 87th Cong., 2nd sess., 1962 (hereafter cited as Military Personnel Hearings, 1962).

45. James Batten, "U.S. Servicemen May Get Rights They Are Defending," *Charlotte Observer*, 20 August 1967, Ervin Papers, box 469. For a discussion of the legal aspects of the bill, see William A. Creech, "Congress Looks at the Serviceman's Rights," *American Bar Association Journal* 49 (November 1963): 1070–74. A critique of the trend toward granting military personnel constitutional rights can be found in "Constitutional Rights of Servicemen Before Courts-Martial," *Columbia Law Review* 64 (January 1964): 127–49.

46. James Batten, "U.S. Servicemen May Get Rights They are Defending," *Charlotte Observer*, 20 August 1967, Ervin Papers, box 469.

47. Fred P. Graham, "Reforms Sought in Military Code," *New York Times*, 18 May 1967; Roy Parker, "Ervin and Henderson Trying to Aid Soldiers," *Greensboro Daily News*, 6 March 1966, Ervin Notebooks, s-12; "Bill To Protect GIs of Coercion Gets Senate OK," *Durham Morning Herald*, 23 November 1967, Ervin Papers, box 469.

48. For example, if one Indian assaulted another on a reservation, the case had to be tried in a tribal court, but that court could not imprison the attacker for more than six months, no matter how badly the victim had been hurt. See "Constitutional Rights of the American Tribal Indian," *Virginia Law Review* 51 (January 1965): 121–26.

49. Ervin, *Preserving the Constitution*, 203; Theda Purdue, *Native Carolinians: The Indians of North Carolina* (Raleigh: North Carolina Division of Archives and History, 1983).

50. *Congressional Record*, 87th Cong., 1st sess., 25 August 1961, 17121; "Rights Denial to Indians Investigated," *Washington Post*, 30 August 1961; "Senate Unit to Check Indians' Civil Rights," *Twin City Sentinel*, 28 August 1961, Ervin Notebooks, s-6.

51. U.S. Congress, Senate, Committee on the Judiciary, Hearings before the Subcommittee on Constitutional Rights, *Constitutional Rights of the American Indian*, 87th Cong., 1st sess., 1961, Part 1 and Part 2; 1962, Part 3; 1963, Part 4. U.S. Congress, Senate, Committee

on the Judiciary, Hearings before the Subcommittee on Constitutional Rights, *Constitutional Rights of the American Indian; on S.961, S.962, S.963, S.964, S.966, S.967, S.968 and Senate Joint Resolution 40*, 89th Cong., 1st sess., 1965.

52. Ervin collected this and other stories relating to Native Americans on typed note cards found in Ervin Papers, box 404, folder 393.

53. Ibid.

54. "Ervin Urges More Rights for Indians," *Charlotte Observer*, 22 June 1965, Ervin Notebooks, s-11.

55. For a complete text of the bill and a discussion of its legislative history, see Ervin, *Preserving the Constitution*, 195–204. "Bill for Indians Introduced," *Greensboro Daily News*, 30 July 1964, Ervin Notebooks, s-10; "Rights Bill for Indians Introduced," *Asheville Citizen*, 31 July 1964, Ervin Notebooks, s-10; "Ervin Urges More Rights for Indians," *Charlotte Observer*, 22 June 1965, Ervin Notebooks, s-11. For a discussion of the legal aspects of the bill, see "The Indian Bill of Rights and the Constitutional Status of Tribal Governments," *Harvard Law Review* 82 (April 1969): 1343–73; "Title II of the 1968 Civil Rights Act: An Indian Bill of Rights," *North Dakota Law Review* 45 (Spring 1969): 337–52.

56. Subcommittee on Constitutional Rights, press release, 10 October 1967, Ervin Papers, box 455, folder 317.

57. "Five Bills by Ervin Aid Indians," *Winston-Salem Journal*, 24 May 1967, Ervin Papers, box 469; Ervin, "Senator Sam Ervin Says," no. 675, 14 December 1967, Ervin Papers, box 451; Subcommittee on Constitutional Rights, press release, 10 October 1967, Ervin Papers, box 455, folder 317; Ervin press release, 25 October 1967, Ervin Papers, box 455, folder 323. Ervin's attempt to defeat the bill to protect civil rights workers by expanding it is discussed in chapter 5.

58. "Indian Bill Cut Upsets Sen. Ervin," *Charlotte News*, 26 October 1967, Ervin Papers, box 469.

59. Ibid.

60. "Backup Material for Indian Message," WHCF, box SP 122, LBJL; Ervin Press Release, 6 March 1968, Ervin Papers, box 455, folder 352. President Johnson's staff had followed the progress of Ervin's Indian Bill of Rights for several years and had confidence that it was a legitimate legislative effort to help Native Americans. See Warren Christopher to Charles J. Zwick, 12 April 1968, WHCF, Enrolled Legislation, P.L. 90-264, LBJL; Memorandum, [Joseph] Califano to the President, 8 March 1968, WHCF, Enrolled Legislation, P.L. 90-284, LBJL; Memorandum, Secretary of the Interior to Charles J. Zwick, 11 April 1968, WHCF, Enrolled Legislation, P.L. 90-284, LBJL.

61. George Carmack, "Bill of Rights for Indians Stirs Up Storm," *Pittsburgh Press*, 14 April 1968, Ervin Papers, box 469; Ervin, *Preserving the Constitution*, 202.

62. Congressional Quarterly Almanac, 1968, 162; Ervin, *Preserving the Constitution*, 202–3.

63. *Congressional Record*, 90th Cong., 2nd sess., 8 March 1968, 5837.

64. George Carmack, "Bill of Rights for Indians Stirs Up Storm," *Pittsburgh Press*, 14 April 1968, Ervin Papers, box 469.

65. Watson, *Lion in the Lobby*, 697.

66. Arthur Lazarus Jr., "Title II of the 1968 Civil Rights Act: An Indian Bill of Rights," *North Dakota Law Review* 45 (Spring 1969): 337.

67. Ervin, *Preserving the Constitution*, 203; Clancy, *Just a Country Lawyer*, 205–6. The Congress of American Indians also awarded Ervin its highest distinction, The William Teller Award.

68. "Lawyers Criticized by ADA Speaker," *Charlotte Observer*, 17 April 1961, Ervin Notebooks, s-6; James K. Batten, "Sam Ervin and the Privacy Invaders," *New Republic*, 8 May 1971, 19. Ervin's reputation as a civil libertarian grew in jumps and spurts throughout the 1960s, peaking in 1970 with his opposition to Nixon's D.C. crime bill. See "The Hon. Sam J. Ervin, U.S. Senator—Lawyer, Jurist, and Legislator," *Federal Bar News* (January 1965); Lloyd Preslar, "Presenting the Notched Ears Awards for 1966," *Winston-Salem Journal*, 1 January 1967, Ervin Papers, box 469; John Herbers, "Senator Ervin Thinks the Constitution Should Be Taken Like Mountain Whiskey—Undiluted and Untaxed," *New York Times Magazine*, 17 November 1970.

69. Richard Russell, press release, 2 December 1967, Ervin Papers, box 455, folder 335. See also Luther J. Carter, "Sam Ervin: Constitutional Watchdog," *Virginian-Pilot*, 12 August 1964, Ervin Notebooks, s-8; Jay Hensley, "Ervin Says Freedoms Are Being Destroyed," *Asheville Citizen*, 22 December 1965, Ervin Notebooks, s-11.

70. James K. Batten, "Sam Ervin and the Privacy Invaders," *New Republic*, 8 May 1971, 21; Ervin, *Preserving the Constitution*, 151–85.

71. "Under the Dome," *Raleigh News and Observer*, 11 August 1958; "N.C. Senator Urges Rival To Teamsters," *Greensboro Daily News*, 10 August 1958; "Sen. Ervin Unlooses Blast at Teamsters' Super Law," *Charlotte Observer*, 30 November 1958, Ervin Notebooks, s-4.

72. The Kennedy-Ervin bill eventually became the Labor-Management Reporting Act of 1959, after significant amendments. For Ervin's view of the bill see Sam Ervin Jr., Oral History Interview by Ronald J. Grele, 17 May 1966, for the John F. Kennedy Presidential Library, found in Sam J. Ervin Papers, Subgroup B: Private Papers, 3847B, Southern Historical Collection, Wilson Library, University of North Carolina at Chapel Hill (hereafter cited as Ervin Papers, B.), folder 693; and Ervin's lengthy letter to the Chamber of Commerce of the United States, 29 May 1959, Ervin Papers, box 357, folder 14707.

73. Ervin led the Subcommittee on Separation of Powers, which he chaired, in hearings against the NLRB between 1968 and 1970. See Report of the Subcommittee on Separation of Powers, printed by Industrial Relations Department, National Association of Manufacturers, 1970, Ervin Papers, B., folder 695. On his filibuster against repealing section 14-B of the Taft-Hartley Act, see the transcript of his appearance on a television program called "Opinion in the Capital," WTTG, Washington, D.C., 5 September 1965, Ervin Papers, box 358, folder 14728.

74. For a brief but critical overview of Ervin's appearance in *National Labor Relations Board v. Darlington Manufacturing Company, et al.*, see Stephen Klitzman, "Sam Ervin," Ralph Nader Congress Project, 1972, 24. 22–25. See also "Ought to Reconsider," *Raleigh News and Observer*, 1 November 1954, Ervin Notebooks, s-10; "Ervin Defends 'Unusual' Role," *Winston-Salem Journal*, 10 December 1964, Ervin Notebooks, s-10.

75. Theron L. Caudle to Ervin, 19 September 1946, Ervin Papers, B., Folder 872.

76. Those cases are *Flast v. Cohen* (1967), *Tatum v. Laird* (1972), and *Gravel v. U.S.* (1972). See Klitzman, "Sam Ervin," 24.

77. Klitzman, "Sam Ervin," 24.

78. Ervin's fee is revealed in his income tax records for 1964–66, Ervin Papers, B., folder

1041. Ervin always defended his participation in the Darlington case, and all of his other anti-labor actions, to just be part of his larger crusade to defend the Constitution and rein in runaway government. "I do believe in voluntary unionism," Ervin insisted to Dick Dabney, "but I am opposed to compulsory unionism which drafts men into organizations they do not wish to join." See Ervin Corrections to Dabney, Ervin Papers, B., Folder 1162. For Ervin's most extensive defense of his role in the Darlington case, see *Congressional Record*, 91st Cong., 1st sess., 1969, 27283–87.

79. The best analysis of Ervin's role in defeating the ERA is found in Donald G. Mathews and Jane Sherron De Hart, *Sex, Gender, and the Politics of the ERA: A State and a Nation* (New York: Oxford University Press, 1990), 28–53.

80. "Federal Controls over Marriages and Births," *U.S. News and World Report*, 29 July 1963, 10; Ervin press release, "The Equal Rights Amendment: An Atomic Mousetrap," 23 March 1971, Ervin Papers, box 337, folder 13392.

81. Doug Moore, "Senator Ervin Doesn't Believe in Arguing," *Appalachian*, 2 April 1971, Ervin Papers, box 470.

82. "Equal Rights: Amendment Passed over Ervin Opposition," *Congressional Quarterly Almanac*, 1972, quotes on 199, 200, and 202.

83. Mathews and De Hart, *Sex, Gender, and the Politics of the ERA*, 51.

84. Susie Sharp, interview, transcript, *Senator Sam* (film), New Atlantic Productions, 12.

85. "Women Rightists Angered by Ervin," *Greensboro Daily News*, 22 August 1970, Ervin Papers, box 470; Greg Herrington, "'Sam's Exactly Right,' Says Sen. Ervin's Wife," *Charlotte Observer*, 19 September 1970, Ervin Papers, box 470; Jean Ervin interview, transcript, *Senator Sam* (film); "Senator Sam Ervin is opposed to ERA, but not all the women in his family share his views," *People of North Carolina*, May 1972, North Carolina Collection Clipping File, 1976–1989, North Carolina Collection, Wilson Library, University of North Carolina at Chapel Hill; Clancy, *Just a Country Lawyer*, 130. Ervin's views on the ERA are summarized in his autobiography, *Preserving the Constitution*, 240–79.

86. Lloyd Preslar, "It Isn't Easy to Put a Label on Sam Ervin," *Winston-Salem Journal*, 26 September 1965, Ervin Notebooks, s-11.

87. Davis Merritt, "Ervin Turns Meat Grinder on Mitchell," *Charlotte Observer*, 10 February 1970, Ervin Papers, box 470; "The Hon. Sam J. Ervin, U.S. Senator—Lawyer, Jurist, and Legislator," *Federal Bar News* (January 1965); James K. Batten, "Sam J. Ervin Just Won't Fit the Mold," *Charlotte Observer*, 2 April 1967; Herbers, "Like Mountain Whiskey"; "Senator Ervin Defends Right of Free Speech," *Asheville Citizen*, 6 February 1970, Ervin Papers, box 470; Clancy, *Just a Country Lawyer*, 201–2; Klitzman, "Sam Ervin," 1–2.

CHAPTER SEVEN

1. Ervin, "Privacy and the False Prophets," an address before the "People's Forum on Privacy," 15 June 1971, Washington, D.C., box 408, folder 461, in Sam J. Ervin Papers, Subgroup A: Senate Papers, 3847A, Southern Historical Collection, Wilson Library, University of North Carolina at Chapel Hill (hereafter cited as Ervin Papers). Ervin published an abbreviated version of his speech under the title "The Most Precious Freedom," *New York Times*, 21 June 1971.

2. Ibid.

3. Tom Wicker, "Sen. Ervin and Individual Rights," *New York Times*, 29 March 1970.

4. "Plans and Programs, Subcommittee on Constitutional Rights, 1 February 1959 Through 31 January 1960," Thomas Hennings Jr. Papers, folder 5223, Joint Collection, University of Missouri Western Historical Manuscript Collection—Columbia and State Historical Society of Missouri Manuscripts (hereafter cited as Hennings Papers).

5. Ervin, *Preserving the Constitution: The Autobiography of Senator Sam Ervin* (Charlottesville, Va.: Michie, 1984), 296; Lloyd Preslar, "It Isn't Easy to Put a Label on Sam Ervin," *Winston-Salem Journal*, 26 September 1965, Sam Ervin newspaper clipping notebooks, s-11, in Sam J. Ervin Papers, Subgroup A: Senate Papers, 3847A, Southern Historical Collection, Wilson Library, University of North Carolina at Chapel Hill (hereafter cited as Ervin Notebooks). Beginning in the mid-1960s a series of newspaper and magazine articles tried to resolve the apparent contradictions in Ervin's political philosophy. See Roy Parker Jr., "Busy Sen. Ervin Is Rivaling Johnson in Long List of Legislative Interests," *Greensboro Daily News*, 25 September 1965, s-11, Ervin Notebooks, s-6; James K. Batten, "Sam J. Ervin Just Won't Fit in a Mold," *Charlotte Observer*, 2 April 1967; Tom Wicker, "Sen. Ervin and Individual Rights," *New York Times*, 29 March 1970.

6. Ervin proposed a bill that would make all voluntary confessions valid as evidence in federal courts irrespective of the length of time a suspect was held before arraignment. See "Ervin Asks Revision of Mallory Rule," *Washington Post*, 14 June 1961; "4 Senators Join Fight to Upset Mallory Rule," *Washington Evening Star*, 8 March 1963, Ervin Notebooks, s-8; "Senator Ervin Urges Mallory Rule Change," *Washington Post*, 24 October 1963.

7. *Congressional Record*, 85th Cong., 2nd sess., 19 August 1958, 18481.

8. "Ervin Asks Revision of Mallory Rule," *Washington Post*, 14 June 1961.

9. *Escobedo v. Illinois*, 378 U.S. 500 (1964); *Miranda v. Arizona*, 384 U.S. 436 (1966).

10. *Congressional Record*, 90th Cong., 1st sess., 23 January 1967, 5635–39; Ervin to John L. McClellan, 13 January 1967, Ervin Papers, box 205.

11. Ervin to John L. McClellan, 13 January 1967, Ervin Papers, box 205; Ervin, "The Ervin Amendment," *Charlotte News*, 2 August 1966.

12. *Congressional Record*, 85th Cong., 2nd sess., 19 August 1958, 18481.

13. Ibid.; UPI Release 163, 19 August 1958, Hennings Papers, folder 5157-B.

14. U.S. Congress, Senate, Committee on the Judiciary, Hearings before the Subcommittee on Constitutional Rights, *Nomination of Thurgood Marshall*, 90th Cong., 1st sess., 1967, 53. Ervin's comment is not recorded in the official transcript and must have been an aside heard and recorded by John P. MacKenzie, "Southerners Delay Action on Marshall," *Washington Post*, 15 July 1967, and in "Senator Ervin Discounts Police Brutality Talk," *Charlotte Observer*, 17 August 1967, Ervin Papers, box 469.

15. Ted Lewis, "Capital Circus," *Greensboro Daily News*, 16 November 1961, Ervin Notebooks, s-6.

16. John A. Carroll and Edward V. Long to Ervin, 11 August 1961, box 20, folder 120b, Edward V. Long Papers, Joint Collection, University of Missouri Western Historical Manuscript Collection—Columbia and State Historical Society of Missouri Manuscripts (hereafter cited as Long Papers); U.S. Senate, Committee on the Judiciary, Hearings before the Subcommittee on Constitutional Rights, *Wiretapping and Eavesdropping Legislation*, 87th Cong., 1st sess., 1961; James Deakin, "Long Carries on Hennings's Fight Against Legalizing Wiretapping to Get Evidence," *St. Louis Post-Dispatch*, 18 March 1962, box 25,

Richard Bolling Papers, Joint Collection, University of Missouri Western Historical Manuscript Collection—Columbia and State Historical Society of Missouri Manuscripts (hereafter cited as Bolling Papers). Edward Long rivaled Ervin for the title of most active civil libertarian in the Senate in the 1960s. It was his efforts to restrict wiretapping, not Ervin's, that led to the unsuccessful introduction of the Right of Privacy Bill of 1967.

17. "Congress Urged to Take Action on Wire-tapping," *Greensboro Daily News*, 8 November 1961, Ervin Notebooks, s-6; Lloyd Preslar, "Wire-tap Bills Set for Hearing," *Winston-Salem Journal*, 19 April 1961. In reality, undisclosed wiretapping by the federal government was widespread. In May 1961 the FBI reported that it presently operated eighty-five wiretaps, all involving national security. *Congress and the Nation: 1954–1964* (Washington, D.C.: Congressional Quarterly Services, 1965), 1661.

18. Senator Edward Long suggested, "*Now* the law does not permit law enforcement officials to go over the line," and he wondered why Congress should authorize a broad expansion of wiretapping and be reduced to trusting "Bobby's assurances that safeguards would be made to protect our citizen's *inherent rights*" (emphasis in the original). Long, who remembered how past attorneys general had abused their powers, eerily predicted Watergate when he added, "What happens when the next Atty Gen performs like some of the 'irresponsible ones.'" Long's notes are written on an editorial clip sheet found in Bolling Papers, box 25.

19. J. W. Davis, "Washington To Get Earful About the Electronic Ear," *Charlotte Observer*, 16 April 1961, Ervin Notebooks, s-6; Ted Lewis, "Capital Circus," *Greensboro Daily News*, 16 November 1961, Ervin Notebooks, s-6; Ervin's opening statement, U.S. Congress, Senate, Committee on the Judiciary, Hearings before the Subcommittee on Criminal Laws and Procedures, *Controlling Crime Through More Effective Law Enforcement*, 90th Cong., 1st sess., 1967, 5–6.

20. Lyndon Johnson, "Message on Crime in America," 6 February 1967, *Public Papers of the Presidents: Lyndon B. Johnson, 1967*, vol. 1 (Washington, D.C.: U.S. Government Printing Office, 1968), 144. Johnson proposed the Safe Streets Act of 1967 to combat crime and asked Congress to pass the Right of Privacy Act of 1967 to outlaw all wiretapping except in cases of national security. Memorandum for the Heads of Executive Departments and Agencies, from Lyndon B. Johnson, 30 June 1965, WHCF, LE/JL, box 79, Lyndon Baines Johnson Presidential Library (LBJL); Memorandum, Joe Califano and Lee White to the President, 9 February 1966, WHCF, LE/JL, box 79, LBJL.

21. When President Johnson signed the crime bill he complained, "I urged that Congress outlaw all wiretapping and electronic eavesdropping, public and private, wherever and whenever it occurs. The only exceptions would be those instances where the security of the Nation itself was at stake. . . . But Congress, in my judgment, had taken an unwise and potentially dangerous step." See "Safe Streets Act Signing Statement," 19 June 1968, WHCF, legislative background, box 7, LBJL.

22. "Ervin Endorses Johnson's Bill Against Wiretap," *Greensboro Daily News*, 24 February 1967, Ervin Papers, box 469; "Sen. Ervin's Choices," *Winston-Salem Twin City Sentinel*, 4 June 1968, Ervin Papers, box 469; Clancy, *Just a Country Lawyer*, 204; Dick Dabney, *A Good Man: The Life of Sam J. Ervin* (Boston: Houghton Mifflin, 1976), 199.

23. "Plans and Programs, Subcommittee on Constitutional Rights, 1 February 1959 Through 31 January 1960," Hennings Papers, folder 5223.

24. Ibid.

25. Memorandum, John W. Douglass to Joseph Califano, 11 April 1966, WHCF, LE/JL 2, LBJL. These four reform bills were originally sponsored by the Justice Department, but the Johnson administration singled out Ervin and two members of the House as the "primary movers in getting the bills through." Memorandum, Joe Califano to the President, 15 July 1966, WHCF, LE/JL 2, LBJL.

26. *Congress and the Nation: 1954–1964* (Washington, D.C.: Congressional Quarterly Services, 1965), 1674.

27. President Kennedy said: "The right to compensated counsel must be assured to every man accused of a crime in the federal courts, regardless of his means." "State of the Union Address," 14 January 1963, *Papers of the Presidents: John F. Kennedy, 1963* (Washington, D.C.: Government Printing Office, 1964), 14. Ervin had sponsored the same bill the preceding year. It passed the Senate but died in a House committee.

28. Ervin, "Uncompensated Counsel: They Do Not Meet the Constitutional Mandate," *American Bar Association Journal* 49 (May 1963): 436.

29. Ibid., 436.

30. U.S. Congress, Senate, Committee on the Judiciary, Subcommittee on Constitutional Rights, *Legal Counsel for Indigent Defendants in Federal Courts*, 87th Cong., 1st sess., 1961, Committee Print; U.S. Congress, Senate, Committee on the Judiciary, Joint Hearings before the Subcommittee on Constitutional Rights and Subcommittee on Improvements in Judicial Machinery, 88th Cong., 2nd sess., 1964. In 1964 Ervin wrote to every governor to ask how their state planned to respond to the Supreme Court's ruling in *Gideon v. Wainwright* 372 U.S. 335 (1963), which applied the right to counsel to state proceedings. Ervin to John M. Dalton, 30 January 1964, container 2417, folder 3350, John Dalton Papers, Joint Collection, University of Missouri Western Historical Manuscript Collection—Columbia and State Historical Society of Missouri Manuscripts. By 1968, the subcommittee estimated that over 24,000 federal indigent defendants a year benefited from the act. See a draft of a report of the Subcommittee on Constitutional Rights to accompany S. 1461, 23 April 1970, box 126, Roman L. Hruska Papers, State Archives, Nebraska State Historical Society (hereafter cited as Hruska Papers).

31. On the bail reform movement see Charles E. Ares, Anne Rankin, and Herbert Sturz, "The Manhattan Bail Project: An Interim Report on the Use of Pre-Trial Parole," *New York University Law Review* 38 (1963): 67–72; *National Conference on Bail and Criminal Justice* (Washington, D.C.: U.S. Department of Justice and the Vera Foundation, Inc., 1975); Robert F. Kennedy, "Address to the National Conference on Bail and Criminal Justice," Washington, D.C., 29 May 1964, Robert F. Kennedy Papers, Attorney General Files, speeches, box 3, folder "Senate Judiciary Committee, 8-4-64" (hereafter cited as Robert Kennedy Papers), John F. Kennedy Presidential Library (JFKL); Calab Foote, "The Coming Constitutional Crisis in Bail," *University of Pennsylvania Law Review* 113, Part I (May 1965): 959–99; Part II (June 1965): 1125–85; Ronald L. Goldfarb, *Ransom: A Critique of the American Bail System* (New York: Harper and Row, 1965); Wayne H. Thomas Jr., *Bail Reform in America* (Berkeley: University of California Press, 1976); "Release Without Bail," *Washington Post*, 9 August 1964.

32. "U.S. System of Bonding Criticized," *Greensboro Daily News*, 5 August 1964, Ervin Notebooks, s-8.

33. U.S. Congress, Senate, Committee on the Judiciary, Hearings before the Subcommittee on Constitutional Rights and Subcommittee on Improvements in Judicial Machinery, *Federal Bail Procedures*, 88th Cong., 2nd sess., 1964, 37 (hereafter cited as Bail Hearings, 1964); Roy Parker Jr., "Ervin Bill Gets Kennedy Praise," *Raleigh News and Observer*, 5 August 1964, Ervin Notebooks, s-10. Ervin's Subcommittee on Constitutional Rights had been studying the subject of bail reform since 1961. For Kennedy's testimony see "Testimony by Attorney General Robert Kennedy on Bail Legislation," 4 August 1964, Robert Kennedy Papers, Attorney General Files, speeches, box 3, folder "Senate Judiciary Committee, 8-4-64," JFKL. See also U.S. Congress, Senate, Committee on the Judiciary, Hearings before the Subcommittee on Constitutional Rights and Subcommittee on Improvements in Judicial Machinery, *Constitutional Rights and Federal Bail Procedures*, 89th Cong., 1st sess., 1965 (hereafter cited as Bail Hearings, 1965); Goldfarb, *Ransom*, 33–34.

34. The Bail Reform Act of 1966 provided that if a judge had a reasonable fear that a defendant might flee, he should first consider a conditional release tailored to the defendant's situation, and only as a last resort rely on a deposit bond. Of course, if the judge found that a significant risk of flight or danger existed, then the defendant could still be detained before trial. The act contained additional measures that reflected the findings of the Manhattan Project, the National Bail Conference, and the subcommittee's own five-year study. See Ervin, "The Legislative Role in Bail Reform," *George Washington Law Review* 35 (March 1968): 429–54; "The Bail Reform Act of 1966," *Iowa Law Journal* 53 (August 1967): 170–94; Ervin, *Preserving the Constitution*, 293–302; James J. Kilpatrick, "A Step Toward Equal Justice," *Winston-Salem Journal*, 20 November 1965, Ervin Notebooks, s-11.

35. Memorandum, Joe Califano to the President, 14 June 1966, WHCF, LBJ appointment file, diary backup, box 37, LBJL.

36. A White House memorandum stated that "Ervin is largely responsible for this legislation." See "List of Prominent and Interesting People Who Will Be at the Bail Act Signing Ceremony," WHCF, LBJ appointment file, diary backup, box 37, LBJL. Another White House memorandum stated, "The Department of Justice believes that the Bail Reform Act of 1966 represents an historic step toward achieving the fair and equal administration of our criminal laws." Memorandum, Ramsey Clark to Mr. Schultz, 14 June 1966, WHCF, enrolled legislation, P.L. 89-465, LBJL. "Under the Dome," *Raleigh News and Observer*, 27 June 1966, Ervin Notebooks, s-12; "Johnson Signs Bail Reform Measure," *Washington Star*, 22 June 1966, Ervin Notebooks, s-12. One legal scholar has written: "Undoubtedly the most significant legislation to date in the bail reform effort has been the Federal Bail Reform Act of 1966." Thomas, *Bail Reform in America*, 161.

37. "Under the Dome," *Raleigh News and Observer*, 27 June 1966, Ervin Notebooks, s-12; Lloyd Preslar, "Presenting the Notched Ears Awards for 1966," *Winston-Salem Journal*, 1 January 1967, Ervin Papers, box 469.

38. Ervin, *Preserving the Constitution*, 302.

39. Ervin, "The Ervin Amendment," *Charlotte News*, 2 August 1966, Ervin Notebooks, s-12.

40. Ervin, "Senator Sam Ervin Says," no. 428, 21 March 1963, Ervin Papers, box 450; "Ervin Bill Aims at Crime in Washington," *Raleigh News and Observer*, 20 March 1963, Ervin Notebooks, s-9; Ervin, "Uncompensated Counsel: They Do Not Meet the Constitu-

tional Mandate," *American Bar Association Journal* 49 (May 1963): 438; Ervin, *Preserving the Constitution*, 302–3.

41. "Mallory Bill Notes U.S. Courts Changed Approach," [unidentified source, n.d.] 1958, Ervin Papers, box 469, folder 2c.

42. *A Book Named John Cleland's Memoirs of a Woman of Pleasure v. Massachusetts*, 383 U.S. 413 (1966); *Harper v. Virginia Board of Elections*, 383 U.S. 663 (1966); *United States v. Wade*, 388 U.S. 218 (1967); *Gilbert v. California*, 388 U.S. 263 (1967); *Baker v. Carr*, 369 U.S. 186 (1962); *National Association for the Advancement of Colored People v. Button*, 371 U.S. 415 (1963); *Reitman v. Mulkey*, 387 U.S. 369 (1967); *Engel v. Vitale*, 370 U.S. 421 (1962); *Abingdon School District v. Schempp*, 374 U.S. 203 (1963); and *Murray v. Curlett*, 374 U.S. 203 (1963). Ervin's views on these and other Supreme Court rulings can be found in Ervin, *Preserving the Constitution*, 125–50.

43. Ervin, *Humor of a Country Lawyer* (Chapel Hill: University of North Carolina Press, 1983), 182.

44. Ibid.

45. Ervin, *Humor of a Country Lawyer*, 182–83. Slightly different versions of the story can be found in "Echoes from Capitol Hill," *Sacramento Bee*, 8 February 1966, Ervin Notebooks, s-12; Blake Clark to *Reader's Digest*, 9 July 1969, Ervin Papers, box 455, folder 308.

46. *Engel v. Vitale*, 370 U.S. 421 (1962); *School District of Abingdon Township v. Schempp*, 374 U.S. 203 (1963); *Murray v. Curlett*, 374 U.S. 203 (1963).

47. Robert S. Alley, *School Prayer* (Buffalo: Prometheus Books, 1994), 109.

48. Bernard Schwartz, *Super Chief: Earl Warren and His Supreme Court—A Judicial Biography* (New York: New York University Press, 1983), 442.

49. Bruce Jolly, "Supreme Court's Decision Brings Shock, Action," *Greensboro Daily News*, 27 June 1962, Ervin Notebooks, s-7; Ervin to Frank Winston Moore, 6 February 1963, Ervin Papers, box 96, folder 184; Ervin, "Senator Sam Ervin Says," no. 392, 12 July 1962, Ervin Papers, box 450; Charles Richards, "Ruling on Prayers Shocks Tar Heel Congressmen," *Winston-Salem Journal*, 27 June 1962, Ervin Notebooks, s-7.

50. Joseph Hearst, "College Aid Hits Religion Snag," *Chicago Daily Tribune*, 3 February 1962; David Stephens, "Sen. Ervin Argues Church-State Separation," *Nashville Tennessean*, 18 March 1966, Ervin Notebooks, s-9; "College Aid Chances," *St. Paul Dispatch*, [n.d.] October 1963, Ervin Notebooks, s-9; David Lawrence, "Way Found to Test Church School Aid," *Detroit Free Press*, 24 October 1963, Ervin Notebooks, s-9. Both the Kennedy and Johnson administrations opposed Ervin's judicial review bills; see Norbert A. Schlei Oral History Interview, by John Stewart, 20 February 1968, Oral History Project, 79 (JFKL); Memorandum, Ralph K. Huitt to Douglass Cater, 31 August 1966, WHCF, LE/JL-2 (LBJL); Bill Connelly, "Justice Department Maneuver on School Aid Stings Senate," *Winston-Salem Journal*, 20 December 1967, Ervin Papers, box 469. The issue addressed by Ervin's judicial review bill was decided by the Supreme Court in *Flask v. Cohen*, 392 U.S. 83 (1968); see Leo Pfeffer, *God, Caesar, and the Constitution* (Boston: Beacon Press, 1975), 264–67; Frank J. Sorauf, *The Wall of Separation* (Princeton: Princeton University Press, 1976), 352–53. For a complete record of Ervin's hearings, *Congressional Record* statements, amendments to pending legislation, and a bibliography, see U.S. Congress, Senate, Committee on the Judiciary, Hearings before the Subcommittee on Constitutional Rights, *Judicial Review*, 89th Cong., 2nd sess., 1966.

51. Ervin, Press Release, 27 September 1960, Ervin Papers, box 453, folder 75.

52. "What Presbyterian Congressmen Say about Christians and Politics," *Presbyterian Survey*, July 1960, 10.

53. Ibid. Ervin, Press Release, 27 September 1960, Ervin Papers, box 453, folder 75.

54. Ervin, "Senator Ervin and Private School Aid," *The Sampsonian* (North Carolina), 6 April 1961, Ervin Notebooks, s-6. For an overview of the debate on the wisdom of Ervin's judicial review bills see Drew Pearson, "Senate in for School-Aid Battle," *Washington Post*, 12 November 1963; David Lawrence, "Aid for Church-Affiliated Schools," *Washington Post*, 23 October 1963; William C. Selover, "Illegal Aid," *Christian Science Monitor*, 16 January 1967; and two contrasting editorials, "Buck Passing," *Washington Post*, 28 October 1963, and "Weighing the Law," *Washington Post*, 7 April 1967.

55. Lloyd Preslar, "Sam Ervin Had the Senate with Him in Stand Against Prayer Amendment," *Winston-Salem Journal*, 25 September 1966, Ervin Notebooks, s-12.

56. Richard Russell to David Goldwater, 16 July 1966, Richard B. Russell Papers, box 233, folder 6, Richard B. Russell Memorial Library, University of Georgia Libraries, Athens (hereafter cited as Russell Papers). Russell also wrote: "I am frank to say that I regard the Supreme Court decision in this case to be more consistent with the Constitution and precedent than I do their decisions in a number of other cases, including the 1954 *Brown* case." Richard Russell to Frederick Davis, 12 November 1963, Russell Papers, box 233, folder 18.

57. Interview with George Autry, [n.d.] 1987, for "Senator Sam," a documentary film produced by Mainstreet Productions for North Carolina Public Television, 1988, transcript in possession of author.

58. Dabney, *Good Man*, 241.

59. Clancy, *Just a Country Lawyer*, 217.

60. See George Autry Interview Transcript, "Senator Sam," 26–29; George B. Autry, "Sam Ervin: The Book By and About Him," *Duke Law Journal* 1985 (December 1985), 1246–48; Dabney, *Good Man*, 241–42; and to a lesser degree Clancy, *Just a Country Lawyer*, 212–17.

61. Ervin, *Preserving the Constitution*, 241–42.

62. Ibid., 247.

63. John R. Schmidhauser and Larry L. Berg, *The Supreme Court and Congress: Conflict and Interaction, 1945–1968* (New York: Free Press, 1972), 164.

64. *Congressional Record*, 89th Cong., 2nd sess., 20 September 1966, 23122–34, also in Ervin Papers, box 447, folder 7.

65. Ibid.

66. Ibid.

67. Bruce H. Kalk, "The Machiavellian Nominations: Richard Nixon's Southern Strategy and the Struggle for the Supreme Court, 1968–1970" (Ph.D. dissertation, University of North Carolina at Chapel Hill, 1992); Michael W. LaMorte and Fred N. Dorminy, "Compliance with the *Schempp* Decision: A Decade Later," *Journal of Law and Education* 3 (July 1974): 406–7; Ellis Katz, "Patterns of Compliance with the *Schempp* Decision," *Journal of Public Law* 14 (1965): 396–408.

68. Ervin's constituent mail discussing the school prayer amendment can be found in Ervin Papers, boxes 96, 125, and 161. The response to his Senate speech ran about equally

positive and negative. For an informed debate between Ervin and an angry constituent see a series of letters between Ervin and Charles H. Crutchfield, Ervin Papers, box 161, folder 573d.

69. "Amen, Senator," *Charlotte Observer*, 22 September 1966, Ervin Notebooks, s-12; Lloyd Preslar, "Sam Ervin Had the Senate with Him in Stand Against Prayer Amendment," *Winston-Salem Journal*, 25 September 1966, Ervin Notebooks, s-12; "Prayer, Yes; Amendment, No," *Richmond News Leader*, 22 September 1966, Ervin Notebooks, s-12; "Amen," *Washington Post*, 23 September 1966. Ervin was also favorably portrayed in "A Victory for Religious Freedom," *Louisville Times*, 24 September 1966, Ervin Notebooks, s-12; "Deserved Defeat," *Indianapolis News*, 27 September 1966, Ervin Notebooks, s-12; "Prayer," *Chicago Sun-Times*, 21 September 1966, Ervin Notebooks, s-12; "2 Prayer Proposals Assailed by Ervin," *New York Times*, 21 September 1966; "Without a Prayer," *Time*, 30 September 1966, 20.

70. Constitutional scholar Philip B. Kurland was so impressed by the senator's courageous stand on school prayer, as well as his defense of the wall of separation between church and state, that he dedicated his book *Church and State* to Ervin. See Philip B. Kurland, *Church and State: The Supreme Court and the First Amendment* (Chicago: University of Chicago Press, 1975).

71. Ervin's opposition to civil rights remained unchanged, but he did alter his defensive philosophical position from defending racial segregation against the color-blind principle of *Brown* to accepting the color-blind ideal as a way of combating new color-conscious affirmative action programs. See chapter 5.

72. Jay Hensley, "Ervin Says Freedoms Are Being Destroyed," *Asheville Citizen*, 22 December 1965, Ervin Notebooks, s-11; Ervin's opening statement, U.S. Congress, Senate, Committee on the Judiciary, Hearings before the Subcommittee on Antitrust and Monopoly, *Professional Basketball*, 92nd Cong., 1st sess., 1971, 12; editorial, "Tampering with Work Release," *Raleigh News and Observer*, 22 November 1967, Ervin Papers, box 469; James K. Batten, "Social Security Benefits and Prison Work Release," *Charlotte Observer*, 21 November 1967, Ervin Papers, box 469.

73. Ervin had been a consistent supporter of the Freedom of Information bill for several years and had worked with both Democrats and Republicans to achieve its passage. See Ervin to John F. Kennedy, 26 June 1961, WHCF, ND14-2, box 633, folder "censorship," JFKL; Roman Hruska press release, 3 November 1963, box J, working papers, Hruska Papers; "Public Is Entitled to Full Information," *Asheville Citizen*, 3 November 1963, Ervin Notebooks, s-9; "Ervin Co-Sponsors Freedom of Information Bill," *Waynesville Mountaineer*, 22 February 1965, Ervin Notebooks s-11; "Ervin Comments on Justice Department," *Greensboro Daily News*, 22 June 1967, Ervin Papers, box 469. The Narcotic Addict Treatment and Rehabilitation Act of 1966 originated in the Johnson administration and was pushed by liberals in the Senate such as Thomas J. Dodd and Robert F. Kennedy. Ervin willingly cooperated by cosponsoring the bill and even helping to redraft it. See Robert F. Kennedy to Ervin, 4 June 1965, Ervin Papers, box 161, folder 565; Thomas J. Dodd to Ervin, 17 June 1965, Ervin Papers, box 161, folder 565; John L. McClellan to Ervin, 13 July 1966, Ervin Papers, box 161, folder 565. Editorial, "An Unwarranted Insult," *Winston-Salem Journal*, 23 July 1965, Ervin Notebooks, s-11.

74. Roy Parker Jr., "Busy Sen. Ervin Is Rivaling Johnson in Long List of Legislative Interests," *Greensboro Daily News*, 25 September 1965, Ervin Notebooks, s-11.

75. Jerry Kluttz, "Policy on Jobs Stirs Hill Clash," *Washington Post*, 4 October 1966; Joseph Young, "Administration Denies It Plans Job Quota System Based on Race," *Washington Star*, 4 October 1966, Ervin Notebooks, s-12.

76. "Senate Subcommittee Probes Personal Questions," *Government Employees' Exchange*, 12 August 1964, Ervin Notebooks, s-12; "The Psyche Snoopers," *Washington Post*, 14 December 1964; Phil Casey, "Psychology Test Shocks Sen. Ervin," *Washington Post*, 9 December 1964; Willard Clopton, "Personality X-Rays or Peeping Toms?" *Washington Post*, 4 July 1965; "Federal Sex Quiz for Employees Hit," *Charlotte Observer*, 18 October 1966, Ervin Notebooks, s-12; Art Buchwald, "Psyching Out," *Washington Post*, 20 June 1965. Much of the controversy surrounded the government's use of the Minnesota Multiphasic Personality Inventory, which contained approximately 550 questions. Defenders of the test argue that overall performance and patterns of response, not the answers to specific questions, reveal emotional fitness. Ervin invited experts to debate the value and the dangers of these types of tests in 1966. See U.S. Congress, Senate, Committee on the Judiciary, Hearings before the Subcommittee on Constitutional Rights, *Psychological Tests and Constitutional Rights*, 89th Cong., 1st sess., 1965.

77. U.S. Congress, Senate, Committee on the Judiciary, Hearings before the Subcommittee on Constitutional Rights, *Privacy and the Rights of Federal Employees*, 89th Cong., 2nd sess., 1966 (hereafter cited as Privacy Hearings, 1966). James K. Batten, "Treasury Mulls Directing Its Execs to Push Rights," *Durham Herald*, 1 October 1966, Ervin Notebooks, s-12; Joseph Young, "Sen. Ervin Assails U.S. Perusal of Employees' Financial Affairs," *Washington Star*, 7 July 1966, Ervin Notebooks, s-12; "Coercion Charged in U.S. Bond Drive," *Christian Science Monitor*, 11 January 1967.

78. John Macy's testimony can be found in Privacy Hearings, 1966, 115–83. See John Cramer, "Macy Rips Ervin Bill Apart," *Washington Daily News*, 4 October 1966, Ervin Notebooks, s-12; Jerry Kluttz, "Policy on Jobs Stirs Hill Clash," *Washington Post*, 4 October 1966.

79. Privacy Hearings, 1966, 7; James K. Batten, "Ervin-Bill Hearing Depicts Federal Bosses as Snoopy," *Charlotte Observer*, 24 September 1966, Ervin Notebooks, s-12.

80. Lloyd Preslar, "Ervin Outlines Bill on Right to Privacy," *Winston-Salem Journal*, 10 August 1966, Ervin Notebooks, s-12; Alfred Friendly, "Protection for Whom? Ervin's Bill of Rights," *Washington Post*, 11 August 1966; "Now: A Bill to Outlaw Government Snooping," *U.S. News and World Report*, 22 August 1966, 9.

81. For more information on the National Data Bank, see Ervin's handwritten notes, Ervin Papers, box 411, folder 520; Arthur R. Miller, *The Assault on Privacy: Computers, Data Banks and Dossiers* (Ann Arbor: University of Michigan Press, 1971), 163, 317–20, 396.

82. Lloyd Preslar, "Ervin and Computer Meet, Become Friends," *Winston-Salem Journal*, 8 March 1967, Ervin Papers, box 469; Ervin, "Computers and Individual Privacy," an address to the Wharton School of Finance and Commerce, University of Pennsylvania Conference on Management, Science, and Information Systems, 6 November 1969, Ervin Papers, box 408, folder 461 (hereafter cited as Wharton School Address, 1969).

83. Ervin, "The Computer and Individual Privacy," address to the American Management Association, New York City, 6 March 1967, Ervin Papers, box 408, folder 461 (hereafter cited as American Management Association Speech, 1967).

84. Constituent complaints about government questionnaires and the census can be

found in U.S. Congress, Senate, Committee on the Judiciary, Hearings before the Subcommittee on Constitutional Rights, *Privacy, the Census, and Federal Questionnaires*, 91st Cong., 1st sess., 1969, 327–457 (hereafter cited as Census Hearings, 1969). See also Wharton School Address, 1969.

85. Wharton School Address, 1969; Census Hearings, 1969, 327–457; Roscoe Drummond, "The Census Monster," *Los Angeles Times*, 23 October 1967; "Replies to 1970 Census Forms," *New York Times*, 29 October 1967; "Big Brother, 1970 Model," *Wall Street Journal*, 10 October 1967.

86. See Ervin, "Privacy and the Constitution," address delivered at Thiel College, 5 January 1972, Ervin Papers, box 411, folder 522. Louis D. Brandeis is quoted from *Olmstead v. United States*, 277 U.S. 438, 478 (1928), dissenting opinion. For a discussion of the legal and constitutional aspects of the right to privacy, see Alan F. Westin, *Privacy and Freedom* (New York: Atheneum, 1967), 330–64; Arthur R. Miller, *The Assault on Privacy* (New York: Times Mirror, 1971), 205–20; Gerald Dworkin, "Privacy and the Law," in *Privacy*, ed. John B. Young (New York: John Wiley and Sons, 1978), 113–36; Darien A. McWhirter and Jon D. Bible, *Privacy as a Constitutional Right* (New York: Quorum Books, 1992); and the landmark essay by Samuel D. Warren and Louis D. Brandeis, "The Right To Privacy," *Harvard Law Review* 4 (1890): 193–220.

87. "Sen. Sam—Nation's Best Trout Catcher," *Greensboro Daily News*, 2 June 1974, North Carolina Clipping File, North Carolina Collection, Wilson Library, University of North Carolina at Chapel Hill.

88. Eventually the senator expanded his concept of the "false prophets" to serve as a defining metaphor of his expanding crusade against the government's threat to the right to privacy. See Ervin, "Privacy and the False Prophets," 1971; Ervin, "Privacy and Government Investigations," a speech delivered to the College of Law, University of Illinois, Urbana-Champaign, 7 May 1971, Ervin Papers, box 411, folder 525; Ervin, draft of a speech to the Dickinson College Symposium, 10 February 1970, Ervin Papers, box 411, folder 525; Ervin press release, "Ervin Attacks School Desegregation Guidelines," 31 March 1966, Ervin Papers, box 454, folder 221. Ervin's dislike of the behavioral sciences may also have reflected the South's frustration with the fact that after the 1940s social scientists no longer upheld popular theories about the inferiority of African Americans. See Richard Kluger, *Simple Justice: The History of Brown v. Board of Education and Black America's Struggle for Equality* (New York: Alfred A. Knopf, 1976), 310–14.

89. Dabney, *Good Man*, 235–24; Clancy, *Just a Country Lawyer*, 207; Ervin, "In Defense of Individuality," Elon College Commencement Address, 27 May 1957, Ervin Papers, box 453, folder 27a.

90. Alan Westin, *Privacy and Freedom* (New York: Atheneum, 1967), 26–28; Kermit L. Hall and James W. Ely Jr., eds., *An Uncertain Tradition: Constitutionalism and the History of the South* (Athens: University of Georgia Press, 1989), 3–59. Ervin also cited the Bible (Micah), English common law, his reading of the history of the American Revolution, and the Fourth Amendment as sources for his commitment to the right to privacy. See Ervin, *Preserving the Constitution*, 281–85.

91. Alfred Friendly, "Protection for Whom?" *Washington Post*, 11 August 1966; Jerry Kluttz, "Policy on Jobs Stirs Hill Clash," *Washington Post*, 4 October 1966; Joseph Young, "Administration Denies It Plans Job Quota System Based on Race," *Washington Star*, 4

October 1966, Ervin Notebooks, s-12. The Ervin-Macy exchange over the racial question-naires can be found in "Privacy Hearings, 1966," 126–38.

92. Russell Long, draft of amendment to H.R. 8315, 15 February 1960, box RO 92, Russell Long Papers, Louisiana and Lower Mississippi Valley Collections, LSU Libraries, Louisiana State University, Baton Rouge.

93. Allen Ellender to George R. Heine, 1 July 1965, box 837, folder "Legislation, 1965, Civil Rights," Allen J. Ellender Papers, Allen J. Ellender Library, Nicholls State University, Thibodaux, Louisiana.

94. John Cramer, "Quit Your Kidding Mr. Macy!" *Washington Daily News*, 9 June 1966, Ervin Notebooks, s-12; Charles Bartlett, "Ervin's Bill Has Some Non-Jeffersonian Aspects," *Greensboro Record*, 15 September 1967, Ervin Papers, box 469. Several Tar Heel editorials politely complained that Ervin's reputation as an ally of "the hardnosed racist of the Deep South in defense of discrimination" weakened the moral force of his struggle for privacy. "Ervin is too often identified as a satellite of the stern, unbending tories on civil rights and too little identified with his fine work in behalf of constitutional rights," the *Greensboro Daily News* lamented. But the editors also admitted that while "Senator Ervin's opposition to various civil rights measures has been definitely more constructive than that of most of the Deep South spokesmen with whom he chooses to team up, it has been unbroken and unrelenting all the same." See "Senator Ervin's Niche," *Greensboro Daily News*, 12 May 1966, Ervin Notebooks, s-12; "Big Brother Stalks Capitol Hill," *Asheville Citizen*, 8 October 1966, Ervin Notebooks, s-12. A similar debate over Ervin's underlying racial motivations accompanied his attacks on Thurgood Marshall during the justice's confirmation hearings in 1967. The *Greensboro Daily News* suggested: "There is prejudice in theory, and there is prejudice in practice, and there is possibly a condescension far more galling than naked racism in the virtually insuperable qualifications Senator Ervin would set up for a new Supreme Court justice." "Pride and Prejudice," *Greensboro Daily News*, 25 August 1967, Ervin Notebooks-12.

95. Stephen Klitzman, "Sam Ervin: Principle Not Politics," in *Citizens Look at Congress*, Ralph Nader Congress Project, 1972, 15, 28.

96. James K. Batten, "Sam Ervin and The Privacy Invaders," *New Republic*, 8 May 1971, 20.

97. Ervin refused to condemn or defend state and local government practices requiring racial information on government forms, and he had no comment on reports that North Carolina public schools and even the University of North Carolina at Chapel Hill gave their students the controversial personality tests. Ervin cited his personal "non-interference rule" with state issues. Richard Corrigan, "N.C. Pupils Have Taken Banned Test," *Charlotte Observer*, 11 June 1965, Ervin Papers, box 469; David Rothman, "UNC Routinely gives Controversial Test," *Charlotte Observer*, 30 January 1967, Ervin Papers, box 469; "Sen. Ervin Won't Get Involved," *Greensboro Daily News*, 10 August 1966, Ervin Notebooks, s-12.

98. Lawrence Speiser's comments are reported in *Role of the Supreme Court: Policy Maker of Adjudicator?* (Washington, D.C.: American Enterprise Institute, 1970), 65. William O. Douglas referred to Ervin as "a hero of mine," in *The Court Years: 1939–1975* (New York: Random House, 1980), 11.

99. Ervin's bill had fifty-four cosponsors. See Ervin to Philip Hart, 15 August 1966, Philip Hart Papers, box 534, folder "congressional correspondence, E," Michigan Histor-

ical Collection, Bentley Library, University of Michigan, Ann Arbor. For the official positions of the ADA, ACLU, and other organizations see their testimony in the Privacy Hearings, 1966.

100. Subcommittee on Constitutional Rights, Press Release, 29 August 1967, Ervin Papers, box 399, folder 280; James K. Batten, "Ervin Blisters CIA's 'Above the Law' Stand," *Charlotte Observer*, 30 August 1967, Ervin Papers, box 469; "Ervin Bill Goes Too Far," *Winston-Salem Journal*, 22 July 1968, Ervin Papers, box 469. The FBI had managed to earn a partial exemption from the Employee's Bill of Rights on national security grounds during hearings in the Judiciary Committee. The CIA, which had declined to testify in Ervin's hearings, asked for even stronger exemptions during the floor debate on the bill. Ervin finally accepted two amendments that granted special latitude to both agencies but kept them under the bill's jurisdiction. Senators Roman Hruska and Daniel Inouye both shared Ervin's anger at the CIA's last-minute maneuver. See Roman Hruska Press Release, 2 July 1964, Hruska Papers, Working files, C; *Congressional Record*, 90th Cong., 1st sess., 1967, 12390–94; Daniel Inouye to Ervin, 1 September 1967, Ervin Papers, box 399, folder 281. Senator Birch Bayh reversed himself and supported the CIA. He wrote to Ervin, "I have always supported your efforts, . . . but I have reservations regarding the FBI, CIA, and NSA." Birch Bayh to Ervin, 28 June 1967, Ervin Papers, box 399, folder 281.

101. Ervin's comments before the Subcommittee on Manpower and Civil Service of the Post Office and Civil Service Committee are quoted in Subcommittee on Constitutional Rights, Press Release, 2 July 1968, Ervin Papers, box 399, folder 282.

102. Lawrence Speiser to Ervin, 29 August 1967, Ervin Papers, box 399, folder 280; "Privacy Bill Shields Red Agents," *Tactics*, 20 August 1970, found in Wilson C. Lucom to Ervin, 9 September 1970, Ervin Papers, box 399, folder 281.

103. "Ervin Blasts Law 'Favoring' Foreign-Born," *Winston-Salem Journal*, 6 August 1955, Ervin Notebooks, s-2; "Senator Ervin Attacks Laws Favoring Foreign Born," *Asheville Citizen*, 6 August 1955, Ervin Notebooks, s-2.

CHAPTER EIGHT

1. Sam Ervin, interview by Paul Clancy, [n.d.] 1973, tape 4 side 2, tape 6 side 2, tape 8 side 1, Sam J. Ervin Papers, Subgroup A: Senate Papers, 3847A, Southern Historical Collection, Wilson Library, University of North Carolina at Chapel Hill (hereafter cited as Ervin Papers); Richard Russell to Ester Barber, 27 January 1958, Richard B. Russell Papers, Series I, Box 18, file 5, Richard B. Russell Memorial Library, University of Georgia Libraries, Athens (hereafter cited as Russell Papers).

2. Paul R. Clancy, *Just a Country Lawyer* (Bloomington: Indiana University Press, 1974), 155.

3. On the election of 1968, see Tom Wicker, *One of Us: Richard Nixon and the American Dream* (New York: Random House, 1991), 300–386; Stephen E. Ambrose, *Nixon*, vol. 2: *The Triumph of a Politician, 1962–1972* (New York: Simon and Schuster, 1989), 102–222; Herbert S. Parmet, *Richard Nixon and His America* (Boston: Little, Brown, 1990), 502–28; Joe McGinniss, *The Selling of the President 1968* (New York: Trident Press, 1969); Dan T. Carter, *George Wallace, Richard Nixon, and the Transformation of American Politics*, The Charles Edmondson Historical Lectures, Baylor University (Waco, Tex.: Baylor University Press, 1992).

4. "The Ervin-Sanford Exchange," *Winston-Salem Journal*, 19 June 1964, Sam Ervin newspaper clipping notebooks, in Sam J. Ervin Papers, Subgroup A: Senate Papers, 3847A, Southern Historical Collection, Wilson Library, University of North Carolina at Chapel Hill (hereafter cited as Ervin Notebooks), s-10. For a discussion of the historic divisions in North Carolina politics, see Paul Luebke, *Tar Heel Politics 2000: Myths and Realities* (Chapel Hill: University of North Carolina Press, 2000).

5. The comments of both B. Everett Jordan and Ervin to the White House are recorded in Memorandum, Marvin [?] to the President, 16 July 1966, FO2, WHCF, Lyndon B. Johnson Presidential Library (LBJL), Austin, Texas. Two other incidents are worth noting. One occurred ten days before the Democratic primary in the gubernatorial race of 1964 (which pitted the traditionalist Dan K. Moore against the modernizer L. Richardson Preyer) when Sanford and Ervin publicly exchanged harsh words over each other's strategy for protecting the state's tobacco interests. The content of the debate was not as important as the fact that it occurred in public. See David Cooper, "Political Notebooks: Sanford-Ervin Clash Outgrowth of Campaign," *Winston-Salem Journal*, 19 June 1964, Ervin Notebooks, s-10; "Ervin-Sanford Exchange," *Winston-Salem Journal*, 19 June 1964, Ervin Notebooks, s-10. The second incident occurred two years later, in 1966, when some of Sanford's friends secretly circulated lapel pins reading "Moore for U.S. Senate" at a Democratic gathering—clearly trying to embarrass Senator Ervin and cause dissension within his traditional wing of the party. Moore recognized the trick, and quickly squelched any move to forward his name as a candidate for the Senate. But most political observers interpreted the political stunt as more proof that Sanford was preparing to challenge Ervin in 1968. See William A. Shires, "Factionalism Runs High in Party Circles in State," *Raleigh Times*, 2 November 1966, Ervin Notebooks, s-12.

6. Oliver Quayle and Company, Political Climate in North Carolina, Study 1047, November 1967, Terry Sanford Papers, Subseries 4.1, Box 113, Southern Historical Collection, Wilson Library, University of North Carolina at Chapel Hill (hereafter cited as Sanford Papers); Terry Sanford Oral History Interview, by Joe B. Frantz, 15 May 1971, 17–18, OH II, LBJL (hereafter cited as Sanford Oral History Interview); Sanford to Donald H. Kline, 2 January 1968, Sanford Papers, subseries 4.1, Folder 1570; "Ervin May Face a Grueling Race," *Winston-Salem Journal*, 10 December 1967, Ervin Papers, Box 469; James K. Batten, "Sam Warns Terry: You'll Be Sorry," *Charlotte Observer*, 9 November 1967, Ervin Papers, Box 469.

7. "Pieces Won't Quite Fit for Terry," *Charlotte Observer*, 2 November 1967, Ervin Papers, Box 469; Michael Putzel, "Sanford's Aspirations No Surprise to Ervin," *Durham Morning Herald*, 5 November 1967, Ervin Papers, Box 469; "Terry Sanford's Senate Gambit," *Chapel Hill Weekly*, 8 November 1967, Ervin Papers, Box 469; "Drastically Divisive," *Fayetteville Observer*, 12 February 1968, Ervin Papers, Box 469; Sanford Oral History Interview, 17–18; Sanford's handwritten notes titled "One way to handle the race issue," Sanford Papers, subseries 4.1, Folder 1590.

8. "Drastically Divisive," *Fayetteville Observer*, 12 February 1968, Ervin Papers, Box 469; Oliver Quayle and Company, "Political Climate in North Carolina," Study 1081, February 1968, Sanford Papers, subseries 4.1, Box 113; "Under the Dome," *Raleigh News and Observer*, 13 February 1968, Ervin Papers, Box 469; Sanford Oral History Interview, 19.

9. David Cooper, "Sanford and Those Lightning Rods," *Winston-Salem Journal*, 5

November 1967, Ervin Papers, Box 469; "Pieces Won't Quite Fit for Terry," *Charlotte Observer*, 2 November 1967, Ervin Papers, Box 469; James K. Batten, "Jordan Asks Terry to Stay Out in '68,'" *Charlotte Observer*, 29 November 1967, Ervin Papers, Box 469; "High Price for Party Unity," *Greensboro Daily News*, 13 February 1968, Ervin Papers, Box 469; Jay Jenkins, "Sanford Says 'No' to 68 Senate Race," *Charlotte Observer*, 11 February 1968, Ervin Papers, Box 469; Walter Rugaber, "North Carolina Awaits Stiff Primaries," *New York Times*, 14 January 1968.

10. Sanford Oral History Interview, 17.

11. John H. Averill, "Not the Session for Civil Rights, but . . . ," *Raleigh News and Observer*, 15 March 1968, Ervin Papers, Box 469; "Rights Bill Is Debated in Senate," *Washington Post*, 19 January 1968; "Senator Ervin Is Leading the Opposition," *Virginian Pilot*, 7 February 1968, Ervin Papers, Box 469; "Filibuster on Rights Is Winning, Ervin Says," *Winston-Salem Journal*, 21 February 1968, Ervin Papers, Box 469.

12. "Crime Control Bill Loses Court Limit," *Asheville Citizen*, 22 May 1968, Ervin Papers, Box 469; Fred P. Graham, "Senate Upholds Supreme Court on Review Issue," *New York Times*, 22 May 1968; Fred P. Graham, "Congress Still Battling the Court," *New York Times*, 26 May 1968.

13. Seven members of the Judiciary Committee issued a statement saying that Ervin's amendments "would roll back a century of progress in American constitutional law and restore American criminal procedure to the dark ages of the early 1900s." See Dana Bullen, "McClellan Asks Prompt Passage of Crime Bill," *Washington Star*, 2 May 1968, Ervin Papers, Box 469; Richard Harris, *The Fear of Crime* (New York: Frederick A. Praeger, 1969), 58–59; John R. Schmidhauser and Larry L. Berg, *The Supreme Court and Congress: Conflict and Interaction, 1945–1968* (New York: Free Press, 1972), 164–67.

14. Carl T. Curtis to Ervin, 14 May 1968, Ervin Papers, Box 395, Folder 196; Ervin to Carl T. Curtis, 15 May 1968, Ervin Papers, Box 395, Folder 196.

15. Roy Parker Jr., "Nixon Uses Ervin's 'Bill of Rights,'" *Greensboro Daily News*, 5 October 1968, Ervin Papers, Box 470.

16. Alexander P. Lamis, *The Two-Party South* (New York: Oxford University Press, 1984), note 278, p. 134.

17. Thad L. Beyle and Peter B. Harkins, "Down the Ballot in 1968," in *Politics and Policy in North Carolina*, ed. Thad Beyle and Merle Black (New York: MSS Information Corporation, 1975), 99; Numan V. Bartley and Hugh D. Graham, *Southern Politics and the Second Reconstruction* (Baltimore: Johns Hopkins University Press, 1975), 127–32; Stephen Klitzman, "Sam Ervin: Principle Not Politics," in *Citizens Look at Congress* (Washington, D.C.: Ralph Nader Congress Project, 1972), 15–16.

18. *Congressional Quarterly Almanac*, 92nd Cong., 1st sess., 1971 (Washington, D.C.: Congressional Quarterly, 1972), 81–110; *Congressional Quarterly Almanac*, 91st Cong., 1st sess., 1969 (Washington, D.C.: Congressional Quarterly, 1970), 1037–70; Klitzman, "Sam Ervin," 13.

19. "The Crime Buster," *Newsweek*, 10 February 1969, 22–23; Wicker, *One of Us*, 616; Memorandum, Richard Nixon to Ehrlichman, 22 January 1969, President's Office Files, President's Handwriting File, Box 1, WHSF, Nixon Presidential Materials Staff (NPMS), National Archives and Records Administration's Office of Presidential Libraries, National Archives II, College Park, Maryland.

20. "Statement Outlining Actions and Recommendations for the District of Columbia," 31 January 1969, *Public Papers of the Presidents of the United States: Richard Nixon, 1969* (Washington, D.C.: Government Printing Office, 1971), 40–48; "Crime in the Nation's Capital," *Time*, 7 February 1969, 14.

21. Ervin believed the Nixon administration pulled a "fast shuffle" in its handling of the bill. In spite of personal assurances made directly to Ervin that the 322-page bill did not contain any substantive changes except of the most technical nature, the senator later discovered several very controversial revisions of existing criminal law that he charged had been "squirreled away in the recesses of the bill." In addition to the preventive detention and no-knock measures discussed below, the administration bill would have reversed most of Ervin's prized Mental Health Bill of Rights. See Ervin, "The Department of Justice Fast Shuffle on the Bill of Rights," remarks prepared for delivery on the Senate floor, [n.d.], Ervin Papers, Box 394, Folder 190.

22. Nixon's "law and order" program is outlined in *Nixon: The First Year of His Presidency* (Washington, D.C.: Congressional Quarterly, 1970), 53–54; and discussed at length in Richard Harris, *Justice: The Crisis of Law, Order, and Freedom in America* (New York: Dutton, 1969).

23. Ervin's quotations are taken from James K. Batten, "Sam Ervin and the Privacy Invaders," *New Republic*, 8 May 1971, 20. U.S. Congress, Senate, Committee on the Judiciary, *Amendments to the Bail Reform Act of 1966*, Hearings before the Subcommittee on Constitutional Rights, 91st Cong., 1st sess., 1969 (hereafter cited as Amendments to the Bail Reform Act Hearings, 1969); U.S. Congress, Senate, Committee on the Judiciary, *Preventive Detention*, Hearings before the Subcommittee on Constitutional Rights, 91st Cong., 2nd sess., 1970 (hereafter cited as Preventive Detention Hearings, 1970). For a discussion of Ervin's opposition, see Erwin Knoll, "Sam Ervin's Thunder and the 'Ominous' Crime Bill," *Progressive*, September 1970, 19–22; Wicker, *One of Us*, 619–23.

24. John N. Mitchell, "Bail Reform and the Constitutionality of Pretrial Detention," *Virginia Law Review* 55 (November 1969): 1223–42; Laurence H. Tribe, "An Ounce of Detention: Preventive Justice in the World of John Mitchell," *Virginia Law Review* (1970): 371–82; Harry Sabin, "Bail for the Rich, Jail for the Poor," *Nation*, 24 March 1969, 363–66. The bank robber story is recounted in Preventive Detention Hearings, 1970, 333. Realizing that "preventive detention" was a controversial phrase, the Nixon administration tried, unsuccessfully, to convince their allies to replace it with "temporary pretrial detention." Donald E. Santarelli to John Gail, 17 September 1969, Roman Hruska Manuscript Collection, W.F., G, Nebraska State Historical Society (hereafter cited as Hruska Papers).

25. Alan M. Dershowitz, "Preventing 'Preventive Detention,' " *New York Review of Books*, 13 March 1969. The debate over preventive detention is discussed in Wayne H. Thomas Jr., *Bail Reform in America* (Berkeley: University of California Press, 1976), 227–48.

26. U.S. Congress, Senate, Committee on the Judiciary, *Speedy Trial*, Hearings before the Subcommittee on Constitutional Rights, 92nd Cong., 1st Sess., 1971 (hereafter cited as Speedy Trial Hearings, 1971), and 93rd Cong., 1st sess., 1973. Ervin's quotation is taken from Speedy Trial Hearings, 1971, 777. See also "As We See It—Fast Trial, Not Detention, A Way to Fight Crime," *Detroit Free Press*, 29 May 1971, Ervin Papers, Box 469; Memorandum, Constitutional Rights Subcommittee Staff, to Ervin, 16 April 1973, Ervin Papers, Box 396, Folder 211; *Congressional Record*, 91st Cong., 2nd sess., 9 June 1970, 18845–46.

27. Ervin's arguments against preventive detention are clearly outlined in his opening statement for the Preventive Detention Hearings, 1970, 1–16. The senator had been building a record against preventive detention for several years; see Ervin to the editor, *Evening Star*, 1 December 1966, copy found in Roman Hruska Papers, W.F., C; "Easy Bail Called Public Hazard," *Washington Post*, 1 January 1967. Ervin discussed the crime statistics in Preventive Detention Hearings, 1970, 12–13, 339–41; see *National Bureau of Standards Compilation and Use of Criminal Court Data in Relation to Pre-Trial Release of Defendants: Pilot Study*, reprinted in Preventive Detention Hearings, 1970, 765.

28. Preventive Detention Hearings, 1971, 3.

29. "Hruska Says Nixon to Get Aid V. Crime," *Omaha World Herald*, 12 February 1969; Tom Wicker, "Rights of Criminals Are Rights of All Americans," *New York Times*, 1 January 1970; William F. Buckley Jr., *National Review*, 24 February 1970, 220.

30. Staff Memorandum, Subcommittee on Constitutional Rights, "Proposals for 'No-Knock' Entry," 5 June 1970, Ervin Papers, Box 394, Folder 190; Tom Wicker, " 'No-Knock' Opponents Were Right," *New York Times*, 8 July 1973; "Ominous Crime Bill," *Time*, 8 March 1971; "Sen. Sam's Dissent," *Winston-Salem Journal*, 8 January 1970, Ervin Papers, Box 469; *Congressional Record*, 91st Cong., 2nd sess., 2 April 1970, 17591–96; Ervin, *Preserving the Constitution*, 275–79.

31. Subcommittee on Constitutional Rights Press Release, "Ervin Calls D.C. Crime Bill a Blue-Print for a Police State," 23 March 1970, Ervin Papers, Box 395, Folder 202; Speedy Trial Hearings, 1971, 777; Klitzman, "Sam Ervin," 15, 17; Lawrence Leamer, "The Sam Ervin Show," *Harpers* (March 1972): 80–86; James K. Batten, "Sam Ervin and the Privacy Invaders," *New Republic* (8 May 1971): 19–23; John Herbers, "Sam Ervin Thinks the Constitution Should Be Taken Like Mountain Whiskey—Undiluted and Untaxed," *New York Times Magazine* (15 November 1970); Erwin Knoll, "Sam Ervin's Thunder," *Progressive* (September 1970): 19–22; Robert Sherrill, "Big Brother Watching You? See Sam Ervin," *Playboy* (December 1971): 127.

32. David Brinkley, transcript of closing commentary, NBC News, 23 July 1970, Ervin Papers, Box 470.

33. The legislative history of preventive detention and the D.C. crime bill is discussed in Paul D. Borman, "The Selling of Preventive Detention 1970," *Northwest Law Review* 65 (January–February 1971): 879–931; Tom Wicker, *One of Us*, 615–23; Ervin, *Preserving the Constitution*, 275–79. At least one commentator thought that the passage of this bill empowered Richard Nixon to legally set up the Plumbers, spy on Ellsberg, and execute the Huston Plan. See the comments of Howard K. Smith as recounted in Memorandum, Bruce Kehrli to Al Haig, 11 July 1973, President's Office Files, Annotated News Summaries, Box 50, WHSF, NPMS.

34. Thomas, *Bail Reform in America*, 232, 244; "No-Knock Officer Slain At Bedroom Door," *Baltimore Afro-American*, 3 June 1972; Tom Wicker, " 'No-Knock' Opponents Were Right," *New York Times*, 8 July 1973; Stephen Green, "Repeal of No-Knock Is Voted by Senate in Dramatic Shift," *Washington Post*, 12 July 1974; "Senate Votes to Repeal No-Knock Drug Law Rule," *New York Times*, 12 July 1974; Ervin, *Preserving the Constitution*, 278–79; Memorandum, Wilfred H. Rommel to the President, 23 October 1974, Legislative Case Files, Box 11, WHCF, Gerald R. Ford Presidential Library (GRFL), Ann Arbor, Michigan.

35. Ervin, "Origin and Purpose of the First Amendment," remarks prepared for the California Bar Association, September 1971, Ervin Papers, Box 400, Folder 306; Tom Hall, "Nixon Gives Way to Fear," *San Francisco Examiner*, 16 September 1971, Ervin Papers, Box 396; Ervin, "Constitutional Casualties in the War on Crime," *Denver Law Journal* special edition (1971): 1–11; Wicker, *One of Us*, 623; Clancy, *Just a Country Lawyer*, 224.

36. Ervin to David M. Kennedy, 9 July 1970, Ervin Papers, Box 411, Folder 520; George Lardner Jr., "Ervin Decries U.S. Probe of 'Subversive' Readers," *Washington Post*, 10 July 1970; "Sen. Ervin Hits Plan to Open Mail," *Charlotte News*, 27 April 1970, Ervin Papers, Box 470. The Treasury Department defended itself by arguing that it only sought the names of those who had checked out books on bombs and explosives. But Ervin complained about the lack of standards in deciding who would be listed in the department's files, and he asked how persons included on such a list could learn of and challenge the government's suspicions about them.

37. Mike Causey, "Secret Service Seeks Information," *Washington Post*, 12 November 1969; "Ervin Raps Request of Secret Service," *Durham Herald*, 13 January 1970, Ervin Papers, Box 470; Ervin, "Computers and Individual Privacy," an address to the Wharton School of Finance and Commerce, University of Pennsylvania, Conference on Management, Science, and Information Systems, 6 November 1969, Ervin Papers, Box 408, Folder 461.

38. Ervin discussed the blacklist in his address before the Dickenson College Public Affairs Symposium, 16 March 1971, Ervin Papers, Box 453, Folder 532; and it was reported in the *Greensboro Daily News*, 16 March 1970, *Winston-Salem Journal*, 8 January 1970, and by Davis Merritt, "HEW: What Blacklist?" *Charlotte Observer*, 29 September 1969, Ervin Papers, Box 470. The actions of the Post Office are discussed in Dick Dabney, *A Good Man: The Life of Sam J. Ervin* (Boston: Houghton Mifflin, 1976), 248–49.

39. Huston, an aide of Nixon's throughout the 1960s, had urged the CIA deputy director in June 1969 to expand its admittedly illegal domestic political surveillance of antiwar protesters and other critics of the Nixon administration. The enthusiastic Huston had also called an assistant to the Internal Revenue Service commissioner that July and encouraged the creation of the Special Services Staff to investigate leftist political organizations as well as personal enemies of Richard Nixon. See Athan Theoharis, *Spying on Americans: Political Surveillance from Hoover to the Huston Plan* (Philadelphia: Temple University Press, 1978), 189–90; Stanley I. Kutler, *The Wars of Watergate: The Last Crisis of Richard Nixon* (New York: Alfred A. Knopf, 1990), 105.

40. Tom Charles Huston to H. R. Haldeman, 10 July 1970, H. R. Haldeman Files, Office and Memo Files, Box 70, Folder "Brown Follow Up," WHSF, NPMS.

41. Ibid.

42. Ervin expressed this belief in an interview with Paul Clancy, [n.d.] 1973, tape 8, side 1, Ervin Papers. See also Kutler, *Wars of Watergate*, 96–101; Frank J. Donner, *The Age of Surveillance: The Aims and Methods of America's Political Intelligence System* (New York: Random House, 1981), 263–68; J. Anthony Lukas, *Nightmare: The Underside of the Nixon Years* (New York: Viking Press, 1976), 30–40; and for a different interpretation, see Ambrose, *Nixon*, vol. 1: *Education*, 367–69.

43. Joseph C. Spear, *Presidents and the Press: The Nixon Legacy* (Cambridge, Mass.: MIT Press, 1984), 39; William Safire, *Before the Fall* (Garden City, N.Y.: Doubleday, 1975), 352.

44. Presidential Office Files, Annotated News Summaries, 27 December 1970, p. 9, WHSF, NPMS; Ambrose, *Nixon: Education*, 409–12. An excellent discussion of the roots of Nixon's hatred of the press can be found in Wicker, *One of Us*, 436–46.

45. Spear, *Presidents and the Press*, 39; Marilyn A. Lashner, *The Chilling Effect in TV News: Intimidation by the Nixon White House* (New York: Praeger, 1984), 5; William E. Porter, *Assault on the Media: The Nixon Years* (Ann Arbor: University of Michigan Press, 1976), 4–5.

46. Arthur Johnsey, "Sen. Ervin Scores News Suppression," *Greensboro Daily News*, 21 January 1955, Ervin Notebooks, S-1; Al G. Dickenson, "Ervin Spells Out Press Freedom," *Wilmington Star-News*, 23 January 1955, Ervin Notebooks, s-1; "Press Trial Conflict To Be Aired," *Greensboro Daily News*, 26 August 1965, Ervin Notebooks, s-11; "Free Press Defended, Berated," *Asheville Citizen*, 20 August 1965, Ervin Notebooks, s-11; U.S. Congress, Senate, Committee on the Judiciary, *Free Press and Fair Trial*, Hearings before the Subcommittee on Constitutional Rights, 89th Cong., 1st sess., 1965; U.S. Congress, Senate, Committee on the Judiciary, *Freedom of the Press*, Hearings before the Subcommittee on Constitutional Rights, 92nd Cong., 1st and 2nd sess., 1971–72 (hereafter cited as Freedom of the Press Hearings, 1971–72). Ervin also believed that the government's attempts to restrict advertising—especially of North Carolina's tobacco products—represented an unconstitutional restriction of the freedom of the press. See Ervin, "Advertising—The Stepchild of the First Amendment," remarks before the Proprietary Association Annual Meeting, 16 May 1972, American Civil Liberties Union Papers, vol. 2, General Correspondence, A. 1300, Seeley G. Mudd Manuscripts Library, Princeton University (hereafter cited as ACLU Papers).

47. For an excellent discussion of Ervin's Freedom of the Press Hearings in 1971–72, see Lawrence Leamer, "Sam Ervin Show," in *Congress and the News Media*, ed. Robert O. Blanchard (New York: Hastings House, 1974), 356–67. *Caldwell v. United States*, 408 U.S. 665 (1972). For the response of the press, see a series of articles by Norman E. Isaacs, Benno C. Schmidt Jr., and Fred W. Friendly, "Beyond the *Caldwell* Decision," *Columbia Journalism Review* (September/October 1972): 18–37; Brit Hume, "A Chilling Effect on the Press," *New York Times Magazine*, 17 December 1972; and, for a different opinion, Vermont Royster, "Dubious Shield," *Wall Street Journal*, 28 February 1973. Commenting on *Caldwell*, Ervin suggested that "the Supreme Court's majority has overlooked the philosophy of the First Amendment's guarantee of a free press. . . . The Majority has apparently forgotten the historic dangers always implicit when government, even for the most noble of purposes, interferes with and restricts the operation of the press." Staff Report of the Senate Subcommittee on Constitutional Rights, August, 1972, ACLU Papers, vol. 2, General Correspondence, A 1300. Ervin's enthusiasm for a newsmen's privilege bill led him to draft one version of a shield law that relied on Section 5 of the Fourteenth Amendment to cover reporters in the states as well—a clear violation of the states' rights philosophy he utilized so well to fight civil rights legislation. See Memorandum, Larry Baskir to Ervin, 26 February 1973, Ervin Papers, Box 400, Folder 297. After the *Caldwell* decision, Ervin held a second set of hearings in 1973: U.S. Congress, Senate, Committee on the Judiciary, *Newsmen's Privilege*, Hearings before the Subcommittee on Constitutional Rights, 93rd Cong., 1st sess., 1973 (hereafter cited as Newsmen's Privilege Hearings, 1973). Ervin suggested in his opening statement that "the administration's stance with regard to newsmen's privilege, while not one of vehement hostility, has nonetheless been one of resistance," and he

pointed out that CBS and NBC alone received 121 subpoenas in the first thirty months of the Nixon administration. Newsmen's Privilege Hearings, 1973, 5.

48. Ervin quoted the *Newsweek* story in "Is the Press Being Hobbled?" remarks before the North Carolina Press Association, 19 January 1973, Ervin Papers, Box 458 (hereafter cited as "Is the Press Being Hobbled?"). See also Ervin, "The President and the Press," remarks made at Texas Tech University, 16 February 1972, Ervin Papers, Box 457 (hereafter cited as "President and the Press"); and Spear, *Presidents and the Press*, 150–53.

49. Dr. Clay Whitehead, Director of the White House Office of Telecommunications Policy, made the threat of FCC censorship that had been hinted at earlier by Spiro Agnew even more explicit when he announced a new administration proposal to condition the renewal of broadcast licenses of local television stations on whether they "act to correct imbalance or consistent bias from the networks." See Ervin, "Is the Press Being Hobbled?"; Clay T. Whitehead to Ervin, 9 April 1973, Ervin Papers, Box 400, Folder 296. The White House encouraged their supporters in North Carolina to lobby Ervin to drop his objections to the FCC's new policy. See Richard Nixon to Charles H. Crutchfield, 19 April 1973, EX VT1-1, Box 17, WHCF, NPMS.

50. *New York Times Co. v. United States* 403 U.S. 713. Ervin's quotation on the Pentagon Papers case came in his opening remarks, Freedom of the Press Hearings, 1971–1972, 5. See also "The Pentagon Papers: Free at Last," *Washington Post*, 1 July 1971; Peter D. Junger, "Down Memory Lane: The Case of the Pentagon Papers," *Case Western Reserve Law Review* 23 (November 1971): 3–75; "The Right of the Press to Gather Information," *Columbia Law Review* 71 (May 1971): 838–64; Ervin, "President and the Press."

51. Donald Wise, *The Politics of Lying* (New York: Random House, 1973), 392n; Porter, *Assault on the Media*, 144; Spear, *Presidents and the Press*, 148–49; Ken W. Clawson, "FBI Probes Newsman Critical of President," *Washington Post*, 11 November 1971; Carroll Kilpatrick, "White House Weighed Job for Schorr," *Washington Post*, 1 February 1972; Daniel Schorr, *Clearing the Air* (New York: Berkeley Publishing, 1978), 69–74.

52. Daniel Schorr testimony, Freedom of the Press Hearings, 1971–72, 416–31; Memorandum, John Dean to John Ehrlichman et al., 9 December 1971, John Dean Files, Subject Files, Box 65, Folder "Schorr," WHSF, NPMS (hereafter cited as Dean Files); Memorandum, John Dean to Clark MacGregor, 20 December 1971, Dean Files, Box 65, Folder "Schorr"; John Dean to Ervin, 22 November 1971, Ervin Files, Box 400, Folder 304; Ervin to Richard Nixon, 12 November 1971, and 3 December 1971, Ervin Papers, Box 400, Folder 296; Spear, *Presidents and the Press*, 149; H. R. Haldeman and Joseph DiMona, *Ends of Power* (New York: Times Books, 1978), 184–85.

53. Ervin, "Is the Press Being Hobbled?"; Transcript of Conversation, White House Tapes, Watergate Special Prosecution Force Segment, 28 February 1973, Conversation No.: 865-014, NPMS.

54. Statement by former Vice President Richard Nixon on the equal rights amendment, released July 1968, Campaign Files, Ex HU 2-5, Box 21, WHCF, NPMS; "Ervin to Protect Women," *Greensboro Daily News*, 18 August 1970, Ervin Papers, Box 470.

55. Memorandum, Leonard Garment to Ken Cole, 24 September 1970, EX-HU 2-5, Box 21, WHCF, NPMS.

56. Memorandum, Rita E. Hauser to John Ehrlichman and Leonard Garment, 14 September 1970, EX-HU 2-5, Box 21, WHCF, NPMS.

57. Memorandum, John Dean, through John Ehrlichman, to the President, 14 March 1972, EX-HU 2-5, Box 21, WHCF, NPMS.

58. Paul Clancy, "Ervin Plea on Women Rejected," *Charlotte Observer*, 22 March 1972, Ervin Papers, box 470. For an excellent overview and analysis of Ervin's opposition to the ERA see "Physiological and Functional Differences: Sam Ervin on Classification by Sex," in *Sex, Gender, and the Politics of the ERA*, ed. Donald G. Mathews and Jane Sherron De Hart (Oxford: Oxford University Press, 1990), 28–53.

59. Transcript, interview with Richard Nixon, WBTV, Charlotte, 11 September 1968, attached to Memorandum, Chuck Stewart to Jim Keogh, 7 April 1969, John D. Ehrlichman Files, Box 30, Folder 105, WHSF, NPMS (hereafter cited as Ehrlichman Files); Paul Jablow, "Nixon Raps HEW on Schools," *Charlotte Observer*, 13 September 1968, Ervin Papers, Box 387, Folder 54; "Nixon Stand on Schools Is Poor Logic, Strong Politics," *Charlotte Observer*, 15 September 1968, Ervin Papers, Box 387, Folder 54.

60. Robert Finch and John Mitchell, "Statement on Schools: 'Our Aim is to Educate, Not Punish,'" *Washington Post*, 4 July 1969; Leadership Conference on Civil Rights Memorandum no. 5-69, 20 March 1969, Leadership Conference on Civil Rights Papers, Series D, Box 3, Folder "Memos 1969," Manuscript Division, Library of Congress, Washington, D.C. (hereafter cited as LCCR Papers); President's Office Files, Annotated News Summaries, 12 October 1969, Box 31, NPMS; Gary Orfield, "President Keeps Promise of his 'Southern Strategy,'" *Washington Post*, 6 July 1969. See also Joan Hoff, *Nixon Reconsidered* (New York: Basic Books, 1994), 83–90; Wicker, *One of Us*, 490–94; and Parmet, *Richard Nixon and His America*, 594–97.

61. Theodore M. Hesburgh, Chairman of the U.S. Commission on Civil Rights, is quoted in *Nixon: The First Year of His Presidency* (Washington, D.C.: Congressional Quarterly, 1970), 50; Roy Wilkins to Richard Bolling, 9 December 1969, Richard Bolling Papers, Box 65, Joint Collection, Western Historical Manuscript Collection—Columbia and State Historical Society of Missouri Manuscripts (hereafter cited as Bolling Papers); Ervin's opening statement, U.S. Congress, Senate, Committee on the Judiciary, *Amendments to the Voting Rights Act of 1965*, Hearings before the Subcommittee on Constitutional Rights, 91st Cong., 1st and 2nd sessions, 1969–70, 1 (hereafter cited as Amendments to Voting Rights Act Hearings, 1969–1970); "Senator Ervin Fights Voting Rights Law," *Raleigh News and Observer*, 10 July 1969, Ervin Papers, Box 470; Telegram, Clarence Mitchell to Thomas Eagleton, 6 March 1970, 9 March 1970, Thomas Eagleton Papers, Box 87, Joint Collection, University of Missouri Western Historical Manuscript Collection—Columbia and State Historical Society of Missouri Manuscripts (hereafter cited as Eagleton Papers); Spencer Rich, "Ervin Hints Filibuster on Voting Rights Bill," *Washington Post*, 19 February 1970.

62. Memorandum to Bryce Harlow, 1 July 1969, "Congressional Support for the Administration Position on Voting Rights," Dean Files, Subject Files, Box 72, WHSF, NPMS; Ervin to Stuart Symington, 6 March 1970, Stuart Symington Papers, Box 198, Joint Collection, University of Missouri Western Historical Manuscript Collection—Columbia and State Historical Society of Missouri Manuscripts (hereafter cited as Symington Papers); Amendments to the Voting Rights Act Hearings, 1969–70; Hoff, *Nixon Reconsidered*, 94.

63. Ervin to L. B. Hollowell Jr., 10 June 1969, Ervin Papers, Box 392, Folder 154; Ervin to Richardson Preyer, 20 March 1970, Ervin Papers, Box 387, Folder 42; Bruce Kalk, "The

Machiavellian Nominations: Richard Nixon's Southern Strategy and the Struggle for the Supreme Court, 1968–70" (Ph.D. diss., University of North Carolina at Chapel Hill, 1992).

64. *Alexander v. Holmes County Board of Education* 396 U.S. 19 (1960). In December 1969, the Nixon administration once again sided with southern school districts in asking for a delay, and once again the Supreme Court ordered immediate integration in *Carter v. West Feliciana Parish School Board*, 396 U.S. 290 (1970). The federal court's rejection of "all deliberate speed" began in the Fifth Circuit Court with *United States v. Jefferson County Board of Education*, 372 U.S. F.2dd 836 (5th Cir. 1966), and is best seen in the landmark case *Green v. County School Board*, 391 U.S. 430 (1968). See J. Harvie Wilkinson III, *From Brown to Bakke: The Supreme Court and School Desegregation, 1954–1978* (New York: Oxford University Press, 1979), 116–27; and Hugh Davis Graham, *The Civil Rights Era: Origins and Development of National Policy, 1960–1972* (New York: Oxford University Press, 1990), 372–75.

65. The historiography of Nixon and civil rights is contentious. For sympathetic treatments of Nixon see Wicker, *One of Us*, 484–507; and Hoff, *Nixon Reconsidered*, 77–114. The best critical evaluation can be found in Graham, *Civil Rights Era*, 301–449.

66. *Swann v. Charlotte Mecklenburg Board of Education*, 402 U.S. 1 (1971); Ervin, "Amicus Curiae Brief for the Classroom Teachers Association of the Charlotte-Mecklenburg School System, Inc.," Ervin Papers, Box 387, Folder 49; Ervin to Margery Alexander Thompson, 12 November 1970, Ervin Papers, Box 387, Folder 53; Roy Parker Jr., "Ervin Represents Teachers in Charlotte School Case," *Raleigh News and Observer*, 22 September 1970, Ervin Papers, Box 470; "Ervin Blasts Court Decision on Busing," *Charlotte Observer*, 26 April 1971, Ervin Papers, Box 470.

67. Howard Covington, "Sam Ervin Raps Nixon, Backs Bahakel in Race," *Charlotte Observer*, 24 October 1970; Ervin to The President, 2 August 1971, EX HU 2-1, Box 9, WHCF, NPMS; Transcript, "Excerpts from Taped Interview with Senator Sam J. Ervin, Jr., on Neighborhood Schools," n.d., Ervin Papers, Box 456, Folder 507. Ervin added: "Every time an election comes and President Nixon wants to get votes, for Republican candidates or for himself, he comes to North Carolina as he did in 1968 or as he did the other day in Asheville, and comes out for neighborhood schools and against busing. But every time a proposal is made to carry out that policy, he is silent and his Man Friday, the Secretary of Health, Education, and Welfare, comes out and fights it." See also "Ervin Sees Hope in Nixon's Actions," *Raleigh News and Observer*, 13 February 1970, Ervin Papers, Box 470.

68. H. R. Haldeman to John Ehrlichman, 19 May 1972, Ehrlichman Files, Box 66, WHSF, NPMS.

69. *Congressional Record*, 91st Cong., 2nd sess., 10 February 1970, 3077–78; Larry Cheek, "At the Senate Theater: Lyrics by Sam Ervin Jr.," *Greensboro Daily News*, 15 February 1970, Ervin Papers, Box 470; "Ervin Says U.S. Has a 'Double Standard,'" *Morganton News Herald*, 15 January 1970, Ervin Papers, Box 470; Ervin Press Release, "Ervin Solicits Support for Freedom of Choice Legislation," 29 August 1973, Ervin Papers, Box 458, Folder 1001. Ervin explained to a colleague: "Despite the fact that I happen to reside in the South, I was able to obtain the votes of 36 Senators for an amendment to the school bill which would have absolutely prohibited all busing. . . . This is at least 16 votes more than I could have possibly procured for such an amendment two years ago." Ervin to Richardson

Preyer, 20 March 1970, Ervin Papers, Box 387, Folder 42. The LCCR warned that "hysteria over school busing is sweeping the nation." LCCR Press Release, 25 May 1972, LCCR Papers, Series E, Box 3, Folder "Busing, Press Conferences"; Roy Wilkins concluded that "the dangers we face are broader and graver than mere restrictions on busing. What we are confronted with is an attempt to use 'busing' to turn back the clock on desegregation." Roy Wilkins to Jacob S. Potofsky, 9 June 1972, LCCR Papers, Series E, Box 1, Folder "Statement on the Anti-Busing Assault."

70. Ervin press release, "Ervin Praises Freedom of Choice Committee," 13 February 1970, Ervin Papers, Box 456, Folder 463.

71. Nina Totenberg, "Foes of Busing near Victory in Campaign to Curb Courts," *National Observer*, 5 February 1972, Ervin Papers, Box 470; Clancy, *Just a Country Lawyer*, 197. So many northern politicians shifted positions on busing in the House that when combined with southerners they constituted a new antibusing majority. Two examples are James G. O'Hara, a Democrat from Michigan, and Roman C. Pucinski, a Democrat from Illinois. See *Congressional Quarterly Almanac*, 1971, 110–11; Wilkinson, *From Brown to Bakke*, 218–19.

72. *Congressional Record*, 92nd Cong., 2nd sess., 18 February 1972, 4608–16; Marjorie Hunter, "Nixon's Plan Splits Rivals; Ervin Asks End to Busing," *New York Times*, 18 March 1972; Paul Clancy, "Nixon May Back Amendment If Busing Bills Fail," *Charlotte Observer*, 4 April 1972; Memorandum, John D. Ehrlichman to the President, 30 May 1972, Ehrlichman Files, Alphabetical Subject File, Box 26, WHSF, NPMS. As Ervin left the Senate, he was still trying to pass a bill or amendment to end school busing. See Ervin to Dear Colleague, 2 May 1974, Ervin Papers, Box 387, Folder 45.

73. *Congressional Record*, 92nd Cong., 2nd sess., 21 January 1972, 700–703; *Congressional Record*, 92nd Cong., 2nd sess., 24 January 1972, 929–33, 941–42; Graham, *Civil Rights Era*, 420–49; Hoff, *Nixon Reconsidered*, 93–94. Ervin had long opposed giving any enforcement power to the EEOC. The Nixon administration engaged in a protracted internal debate before deciding to favor the court-enforced approach over granting the EEOC cease-and-desist powers. See John Dean to Richard G. Kleindienst, [n.d.] 1969, Dean Files, Subject files, Box 33, WHSF, NPMS.

74. Graham, *Civil Rights Era*, 440. Ervin discussed his rise to a position of leadership in the southern caucus during an interview in 1971: "[Richard Russell] always headed up our opposition to laws of this kind, and since he's gone, I've had to try on some occasions to try to substitute for him." Ervin Oral History Interview, by Hugh Cates, 28 April 1971, Oral History Interview no. 65, Richard Russell Library. See also Jack Spain Oral History Interview, by Hugh Cates, 28 April 1971, Oral History Interview 148, Richard Russell Library.

75. Ehrlichman, Notes of Meetings with the President, 22 December 1969, Ehrlichman Files, Box 3, WHSF, NPMS; Ehrlichman's quote is cited in Parmet, *Richard Nixon and His America*, 600. Nixon's consistency is defended in Hoff, *Nixon Reconsidered*, 90–94. Nixon's political motives are stressed in Graham, *Civil Rights Era*, 325, 340.

76. U.S. Congress, Senate, Committee on the Judiciary, *The Philadelphia Plan: Congressional Oversight of Administrative Agencies*, Hearings before the Subcommittee on Separations of Powers, 91st Cong., 1st sess., 1969 (hereafter cited as Philadelphia Plan Hearings, 1969); Subcommittee on Separation of Powers Press Release, "Senate Report Condemns Philadelphia Plan," 26 April 1971, Ervin Papers, Box 56, Folder 545; Ervin Press

Release, "Ervin Calls for Abolition of Minority Hiring Quotas," 8 September 1972, Ervin Papers, Box 457, Folder 674.

77. Philadelphia Plan Hearings, 1969, 1–5, 100–111; Subcommittee on Separation of Powers Press Release, "Senate Report Condemns Philadelphia Plan," 26 April 1971, Ervin Papers, Box 56, Folder 545; Larry Cheek, "Sen. Sam Almost Blocked Nixon's Philadelphia Plan," *Greensboro Daily News*, 28 December 1969, Ervin Papers, Box 470; William Chapman, "Ervin Assails Plan on Minority Hiring," *Washington Post*, 28 October 1969; John Herbers, "Nixon Aides Explain the Goal of Job Plan," *New York Times*, 29 October 1969.

78. Ehrlichman, Notes of Meetings with the President, 22 November 1969, Ehrlichman Files, Box 3, WHSF, NPMS; *Congressional Record*, 91st Cong., 1st sess., 18 December 1969, 39948–49, 39973. Both Ervin and Comptroller General Elmer R. Staats had written to Robert Byrd urging that he introduce the rider to a minor supplemental appropriation in the Senate Appropriations Committee, which he did on 15 December 1969. See Elmer Staats to Robert Byrd, 2 December 1969, Ervin Papers, Box 407, Folder 440. See also Graham, *Civil Rights Era*, 322–45.

79. Ervin described his constitutional theory of limited government in his opening statement during the first public hearings of the Separation of Powers Subcommittee. See U.S. Congress, Senate, Committee on the Judiciary, *Separation of Powers*, Hearings before the Separation of Powers Subcommittee, 90th Cong., 1st sess., 1967, 1–3 (hereafter cited as Separation of Powers Hearings, 1967). See also Clifford Kenneth Van Sickle, "The Oral Communication of Senator Sam Ervin: A Study in Consistency" (Ph.D. dissertation, Department of Speech, Michigan State University, 1976).

80. Bill Graves, "Senator Ervin Will Introduce Measure To Probe Congress 'Encroachments,'" *Winston-Salem Journal*, 19 May 1956, Ervin Notebooks, s-3; "Senator Sam Ervin Says," Weekly Newspaper Column, no. 72, 24 May 1956, Ervin Papers, Box 449.

81. Ervin to Edmond W. Price, 25 September 1957, Ervin Papers, Box 26, Folder 220; Wilber M. Brucker to Ervin, 4 October 1957, Ervin Papers, Box 26, Folder 220; Ervin Press Release, "Excerpts from Jefferson-Jackson Day Speech at Little Rock, Arkansas," 29 March 1958, Ervin Papers, Box 453; Ervin television interview transcript, "Capital Cloakroom," CBS, 9 March 1956, Ervin Papers, Box 392, Folder 159; "Administration 'Covering Up' Ervin Says," *Charlotte Observer*, 17 February 1956; U.S. Congress, Senate, Committee on the Judiciary, *Executive Privilege and Freedom of Information*, Hearings before the Subcommittee on Constitutional Rights, 86th Cong., 1st sess., 1959. In spite of Ervin's interest in the question of separation of powers, he only attended four out of twenty-six meetings between December 1959 and December 1967 of the Advisory Commission on Intergovernment Relations on which he served as the Senate's representative. See Farris Bryant to John Macy, 26 December 1967, WHCF, Ervin Name File, LBJL.

82. Ervin to John F. Kennedy, 24 September 1962, FE 4-1, Box 100, Folder "Pres. Powers," WHCF, John F. Kennedy Presidential Library (JFKL), Boston; Ervin, "Freedom in Peril," Remarks prepared for the Tennessee Bar Association, Johnson City, Tennessee, 24 January 1964, Ervin Papers, Box 391, Folder 126; Richard Russell, John Stennis, and Sam Ervin to Lyndon B. Johnson, 2 May 1966, HU, Box 50, Folder "HU 2-55-4-66," WHCF, LBJL.

83. Roy Parker Jr., "Sen. Ervin Heads Constitution Study," *Raleigh News and Observer*, 1 December 1966, Ervin Notebooks, s-12; "Still Human Nature," *Charlotte News*, 2 Decem-

ber 1966; John R. Schmidhauser and Larry L. Berg, *The Supreme Court and Congress: Conflict and Interaction, 1945–1968* (New York: Free Press, 1972). One scholar believes that the formation of the Separation of Powers Subcommittee was directly related to Ervin's crusade against the nomination of Justice Abe Fortas. See Alpheus T. Mason, "Pyrrhic Victory: The Defeat of Abe Fortas," *Virginia Quarterly* 45 (Winter 1968): 20–23.

84. Paul Woodward is quoted in Clancy, *Just a Country Lawyer*, 248; James K. Batten, "Sen. Ervin May Be Shaping History Without Fanfare," *Charlotte Observer*, 2 October 1966, Ervin Notebooks, s-12.

85. Ervin's opening statement, Separation of Powers Hearings, 1967. U.S. Congress, Senate, Committee on the Judiciary, *The Supreme Court*, Hearings before the Subcommittee on Separation of Powers, 90th Cong., 2nd sess., 1968; U.S. Congress, Senate, Committee on the Judiciary, *Federal Constitutional Convention*, Hearings before the Subcommittee on Separation of Powers, 90th Cong., 1st sess., 1967; U.S. Congress, Senate, Committee on the Judiciary, *Congressional Oversight of Administrative Agencies (National Labor Relations Board)*, 90th Cong., 2nd sess., 1968. See also Memorandum, Separation of Powers Subcommittee, "Suggested Long-term Goals," [n.d.], Ervin Papers, Box 406, Folder 418; Ervin to James O. Eastland, 16 January 1969, Ervin Papers, Box 405, Folder 408; "Congress May Reach for Lost Initiative," *Christian Science Monitor*, 17 January 1968; Philip Kurland, "The Court Should Decide Less and Explain More," *New York Times Magazine*, 9 June 1968. Kurland served as a consultant to the subcommittee along with Alexander Bickel, Robert McCloskey, and Arthur S. Miller.

86. U.S. Congress, Senate, Committee on the Judiciary, *Report* of the Separation of Powers Subcommittee, 92nd Cong., 2nd sess., 1972, 4–5 (hereafter cited as Separation of Powers Report, 1972); Arthur M. Schlesinger Jr., *The Imperial Presidency* (Boston: Houghton Mifflin, 1973), 342–45, 400.

87. Ervin was joined by Senators Ralph W. Yarborough of Texas and Edward M. Kennedy of Massachusetts at the press conference. See Eric Redman, *The Dance of Legislation* (New York: Simon and Schuster, 1973), 273–80; Fred Graham, "Nixon Accused of Misusing 'Pocket Veto Power,'" *New York Times*, 31 December 1970.

88. U.S. Congress, Senate, Committee on the Judiciary, *Constitutionality of the President's "Pocket Veto" Power*, Hearings before the Subcommittee on Separation of Powers, 92nd Cong., 1st sess., 1971; Ervin, "Latest Presidential Use of Pocket Veto Violates the Separation of Powers Doctrine," draft of remarks, [n.d.] 1971, Ervin Papers, Box 411, Folder 512; Larry Cheek, "Nixon Veto of Health Bill Riled Ervin and Preyer," *Greensboro Daily News*, 10 January 1971, Ervin Papers, Box 470; "Ervin Spells Out Pocket Veto," *Morganton News Herald*, 26 April 1971, Ervin Papers, Box 470; Ken W. Clawson, "Justice Department Cites Pocket Veto Precedents," *Washington Post*, 1 January 1971; James M. Naughton, "Kennedy and Ervin Planning a Test in Supreme Court of President's Pocket Veto Powers," *New York Times*, 27 January 1971. See also Arthur S. Miller, "Congressional Power to Define the Presidential Pocket Veto Power," *Vanderbilt Law Review* 25 (March 1972): 557–72.

89. Separation of Powers Subcommittee Report, 1972, 5–6; "'Impounded' Cash Listed by Ervin," *Charlotte Observer*, 19 March 1971, Ervin Papers, Box 470; Schlesinger, *Imperial Presidency*, 225–40, 397–400; Kutler, *Wars of Watergate*, 133–37; Hoff, *Nixon Reconsidered*, 24–27; Louis Fisher, "Presidential Spending Discretion and Congressional Controls," *Law and*

Contemporary Problems 37 (Winter 1972): 135–72. One legal scholar concluded: "There is no basis for a general impounding power, by express terms or by implication, either in the Constitution or in any general statute." See Warren J. Archer, "Presidential Impounding of Funds: The Judicial Response," *University of Chicago Law Review* 40 (Winter 1973): 328–56.

90. Subcommittee on Separation of Powers Press Release, 18 March 1971, Ervin Papers, Box 404; Schlesinger, *Imperial Presidency*, 237–40.

91. Subcommittee on Separation of Powers Press Release, 18 March 1971, Ervin Papers, Box 404; U.S. Congress, Senate, Committee on the Judiciary, *Executive Impoundment of Appropriated Funds*, Hearings before the Subcommittee on Separation of Powers, 92nd Cong., 1st sess., 1971; *Congressional Record*, 92nd Cong., 1st sess., 23 April 1971, 11702–3; James J. Kilpatrick, "The President vs. The Congress: Fund Impounding Raises Eternal Question of Power," *Raleigh News and Observer*, 4 April 1971, Ervin Papers, Box 470; Spencer Rich, "Nixon's $12 Billion Freeze Angers Key Hill Democrats," *Washington Post*, 5 April 1971; "Ervin Challenges Nixon on Funds," *New York Times*, 24 March 1971. Joan Hoff suggests that Nixon's critics were motivated by partisan political interests, but Stanley Kutler describes Ervin's actions against impoundment as "a rare outburst of principled concern." See Hoff, *Nixon Reconsidered*, 25–27; Kutler, *Wars of Watergate*, 136.

92. Memorandum, Subcommittee on Constitutional Rights, "Suggested Long-Term Goals," [n.d.] 1967, Ervin Papers, Box 406, Folder 418; Subcommittee on Separation of Powers Press Release, "Ervin Sets Hearings on Executive Privilege," 23 June 1971, Box 9, Papers of the Subcommittee on Separation of Powers, Senate Committee on the Judiciary, Records of the U.S. Senate, Record Group 46, National Archives, Washington, D.C. (hereafter cited as Papers of the Subcommittee on Separation of Powers). On executive privilege, see Ervin, "Controlling 'Executive Privilege,'" *Loyola Law Review* 20 (1974): 11–32; Luis Kutner, "Executive Privilege . . . Growth of Power over a Declining Congress," *Loyola Law Review* 20 (1974): 33–44; Schlesinger, *Imperial Presidency*, 246–53; Raoul Berger, *Executive Privilege: A Constitutional Myth* (Cambridge, Mass.: Harvard University Press, 1974); and Mark J. Rozell, "Executive Privilege: A Bibliographic Essay," *Law and Politics* 4 (Winter 1988): 639–51.

93. Memorandum, Richard Nixon to The Heads of Executive Departments and Agencies, 24 March 1969, Papers of the Subcommittee on Separation of Powers, Box 8; testimony of William H. Rehnquist, U.S. Congress, Senate, Committee on the Judiciary, *Executive Privilege: The Withholding of Information by the Executive*, Hearings before the Subcommittee on Separation of Powers, 92nd Cong., 1st sess., 1971 (hereafter cited as Executive Privilege Hearings, 1971), 420–43. For a thorough review of the testimony in Ervin's 1971 Executive Privilege Hearings, see Philip B. Kurland, *Watergate and the Constitution* (Chicago: University of Chicago Press, 1978), 37–42. Ervin's definition came in his opening statement, Executive Privilege Hearings, 1971, 1. At the beginning of Nixon's second term, the administration claimed that it had only evoked executive privilege "on three occasions in the past four years." See John W. Dean III to Michael Mansfield, 25 January 1973, Ervin Papers, Box 399, Folder 274. Ervin, however, cited a study by the Subcommittee on Separation of Powers that turned up more than one hundred incidents in which information requested by Congress had been denied. See Ervin, "Executive Privilege: The Need for Congressional Action," address before the Illinois State Bar Association, Chicago, 15 June 1973, Ervin Papers, Box 399, Folder 275.

94. Ervin, opening statement, Executive Privilege Hearings, 1971, 1, 7; Ervin to Edward J. Gurney, 22 June 1971, Papers of the Subcommittee on Separation of Powers, Box 12; Murrey Marder, "Senators Accuse the Executive Branch of Contempt for Hill," *Washington Post*, 28 July 1971; Marjorie Hunter, "President v. Congress, Nixon's Refusal to Furnish Data Deepens Constitutional Struggle," *New York Times*, 3 September 1971. The bill proposed by Senator Fulbright caused an intense internal debate within the subcommittee staff. See Memorandum, to Rufus [Edmisten], from Irene, 19 October 1971, Papers of the Subcommittee on Separation of Powers, Box 11, Raoul Berger to Ervin, 27 April 1972, Papers of the Subcommittee on Separation of Powers, Box 11.

95. Memorandum, Tod R. Hullin to Bob Haldeman, "Senator Ervin's Hearings on the Daniel Schorr Incident," 17 January 1971, Ex FG 36-12, box 21, WHCF, NPMS; H. R. Haldeman's Handwritten Notes of Meetings with the President, H. R. Haldeman Files, Box 45, 12 April 1972, and 17 April 1972, Box 45, WHSF, NPMS (hereafter cited as Haldeman Notes); Ervin to Raoul Berger, 6 June 1972, Subcommittee on Separation of Powers Papers, Box 11.

96. Ervin's opening statement, Executive Privilege Hearings, 1971, 3; Ervin, "Secrecy in a Free Society," *Nation*, 8 November 1971, 455.

97. Memorandum, Charles Tom Huston to H. R. Haldeman, 15 September 1970, Dean Files, Subject Files, Box 70, Folder "SACB," WHSF, NPMS; Executive Order 11605, issued 2 July 1971, Ervin Papers, Box 413, Folder 551; "Executive Order 11605," *Washington Post*, 17 July 1971; "Nothing to Do," *New York Times*, 25 July 1971.

98. Clancy, *Just a Country Lawyer*, 225; "'Inherent Powers' and Presidential Government," *Washington Post*, 3 August 1971; U.S. Congress, Senate, Committee on the Judiciary, *President Nixon's Executive Order 11605 Relating to the Subversive Activities Control Board*, Hearings before the Subcommittee on Separation of Powers, 92nd Cong., 1st sess., 1971; "Subversive Board Funds Ban Proposed," *Winston-Salem Journal*, 17 July 1971, Ervin Papers, Box 470; Dana Adams Schmidt, "Ervin Denounces Nixon Revival of Subversives Board," *New York Times*, 6 October 1971. Ervin introduced a bill to make it unlawful for any employee of the Department of Justice or the SACB to carry out Nixon's executive order. He also proposed a resolution to express the will of the Senate that the executive order represented an unconstitutional attempt to usurp the legislative power of Congress. After a year of political wrangling, Congress agreed in 1972 to withhold any funds necessary for the Board to carry out Nixon's executive order. See Schlesinger, *Imperial Presidency*, 245–46.

99. *Congressional Record*, 92nd Cong., 1st sess., 20 September 1971, 32445–63; *Gravel v. U.S.* 408 US 606, 1972; Ervin's brief can be found in Ervin to "Colleague," 10 April 1972, Papers of the Subcommittee on Constitutional Rights, Box 13A, Records of the U.S. Senate, Record Group 46, National Archives, Washington D.C. (hereafter cited as Papers of the Subcommittee on Constitutional Rights). Ervin's legislation is discussed in Ervin to Henry M. Jackson, 14 March 1973, Papers of the Subcommittee on Constitutional Rights, Box 13A; and Mike Gravel to Ervin, 24 March 1972, Papers of the Subcommittee on Constitutional Rights, Box 13A. See also Ervin, "The Freedom to Speak," *New York Times*, 3 October 1971; Ervin, "The Gravel and Brewster Cases: An Assault on Congressional Independence," *Virginia Law Review* 59 (February 1973): 175–95; Robert J. Reinstein and Harvey A. Silverglate, "Legislative Privilege and the Separation of Powers," *Harvard Law*

Review 86 (May 1973): 1113–82; Henry Steele Commager, "A Senator's Immunity," *New York Times*, 15 October 1971; Larry Cheek, "Ervin an Exception to His Own Words: He Defends Gravel in Court," *Greensboro Daily News*, 20 April 1972, Ervin Papers, Box 470; Marquis Childs, "Sam Ervin: Constitutionalist," *Washington Post*, 18 April 1972. The legislative immunity is explicitly stated in Article I, Section 6, of the Constitution, which provides that "for any Speech or Debate in either House, they shall not be questioned in any other Place."

100. U.S. Congress, Senate, Committee on the Judiciary, *Congressional Oversight of Executive Agreements*, Hearings before the Separation of Powers Subcommittee, 92nd Cong., 2nd sess., 1972; Bill Connelly, "Ervin to Challenge President's Power," *Winston-Salem Journal*, 6 January 1972, Ervin Papers, Box 470; "Congress Urged to Curb Use of Executive Accords," *New York Times*, 25 April 1972. Ervin's bill would have provided for congressional review of all international agreements and empowered Congress to nullify any agreement within sixty days by concurrent resolution of both the House and Senate. If not disapproved, the executive agreement would stand.

101. Schlesinger, *Imperial Presidency*, 392. Philip Kurland coined a similar name for the Nixon administration's controversial conclusions about its "inherent" constitutional powers—"the Plebiscitary Presidency." See Kurland, *Watergate and the Constitution*, 200–224. Stephen Ambrose, however, calls such historians "double-standard spokesmen," charging that they "idolized a strong Presidency when FDR, Harry Truman, and John F. Kennedy occupied the White House, but viciously turned against it when the strong President was Dick Nixon." Ambrose, though, does agree that "had there never been a Watergate, there still would have been a war between Nixon and Congress." He adds, "Most Americans recalled the epic battle between Nixon and the Congress as one that revolved solely around Watergate. But in fact both sides had drawn their troops up in a battle line, established their strategy, and geared themselves for war *before* almost anything was known about Watergate beyond the bare fact of the break-in" (emphasis in the original). See Stephen E. Ambrose, *Nixon*, vol. 3: *Ruin and Recovery, 1973–1990* (New York: Simon and Schuster, 1991), 60–61.

102. Joseph P. Fried, "Allen J. Ellender of Louisiana Dies," *New York Times*, 28 July 1972; Clancy, *Just a Country Lawyer*, 253–54. Ellender had been the chairman of the Appropriations Committee. In order for John McClellan to take over that position, he had to give up his leadership of Government Operations since a senator can only hold one chairmanship of a full committee at a time. Henry Jackson was next in line for Government Operations, but he did not want to surrender his chairmanship of the Interior Committee. Ervin was the third ranking Democrat on Government Operations, so he inherited the chair.

103. Editorial, *Washington Post*, 24 August 1972; U.S. Congress, Senate, *Impoundment of Appropriated Funds by the President*, Hearings before the Ad Hoc Subcommittee on Impoundment of Funds of the Committee on Government Operations and the Subcommittee on Separation of Powers of the Committee on the Judiciary, 93rd Cong., 1st sess., 1973; Tom Wicker, "Impounding and Implying," *New York Times*, 8 February 1973; "The Impoundment Battle," *Washington Post*, 6 February 1973; U.S. Congress, Senate, *Executive Privilege, Secrecy in Government, Freedom of Information*, Hearings before the Subcommittee on Intergovernmental Relations on the Committee on Government Operations and the Subcommittees on Separation of Powers and Administrative Practice and Pro-

cedure of the Committee on the Judiciary, 93rd Cong., 1st sess., 1973, Vols. 1–3; Arthur S. Miller, "The New Constitutional Crisis," *Progressive* (March 1973): 15–18; James M. Naughton, "Ervin Assuming Leadership in Effort to Reassert the Authority of Congress," *New York Times*, 4 February 1973.

104. Ehrlichman's Notes, 8 January 1973, Ehrlichman Files, Box 14, NPMS; Ehrlichman's notes of a meeting with the President and Vice President, [n.d.] 1973, Ehrlichman Files, Speech and Briefing Files, Box 68, WHSF, NPMS.

105. Memorandum, from John Ehrlichman, "The New Minority," [n.d.] 1973, Ehrlichman Files, Speech and Briefing Files, Box 68, WHSF, NPMS; Memorandum, Bill Baroody Jr. to Roy L. Ash et al., "Overall Strategy—Battle of the Budget," 8 March 1973, Ehrlichman Files, Speech and Briefing Files, Box 68, WHSF, NPMS; "Press Conference of John Ehrlichman," 9 March 1973, 12:40 pm, Ehrlichman Files, Speech and Briefing Files, Box 68, WHSF, NPMS; John D. Ehrlichman to Charles Percy, 12 January 1973, Ervin Papers, Box 399, Folder 274.

106. U.S. Congress, Senate, the Select Committee on Presidential Campaign Activities, *Hearings*, 93rd Cong., 1st and 2nd sess., 1973, 1974; James J. Kilpatrick, "Sam Ervin, a Founding Father," *Winston-Salem Journal*, 29 May 1970, is the first reference to Ervin as a "founding father."

CHAPTER NINE

1. Christopher H. Pyle, "CONUS Intelligence: The Army Watches Civilian Politics," *Washington Monthly*, January 1970, 4; reproduced in *Congressional Record*, 91st Cong., 2nd sess., 1970, 2227–31. Pyle remains the leading authority on the military domestic intelligence system of the 1960s, and this chapter leans heavily on his pathbreaking research. After serving as a special adviser to the Subcommittee on Constitutional Rights during Ervin's hearings in 1971, he earned his Ph.D. in political science from Columbia University with "Military Surveillance of Civilian Politics, 1967–1970" (Ph.D. diss., Columbia University, 1974; Ann Arbor, Mich.: University Microfilms, 1974). He also published an extensive article on the topic, "Military Intelligence Overkill," in *Uncle Sam Is Watching You: Highlights from the Hearings of the Subcommittee on Constitutional Rights*, ed. Alan Barth (Washington, D.C.: Public Affairs Press, 1971).

2. Pyle, "CONUS Intelligence," 5–6. The Army's domestic intelligence system was actually an ill-defined collection of information-gathering agencies under several different titles. Some agencies did not even know they were duplicating the activities of other military intelligence units. For the sake of clarity I shall call the system "CONUS" (Continental U.S.). For more information on the breakdown of the various agencies see any of the above mentioned articles by Pyle, or Frank J. Donner, *The Age of Surveillance: The Aims and Methods of America's Political Intelligence System* (New York: Vintage Books, 1981), 293–309.

3. Ibid.

4. Ibid., 7, 16.

5. Typical was the North Carolinian who wrote to Ervin: "I hope you will investigate this situation and bring the power of the Senate to act to protect the citizens of this nation from further encroachment of their rights." *Congressional Record*, 91st Cong., 2nd sess., 1970, 2226. See U.S. Congress, Senate, Committee on the Judiciary, *Military Surveillance of*

Civilian Politics, a report of the Subcommittee on Constitutional Rights, 93rd Cong., 1st sess., 1973, 2 (hereafter cited as Military Surveillance Report, 1973).

6. Ervin to Stanley R. Resor, 22 January 1970, Sam J. Ervin Papers, Subgroup A: Senate Papers, 3847A, Southern Historical Collection, Wilson Library, University of North Carolina at Chapel Hill (hereafter cited as Ervin Papers), box 408, folder 458. This letter and additional correspondence between the senator and the Departments of Defense and Justice concerning military surveillance may also be found in *Congressional Record*, 91st Cong., 2nd sess., 1970, 26333–26350; and in U.S. Congress, Senate, Committee on the Judiciary, *Federal Data Banks, Computers, and the Bill of Rights*, Hearings before the Subcommittee on Constitutional Rights, Part II, Documentary Analysis, 92nd Cong., 1st sess., 1971 (hereafter cited as Documentary Analysis). *Congressional Record*, 91st Cong., 2nd sess., 1970, 2227.

7. Christopher H. Pyle, "CONUS Revisited: The Army Covers Up," *Washington Monthly* 2 (July 1970): 50. Pyle combined this article with his January article to form the basis of his testimony before the committee's hearings in 1971 (hereafter cited as Pyle Testimony). See U.S. Congress, Senate, Committee on the Judiciary, *Federal Data Banks, Computers, and the Bill of Rights*, Hearings before the Subcommittee on Constitutional Rights, Part I, 92nd Cong., 1st sess., 1971 (hereafter cited as Ervin Hearings, 1971); Military Surveillance Report, 1973, 98; *Laird v. Tatum*, 408 U.S. 1 (1972); Donner, *Age of Surveillance*, 317; Edward Sohier, Testimony before the Subcommittee on Constitutional Rights, 24 February 1971, Ervin Hearings, 1971, 278–79. Sohier's testimony, along with sections of other ex-intelligence agents' testimony, appears in Barth, *Uncle Sam Is Watching You*.

8. Military Surveillance Report, 1973, 99, 100; Donner, *Age of Surveillance*, note 78, 508; Joseph Hanlon, "Army Drops Data Banks but Keeps Data Banks," *Computerworld*, 11 March 1970, Documentary Analysis, 1646.

9. Robert Jordan to Ervin, 25 February 1970, Ervin Papers, box 408, folder 458.

10. Robert Jordan to Ervin, 25 February 1970, Ervin Papers, box 408, folder 548; and discussed in Morton Kondracke, "Civilian Data Banks Continue, Despite Army Disavowal," *Chicago Sun-Times*, 27 February 1970. In spite of Ervin's growing concern about all of the Nixon administration's domestic surveillance practices, he did not believe the Republicans had expanded the Army's domestic intelligence system. When Edwin Newman of NBC News asked him: "Has it made much difference over the years which administration is in office?" Ervin answered, "No, I don't think that it has. As a rule, as far as the military is concerned, it stays about the same." NBC News, "Speaking Freely," filmed 8 December 1970, Ervin Papers, box 41, folder 518.

11. "U.S to Tighten Its Surveillance of Left-Wing Groups and Individuals in an Effort to Prevent Violence," *New York Times*, 12 April 1970, 1, 69; Memorandum, "Bombing and Arson Attacks in the United States," [n.d.], H. R. Haldeman Files, Office and Memo Files, Box 70, folder "Brown Follow-up," Richard Nixon Presidential Materials Project, Nixon Presidential Materials Staff (NPMS), National Archives, College Park, Maryland (hereafter cited as Haldeman Files).

12. Jared Stout, "Mitchell Defends Justice Department's Big Brother Role," Newhouse News Services, in *Staten Island Advance*, 19 July 1970, Documentary Analysis, 1660. This claim echoed the administration's argument for wiretapping before the Chicago 7 trial one year earlier. See Pyle, "Military Surveillance" (diss.), 217. Nixon expanded the ques-

tionable wiretapping policies practiced by previous administrations to a new level of disregard for the law. See Kutler, *Wars of Watergate*, 123–25; Theoharis, *Spying on Americans*, 192–95.

13. The Lynch policy statement was released to the Army on 9 June 1970. Ervin received a copy in a letter from Thaddeus R. Beal, 23 June 1970, Ervin Papers, box 411, folder 570; *Congressional Record*, 91st Cong., 2nd sess., 29 July 1970, 26327; Ervin to Stanley R. Resor, 27 July 1970, Ervin Papers, box 408, folder 458.

14. Lynch's policy statement was included in Thaddeus R. Beal to Ervin, 23 June 1970, Ervin Papers, box 411, folder 570.

15. The development of the Huston Plan is thoroughly described in Theoharis, *Spying on Americans*, 13–39. The text of the Huston Plan is in Tyrus G. Fain et al., eds., *The Intelligence Community: History, Organization, and Issues* (New York: Bowker, 1977), 817–66.

16. Kutler, *Wars of Watergate*, 97.

17. Ibid., 34. Hoover had opposed the Huston Plan from the start, attaching footnotes to the official memorandum of 23 July that basically killed the plan before it began. Hoover then met with the attorney general and followed this meeting with another memorandum dated 27 July 1970 that finally forced Nixon to rescind the plan. Theoharis, *Spying on Americans*, 28–34.

18. Kutler, *Wars of Watergate*, 101–3. Stanley Kutler has written that "the Huston Plan was only one corner of a more general design for dealing with political enemies of all kinds."

19. During Watergate Ervin described Huston and his plan with harsh language: "Whenever you start . . . to set up methods of spying on American citizens and having them more or less supervised by the White House, to my mind it exhibits . . . a gestapo mentality." Ervin interview, n.d., by Paul R. Clancy, tape 8, side 1, Ervin Papers.

20. *Congressional Record*, 91st Cong., 2nd sess., 1970, 26321.

21. Ibid.; Samuel J. Ervin Jr., *Preserving the Constitution* (Charlottesville, Va.: Michie, 1984), 89.

22. Interview with Rufus Edmisten, 25 February 1986, by the author; Clancy, *Just a Country Lawyer*, 1–17.

23. Ibid.

24. Telephone interview with Lawrence Baskir, 11 March 1986, by the author.

25. For more on the constitutional concept of a "chilling effect," see Frank Askin, "Surveillance: The Social Science Perspective," in Staff of the Columbia Human Rights Law Review Symposium, ed., *Surveillance, Dataveillance, and Personal Freedom* (Fair Lawn, N.J.: R. E. Burdick, 1973), 69–98. For a legal analysis of the chilling effect doctrine, see "Notes: The Chilling Effect in Constitutional Law," *Columbia Law Review* 69 (1969): 808–42.

26. *Laird v. Tatum et al.*, 444 F.2d 947 (D.C. Cir.); Pyle Testimony, Ervin Hearings, 1971, 213. The story was carried in numerous newspapers, including the following that may be found in Documentary Analysis, 1654–57: "Army Check on Civilians is Upheld," *Washington Post*, 23 April 1970; Morton Kondracke, "Dismiss Suit on Army Civilian Data File," *Chicago Sun-Times*, 23 April 1970; "Judge Dismisses Suit to Bar Army's Civilian Surveillance," *Washington Evening Star*, 22 April 1970.

27. Robert Gruenberg, *Chicago Daily News*, 18 December 1970, Documentary Analysis, 1719–20; President's Office Files, Annotated News Summaries, Box 32, 17 December 1970, NPMS.

28. For Mitchell's claim see Jared Stout, "Mitchell Defends Justice Department's Big Brother Role," Newhouse News Service, 19 July 1970, Documentary Analysis, 1971, 1660; Pyle, "Military Surveillance" (diss.), 217. One example of this consolidation was the new InterDivisional Information Unit. This agency provided a computer link-up of all federal law enforcement programs. Once again national security considerations outweighed concern for civil liberties. When the chief of the new agency was asked by reporters if it would threaten civil liberties, he confessed that no guidelines had been incorporated to protect privacy but he promised, "It's not a register of 'good guys' and 'bad guys.' . . . It's simply a list of who participated in demonstrations, rallies, and the like." Jared Stout, "Police Tool or Dangerous Weapon?," *Staten Island Advance*, 15 November 1970, Documentary Analysis, 1805. See also John MacKenzie, "FBI Awarded Control of Crime Bank," *Washington Post*, 17 December 1970.

29. "Justice to Beef Up Internal Security Division," *Human Events*, 30 January 1970, 5; *National Review*, 25 August 1970, 875. Father Berrigan and the nuns were found not guilty later that year. For information on the indictment, see *Human Events*, 23 January 1971, 4.

30. *National Review*, 12 April 1970, 400; Francis J. McNamara, "Putting Army Spying in Perspective," *Human Events*, 30 January 1971, 9; "When Called On to Preserve Peace You Must Know Who Threatens It," *Army*, February 1971, 7.

31. Department of Defense Press Release, 23 December 1970, Ervin Papers, box 408, folder 461.

32. Pyle, "Military Surveillance" (diss.), 294–301; Pyle Testimony, Ervin Hearings, 1971, 202–4; Christopher Pyle, "Military Surveillance of Civilian Politics," unpublished manuscript, 29–30.

33. *Congressional Record*, 92nd Cong., 1st sess., 1971, 2024.

34. Theoharis, *Spying on Americans*, 88.

35. The description of the Old Senate Caucus Chamber is from Pyle, "Military Surveillance" (unpublished ms.), 1; and Samuel Dash, *Chief Counsel: Inside the Ervin Committee—The Untold Story of Watergate* (New York: Random House, 1976), 125–26.

36. This description of Ervin comes from a telephone interview with Marcia Mc-Naughton, staff member on the Subcommittee on Constitutional Rights, 9 March 1986, by the author.

37. Ervin's opening statement, Ervin Hearings, 1971, 1.

38. Ibid., 2.

39. Ibid., 7.

40. On Ervin's use of hearings see Lawrence Leamer, "The Sam Ervin Show," *Harper's Magazine* (March 1972): 80–86; Tom Wicker, "The Watergate Committee Chairman's New Clothes," *Southern Voices*, March–April 1974, 7–8; Gladys Engel Lang and Kurt Lang, *The Battle for Public Opinion: The President, the Press and the Polls During Watergate* (New York: Columbia University Press, 1983).

41. *Charlotte Observer*, 5 January 1971, Documentary Analysis, 1948; "Army Doesn't Think So: Ex-GI Says Local Spy Duty on Civilian Group Ordered," *Colorado Springs Gazette-Telegraph*, 3 May 1970, Documentary Analysis, 1657; Michael J. Satchell, *Kansas*

City Times, 22 January 1971, Documentary Analysis, 1747–51. The retired military officers named were Rear Adm. Arnold E. True and Brig. Gen. Hugh B. Hester.

42. Pyle, "Military Surveillance" (unpublished ms.), 5; Jared Stout, "Keeping Tabs on Civilians," *Nation*, 28 December 1970, 681–83; Pyle Testimony, Ervin Hearings, 1971, 198–200; *Congressional Record*, 91st Cong., 2nd sess., 1970, 41751–52; "Army Net to Spy on War Foes Reported," *Washington Star*, 3 December 1970, Documentary Analysis, 1769; and Persons of Interest, *Life*, 26 March 1971, 21–27. Much of the credit for the press coverage of the Army spy scandal belongs to Christopher Pyle. It was Pyle who contacted NBC, which paid him $3,500 for his services. Pyle, "Military Surveillance" (unpublished ms.), 5. Pyle later explained that he followed a three-prong strategy to uncover the full workings of the CONUS system, including Ervin's subcommittee investigation, the ACLU's court case *Laird v. Tatum*, and the investigations and reporting of the press. See Joan M. Jensen, *Army Surveillance in America* (New Haven: Yale University Press, 1991), 250.

43. Ibid., 14, 21.

44. The atmosphere in the hearing room was described in the *Greensboro Daily News*, 3 March 1971, Ervin Papers, box 470.

45. Ervin Hearings, 1971, 372–74.

46. Ervin Hearings, 1971, 374–75; interview with Baskir by the author, 11 March 1986. The Kerner Commission had suggested the need for "adequate intelligence," and it recommended improving police information gathering systems, but it said nothing about military intelligence. See *The Kerner Report* (New York: Bantam Books, 1968), 487.

47. Ervin was especially critical of the Johnson administration for its lack of concern for privacy in civil rights legislation and the National Data Center proposal. For a brief review of Ervin's frequent attacks on Johnson, as well as other recent presidents, see U.S. Congress, Senate, Committee on the Judiciary, *Federal Data Banks and Constitutional Rights: Summary and Conclusions*, a report of the Subcommittee on Constitutional Rights, 93rd Cong., 2nd sess., 1974, 7–25 (hereafter cited as Report, 1974).

48. Baskir, interview by author, 11 March 1986.

49. "Ervin Views Army Spying as Illegal," *Washington Post*, 3 March 1971.

50. These rumors were reported by Richard Halloran, "Senate Panel Holds Vast 'Subversives' File Amassed by Ex-Chief of Army Intelligence," *New York Times*, 7 September 1971.

51. Ervin Hearings, 1971, 160.

52. Pyle, "Military Surveillance" (unpublished ms.), 12; Halloran, *New York Times*, 7 September 1971.

53. Pyle, "Military Surveillance" (unpublished ms.), 13.

54. See Froehlke's prepared statement, Ervin Hearings, 1971, 375–410; "Keeping Tabs on Civilians," *Nation*, 28 December 1970, 681–83; Jared Stout, "Military Agents Had Secret Role at 1968 Conventions," Newhouse News Service, 2 December 1970, Documentary Analysis, 1761.

55. "Johnson and Clark Linked to Surveillance Planning," *New York Times*, 17 April 1971. During his confirmation hearings to become President Clinton's secretary of state in 1993, Warren Christopher had to answer questions raised after investigators found a military domestic intelligence report from 1968 that carried his handwritten initials.

Christopher had served as Johnson's deputy attorney general. *Los Angeles Times*, 12 January 1993; *New York Times*, 12 January 1993.

56. *Greensboro Daily News*, 3 March 1971; *New York Times*, 22 June 1971; Ervin Hearings, 1971, 398. The Information Collection Plan was printed in the *Congressional Record*, 91st Cong., 2nd sess., 1970, 4553–55.

57. Ibid., 431.

58. "Ervin Views Army Spying as Illegal," *Washington Post*, 3 March 1971.

59. Ervin Hearings, 1971, 597–604.

60. The first Rehnquist-Ervin exchange is found in Ervin Hearings, 1971, 614–24, especially 620.

61. The second Rehnquist-Ervin exchange is found in Ervin Hearings, 1971, 860–66.

62. Ibid., 863.

63. "Ervin to Quiz Army on Files," *Washington Post*, 12 March 1971; Editorial, *Washington Post*, 17 March 1971; Tom Wicker, *New York Times*, 11 March 1971; *Chattanooga Times*, 21 March 1971, Documentary Analysis, 2007; "Restraining Big Brother," *Albany Times-Union*, 24 March 1971, Documentary Analysis, 1923.

64. Ervin's desire to continue the hearings was reported in "Two Army Nets Suspected," *Washington Post*, 23 March 1971. By the time the hearings ended, Ervin's chief distraction was the legal brief he was preparing to deliver in the upcoming *Swann v. Charlotte-Mecklenburg Board of Education* busing case. Ervin and the Defense Department exchanged a series of letters between March and September 1971 in which they fought over the testimony of the missing generals and the declassification of Army documents. See Documentary Analysis, 1217–68.

65. "Drifting Toward 1984," *Time*, 29 March 1971.

66. "Project MUM," *New Republic*, 13 November 1971, 9; "Snooping Out the Snoopers," *Progressive* 35 (May 1971): 9.

67. Answering a question during his testimony, Froehlke explained that "under certain extreme circumstances the Army might again have to [conduct domestic intelligence]." Ervin Hearings, 1971, 436. His statement was reported in the *Greensboro Daily News*, 3 March 1971.

68. Pyle, "Military Surveillance" (unpublished ms.), 14. An unidentified source on the subcommittee staff, cited in Stephen Klitzman, "Sam Ervin: Principles Not Politics," in *Citizens Look at Congress* (Washington, D.C.: Ralph Nader Congress Project, 1972), 36. Kennedy's attempt to move the hearings was reported in the *Washington Post*, 8 April 1971.

69. Frederick Nelson, "Can We Stop Surveillance of Radicals," *Human Events*, 17 April 1971, 14.

70. Mrs. Elrod to Ervin, 8 April 1971, Ervin Papers, box 408, folder 458.

71. In March 1971, the Harris Poll found that 43 percent of the public agreed that "the Army has overstepped its bounds by spying on civilians here at home." Only 30 percent disagreed, while 27 percent were not sure. *Harris Survey Yearbook of Public Opinion*, 1971.

72. *New York Times*, 21 March 1971, 6 April 1971; *Washington Post*, 6 April 1971. A *Washington Post* survey conducted in December 1970, but not published until 7 April 1971, found that "about one quarter of the Members of Congress . . . said they suspected or believed their phones were tapped or their offices bugged" by the FBI. Majority Leader

Hale Boggs called for FBI chief Hoover's resignation. *Congressional Record*, 92nd Cong., 1st sess., 5 April 1971, 9470.

73. *Washington Post*, 22 March 1971, 24 March 1971. On the Media papers see Athan Theoharis, *Spying on Americans: Political Surveillance from Hoover to the Huston Plan* (Philadelphia: Temple University Press, 1978), 148–51; Morton H. Halperin et al., *The Lawless State: The Crimes of the U.S. Intelligence Agencies* (New York: Penguin, 1976), 90–132; Frank J. Donner, *The Age of Surveillance: The Aims and Methods of America's Political Intelligence System* (New York: Vintage Books, 1981), 57–59, 167, 169.

74. The FBI's secret counterintelligence agency was called "COINTELPRO." While the existence of this agency was revealed in the Media papers, the full extent of the program was not discovered until 1972. See Cathy Perkus, ed., *COINTELPRO: The FBI's Secret War on Political Freedom* (New York: Monad Press, 1975); James Kirkpatrick Davis, *Spying on America: The FBI's Domestic Counterintelligence Program* (New York: Praeger, 1992); Ward Churchill and Jim Vander Wall, eds., *The COINTELPRO Papers: Documents from the FBI's Secret Wars Against Domestic Dissent* (Boston: South End Press, 1990).

75. A form letter from "The Citizens' Committee to Investigate the FBI," 3 May 1971, Box 8, H. Hubert Wilson Collection, Seeley G. Mudd Manuscript Library, Princeton University. The Citizens' Committee offered the following breakdown of the content of all the Media papers: 40 percent, political surveillance; 25 percent, bank robberies; 20 percent, murder, rape, theft; 7 percent, draft resistance; 1 percent, organized crime.

76. For instance, one COINTELPRO memorandum expressed concern about "the AFSC [American Friends Service Committee], a religious org., which could conceivably embarrass the Bureau," and proposed actions that "may have the additional benefit of stifling criticism of the President's policies from within his own church." Airtel memorandum from SAC, San Antonio, to Director, 3 March 1971, American Friends Service Committee Archives, The Friends' Center, Philadelphia (hereafter cited as AFSC Papers). Since Johnson was not a Quaker, exactly how disrupting the AFSC would reduce criticism within his church was unclear. In another memo Hoover ordered a COINTELPRO unit to list the name of an AFSC worker who helped organize antiwar protests in its "Key Activist Program." The director reminded his agents that "the main objective of the Key Activist Program is to neutralize influence of important subjects," and he asked that they "recommend possible counterintelligence measures" that could be taken against them. Airtel memorandum from "Director," to "SAC New York, New Haven, Phili.," 8 December 1969, AFSC.

77. Baskir, interview by author, 11 March 1986. Senator Edward Kennedy was an especially strong advocate of carrying the subcommittee's investigation into the FBI, and he tried unsuccessfully to continue the hearings in his own Subcommittee on Administrative Practices. *Washington Post*, 8 April 1971.

78. *Washington Post*, 12 April 1971; *New York Times*, 21 April 1976; William W. Keller, *The Liberals and J. Edgar Hoover: Rise and Fall of a Domestic Intelligence State* (Princeton, N.J.: Princeton University Press, 1989), 149–51; "Congress and the FBI," *Washington Post*, 28 April 1971.

79. *Washington Post*, 9 April 1971; "Ervin Rules Out Inquiry into FBI Now," *New York Times*, 19 April 1971.

80. "Privacy and Government Investigations," an address delivered by Ervin to the College of Law, University of Illinois, Urbana-Champaign, 7 May 1971, Ervin Papers, box 411, folder 525.

81. The senator was also busy with the unfinished business from his military surveillance hearings. Ervin's continuing fight with the Defense and Justice departments over their refusal to surrender the information they had promised consumed much of his time. He also had to force the administration to declassify the documents obtained by the subcommittee so that he could publish its final report. It would eventually take over a year of prodding, and the threat of a subpoena, to coerce the administration into declassifying the documents for public inspection. The subcommittee's final report was not issued until the summer of 1973. It is titled *Military Surveillance of Civilian Politics*, a report of the Subcommittee on Constitutional Rights, 93rd Cong., 1st sess., 1973. Indices to Ervin's correspondence with the Army, the Defense Department, and the Justice Department can be found in Documentary Analysis, 1046, 1180, and 1311.

82. Chief of Staff Baskir had approached Ervin earlier with the possibility of including the FBI's surveillance practices in the hearings, but the senator, who admired Hoover, refused to consider it. Baskir, interview by author, 11 March 1986. The special treatment many members of Congress afforded the FBI is discussed in Keller, *Liberals and J. Edgar Hoover*, 145–49, 192–99. After the Watergate revelations Ervin did begin to question the FBI. See Davis, *Spying on America*, 165–69. But even then Ervin was reluctant to push an investigation of COINTELPRO. See Memorandum, Larry Baskir to Ervin, [n.d.] 1974, Ervin Papers, box 411, folder 527. It later was revealed that the FBI had kept a file on Ervin and had taken notes on his speeches. See Alex Charns, "FBI Had Sam Ervin Wondering," *Durham Morning-Herald*, 17 May 1987.

83. See "Privacy and the False Prophets," an address Ervin delivered to "The People's Forum on Privacy," Washington, D.C., 15 June 1971, Ervin Papers, box 411; "Army Surveillance and the Constitution," an address delivered to the Philadelphia Bar Association, 25 March 1971, and to The Impact Symposium at Vanderbilt University, Nashville, 17 April 1971, and to the Region III Convention of the Sigma Delta Chi, Chapel Hill, 24 April 1971, Ervin Papers, box 411. To get his message to the widest possible audience, Ervin published the final version of his speech, titled "The Most Important Freedom," as an editorial in the *New York Times*, 21 June 1971.

84. "Army Surveillance and the Constitution," an address Ervin delivered to the Philadelphia Bar Association, 25 March 1971, Ervin Papers, box 411.

85. The letter appears in Ervin's speech "Army Surveillance and the Constitution," an address delivered to the Philadelphia Bar Association, 25 March 1971, Ervin Papers, box 411. He did not name the author.

86. Baskir, interview by author, 11 March 1986. Stanley I. Kutler, *The Wars of Watergate* (New York: Alfred A. Knopf, 1990), 122.

87. *Laird v. Tatum et al.*, 408 U.S. 1 (1972). The ruling is reproduced in Morton H. Halperin and Daniel Hoffman, *Freedom vs. National Security* (New York: Chelsea House Publishers, 1977), 576–83. See "The Supreme Court, 1971 Term," *Harvard Law Review* 86 (November 1972): 130–37; and Military Surveillance Report, 1973, 102–16. Ervin's oral arguments before the Court as amicus curiae on 27 March 1971 may be found in Philip B.

Kurland and Gerhard Casper, eds., *Landmark Briefs and Arguments of the Supreme Court of the United States: Constitutional Law* (Arlington, Va.: University Publications of America, 1975), 347–50.

88. "Senator Sam Ervin Says," Weekly Newspaper Column, 13 July 1972, Ervin Papers, box 452. Ervin's reaction to *Laird v. Tatum* is discussed in Paul R. Clancy, *Just a Country Lawyer: A Biography of Sam Ervin* (Bloomington: Indiana University Press, 1974), 233.

89. Melvin L. Wulf to Gilbert Harrison, 1 November 1972, American Civil Liberties Union Collection, G. 7100 (1976), Vol. 15, Seeley G. Mudd Manuscript Library, Princeton University (hereafter cited as ACLU Papers). ACLU legal files on *Tatum v. Laird* may be found in A. 1425 (1976), Vol. 20, ACLU Papers.

90. The *Columbia Law Review* concluded: "Although [Rehnquist's] judgment might have been impartial, his participation in *Laird* lacked the appearance of impartiality necessary to maintain public confidence in the Supreme Court." See "Justice Rehnquist's Decision to Participate in *Laird v. Tatum*," *Columbia Law Review* 73 (January 1973): 106–24, quote at 124; Fred Graham, "Rehnquist Determined Not To 'Bend over Backward,' " *New York Times*, 15 October 1972; David S. Broder, "Those Memos Will Tell," *Washington Post*, 6 August 1986; "Lawyer Raps Rehnquist for Role in Army Spying Case," *Los Angeles Times*, 5 September 1986; Kutler, *Wars of Watergate*, 122–23. Rehnquist presented his defense in an editorial that appeared in the *New York Times*, 18 October 1972.

91. The Senate bill was numbered 3750. See Congressional Index, 92nd Cong., 2nd sess., 1972, p. 1971. Ervin reintroduced the same bill in each session of Congress after 1972. See "Senator Sam Ervin Says," Weekly Newspaper Column, 18 July 1974, Ervin Papers, box 449. For information on Ervin's activities in the summer of 1972, see Arthur M. Schlesinger Jr., *Imperial Presidency* (Boston: Houghton Mifflin, 1973), 392–411; and Clancy, *Just a County Lawyer*, 245–55. Senators Hruska and Thurmond shared their opinions under the title "Additional Views," in Military Surveillance Report, 1973.

92. U.S. Congress, Senate, Committee on the Judiciary, *Hearings on S. 2318*, Hearings before the Subcommittee on Constitutional Rights, 93rd Cong., 2nd sess., 9 and 10 April, 1974 (hereafter cited as Hearings on S. 2318, 1974). See Ervin to John L. McClellan, 6 May 1974, Ervin Papers, box 411, folder 527; "Senator Sam Ervin Says," Weekly Newspaper Column, 4 October 1974, Ervin Papers, box 411, folder 527. Ervin mentioned the number of cosponsors in his opening statement, Hearings on S. 2318, 1974, 1. Some members of Ervin's staff blamed the bill's failure on the senator's poor political leadership. See memorandum from Dorothy Glass, [n.d.] 1974, Ervin Papers, box 411, folder 527.

93. Basing his conclusions on Ervin's hearings on military domestic surveillance in 1974, as well as other sources, Morton Halperin observed in 1976: "It thus seems clear that military intelligence operations against American citizens did not end with the 1971 revelations. The practices have continued—though reduced—and the bureaucratic structure remains in place." Halperin, *Lawless State*, 170.

CHAPTER TEN

1. Though it is certainly true that Ervin seldom passed up an opportunity to take a political potshot at the Republican party, the evidence simply does not support Nixon's contention that the senator was primarily motivated by partisanship. Mike Mansfield chose Ervin as the chairman of the Watergate Committee because he regarded him to be

the most nonpartisan Democrat in the Senate. In addition, Ervin had one of the most independent voting records in Congress. See *Congressional Quarterly Almanac, 1971* (Washington, D.C.: Congressional Quarterly, 1972), 81–110; John Ehrlichman, *Witness to Power: The Nixon Years* (New York: Simon and Schuster, 1982), 366–67; Stephen E. Ambrose, *Nixon*, vol. 3: *Ruin and Recovery, 1973–1990* (New York: Simon and Schuster, 1991), 69; Bob Woodward and Carl Bernstein, "Nixon and His Aides Believe Hearings is a Witchhunt," *Washington Post*, 21 July 1973.

2. Bruce Tindall, "Down Home Truths: The Wit and Wisdom of Senator Sam Ervin," unpublished manuscript, 1974, folder 1171, in the Sam J. Ervin Papers, Subgroup B: Private Papers, 3847B, Southern Historical Collection, Wilson Library, University of North Carolina at Chapel Hill (hereafter cited as Ervin Papers, B.); Rufus Edmisten's phrase "the academic period" is cited in Paul R. Clancy, *Just a Country Lawyer: A Biography of Senator Sam Ervin* (Bloomington: Indiana University Press, 1974), 11; Edmisten's full quote is taken from his interview with the author, 25 February 1986; Lawrence Baskir, interview with author, 11 March 1986.

3. Stanley I. Kutler, *The Wars of Watergate: The Last Crisis of Richard Nixon* (New York: Alfred A. Knopf, 1990), 616; Joan Hoff, *Nixon Reconsidered* (New York: Basic Books, 1994), 1–16; J. Anthony Lukas, *Nightmare: The Underside of the Nixon Years* (New York: Viking Press, 1976), viii. Kutler's traditional analysis builds on the earlier interpretations of Lukas, *Nightmare*, and Arthur M. Schlesinger Jr., *The Imperial Presidency* (Boston: Houghton Mifflin, 1973), among others. Hoff's revisionist perspective is shared, to varying degrees, by Richard Reeves, *Richard Nixon: Alone in the White House* (New York: Simon and Schuster, 2001); Richard M. Nixon, *RN: The Memoirs of Richard Nixon* (New York: Grosset and Dunlop, 1978); Herbert S. Parmet, *Richard Nixon and His America* (Boston: Little, Brown, 1990), which devotes only six pages to Watergate; and, to a lesser extent, Tom Wicker, *One of Us: Richard Nixon and the American Dream* (New York: Random House, 1991), which reverses the typical Nixon defense by criticizing the president's foreign policy while praising his domestic achievements on issues ranging from desegregation to the environment. For an excellent overview of Watergate historiography see Michael Schudson, *Watergate in American Memory: How We Remember, Forget and Reconstruct the Past* (New York: Basic Books, 1992).

4. Henry Mitchell, *Washington Post*, 19 December 1982.

5. Ervin, *The Whole Truth: The Watergate Conspiracy* (New York: Random House, 1980), xii.

6. Two books that further chronicle the history of the Ervin Committee are Samuel Dash, *Chief Counsel: Inside the Ervin Committee—The Untold Story of Watergate* (New York: Random House, 1976); Fred D. Thompson, *At This Point in Time: The Inside Story of the Watergate Committee* (New York: Quadrangle/New York Times Book Company, 1975).

7. Mansfield and Ervin discussed several different ways in which the Senate could investigate Watergate during the fall of 1972, including the possibility that Ervin's Subcommittee on Constitutional Rights might take the lead. See Mike Mansfield to Ervin, 17 November 1972, box 371, folder 14197, in Sam J. Ervin Papers, Subgroup A: Senate Papers, 3847A, Southern Historical Collection, Wilson Library, University of North Carolina at Chapel Hill (hereafter cited as Ervin Papers); Mike Mansfield to James O. Eastland, 17 November 1972, Ervin Papers, box 371, folder 14197.

8. Ervin, *Whole Truth*, 18; "Why Ervin Heads The Senate Inquiry," *U.S. News & World Report*, 28 May 1973.

9. John Dean interview, transcript, *Senator Sam* (film), New Atlantic Productions, 4.

10. Staff of the *New York Times*, *The Watergate Hearings* (New York: Bantam Books, 1973), cited in Ervin, *Whole Truth*, 18.

11. Bruce McGarrity Tindall, "Down Home Truths from Senator Sam Ervin," unpublished manuscript, Sam J. Ervin Papers, Subgroup B: Private Papers, 3847B, Southern Historical Collection, Wilson Library, University of North Carolina at Chapel Hill (hereafter cited as Ervin Papers, B.), folder 1171.

12. Bob Woodward and Carl Bernstein, "Senate Votes Watergate Probe," *Washington Post*, 8 February 1973; James Naughton, "Ervin Assuming Leadership in Effort to Reassert the Authority of Congress," *New York Times*, 4 February 1973. In addition to Ervin and Baker, the other senators appointed to the Watergate Committee included Herman Talmadge, Daniel Inouye, Joseph Montoya, Edward Gurney, and Lowell Weicker Jr. All of the senators on the committee were considered either conservative or moderate, all seven were lawyers, and each had served in the military, making it very difficult for President Nixon to attack the committee as liberal, unpatriotic, or inexperienced.

13. Ervin, *Whole Truth*, 24.

14. Haldeman's quote is cited from Ehrlichman's private White House notes in Kutler, *Wars of Watergate*, 345.

15. Ervin, *Whole Truth*, 25–26.

16. Address by the Vice President to the National Association of Attorneys General, 13 June 1973, Ervin Papers, box 371, folder 14198; Jack Aulis, "Most Newsmen Deny Senator Sam Is Senile," *Raleigh News and Observer*, 8 July 1973.

17. "Helms Hits Democrats on Watergate," Ervin Papers, Box 372, folder 14219; "Helms Attacks Watergate Panel," *Raleigh News and Observer*, 16 July 1973.

18. James M. Naughton, "Constitutional Ervin," *New York Times Magazine*, 13 May 1973.

19. Hugh Sidey, "The Country Lawyer and Friends," *Time*, 6 August 1973, 27.

20. Lukas, *Nightmare*, 297.

21. Ibid., 293.

22. Ibid., 290.

23. Ervin, *Whole Truth*, 59–61.

24. "Defying Nixon's Reach for Power," *Time*, 16 April 1973; Ervin, *Whole Truth*, 32–36.

25. Paul Clancy, " 'The Sam Ervin Show' Is Favorite of the Media," *Charlotte Observer*, 8 April 1973.

26. Ibid.

27. Tindall, "Down Home Truths," Ervin Papers, B., folder 1171. Ervin appeared on the cover of *Newsweek* just over a week later, "Uncovering the Watergate Cover-up," *Newsweek*, 28 May 1973.

28. "Defying Nixon's Reach for Power," *Time*, 16 April 1973.

29. Ibid.

30. One reporter even predicted that Ervin would be "the hottest thing to hit the tube since Archie Bunker." Rem Rieder, "Ervin in Dazzling Form Limbering Up for Probe," Evening and Sunday *Philadelphia Bulletin*, April 1973, Ervin Papers, Clippings files, box

47\. The phrase "The Sam Ervin Show" appeared in several newspaper articles, including Paul Clancy, " 'The Sam Ervin Show' Is Favorite of the Media," *Charlotte Observer*, 8 April 1973; and Stewart Alsop, "The Sam Ervin Show," *Newsweek*, 2 April 1973.

31\. Olin Robison, "Speaking the Truth to Our Children," *Christian Century*, 3 December 1986, 1092.

32\. The full record of the Ervin hearings can be found in U.S. Congress, Senate, Hearings before the Select Committee on Presidential Campaign Activities, 93rd Cong., 1st sess., 1973. The opening day is best described in Ervin, *Whole Truth*, 124–27; Dick Dabney, *A Good Man: The Life of Sam J. Ervin* (Boston: Houghton Mifflin, 1976), 267, 262; Kutler, *Wars of Watergate*, 346–47.

33\. *Watergate: Chronology of a Crisis* (Washington, D.C.: *Congressional Quarterly*, 1973), 1:47.

34\. Ibid., 278.

35\. Clancy, *Just a Country Lawyer*, 272; Dabney, *Good Man*, 269–70.

36\. Dean received "use immunity," meaning that he could not be prosecuted solely on the uncollaborated basis of what he said during the hearings.

37\. *Watergate: Chronology of a Crisis*, 152.

38\. Dean's testimony is reviewed in detail in Ervin, *Whole Truth*, 161–71.

39\. Gladys Engel Lang and Kurt Lang, *The Battle for Public Opinion: The President, the Press and the Polls During Watergate* (New York: Columbia University Press, 1983), 76.

40\. Ibid., 78.

41\. "Sam Ervin, Saving the Republic, and Show Business," *New Times*, 19 October 1973; Dabney, *Good Man*, 266.

42\. Ervin, *Whole Truth*, 19.

43\. Clancy, *Just a Country Lawyer*, 275; Fred Emery, *Watergate: The Corruption of American Politics and the Fall of Richard Nixon* (New York: Simon and Schuster, 1994), 364–66.

44\. Lou Harris and Associates, *The Harris Survey Yearbook of Public Opinion 1973: A Compendium of Current American Attitudes* (New York: Harris and Associates, 1976), 147.

45\. Jules Archer, *Watergate: America in Crisis* (New York: Thomas Y. Crowell, 1975), 180.

46\. As Fred Emery, a reporter for *The Times* of London, concluded, "At the touch of a button John Dean could now be contradicted by the President—or corroborated." Emery, *Watergate*, 369. This description of Butterfield's testimony and the reaction to it relies on Lukas, *Nightmare*, 369–75; Theodore H. White, *Breach of Faith: The Fall of Richard Nixon* (New York: Scribner, 1975), cited in Ervin, *Preserving the Constitution*, 321.

47\. President Nixon to Chairman Ervin, 23 July 1973, Ervin Papers, box 371, folder 14199.

48\. For clarity's sake the reference to the tapes here is meant generally to cover all the presidential tapes and not just the actual tapes Ervin and Cox requested at that time. While the specific tapes that Ervin and Cox requested in August would deeply harm Nixon's credibility and political standing, it was other tapes subpoenaed by the Special Prosecutor and House Judiciary Committee that would produce the smoking gun that finally drove Nixon from office.

49\. Lou Harris and Associates, *The Harris Survey*, 24 July 1973. The quotes come from constituent mail that can be found in Ervin Papers, box 355, 27 July–30 July.

50. Ervin to Dick Dabney, Corrections to Dabney manuscript, Ervin Papers, B., folder 1162.

51. Ervin, *Whole Truth*, 122–23.

52. Lukas, *Nightmare*, 390; "Can Public Confidence Be Restored?" *Time*, 20 August 1973, 9–22.

53. Clancy, *Just a Country Lawyer*, 283; Miles Benson, "It Was Simpler in Tom Dooley's Day," *Greensboro Record*, 4 September 1973, Ervin Papers, B., folder 1184.

54. White, *Breach of Faith*, 239. Other historians share the view of the significance of the Ervin hearings; see Kutler, *Wars of Watergate*, 381–82.

55. Ervin is quoting from Deuteronomy 34:7. "A Hero Steps Down," [n.d.] news clipping, Ervin Papers, box 471; Ervin to Graham Bell, 29 January 1974, Ervin Papers, box 336, folder 13343.

56. Ervin, "Senator Sam Ervin Says," 24 October 1974, Ervin Papers, B., folder 1298. For information on these pieces of legislation, see *Review: 1974 Session of the Congress* (Washington, D.C.: American Enterprise Institute for Public Policy Research, 1975); and *Congressional Quarterly Almanac*, 1974.

57. Ervin Press Release, "The Privacy Act of 1974," Ervin Papers, B., folder 787.

58. Donald G. Mathews and Jane Sherron De Hart, *Sex, Gender, and the Politics of ERA: A State and the Nation* (New York: Oxford University Press, 1990); U.S. Congress, Senate, Subcommittee on Constitutional Rights of the Committee on the Judiciary, *Busing of Schoolchildren*, 93rd Cong., 2nd sess., 1974, 1. For information on Ervin's legislative actions in 1974, see *Review: 1974 Session of the Congress*, American Enterprise Institute for Public Policy Research, 1975; and *Congressional Quarterly Almanac*, 1974.

59. Senator Helms confided to the author that Ervin called him several days a week until he finally had to stop taking all of his calls. On retirement, see Ervin, *Preserving the Constitution*, 341–43; Dabney, *Good Man*, 285–87.

60. Phillip Finch, "Senator Sam Comes To Town," *San Francisco Sunday Examiner & Chronicle*, 23 March 1975, Ervin Papers, B., folder 1131.

61. Ervin's quote is taken from "Ex-U.S. Sen. Sam Ervin Dies at 88," *Charlotte Observer*, 24 April 1985. On his speaking engagements see Dabney, *Good Man*, 286. Ervin's financial records during retirement are found in Ervin Papers, B., box 90, folders 1070–1081.

62. "A Most Unlikely Hero," *San Diego Union*, 27 April 1985, Ervin Papers, B., folder 1233; "Not Quite Just a Country Lawyer," *Time*, 6 May 1985.

63. James J. Kilpatrick, "Sam Ervin, Founding Father," *Winston-Salem Journal*, 29 May 1970, is the first of many times that Kilpatrick referred to Ervin as a "founding father"; Tom Wicker, "The Watergate Committee Chairman's New Clothes," *Southern Voices* 1 (March–April 1974): 7. After Watergate, the two standard interpretations of Ervin's career —the consistent constitutional libertarian v. the inconsistent southern obstructionist— found expression in several major articles, dissertations, and books. For a sampling of the consistent constitutional libertarian view, see Clifford Kenneth Van Sickle, "The Oral Communication of Senator Sam Ervin: A Study in Consistency" (Ph.D. diss., Department of Speech, Michigan State University, 1976); Clancy, *Just a Country Lawyer*; David Leon Chandler, *The Natural Superiority of Southern Politicians: A Revisionist History* (Garden City, N.Y.: Doubleday, 1977), 306–18. Examples of the more critical analysis of Ervin as an inconsistent southern obstructionist can be found in Stephen Klitzman, "Sam Ervin:

Principle Not Politics," in *Citizens Look at Congress* (Washington, D.C.: Ralph Nader Congress Project, 1972); and Dabney, *Good Man.*

64. Ervin's story is recounted in William O. Douglas, *The Court Years, 1939–1975* (New York: Random House, 1980), 11. Ervin's autobiography is titled *Preserving the Constitution* (Charlottesville, Va.: Michie, 1984).

65. William Chafe, *Civilities and Civil Rights: Greensboro, North Carolina, and the Black Struggle for Freedom* (New York: Oxford University Press, 1980). See also V. O. Key, *Southern Politics in State and Nation* (New York: Alfred A. Knopf, 1949), 205–28; H. G. Jones, "North Carolina, 1946–1976: Where Historians Fear to Tread," in *Writing North Carolina History*, ed. Jeffrey J. Crow and Larry E. Tise (Chapel Hill: University of North Carolina Press, 1979), 211–18; Thad L. Beyle, "The Paradox of North Carolina," in *Politics and Policy in North Carolina*, ed. Thad L. Beyle and Merle Black (New York: MSS Information Corporation, 1975), 1–12; Raymond Gavins, "A 'Sin of Omission': Black Historiography in North Carolina," in *Black Americans in North Carolina and the South*, ed. Jeffrey J. Crow and Flora J. Hatley (Chapel Hill: University of North Carolina Press, 1984), 11–56. The Tar Heel State's progressive mystique and moderate strategy to delay the civil rights revolution proved to be so successful that in 1976 Jack Bass and Walter DeVries characterized North Carolina as "perhaps the least changed of the old Confederate states," in *The Transformation of Southern Politics: Social Change and Political Consequences since 1945* (New York: Basic Books, 1976), 218–47.

66. See Key, *Southern Politics in State and Nation*, 9; Kermit L. Hall and James W. Ely Jr., eds., *An Uncertain Tradition: Constitutionalism and the History of the South* (Athens: University of Georgia Press, 1989), 3–59; Edmund S. Morgan, *American Slavery—American Freedom: The Ordeal of Colonial Virginia* (New York: W. W. Norton, 1975); Gordon S. Wood, *The Creation of the American Republic, 1776–1787* (Chapel Hill: University of North Carolina Press, 1969).

67. Arthur Schlesinger Jr. suggested that "Sam Ervin was of the pure Jeffersonian school, like the old Tertium Quids who felt that Jefferson and Madison, in strengthening the Presidency and seeing the national government as an instrument of the general welfare, had deserted the true faith." Schlesinger, *Imperial Presidency*, 403–4.

INDEX

Abington Township Pa. v. Schempp, 193, 198
Acheson, Dean, 87
ACLU. *See* American Civil Liberties Union
ADA. *See* Americans for Democratic Action
Adams, Sherman, 120
Affirmative action, 160, 205, 232, 279, 368 (n. 71)
AFL-CIO, 153, 185, 207
African Americans. *See* Civil rights; Education; Integration; NAACP; Racism; Segregation; Violence; Voting rights
AFSC. *See* American Friends Service Committee
Agnew, Spiro, 221–22, 284, 379 (n. 49)
Agriculture Department, U.S., 201
Aiken, George D., 323 (n. 36)
Alabama and civil rights, 110, 118, 130, 136, 139–40, 147, 148
Albany Times-Union, 270
Alcohol. *See* Prohibition
Alexander, Holmes, 339 (n. 115)
Alexander v. Holmes County Board of Education, 228
Allen, James B., 231
Ambrose, Stephen, 387 (n. 101)
American Civil Liberties Union, 119, 185, 207, 247, 255–56, 266, 275, 277, 392 (n. 42)
American Friends Service Committee (AFSC), 394 (n. 76)
American Indians. *See* Native Americans
American Revolution, 25, 302, 370 (n. 90)
Americans for Democratic Action (ADA), 118, 161–62, 207
Anderson, Clinton P., 176
Andrews, George W., 193
Anticommunism, 86–96, 210–11, 240, 257. *See also* Communist Party

Anti-war protesters: domestic surveillance of, 247, 250, 261, 377 (n. 39); Ervin's defense of rights of, 9; and Johnson administration, 266; violence against, 249; violence and property damage by, 250, 257. *See also* Vietnam War
Arkansas and civil rights, 114, 125–26, 136
Army. *See* Military draft; Military personnel
Army domestic intelligence system. *See* Government domestic spying
Army-McCarthy hearings, 86–87, 89, 91, 92, 235, 259, 260–61
Asheville Citizen, 96, 105
Asheville Citizen Times, 86
Autry, George B., 133, 195, 196
Avery, William Waightstill, 15–16

Bacot, Daniel Huger, 35
Bail Reform Act (1966), 186, 190–91, 216, 365 (n. 36)
Bail system, 189–91, 216, 365 (n. 36)
Baker, Howard, 3, 6, 283, 287, 398 (n. 12)
Baker, Russell, 127
Baltimore Sun, 113
Barnard, Bob, 355–56 (n. 25)
Barnett, Ross, 134, 136
Barry, Marion S., Jr., 131
Bartley, Numan, 102
Baskir, Lawrence, 254–55, 264, 280, 395 (n. 82)
Bass, Jack, 115, 401 (n. 65)
Batten, James K., 236
Bayh, Birch, 264, 372 (n. 100)
Becker, Frank, 193
Behavioral sciences, 204, 370 (n. 88)
Bell, Margaret. *See* Ervin, Margaret Bell
Bernstein, Carl, 8, 282
Berrigan, Daniel, 257, 391 (n. 29)

Bible quotations, 1, 29, 117, 148, 161, 184, 197, 226, 370 (n. 90)

Bickel, Alexander, 346 (n. 44)

Bilbo, Theodore, 130

Billings, Josh, 135, 192

Birmingham violence and riot, 139–40, 144–45

Black, Hugo L., 316 (n. 93)

Black Panthers, 273

Black Power, 153, 273, 350 (n. 89)

Blacks. *See* Civil rights; Education; Integration; NAACP; Racism; Segregation; Violence; Voting rights

Blackstone, William, 49

Bloch, Charles J., 336 (n. 77)

Blue Ridge Mountains, 14, 76, 81, 204

Boggs, Hale, 272, 393–94 (n. 72)

Bolling, Richard, 331 (n. 21), 332 (n. 24)

Bond, Julian, 261

Brandeis, Louis D., 151, 204

Brauer, Carl, 140

Brezhnev, Leonid, 288

Bricker, John W., 325 (n. 64)

Bridges, Edwin B., 60, 61

Briggs v. Elliot, 97–98, 159

Brinkley, David, 220

Brogden, Willis J., 81

Brooke, Edward F., 156

Broughton, J. Melville, 62

Brown, Rap, 153

Brownell, Herbert, 113–15, 125, 332 (nn. 28–29), 332 (n. 33), 334 (n. 62), 336 (n. 77)

Brown II, 97, 98

Brown v. Board of Education: Carlyle's moderate approach to, 83–84; and Civil Rights Act (1960), 128; Ervin's opposition to, 82, 83, 97–106, 125, 159, 326 (n. 84), 326–27 (n. 86), 327 (n. 88); Ervin's rethinking of, 158–60, 228, 229, 279; Hoey on, 320 (n. 4); legal precedents for, 328 (n. 95); and Little Rock school desegregation, 125–26, 168, 234, 338 (n. 105); and NAACP, 110; Nixon on, 226; Alan Wright on, 119

Buchanan, Patrick, 221–22, 280

Burger, Warren E., 227–28, 275

Burke County, N.C., 13–17, 28, 53–55, 68–69, 76. *See also* Morganton, N.C.

Burke, Edmund, 154

Burleson, Commodore, 61

Burnham, James, 257–58

Busing, 151, 152, 160, 226, 228–31, 274, 279, 296, 381 (n. 67), 381–82 (n. 69), 382 (n. 71)

Butler, John Marshall, 167, 355 (n. 18)

Butterfield, Alexander, 290–91, 294

Buzhardt, J. Fred, 258, 265–68, 270, 276

Byrd, Harry F., 98, 105, 109, 110, 340 (n. 130)

Byrd, Robert, 383 (n. 78)

Byrnes, James, 328 (n. 102)

Caldwell v. United States, 223, 378 (n. 47)

Calhoun, John C., 25

Campaign contribution limits, 295

Cannon, Charles A., 75

Cardozo, Benjamin, 191

Carlson, Frank, 90

Carlyle, Irving, 83–84

Carmichael, Stokely, 153

Carnegie, Dale, 72

Carolinian, 86

Carroll, Lewis, 217–18

Carswell, G. Harrold, 228

Carter v. West Feliciana Parish School Board, 381 (n. 64)

Case, Francis, 90

Cash, W. J., 24

Caulfield, John, 287

Cavett, Dick, 286

Census questionnaires, 203–4, 209, 224

Central Intelligence Agency, 207, 208, 251, 252, 284–85, 372 (n. 100), 377 (n. 39)

Chafe, William, 301

Chafe, Zechariah, Jr., 47–48

Charlotte Observer, 199, 219, 236, 283–84, 285, 355 (n. 24)

Chase, Harry Woodburn, 58

Cherry, R. Gregg, 62, 77

Christopher, Warren, 392–93 (n. 55)

Church-state separation, 193–94, 296, 368 (n. 70)

CIA. *See* Central Intelligence Agency

Civil Aeronautics Administration, 234

Civil disobedience, 135

Civil liberties: of criminal defendants, 165–66, 185–87, 189–91, 192; Ervin's defense of, generally, 9–10, 83, 133, 162, 164, 169, 177, 182–83, 185, 199–200, 279, 299, 302, 360 (n. 68); Ervin Sr. on, 28; Ervin's voting record on, 162; of federal government workers, 200–202, 205–9, 214, 224–25, 369 (n. 76); and Freedom of Information Act (1966), 169, 200, 368 (n. 73); and freedom of the press, 169, 222–24, 279, 378–79 (n. 46); and government secrecy, 169; Harvard Law School on, 47–48; and individual freedom, 182; and Jencks bill, 169; and McCarthy censure by Senate, 89–96, 106; of mentally ill, 171–72, 177, 357–58 (nn. 42–43); of military personnel, 172–73, 201; and Narcotic Addict Rehabilitation Act (1966), 200; of Native Americans, 156, 162, 173–76, 177, 352 (n. 109), 358 (n. 48), 359 (n. 60); and Nixon administration, 185, 220–25, 245, 279; and prisoner work release programs, 199; and school prayer, 192–99, 235, 367 (n. 56), 368 (n. 70); and Senate Subcommittee on Constitutional Rights, 169–77, 279, 356 (n. 31), 357 (n. 34); and sports, 9, 199; and Warren Court, 164–68, 192. *See also* Government domestic spying; Privacy rights

Civil rights: and affirmative action, 160, 205, 232, 279, 368 (n. 71); and attorney general's power, 112, 115–16, 120, 140, 346 (n. 43); and Democratic platform (1960), 132–33, 341 (n. 1); and EEOC, 206, 231–32, 233, 350 (n. 91), 382 (n. 73); and Eisenhower administration, 112–25; Ervin on groups involved in, 134–

35; and Ervin's color-blind approach to, 159–60, 228, 229, 279, 368 (n. 71); Ervin's opposition to, generally, 10, 83, 86, 110, 130, 132–33, 143–44, 160, 162, 164, 177, 205, 233–35, 299, 302, 320 (n. 3), 344 (n. 28), 371 (n. 94); Ervin's opposition to *Brown v. Board of Education*, 82, 83, 97–106, 125, 278–79, 326 (n. 84), 326–27 (n. 86), 327 (n. 88); goals of legislation on, 149; and housing, 153–56, 176, 213, 350 (n. 94), 350 (n. 96), 351 (n. 103); and Lyndon Johnson, 331 (n. 21); and Kennedy administration, 136–45, 345 (n. 33); and Little Rock school desegregation, 114, 125–26, 168, 234, 338 (n. 105); NAACP on federal legislation on, in 1950s, 108, 110; NAACP on federal legislation on, in 1940s, 76; and Nixon administration, 226–33, 279, 381 (n. 67); and Philadelphia Plan, 232–33, 236; racist approach against, 99, 105, 110, 130, 335 (n. 71); and school desegregation, 82–84, 97–106, 125–26, 226–31, 320 (n. 4), 328 (n. 95), 381 (n. 64); and Senate Subcommittee on Constitutional Rights, 107, 110, 113–16, 119, 137, 139, 150–51, 169, 170, 339 (n. 115); separation of powers doctrine in Ervin's opposition to, 233–35; soft southern strategy against, 110, 113–20, 122, 124, 127–31, 137–38, 146, 160, 168, 205, 335 (n. 71), 336 (nn. 83, 87), 338–39 (n. 113); white backlash against, 152–54, 350 (nn. 87, 89); white liberals' and intellectuals' support for, 110–11, 118. *See also* Busing; Civil rights movement; Integration; Privacy rights; Voting rights; *specific civil rights and voting acts*

Civil Rights Act (1957): African Americans' call for presidential veto of, 337 (n. 90); and Eisenhower, 112, 114, 119, 122, 124, 333 (n. 34); Ervin on, 124, 336 (n. 83); Ervin's arguments against, 112–25, 333 (n. 38), 333 (n. 43), 333–34

(n. 50), 335 (n. 73), 336 (nn. 77, 83); filibuster against, 122; and Lyndon Johnson, 122, 124; jury trial amendment to,
119, 122–24; and jury trial issue, 116,
117–19, 122, 124, 333 (n. 43), 333–34
(n. 50), 334 (n. 58), 334–35 (nn. 62–63);
NAACP on, 117–18, 125, 338 (n. 103);
newspapers on, 113, 114–15, 122, 124;
provisions of, 112; Senate debate on,
120, 122; and Senate Judiciary Committee, 119–20; Senate passage of, 122; Senate subcommittee hearings on, 113–17,
119; soft southern strategy against, 113–
20, 122, 124, 168, 335 (n. 71), 336 (n. 83);
southern senators' success in weakening, 124, 130, 338 (n. 103); and voting
rights, 112, 116
Civil Rights Act (1960), 127–31, 205, 339
(n. 118), 339–40 (nn. 121–23)
Civil Rights Act (1964): cloture vote on filibuster against, 149; Ervin's amendments to, 146–47, 149; Ervin's opposition to, 140–47, 157, 235, 346 (n. 43);
Ervin's concern about enforcement of,
149, 150–52; filibuster against, 146;
hearings on, 140–45, 157, 161; HEW
guidelines on integration of public
schools, 149–52, 159–60, 205, 206, 226–
27, 235, 349 (n. 74); newspapers on,
146, 161; and Philadelphia Plan, 233;
president's signature for, 147; provisions of, 140, 233, 349 (n. 81); Senate
passage of, 147; and sex discrimination,
175; significance of, 149; soft southern
strategy against, 146
Civil Rights Act (1968), 155–58, 176, 353
(n. 115)
Civil Rights Commission, 127, 227, 336–37
(n. 88), 339 (n. 121), 345 (n. 33)
Civil rights movement: Birmingham violence and rioting, 139–40, 144–45; and
Black Power, 153, 273, 350 (n. 89);
"Bloody Sunday" in Alabama, 147; and
Communist Party, 109; Freedom Rides,
135, 136; Freedom Summer, 147; March

on Washington (1963), 144; and Montgomery bus boycott, 110, 118; and nonviolent civil disobedience, 135; and
protection of civil rights workers, 155–
57; and riots, 139, 152, 261, 350 (n. 89),
350–51 (n. 97), 352 (n. 108); sit-ins, 131,
135; and student activism in North
Carolina, 131, 135; violence against civil
rights protesters, 118, 135, 136, 138–39,
144–45, 147, 330–31 (n. 10). See also
Civil rights
Civil Service Commission, 201–2, 205,
206
Civil War, 12, 24–26, 46, 55
"Claghorn's Hammurabi," 133
Clancy, Paul, xv, 24, 219, 285
Clark, Jim, 340 (n. 130)
Clark, Joseph, 129
Clark, Ramsey, 192
Clements, Earle, 90
Cloture vote against filibusters, 138, 147,
149, 340 (n. 126)
Coates, Albert, 44
Cobb, Collier, 32
Cold War Cases, 164–65, 166, 208, 354
(n. 7)
Coleman, James, 124
Coleman, J. P., 329 (n. 119)
Cole v. Young, 355 (n. 18)
Colson, Charles, 2
Commerce Clause, 141, 155, 157, 346 (n. 44)
Committee to Reelect the President
(CRP), 281, 282, 288
Communist Party, 109, 164–65, 279. See
also Anticommunism
Computerized data banks, 202–3, 209,
224, 247, 253–54, 263, 268
Congress. See House of Representatives,
U.S.; Senate, U.S.; specific members of
Congress
Congressional Budget and Impoundment
Control Act, 295
Congressional districts, reapportionment
of, 192
Congressional Office of the Budget, 295

Congress of Racial Equality (CORE), 135, 153

Connor, Eugene ("Bull"), 130, 139, 340 (n. 130)

Constitution, U.S.: amendment process in, 327 (n. 88); and *Brown v. Board of Education*, 97–106, 326 (n. 84), 326–27 (n. 86), 327 (n. 88); and busing, 230; and Civil Rights Act (1957), 116–17, 124, 333–34 (n. 50), 336 (n. 83); and Civil Rights Act (1960), 128, 339 (n. 121); and Civil Rights Act (1964), 141–43, 146, 151, 157, 346 (nn. 43–44); and Civil Rights Act (1968), 155–58; Commerce Clause in, 141, 155, 157, 346 (n. 44); due process clause in, 128, 218, 334 (n. 50); equal protection clause of, 101, 102; and ERA, 179–80, 226; Ervin as constitutional scholar, 9–10, 101–2, 133, 138, 158, 300, 301, 305–6 (n. 22), 341 (n. 5); and government domestic spying, 248, 255, 256, 263, 269–70; and jury trial, 116, 117, 333–34 (n. 50); and literacy tests, 137–38, 344 (n. 27); and open-housing legislation, 154; and privacy rights, 204, 370 (n. 90); and southern constitutional tradition, 204–5, 301–2; on "Speech or Debate" immunity of members of Congress, 387 (n. 99); and Voting Rights Act (1965), 148, 342 (n. 7), 348 (n. 64). *See also specific amendments*

Constitutional Rights Subcommittee. *See* Senate Subcommittee on Constitutional Rights

Consumer protection, 8, 296

Consumer Protection Agency, 296

Cooley, Thomas M., 327 (n. 86)

Cooper, David, 213

Cooper, John Sherman, 138

CORE. *See* Congress of Racial Equality

Coughlan, Rob, 4

Court procedures reforms, 188–89, 364 (n. 25)

Cox, Archibald, 8, 291, 294

Cramer, John, 206

Craven, James Braxton, Jr., 51, 69, 78, 316 (n. 89)

Crime control: Ervin on, 9, 213–14; and Johnson administration, 363 (n. 20); and Nixon administration, 9, 214, 215–20, 257, 295, 360 (n. 68), 375 (n. 21), 375 (n. 24), 376 (n. 33); and no-knock searches by police, 217, 218–19, 220, 375 (n. 21); and preventive detention, 217–18, 220, 295, 375 (nn. 21, 24); and Speedy Trial Act, 295–96; and wiretapping, 187–88, 191, 208, 213, 217, 257, 363 (nn. 17–18), 363 (nn. 20–21), 389–90 (n. 12). *See also* Criminal defendants

Criminal defendants: and bail system, 189–91, 216, 365 (n. 36); confessions of, 213, 362 (n. 6); legal aid for, 189, 364 (n. 27), 364 (n. 30); rights of, 165–66, 185–87, 191, 192, 213–14, 227, 279. *See also* Crime control

Criminal Justice Act (1964), 186, 189

Crouse, Floyd, 44

CRP. *See* Committee to Reelect the President

Curtis, Carl T., 214

Dabney, Dick, xv, 310 (n. 73), 361 (n. 78)

Dabney, Virginius, 119

Darwinism. *See* Evolution debate

Davis, David, 6

Dean, John, 224, 225, 282–85, 287–89, 291, 293, 399 (nn. 36, 46)

Death penalty, 52, 80, 316 (n. 93)

Deaton v. Deaton, 79

Defense Department, U.S., 251, 253, 255, 258, 259, 265, 266, 270–71, 276, 393 (n. 64), 395 (n. 81). *See also* Government domestic spying

Democratic Party: and civil rights in 1950s, 126–27; and Ervin's election to North Carolina legislature, 48, 57; national conventions of, 132, 261, 266; in North Carolina, 48, 56, 61–63, 66, 211–13, 373 (n. 5); and presidential election of 1928, 61–63; and presidential election of 1960, 138; and presidential election of 1968, 214–15, 350 (n. 87); during Reconstruction, 27–28

Desegregation. *See* Integration

DeVries, Walter, 115, 401 (n. 65)

Dirksen, Everett, 140, 155, 156, 194–99, 231, 235, 352 (n. 108)

District of Columbia: crime control legislation for, 215–20; Mental Health Bill for, 172, 357–58 (n. 42)

Dodd, Thomas J., 368 (n. 73)

Domestic spying. *See* Government domestic spying

Douglas, Helen Gahagan, 210

Douglas, Paul, 127, 168, 334 (n. 63)

Douglas, William O., 316 (n. 93)

Drug addiction, 200, 368 (n. 73)

Due process clause, 128, 218, 334 (n. 50)

Duke, James B., 54

Duke University, 166

Durham Morning Herald, 86, 145

Eagleton, Thomas, 130

Eastland, James O.: on *Brown v. Board of Education*, 99; and Civil Rights Act (1957), 113, 119; and Civil Rights Act (1960), 129; and Civil Rights Act (1964), 142, 144; on civil rights movement and Communist Party, 99, 109; and Ervin's hearings on government domestic spying, 265–66, 274; as Senate Judiciary Committee chair, 107, 109, 119; significance of, 130, 340 (n. 130)

Edmisten, Rufus, 254, 280

Education: of African Americans, 57, 76, 98, 130, 134, 143, 149–52, 228, 337 (n. 98); and busing, 151, 152, 160, 226, 228–31, 274, 279, 296, 381 (n. 67), 381–82 (n. 69), 382 (n. 71); and desegregation of public schools, 82–84, 97–106, 125–26, 130, 150, 226–27, 228, 320 (n. 4), 328 (n. 95), 337 (n. 98), 381 (nn. 64, 67); Ervin on, 77; and evolution debate, 58,

59; federal aid for, 128, 151, 193–94, 226–27, 349 (n. 81); and integration of public schools under Civil Rights Act (1964), 149–52; and integration of universities, 136, 139, 140; Little Rock school desegregation, 114, 125–26, 168, 234, 338 (n. 105); and Nixon and school desegregation, 226–31, 381 (n. 67); in North Carolina, 29, 55, 143, 313 (n. 50); northern school districts and desegregation, 230; and Pearsall Plan, 98; private schools, 205; and school prayer, 192–99, 235, 367 (n. 56), 368 (n. 70); and southern opposition to *Brown v. Board of Education*, 97–106, 326 (n. 84), 326–27 (n. 86), 327 (n. 88); and statistics on school integration, 150, 151, 228

Education Amendments (1974), 296

Edwards v. California, 328 (n. 102)

EEOC. *See* Equal Employment Opportunity Commission

Ehringhaus, J. C. B., 62, 63, 65, 68

Ehrlichman, John D.: and crime control bill, 216; and ERA, 225; on Philadelphia Plan, 232; resignation of, 285; on Schorr, 223; and separation of power issues, 244; and Watergate Committee, 283; and Watergate hearings, 4–6, 287, 291–92, 293

Eighth Amendment, 189

Eisenhower, Dwight D.: and Civil Rights Act (1957), 112, 114, 119, 122, 124, 333 (n. 34), 337 (n. 90); election of, 111; Ervin on, 104; and executive agreements, 235; and executive power and privilege, 125, 169, 235; and literacy tests for voting, 138; and Little Rock school desegregation, 114, 125–26, 234

Elections. *See* Electoral campaigns of Ervin; Presidential election entries

Electoral campaigns of Ervin: for district solicitor, 57; for North Carolina legislature, 48, 57; for U.S. House of Representatives, 73; U.S. Senate (1954), 106;

for U.S. Senate, (1956) 106, 330–31
(n. 120); for U.S. Senate (1962), 138, 344
(n. 28); for U.S. Senate (1968), 211–15,
373 (n. 5)

Electronic surveillance. *See* Wiretapping

Elementary and Secondary Education Act
(1965), 194, 349 (nn. 81, 83)

Ellender, Allen, 205–6, 243, 387 (n. 102)

Ellsberg, Daniel, 4, 281, 292, 376 (n. 33)

Ely, Hanson E., 38, 42

Emery, Fred, 399 (n. 46)

Engel v. Vitale, 193, 198

Equal Employment Opportunity Commission (EEOC), 75, 206, 231–32, 233,
350 (n. 91), 382 (n. 73)

Equal protection clause, 101, 102

Equal rights amendment (ERA), 9, 179–
80, 214, 225–26, 296

Ervin, Betty, 87

Ervin, Catharine ("Cat"), 22, 23, 29, 43–
44, 71

Ervin, Edward, 20, 30, 71

Ervin, Eunice, 23, 53

Ervin, James Robert, 25

Ervin, Jean, 19, 21, 22, 27, 31, 40, 42, 53, 60

Ervin, Joe, 15, 20, 30, 71, 72–73

Ervin, John, 25

Ervin, John Witherspoon, 24, 25–27

Ervin, Laura (daughter), 53, 76, 87

Ervin, Laura (sister), 23

Ervin, Laura Powe (mother), 18–20, 22,
40–42

Ervin, Leslie, 53, 76, 87, 180

Ervin, Margaret (sister), 20

Ervin, Margaret Bell: children of, 53, 71,
76, 159; courtship of, 44, 46, 48; and
Great Depression, 66; home of, 48;
marriage of, 48, 53, 215; on McCarthy,
86, 87, 89, 92; photographs of, 23, 45,
87, 300; and retirement of Sam Ervin,
295, 297; and servants, 53; as teacher,
48; and Watergate, 285, 293; and
women's role, 159

Ervin, Sam: African Americans on, 86, 114,
215, 331 (n. 23); autobiography by, xii,
19, 38, 158, 195–96, 254, 301, 341 (n. 3);
Bible quotes by, 1, 29, 117, 148, 161, 184,
197, 226, 370 (n. 90); biographies of,
xiii, xv, 38, 320 (n. 3); birth of, xii, 13;
childhood and youth of, 18–24, 29–42;
children of, 53, 71, 76, 159; and Civil
War battlefields, 24; and "Claghorn's
Hammurabi," 133; community service
and professional activities by, 56, 62,
66, 72; courtship of Margaret Bell by,
44, 46, 48; critics of, 10, 86, 114, 133, 138,
162, 207, 208, 271–72, 292, 300, 305–6
(n. 22), 331 (n. 23); death of, xii, 11, 299;
and deaths of siblings, 71, 72, 73; education of, 29–36, 44, 85; and etiquette of
civility, 68, 99, 130, 138, 301; family
background of, 24–29; Fan Club for, 4;
and father's death, 72; finances of, 66,
77, 179, 297; as Freemason, 58; and
genealogy, 24, 75–76; health problems
of, 36, 71, 299, 332 (n. 31); homes of, 20,
48; on Kennedy assassination, 145;
marriage of, 48, 53, 215; and Native
Americans, 174; parents of, 17–20, 43,
44; personality and character of, 22–23,
49, 70, 71, 284, 319 (n. 137); photographs of, 3, 5, 23, 32, 33, 37, 67, 87, 88,
100, 109, 121, 163, 181, 196, 216, 293, 299,
300; physical appearance of, 1, 161;
poetry quotations by, 69, 96, 161; as
Presbyterian, 21–22, 24–25, 58, 72, 76,
194, 292, 299; racism charges against,
53, 57, 83, 133–34, 331 (n. 23); reading
by, 22, 23, 72; retirement of, 8, 24, 295,
296–99; sense of humor of, 22–23, 29,
49, 59, 70, 74, 78, 93–94, 104, 113–14,
156, 174, 202–3; and servants, 21, 51, 53;
Shakespeare quotations by, 146, 154; as
storyteller, 7, 46, 49, 50–51, 70, 74, 93–
94, 104, 113–14, 129, 130, 134, 135, 137,
141, 142, 156, 161, 179, 192, 226, 229–30,
254, 300–301, 319 (n. 137); and World
War I, 36–40, 42; and World War II, 21;
writings by, xii, xv, 281, 308 (n. 41)
—career of: as Burke County Criminal

Court judge, 68–69; cartoons on, 33, 95, 123, 145, 197, 241, 262, 298; and constitutional philosophy, 9–10, 101–2, 305–6 (n. 22); FBI file on, 395 (n. 82); as "founding father," 244, 286, 299, 302, 388 (n. 106), 400 (n. 63); as gubernatorial candidate, 80–81, 86, 319 (n. 136); and Harvard Law School, 43–44, 46–48, 69, 316 (n. 89); in House of Representatives, 73–75, 178–79, 210; as lawyer, 43, 48–53, 66, 67, 71–72, 75, 76–77, 172, 189, 254–55, 312 (n. 22); as lobbyist for educators, 77; and murder cases, 51–52, 59–61, 80, 316 (n. 93); in North Carolina legislature, 48, 57–59, 76, 143, 189, 313 (n. 50); on North Carolina special commission on court system, 77; as North Carolina Superior Court judge, 66, 69–71, 84, 316 (n. 93), 321 (n. 19); as North Carolina Supreme Court judge, 77–81, 84, 85–86, 102–3, 117, 318–19 (n. 131), 319 (n. 137); paradoxes and contradictory career of, xii–xiii, 9–10, 162, 186, 191, 299–301, 400–401 (n. 63); and political philosophy, 1–2, 4–6, 11–13, 80, 86, 99, 177, 182, 184, 193–94, 234, 278–79, 296, 301–2, 355 (n. 19); significance of, xii–xiii, 340 (n. 130); and speeches, 93–94, 104–5, 125–26, 132, 155, 184–85, 192, 195–99, 223, 226, 286, 297, 395 (n. 83); stereotypes of, as country lawyer and conservative southern senator, 161–62, 182, 254–55; and textile strike (1934), 63–66, 177

Ervin, Samuel, III, 53, 71, 72, 76, 87, 319 (n. 137)

Ervin, Samuel James, Sr.: childhood and youth of, 17, 27; church membership of, 21–22, 59; civic and business contributions of, 28–29; clothing worn by and physical appearance of, 17, 22; daily schedule of, 17; death of, 72; and Democratic Party, 27–28, 62; and election violence in 1898, 28; family background of, 17, 24–26; on judges, 68; as lawyer, 17–18, 43, 44, 48, 49, 51–52, 66; marriage of, 18; personality of, 17, 49; photograph of, 18; and privacy rights, 204; and Prohibition, 58–59, 204; reading by, 17–18; and Reconstruction, 26–27, 27–28, 47; and Sam's education, 30; and Sam's wedding, 48

Ervin, Susan Graham, 15, 54–55, 307 (n. 11)

Escobedo v. Illinois, 186

Evolution debate, 58, 59

Executive power and privilege: definition of, 238–39; and Eisenhower, 125, 169, 235; Ervin on, 238–39, 285–86; Ervin's conflict with Nixon over, 238–43; and Kennedy, 235; and Nixon, 185, 238–43, 279, 285–86, 385 (n. 93), 387 (n. 101); and withholding of information by administrative departments, 236

Ex parte Milligan, 5–6

Fairman, Charles, 102–3, 328 (n. 102)

Family Practice of Medicine Act, 236–37

Faubus, Orval, 125, 168, 340 (n. 130)

Faulkner, William, 24

FBI. See Federal Bureau of Investigation

FCC. See Federal Communications Commission

Federal Bureau of Investigation: domestic spying by, 251, 272–74, 363 (n. 17), 393 (n. 72), 394 (nn. 74–77), 395 (n. 82); and Ervin file, 395 (n. 82); Ervin's criticism of, 208; Ervin's refusal to investigate, 273–74; and Government Employees Bill of Rights, 372 (n. 100); and Huston Plan, 252; intelligence gathering on members of Congress by, 393 (n. 72); Schorr investigation by, 223–24; Supreme Court on access to records of, 164, 169

Federal Communications Commission (FCC), 223, 379 (n. 49)

Federal Election Campaign Act (1974), 295

The Federalist, 151

Fifteenth Amendment, 117, 158

Fifth Amendment, 128, 218

Filibusters: and Civil Rights Act (1957), 122, 335 (n. 73); and Civil Rights Act (1960), 128–31, 339 (n. 114), 340 (n. 123); and Civil Rights Act (1964), 146, 147; against civil rights bills generally, 112; cloture vote against, 138, 147, 149, 340 (n. 126); against drafting strikers (1946), 75; by Ervin, 128–29, 137–38, 146, 296, 340 (n. 123); against Fortas's appointment to Supreme Court, 155; on literacy tests, 137; against open housing, 155; by Thurmond, 122

First Amendment: and freedom of the press, 223, 378 (n. 47); and government domestic spying, 248, 255, 256, 263, 269–70, 274–75; and privacy rights, 204; and school prayer, 193, 195, 196, 198

Flanigan, Peter, 240

Fleming, Clara, 51

Fleming, Samuel, 16

Fortas, Abe, 154–55, 351 (n. 102)

Fourteenth Amendment: and *Brown v. Board of Education*, 83, 101, 102, 158, 159, 326 (n. 84), 327 (n. 88), 328 (n. 96); and Civil Rights Act (1957), 117; and Civil Rights Act (1964), 141; and Civil Rights Act (1968), 155, 157; and ERA, 179; Ervin's interpretation of, 158; and privacy rights, 204; and shield law for reporters, 378 (n. 47)

Fourth Amendment, 188, 219, 357 (n. 34), 370 (n. 90)

Franklin, Beau, 52

Freedom of Information Act (1966), 169, 200, 368 (n. 73)

Freedom of the press, 169, 222–24, 279, 378–79 (n. 46)

Freedom Rides, 135, 136

Freedom Summer, 147

Freemasons, 58

Freund, Paul, 305–6 (n. 22)

Froehlke, Robert F., 258, 266–68, 270, 271, 393 (n. 67)

Fulbright, J. William, 144–45, 195, 196, 239

Gardner, O. Max, 62, 69

Garrison, Lum, 57

Gatton, Harry, 93

Genealogy, 24, 75–76

General Services Administration, 295

Genocide treaty, 296

George, Walter, 89, 90, 105–6, 108–9

Georgia and civil rights, 99, 148, 150

Gibbon, Edward, xi

Gideon v. Wainwright, 364 (n. 30)

Goldwater, Barry, 284

Government domestic spying: ACLU's suit against, 255–56, 275, 277; on anti-war protesters, 247, 250, 261, 377 (n. 39); Army cover-up of, 248–51, 253, 256, 259, 276; and civil liberties, 391 (n. 28); conservatives' support for, 271–72; and CONUS system, 247–49, 251, 253, 388 (n. 2), 392 (n. 42); critics of Ervin's hearings on, 271–72; and Ervin's bill prohibiting military surveillance of civilians, 275–76, 396 (n. 92); Ervin's hearings on, 246–48, 253–54, 258–72, 276–77, 279, 393 (n. 67), 395 (n. 81); Ervin's opposition to, 9, 388 (n. 5), 389 (n. 10), 390 (n. 19); Ervin's speeches on, 274–75; by FBI, 272–74, 394 (nn. 74–77), 395 (n. 82); and First Amendment, 248, 255, 256, 263, 269–70, 274–75; Halperin on, 396 (n. 93); and HEW blacklist of scientists, 221; and Huston Plan, 221, 251–53, 289, 376 (n. 33), 390 (nn. 17, 19); and InterDivisional Information Unit, 391 (n. 28); and Justice Department, 250, 251, 257, 259, 268–70, 272; and library records, 221, 377 (n. 36); on members of Congress by FBI, 272, 393 (n. 72); national security argument on, 256–58; and news media, 254–60, 268, 270, 271, 273, 276–77; and Nixon administration, 220–21, 250–54,

256–58, 264–65, 279; and Post Office
Department, 221; and privacy rights,
258–60, 271, 273; public opinion on,
272, 393 (n. 71); Pyle on, xv, 246–50,
259, 261, 265, 271, 388 (n. 1), 389 (n. 7),
392 (n. 42); and Secret Service pro-
gram, 221; Supreme Court on, 256,
275, 277; Watergate hearings com-
pared with hearings on, 246–47, 276–
77
Government Employees Bill of Rights,
202, 207–8, 214, 224–25, 372 (n. 100)
Government workers, privacy rights of,
200–202, 205–9, 214, 224–25, 369
(n. 76)
Graham, Billy, 196
Graham, Edward Kidder, 35–36
Graham, Frank, 212, 325 (n. 62)
Graham, Hugh Davis, 231–32
Gravel, Mike, 242
Great Depression, 63–66
Greene, Claude E., 344 (n. 28)
Greene, Lorne, 286
Greensboro Daily News, 95, 123, 371 (n. 94)
*Green v. County School Board of New Kent
County*, 349 (n. 84), 381 (n. 64)
Gregory, Dick, 290
Griffin, Robert, 230
Gurney, Edward, 3, 43, 398 (n. 12)
Guthrie, Arlo, 261

Haig, Alexander, 2
Haldeman, H. R. (Bob): and attempts to
discredit Ervin as chair of Watergate
Committee, 283; on busing, 229; on
Ervin as chair of select committee to
investigate Watergate, 2; and govern-
ment domestic spying, 221, 256; resig-
nation of, 285; on Schorr, 223; and
Watergate Committee, 283; and Water-
gate hearings, 287, 292, 293
Hallyburton, J. J., 60, 61
Halperin, Morton, 396 (n. 93)
Hamilton, Alexander, 105, 155
Hamilton, J. G. De Roulhac, 34–35

Hand, Learned, 48, 167
Harlan, John Marshall, 158
Hart, George L., Jr., 256
Hart, Philip, 136, 153, 207, 337 (n. 88), 351
(n. 103)
Harvard Law School, 43–44, 46–48, 69,
102–3, 316 (n. 89)
Hauser, Charlie, 76
Hawkins, Joshua, 50–51
Haynsworth, Clement F., 228
Health and safety regulations, 8–9
Health, Education, and Welfare Depart-
ment, U.S.: and blacklist of scientists,
221; computerized files of, 202, 268;
and enforcement of school integration,
149–52, 159–60, 205, 206, 226–27, 235,
349 (n. 74); and funding cuts for
enforcement of school desegregation,
151, 226–27; and funds for desegregated
schools, 128
Helms, Jesse, 284, 400 (n. 59)
Helms, Richard, 252
Hennings, Thomas, 94, 113, 120, 127, 167,
169–70, 172, 243, 356 (n. 31)
Herbers, John, 182
Hertz v. Woodman, 102
Hicks, James, 337 (n. 90)
Higher Education Act (1965), 194
Higher Education Facilities Act (1963),
193–94
Hobbes, Thomas, 9
Hobson, Fred, 24
Hodges, Luther, 126
Hoey, Clyde R., 62, 69, 82, 84, 170, 243, 320
(n. 4), 321 (n. 19)
Hoff, Joan, 385 (n. 91), 397 (n. 3)
Hoffa, James, 178, 280
Holland, Spessard, 136
Holmes, Oliver Wendell, 47
Hoover, Herbert, 62
Hoover, J. Edgar, 252–53, 272, 274, 390
(n. 17), 394 (nn. 72, 76)
Horwitz, Morton J., 102
Hospitals: and labor unions, 296; segrega-
tion of, 350 (n. 89)

House Committee on Un-American Activities, 74, 258, 265

House of Representatives, U.S.: and busing, 382 (n. 71); Joe Ervin's term in, 71, 72–73; Sam Ervin's term in, 73–75, 178–79, 210. *See also specific members of Congress*

Housing, 153–56, 176, 213, 296, 350 (nn. 94, 96), 351 (n. 51)

Housing and Urban Development Department (HUD), 154

Housing Authority, In re, 79

Howe, George, 32

Howe, Harold, 150, 151

Hruska, Roman, 219, 242, 263–64, 276, 372 (n. 100)

HUD. *See* Housing and Urban Development Department

Hughes, Charles Evans, 101

Human Affairs, 271

Humphrey, Hubert H., 119, 151, 211, 214–15, 238, 283

Huston, Tom Charles, 221, 242, 251–52, 377 (n. 39), 390 (n. 19)

Huston Plan, 251–53, 289, 376 (n. 33), 390 (nn. 17, 19)

Immigration, 133, 162, 342 (n. 6)

Impoundment of funds, 237–38, 243, 274, 279, 295

Impoundment Procedures Act, 238, 243, 244

Indian Bill of Rights, 156, 175–76, 352 (n. 109), 359 (n. 60)

Inouye, Daniel, 3, 292, 372 (n. 100), 398 (n. 12)

In re Housing Authority, 79

Integration: and busing, 151, 152, 160, 226, 228–31, 274, 279, 296, 381 (n. 67), 381–82 (n. 69), 382 (n. 71); court cases against, 152; and housing, 153–56, 176, 213, 350 (nn. 94, 96), 351 (n. 103); of Little Rock schools, 114, 125–26, 168, 234, 338 (n. 105); of Montgomery bus system, 110, 118; Nixon and school deseg-

regation, 226–31, 381 (n. 67); northern school districts and desegregation, 230; public opinion on, 152; of public schools, 82–84, 97–106, 130, 149–52, 159–60, 205, 206, 226–31, 320 (n. 4), 328 (n. 95), 337 (n. 98), 381 (nn. 64, 67); statistics on, of schools, 150, 151, 228; of universities, 136, 139, 140. *See also* Civil rights; Education; Segregation

InterDivisional Information Unit, 391 (n. 28)

Internal Revenue Service, 201, 377 (n. 39)

Interstate Commerce Clause, 141, 155, 157, 346 (n. 44)

ITT affair, 240

Jackson, Henry, 387 (n. 102)

Jackson, LeRoy, 52

Javits, Jacob, 130, 351 (n. 103), 355 (n. 25)

Jaworski, Leon, 8, 294

Jefferson, Thomas, 193, 237, 301, 302, 401 (n. 67)

Jencks v. United States, 164, 169

Jenner, William E., 164–66

Jenner Bill, 166–68, 354–55 (n. 15), 355 (n. 18), 355–56 (nn. 24–25)

Johnson, Edwin C., 89–92

Johnson, Lady Bird, 89

Johnson, Lyndon: and Bail Reform Act, 190–91; and Civil Rights Act (1957), 122, 124; and Civil Rights Act (1960), 129; and Civil Rights Act (1964), 141, 146, 147, 150, 151; and Civil Rights Act (1968), 156; and civil rights bills after 1965, 152–54, 175; and civil rights in 1950s, 122, 124, 126–27, 331 (n. 21); and crime control legislation, 363 (nn. 20–21); on Ervin, 94, 124; Ervin's criticisms of generally, 264; Ervin's support of presidential programs of, 215; and McCarthy censure by Senate, 89–90, 94; and mental health bill, 172; and presidential election of 1960, 138; and presidential election of 1964, 147; and privacy rights, 392 (n. 47); public opin-

ion on presidency of, 152; Supreme
Court appointments by, 154–55, 351
(nn. 99, 102), 371 (n. 94); as vice president, 141; and Voting Rights Act (1965),
147–49, 152; and wiretapping, 187–88,
363 (nn. 20–21)

Johnston, Olin, 170

Jonas, Charles R., Jr., 283–84

Jordan, B. Everett, 198, 344 (n. 31)

Jordan, Robert E., III, 248–50, 258

Journalists. *See* News media; Television;
specific newspapers and magazines

Judicial temperament, 69

Judiciary Committee. *See* Senate Judiciary
Committee

Jury selection, 155, 352 (n. 104)

Jury trial: and Civil Rights Act (1957)
amendment, 119, 122–24; and Constitution, 116, 117, 333–34 (n. 50); Ervin
on importance of, 146; and Ervin's
objections to civil rights bills (1963 and
1964), 346 (n. 43); and Ervin's objections to Civil Rights Act (1957), 116,
117–19, 122, 124, 333 (n. 43), 333–34
(n. 50), 334 (n. 58), 334–35 (nn. 62–63),
356 (n. 28); O'Mahoney's compromise
on, in Civil Rights Act (1957), 356
(n. 28); Speedy Trial Act, 295–96

Justice Department, U.S.: and Civil Rights
Act (1957), 338 (n. 103); and civil rights
and attorney general's power, 112, 115–
16, 120, 140, 346 (n. 43); and civil rights
bill (1963), 140; Civil Rights Section of,
112; and court procedures reforms, 364
(n. 25); domestic surveillance by, 250,
251, 257, 259, 268–70, 272; and ITT
affair, 240; and literacy tests for voting,
137; and news media, 222; and Nixon's
crime control program, 217, 218; and
Nixon's executive orders, 386 (n. 98);
and preventive detention, 218; on
problems in criminal justice, 188; and
school desegregation, 120, 227, 228–29;
and "Speech or Debate" immunity of
members of Congress, 242; and suits

against poll tax, 148; on violence
against African Americans, 126; and
Voting Rights Act, 227; and Watergate
hearings, 277

Katzenbach, Nicholas, 150, 192, 349 (n. 74)

Keating, Kenneth B., 339 (n. 114)

Kennedy, Edward, 271, 394 (n. 77)

Kennedy, John F.: assassination of, 145–46,
152; and civil rights legislation, 136–37,
139–40, 334 (n. 63), 345 (n. 33); and
Democratic National Convention
(1960), 132; Ervin on, 141, 145; and
executive power, 235; and legal aid, 189,
364 (n. 27); and presidential election of
1960, 138, 194, 211; in Senate, 141, 178,
334 (n. 63); and wiretapping, 187

Kennedy, Robert: and bail system, 190; and
Civil Rights Bill (1963), 139–45, 157, 159,
161; Ervin on, 141; and literacy test for
voting, 137; and Narcotic Addict Treatment and Rehabilitation Act, 368 (n. 73);
and Senate Rackets Committee, 141,
178; and wiretapping, 187, 363 (n. 18)

Kennedy-Ervin bill, 178, 360 (n. 72)

Kerner, Otto, 261

Kerner Commission, 261, 264, 392 (n. 46)

Key, V. O., 56, 321 (n. 13)

Kilpatrick, James J., 299, 302, 400 (n. 63)

Kincaid, Gladys, 59–60

King, Coretta Scott, 261

King, Martin Luther, Jr., 118, 125, 135, 139,
144, 261, 292

*Kingsley International Pictures v. New York
State Board of Regents*, 354 (n. 10)

Kinston Free Press, 70

Kissinger, Henry, 257

Kleindienst, Richard, 239–40, 285

Knowland, William, 323 (n. 44)

Ku Klux Klan, 34, 83

Kurland, Philip B., 368 (n. 70), 387 (n. 101)

Kutler, Stanley, 280, 385 (n. 91), 397 (n. 3)

Labor-Management Reporting Act, 360
(n. 72)

Labor unions: and *Darlington* case, 178–79, 351 (n. 102), 360–61 (n. 78); Ervin's opposition to, 9, 75, 177–79; federal bill against strikes, 74–75; and hospitals, 296; and jury trials, 119, 334 (n. 62); and Kennedy-Ervin bill, 178, 360 (n. 72); and Landrum-Griffin Act, 141; and LCCR, 153; and miners' strike, 75; and Senate investigation of labor racketeering, 178; and Taft-Hartley Act, 178; and textile strikes, 63–66, 117, 177; and Wagner Act, 75

Laird, Melvin, 255, 258

Laird v. Tatum, 270, 275, 277, 392 (n. 42), 396 (n. 90)

Lazarus, Arthur, Jr., 176

Leadership Conference on Civil Rights (LCCR): and AFL-CIO, 153; and civil rights legislation, 110, 149, 155–56, 339 (n. 114); on Ervin, 170, 351 (n. 104); and Indian Bill of Rights, 176; and presidential election of 1956, 111; Rauh as general counsel for, 305 (n. 22), 341 (n. 5); and school desegregation, 227

Lee, George, 330 (n. 10)

Lee, Howard, 144

Legal aid to poor defendants, 189, 364 (nn. 27, 30)

Legal Realist School, 328 (n. 95)

Lennon, Alton A., 88, 319 (n. 1), 321 (n. 14)

Lewis, John L., 75, 119

Library records, 221, 377 (n. 36)

Liddy, Gordon, 283

Lincoln, Abraham, 6, 342 (n. 8)

Lincoln, Benjamin, 174

Literacy tests, 136–38, 147–48, 343 (n. 24)

Little Rock, Ark., school desegregation, 114, 125–26, 168, 234, 338 (n. 105)

Llewellyn, Karl, 316 (n. 89)

London *Times*, 399 (n. 46)

Long, Edward V., 187, 188, 363 (n. 16)

Long, Russell, 131, 139, 147, 205

Look, 134

Los Angeles Times, 6–7, 146

Louisiana, 131, 338 (n. 101)

Lukas, J. Anthony, 280, 397 (n. 3)

Lynching, 60, 61. *See also* Violence

MacNeil, Neil, 286

Macy, John, 201–2, 205

Madison, James, 151, 169, 401 (n. 67)

Magruder, Jeb Stuart, 288

Mailer, Norman, 286

Malindy, Polly, 15

Mallory, Andrew, 165–66, 186

Mallory v. United States, 165–66, 186, 191, 213

Malone, Walter, 69

Manhattan Bail Project, 189–90

Mansfield, Mike, 147, 148, 176, 278, 282, 283, 396–97 (n. 1), 397 (n. 7)

Mardian, Robert, 242

Marion, Francis, 25

Marshall, John, 101, 102, 371 (n. 94)

Marshall, Thurgood, 154, 187, 351 (n. 99)

McCarthy, Joe: and Army-McCarthy hearings, 86–87, 89, 91, 92, 235, 259, 260–61; censure of, by Senate, 82, 89–96, 106, 278, 286, 302, 323 (n. 44), 323–24 (nn. 47–49), 324 (nn. 52–53), 324–25 (n. 62), 325 (nn. 64–65); and government domestic spying, 265; Margaret Ervin on, 86, 87, 89, 92; newspapers on, 94–96, 324 (n. 52); and Nixon, 210–11, 240

McCarthy, Mary, 7

McClellan, John, 170, 387 (n. 102)

McCord, James, 283, 284–85, 287

McGovern, George, 207

McKay, Martha, 305 (n. 22), 341 (n. 5)

McLean, A. W., 60

McMichael, Jule, 70

McMillan, James B., 324–25 (n. 62)

McNamara, Francis J., 258

Media. *See* News media; Television; *specific newspapers and magazines*

Medicaid and Medicare, 8

Mental Health Bill for District of Columbia, 172, 357–58 (n. 42)

Mentally ill, 171–72, 177, 357–58 (nn. 42–43), 375 (n. 21)

Meredith, James, 139

Metcalf, Lee, 176

Michaux, Dick, 48

Mikva, Abner, 261, 266

Military domestic surveillance. *See* Government domestic spying

Military draft, 74

Military Justice Act, 173

Military personnel, civil liberties of, 172–73, 201

Miller, Arthur S., 328 (n. 97)

Miller, Broadus, 60–61

Milligan, Ex parte, 5–6

Mills, Joe ("Captain"), 28

Miners' strike, 75

Minimum wage, 8

Minority business opportunities, 231–32

Minority identification questionnaires, 205, 206, 371 (n. 97)

Miranda v. Arizona, 186, 187, 191, 207, 213, 214, 255

Mississippi and civil rights, 99, 109, 126, 136, 139, 145, 147, 148, 228

Mitchell, Clarence, 111, 146, 170, 176

Mitchell, John: and crime control, 216, 217; and CRP, 281; and government domestic spying, 250–51, 257, 272, 273; Kleindienst as replacement for, 239–40; and Philadelphia Plan, 233; and Watergate hearings, 287, 290, 293; and Watergate scandal, 280, 288

Mitchell, Juanita, 111

Mitchell, Margaret, 27

Mondale, Walter F., 156

Montague, Arthur, 51–52

Montgomery, Ala., bus boycott, 110, 118

Montoya, Joseph, 398 (n. 12)

Moore, Dan K., 78, 373 (n. 5)

Morganton, N.C.: African Americans in, 21, 53, 54; community service by Ervin in, 56, 62, 66, 72; court cases in, during nineteenth century, 15–16; courthouse in, 15–17; cultural events in, 55; economy of, 13–14, 28–29, 54–55, 63, 76; Ervin family's move to, 17, 26; homes of Sam Ervin in, 20, 48; local government of, 55; and mountains in Burke County, 14–15; murder cases in, 51–52, 59–61; population of, 13, 53–54; Presbyterian Church in, 21–22, 76, 299; race relations in, 21, 53, 54, 76; retirement of Ervin in, 296–99; schools in, 29, 55, 57, 76, 143; white leaders of, 55–56

Morganton News-Herald, 60, 61, 72

Murder cases, 51–52, 59–61, 80, 316 (n. 93)

Murphy, Bruce Allen, 351 (n. 102)

Murphy, Carl, 337 (n. 90)

Murray v. Curlett, 193

Muskie, Edmund, 296

NAACP. *See* National Association for the Advancement of Colored People

Narcotic Addict Rehabilitation Act (1966), 200, 368 (n. 73)

National Archives, 295

National Association for the Advancement of Colored People: on Black Power advocates, 153; on black voter registration in South, 331 (n. 16); on civil rights legislation in 1950s, 108, 110, 117–18, 125–27, 388 (n. 103); on Eisenhower administration, 126; on Ervin, 110, 117–18, 141; and Johnson administration, 266; and Kennedy administration, 136; and "kissing case," 337 (n. 99); military surveillance of, 247; in North Carolina, 126, 139; Pohlhaus as general counsel for, 305 (n. 22), 341 (n. 5); and school desegregation, 227; Supreme Court on, 192. *See also* Wilkins, Roy

National Election Commission, 295

National Guard, 63–66

National Labor Relations Board (NLRB), 75, 178–79, 236, 296, 360 (n. 73)

National Labor Relations Board v. Darlington Manufacturing Company et al., 178–79, 351 (n. 102), 360–61 (n. 78)

National Review, 257–58

National security argument, 4, 6, 256–58, 291

National Women's Political Caucus, 305
(n. 22), 341 (n. 5)

Native Americans, 156, 162, 173–76, 177, 352
(n. 109), 358 (n. 43), 359 (n. 60)

Naval Academy Preparatory School, 29–30

Newby, I. A., 129

New Deal, 62

Newman, Edwin, 389 (n. 10)

New Republic, 124, 207, 219, 271, 336 (n. 87)

News and Observer. See *Raleigh News and Observer*

News media: freedom of, 169, 222–24, 279,
378–79 (n. 46); and shield law for
reporters, 378 (n. 47). *See also* Television; *specific newspapers and magazines*

New South, 12–14, 28–29, 55–56

Newspaper cartoons, 95, 123, 145, 197, 241,
262, 298

Newsweek, 111, 223

Newton, Adrian, 319 (n. 137)

New York Times: on Civil Rights Act
(1957), 333 (n. 43); on Ervin during
Watergate hearings, 6, 9; Ervin on freedom in, 395 (n. 83); on Ervin's defense
of civil liberties, 182; and Ervin's hearings on government domestic spying,
270; on Ervin's opposition to Democratic Party platform on civil rights,
341 (n. 1); on Ervin's voting record in
U.S. Senate, 8–9; on government
domestic spying, 250, 270, 273; on
Hennings, 170; on Nixon-Ervin conflicts, 282; on Nixon's anticrime bill,
220; and Pentagon Papers, 223; Rehnquist's editorial in, 396 (n. 90); on
World War I, 40

New York Times Magazine, 7, 219, 304
(n. 15)

New York Times v. United States, 223

Nixon, Richard M.: and anticommunism,
210–11, 265; and busing, 226, 228–31,
381 (n. 67); civil rights policy of, and
Ervin, 226–33, 245, 279, 381 (n. 67); and
control of his presidential tapes and
documents, 295; and crime control, 9,

214, 215–20, 257, 295, 360 (n. 68), 375
(nn. 21, 24), 376 (n. 33); and ERA, 214,
225–26; Ervin's conflicts with, over
civil liberties, 185, 220–25, 245, 279;
Ervin's conflicts with, over separation
of powers, 233–45, 279, 386 (n. 98);
Ervin's support of presidential programs of, 215; and executive agreements, 243; and executive power and
privilege, 185, 238–43, 279, 285–86, 291,
385 (n. 93), 387 (n. 101); foreign policy
of, 243, 387 (n. 100); and government
domestic spying, 220–21, 250–54, 256–
58, 264–65, 279; and Government
Employees Bill of Rights, 224–25; and
Huston Plan, 251–53, 289, 390 (nn. 17,
19); imperial presidency of, 4, 7, 242,
243, 244, 276, 279, 285; and impoundment of funds, 237–38, 274, 279; and
McCarthy, 210–11, 240; memoirs by,
280–81; and minority business opportunities, 231–32; national security argument by, 4, 256–58, 291; and news
media, 8, 219, 220, 221–24, 227, 256–58,
279, 378–79 (n. 47); and Pentagon
Papers, 238, 242, 281; and Philadelphia
Plan, 232–33, 236; photographs of, 88,
216; pocket veto by, 236–37; and presidential election of 1960, 211, 214; and
presidential election of 1968, 10, 211,
214–15; public opinion on, during
Watergate hearings, 4, 290, 294; reelection of, 4, 282; refusal of, to surrender
tapes, 6, 291, 293–94; resignation of, 8,
244, 294; Russell on, 211; and SACB,
240, 242, 257, 279, 386 (n. 98); and
school desegregation, 226–31, 381
(n. 67); in Senate, 210–11, 240; Southern Strategy of, 226–27; and Supreme
Court, 214, 226, 227–29; and surrender
of White House tapes, 277, 294; vetoes
by, 244; as vice president, 86, 88, 90,
211; and Vietnam War, 249, 281; and
Voting Rights Act (1970), 227; and
Watergate Committee chaired by

Ervin, 2, 283–84; and Watergate scandal, 6, 280–85, 289–91, 293–94; and wiretapping, 257, 389–90 (n. 12). *See also Watergate headings*

NLRB. *See* National Labor Relations Board

No-knock searches by police, 217, 218–19, 220, 375 (n. 21)

Nonviolent civil disobedience, 135

North Carolina legislature, 48, 57–59, 76, 143, 189, 313 (n. 50)

North Carolina Superior Court, 66, 68–71, 84, 316 (n. 93), 321 (n. 19)

North Carolina Supreme Court, 52, 70, 77–81, 85–86, 102–3, 117, 318–19 (n. 131), 319 (n. 137)

Oberdorfer, Don, 355 (n. 24)

Obscenity and pornography, 165, 192, 354 (n. 10)

O'Hara, Barratt, 168

O'Hara, James G., 382 (n. 71)

Omaha World-Herald, 154

O'Mahoney, Joseph, 356 (n. 28)

Omnibus Crime Control and Safe Streets Act (1968), 188, 213–14, 220, 363 (nn. 20–21), 375 (n. 21)

Orwell, George, 246

Palmer, Jim, 80

Parker, John J., 97–98, 159

Parker, Samuel I., 39–40, 42, 310 (n. 73)

Parmet, Herbert S., 397 (n. 3)

Paternalism, 56, 57–58, 63, 68, 115, 138, 143–44, 177, 301

Patterson, John, 340 (n. 130)

Pearsall Plan, 98

Pennsylvania v. Nelson, 164

Pentagon Papers, 223, 238, 242, 281

Percy, Charles, 244, 296

Personality tests, 369 (n. 76), 371 (n. 97)

Philadelphia Plan, 232–33, 236

Pitt, William, the Elder, 5

Plessy v. Ferguson, 86, 158

Plumbers. *See* White House "Plumbers"

Pocket Veto Act, 237, 243

Pohlhaus, J. Francis, 305 (n. 22), 341 (n. 5)

Police, 186–87, 217, 218–19, 220. *See also* Crime control

Pollitt, Daniel H., 166

Poll tax, 136, 148, 192, 343 (n. 22)

Poole, David Scott, 58–59

Pornography and obscenity, 165, 192, 354 (n. 10)

Post Office Department, 221

Pound, Roscoe, 47

Powell, Betty, 21, 51, 53

Powell, Polly, 21, 53

Prayer. *See* School prayer

Presbyterian Church, 21–22, 24–25, 58, 59, 72, 76, 86, 194, 292, 299

Preserving the Constitution (Ervin), xii, 301, 341 (n. 3)

Presidential election of 1928, 61–63

Presidential election of 1956, 111, 331 (n. 21)

Presidential election of 1960, 127, 138, 194, 211, 214

Presidential election of 1964, 147

Presidential election of 1968, 10, 211, 214–15, 226, 350 (n. 87)

Presidential election of 1972, 4, 231, 282

Preslar, Lloyd, 186

Preventive detention, 217–18, 220, 295, 375 (nn. 21, 24)

Preyer, L. Richardson, 373 (n. 5)

Price controls, 74

Prisoner work release programs, 199

Pritchett, Herman, 354 (n. 7), 356 (n. 25)

Privacy Act (1975), 296

Privacy rights: and census questionnaires, 203–4, 209, 224; and computerized data banks, 202–3, 209, 224, 247, 253–54, 263, 268; conservatives' support for, 206; and Constitution, 204, 307 (n. 90); Ervin's bill on, 296; Ervin's speech on, 184–85; and false prophets, 184–85, 204, 370 (n. 88); for federal government workers, 200–202, 205–9, 214, 224–25, 369 (n. 76); and Johnson administration, 392 (n. 47); liberals' support for, 206–7; and minority identification questionnaires, 205, 206, 371 (n. 97); newspapers on, 206, 371 (n. 94); reasons for Ervin's commitment to, 204–6; and southern constitutional tradition, 204–5; and southern opposition to civil rights, 205–7; and wiretapping, 187–88, 191, 208, 213, 217, 257, 363 (nn. 16–18, 20–21), 389–90 (n. 12). *See also* Civil liberties; Government domestic spying

Progressive, 219, 271

Progressive mystique, 301, 344 (n. 28), 401 (n. 65)

Progressive Plutocracy, 56–59, 62–63, 66, 80–81, 85, 115

Prohibition, 58–59, 62, 204

Proxmire, William, 242

Pucinski, Roman C., 382 (n. 71)

Pyle, Christopher, xv, 246–50, 255, 259, 261, 265, 271, 388 (n. 1), 389 (n. 7), 392 (n. 42)

Race relations. *See* Civil rights; Integration; Racism; Segregation

Race relations in North Carolina, 21, 53, 54, 76, 115, 134, 139, 142–43

Racism: charges of, against Ervin, 53, 57, 83, 133–34, 220, 331 (n. 23); Ervin on, 342 (n. 7); and paternalism, 56, 57–58, 63, 68, 115, 138, 143–44, 301; rhetoric against civil rights, 99, 105, 110, 130, 335 (n. 71); and violence against African Americans, 98, 118, 126, 135, 136, 138–39; and whites' "nigra jokes," 74, 104

Rackets Committee, 141, 178

Railroad pensions, 296

Raleigh, Sir Walter, xi

Raleigh News and Observer, 60, 137–38, 191

Raleigh Times, 59

Randolph, A. Phillip, 337 (n. 90)

Raper, Charles Lee, 32, 34

Rather, Dan, 223

Rauh, Joseph, Jr., 118, 140, 161–62, 177, 305 (n. 22), 334–35 (n. 63), 341 (n. 5)

Reapportionment of congressional districts, 192

Reconstruction, 12, 24–27, 34–35, 47, 108, 115, 333 (n. 38)

Red Shirt Brigades, 28, 34

Reedy, George E., 90–91

Reeves, Richard, 397 (n. 3)

Rehnquist, William H., 268–70, 275, 396 (n. 90)

Republican Party: and African Americans, 111; and civil rights in 1950s, 126, 127, 338 (n. 105); funds for, 240; 1968 national convention of, 261, 266; in North Carolina, 62; and presidential election of 1928, 62; and presidential election of 1968, 226, 350 (n. 87); during Reconstruction, 28

Retirement pensions, 296

Ribicoff, Abraham, 296

Richmond News Leader, 199

Richmond Times-Dispatch, 119

Right of Privacy Act (1967), 363 (nn. 16, 20)

Right to privacy. *See* Privacy rights

Riley, Ernest, 65–66

Riots. *See* Violence

Rogers, William, 124, 126, 127

Rooney, John, 193

Roosevelt, Franklin D., 75

Roth v. United States, 165, 354 (n. 10)

Royster, Wilbur, 32

Russell, Richard: and Civil Rights Act (1957), 120–22, 124; and Civil Rights Act (1960), 128, 340 (n. 123); and Civil Rights Act (1964), 146, 147, 150; death of, 231; on Ervin and civil liberties, 177; and literacy tests for voting, 137; and McCarthy censure, 89; on Nixon, 211; and open housing bill (1968), 213; and school prayer, 194, 367 (n. 56); significance of, 340 (n. 130); and Southern Manifesto, 106, 150; and southern strategy against civil rights generally, 109, 335 (n. 71), 382 (n. 74); stereotype of, 161

SACB. *See* Subversive Activities Control Board

Safe Streets and Crime Prevention Act (1968), 188, 213–14, 220, 363 (nn. 20–21), 375 (n. 21)

Safety regulations, 8–9

Sanford, Terry, 138, 211–13, 344 (nn. 30–31), 373 (n. 5)

San Francisco Chronicle, 197

Scheirbeck, Helen Maynor, 173

Schlafly, Phyllis, 226, 296

Schlei, Norbert, 346 (n. 44)

Schlesinger, Arthur, Jr., 243, 276, 397 (n. 3), 401 (n. 67)

School prayer, 192–99, 235, 367 (n. 56), 368 (n. 70)

Schools. *See* Busing; Education; Integration

Schorr, Daniel, 223–24, 239

SCLC. *See* Southern Christian Leadership Conference

Scopes trial, 59

Scott, Kerr, 321 (n. 14)

Seawell, A. A. F., 78

Secret Service, 221

Segregation: African Americans' views of, 134, 337 (n. 98); and *Briggs v. Elliot*, 97–98, 159; Ervin on, 134; of hospitals, 350 (n. 89); and Montgomery bus boycott, 110, 118; in North Carolina, 12, 126; and opposition to *Brown v. Board of Education*, 97–106; senatorial defenders of, 96–107, 109–10; and separate but equal doctrine, 76, 82, 86, 158. *See also* Civil rights; Integration

Senate, U.S.: and busing, 229–31, 381 (n. 69); censure of McCarthy by, 82, 89–96, 106, 286, 323 (n. 44), 323–24 (nn. 47–49), 324 (nn. 52–53), 324–25 (n. 62), 325 (nn. 64–65); and civil rights bills after 1965, 153–54, 350–51 (n. 97); committee assignments for Ervin in, 88, 107, 108, 110, 113, 141, 162, 170, 235, 243, 339 (n. 115), 360 (n. 73), 387 (n. 102); and EEOC, 231–32; elec-
tion and reelections of Ervin to, 106, 138, 211–13, 215, 330 (n. 120), 373 (n. 5); and ERA, 9, 179–80, 225, 226; Ervin's appointment to, 82–86, 170, 243; Ervin's voting record in, xii–xiii, 8–9, 162, 397 (n. 1); and genocide treaty, 296; and international agreements, 243, 387 (n. 100); and Johnson's Supreme Court appointments, 154–55, 351 (nn. 99, 102), 371 (n. 94); and literacy tests, 136–38, 147–48, 343 (n. 24), 344 (n. 27); McCarthy's Permanent Investigations Subcommittee of, 88–89; and Nixon's impoundment of funds, 237–38, 279; and Pentagon Papers, 242; and Philadelphia Plan, 232–33, 233; and pocket veto by Nixon, 236–37; and poll tax, 136, 148; retirement of Ervin from, 295, 296–99; salary of Senators, 179; and school prayer, 194–99; and soft southern strategy against civil rights, 110, 113–20, 122, 124, 127–31, 137–38, 146, 160, 168, 205, 335 (n. 71), 336 (nn. 83, 87), 338–39 (n. 113); Southern Caucus in, 108–9; southern control of committees in, 108, 330 (n. 2); southern Democratic senators' blocking of civil rights bills in, 108–12; and Southern Manifesto, 105–7, 150, 234, 329 (n. 119); and "Speech or Debate" immunity of members of, 242, 243, 387 (n. 99); and SACB, 240, 242; voting record of Ervin in, xii–xiii, 8–9, 162; and Watergate scandal, 282; and Watergate special committee, 282, 283; Watkins Committee of, 91–92, 96, 323 (n. 44), 323–24 (nn. 47–49). *See also* Filibusters; Senate Judiciary Committee; Senate Subcommittee on Constitutional Rights; Watergate hearings; *specific laws and senators*

Senate Appropriations Committee, 242, 387 (n. 102)

Senate Government Operations Committee, 88, 243–44, 282, 295, 387 (n. 102)

Senate Judiciary Committee: and civil rights, 107, 108, 109–10, 113, 119–20, 175, 339 (n. 115); and crime bill (1968), 213–14, 374 (n. 13); Eastland as chair of, 107, 109, 119; and Fortas's appointment to Supreme Court, 155; and Hennings's death, 170; and Jenner Bill, 167; and Watergate scandal, 282, 399 (n. 48)

Senate Rackets Committee, 141, 178

Senate Rules Committee, 339 (n. 115)

Senate Subcommittee on Administration Practices, 271

Senate Subcommittee on Constitutional Rights: and bail system, 190; and civil liberties, 169–77, 185, 279, 356 (n. 31), 357 (n. 34); and civil rights, 107, 110, 113–16, 119, 137, 139, 150–51, 169, 170, 339 (n. 115); and computerized data banks, 202, 224, 247, 253–54, 263, 268; Ervin as chair of, 162, 170–71, 185, 188, 208, 243, 279; and freedom of the press, 222–24; Hennings as chair of, 167, 169–70, 357 (n. 34); and legal aid, 189, 364 (n. 30); and military domestic surveillance, 246–50, 253–54, 258–72, 276, 279, 393 (n. 67), 395 (nn. 81–82); and Nixon's anticrime proposals, 217, 224; and privacy rights of government workers, 200–202, 205, 208; and voting rights, 227; and Watergate scandal, 397 (n. 7)

Senate Subcommittee on Separation of Powers, 232–33, 235–40, 242, 243, 279, 360 (n. 73), 383 (n. 79), 385 (n. 93)

Separation of powers doctrine, 232–45, 279, 386 (n. 98)

Service v. Dulles, 164

Settlemyre, Uncle, 21

Shakespeare, William, 146, 154

Shannon, Jasper Barry, 55

Sharp, Susie, 70, 76, 180

Sherrill, Robert, 305 (n. 22), 341 (n. 5)

Sidey, Hugh, 284

Silver, Frankie, 15

Simmons, Furnifold, 57, 62

Sirica, John J., 281, 283, 284

Sixth Amendment, 189, 295

Slavery, 25, 26

Smith, Al, 62

Smith, Lamar, 330 (n. 10)

Smith, Willis, 212

Smith Act, 164

SNCC. See Student Nonviolent Coordinating Committee

Sorensen, Theodore, 140

Southern Christian Leadership Conference (SCLC), 135, 153, 247

Southern Manifesto, 105–7, 150, 234, 329 (n. 119)

Southern Strategy, 226–27

Spaulding, Asa T., 337 (n. 90)

"Speech or Debate" immunity of members of Congress, 242, 243, 387 (n. 99)

Speedy Trial Act, 295–96

Speiser, Lawrence, 207, 208

Sports' antitrust exemption, 9, 199

Spying. See Government domestic spying

Staats, Elmer, 233, 383 (n. 78)

Stacy, Walter P., 52, 77–78

Stans, Maurice, 287

Stare decisis legal doctrine, 101, 102–3

States' rights, 191, 302, 326 (n. 84), 378 (n. 47)

State v. Ballance, 328 (n. 99)

State v. Bridges, 79

State v. Hart, 79

State v. Palmer, 80

State v. Scoggin, 79

Stennis, John: and Civil Rights Act (1957), 120, 121, 122; and Civil Rights Act (1964), 150; and McCarthy censure, 90–92; significance of, 340 (n. 130); and soft southern strategy against civil rights, 335 (n. 71); and Southern Manifesto, 106, 150; stereotype of, 161

Stevenson, Adlai, III, 261, 266

Stewart, Potter, 69

Strikes. See Labor unions

Student Nonviolent Coordinating Committee (SNCC), 131, 135, 153

Subversive Activities Control Board
(SACB), 240, 242, 243, 257, 279, 386
(n. 98)
Sullivan, William, 252–53
Supreme Court, U.S.: appeal of *Williams v.
North Carolina* to, 316 (n. 93); and
Brown II, 97, 98; and *Caldwell* case, 223,
378 (n. 47); and civil liberties, 164–68,
192, 279; and Cold War Cases, 164–65,
166, 208, 354 (n. 7); on Commerce
Clause, 141–42; and *Darlington* case,
178–79, 351 (n. 102), 360–61 (n. 78);
Ervin on Nixon's appointments to, 228;
Ervin's criticisms of, 117, 129, 164–69,
191–93, 208, 235; Ervin Sr. on, 18; and
First Amendment, 196; on freedom of
the press, 223, 378 (n. 47); on government domestic spying, 256, 275, 277;
and *Jencks* decision, 164, 169; and Jenner Bill, 166–68, 354–55 (n. 15), 355
(n. 18), 355–56 (nn. 24–25); Johnson's
appointments to, 154–55, 351 (nn. 99,
102), 371 (n. 94); on NAACP, 192; and
Nixon, 214, 226, 227–29; on Nixon's
surrender of White House tapes, 294;
and obscenity and pornography cases,
165, 192, 354 (n. 10); and Pentagon
Papers, 242; on poll tax, 192; public
awareness of decisions by, 98–99; and
rights of criminal defendants, 165–66,
186–87, 192, 213–14, 227, 279; and
school desegregation, 82–84, 97–106,
164, 227, 228, 320 (n. 4), 328 (n. 95), 349
(n. 84), 381 (n. 64); on school prayers,
192–94, 198, 199, 235, 367 (n. 56); and
separate but equal doctrine, 76, 82, 86,
158; on "Speech or Debate" immunity
of members of Congress, 242; on *stare
decisis*, 102. *See also specific cases and
Supreme Court justices*
Supreme Court of North Carolina. *See*
North Carolina Supreme Court
*Swann v. Charlotte Mecklenburg Board of
Education*, 229, 274, 381 (n. 66), 393
(n. 64)

Sweezy v. New Hampshire, 164
Swink, Ephraim, 94

Taft, Robert, 75
Taft-Hartley Act, 178
Talmadge, Herman, 150, 340 (n. 130), 398
(n. 12)
Tanner, Miles, 21
Tate, Essie, 53, 66, 72
Tatum, Arlo, 255
Teamsters, 178
Television: Army-McCarthy hearings on,
89; Brinkley on Ervin, 220; Ervin's
appearances on, after retirement, 297;
and Ervin's hearings on government
domestic spying, 259–60; and FBI
investigation of Schorr, 223–24; and
FCC censorship, 379 (n. 49); and Jenner Bill, 167; and Nixon on school
desegregation and busing, 229, 231;
Nixon's speech on Watergate scandal
on, 293–94; violent reaction to civil
rights movement on, 135, 139;
Watergate hearings on, 1–6, 294,
398 (n. 30)
Tenth Amendment, 326 (n. 84)
Textile strikes, 63–66, 117, 177
Thirteenth Amendment, 74, 158
Thompson, Fred, 291
Thurmond, Strom: and Civil Rights Act
(1957), 122; and Civil Rights Act (1964),
147; and defense of segregation gener-
ally, 109; filibuster by, 122; and govern-
ment domestic spying, 276; as presi-
dential candidate, 109; and approach
against civil rights, 105, 110, 130; signifi-
cance of, 340 (n. 130); on Supreme
Court, 166
Till, Emmett, 330 (n. 10)
Tillet, Gladys, 22–23, 132–33
Time, 7, 111, 138, 271, 284, 285–86
Tindall, Bruce, 78–79
Tocqueville, Alexis de, 49
Treasury Department, U.S., 201, 221, 377
(n. 36)

Truman, Harry, 74
Turlington Act, 58
Twenty-fourth Amendment, 136
Tydings, Millard, 87

Umstead, William B., 80, 82–86, 321
(nn. 14, 19)
Unions. *See* Labor unions
United Mine Workers, 75, 119
U.S. Congress. *See* House of Represen-
tatives, U.S.; Senate, U.S.; Water-
gate hearings; *specific members of
Congress*
*United States v. Jefferson County Board of
Education,* 349 (n. 84), 381 (n. 64)
United Textile Workers Union, 63–66
University of Alabama, 140
University of Mississippi, 136, 139
University of North Carolina, 30–36, 44,
58, 66, 85, 150, 166, 371 (n. 97)

Van Deman, Ralph H., 265–66
Vanocur, Sander, 222
Vera Foundation, 189–90
Vietnam War, 9, 201, 211, 214, 221, 223,
249, 259, 281. *See also* Anti-war
protesters
Violence: against African Americans, 98,
118, 126, 135, 136, 138–39; and African
Americans' murders of whites, 51, 59–
61; and anti-war protesters, 249, 250; in
Birmingham, 139–40, 144–45; against
civil rights protesters, 118, 135, 136, 138–
39, 144–45, 147, 330–31 (n. 10); Ervin's
denunciation of, 136; and riots, 28, 139,
152, 261, 350 (n. 89), 350–51 (n. 97), 352
(n. 108)
Virginian-Pilot, 7
Voorhis, Jerry, 210, 265
Voting rights: black voter registration in
1950s, 126, 331 (n. 16); black voter registration in 1960s, 130, 147, 149; and Civil
Rights Act (1957), 112, 116; and Civil
Rights Act (1960), 128, 339 (n. 118); and
disenfranchisement of African Ameri-

cans, 28, 34, 126, 338 (n. 101); and Freedom Summer in Mississippi, 147; and
literacy tests, 136–38, 147–48, 343
(n. 24), 344 (n. 27); and Nixon administration, 227; and poll tax, 136, 148,
192, 343 (n. 22); during Reconstruction,
28. *See also* Civil rights; *specific voting
rights acts*
Voting Rights Act (1965), 147–49, 152, 227,
342 (n. 7), 348 (n. 64)
Voting Rights Act (1970), 227

Wagner, Lori, 163
Wagner Act, 75
Walker, Daniel, 190
Wallace, George, 130, 136, 140, 211, 214, 215,
226, 231, 340 (n. 130)
Warren, Earl, 129, 154, 164–68, 191–92, 214,
227
Warren, Edward "Bull," 46–47
Washington, George, 327 (n. 88)
Washington, D.C. *See* District of
Columbia
Washington Daily News, 206
Washington Monthly, 246, 247
Washington Post, 199, 221, 223, 241, 243–
44, 268, 270, 273, 282, 298, 393
(n. 72)
Washington Star, 122
Watergate Committee, 282, 283–84, 287,
294, 396–97 (n. 1), 398 (n. 12)
Watergate hearings: applause for Ervin
during, 2, 43; Butterfield's testimony
during, 290–91, 294; compared with
government domestic spying hearings,
246–47, 276–77; Dean's testimony during, 288–89, 291, 293, 399 (n. 36), 399
(n. 46); death threats against Ervin and
other committee members, 292; Ehrlichman's testimony during, 4–6, 291–
92, 293; end of, 294; Ervin as committee
chair for, 2, 278, 282–83, 396–97 (n. 1);
Ervin on, 286; Ervin's impromptu
political sermons during, 1–2, 4–6;
Ervin's personal mannerisms and phys-

ical appearance on television, 1, 6–7, 71, 286, 287; Ervin's press conference before, 285–86; Ervin's response to Ehrlichman's testimony during, 4–6, 292; events preceding, 279–80; and executive privilege evoked by Nixon, 285–86, 291; goal of, 287; Gurney's criticism of Ervin during, 43; Haldeman's testimony during, 292, 293; information uncovered by, 2, 294; Magruder's testimony during, 288; McCord's testimony during, 287; Mitchell's testimony during, 290, 293; newspaper and news magazine coverage of, 1–8, 260–61, 276–77, 285–86, 304 (n. 15); and Nixon's knowledge of Watergate scandal, 6; and Nixon's refusal to surrender tapes, 6, 291, 293–94; in Old Senate Caucus Chamber, 259, 286; opening of, by Ervin, 286–87; photographs of, 3, 5, 293; public opinion on, 4, 292; stages of, 287; Stans's testimony during, 287; and surrender of White House tapes, 277, 294; and tapes from Nixon's Oval Office, 6, 277, 291, 294, 399 (n. 48); television coverage of, 1–6, 294, 398 (n. 30). *See also* Watergate scandal

Watergate scandal: and attempts to discredit Ervin as chair of Watergate Committee, 283–84; and break-in at Democratic National Committee headquarters by White House "Plumbers," 4, 253, 281; and break-in at Ellsberg's psychiatrist's office, 4, 281, 292, 376 (n. 33); and CIA, 284–85; complexity of, 7, 8; conspiracies involved in, 281–82, 284–85; criminal trial on, in Sirica's courtroom, 281, 282, 283; and CRP, 281, 282, 288; Ervin on, 280–81; and Huston Plan, 253, 289; McCord's letter on, 284–85; Mitchell on, 280; national security argument on, 257, 291; newspaper coverage of generally, 7–8; and Nixon, 6, 280–85, 289–91, 293–94; Nixon's televised speeches on,

285, 293–94; Woodward and Bernstein's investigation of, 282. *See also* Watergate hearings

Watkins, Arthur V., 90–91, 93
Watkins Committee, 91–92, 96, 323 (n. 44), 323–24 (nn. 47–49)
Watkins v. United States, 164
Webster, Daniel, 151
Weicker, Lowell, Jr., 3, 398 (n. 12)
Westin, Alan, 205
Whisenant, Mrs., 59–60
White, Theodore H., 294
White, Walter S., 323 (n. 44)
White, William S., 355 (n. 19)
Whitehead, Clay, 379 (n. 49)
White House "Plumbers," 2, 4, 253–54, 281, 376 (n. 33)
White supremacy, 34–35, 134, 302, 342 (n. 8)
The Whole Truth: The Watergate Conspiracy (Ervin), xii, 281
Wicker, Tom, 8–9, 185, 270, 299, 397 (n. 3)
Wiley, Alex, 127
Wilhoit, Francis M., 327 (n. 91), 330 (n. 7)
Wilkins, Roy: on black voters, 111; on busing, 382 (n. 69); on Civil Rights Act (1957), 117, 125, 338 (n. 103); and Civil Rights Act (1960), 129; on federal civil rights bills before 1957, 108; and political parties and civil rights issue, 126–27. *See also* NAACP
Wilkens v. Finance Co., 79
Williams, Horace, 34
Williams v. North Carolina, 316 (n. 93)
Willis, Edwin E., 339–40 (n. 122)
Wilmington Race Riot, 28
Wilson, Woodrow, 35, 103–4, 239
Winston-Salem Journal, 124, 186, 191, 199, 213, 355–56 (n. 25)
Wiretapping, 187–88, 191, 208, 213, 217, 257, 363 (nn. 16–18, 20–21), 389–90 (n. 12). *See also* Government domestic spying
Witherspoon, John and Jane, 25
Wolfe, Thomas, 44

Women's rights. *See* Equal rights
    amendment
Woodward, Bob, 8, 282
Woodward, Paul L., 236
World War I, 35–40, 42, 47, 68
World War II, 21, 71, 72, 74, 76
Wright, Charles Alan, 119

Yarborough, Ralph W., 196
Yates v. United States, 164
Young, Robert, 332 (n. 33)
Younts, Paul R., 63–64

Ziegler, Ron, 221, 256
Zwicker, Ralph, 91